C++ GUI Programming with Qt 4

Second Edition

C++ GUI Programming with Qt 4

Second Edition

Jasmin Blanchette
Mark Summerfield

In association with Trolltech Press

Upper Saddle River, NJ · Boston · Indianapolis · San Francisco
New York · Toronto · Montreal · London · Munich · Paris · Madrid
Capetown · Sydney · Tokyo · Singapore · Mexico City

The publisher offers excellent discounts on this book when ordered in quantity for bulk purchases or special sales, which may include electronic versions and/or custom covers and content particular to your business, training goals, marketing focus, and branding interests. For more information, please contact:

U.S. Corporate and Government Sales
(800) 382-3419
corpsales@pearsontechgroup.com

For sales outside the United States, please contact:

International Sales
international@pearsoned.com

Visit us on the Web: www.prenhallprofessional.com

This Book Is Safari Enabled

The Safari® Enabled icon on the cover of your favorite technology book means the book is available through Safari Bookshelf. When you buy this book, you get free access to the online edition for 45 days.

Safari Bookshelf is an electronic reference library that lets you easily search thousands of technical books, find code samples, download chapters, and access technical information whenever and wherever you need it.

To gain 45-day Safari Enabled access to this book:

- Go to http://www.prenhallprofessional.com/safarienabled
- Complete the brief registration form
- Enter the coupon code S1F3-5NDG-9Z64-LNGX-K8F2

If you have difficulty registering on Safari Bookshelf or accessing the online edition, please e-mail customer-service@safaribooksonline.com.

Library of Congress Cataloging-in-Publication Data

Blanchette, Jasmin.
C++ GUI programming with Qt 4 / Jasmin Blanchette, Mark Summerfield.–2nd ed.
p. cm.
Includes index.
ISBN-13: 978-0-13-235416-5 (hardcover : alk. paper)
1. Qt (Electronic resource) 2. Graphical user interfaces (Computer systems) 3. C++ (Computer program language) I. Summerfield, Mark. II. Title.

QA76.9.U83B532 2008
005.13'3—dc22

2008000243

ISBN-13: 978-0-13-235416-5
ISBN 0-13-235416-0

Text printed in the United States on recycled paper at Courier Westford in Westford, Massachusetts.

3rd Printing February 2009

Contents

Part III: Advanced Qt

Appendixes

Series Editor's Note

Dear Reader,

As a working programmer, I use Qt every day, and I am really impressed by the organization, design, and power that Qt brings to the C++ programmer.

While Qt began life as a cross-platform GUI toolkit, it has expanded to include portable facilities for just about every aspect of day-to-day programming: files, processes, networking, and database access, to name just a few. Because of Qt's broad applicability, you really can write your code once and just recompile it on a different platform in order to have it work out of the box. This is extraordinarily valuable when your customer base requires your product to run on different platforms.

Of course, because Qt is also available with an open source license, if you're an open source developer, you too can benefit from everything Qt has to offer.

While Qt comes with extensive online help, that help is primarily reference oriented. The example programs are useful, but it can be hard to reverse engineer correct use of Qt for your programs just by reading the examples. And that is where this book comes into the picture.

This is a really neat book. First, it's the official book on Qt from Trolltech, which says a lot. But it's also a great book: well organized, well written, and easy to follow and learn from. The combination of a great book about a great technology makes for a real winner, and that is why I am very proud and excited to have this book in the Prentice Hall Open Source Software Development Series.

I hope you will enjoy reading this book and that you will learn a lot from it; I certainly did.

Arnold Robbins
Nof Ayalon, Israel
November 2007

Foreword

Why Qt? Why do programmers like us choose Qt? Sure, there are the obvious answers: Qt's single-source compatibility, its feature richness, its C++ performance, the availability of the source code, its documentation, the high-quality technical support, and all the other items mentioned in Trolltech's glossy marketing materials. This is all very well, but it misses the most important point: Qt is successful because programmers *like* it.

How come programmers like one technology, but dislike another? Personally, I believe software engineers enjoy technology that feels right, but dislike everything that doesn't. How else can we explain that some of the brightest programmers need help to program a video recorder, or that most engineers seem to have trouble operating the company's phone system? I for one am perfectly capable of memorizing sequences of random numbers and commands, but if these are required to control my answering machine, I'd prefer not to have one. At Trolltech, our phone system forces us to press the '*' for two seconds before we are allowed to enter the other person's extension number. If you forget to do this and start to enter the extension immediately, you have to dial the entire number again. Why '*'? Why not '#', or '1', or '5', or any of the other 20 keys on the phone? Why two seconds and not one, or three, or one and a half? Why anything at all? I find the phone so irritating that I avoid using it whenever I can. Nobody likes having to do random things, especially when those random things apparently depend on some equally random context you wish you didn't have to know about in the first place.

Programming can be a lot like using our phone system, only worse. And this is where Qt comes to the rescue. Qt is different. For one thing, Qt makes sense. And for another, Qt is fun. Qt lets you concentrate on your tasks. When Qt's original architects faced a problem, they didn't just look for a good solution, or a quick solution, or the simplest solution. They looked for the *right* solution, and then they documented it. Granted, they made mistakes, and granted, some of their design decisions didn't pass the test of time, but they still got a lot of things right, and what wasn't right could and can be corrected. You can see this by the fact that a system originally designed to bridge Windows 95 and Unix/Motif now unifies modern desktop systems as diverse as Windows Vista, Mac OS X, and GNU/Linux, as well as small devices such as mobile phones.

Long before Qt became so popular and so widely used, the dedication of Qt's developers to finding the right solutions made Qt special. That dedication is just as strong today and affects everyone who maintains and develops Qt. For us, working on Qt is a responsibility and a privilege. We are proud of helping to make your professional and open source lives easier and more enjoyable.

One of the things that makes Qt a pleasure to use is its online documentation. But the documentation's focus is primarily on individual classes, with little said about how to build sophisticated real-world applications. This excellent book fills that gap. It shows you what Qt has to offer, how to program Qt the "Qt way", and how to get the best from Qt. The book will teach a C++, Java, or C# programmer how to program Qt, and provides enough advanced material to satisfy experienced Qt programmers. The book is packed with good examples, advice, and explanations—and it is the text that we use to induct all new programmers who join Trolltech.

Nowadays, a vast number of commercial and free Qt applications are available for purchase or download. Some are specialized for particular vertical markets, while others are aimed at the mass-market. Seeing so many applications built with Qt fills us with pride and inspires us to make Qt even better. And with the help of this book, there will be more and higher-quality Qt applications than ever before.

Matthias Ettrich
Berlin, Germany
November 2007

Preface

Qt is a comprehensive C++ application development framework for creating cross-platform GUI applications using a "write once, compile anywhere" approach. Qt lets programmers use a single source tree for applications that will run on Windows 98 to Vista, Mac OS X, Linux, Solaris, HP-UX, and many other versions of Unix with X11. The Qt libraries and tools are also part of Qt/Embedded Linux, a product that provides its own window system on top of embedded Linux.

The purpose of this book is to teach you how to write GUI programs using Qt 4. The book starts with "Hello Qt" and quickly progresses to more advanced topics, such as creating custom widgets and providing drag and drop. The text is complemented by a set of examples that you can download from the book's web site, `http://www.informit.com/title/0132354160`. Appendix A explains how to download and install the software, including a free C++ compiler for those using Windows.

The book is divided into three parts. Part I covers all the fundamental concepts and practices necessary for programming GUI applications using Qt. Knowledge of this part alone is sufficient to write useful GUI applications. Part II covers central Qt topics in greater depth, and Part III provides more specialized and advanced material. You can read the chapters of Parts II and III in any order, but they assume familiarity with the contents of Part I. The book also includes several appendixes, with Appendix B showing how to build Qt applications and Appendix C introducing Qt Jambi, the Java version of Qt.

The first Qt 4 edition of the book built on the Qt 3 edition, although it was completely revised to reflect good idiomatic Qt 4 programming techniques and included new chapters on Qt 4's model/view architecture, the new plugin framework, embedded programming with Qt/Embedded Linux, and a new appendix. This extended and revised second edition has been thoroughly updated to take advantage of features introduced in Qt versions 4.2 and 4.3, and includes new chapters on look and feel customization and application scripting as well as two new appendixes. The original graphics chapter has been split into separate 2D and 3D chapters, which between them now cover the new graphics view classes and `QPainter`'s OpenGL back-end. In addition, much new material has been added to the database, XML, and embedded programming chapters.

This edition, like its predecessors, emphasizes explaining Qt programming and providing realistic examples, rather than simply rehashing or summarizing Qt's extensive online documentation. Because the book teaches solid Qt 4 programming principles and practices, readers will easily be able to learn the new Qt modules that come out in Qt 4.4, Qt 4.5, and later Qt 4.*x* versions. If you are using one of these later versions, be sure to read the "What's New in Qt 4.*x*" documents in the reference documentation to get an overview of the new features that are available.

We have written the book with the assumption that you have a basic knowledge of C++, Java, or C#. The code examples use a subset of C++, avoiding many C++ features that are rarely needed when programming Qt. In the few places where a more advanced C++ construct is unavoidable, it is explained as it is used. If you already know Java or C# but have little or no experience with C++, we recommend that you begin by reading Appendix D, which provides sufficient introduction to C++ to be able to use this book. For a more thorough introduction to object-oriented programming in C++, we recommend *C++ How to Program* by P. J. Deitel and H. M. Deitel (Prentice Hall, 2007), and *C++ Primer* by Stanley B. Lippman, Josée Lajoie, and Barbara E. Moo (Addison-Wesley, 2005).

Qt made its reputation as a cross-platform framework, but thanks to its intuitive and powerful API, many organizations use Qt for single-platform development. Adobe Photoshop Album is just one example of a mass-market Windows application written in Qt. Many sophisticated software systems in vertical markets, such as 3D animation tools, digital film processing, electronic design automation (for chip design), oil and gas exploration, financial services, and medical imaging, are built with Qt. If you are making a living with a successful Windows product written in Qt, you can easily create new markets in the Mac OS X and Linux worlds simply by recompiling.

Qt is available under various licenses. If you want to build commercial applications, you must buy a commercial Qt license from Trolltech; if you want to build open source programs, you can use the open source (GPL) edition. The K Desktop Environment (KDE) and most of the open source applications that go with it are built on Qt.

In addition to Qt's hundreds of classes, there are add-ons that extend Qt's scope and power. Some of these products, like the Qt Solutions components, are available from Trolltech, while others are supplied by other companies and by the open source community; see `http://www.trolltech.com/products/qt/3rdparty/` for a list of available add-ons. Trolltech's developers also have their own web site, Trolltech Labs (`http://labs.trolltech.com/`), where they put unofficial code that they have written because it is fun, interesting, or useful. Qt has a well-established and thriving user community that uses the `qt-interest` mailing list; see `http://lists.trolltech.com/` for details.

If you spot errors in the book, have suggestions for the next edition, or want to give us feedback, we would be delighted to hear from you. You can reach us at `qt-book@trolltech.com`. The errata will be placed on the book's web site (`http://www.prenhallprofessional.com/title/0132354160`).

Acknowledgments

Our first acknowledgment is of Eirik Chambe-Eng, Trolltech's Chief Troll and one of Trolltech's two founders. Eirik not only enthusiastically encouraged us to write the Qt 3 edition of the book, he also allowed us to spend a considerable amount of our work time writing it. Eirik and Trolltech CEO Haavard Nord both read the manuscript and provided valuable feedback. Their generosity and foresight were aided and abetted by Matthias Ettrich, who cheerfully accepted our neglect of duty as we obsessed over the writing of this book, and gave us a lot of advice on good Qt programming style.

For the Qt 3 edition, we asked two Qt customers, Paul Curtis and Klaus Schmidinger, to be our external reviewers. Both are Qt experts with an amazing attention to technical detail, which they proved by spotting some very subtle errors in our manuscript and suggesting numerous improvements. And within Trolltech, alongside Matthias, our most stalwart reviewer was Reginald Stadlbauer. His technical insight was invaluable, and he taught us how to do some things in Qt that we didn't even know were possible.

For this Qt 4 edition, we have continued to benefit from the unstinting help and support of Eirik, Haavard, and Matthias. Klaus Schmidinger continued to give valuable feedback, and we also benefitted from Qt customer Paul Floyd's careful reviewing of some of the new material. Thanks also to David García Garzón for help on SCons in Appendix B. Within Trolltech, our key reviewers were Carlos Manuel Duclos Vergara, Andreas Aardal Hanssen, Henrik Hartz, Martin Jones, Vivi Glückstad Karlsen, Trond Kjernåsen, Trenton Schulz, Andy Shaw, Gunnar Sletta, and Pål de Vibe.

In addition to the reviewers mentioned above, we received expert help from Eskil Abrahamsen Blomfeldt (Qt Jambi), Frans Englich (XML), Harald Fernengel (databases), Kent Hansen (application scripting), Volker Hilsheimer (ActiveX), Bradley Hughes (multithreading), Lars Knoll (2D graphics and internationalization), Anders Larsen (databases), Sam Magnuson (qmake), Marius Bugge Monsen (item view classes), Dimitri Papadopoulos (Qt/X11), Girish Ramakrishnan (style sheets), Samuel Rødal (3D graphics), Rainer Schmid (networking and XML), Amrit Pal Singh (introduction to C++), Paul Olav Tvete (custom widgets and embedded programming), Geir Vattekar (Qt Jambi), and Thomas Zander (build systems).

Extra thanks are due to Trolltech's documentation and support teams for handling documentation-related issues while the book consumed so much of our time, and to Trolltech's system administrators for keeping our machines running and our networks communicating throughout the project.

On the production side, Jeff Kingston, author of the Lout typesetting tool, continued to add enhancements to the tool, many in response to our feedback. Also thanks to James Cloos for providing a condensed version of the DejaVu Mono font that we used as the basis for our monospaced font. Trolltech's Cathrine Bore handled the contracts and legalities on our behalf. Thanks also to Nathan Clement for the troll illustrations, and to Audrey Doyle for her careful proofreading. And finally, thanks to our editor, Debra Williams-Cauley, both for her support and for making the process as hassle-free as possible, and to Lara Wysong for handling the production practicalities so well.

A Brief History of Qt

The Qt framework first became publicly available in May 1995. It was initially developed by Haavard Nord (Trolltech's CEO) and Eirik Chambe-Eng (Trolltech's Chief Troll). Haavard and Eirik met at the Norwegian Institute of Technology in Trondheim, where they both graduated with master's degrees in computer science.

Haavard's interest in C++ GUI development began in 1988 when he was commissioned by a Swedish company to develop a C++ GUI framework. A couple of years later, in the summer of 1990, Haavard and Eirik were working together on a C++ database application for ultrasound images. The system needed to be able to run with a GUI on Unix, Macintosh, and Windows. One day that summer, Haavard and Eirik went outside to enjoy the sunshine, and as they sat on a park bench, Haavard said, "We need an object-oriented display system." The resulting discussion laid the intellectual foundation for the object-oriented cross-platform GUI framework they would soon go on to build.

In 1991, Haavard started writing the classes that eventually became Qt, collaborating with Eirik on the design. The following year, Eirik came up with the idea for "signals and slots", a simple but powerful GUI programming paradigm that has now been embraced by several other toolkits. Haavard took the idea and produced a hand-coded implementation. By 1993, Haavard and Eirik had developed Qt's first graphics kernel and were able to implement their own widgets. At the end of the year, Haavard suggested that they go into business together to build "the world's best C++ GUI framework".

The year 1994 began inauspiciously with the two young programmers wanting to enter a well-established market, with no customers, an unfinished product, and no money. Fortunately, their wives were employed and therefore able to support their husbands for the two years Eirik and Haavard expected to need to develop the product and start earning an income.

The letter 'Q' was chosen as the class prefix because the letter looked beautiful in Haavard's Emacs font. The 't' was added to stand for "toolkit", inspired by Xt, the X Toolkit. The company was incorporated on March 4, 1994, originally as Quasar Technologies, then as Troll Tech, and today as Trolltech.

In April 1995, thanks to a contact made through one of Haavard's university professors, the Norwegian company Metis gave them a contract to develop software based on Qt. Around this time, Trolltech hired Arnt Gulbrandsen, who during his six years at Trolltech devised and implemented an ingenious documentation system as well as contributing to Qt's code.

On May 20, 1995, Qt 0.90 was uploaded to `sunsite.unc.edu`. Six days later, the release was announced on `comp.os.linux.announce`. This was Qt's first public release. Qt could be used for both Windows and Unix development, offering the same API on both platforms. Qt was available under two licenses from day one: A commercial license was required for commercial development, and a free software edition was available for open source development. The Metis contract kept Trolltech afloat, while for ten long months no one bought a commercial Qt license.

In March 1996, the European Space Agency became the second Qt customer, with a purchase of ten commercial licenses. With unwavering faith, Eirik and Haavard hired another developer. Qt 0.97 was released at the end of May, and on September 24, 1996, Qt 1.0 came out. By the end of the year, Qt had reached version 1.1; eight customers, each in a different country, had bought 18 licenses between them. This year also saw the founding of the KDE project, led by Matthias Ettrich.

Qt 1.2 was released in April 1997. Matthias Ettrich's decision to use Qt to build KDE helped Qt become the de facto standard for C++ GUI development on Linux. Qt 1.3 was released in September 1997.

Matthias joined Trolltech in 1998, and the last major Qt 1 release, 1.40, was made in September of that year. Qt 2.0 was released in June 1999. Qt 2 had a new open source license, the Q Public License (QPL), which complied with the Open Source Definition. In August 1999, Qt won the LinuxWorld award for best library/tool. Around this time, Trolltech Pty Ltd (Australia) was established.

Trolltech released Qt/Embedded Linux in 2000. It was designed to run on embedded Linux devices and provided its own window system as a lightweight replacement for X11. Both Qt/X11 and Qt/Embedded Linux were now offered under the widely used GNU General Public License (GPL) as well as under commercial licenses. By the end of 2000, Trolltech had established Trolltech Inc. (USA) and had released the first version of Qtopia, an application platform for mobile phones and PDAs. Qt/Embedded Linux won the LinuxWorld "Best Embedded Linux Solution" award in both 2001 and 2002, and Qtopia Phone achieved the same distinction in 2004.

Qt 3.0 was released in 2001. Qt was now available on Windows, Mac OS X, Unix, and Linux (desktop and embedded). Qt 3 provided 42 new classes and its code exceeded 500 000 lines. Qt 3 was a major step forward from Qt 2, including considerably improved locale and Unicode support, a completely new text viewing and editing widget, and a Perl-like regular expression class. Qt 3 won the Software Development Times "Jolt Productivity Award" in 2002.

In the summer of 2005, Qt 4.0 was released. With about 500 classes and more than 9 000 functions, Qt 4 is larger and richer than any previous version, and it has been split into several libraries so that developers only need to link against the parts of Qt that they need. Qt 4 is a huge advance on previous versions with improvements that include a completely new set of efficient and easy-to-use template containers, advanced model/view functionality, a fast and flexible 2D painting framework, and powerful Unicode text viewing and editing classes, not to mention thousands of smaller enhancements across the complete range of Qt classes. Qt 4's feature set is now so broad that it has taken Qt beyond being a GUI toolkit and made it into a full-blown application development framework. Qt 4 is also the first Qt edition to be available for both commercial and open source development on all the platforms it supports.

Also in 2005, Trolltech opened a representative office in Beijing to provide customers in China and the region with sales services, training, and technical support for Qt/Embedded Linux and Qtopia.

Qt has long been available to non-C++ programmers through the availability of unofficial language bindings, in particular PyQt for Python programmers. In 2007, the Qyoto unofficial bindings were released for C# programmers. Also in 2007, Trolltech launched Qt Jambi, an officially supported Java version of the Qt API. Appendix C provides an introduction to Qt Jambi.

Since Trolltech's birth, Qt's popularity has grown unabated and continues to grow to this day. This success is a reflection both of the quality of Qt and of how enjoyable it is to use. In the past decade, Qt has gone from being a product used by a select few "in the know" to one that is used daily by thousands of customers and tens of thousands of open source developers all around the world.

Part I

Basic Qt

- *Hello Qt*
- *Making Connections*
- *Laying Out Widgets*
- *Using the Reference Documentation*

1. Getting Started

This chapter shows how to combine basic C++ with the functionality provided by Qt to create a few small graphical user interface (GUI) applications. This chapter also introduces two key Qt ideas: "signals and slots" and layouts. In Chapter 2, we will go into more depth, and in Chapter 3, we will start building a more realistic application.

If you already know Java or C# but have limited experience with C++, you might want to start by reading the C++ introduction in Appendix D.

Hello Qt

Let's start with a very simple Qt program. We will first study it line by line, and then see how to compile and run it.

```
1 #include <QApplication>
2 #include <QLabel>

3 int main(int argc, char *argv[])
4 {
5     QApplication app(argc, argv);
6     QLabel *label = new QLabel("Hello Qt!");
7     label->show();
8     return app.exec();
9 }
```

Lines 1 and 2 include the definitions of the `QApplication` and `QLabel` classes. For every Qt class, there is a header file with the same name (and capitalization) as the class that contains the class's definition.

Line 5 creates a `QApplication` object to manage application-wide resources. The `QApplication` constructor requires `argc` and `argv` because Qt supports a few command-line arguments of its own.

Line 6 creates a `QLabel` widget that displays "Hello Qt!". In Qt and Unix terminology, a *widget* is a visual element in a user interface. The term stems from "window gadget" and is the equivalent of both "control" and "container" in Windows terminology. Buttons, menus, scroll bars, and frames are all examples of widgets. Widgets can contain other widgets; for example, an application window is usually a widget that contains a `QMenuBar`, a few `QToolBar`s, a `QStatusBar`, and some other widgets. Most applications use a `QMainWindow` or a `QDialog` as the application window, but Qt is so flexible that any widget can be a window. In this example, the `QLabel` widget is the application window.

Line 7 makes the label visible. Widgets are always created hidden so that we can customize them before showing them, thereby avoiding flicker.

Line 8 passes control of the application on to Qt. At this point, the program enters the event loop. This is a kind of stand-by mode where the program waits for user actions such as mouse clicks and key presses. User actions generate *events* (also called "messages") to which the program can respond, usually by executing one or more functions. For example, when the user clicks a widget, a "mouse press" and a "mouse release" event are generated. In this respect, GUI applications differ drastically from conventional batch programs, which typically process input, produce results, and terminate without human intervention.

For simplicity, we don't bother calling `delete` on the `QLabel` object at the end of the `main()` function. This memory leak is harmless in such a small program, since the memory will be reclaimed by the operating system when the program terminates.

It is now possible to try the program on your own machine. It should look like the one shown in Figure 1.1. First, you will need to install Qt 4.3.2 (or a later Qt 4 release), a process that is explained in Appendix A. From now on, we will assume that you have a correctly installed copy of Qt 4 and that Qt's `bin` directory is in your `PATH` environment variable. (On Windows, this is done automatically by the Qt installation program.) You will also need the program's code in a file called `hello.cpp` in a directory called `hello`. You can type in `hello.cpp` yourself or copy it from the examples that accompany this book, where it is available as `examples/chap01/hello/hello.cpp`. (All the examples are available from the book's web site, `http://www.informit.com/title/0132354160`.)

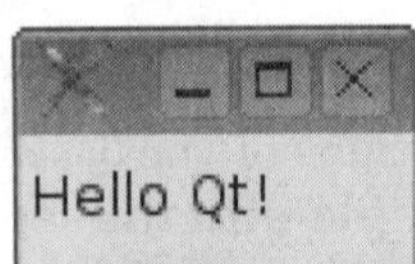

Figure 1.1. Hello on Linux

From a command prompt, change the directory to `hello`, and type

```
qmake -project
```

to create a platform-independent project file (`hello.pro`), and then type

```
qmake hello.pro
```

to create a platform-specific makefile from the project file. (The `qmake` tool is covered in more detail in Appendix B.) Type `make` to build the program. Run it by typing `hello` on Windows, `./hello` on Unix, and `open hello.app` on Mac OS X. To terminate the program, click the close button in the window's title bar.

If you are using Windows and have installed the Qt Open Source Edition and the MinGW compiler, you will have a shortcut to an MS-DOS Prompt window that has all the environment variables correctly set up for Qt. If you start this window, you can compile Qt applications within it using `qmake` and `make` as described previously. The executables produced are put in the application's `debug` or `release` folder (e.g., `C:\examples\chap01\hello\release\hello.exe`).

If you are using Microsoft Visual C++ with a commercial version of Qt, you will need to run `nmake` instead of `make`. Alternatively, you can create a Visual Studio project file from `hello.pro` by typing

```
qmake -tp vc hello.pro
```

and then build the program in Visual Studio. If you are using Xcode on Mac OS X, you can generate an Xcode project using the command

```
qmake -spec macx-xcode hello.pro
```

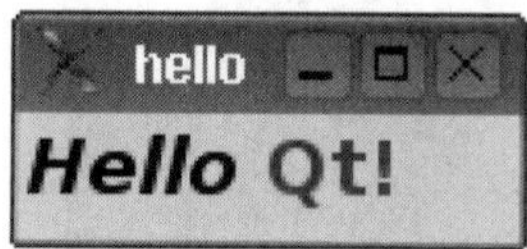

Figure 1.2. A label with basic HTML formatting

Before we go on to the next example, let's have some fun: Replace the line

```
QLabel *label = new QLabel("Hello Qt!");
```

with

```
QLabel *label = new QLabel("<h2><i>Hello</i> "
                           "<font color=red>Qt!</font></h2>");
```

and rebuild the application. When run, it should look like Figure 1.2. As the example illustrates, it's easy to brighten up a Qt application's user interface using some simple HTML-style formatting.

Making Connections

The second example shows how to respond to user actions. The application consists of a button that the user can click to quit. The source code is very similar to Hello, except that we are using a `QPushButton` instead of a `QLabel` as our main widget, and we are connecting a user action (clicking a button) to a piece of code.

This application's source code is in the book's examples, in the file examples/chap01/quit/quit.cpp; the running application is shown in Figure 1.3. Here's the contents of the file:

```
#include <QApplication>
#include <QPushButton>

int main(int argc, char *argv[])
{
    QApplication app(argc, argv);
    QPushButton *button = new QPushButton("Quit");
    QObject::connect(button, SIGNAL(clicked()),
                     &app, SLOT(quit()));
    button->show();
    return app.exec();
}
```

Qt's widgets emit *signals* to indicate that a user action or a change of state has occurred.* For instance, QPushButton emits a clicked() signal when the user clicks the button. A signal can be connected to a function (called a *slot* in that context) so that when the signal is emitted, the slot is automatically executed. In our example, we connect the button's clicked() signal to the QApplication object's quit() slot. The SIGNAL() and SLOT() macros are part of the syntax.

Figure 1.3. The Quit application

We will now build the application. We assume that you have created a directory called quit containing quit.cpp. Run qmake in the quit directory to generate the project file, and then run it again to generate a makefile, as follows:

```
qmake -project
qmake quit.pro
```

Now build the application, and run it. If you click Quit, or press Space (which presses the button), the application will terminate.

Laying Out Widgets

In this section, we will create a small example application that demonstrates how to use layouts to manage the geometry of widgets in a window and how to use signals and slots to synchronize two widgets. The application—shown in Figure 1.4—asks for the user's age, which the user can enter by manipulating either a spin box or a slider.

---

*Qt signals are unrelated to Unix signals. In this book, we are only concerned with Qt signals.

The application consists of three widgets: a `QSpinBox`, a `QSlider`, and a `QWidget`. The `QWidget` is the application's main window. The `QSpinBox` and the `QSlider` are rendered inside the `QWidget`; they are *children* of the `QWidget`. Alternatively, we can say that the `QWidget` is the *parent* of the `QSpinBox` and the `QSlider`. The `QWidget` has no parent itself because it is being used as a top-level window. The constructors for `QWidget` and all of its subclasses take a `QWidget *` parameter that specifies the parent widget.

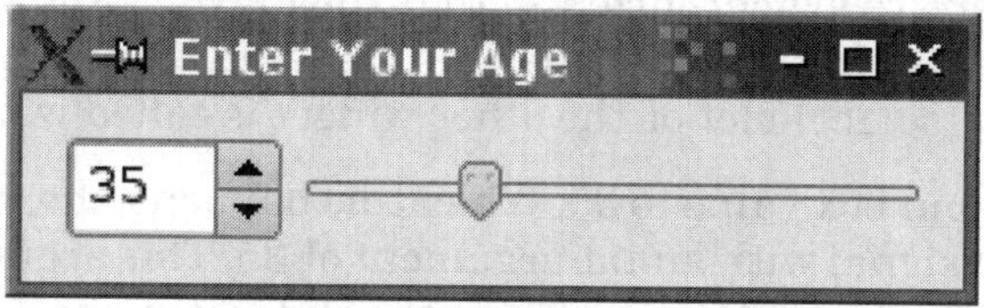

Figure 1.4. The Age application

Here's the source code:

```
1  #include <QApplication>
2  #include <QHBoxLayout>
3  #include <QSlider>
4  #include <QSpinBox>

5  int main(int argc, char *argv[])
6  {
7      QApplication app(argc, argv);

8      QWidget *window = new QWidget;
9      window->setWindowTitle("Enter Your Age");

10     QSpinBox *spinBox = new QSpinBox;
11     QSlider *slider = new QSlider(Qt::Horizontal);
12     spinBox->setRange(0, 130);
13     slider->setRange(0, 130);

14     QObject::connect(spinBox, SIGNAL(valueChanged(int)),
15                      slider, SLOT(setValue(int)));
16     QObject::connect(slider, SIGNAL(valueChanged(int)),
17                      spinBox, SLOT(setValue(int)));
18     spinBox->setValue(35);

19     QHBoxLayout *layout = new QHBoxLayout;
20     layout->addWidget(spinBox);
21     layout->addWidget(slider);
22     window->setLayout(layout);

23     window->show();

24     return app.exec();
25 }
```

Lines 8 and 9 set up the `QWidget` that will serve as the application's main window. We call `setWindowTitle()` to set the text displayed in the window's title bar.

Lines 10 and 11 create a QSpinBox and a QSlider, and lines 12 and 13 set their valid ranges. We can safely assume that the user is at most 130 years old. We could pass window to the QSpinBox and QSlider constructors, specifying that these widgets should have window as their parent, but it isn't necessary here because the layout system will figure this out by itself and automatically set the parent of the spin box and the slider, as we will see shortly.

The two QObject::connect() calls shown in lines 14 to 17 ensure that the spin box and the slider are synchronized so that they always show the same value. Whenever the value of one widget changes, its valueChanged(int) signal is emitted, and the setValue(int) slot of the other widget is called with the new value.

Line 18 sets the spin box value to 35. When this happens, the QSpinBox emits the valueChanged(int) signal with an int argument of 35. This argument is passed to the QSlider's setValue(int) slot, which sets the slider value to 35. The slider then emits the valueChanged(int) signal because its own value changed, triggering the spin box's setValue(int) slot. But at this point, setValue(int) doesn't emit any signal, since the spin box value is already 35. This prevents infinite recursion. Figure 1.5 summarizes the situation.

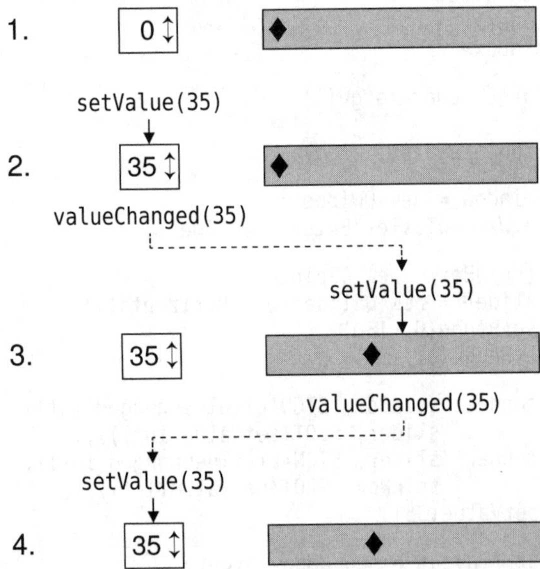

Figure 1.5. Changing one widget's value changes both

In lines 19 to 22, we lay out the spin box and slider widgets using a *layout manager*. A layout manager is an object that sets the size and position of the widgets that lie under its responsibility. Qt has three main layout manager classes:

- QHBoxLayout lays out widgets horizontally from left to right (right to left for some cultures).
- QVBoxLayout lays out widgets vertically from top to bottom.

Widget Styles

The screenshots we have seen so far have been taken on Linux, but Qt applications look native on every supported platform. Qt achieves this by emulating the platform's look and feel, rather than wrapping a particular platform or toolkit's widget set.

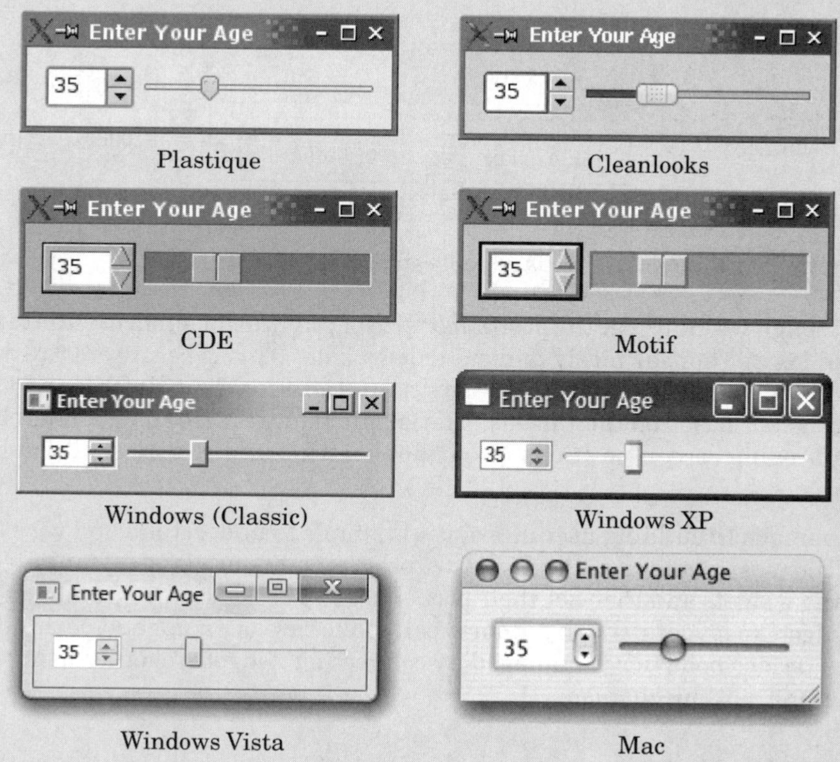

Figure 1.6. Predefined styles

The Plastique style is the default style for Qt/X11 applications running under KDE, and Cleanlooks is the default under GNOME. These styles use gradients and anti-aliasing to provide a modern look and feel. Qt application users can override the default style by using the `-style` command-line option. For example, to launch the Age application using the Motif style on X11, simply type the following command:

```
./age -style motif
```

Unlike the other styles, the Windows XP, Windows Vista, and Mac styles are available only on their native platforms, since they rely on the platforms' theme engines.

An additional style, *QtDotNet*, is available from Qt Solutions. It is also possible to create custom styles, as explained in Chapter 19.

- `QGridLayout` lays out widgets in a grid.

The call to `QWidget::setLayout()` on line 22 installs the layout manager on the window. Behind the scenes, the `QSpinBox` and `QSlider` are "reparented" to be children of the widget on which the layout is installed, and for this reason we don't need to specify an explicit parent when we construct a widget that will be put in a layout.

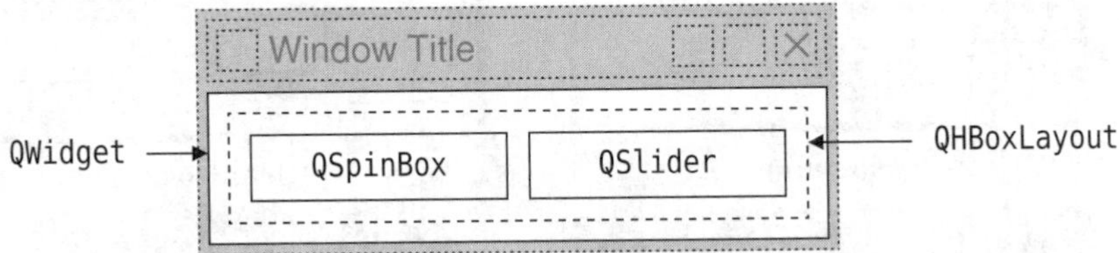

Figure 1.7. The Age application's widgets and layout

Even though we didn't set the position or size of any widget explicitly, the `QSpinBox` and `QSlider` appear nicely laid out side by side. This is because `QHBoxLayout` automatically assigns reasonable positions and sizes to the widgets for which it is responsible, based on their needs. The layout managers free us from the chore of hard-coding screen positions in our applications and ensure that windows resize smoothly.

Qt's approach to building user interfaces is simple to understand and very flexible. The most common pattern that Qt programmers use is to instantiate the required widgets and then set their properties as necessary. Programmers add the widgets to layouts, which automatically take care of sizing and positioning. User interface behavior is managed by connecting widgets together using Qt's signals and slots mechanism.

Using the Reference Documentation

Qt's reference documentation is an essential tool for any Qt developer, since it covers every class and function in Qt. This book makes use of many Qt classes and functions, but it does not cover all of them, nor does it provide every detail of those that are mentioned. To get the most benefit from Qt, you should familiarize yourself with the Qt reference documentation as quickly as possible.

The documentation is available in HTML format in Qt's `doc/html` directory and can be read using any web browser. You can also use *Qt Assistant*, the Qt help browser, which has powerful searching and indexing features that make it quicker and easier to use than a web browser.

To launch *Qt Assistant*, click Qt by Trolltech v4.x.y|Assistant in the Start menu on Windows, type `assistant` on the command line on Unix, or double-click Assistant in the Mac OS X Finder. The links in the "API Reference" section on the home page provide different ways of navigating Qt's classes. The "All Classes" page lists every class in Qt's API. The "Main Classes" page lists only the most

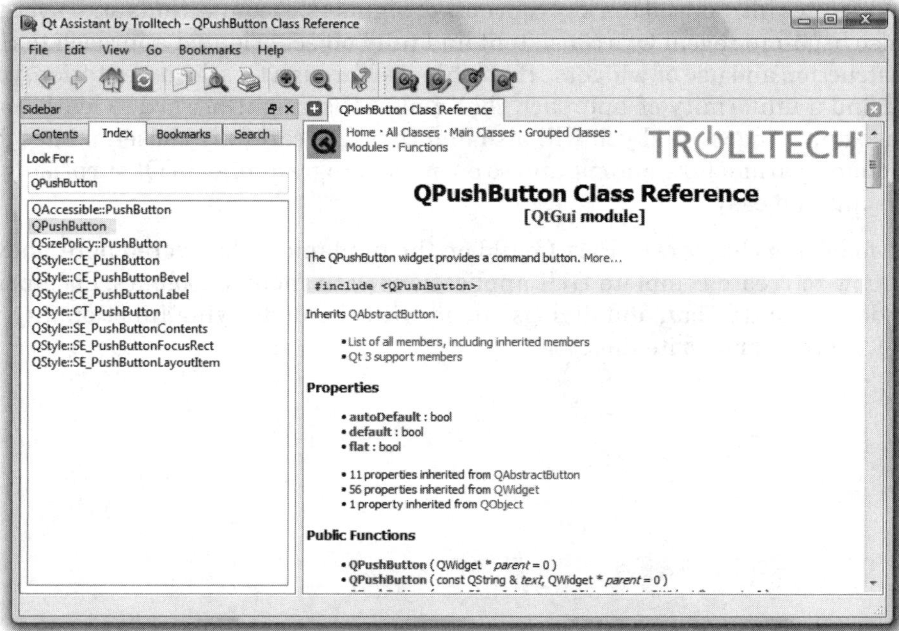

Figure 1.8. Qt's documentation in *Qt Assistant* on Windows Vista

commonly used Qt classes. As an exercise, you might want to look up the classes and functions that we have used in this chapter.

Note that inherited functions are documented in the base class; for example, `QPushButton` has no `show()` function of its own, but it inherits one from `QWidget`. Figure 1.9 shows how the classes we have seen so far relate to each other.

The reference documentation for the current version of Qt and for some earlier versions is available online at `http://doc.trolltech.com/`. This site also has selected articles from *Qt Quarterly*, the Qt programmers' newsletter sent to all commercial licensees.

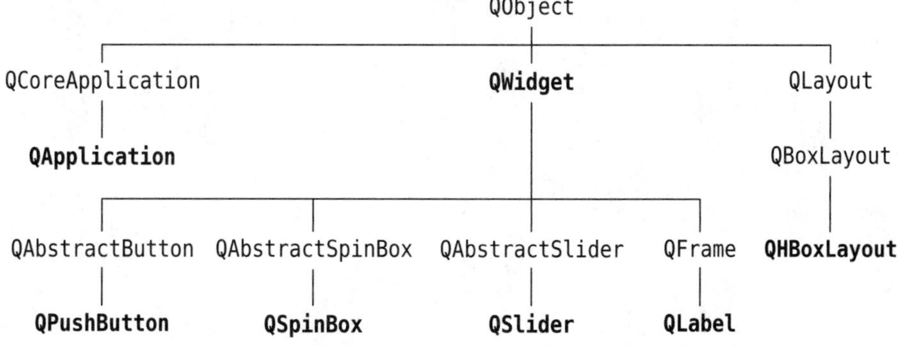

Figure 1.9. Inheritance tree for the Qt classes seen so far

This chapter introduced the key concepts of signal–slot connections and layouts. It also began to reveal Qt's consistent and fully object-oriented approach to the construction and use of widgets. If you browse through Qt's documentation, you will find a uniformity of approach that makes it straightforward to learn how to use new widgets, and you will also find that Qt's carefully chosen names for functions, parameters, enums, and so on, make programming in Qt surprisingly pleasant and easy.

The following chapters of Part I build on the fundamentals covered here, showing how to create complete GUI applications with menus, toolbars, document windows, a status bar, and dialogs, along with the underlying functionality to read, process, and write files.

- *Subclassing QDialog*
- *Signals and Slots in Depth*
- *Rapid Dialog Design*
- *Shape-Changing Dialogs*
- *Dynamic Dialogs*
- *Built-in Widget and Dialog Classes*

2. Creating Dialogs

This chapter will teach you how to create dialog boxes using Qt. Dialog boxes present users with options and choices, and allow them to set the options to their preferred values and to make their choices. They are called dialog boxes, or simply "dialogs", because they provide a means by which users and applications can "talk to" each other.

Most GUI applications consist of a main window with a menu bar and toolbar, along with dozens of dialogs that complement the main window. It is also possible to create dialog applications that respond directly to the user's choices by performing the appropriate actions (e.g., a calculator application).

We will create our first dialog purely by writing code to show how it is done. Then we will see how to build dialogs using *Qt Designer*, Qt's visual design tool. Using *Qt Designer* is a lot faster than hand-coding and makes it easy to test different designs and to change designs later.

Subclassing QDialog

Our first example is a Find dialog written entirely in C++. It is shown in Figure 2.1. We will implement the dialog as a class in its own right. By doing so, we make it an independent, self-contained component, with its own signals and slots.

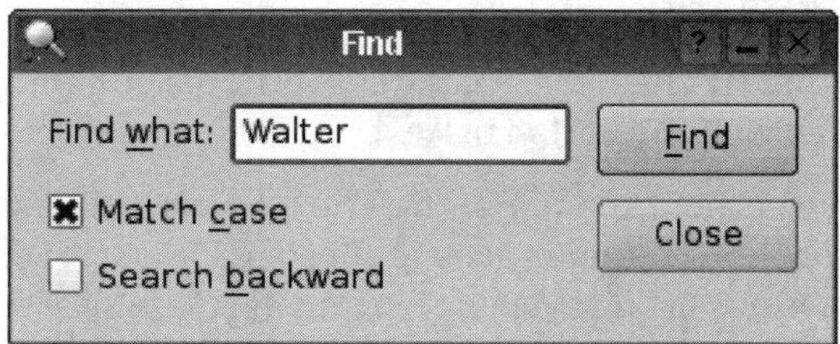

Figure 2.1. The Find dialog

The source code is spread across two files: `finddialog.h` and `finddialog.cpp`. We will start with `finddialog.h`.

```
1 #ifndef FINDDIALOG_H
2 #define FINDDIALOG_H

3 #include <QDialog>

4 class QCheckBox;
5 class QLabel;
6 class QLineEdit;
7 class QPushButton;
```

Lines 1 and 2 (and 27) protect the header file against multiple inclusions.

Line 3 includes the definition of `QDialog`, the base class for dialogs in Qt. `QDialog` is derived from `QWidget`.

Lines 4 to 7 are forward declarations of the Qt classes that we will use to implement the dialog. A *forward declaration* tells the C++ compiler that a class exists, without giving all the detail that a class definition (usually located in a header file of its own) provides. We will say more about this shortly.

Next, we define `FindDialog` as a subclass of `QDialog`:

```
8 class FindDialog : public QDialog
9 {
10     Q_OBJECT

11 public:
12     FindDialog(QWidget *parent = 0);
```

The `Q_OBJECT` macro at the beginning of the class definition is necessary for all classes that define signals or slots.

The `FindDialog` constructor is typical of Qt widget classes. The `parent` parameter specifies the parent widget. The default is a null pointer, meaning that the dialog has no parent.

```
13 signals:
14     void findNext(const QString &str, Qt::CaseSensitivity cs);
15     void findPrevious(const QString &str, Qt::CaseSensitivity cs);
```

The `signals` section declares two signals that the dialog emits when the user clicks the Find button. If the Search backward option is enabled, the dialog emits `findPrevious()`; otherwise, it emits `findNext()`.

The `signals` keyword is actually a macro. The C++ preprocessor converts it into standard C++ before the compiler sees it. `Qt::CaseSensitivity` is an enum type that can take the values `Qt::CaseSensitive` and `Qt::CaseInsensitive`.

```
16 private slots:
17     void findClicked();
18     void enableFindButton(const QString &text);

19 private:
```

```
    QLabel *label;
    QLineEdit *lineEdit;
    QCheckBox *caseCheckBox;
    QCheckBox *backwardCheckBox;
    QPushButton *findButton;
    QPushButton *closeButton;
};

#endif
```

In the class's private section, we declare two slots. To implement the slots, we will need to access most of the dialog's child widgets, so we keep pointers to them as well. The slots keyword is, like signals, a macro that expands into a construct that the C++ compiler can digest.

For the private variables, we used forward declarations of their classes. This was possible because they are all pointers and we don't access them in the header file, so the compiler doesn't need the full class definitions. We could have included the relevant header files (<QCheckBox>, <QLabel>, etc.), but using forward declarations when it is possible makes compiling somewhat faster.

We will now look at finddialog.cpp, which contains the implementation of the FindDialog class.

```
#include <QtGui>

#include "finddialog.h"
```

First, we include <QtGui>, a header file that contains the definition of Qt's GUI classes. Qt consists of several modules, each of which lives in its own library. The most important modules are *QtCore*, *QtGui*, *QtNetwork*, *QtOpenGL*, *QtScript*, *QtSql*, *QtSvg*, and *QtXml*. The <QtGui> header file contains the definition of all the classes that are part of the *QtCore* and *QtGui* modules. Including this header saves us the bother of including every class individually.

In finddialog.h, instead of including <QDialog> and using forward declarations for QCheckBox, QLabel, QLineEdit, and QPushButton, we could simply have included <QtGui>. However, it is generally bad style to include such a big header file from another header file, especially in larger applications.

```
FindDialog::FindDialog(QWidget *parent)
    : QDialog(parent)
{
    label = new QLabel(tr("Find &what:"));
    lineEdit = new QLineEdit;
    label->setBuddy(lineEdit);

    caseCheckBox = new QCheckBox(tr("Match &case"));
    backwardCheckBox = new QCheckBox(tr("Search &backward"));

    findButton = new QPushButton(tr("&Find"));
    findButton->setDefault(true);
    findButton->setEnabled(false);

    closeButton = new QPushButton(tr("Close"));
```

On line 4, we pass on the `parent` parameter to the base class constructor. Then we create the child widgets. The `tr()` function calls around the string literals mark them for translation to other languages. The function is declared in `QObject` and every subclass that contains the `Q_OBJECT` macro. It's a good habit to surround user-visible strings with `tr()`, even if you don't have immediate plans for translating your applications to other languages. We cover translating Qt applications in Chapter 18.

In the string literals, we use ampersands ('&') to indicate shortcut keys. For example, line 11 creates a Find button, which the user can activate by pressing Alt+F on platforms that support shortcut keys. Ampersands can also be used to control focus: On line 6 we create a label with a shortcut key (Alt+W), and on line 8 we set the label's buddy to be the line editor. A *buddy* is a widget that accepts the focus when the label's shortcut key is pressed. So when the user presses Alt+W (the label's shortcut), the focus goes to the line editor (the label's buddy).

On line 12, we make the Find button the dialog's default button by calling `setDefault(true)`. The default button is the button that is pressed when the user hits Enter. On line 13, we disable the Find button. When a widget is disabled, it is usually shown grayed out and will not respond to user interaction.

```
15      connect(lineEdit, SIGNAL(textChanged(const QString &)),
16              this, SLOT(enableFindButton(const QString &)));
17      connect(findButton, SIGNAL(clicked()),
18              this, SLOT(findClicked()));
19      connect(closeButton, SIGNAL(clicked()),
20              this, SLOT(close()));
```

The private slot `enableFindButton(const QString &)` is called whenever the text in the line editor changes. The private slot `findClicked()` is called when the user clicks the Find button. The dialog closes itself when the user clicks Close. The `close()` slot is inherited from `QWidget`, and its default behavior is to hide the widget from view (without deleting it). We will look at the code for the `enableFindButton()` and `findClicked()` slots later on.

Since `QObject` is one of `FindDialog`'s ancestors, we can omit the `QObject::` prefix in front of the `connect()` calls.

```
21      QHBoxLayout *topLeftLayout = new QHBoxLayout;
22      topLeftLayout->addWidget(label);
23      topLeftLayout->addWidget(lineEdit);

24      QVBoxLayout *leftLayout = new QVBoxLayout;
25      leftLayout->addLayout(topLeftLayout);
26      leftLayout->addWidget(caseCheckBox);
27      leftLayout->addWidget(backwardCheckBox);

28      QVBoxLayout *rightLayout = new QVBoxLayout;
29      rightLayout->addWidget(findButton);
30      rightLayout->addWidget(closeButton);
31      rightLayout->addStretch();

32      QHBoxLayout *mainLayout = new QHBoxLayout;
```

```
33     mainLayout->addLayout(leftLayout);
34     mainLayout->addLayout(rightLayout);
35     setLayout(mainLayout);
```

Next, we lay out the child widgets using layout managers. Layouts can contain both widgets and other layouts. By nesting `QHBoxLayout`s, `QVBoxLayout`s, and `QGridLayout`s in various combinations, it is possible to build very sophisticated dialogs.

For the Find dialog, we use two `QHBoxLayout`s and two `QVBoxLayout`s, as shown in Figure 2.2. The outer layout is the main layout; it is installed on the `FindDialog` on line 35 and is responsible for the dialog's entire area. The other three layouts are sub-layouts. The little "spring" at the bottom right of Figure 2.2 is a spacer item (or "stretch"). It uses up the empty space below the Find and Close buttons, ensuring that these buttons occupy the top of their layout.

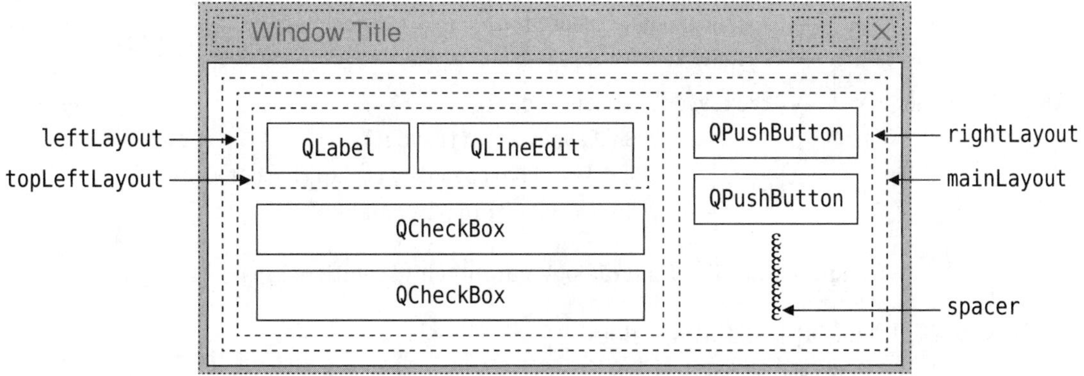

Figure 2.2. The Find dialog's layouts

One subtle aspect of the layout manager classes is that they are not widgets. Instead, they are derived from `QLayout`, which in turn is derived from `QObject`. In the figure, widgets are represented by solid outlines and layouts are represented by dashed outlines to highlight the difference between them. In a running application, layouts are invisible.

When the sublayouts are added to the parent layout (lines 25, 33, and 34), the sublayouts are automatically reparented. Then, when the main layout is installed on the dialog (line 35), it becomes a child of the dialog, and all the widgets in the layouts are reparented to become children of the dialog. The resulting parent–child hierarchy is depicted in Figure 2.3.

```
36     setWindowTitle(tr("Find"));
37     setFixedHeight(sizeHint().height());
38 }
```

Finally, we set the title to be shown in the dialog's title bar and we set the window to have a fixed height, since there aren't any widgets in the dialog that can meaningfully occupy any extra vertical space. The `QWidget::sizeHint()` function returns a widget's "ideal" size.

This completes the review of `FindDialog`'s constructor. Since we used `new` to create the dialog's widgets and layouts, it would seem that we need to write a destructor that calls `delete` on each widget and layout we created. But this isn't necessary, since Qt automatically deletes child objects when the parent is destroyed, and the child widgets and layouts are all descendants of the `FindDialog`.

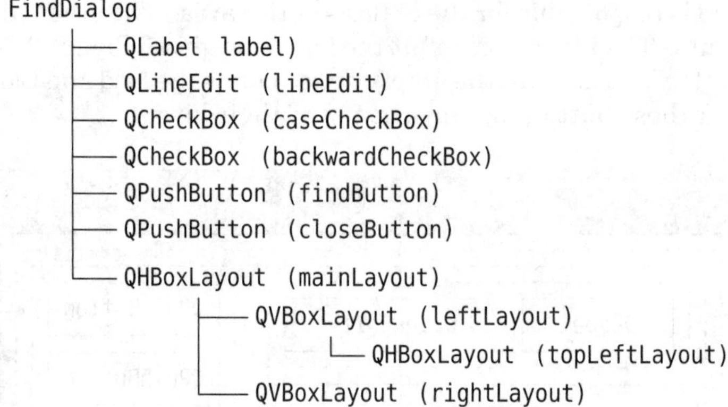

Figure 2.3. The Find dialog's parent–child relationships

Now we will look at the dialog's slots:

```
void FindDialog::findClicked()
{
    QString text = lineEdit->text();
    Qt::CaseSensitivity cs =
            caseCheckBox->isChecked() ? Qt::CaseSensitive
                                      : Qt::CaseInsensitive;
    if (backwardCheckBox->isChecked()) {
        emit findPrevious(text, cs);
    } else {
        emit findNext(text, cs);
    }
}

void FindDialog::enableFindButton(const QString &text)
{
    findButton->setEnabled(!text.isEmpty());
}
```

The `findClicked()` slot is called when the user clicks the Find button. It emits the `findPrevious()` or the `findNext()` signal, depending on the Search backward option. The `emit` keyword is specific to Qt; like other Qt extensions it is converted into standard C++ by the C++ preprocessor.

The `enableFindButton()` slot is called whenever the user changes the text in the line editor. It enables the button if there is some text in the editor, and disables it otherwise.

These two slots complete the dialog. We can now create a `main.cpp` file to test our `FindDialog` widget:

```
#include <QApplication>

#include "finddialog.h"

int main(int argc, char *argv[])
{
    QApplication app(argc, argv);
    FindDialog *dialog = new FindDialog;
    dialog->show();
    return app.exec();
}
```

To compile the program, run `qmake` as usual. Since the `FindDialog` class definition contains the `Q_OBJECT` macro, the makefile generated by `qmake` will include special rules to run `moc`, Qt's meta-object compiler. (We cover Qt's meta-object system in the next section.)

For `moc` to work correctly, we must put the class definition in a header file, separate from the implementation file. The code generated by `moc` includes this header file and adds some C++ boilerplate code of its own.

Classes that use the `Q_OBJECT` macro must have `moc` run on them. This isn't a problem because `qmake` automatically adds the necessary rules to the makefile. But if you forget to regenerate your makefile using `qmake` and `moc` isn't run, the linker will complain that some functions are declared but not implemented. The messages can be fairly obscure. GCC produces error messages like this one:

```
finddialog.o: In function `FindDialog::tr(char const*, char const*)':
/usr/lib/qt/src/corelib/global/qglobal.h:1430: undefined reference to
`FindDialog::staticMetaObject'
```

Visual C++'s output starts like this:

```
finddialog.obj : error LNK2001: unresolved external symbol
"public:~virtual int __thiscall MyClass::qt_metacall(enum QMetaObject
::Call,int,void * *)"
```

If this ever happens to you, run `qmake` again to update the makefile, then rebuild the application.

Now run the program. If shortcut keys are shown on your platform, verify that the shortcut keys Alt+W, Alt+C, Alt+B, and Alt+F trigger the correct behavior. Press Tab to navigate through the widgets with the keyboard. The default tab order is the order in which the widgets were created. This can be changed using `QWidget::setTabOrder()`.

Providing a sensible tab order and keyboard shortcuts ensures that users who don't want to (or cannot) use a mouse are able to make full use of the application. Full keyboard control is also appreciated by fast typists.

In Chapter 3, we will use the Find dialog inside a real application, and we will connect the `findPrevious()` and `findNext()` signals to some slots.

Signals and Slots in Depth

The signals and slots mechanism is fundamental to Qt programming. It enables the application programmer to bind objects together without the objects knowing anything about each other. We have already connected some signals and slots together, declared our own signals and slots, implemented our own slots, and emitted our own signals. Let's take a moment to look at the mechanism more closely.

Slots are almost identical to ordinary C++ member functions. They can be virtual; they can be overloaded; they can be public, protected, or private; they can be directly invoked like any other C++ member functions; and their parameters can be of any types. The difference is that a slot can also be connected to a signal, in which case it is automatically called each time the signal is emitted.

The `connect()` statement looks like this:

```
connect(sender, SIGNAL(signal), receiver, SLOT(slot));
```

where *sender* and *receiver* are pointers to `QObject`s and where *signal* and *slot* are function signatures without parameter names. The `SIGNAL()` and `SLOT()` macros essentially convert their argument to a string.

In the examples we have seen so far, we have always connected different signals to different slots. There are other possibilities to consider.

- **One signal can be connected to many slots:**

  ```
  connect(slider, SIGNAL(valueChanged(int)),
          spinBox, SLOT(setValue(int)));
  connect(slider, SIGNAL(valueChanged(int)),
          this, SLOT(updateStatusBarIndicator(int)));
  ```

  When the signal is emitted, the slots are called one after the other, in an unspecified order.

- **Many signals can be connected to the same slot:**

  ```
  connect(lcd, SIGNAL(overflow()),
          this, SLOT(handleMathError()));
  connect(calculator, SIGNAL(divisionByZero()),
          this, SLOT(handleMathError()));
  ```

  When either signal is emitted, the slot is called.

- **A signal can be connected to another signal:**

```
connect(lineEdit, SIGNAL(textChanged(const QString &)),
        this, SIGNAL(updateRecord(const QString &)));
```

  When the first signal is emitted, the second signal is emitted as well. Apart from that, signal–signal connections are indistinguishable from signal–slot connections.

- **Connections can be removed:**

```
disconnect(lcd, SIGNAL(overflow()),
           this, SLOT(handleMathError()));
```

  This is rarely needed, because Qt automatically removes all connections involving an object when that object is deleted.

To successfully connect a signal to a slot (or to another signal), they must have the same parameter types in the same order:

```
connect(ftp, SIGNAL(rawCommandReply(int, const QString &)),
        this, SLOT(processReply(int, const QString &)));
```

Exceptionally, if a signal has more parameters than the slot it is connected to, the additional parameters are simply ignored:

```
connect(ftp, SIGNAL(rawCommandReply(int, const QString &)),
        this, SLOT(checkErrorCode(int)));
```

If the parameter types are incompatible, or if the signal or the slot doesn't exist, Qt will issue a warning at run-time if the application is built in debug mode. Similarly, Qt will give a warning if parameter names are included in the signal or slot signatures.

So far, we have only used signals and slots with widgets. But the mechanism itself is implemented in `QObject` and isn't limited to GUI programming. The mechanism can be used by any `QObject` subclass:

```
class Employee : public QObject
{
    Q_OBJECT

public:
    Employee() { mySalary = 0; }

    int salary() const { return mySalary; }

public slots:
    void setSalary(int newSalary);

signals:
    void salaryChanged(int newSalary);

private:
    int mySalary;
};
```

Qt's Meta-Object System

One of Qt's major achievements has been the extension of C++ with a mechanism for creating independent software components that can be bound together without any component knowing anything about the other components it is connected to.

The mechanism is called the *meta-object system*, and it provides two key services: signals–slots and introspection. The introspection functionality is necessary for implementing signals and slots, and allows application programmers to obtain "meta-information" about `QObject` subclasses at run-time, including the list of signals and slots supported by the object and its class name. The mechanism also supports properties (used extensively by *Qt Designer*) and text translation (for internationalization), and it lays the foundation for the *QtScript* module. From Qt 4.2, properties can be added dynamically, a feature we will see in action in Chapters 19 and 22.

Standard C++ doesn't provide support for the dynamic meta-information needed by Qt's meta-object system. Qt solves this problem by providing a separate tool, `moc`, that parses `Q_OBJECT` class definitions and makes the information available through C++ functions. Since `moc` implements all its functionality using pure C++, Qt's meta-object system works with any C++ compiler.

The mechanism works as follows:

- The `Q_OBJECT` macro declares some introspection functions that must be implemented in every `QObject` subclass: `metaObject()`, `tr()`, `qt_metacall()`, and a few more.
- Qt's `moc` tool generates implementations for the functions declared by `Q_OBJECT` and for all the signals.
- `QObject` member functions such as `connect()` and `disconnect()` use the introspection functions to do their work.

All of this is handled automatically by `qmake`, `moc`, and `QObject`, so you rarely need to think about it. But if you are curious, you can read the `QMetaObject` class documentation and have a look at the C++ source files generated by `moc` to see how the implementation works.

```
void Employee::setSalary(int newSalary)
{
    if (newSalary != mySalary) {
        mySalary = newSalary;
        emit salaryChanged(mySalary);
    }
}
```

Notice how the `setSalary()` slot is implemented. We emit the `salaryChanged()` signal only if `newSalary != mySalary`. This ensures that cyclic connections don't lead to infinite loops.

Rapid Dialog Design

Qt is designed to be pleasant and intuitive to hand-code, and it is not unusual for programmers to develop entire Qt applications purely by writing C++ source code. Still, many programmers prefer to use a visual approach for designing forms, because they find it more natural and faster than hand-coding, and they want to be able to experiment with and change designs more quickly and easily than is possible with hand-coded forms.

Qt Designer expands the options available to programmers by providing a visual design capability. *Qt Designer* can be used to develop all or just some of an application's forms. Forms that are created using *Qt Designer* end up as C++ code, so *Qt Designer* can be used with a conventional tool chain and imposes no special requirements on the compiler.

In this section, we will use *Qt Designer* to create the Go to Cell dialog shown in Figure 2.4. Whether we do it in code or in *Qt Designer*, creating a dialog always involves the same fundamental steps:

1. Create and initialize the child widgets.
2. Put the child widgets in layouts.
3. Set the tab order.
4. Establish signal–slot connections.
5. Implement the dialog's custom slots.

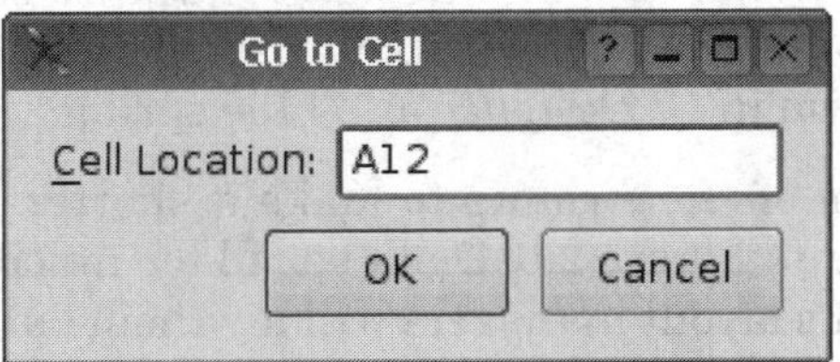

Figure 2.4. The Go to Cell dialog

To launch *Qt Designer*, click Qt by Trolltech v4.x.y|Designer in the Start menu on Windows, type `designer` on the command line on Unix, or double-click Designer in the Mac OS X Finder. When *Qt Designer* starts, it will pop up a list of templates. Click the "Widget" template, then click Create. (The "Dialog with Buttons Bottom" template might look tempting, but for this example we will create the OK and Cancel buttons by hand to show how it is done.) You should now have a window called "Untitled".

By default, *Qt Designer*'s user interface consists of several top-level windows. If you prefer an MDI-style interface, with one top-level window and several subwindows, as shown in Figure 2.5, click Edit|Preferences and set the user interface mode to Docked Window.

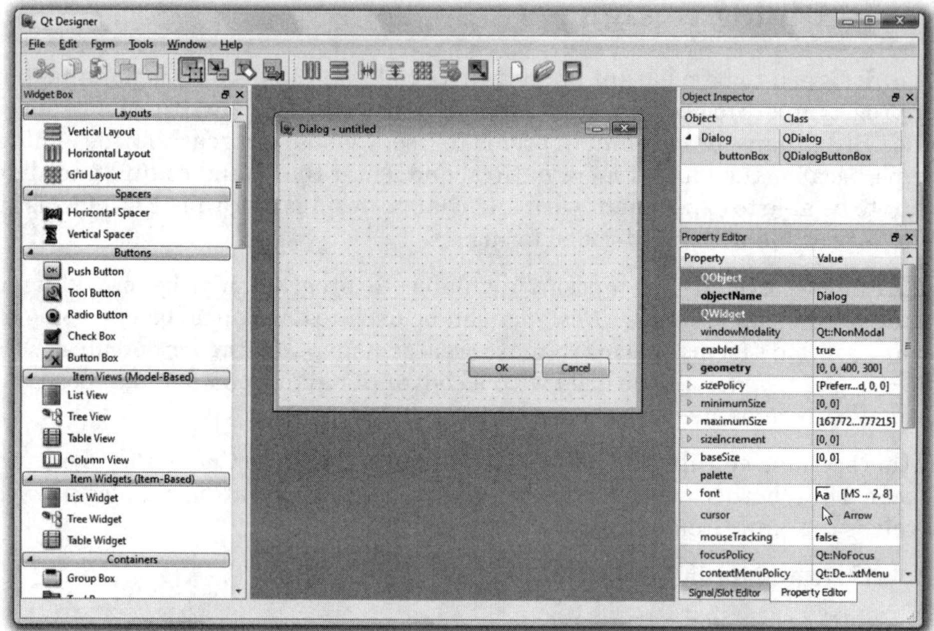

Figure 2.5. *Qt Designer* in docked window mode on Windows Vista

The first step is to create the child widgets and place them on the form. Create one label, one line editor, one horizontal spacer, and two push buttons. For each item, drag its name or icon from *Qt Designer*'s widget box and drop the item roughly where it should go on the form. The spacer item, which is invisible in the final form, is shown in *Qt Designer* as a blue spring.

Now drag the bottom of the form up to make it shorter. This should produce a form that is similar to Figure 2.6. Don't spend too much time positioning the items on the form; Qt's layout managers will lay them out precisely later on.

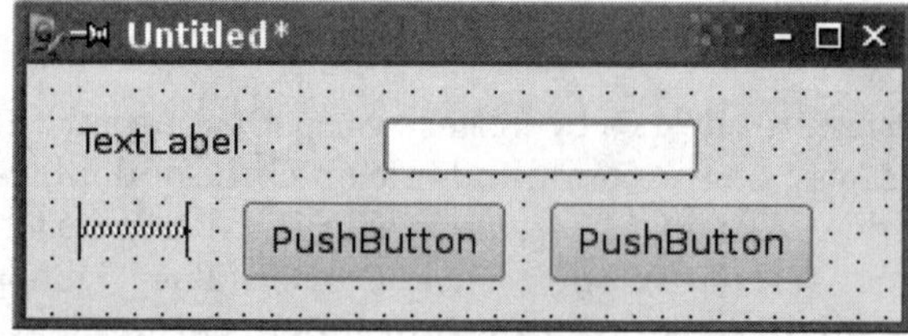

Figure 2.6. The form with some widgets

Set each widget's properties using *Qt Designer*'s property editor:

1. Click the text label. Make sure that its `objectName` property is "label" and set the `text` property to "&Cell Location:".
2. Click the line editor. Make sure that the `objectName` property is "lineEdit".

3. Click the first button. Set the `objectName` property to "okButton", the `enabled` property to "false", the `text` property to "OK", and the `default` property to "true".
4. Click the second button. Set the `objectName` property to "cancelButton" and the `text` property to "Cancel".
5. Click the form's background to select the form itself. Set the `objectName` property to "GoToCellDialog" and the `windowTitle` property to "Go to Cell".

All the widgets look fine now, except the text label, which shows &Cell Location. Click Edit|Edit Buddies to enter a special mode that allows you to set buddies. Next, click the label and drag the red arrow line to the line editor, then release. The label should now appear as Cell Location, as shown in Figure 2.7, and have the line editor as its buddy. Click Edit|Edit Widgets to leave buddy mode.

Figure 2.7. The form with properties set

The next step is to lay out the widgets on the form:

1. Click the Cell Location label and press Shift as you click the line editor next to it so that they are both selected. Click Form|Lay Out Horizontally.
2. Click the spacer, then hold Shift as you click the form's OK and Cancel buttons. Click Form|Lay Out Horizontally.
3. Click the background of the form to deselect any selected items, then click Form|Lay Out Vertically.
4. Click Form|Adjust Size to resize the form to its preferred size.

The red lines that appear on the form show the layouts that have been created, as shown in Figure 2.8. They don't appear when the form is run.

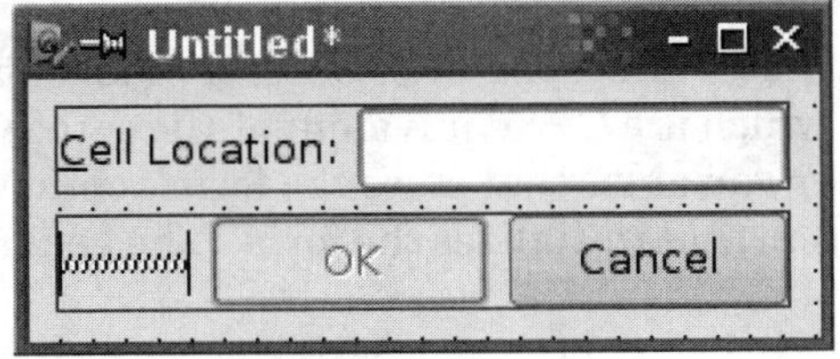

Figure 2.8. The form with the layouts

Now click Edit|Edit Tab Order. A number in a blue rectangle will appear next to every widget that can accept focus, as shown in Figure 2.9. Click each widget in turn in the order you want them to accept focus, then click Edit|Edit Widgets to leave tab order mode.

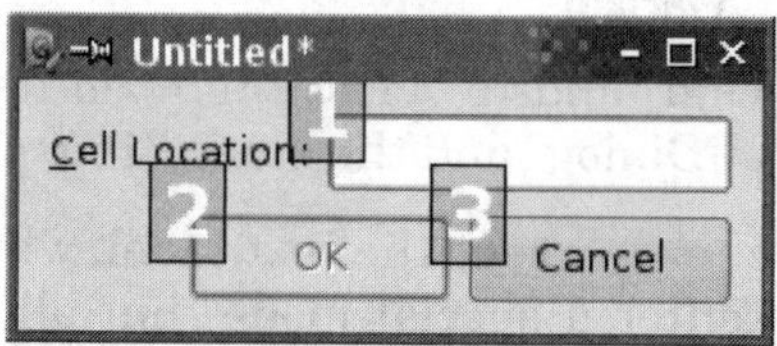

Figure 2.9. Setting the form's tab order

To preview the dialog, click the Form|Preview menu option. Check the tab order by pressing Tab repeatedly. Close the dialog using the close button in the title bar.

Save the dialog as `gotocelldialog.ui` in a directory called `gotocell`, and create a `main.cpp` file in the same directory using a plain text editor:

```
#include <QApplication>
#include <QDialog>

#include "ui_gotocelldialog.h"

int main(int argc, char *argv[])
{
    QApplication app(argc, argv);

    Ui::GoToCellDialog ui;
    QDialog *dialog = new QDialog;
    ui.setupUi(dialog);
    dialog->show();

    return app.exec();
}
```

Now run `qmake` to create a `.pro` file and a makefile (`qmake -project; qmake gotocell.pro`). The `qmake` tool is smart enough to detect the user interface file `gotocelldialog.ui` and to generate the appropriate makefile rules to invoke `uic`, Qt's user interface compiler. The `uic` tool converts `gotocelldialog.ui` into C++ and puts the result in `ui_gotocelldialog.h`.

The generated `ui_gotocelldialog.h` file contains the definition of the `Ui::GoToCellDialog` class, which is a C++ equivalent of the `gotocelldialog.ui` file. The class declares member variables that store the form's child widgets and layouts, and a `setupUi()` function that initializes the form. The generated class looks like this:

```
class Ui::GoToCellDialog
{
public:
    QLabel *label;
```

```
        QLineEdit *lineEdit;
        QSpacerItem *spacerItem;
        QPushButton *okButton;
        QPushButton *cancelButton;
        ...

        void setupUi(QWidget *widget) {
            ...
        }
    };
```

The generated class doesn't have any base class. When we use the form in `main.cpp`, we create a `QDialog` and pass it to `setupUi()`.

If you run the program now, the dialog will work, but it doesn't function exactly as we want:

- The OK button is always disabled.
- The Cancel button does nothing.
- The line editor accepts any text, instead of accepting only valid cell locations.

We can make the dialog function properly by writing some code. The cleanest approach is to create a new class that is derived from both `QDialog` and `Ui::GoToCellDialog` and that implements the missing functionality (thus proving the adage that any software problem can be solved simply by adding another layer of indirection). Our naming convention is to give this new class the same name as the `uic`-generated class but without the `Ui::` prefix.

Using a text editor, create a file called `gotocelldialog.h` that contains the following code:

```
#ifndef GOTOCELLDIALOG_H
#define GOTOCELLDIALOG_H

#include <QDialog>

#include "ui_gotocelldialog.h"

class GoToCellDialog : public QDialog, public Ui::GoToCellDialog
{
    Q_OBJECT

public:
    GoToCellDialog(QWidget *parent = 0);

private slots:
    void on_lineEdit_textChanged();
};

#endif
```

Here, we have used public inheritance because we want to access the dialog's widgets from outside the dialog. The implementation belongs in the `gotocelldialog.cpp` file:

```
#include <QtGui>

#include "gotocelldialog.h"

GoToCellDialog::GoToCellDialog(QWidget *parent)
    : QDialog(parent)
{
    setupUi(this);

    QRegExp regExp("[A-Za-z][1-9][0-9]{0,2}");
    lineEdit->setValidator(new QRegExpValidator(regExp, this));

    connect(okButton, SIGNAL(clicked()), this, SLOT(accept()));
    connect(cancelButton, SIGNAL(clicked()), this, SLOT(reject()));
}

void GoToCellDialog::on_lineEdit_textChanged()
{
    okButton->setEnabled(lineEdit->hasAcceptableInput());
}
```

In the constructor, we call `setupUi()` to initialize the form. Thanks to multiple inheritance, we can access `Ui::GoToCellDialog`'s members directly. After creating the user interface, `setupUi()` will also automatically connect any slots that follow the naming convention `on_`*`objectName`*`_`*`signalName`*`()` to the corresponding *`objectName`*'s *`signalName`*`()` signal. In our example, this means that `setupUi()` will establish the following signal–slot connection:

```
connect(lineEdit, SIGNAL(textChanged(const QString &)),
        this, SLOT(on_lineEdit_textChanged()));
```

Also in the constructor, we set up a validator to restrict the range of the input. Qt provides three built-in validator classes: `QIntValidator`, `QDoubleValidator`, and `QRegExpValidator`. Here we use a `QRegExpValidator` with the regular expression "[A-Za-z][1-9][0-9]{0,2}", which means: Allow one uppercase or lowercase letter, followed by one digit in the range 1 to 9, followed by zero, one, or two digits each in the range 0 to 9. (For an introduction to regular expressions, see the `QRegExp` class documentation.)

By passing `this` to the `QRegExpValidator` constructor, we make it a child of the `GoToCellDialog` object. By doing so, we don't have to worry about deleting the `QRegExpValidator` later; it will be deleted automatically when its parent is deleted.

Qt's parent–child mechanism is implemented in `QObject`. When we create an object (a widget, validator, or any other kind) with a parent, the parent adds the object to the list of its children. When the parent is deleted, it walks through its list of children and deletes each child. The children themselves then delete all of their children, and so on recursively until none remain. The parent–child mechanism greatly simplifies memory management, reducing the risk of memory leaks. The only objects we must call `delete` on are the objects we create with `new` and that have no parent. And if we delete a child object before its parent, Qt will automatically remove that object from the parent's list of children.

For widgets, the parent has an additional meaning: Child widgets are shown within the parent's area. When we delete the parent widget, not only does the child vanish from memory, it also vanishes from the screen.

At the end of the constructor, we connect the OK button to QDialog's accept() slot and the Cancel button to the reject() slot. Both slots close the dialog, but accept() sets the dialog's result value to QDialog::Accepted (which equals 1), and reject() sets the result to QDialog::Rejected (which equals 0). When we use this dialog, we can use the result to see if the user clicked OK and act accordingly.

The on_lineEdit_textChanged() slot enables or disables the OK button, according to whether the line editor contains a valid cell location. QLineEdit::hasAcceptableInput() uses the validator we set in the constructor.

This completes the dialog. We can now rewrite main.cpp to use it:

```
#include <QApplication>

#include "gotocelldialog.h"

int main(int argc, char *argv[])
{
    QApplication app(argc, argv);
    GoToCellDialog *dialog = new GoToCellDialog;
    dialog->show();
    return app.exec();
}
```

Regenerate gotocell.pro using qmake -project (since we have added source files to the project), run qmake gotocell.pro to update the makefile, then build and run the application again. Type "A12" in the line editor, and notice that the OK button becomes enabled. Try typing some random text to see how the validator does its job. Click Cancel to close the dialog.

The dialog works correctly, but for Mac OS X users, the buttons are the wrong way round. We chose to add each button individually, to show how it was done, but really we should have used a QDialogButtonBox, a widget that contains the buttons we specify and that presents them in the correct way for the window system on which the application is being run, as shown in Figure 2.10.

To make the dialog use a QDialogButtonBox, we must change both the design and the code. In *Qt Designer*, there are just four steps to take:

1. Click the form (not any of the widgets or layouts) and then click Form|Break Layout.
2. Click and delete the OK button, the Cancel button, the horizontal spacer, and the (now empty) horizontal layout.
3. Drag a "Button Box" onto the form, below the cell location label and line editor.
4. Click the form and then click Form|Lay Out Vertically.

If we had just been doing design changes, such as changing the dialog's layouts and widget properties, we would be able to simply rebuild the application. But here we have removed some widgets and added a new widget, and in these cases we must usually change the code too.

The changes we must make are all in the file gotocelldialog.cpp. Here is the new version of the constructor:

```
GoToCellDialog::GoToCellDialog(QWidget *parent)
    : QDialog(parent)
{
    setupUi(this);
    buttonBox->button(QDialogButtonBox::Ok)->setEnabled(false);

    QRegExp regExp("[A-Za-z][1-9][0-9]{0,2}");
    lineEdit->setValidator(new QRegExpValidator(regExp, this));

    connect(buttonBox, SIGNAL(accepted()), this, SLOT(accept()));
    connect(buttonBox, SIGNAL(rejected()), this, SLOT(reject()));
}
```

In the previous version, we initially disabled the OK button in *Qt Designer*. We cannot do that with a QDialogButtonBox, so we do so in code, immediately after the setupUi() call. The QDialogButtonBox class has an enum of standard buttons, and we can use this to access particular buttons, in this case the OK button.

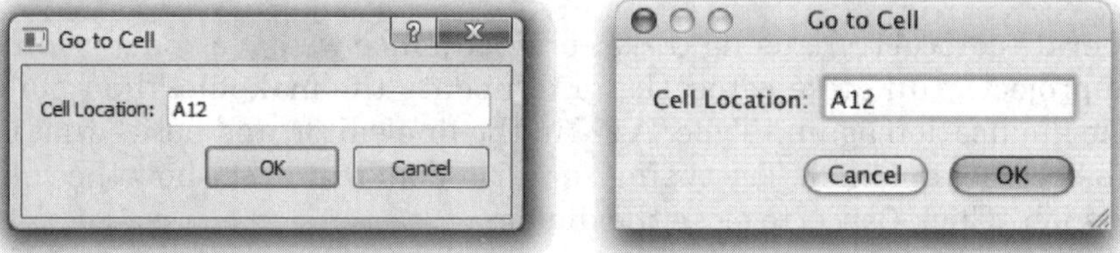

Figure 2.10. The Go to Cell dialog on Windows Vista and Mac OS X

Very conveniently, *Qt Designer*'s default name for a QDialogButtonBox is buttonBox. Both connections are made from the button box rather than from the buttons themselves. The accepted() signal is emitted when a button with the AcceptRole is clicked, and similarly the rejected() signal is emitted by a button with the RejectRole. By default, the standard QDialogButtonBox::Ok button has the AcceptRole, and the QDialogButtonBox::Cancel button has the RejectRole.

Only one more change is required, in the on_lineEdit_textChanged() slot:

```
void GoToCellDialog::on_lineEdit_textChanged()
{
    buttonBox->button(QDialogButtonBox::Ok)->setEnabled(
            lineEdit->hasAcceptableInput());
}
```

The only thing different from before is that instead of referring to a particular button stored as a member variable, we access the button box's OK button.

One of the beauties of using *Qt Designer* is that it allows programmers great freedom to modify their form designs without being forced to change their source code. When you develop a form purely by writing C++ code, changes to the design can be quite time-consuming. With *Qt Designer*, no time is lost since `uic` simply regenerates the source code for any forms that have changed. The dialog's user interface is saved in a `.ui` file (an XML-based file format), while custom functionality is implemented by subclassing the `uic`-generated class.

Shape-Changing Dialogs

We have seen how to create dialogs that always show the same widgets whenever they are used. In some cases, it is desirable to provide dialogs that can change shape. The two most common kinds of shape-changing dialogs are *extension dialogs* and *multi-page dialogs*. Both types of dialog can be implemented in Qt, either purely in code or using *Qt Designer*.

Extension dialogs usually present a simple appearance but have a toggle button that allows the user to switch between the dialog's simple and extended appearances. Extension dialogs are commonly used for applications that are trying to cater to both casual and power users, hiding the advanced options unless the user explicitly asks to see them. In this section, we will use *Qt Designer* to create the extension dialog shown in Figure 2.11.

The dialog is a Sort dialog in a spreadsheet application, where the user can select one or several columns on which to sort. The dialog's simple appearance allows the user to enter a single sort key, and its extended appearance provides for two extra sort keys. A More button lets the user switch between the simple and extended appearances.

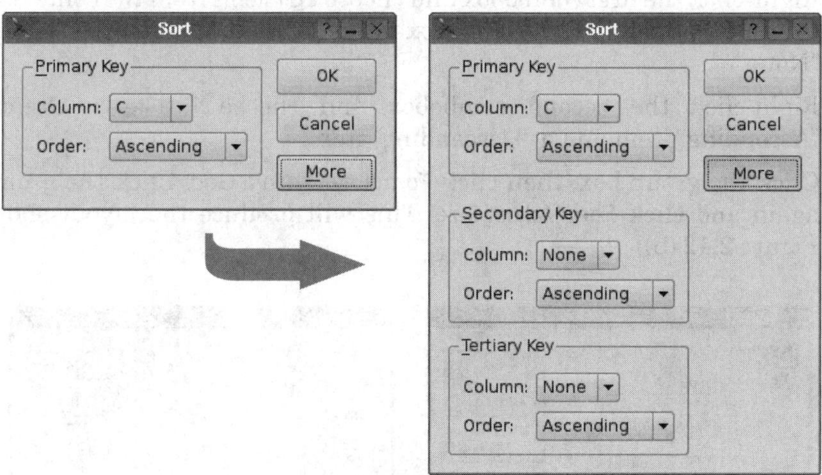

Figure 2.11. The Sort dialog with simple and extended appearances

We will create the widget with its extended appearance in *Qt Designer*, and hide the secondary and tertiary keys at run-time as needed. The widget looks complicated, but it's fairly easy to do in *Qt Designer*. The trick is to do the primary key part first, then duplicate it twice to obtain the secondary and tertiary keys:

1. Click File|New Form and choose the "Dialog without Buttons" template.
2. Create an OK button and drag it to the top right of the form. Change its `objectName` to "okButton" and set its `default` property to "true".
3. Create a Cancel button, and drag it below the OK button. Change its `objectName` to "cancelButton".
4. Create a vertical spacer and drag it below the Cancel button, then create a More button and drag it below the vertical spacer. Change the More button's `objectName` to "moreButton", set its `text` property to "&More", and its `checkable` property to "true".
5. Click the OK button, then Shift+Click the Cancel button, the vertical spacer, and the More button, then click Form|Lay Out Vertically.
6. Create a group box, two labels, two comboboxes, and one horizontal spacer, and put them anywhere on the form.
7. Drag the bottom-right corner of the group box to make it larger. Then move the other widgets into the group box and position them approximately as shown in Figure 2.12 (a).
8. Drag the right edge of the second combobox to make it about twice as wide as the first combobox.
9. Set the group box's `title` property to "&Primary Key", the first label's `text` property to "Column:", and the second label's `text` property to "Order:".
10. Right-click the first combobox and choose Edit Items from the context menu to pop up *Qt Designer*'s combobox editor. Create one item with the text "None".
11. Right-click the second combobox and choose Edit Items. Create an "Ascending" item and a "Descending" item.
12. Click the group box, then click Form|Lay Out in a Grid. Click the group box again and click Form|Adjust Size. This will produce the layout shown in Figure 2.12 (b).

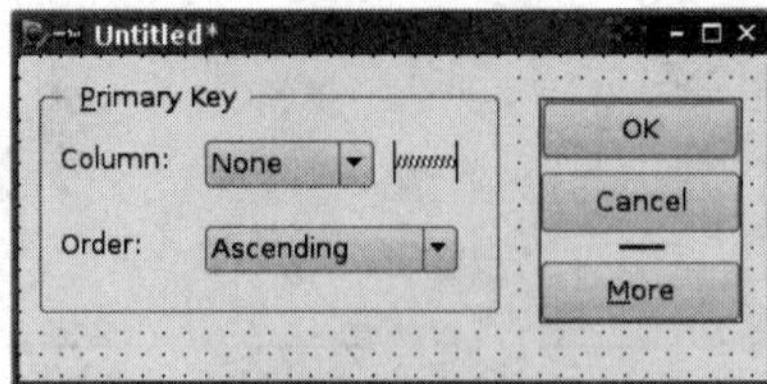

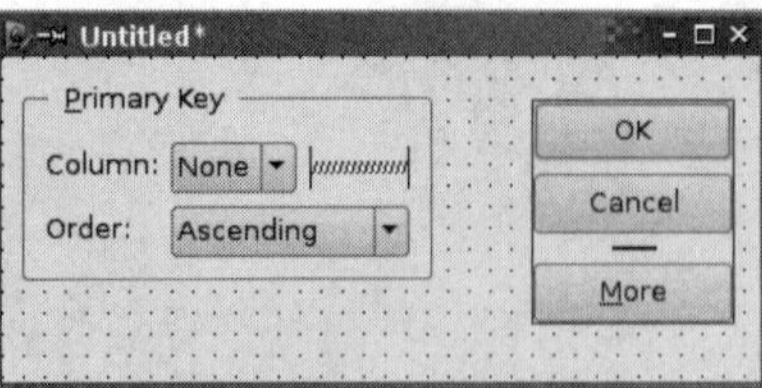

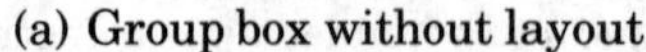
(a) Group box without layout (b) Group box with layout

Figure 2.12. Laying out the group box's children in a grid

If a layout doesn't turn out quite right or if you make a mistake, you can always click Edit|Undo or Form|Break Layout, then reposition the widgets and try again.

We will now add the Secondary Key and Tertiary Key group boxes:

1. Make the dialog window tall enough for the extra parts.
2. Hold down the Ctrl key (Alt on the Mac) and click and drag the Primary Key group box to create a copy of the group box (and its contents) on top of the original. Drag the copy below the original group box, while still pressing Ctrl (or Alt). Repeat this process to create a third group box, dragging it below the second group box.
3. Change their `title` properties to "&Secondary Key" and "&Tertiary Key".
4. Create one vertical spacer and place it between the primary key group box and the secondary key group box.
5. Arrange the widgets in the grid-like pattern shown in Figure 2.13 (a).
6. Click the form to deselect any selected widgets, then click Form|Lay Out in a Grid. Now drag the form's bottom-right corner up and left to make the form as small as it will go. The form should now match Figure 2.13 (b).
7. Set the two vertical spacer items' `sizeHint` property to [20, 0].

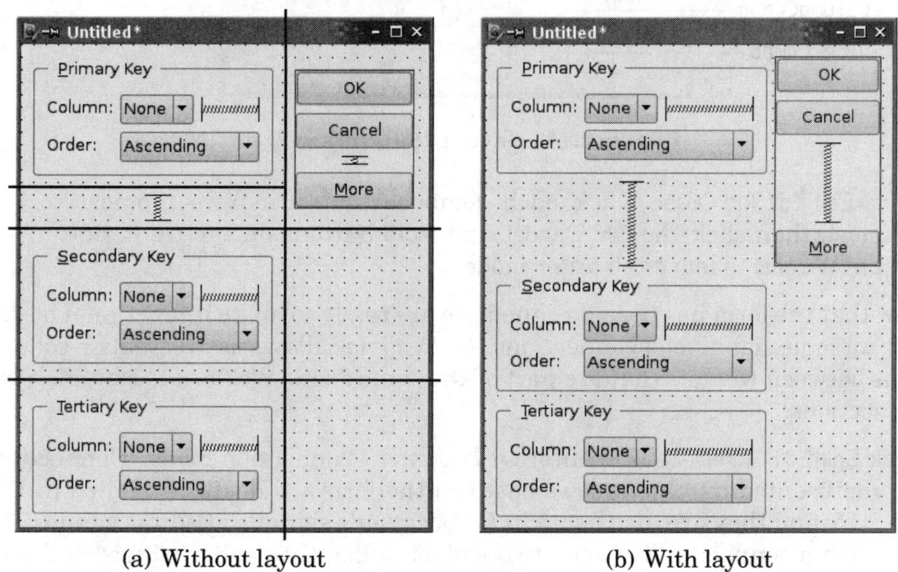

(a) Without layout (b) With layout

Figure 2.13. Laying out the form's children in a grid

The resulting grid layout has two columns and four rows, giving a total of eight cells. The Primary Key group box, the leftmost vertical spacer item, the Secondary Key group box, and the Tertiary Key group box each occupy a single cell. The vertical layout that contains the OK, Cancel, and More buttons occupies two cells.

That leaves two empty cells in the bottom right of the dialog. If this isn't what you have, undo the layout, reposition the widgets, and try again.

Rename the form "SortDialog" and change the window title to "Sort". Set the names of the child widgets to those shown in Figure 2.14.

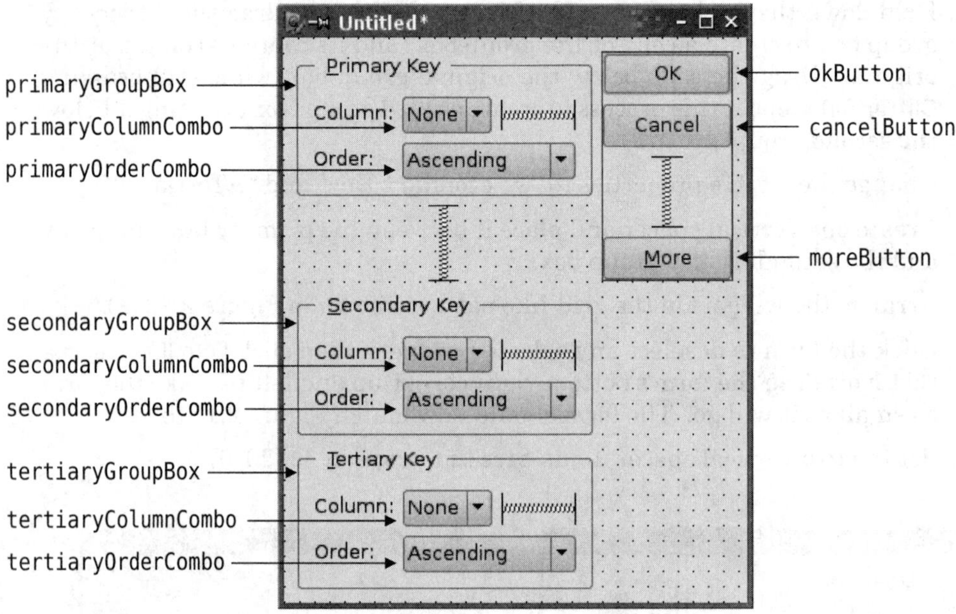

Figure 2.14. Naming the form's widgets

Click Edit|Edit Tab Order. Click each combobox in turn from topmost to bottommost, then click the OK, Cancel, and More buttons on the right side. Click Edit|Edit Widgets to leave tab order mode.

Now that the form has been designed, we are ready to make it functional by setting up some signal–slot connections. *Qt Designer* allows us to establish connections between widgets that are part of the same form. We need to establish two connections.

Click Edit|Edit Signals/Slots to enter *Qt Designer*'s connection mode. Connections are represented by blue arrows between the form's widgets, as shown in Figure 2.15, and they are also listed in *Qt Designer*'s signal/slot editor window. To establish a connection between two widgets, click the sender widget and drag the red arrow line to the receiver widget, then release. This pops up a dialog that allows you to choose the signal and the slot to connect.

The first connection to be made is between the `okButton` and the form's `accept()` slot. Drag the red arrow line from the `okButton` to an empty part of the form, then release to pop up the Configure Connection dialog shown in Figure 2.16. Choose `clicked()` as the signal and `accept()` as the slot, then click OK.

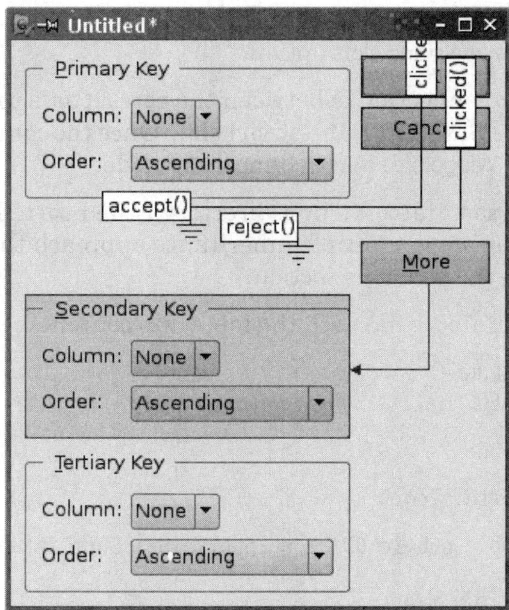

Figure 2.15. Connecting the form's widgets

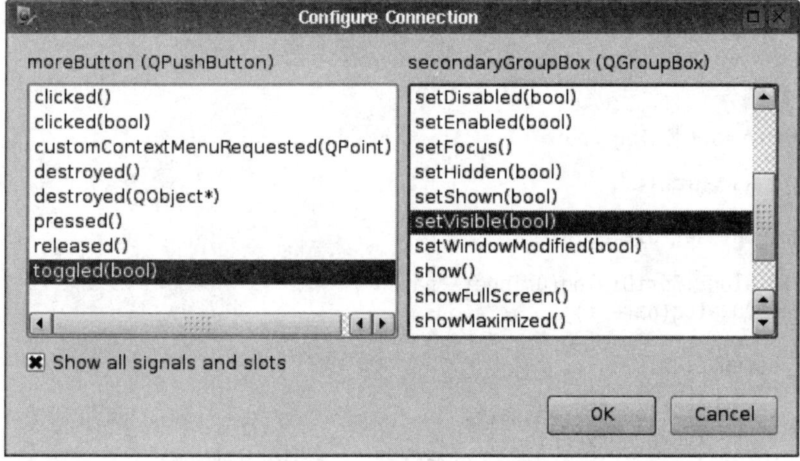

Figure 2.16. *Qt Designer*'s connection editor

For the second connection, drag the red arrow line from the `cancelButton` to an empty part of the form, and in the Configure Connection dialog connect the button's `clicked()` signal to the form's `reject()` slot.

The third connection to establish is between the `moreButton` and the `secondaryGroupBox`. Drag the red arrow line between these two widgets, then choose `toggled(bool)` as the signal and `setVisible(bool)` as the slot. By default, *Qt De-*

signer doesn't list setVisible(bool) in the list of slots, but it will appear if you enable the Show all signals and slots option.

The fourth and last connection is between the moreButton's toggled(bool) signal and the tertiaryGroupBox's setVisible(bool) slot. Once the connections have been made, click Edit|Edit Widgets to leave connection mode.

Save the dialog as sortdialog.ui in a directory called sort. To add code to the form, we will use the same multiple inheritance approach that we used for the Go to Cell dialog in the previous section.

First, create a sortdialog.h file with the following contents:

```
#ifndef SORTDIALOG_H
#define SORTDIALOG_H

#include <QDialog>

#include "ui_sortdialog.h"

class SortDialog : public QDialog, public Ui::SortDialog
{
    Q_OBJECT

public:
    SortDialog(QWidget *parent = 0);

    void setColumnRange(QChar first, QChar last);
};

#endif
```

Now create sortdialog.cpp:

```
#include <QtGui>

#include "sortdialog.h"

SortDialog::SortDialog(QWidget *parent)
    : QDialog(parent)
{
    setupUi(this);

    secondaryGroupBox->hide();
    tertiaryGroupBox->hide();
    layout()->setSizeConstraint(QLayout::SetFixedSize);

    setColumnRange('A', 'Z');
}

void SortDialog::setColumnRange(QChar first, QChar last)
{
    primaryColumnCombo->clear();
    secondaryColumnCombo->clear();
    tertiaryColumnCombo->clear();

    secondaryColumnCombo->addItem(tr("None"));
    tertiaryColumnCombo->addItem(tr("None"));
```

```
19     primaryColumnCombo->setMinimumSize(
20             secondaryColumnCombo->sizeHint());

21     QChar ch = first;
22     while (ch <= last) {
23         primaryColumnCombo->addItem(QString(ch));
24         secondaryColumnCombo->addItem(QString(ch));
25         tertiaryColumnCombo->addItem(QString(ch));
26         ch = ch.unicode() + 1;
27     }
28 }
```

The constructor hides the secondary and tertiary parts of the dialog. It also sets the `sizeConstraint` property of the form's layout to `QLayout::SetFixedSize`, making the dialog non-resizable by the user. The layout then takes over the responsibility for resizing, and resizes the dialog automatically when child widgets are shown or hidden, ensuring that the dialog is always displayed at its optimal size.

The `setColumnRange()` slot initializes the contents of the comboboxes based on the selected columns in the spreadsheet. We insert a "None" item in the comboboxes for the (optional) secondary and tertiary keys.

Lines 19 and 20 present a subtle layout idiom. The `QWidget::sizeHint()` function returns a widget's "ideal" size, which the layout system tries to honor. This explains why different kinds of widgets, or similar widgets with different contents, may be assigned different sizes by the layout system. For comboboxes, this means that the secondary and tertiary comboboxes, which contain "None", end up larger than the primary combobox, which contains only single-letter entries. To avoid this inconsistency, we set the primary combobox's minimum size to the *secondary* combobox's ideal size.

Here is a `main()` test function that sets the range to include columns 'C' to 'F' and then shows the dialog:

```
#include <QApplication>

#include "sortdialog.h"

int main(int argc, char *argv[])
{
    QApplication app(argc, argv);
    SortDialog *dialog = new SortDialog;
    dialog->setColumnRange('C', 'F');
    dialog->show();
    return app.exec();
}
```

That completes the extension dialog. As the example illustrates, an extension dialog isn't much more difficult to design than a plain dialog: All we needed was a toggle button, a few extra signal–slot connections, and a non-resizable layout. In production applications, it is quite common for the button that controls the extension to show the text Advanced >>> when only the basic dialog is visible and Advanced <<< when the extension is shown. This is easy to achieve in Qt by calling setText() on the QPushButton whenever it is clicked.

The other common type of shape-changing dialogs, multi-page dialogs, are even easier to create in Qt, either in code or using *Qt Designer*. Such dialogs can be built in many different ways.

- A QTabWidget can be used in its own right. It provides a tab bar that controls a built-in QStackedWidget.
- A QListWidget and a QStackedWidget can be used together, with the QListWidget's current item determining which page the QStackedWidget shows, by connecting the QListWidget::currentRowChanged() signal to the QStackedWidget::setCurrentIndex() slot.
- A QTreeWidget can be used with a QStackedWidget in a similar way to a QListWidget.

We cover the QStackedWidget class in Chapter 6.

Dynamic Dialogs

Dynamic dialogs are dialogs that are created from *Qt Designer* .ui files at run-time. Instead of converting the .ui file to C++ code using uic, we can load the file at run-time using the QUiLoader class:

```
QUiLoader uiLoader;
QFile file("sortdialog.ui");
QWidget *sortDialog = uiLoader.load(&file);
if (sortDialog) {
    ...
}
```

We can access the form's child widgets using QObject::findChild<T>():

```
QComboBox *primaryColumnCombo =
        sortDialog->findChild<QComboBox *>("primaryColumnCombo");
if (primaryColumnCombo) {
    ...
}
```

The findChild<T>() function is a template member function that returns the child object that matches the given name and type. Because of a compiler limitation, it is not available for MSVC 6. If you need to use the MSVC 6 compiler, call the qFindChild<T>() global function instead, which works in essentially the same way.

The QUiLoader class is located in a separate library. To use QUiLoader from a Qt application, we must add this line to the application's .pro file:

```
CONFIG += uitools
```

Dynamic dialogs make it possible to change the layout of a form without recompiling the application. They can also be used to create thin-client applications, where the executable merely has a front-end form built-in and all other forms are created as required.

Built-in Widget and Dialog Classes

Qt provides a complete set of built-in widgets and common dialogs that cater to most situations. In this section, we present screenshots of almost all of them. A few specialized widgets are deferred until later: We cover main window widgets such as `QMenuBar`, `QToolBar`, and `QStatusBar` in Chapter 3, and we cover layout-related widgets such as `QSplitter` and `QScrollArea` in Chapter 6. Most of the built-in widgets and dialogs are used in the examples presented in this book. In the screenshots shown in Figures 2.17 to 2.26, all the widgets are shown using the Plastique style.

Qt provides four kinds of "buttons": `QPushButton`, `QToolButton`, `QCheckBox`, and `QRadioButton`; they are shown in Figure 2.17. `QPushButton` and `QToolButton` are most commonly used to initiate an action when they are clicked, but they can also behave like toggle buttons (click to press down, click to restore). `QCheckBox` can be used for independent on/off options, whereas `QRadioButton`s are normally mutually exclusive.

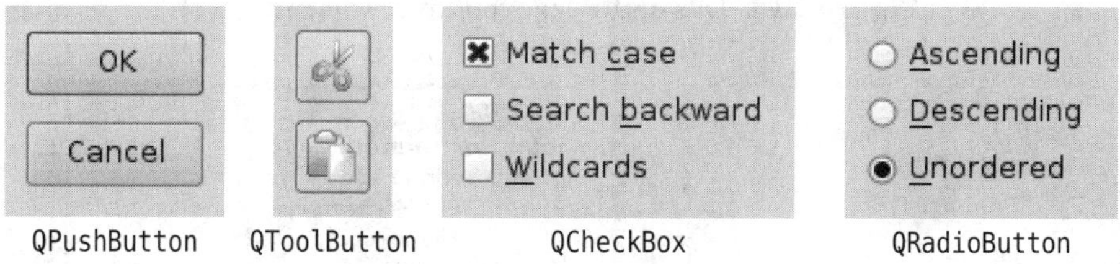

Figure 2.17. Qt's button widgets

Qt's container widgets are widgets that contain other widgets. They are shown in Figure 2.18 and Figure 2.19. `QFrame` can also be used on its own to simply draw lines and serves as the base class for many other widget classes, including `QToolBox` and `QLabel`.

`QTabWidget` and `QToolBox` are multi-page widgets. Each page is a child widget, and the pages are numbered starting from 0. For `QTabWidget`s, both the shape and the position of the tabs can be set.

The item views, shown in Figure 2.20, are optimized for handling large amounts of data and often use scroll bars. The scroll bar mechanism is implemented in `QAbstractScrollArea`, a base class for item views and other kinds of scrollable widgets.

The Qt library includes a rich text engine that can be used for displaying and editing formatted text. The engine supports font specifications, text alignments,

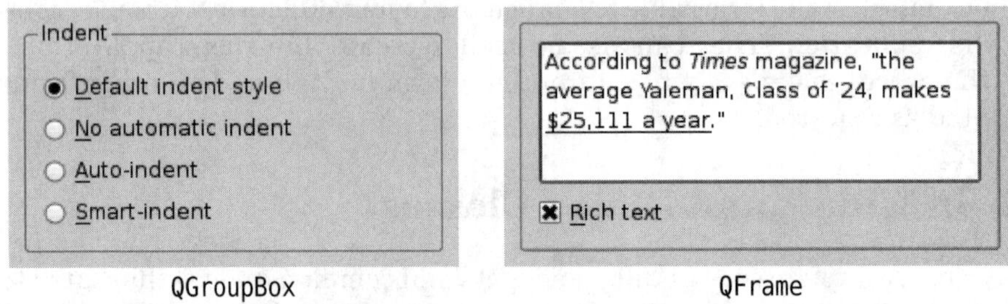

Figure 2.18. Qt's single-page container widgets

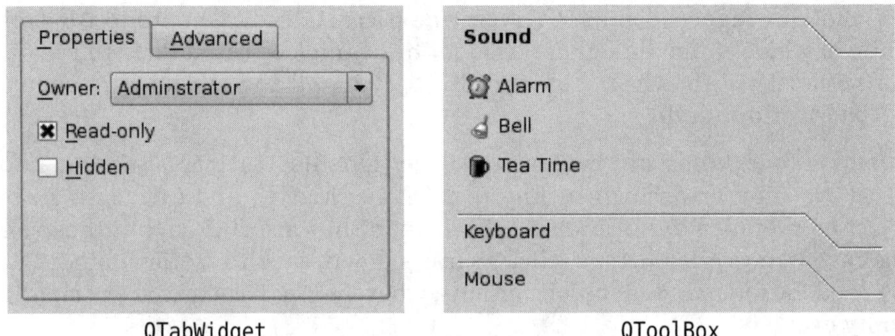

Figure 2.19. Qt's multi-page container widgets

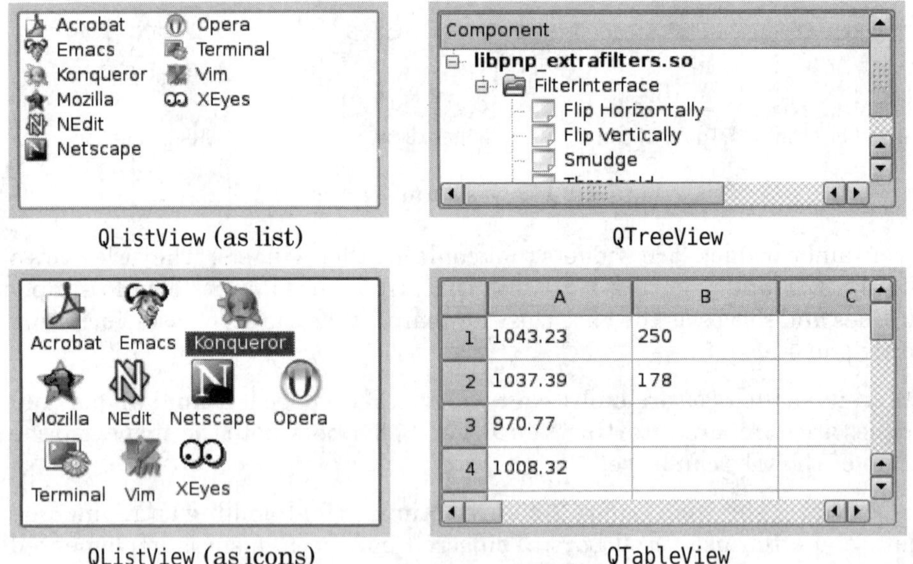

Figure 2.20. Qt's item view widgets

lists, tables, images, and hyperlinks. Rich text documents can be created programmatically element by element or supplied as HTML-formatted text. The precise HTML tags and CSS properties that the engine supports are documented at `http://doc.trolltech.com/4.3/richtext-html-subset.html`.

Qt provides a few widgets that are used purely for displaying information; they are shown in Figure 2.21. `QLabel` is the most important of these, and it can be used for showing plain text, HTML, and images.

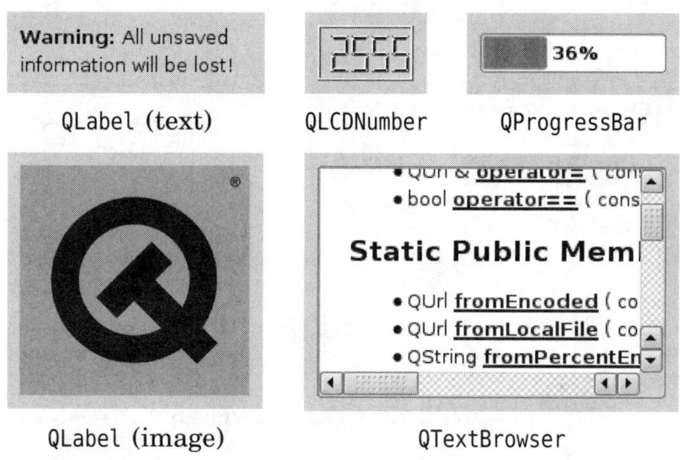

Figure 2.21. Qt's display widgets

`QTextBrowser` is a read-only `QTextEdit` subclass that can display formatted text. This class is used in preference to `QLabel` for large formatted text documents, because unlike `QLabel`, it automatically provides scroll bars when necessary, and also provides extensive support for keyboard and mouse navigation. *Qt Assistant* 4.3 uses `QTextBrowser` to present documentation to the user.

Qt provides several widgets for data entry, as shown in Figure 2.22. `QLineEdit` can restrict its input using an input mask, a validator, or both. `QTextEdit` is a `QAbstractScrollArea` subclass capable of editing large amounts of text. A `QTextEdit` can be set to edit plain text or rich text. In the latter case, it is able to display all of the elements that Qt's rich text engine supports. Both `QLineEdit` and `QTextEdit` are fully integrated with the clipboard.

Qt provides a versatile message box and an error dialog that remembers which messages it has shown—these are shown in Figure 2.23. The progress of time-consuming operations can be indicated using `QProgressDialog` or using the `QProgressBar` shown in Figure 2.21. `QInputDialog` is very convenient when a single line of text or a single number is required from the user.

Qt provides the standard set of common dialogs that make it easy to ask the user to select a color, font, or file, or to print a document. These are shown in Figure 2.24 and Figure 2.25.

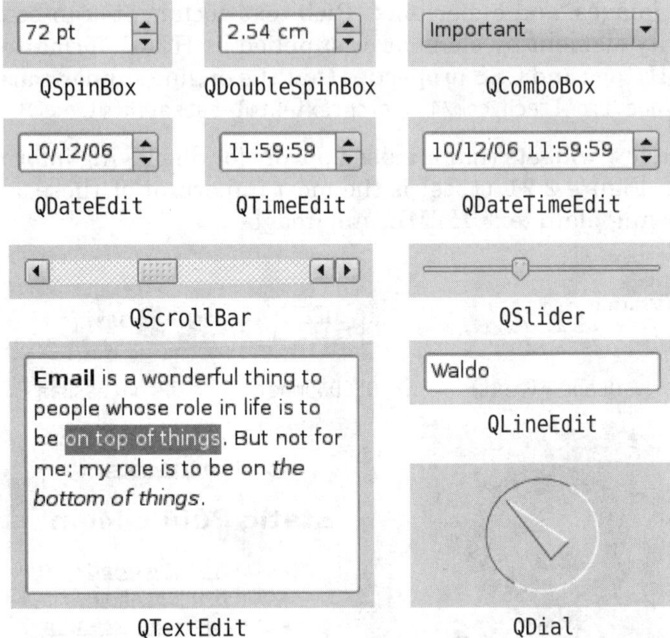

Figure 2.22. Qt's input widgets

On Windows and Mac OS X, Qt uses the native dialogs rather than its own common dialogs when possible. Colors can also be chosen using one of the Qt Solutions color selection widgets, and fonts can be chosen using the built-in QFontComboBox.

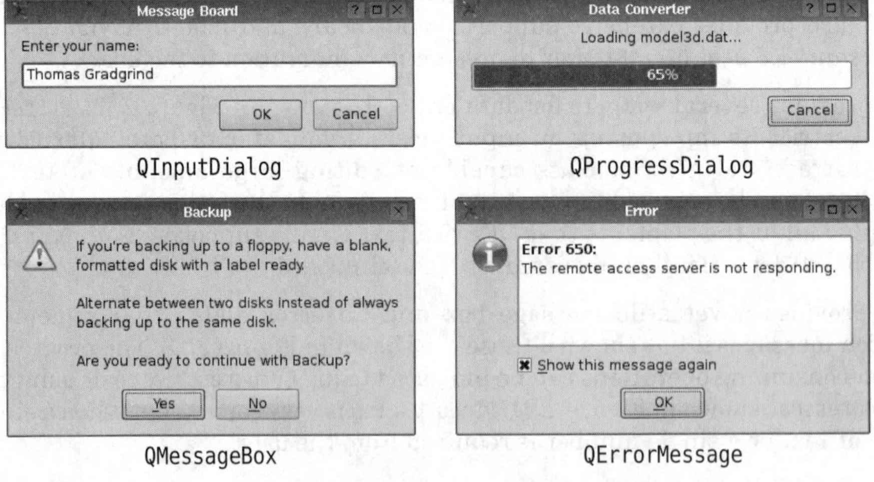

Figure 2.23. Qt's feedback dialogs

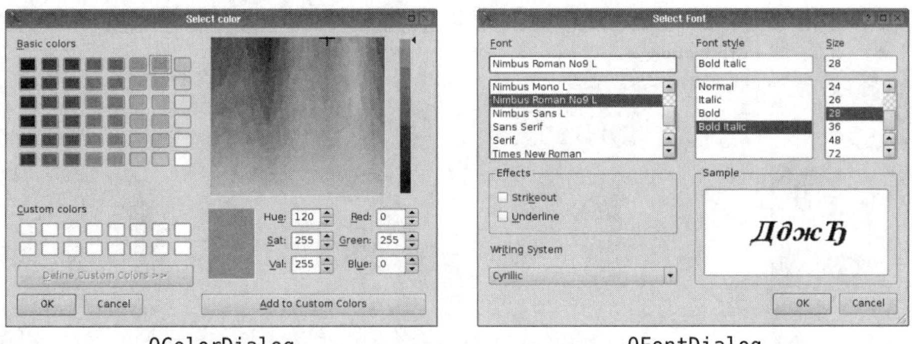

Figure 2.24. Qt's color and font dialogs

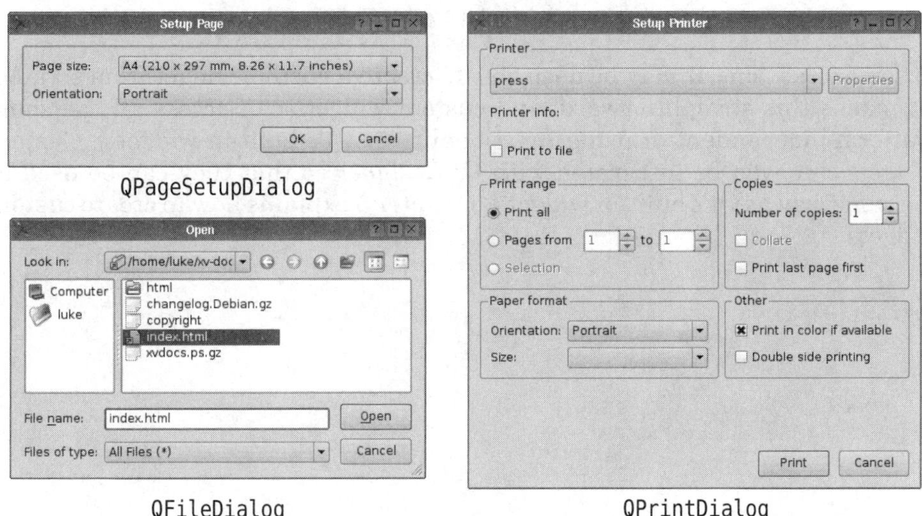

Figure 2.25. Qt's file and print dialogs

Finally, `QWizard` provides a framework for creating wizards (also called assistants on Mac OS X). Wizards are useful for complex or infrequent tasks that users may find difficult to learn. An example of a wizard is shown in Figure 2.26.

A lot of ready-to-use functionality is provided by the built-in widgets and common dialogs. More specialized requirements can often be satisfied by setting widget properties, or by connecting signals to slots and implementing custom behavior in the slots.

If none of the widgets or common dialogs provided with Qt is suitable, one may be available from Qt Solutions, or from a commercial or non-commercial third party. Qt Solutions provides a number of additional widgets, including various color choosers, a thumbwheel control, pie menus, and a property browser, as well as a copy dialog.

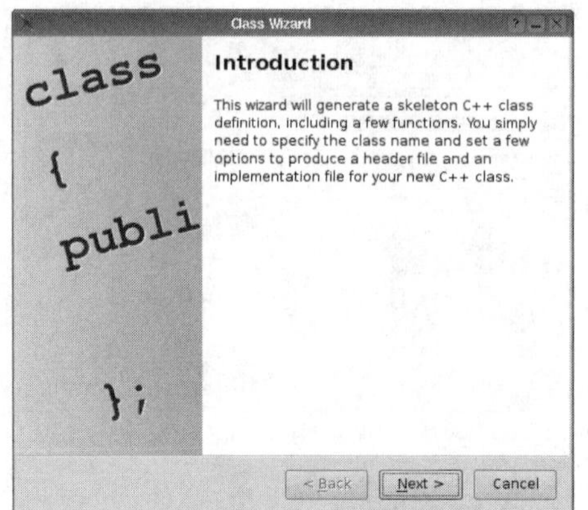

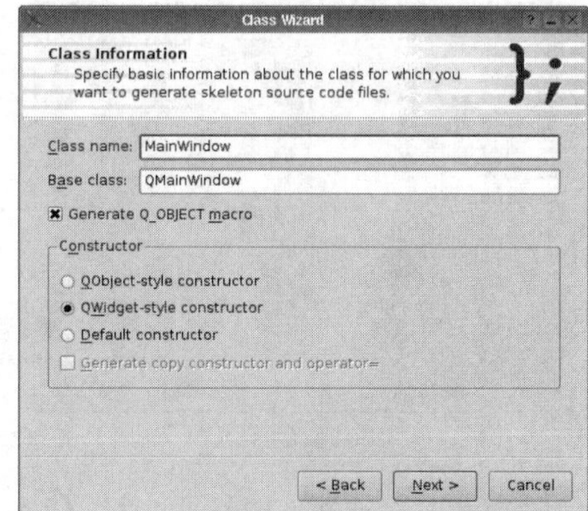

Figure 2.26. Qt's `QWizard` dialog

In some situations, it may be desirable to create a custom widget from scratch. Qt makes this straightforward, and custom widgets can access all the same platform-independent drawing functionality as Qt's built-in widgets. Custom widgets can even be integrated with *Qt Designer* so that they can be used in the same way as Qt's built-in widgets. Chapter 5 explains how to create custom widgets.

- *Subclassing QMainWindow*
- *Creating Menus and Toolbars*
- *Setting Up the Status Bar*
- *Implementing the File Menu*
- *Using Dialogs*
- *Storing Settings*
- *Multiple Documents*
- *Splash Screens*

3. Creating Main Windows

This chapter will teach you how to create main windows using Qt. By the end, you will be able to build an application's entire user interface, complete with menus, toolbars, a status bar, and as many dialogs as the application requires.

An application's main window provides the framework upon which the application's user interface is built. The main window for the Spreadsheet application shown in Figure 3.1 will form the basis of this chapter. The Spreadsheet application makes use of the Find, Go to Cell, and Sort dialogs that we created in Chapter 2.

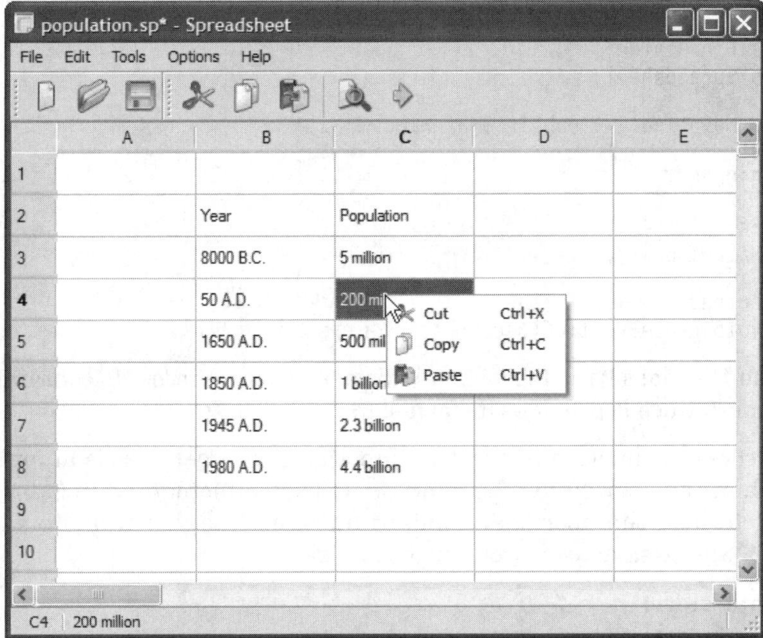

Figure 3.1. The spreadsheet application

Behind most GUI applications lies a body of code that provides the underlying functionality—for example, code to read and write files or to process the data presented in the user interface. In Chapter 4, we will see how to implement such functionality, again using the Spreadsheet application as our example.

Subclassing QMainWindow

An application's main window is created by subclassing QMainWindow. Many of the techniques we saw in Chapter 2 for creating dialogs are also relevant for creating main windows, since both QDialog and QMainWindow are derived from QWidget.

Main windows can be created using *Qt Designer*, but in this chapter we will do everything in code to demonstrate how it's done. If you prefer the more visual approach, see the "Creating Main Windows in *Qt Designer*" chapter in *Qt Designer*'s online manual.

The source code for the Spreadsheet application's main window is spread across mainwindow.h and mainwindow.cpp. Let's start with the header file:

```
#ifndef MAINWINDOW_H
#define MAINWINDOW_H

#include <QMainWindow>

class QAction;
class QLabel;
class FindDialog;
class Spreadsheet;

class MainWindow : public QMainWindow
{
    Q_OBJECT

public:
    MainWindow();

protected:
    void closeEvent(QCloseEvent *event);
```

We define the class MainWindow as a subclass of QMainWindow. It contains the Q_OBJECT macro since it provides its own signals and slots.

The closeEvent() function is a virtual function in QWidget that is automatically called when the user closes the window. It is reimplemented in MainWindow so that we can ask the user the standard question "Do you want to save your changes?" and to save user preferences to disk.

```
private slots:
    void newFile();
    void open();
    bool save();
    bool saveAs();
```

```
    void find();
    void goToCell();
    void sort();
    void about();
```

Some menu options, such as File|New and Help|About, are implemented as private slots in `MainWindow`. Most slots have `void` as their return value, but `save()` and `saveAs()` return a `bool`. The return value is ignored when a slot is executed in response to a signal, but when we call a slot as a function the return value is available to us just as it is when we call any ordinary C++ function.

```
    void openRecentFile();
    void updateStatusBar();
    void spreadsheetModified();

private:
    void createActions();
    void createMenus();
    void createContextMenu();
    void createToolBars();
    void createStatusBar();
    void readSettings();
    void writeSettings();
    bool okToContinue();
    bool loadFile(const QString &fileName);
    bool saveFile(const QString &fileName);
    void setCurrentFile(const QString &fileName);
    void updateRecentFileActions();
    QString strippedName(const QString &fullFileName);
```

The main window needs some more private slots and several private functions to support the user interface.

```
    Spreadsheet *spreadsheet;
    FindDialog *findDialog;
    QLabel *locationLabel;
    QLabel *formulaLabel;
    QStringList recentFiles;
    QString curFile;

    enum { MaxRecentFiles = 5 };
    QAction *recentFileActions[MaxRecentFiles];
    QAction *separatorAction;

    QMenu *fileMenu;
    QMenu *editMenu;
    ...
    QToolBar *fileToolBar;
    QToolBar *editToolBar;
    QAction *newAction;
    QAction *openAction;
    ...
    QAction *aboutQtAction;
};

#endif
```

In addition to its private slots and private functions, MainWindow also has lots of private variables. We will explain all of these as we use them.

We will now review the implementation:

```
#include <QtGui>

#include "finddialog.h"
#include "gotocelldialog.h"
#include "mainwindow.h"
#include "sortdialog.h"
#include "spreadsheet.h"
```

We include the <QtGui> header file, which contains the definition of all the Qt classes used in our subclass. We also include some custom header files, notably finddialog.h, gotocelldialog.h, and sortdialog.h from Chapter 2.

```
MainWindow::MainWindow()
{
    spreadsheet = new Spreadsheet;
    setCentralWidget(spreadsheet);

    createActions();
    createMenus();
    createContextMenu();
    createToolBars();
    createStatusBar();

    readSettings();

    findDialog = 0;

    setWindowIcon(QIcon(":/images/icon.png"));
    setCurrentFile("");
}
```

In the constructor, we begin by creating a Spreadsheet widget and setting it to be the main window's central widget. The central widget occupies the middle of the main window (see Figure 3.2). The Spreadsheet class is a QTableWidget subclass with some spreadsheet capabilities, such as support for spreadsheet formulas. We will implement it in Chapter 4.

We call the private functions createActions(), createMenus(), createContextMenu(), createToolBars(), and createStatusBar() to set up the rest of the main window. We also call the private function readSettings() to read the application's stored settings.

We initialize the findDialog pointer to be a null pointer. The first time MainWindow::find() is called, we will create the FindDialog object.

At the end of the constructor, we set the window's icon to icon.png, a PNG file. Qt supports many image formats, including BMP, GIF, JPEG, PNG, PNM, SVG, TIFF, XBM, and XPM. Calling QWidget::setWindowIcon() sets the icon shown in the top-left corner of the window. Unfortunately, there is no platform-indepen-

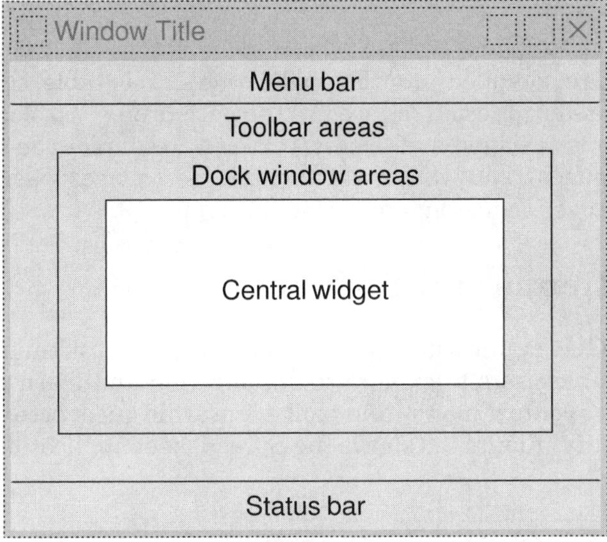

Figure 3.2. QMainWindow's areas

dent way of setting the application icon that appears on the desktop. Platform-specific procedures are explained at `http://doc.trolltech.com/4.3/appicon.html`.

GUI applications generally use many images. There are several methods for providing images to the application. The most common are the following:

- Storing images in files and loading them at run-time.
- Including XPM files in the source code. (This works because XPM files are also valid C++ files.)
- Using Qt's resource mechanism.

Here we use Qt's resource mechanism because it is more convenient than loading files at run-time, and it works with any supported file format. We have chosen to store the images in the source tree in a subdirectory called `images`.

To make use of Qt's resource system, we must create a resource file and add a line to the `.pro` file that identifies the resource file. In this example, we have called the resource file `spreadsheet.qrc`, so we put the following line in the `.pro` file:

```
RESOURCES = spreadsheet.qrc
```

The resource file itself uses a simple XML format. Here's an extract from the one we have used:

```
<RCC>
<qresource>
    <file>images/icon.png</file>
    ...
    <file>images/gotocell.png</file>
```

```
</qresource>
</RCC>
```

Resource files are compiled into the application's executable, so they can't get lost. When we refer to resources, we use the path prefix `:/` (colon slash), which is why the icon is specified as `:/images/icon.png`. Resources can be any kind of file (not just images), and we can use them in most places where Qt expects a file name. We cover them in more detail in Chapter 12.

Creating Menus and Toolbars

Most modern GUI applications provide menus, context menus, and toolbars. The menus enable users to explore the application and learn how to do new things, while the context menus and toolbars provide quick access to frequently used functionality. Figure 3.3 shows the Spreadsheet application's menus.

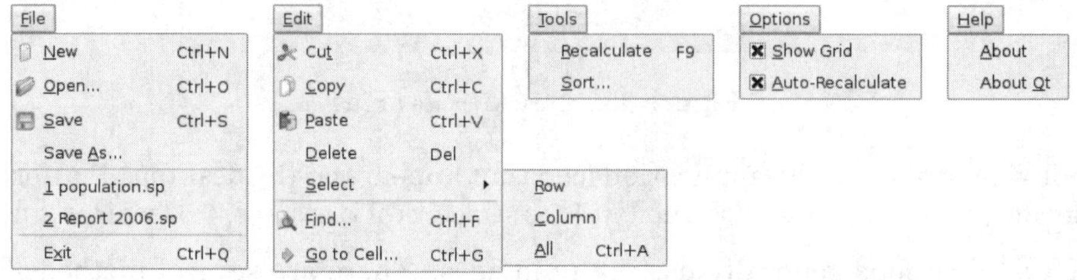

Figure 3.3. The Spreadsheet application's menus

Qt simplifies the programming of menus and toolbars through its action concept. An *action* is an item that can be added to any number of menus and toolbars. Creating menus and toolbars in Qt involves these steps:

- Create and set up the actions.
- Create menus and populate them with the actions.
- Create toolbars and populate them with the actions.

In the Spreadsheet application, actions are created in `createActions()`:

```
void MainWindow::createActions()
{
    newAction = new QAction(tr("&New"), this);
    newAction->setIcon(QIcon(":/images/new.png"));
    newAction->setShortcut(QKeySequence::New);
    newAction->setStatusTip(tr("Create a new spreadsheet file"));
    connect(newAction, SIGNAL(triggered()), this, SLOT(newFile()));
```

The New action has an accelerator (New), a parent (the main window), an icon, a shortcut key, and a status tip. Most window systems have standardized keyboard shortcuts for certain actions. For example, the New action has a shortcut of Ctrl+N on Windows, KDE, and GNOME, and Command+N on Mac OS X. By using the appropriate `QKeySequence::StandardKey` enum value, we ensure that Qt will provide the correct shortcuts for the platform on which the application is running.

We connect the action's `triggered()` signal to the main window's private `newFile()` slot, which we will implement in the next section. This connection ensures that when the user chooses the File|New menu item, clicks the New toolbar button, or presses Ctrl+N, the `newFile()` slot is called.

The Open, Save, and Save As actions are very similar to the New action, so we will skip directly to the "recently opened files" part of the File menu:

```
...
for (int i = 0; i < MaxRecentFiles; ++i) {
    recentFileActions[i] = new QAction(this);
    recentFileActions[i]->setVisible(false);
    connect(recentFileActions[i], SIGNAL(triggered()),
            this, SLOT(openRecentFile()));
}
```

We populate the `recentFileActions` array with actions. Each action is hidden and connected to the `openRecentFile()` slot. Later on, we will see how the recent file actions are made visible and used.

```
exitAction = new QAction(tr("E&xit"), this);
exitAction->setShortcut(tr("Ctrl+Q"));
exitAction->setStatusTip(tr("Exit the application"));
connect(exitAction, SIGNAL(triggered()), this, SLOT(close()));
```

The Exit action is slightly different from the ones we have seen so far. There is no standardized key sequence for terminating an application, so here we specify the key sequence explicitly. Another difference is that we connect to the window's `close()` slot, which is provided by Qt.

We can now skip to the Select All action:

```
...
selectAllAction = new QAction(tr("&All"), this);
selectAllAction->setShortcut(QKeySequence::SelectAll);
selectAllAction->setStatusTip(tr("Select all the cells in the "
                                 "spreadsheet"));
connect(selectAllAction, SIGNAL(triggered()),
        spreadsheet, SLOT(selectAll()));
```

The `selectAll()` slot is provided by one of `QTableWidget`'s ancestors, `QAbstractItemView`, so we do not have to implement it ourselves.

Let's skip further to the Show Grid action in the Options menu:

```
...
showGridAction = new QAction(tr("&Show Grid"), this);
showGridAction->setCheckable(true);
showGridAction->setChecked(spreadsheet->showGrid());
showGridAction->setStatusTip(tr("Show or hide the spreadsheet's "
                                "grid"));
```

```
    connect(showGridAction, SIGNAL(toggled(bool)),
            spreadsheet, SLOT(setShowGrid(bool)));
```

Show Grid is a checkable action. Checkable actions are rendered with a check-mark in the menu and implemented as toggle buttons in the toolbar. When the action is turned on, the `Spreadsheet` component displays a grid. We initialize the action with the default for the `Spreadsheet` component so that they are synchronized at startup. Then we connect the Show Grid action's `toggled(bool)` signal to the `Spreadsheet` component's `setShowGrid(bool)` slot, which it inherits from `QTableWidget`. Once this action is added to a menu or toolbar, the user can toggle the grid on and off.

The Show Grid and Auto-Recalculate actions are independent checkable actions. Qt also supports mutually exclusive actions through the `QActionGroup` class.

```
    ...
    aboutQtAction = new QAction(tr("About &Qt"), this);
    aboutQtAction->setStatusTip(tr("Show the Qt library's About box"));
    connect(aboutQtAction, SIGNAL(triggered()), qApp, SLOT(aboutQt()));
}
```

For the About Qt action, we use the `QApplication` object's `aboutQt()` slot, accessible through the `qApp` global variable. This pops up the dialog shown in Figure 3.4.

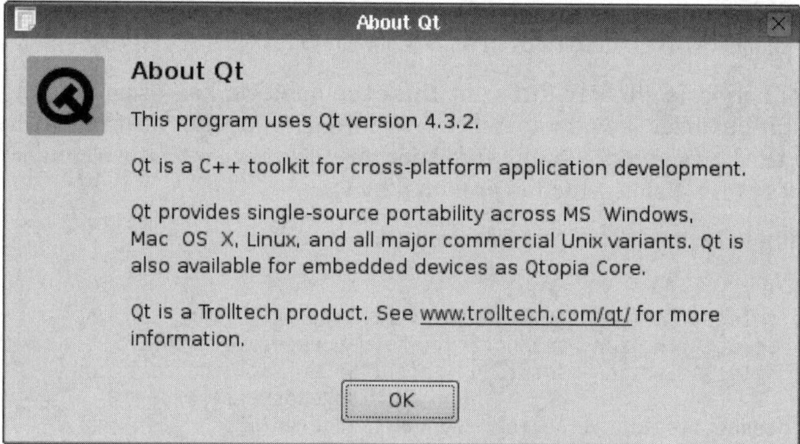

Figure 3.4. About Qt

Now that we have created the actions, we can move on to building a menu system containing them:

```
void MainWindow::createMenus()
{
    fileMenu = menuBar()->addMenu(tr("&File"));
    fileMenu->addAction(newAction);
    fileMenu->addAction(openAction);
    fileMenu->addAction(saveAction);
    fileMenu->addAction(saveAsAction);
```

```
    separatorAction = fileMenu->addSeparator();
    for (int i = 0; i < MaxRecentFiles; ++i)
        fileMenu->addAction(recentFileActions[i]);
    fileMenu->addSeparator();
    fileMenu->addAction(exitAction);
```

In Qt, menus are instances of QMenu. The addMenu() function creates a QMenu widget with the specified text and adds it to the menu bar. The QMainWindow::menuBar() function returns a pointer to a QMenuBar. The menu bar is created the first time menuBar() is called.

We start by creating the File menu and then add the New, Open, Save, and Save As actions to it. We insert a separator to visually group closely related items together. We use a for loop to add the (initially hidden) actions from the recentFileActions array, and then add the exitAction action at the end.

We have kept a pointer to one of the separators. This will allow us to hide the separator (if there are no recent files) or to show it, since we do not want to show two separators with nothing in between.

```
    editMenu = menuBar()->addMenu(tr("&Edit"));
    editMenu->addAction(cutAction);
    editMenu->addAction(copyAction);
    editMenu->addAction(pasteAction);
    editMenu->addAction(deleteAction);

    selectSubMenu = editMenu->addMenu(tr("&Select"));
    selectSubMenu->addAction(selectRowAction);
    selectSubMenu->addAction(selectColumnAction);
    selectSubMenu->addAction(selectAllAction);

    editMenu->addSeparator();
    editMenu->addAction(findAction);
    editMenu->addAction(goToCellAction);
```

Now we create the Edit menu, adding actions with QMenu::addAction() as we did for the File menu, and adding the submenu with QMenu::addMenu() at the position where we want it to appear. The submenu, like the menu it belongs to, is a QMenu.

```
    toolsMenu = menuBar()->addMenu(tr("&Tools"));
    toolsMenu->addAction(recalculateAction);
    toolsMenu->addAction(sortAction);

    optionsMenu = menuBar()->addMenu(tr("&Options"));
    optionsMenu->addAction(showGridAction);
    optionsMenu->addAction(autoRecalcAction);

    menuBar()->addSeparator();

    helpMenu = menuBar()->addMenu(tr("&Help"));
    helpMenu->addAction(aboutAction);
    helpMenu->addAction(aboutQtAction);
}
```

We create the Tools, Options, and Help menus in a similar fashion. We insert a separator between the Options and Help menus. In Motif and CDE styles, the separator pushes the Help menu to the right; in other styles, the separator is ignored. Figure 3.5 shows both cases.

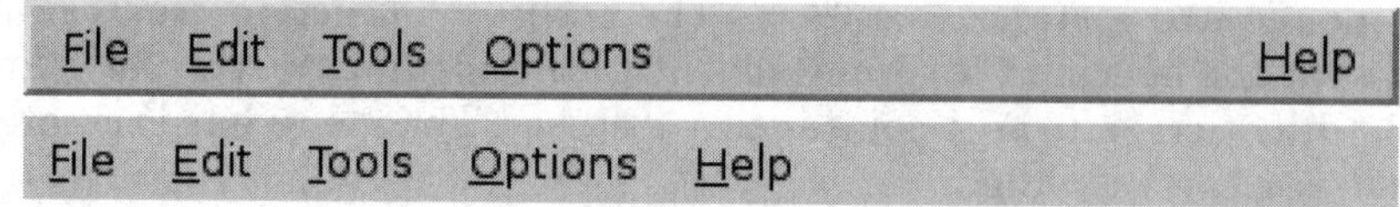

Figure 3.5. The menu bar in Motif and Windows styles

```
void MainWindow::createContextMenu()
{
    spreadsheet->addAction(cutAction);
    spreadsheet->addAction(copyAction);
    spreadsheet->addAction(pasteAction);
    spreadsheet->setContextMenuPolicy(Qt::ActionsContextMenu);
}
```

Any Qt widget can have a list of QActions associated with it. To provide a context menu for the application, we add the desired actions to the Spreadsheet widget and set that widget's context menu policy to show a context menu with these actions. Context menus are invoked by right-clicking a widget or by pressing a platform-specific key. The Spreadsheet's context menu is shown in Figure 3.6.

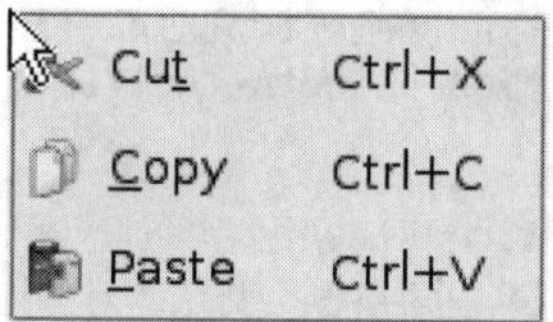

Figure 3.6. The Spreadsheet application's context menu

A more sophisticated way of providing context menus is to reimplement the QWidget::contextMenuEvent() function, create a QMenu widget, populate it with the desired actions, and call exec() on it.

```
void MainWindow::createToolBars()
{
    fileToolBar = addToolBar(tr("&File"));
    fileToolBar->addAction(newAction);
    fileToolBar->addAction(openAction);
    fileToolBar->addAction(saveAction);

    editToolBar = addToolBar(tr("&Edit"));
    editToolBar->addAction(cutAction);
    editToolBar->addAction(copyAction);
    editToolBar->addAction(pasteAction);
    editToolBar->addSeparator();
    editToolBar->addAction(findAction);
```

```
    editToolBar->addAction(goToCellAction);
}
```

Creating toolbars is very similar to creating menus. We create a File toolbar and an Edit toolbar. Just like a menu, a toolbar can have separators, as Figure 3.7 shows.

Figure 3.7. The Spreadsheet application's toolbars

Setting Up the Status Bar

With the menus and toolbars complete, we are ready to tackle the Spreadsheet application's status bar. In its normal state, the status bar contains two indicators: the current cell's location and the current cell's formula. The status bar is also used to display status tips and other temporary messages. Figure 3.8 shows the status bar in each state.

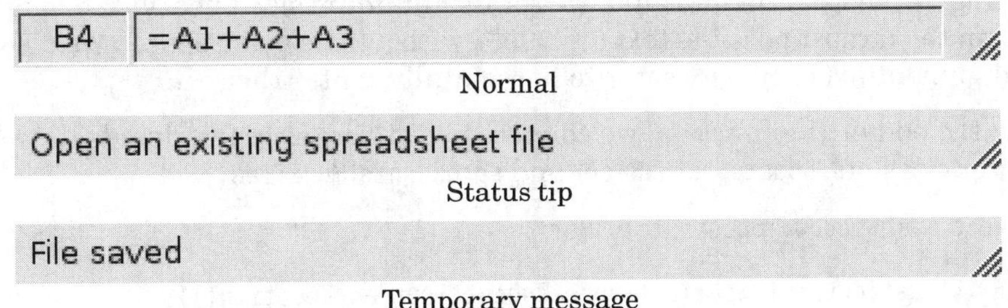

Figure 3.8. The Spreadsheet application's status bar

The `MainWindow` constructor calls `createStatusBar()` to set up the status bar:

```
void MainWindow::createStatusBar()
{
    locationLabel = new QLabel(" W999 ");
    locationLabel->setAlignment(Qt::AlignHCenter);
    locationLabel->setMinimumSize(locationLabel->sizeHint());

    formulaLabel = new QLabel;
    formulaLabel->setIndent(3);

    statusBar()->addWidget(locationLabel);
    statusBar()->addWidget(formulaLabel, 1);

    connect(spreadsheet, SIGNAL(currentCellChanged(int, int, int, int)),
            this, SLOT(updateStatusBar()));
    connect(spreadsheet, SIGNAL(modified()),
            this, SLOT(spreadsheetModified()));
```

```
        updateStatusBar();
    }
```

The QMainWindow::statusBar() function returns a pointer to the status bar. (The status bar is created the first time statusBar() is called.) The status indicators are simply QLabels whose text we change whenever necessary. We have added an indent to the formulaLabel so that the text shown in it is offset slightly from the left edge. When the QLabels are added to the status bar, they are automatically reparented to make them children of the status bar.

Figure 3.8 shows that the two labels have different space requirements. The cell location indicator requires very little space, and when the window is resized, any extra space should go to the cell formula indicator on the right. This is achieved by specifying a stretch factor of 1 in the formula label's QStatusBar::addWidget() call. The location indicator has the default stretch factor of 0, meaning that it prefers not to be stretched.

When QStatusBar lays out indicator widgets, it tries to respect each widget's ideal size as given by QWidget::sizeHint() and then stretches any stretchable widgets to fill the available space. A widget's ideal size is itself dependent on the widget's contents and varies as we change the contents. To avoid constant resizing of the location indicator, we set its minimum size to be wide enough to contain the largest possible text ("W999"), with a little extra space. We also set its alignment to Qt::AlignHCenter to horizontally center the text.

Near the end of the function, we connect two of Spreadsheet's signals to two of MainWindow's slots: updateStatusBar() and spreadsheetModified().

```
void MainWindow::updateStatusBar()
{
    locationLabel->setText(spreadsheet->currentLocation());
    formulaLabel->setText(spreadsheet->currentFormula());
}
```

The updateStatusBar() slot updates the cell location and the cell formula indicators. It is called whenever the user moves the cell cursor to a new cell. The slot is also used as an ordinary function at the end of createStatusBar() to initialize the indicators. This is necessary because Spreadsheet doesn't emit the currentCellChanged() signal at startup.

```
void MainWindow::spreadsheetModified()
{
    setWindowModified(true);
    updateStatusBar();
}
```

The spreadsheetModified() slot sets the windowModified property to true, updating the title bar. The function also updates the location and formula indicators so that they reflect the current state of affairs.

Implementing the File Menu

In this section, we will implement the slots and private functions necessary to make the File menu options work and to manage the recently opened files list.

```
void MainWindow::newFile()
{
    if (okToContinue()) {
        spreadsheet->clear();
        setCurrentFile("");
    }
}
```

The `newFile()` slot is called when the user clicks the File|New menu option or clicks the New toolbar button. The `okToContinue()` private function pops up the "Do you want to save your changes?" dialog shown in Figure 3.9, if there are unsaved changes. It returns `true` if the user chooses either Yes or No (saving the document on Yes), and it returns `false` if the user chooses Cancel. The `Spreadsheet::clear()` function clears all the spreadsheet's cells and formulas. The `setCurrentFile()` private function updates the window title to indicate that an untitled document is being edited, in addition to setting the `curFile` private variable and updating the recently opened files list.

Figure 3.9. "Do you want to save your changes?"

```
bool MainWindow::okToContinue()
{
    if (isWindowModified()) {
        int r = QMessageBox::warning(this, tr("Spreadsheet"),
                        tr("The document has been modified.\n"
                           "Do you want to save your changes?"),
                        QMessageBox::Yes | QMessageBox::No
                        | QMessageBox::Cancel);
        if (r == QMessageBox::Yes) {
            return save();
        } else if (r == QMessageBox::Cancel) {
            return false;
        }
    }
    return true;
}
```

In okToContinue(), we check the state of the windowModified property. If it is true, we display the message box shown in Figure 3.9. The message box has a Yes, a No, and a Cancel button.

QMessageBox provides many standard buttons, and automatically tries to make one button the default (activated when the user presses Enter), and one the escape (activated when the user presses Esc). It is also possible to choose particular buttons as the default and escape buttons, and also to customize the button texts.

The call to warning() may look a bit intimidating at first sight, but the general syntax is straightforward:

```
QMessageBox::warning(parent, title, message, buttons);
```

In addition to warning(), QMessageBox also provides information(), question(), and critical(), each of which has its own particular icon. The icons are shown in Figure 3.10.

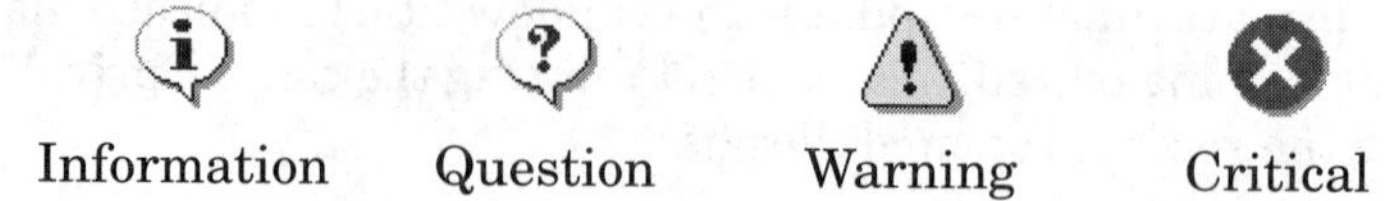

Figure 3.10. Message box icons in Windows style

```
void MainWindow::open()
{
    if (okToContinue()) {
        QString fileName = QFileDialog::getOpenFileName(this,
                                   tr("Open Spreadsheet"), ".",
                                   tr("Spreadsheet files (*.sp)"));
        if (!fileName.isEmpty())
            loadFile(fileName);
    }
}
```

The open() slot corresponds to File|Open. Like newFile(), it first calls okToContinue() to handle any unsaved changes. Then it uses the static convenience function QFileDialog::getOpenFileName() to obtain a new file name from the user. The function pops up a file dialog, lets the user choose a file, and returns the file name—or an empty string if the user clicked Cancel.

The first argument to QFileDialog::getOpenFileName() is the parent widget. The parent–child relationship doesn't mean the same thing for dialogs as for other widgets. A dialog is always a window in its own right, but if it has a parent, it is centered on top of the parent by default. A child dialog also shares its parent's taskbar entry.

The second argument is the title the dialog should use. The third argument tells it which directory it should start from, in our case the current directory.

The fourth argument specifies the file filters. A file filter consists of a descriptive text and a wildcard pattern. Had we supported comma-separated values files and Lotus 1-2-3 files in addition to Spreadsheet's native file format, we would have used the following filter:

```
tr("Spreadsheet files (*.sp)\n"
   "Comma-separated values files (*.csv)\n"
   "Lotus 1-2-3 files (*.wk1 *.wks)")
```

The `loadFile()` private function was called in `open()` to load the file. We make it an independent function because we will need the same functionality to load recently opened files:

```
bool MainWindow::loadFile(const QString &fileName)
{
    if (!spreadsheet->readFile(fileName)) {
        statusBar()->showMessage(tr("Loading canceled"), 2000);
        return false;
    }

    setCurrentFile(fileName);
    statusBar()->showMessage(tr("File loaded"), 2000);
    return true;
}
```

We use `Spreadsheet::readFile()` to read the file from disk. If loading is successful, we call `setCurrentFile()` to update the window title; otherwise, `Spreadsheet::readFile()` will have already notified the user of the problem through a message box. In general, it is good practice to let the lower-level components issue error messages, since they can provide the precise details of what went wrong.

In both cases, we display a message in the status bar for two seconds (2 000 milliseconds) to keep the user informed about what the application is doing.

```
bool MainWindow::save()
{
    if (curFile.isEmpty()) {
        return saveAs();
    } else {
        return saveFile(curFile);
    }
}

bool MainWindow::saveFile(const QString &fileName)
{
    if (!spreadsheet->writeFile(fileName)) {
        statusBar()->showMessage(tr("Saving canceled"), 2000);
        return false;
    }

    setCurrentFile(fileName);
    statusBar()->showMessage(tr("File saved"), 2000);
    return true;
}
```

The save() slot corresponds to File|Save. If the file already has a name because it was opened before or has already been saved, save() calls saveFile() with that name; otherwise, it simply calls saveAs().

```
bool MainWindow::saveAs()
{
    QString fileName = QFileDialog::getSaveFileName(this,
                               tr("Save Spreadsheet"), ".",
                               tr("Spreadsheet files (*.sp)"));
    if (fileName.isEmpty())
        return false;

    return saveFile(fileName);
}
```

The saveAs() slot corresponds to File|Save As. We call QFileDialog::getSaveFileName() to obtain a file name from the user. If the user clicks Cancel, we return false, which is propagated up to its caller (save() or okToContinue()).

If the file already exists, the getSaveFileName() function will ask the user to confirm that they want to overwrite. This behavior can be changed by passing QFileDialog::DontConfirmOverwrite as an additional argument to getSaveFileName().

```
void MainWindow::closeEvent(QCloseEvent *event)
{
    if (okToContinue()) {
        writeSettings();
        event->accept();
    } else {
        event->ignore();
    }
}
```

When the user clicks File|Exit or clicks the close button in the window's title bar, the QWidget::close() slot is called. This sends a "close" event to the widget. By reimplementing QWidget::closeEvent(), we can intercept attempts to close the main window and decide whether we want the window to actually close or not.

If there are unsaved changes and the user chooses Cancel, we "ignore" the event and leave the window unaffected by it. In the normal case, we accept the event, resulting in Qt hiding the window. We also call the private function writeSettings() to save the application's current settings.

When the last window is closed, the application terminates. If needed, we can disable this behavior by setting QApplication's quitOnLastWindowClosed property to false, in which case the application keeps running until we call QApplication::quit().

```
void MainWindow::setCurrentFile(const QString &fileName)
{
    curFile = fileName;
    setWindowModified(false);
```

```
    QString shownName = tr("Untitled");
    if (!curFile.isEmpty()) {
        shownName = strippedName(curFile);
        recentFiles.removeAll(curFile);
        recentFiles.prepend(curFile);
        updateRecentFileActions();
    }

    setWindowTitle(tr("%1[*] - %2").arg(shownName)
                                   .arg(tr("Spreadsheet")));
}

QString MainWindow::strippedName(const QString &fullFileName)
{
    return QFileInfo(fullFileName).fileName();
}
```

In `setCurrentFile()`, we set the `curFile` private variable that stores the name of the file being edited. Before we show the file name in the title bar, we remove the file's path with `strippedName()` to make it more user-friendly.

Every `QWidget` has a `windowModified` property that should be set to `true` if the window's document has unsaved changes, and to `false` otherwise. On Mac OS X, unsaved documents are indicated by a dot in the close button of the window's title bar; on other platforms, they are indicated by an asterisk following the file name. Qt takes care of this behavior automatically, as long as we keep the `windowModified` property up-to-date and place the marker "[*]" in the window title where we want the asterisk to appear when it is required.

The text we passed to the `setWindowTitle()` function was

```
tr("%1[*] - %2").arg(shownName)
                .arg(tr("Spreadsheet"))
```

The `QString::arg()` function replaces the lowest-numbered "*%n*" parameter with its argument and returns the resulting `%n` parameter with its argument and returns the resulting string. In this case, `arg()` is used with two "*%n*" parameters. The first call to `arg()` replaces "%1"; the second call replaces "%2". If the file name is "budget.sp" and no translation file is loaded, the resulting string would be "budget.sp[*] - Spreadsheet". It would have been easier to write

```
setWindowTitle(shownName + tr("[*] - Spreadsheet"));
```

but using `arg()` provides more flexibility for human translators.

If there is a file name, we update `recentFiles`, the application's recently opened files list. We call `removeAll()` to remove any occurrences of the file name in the list, to avoid duplicates; then we call `prepend()` to add the file name as the first item. After updating the list, we call the private function `updateRecentFileActions()` to update the entries in the File menu.

```
void MainWindow::updateRecentFileActions()
{
    QMutableStringListIterator i(recentFiles);
```

```
    while (i.hasNext()) {
        if (!QFile::exists(i.next()))
            i.remove();
    }

    for (int j = 0; j < MaxRecentFiles; ++j) {
        if (j < recentFiles.count()) {
            QString text = tr("&%1 %2")
                           .arg(j + 1)
                           .arg(strippedName(recentFiles[j]));
            recentFileActions[j]->setText(text);
            recentFileActions[j]->setData(recentFiles[j]);
            recentFileActions[j]->setVisible(true);
        } else {
            recentFileActions[j]->setVisible(false);
        }
    }
    separatorAction->setVisible(!recentFiles.isEmpty());
}
```

We begin by removing any files that no longer exist using a Java-style iterator. Some files might have been used in a previous session, but have since been deleted. The `recentFiles` variable is of type `QStringList` (list of `QStrings`). Chapter 11 explains container classes such as `QStringList` in detail, showing how they relate to the C++ Standard Template Library (STL), and the use of Qt's Java-style iterator classes.

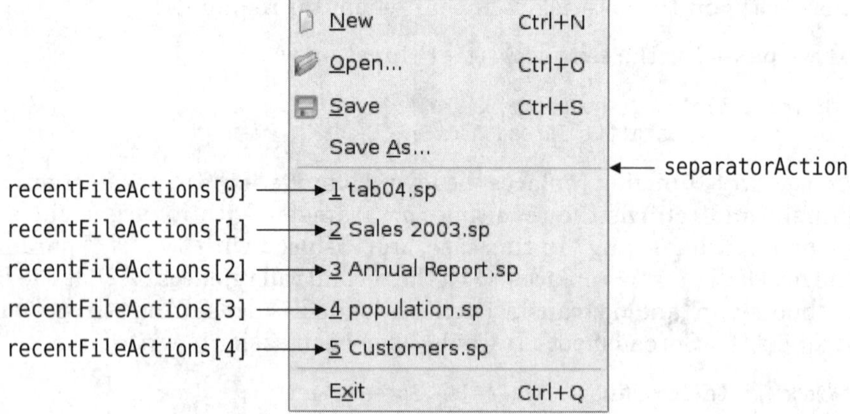

Figure 3.11. The File menu with recently opened files

We then go through the list of files again, this time using array-style indexing. For each file, we create a string consisting of an ampersand, a digit (`j + 1`), a space, and the file name (without its path). We set the corresponding action to use this text. For example, if the first file was `C:\My Documents\tab04.sp`, the first action's text would be "&1 tab04.sp". Figure 3.11 shows the correspondence between the `recentFileActions` array and the resulting menu.

Every action can have an associated "data" item of type `QVariant`. The `QVariant` type can hold values of many C++ and Qt types; we cover it in Chapter 11. Here, we store the full name of the file in the action's "data" item so that we can easily retrieve it later. We also set the action to be visible.

If there are more file actions than recent files, we simply hide the extra actions. Finally, if there is at least one recent file, we set the separator to be visible.

```
void MainWindow::openRecentFile()
{
    if (okToContinue()) {
        QAction *action = qobject_cast<QAction *>(sender());
        if (action)
            loadFile(action->data().toString());
    }
}
```

When the user chooses a recent file, the `openRecentFile()` slot is called. The `okToContinue()` function is used in case there are any unsaved changes, and provided the user did not cancel, we find out which particular action invoked the slot using `QObject::sender()`.

The `qobject_cast<T>()` function performs a dynamic cast based on the meta-information generated by `moc`, Qt's meta-object compiler. It returns a pointer of the requested `QObject` subclass, or 0 if the object cannot be cast to that type. Unlike the Standard C++ `dynamic_cast<T>()`, Qt's `qobject_cast<T>()` works correctly across dynamic library boundaries. In our example, we use `qobject_cast<T>()` to cast a `QObject` pointer to a `QAction` pointer. If the cast is successful (it should be), we call `loadFile()` with the full file name that we extract from the action's data.

Incidentally, since we know that the sender is a `QAction`, the program would still work if we used `static_cast<T>()` or a traditional C-style cast instead. Refer to the "Type Conversions" section of Appendix D for an overview of the different C++ casts.

Using Dialogs

In this section, we will explain how to use dialogs in Qt—how to create and initialize them, run them, and respond to choices made by the user interacting with them. We will make use of the Find, Go to Cell, and Sort dialogs that we created in Chapter 2. We will also create a simple About box.

We will begin with the Find dialog shown in Figure 3.12. Since we want the user to be able to switch between the main Spreadsheet window and the Find dialog at will, the Find dialog must be modeless. A *modeless* window is one that runs independently of any other windows in the application.

When modeless dialogs are created, they normally have their signals connected to slots that respond to the user's interactions.

```
void MainWindow::find()
{
    if (!findDialog) {
        findDialog = new FindDialog(this);
        connect(findDialog, SIGNAL(findNext(const QString &,
                                            Qt::CaseSensitivity)),
                spreadsheet, SLOT(findNext(const QString &,
                                           Qt::CaseSensitivity)));
        connect(findDialog, SIGNAL(findPrevious(const QString &,
                                                Qt::CaseSensitivity)),
                spreadsheet, SLOT(findPrevious(const QString &,
                                               Qt::CaseSensitivity)));
    }

    findDialog->show();
    findDialog->raise();
    findDialog->activateWindow();
}
```

The Find dialog is a window that enables the user to search for text in the spreadsheet. The `find()` slot is called when the user clicks Edit|Find to pop up the Find dialog. At that point, several scenarios are possible:

- This is the first time the user has invoked the Find dialog.
- The Find dialog was invoked before, but the user closed it.
- The Find dialog was invoked before and is still visible.

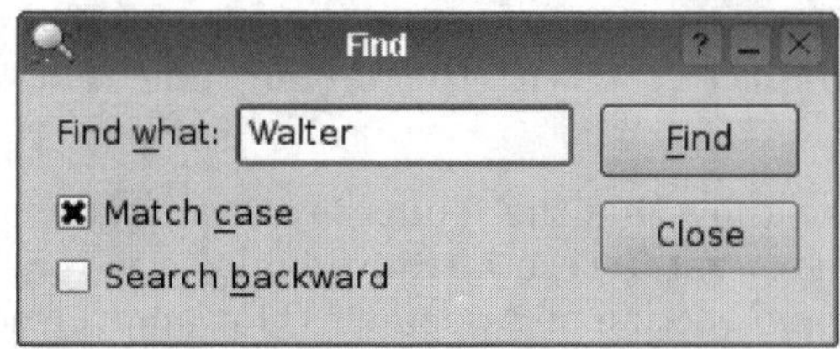

Figure 3.12. The Spreadsheet application's Find dialog

If the Find dialog doesn't already exist, we create it and connect its `findNext()` and `findPrevious()` signals to the corresponding `Spreadsheet` slots. We could also have created the dialog in the `MainWindow` constructor, but delaying its creation makes application startup faster. Also, if the dialog is never used, it is never created, saving both time and memory.

Then we call `show()`, `raise()`, and `activateWindow()` to ensure that the window is visible, on top of the others, and active. A call to `show()` alone is sufficient to make a hidden window visible, on top, and active, but the Find dialog may be invoked when it is already visible. In that case, `show()` does nothing and we must call `raise()` and `activateWindow()` to make the window on top and active. An alternative would have been to write

```
    if (findDialog->isHidden()) {
        findDialog->show();
    } else {
        findDialog->raise();
        findDialog->activateWindow();
    }
```

but this is the programming equivalent of looking both ways before crossing a one-way street.

We will now look at the Go to Cell dialog shown in Figure 3.13. We want the user to pop it up, use it, and close it without being able to switch to any other window in the application. This means that the Go to Cell dialog must be modal. A *modal* window is a window that pops up when invoked and blocks the application, preventing any other processing or interactions from taking place until the window is closed. The file dialogs and message boxes we used earlier were modal.

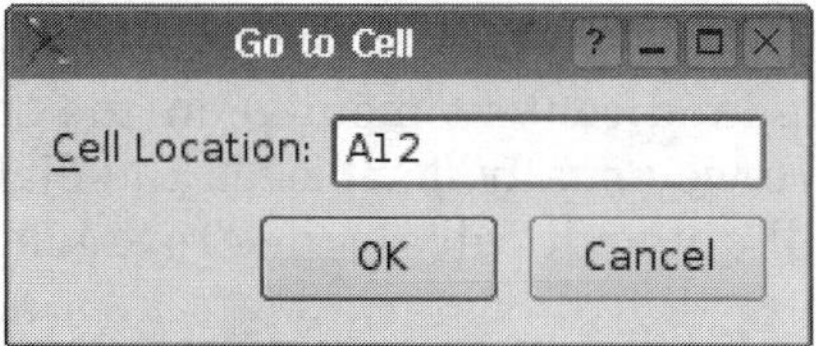

Figure 3.13. The Spreadsheet application's Go to Cell dialog

A dialog is modeless if it's invoked using `show()` (unless we call `setModal()` beforehand to make it modal); it is modal if it's invoked using `exec()`.

```
void MainWindow::goToCell()
{
    GoToCellDialog dialog(this);
    if (dialog.exec()) {
        QString str = dialog.lineEdit->text().toUpper();
        spreadsheet->setCurrentCell(str.mid(1).toInt() - 1,
                                    str[0].unicode() - 'A');
    }
}
```

The `QDialog::exec()` function returns a true value (`QDialog::Accepted`) if the dialog is accepted, and a false value (`QDialog::Rejected`) otherwise. Recall that when we created the Go to Cell dialog using *Qt Designer* in Chapter 2, we connected OK to `accept()` and Cancel to `reject()`. If the user chooses OK, we set the current cell to the value in the line editor.

The `QTableWidget::setCurrentCell()` function expects two arguments: a row index and a column index. In the Spreadsheet application, cell A1 is cell (0, 0) and cell B27 is cell (26, 1). To obtain the row index from the `QString` returned by `QLineEdit::text()`, we extract the row number using `QString::mid()` (which returns a substring from the start position to the end of the string), convert it to an `int` using `QString::toInt()`, and subtract 1. For the column number, we subtract the numeric value of 'A' from the numeric value of the string's uppercased first character. We know that the string will have the correct format because the `QRegExpValidator` we created for the dialog allows the OK button to be enabled only if we have a letter followed by up to three digits.

The `goToCell()` function differs from all the code seen so far in that it creates a widget (a `GoToCellDialog`) as a variable on the stack. At the cost of one extra line, we could just as easily have used `new` and `delete`:

```
void MainWindow::goToCell()
{
    GoToCellDialog *dialog = new GoToCellDialog(this);
    if (dialog->exec()) {
        QString str = dialog->lineEdit->text().toUpper();
        spreadsheet->setCurrentCell(str.mid(1).toInt() - 1,
                                    str[0].unicode() - 'A');
    }
    delete dialog;
}
```

Creating modal dialogs (and context menus) on the stack is a common programming pattern since we usually don't need the dialog (or menu) after we have used it, and it will automatically be destroyed at the end of the enclosing scope.

We will now turn to the Sort dialog. The Sort dialog is a modal dialog that allows the user to sort the currently selected area by the columns they specify. Figure 3.14 shows an example of sorting, with column B as the primary sort key and column A as the secondary sort key (both ascending).

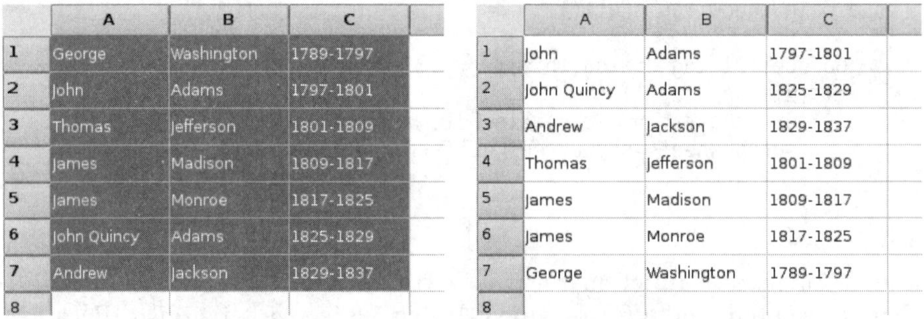

	A	B	C
1	George	Washington	1789-1797
2	John	Adams	1797-1801
3	Thomas	Jefferson	1801-1809
4	James	Madison	1809-1817
5	James	Monroe	1817-1825
6	John Quincy	Adams	1825-1829
7	Andrew	Jackson	1829-1837
8			

(a) Before sort

	A	B	C
1	John	Adams	1797-1801
2	John Quincy	Adams	1825-1829
3	Andrew	Jackson	1829-1837
4	Thomas	Jefferson	1801-1809
5	James	Madison	1809-1817
6	James	Monroe	1817-1825
7	George	Washington	1789-1797
8			

(b) After sort

Figure 3.14. Sorting the spreadsheet's selected area

```
void MainWindow::sort()
{
    SortDialog dialog(this);
    QTableWidgetSelectionRange range = spreadsheet->selectedRange();
    dialog.setColumnRange('A' + range.leftColumn(),
                          'A' + range.rightColumn());
```

```
        if (dialog.exec()) {
            SpreadsheetCompare compare;
            compare.keys[0] =
                  dialog.primaryColumnCombo->currentIndex();
            compare.keys[1] =
                  dialog.secondaryColumnCombo->currentIndex() - 1;
            compare.keys[2] =
                  dialog.tertiaryColumnCombo->currentIndex() - 1;
            compare.ascending[0] =
                  (dialog.primaryOrderCombo->currentIndex() == 0);
            compare.ascending[1] =
                  (dialog.secondaryOrderCombo->currentIndex() == 0);
            compare.ascending[2] =
                  (dialog.tertiaryOrderCombo->currentIndex() == 0);
            spreadsheet->sort(compare);
        }
    }
```

The code in `sort()` follows a similar pattern to that used for `goToCell()`:

- We create the dialog on the stack and initialize it.
- We pop up the dialog using `exec()`.
- If the user clicks OK, we extract the values entered by the user from the dialog's widgets and make use of them.

The `setColumnRange()` call sets the columns available for sorting to the columns that are selected. For example, using the selection shown in Figure 3.14, `range.leftColumn()` would yield 0, giving 'A' + 0 = 'A', and `range.rightColumn()` would yield 2, giving 'A' + 2 = 'C'.

The `compare` object stores the primary, secondary, and tertiary sort keys and their sort orders. (We will see the definition of the `SpreadsheetCompare` class in the next chapter.) The object is used by `Spreadsheet::sort()` to compare two rows. The `keys` array stores the column numbers of the keys. For example, if the selection extends from C2 to E5, column C has position 0. The `ascending` array stores the order associated with each key as a `bool`. `QComboBox::currentIndex()` returns the index of the currently selected item, starting at 0. For the secondary and tertiary keys, we subtract one from the current item to account for the "None" item.

The `sort()` function does the job, but it is a bit fragile. It assumes that the Sort dialog is implemented in a particular way, with comboboxes and "None" items. This means that if we redesign the Sort dialog, we may also need to rewrite this code. While this approach is adequate for a dialog that is called only from one place, it opens the door to maintenance nightmares if the dialog is used in several places.

A more robust approach is to make the `SortDialog` class smarter by having it create a `SpreadsheetCompare` object itself, which can then be accessed by its caller. This simplifies `MainWindow::sort()` significantly:

```
void MainWindow::sort()
{
    SortDialog dialog(this);
    QTableWidgetSelectionRange range = spreadsheet->selectedRange();
    dialog.setColumnRange('A' + range.leftColumn(),
                          'A' + range.rightColumn());

    if (dialog.exec())
        spreadsheet->performSort(dialog.comparisonObject());
}
```

This approach leads to loosely coupled components and is almost always the right choice for dialogs that will be called from more than one place.

A more radical approach would be to pass a pointer to the `Spreadsheet` object when initializing the `SortDialog` object and to allow the dialog to operate directly on the `Spreadsheet`. This makes the `SortDialog` much less general, since it will work only on a certain type of widget, but it simplifies the code even further by eliminating the `SortDialog::setColumnRange()` function. The `MainWindow::sort()` function then becomes

```
void MainWindow::sort()
{
    SortDialog dialog(this);
    dialog.setSpreadsheet(spreadsheet);
    dialog.exec();
}
```

This approach mirrors the first: Instead of the caller needing intimate knowledge of the dialog, the dialog needs intimate knowledge of the data structures supplied by the caller. This approach may be useful where the dialog needs to apply changes live. But just as the caller code is fragile using the first approach, this third approach breaks if the data structures change.

Some developers choose just one approach to using dialogs and stick with that. This has the benefit of familiarity and simplicity since all their dialog usages follow the same pattern, but it also misses the benefits of the approaches that are not used. Ideally, the approach to use should be decided on a per-dialog basis.

We will round off this section with the About box. We could create a custom dialog like we did for the Find dialog or the Go to Cell dialog to present the information about the application, but since most About boxes are highly stylized, Qt provides a simpler solution.

```
void MainWindow::about()
{
    QMessageBox::about(this, tr("About Spreadsheet"),
            tr("<h2>Spreadsheet 1.1</h2>"
               "<p>Copyright &copy; 2008 Software Inc."
               "<p>Spreadsheet is a small application that "
               "demonstrates QAction, QMainWindow, QMenuBar, "
               "QStatusBar, QTableWidget, QToolBar, and many other "
               "Qt classes."));
}
```

The About box is obtained by calling `QMessageBox::about()`, a static convenience function. The function is very similar to `QMessageBox::warning()`, except that it uses the parent window's icon instead of the standard "warning" icon. The resulting dialog is shown in Figure 3.15.

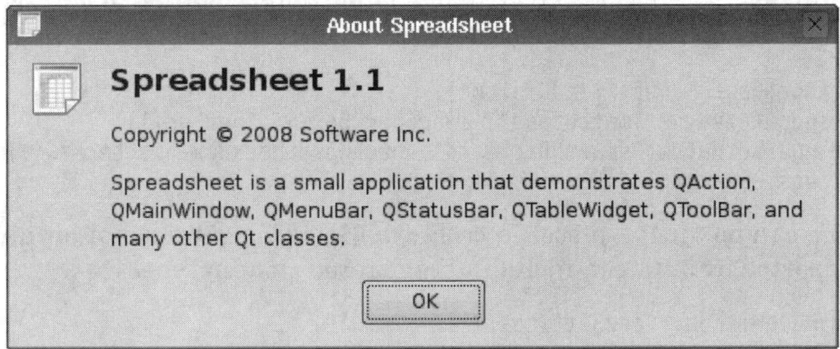

Figure 3.15. About Spreadsheet

So far, we have used several convenience static functions from both `QMessageBox` and `QFileDialog`. These functions create a dialog, initialize it, and call `exec()` on it. It is also possible, although less convenient, to create a `QMessageBox` or a `QFileDialog` widget like any other widget and explicitly call `exec()`, or even `show()`, on it.

Storing Settings

In the `MainWindow` constructor, we called `readSettings()` to load the application's stored settings. Similarly, in `closeEvent()`, we called `writeSettings()` to save the settings. These two functions are the last `MainWindow` member functions that need to be implemented.

```
void MainWindow::writeSettings()
{
    QSettings settings("Software Inc.", "Spreadsheet");

    settings.setValue("geometry", saveGeometry());
    settings.setValue("recentFiles", recentFiles);
    settings.setValue("showGrid", showGridAction->isChecked());
    settings.setValue("autoRecalc", autoRecalcAction->isChecked());
}
```

The `writeSettings()` function saves the main window's geometry (position and size), the list of recently opened files, and the Show Grid and Auto-Recalculate options.

By default, `QSettings` stores the application's settings in platform-specific locations. On Windows, it uses the system registry; on Unix, it stores the data in text files; on Mac OS X, it uses the Core Foundation Preferences API.

The constructor arguments specify the organization's name and the application's name. This information is used in a platform-specific way to find a location for the settings.

`QSettings` stores settings as *key–value* pairs. The *key* is similar to a file system path. Subkeys can be specified using a path-like syntax (e.g., `findDialog/matchCase`) or using `beginGroup()` and `endGroup()`:

```
settings.beginGroup("findDialog");
settings.setValue("matchCase", caseCheckBox->isChecked());
settings.setValue("searchBackward", backwardCheckBox->isChecked());
settings.endGroup();
```

The *value* can be an `int`, a `bool`, a `double`, a `QString`, a `QStringList`, or any other type supported by `QVariant`, including registered custom types.

```
void MainWindow::readSettings()
{
    QSettings settings("Software Inc.", "Spreadsheet");

    restoreGeometry(settings.value("geometry").toByteArray());

    recentFiles = settings.value("recentFiles").toStringList();
    updateRecentFileActions();

    bool showGrid = settings.value("showGrid", true).toBool();
    showGridAction->setChecked(showGrid);

    bool autoRecalc = settings.value("autoRecalc", true).toBool();
    autoRecalcAction->setChecked(autoRecalc);
}
```

The `readSettings()` function loads the settings that were saved by `writeSettings()`. The second argument to the `value()` function specifies a default value, in case there are no settings available. The default values are used the first time the application is run. Since no second argument is given for geometry or for the recent files list, the window will have an arbitrary but reasonable size and position, and the recent files list will be an empty list on the first run.

The arrangement we opted for in `MainWindow`, with all the `QSettings`-related code in `readSettings()` and `writeSettings()`, is just one of many possible approaches. A `QSettings` object can be created to query or modify some setting at any time during the execution of the application and from anywhere in the code.

We have now completed the Spreadsheet's `MainWindow` implementation. In the following sections, we will discuss how the Spreadsheet application can be modified to handle multiple documents and how to implement a splash screen. We will complete its functionality, including handling formulas and sorting, in the next chapter.

Multiple Documents

We are now ready to code the Spreadsheet application's `main()` function:

```
#include <QApplication>

#include "mainwindow.h"

int main(int argc, char *argv[])
{
    QApplication app(argc, argv);
    MainWindow mainWin;
    mainWin.show();
    return app.exec();
}
```

This `main()` function is a little bit different from those we have written so far: We have created the `MainWindow` instance as a variable on the stack instead of using `new`. The `MainWindow` instance is then automatically destroyed when the function terminates.

With the `main()` function just shown, the Spreadsheet application provides a single main window and can handle only one document at a time. If we want to edit multiple documents at the same time, we could start multiple instances of the Spreadsheet application. But this isn't as convenient for users as having a single instance of the application providing multiple main windows, just as one instance of a web browser can provide multiple browser windows simultaneously.

We will modify the Spreadsheet application so that it can handle multiple documents. First, we need a slightly different File menu:

- File|New creates a new main window with an empty document, instead of reusing the existing main window.
- File|Close closes the current main window.
- File|Exit closes all windows.

In the original version of the File menu, there was no Close option because that would have been the same as Exit. The new File menu is shown in Figure 3.16.

This is the new `main()` function:

```
int main(int argc, char *argv[])
{
    QApplication app(argc, argv);
    MainWindow *mainWin = new MainWindow;
    mainWin->show();
    return app.exec();
}
```

With multiple windows, it now makes sense to create `MainWindow` with `new`, because then we can use `delete` on a main window when we have finished with it to save memory.

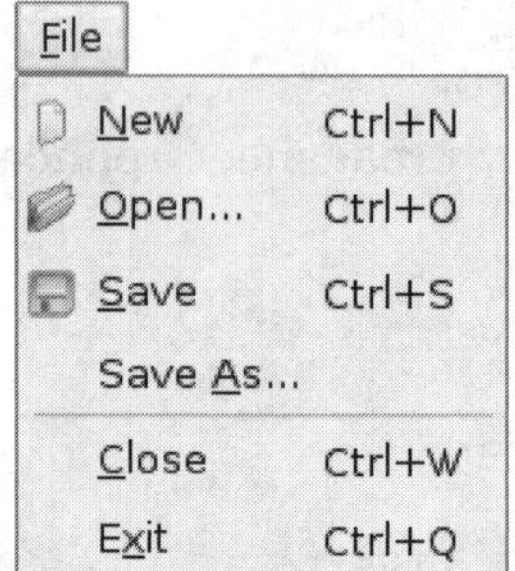

Figure 3.16. The new File menu

This is the new `MainWindow::newFile()` slot:

```
void MainWindow::newFile()
{
    MainWindow *mainWin = new MainWindow;
    mainWin->show();
}
```

We simply create a new `MainWindow` instance. It may seem odd that we don't keep any pointer to the new window, but that isn't a problem since Qt keeps track of all the windows for us.

These are the actions for Close and Exit:

```
void MainWindow::createActions()
{
    ...
    closeAction = new QAction(tr("&Close"), this);
    closeAction->setShortcut(QKeySequence::Close);
    closeAction->setStatusTip(tr("Close this window"));
    connect(closeAction, SIGNAL(triggered()), this, SLOT(close()));

    exitAction = new QAction(tr("E&xit"), this);
    exitAction->setShortcut(tr("Ctrl+Q"));
    exitAction->setStatusTip(tr("Exit the application"));
    connect(exitAction, SIGNAL(triggered()),
            qApp, SLOT(closeAllWindows()));
    ...
}
```

The `QApplication::closeAllWindows()` slot closes all of the application's windows, unless one of them rejects the close event. This is exactly the behavior we need here. We don't have to worry about unsaved changes because that's handled in `MainWindow::closeEvent()` whenever a window is closed.

It looks as though we have finished making the application capable of handling multiple windows. Unfortunately, a hidden problem is lurking: If the user keeps creating and closing main windows, the machine might eventually run out of memory. This is because we keep creating `MainWindow` widgets in `newFile()` but we never delete them. When the user closes a main window, the default

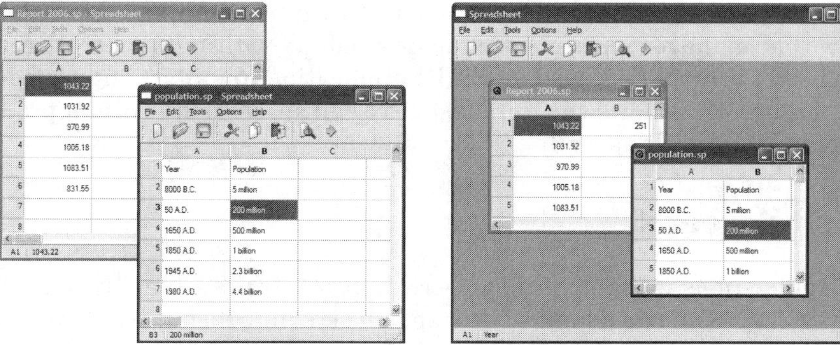

Figure 3.17. SDI versus MDI

behavior is to hide it, so it still remains in memory. With many main windows, this can be a problem.

The solution is to set the `Qt::WA_DeleteOnClose` attribute in the constructor:

```
MainWindow::MainWindow()
{
    ...
    setAttribute(Qt::WA_DeleteOnClose);
    ...
}
```

This tells Qt to delete the window when it is closed. The `Qt::WA_DeleteOnClose` attribute is one of many flags that can be set on a `QWidget` to influence its behavior.

Memory leaking isn't the only problem that we must deal with. Our original application design included an implied assumption that we would have only one main window. With multiple windows, each main window has its own recently opened files list and its own options. Clearly, the recently opened files list should be global to the whole application. We can achieve this quite easily by declaring the `recentFiles` variable static so that only one instance of it exists for the whole application. But then we must ensure that wherever we called `updateRecentFileActions()` to update the File menu, we must call it on all main windows. Here's the code to achieve this:

```
foreach (QWidget *win, QApplication::topLevelWidgets()) {
    if (MainWindow *mainWin = qobject_cast<MainWindow *>(win))
        mainWin->updateRecentFileActions();
}
```

The code uses Qt's `foreach` construct (explained in Chapter 11) to iterate over all the application's windows and calls `updateRecentFileActions()` on all widgets of type `MainWindow`. Similar code can be used for synchronizing the Show Grid and Auto-Recalculate options, or to make sure that the same file isn't loaded twice.

Applications that provide one document per main window are said to be SDI (single document interface) applications. A common alternative on Windows is

MDI (multiple document interface), where the application has a single main window that manages multiple document windows within its central area. Qt can be used to create both SDI and MDI applications on all its supported platforms. Figure 3.17 shows the Spreadsheet application using both approaches. We explain MDI in Chapter 6.

Splash Screens

Many applications present a splash screen at startup, such as the one shown in Figure 3.18. Some developers use a splash screen to disguise a slow startup, while others do it to satisfy their marketing departments. Adding a splash screen to Qt applications is very easy using the `QSplashScreen` class.

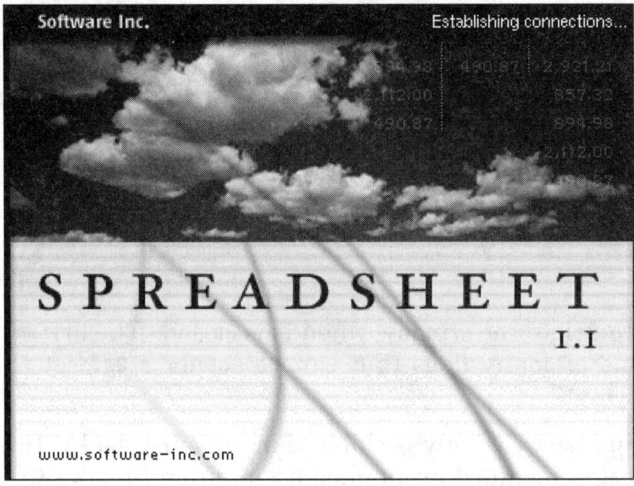

Figure 3.18. A splash screen

The `QSplashScreen` class shows an image before the main window appears. It can also write messages on the image to inform the user about the progress of the application's initialization process. Typically, the splash screen code is located in `main()`, before the call to `QApplication::exec()`.

Next is an example `main()` function that uses `QSplashScreen` to present a splash screen in an application that loads modules and establishes network connections at startup.

```
int main(int argc, char *argv[])
{
    QApplication app(argc, argv);

    QSplashScreen *splash = new QSplashScreen;
    splash->setPixmap(QPixmap(":/images/splash.png"));
    splash->show();

    Qt::Alignment topRight = Qt::AlignRight | Qt::AlignTop;
```

```
    splash->showMessage(QObject::tr("Setting up the main window..."),
                        topRight, Qt::white);
    MainWindow mainWin;

    splash->showMessage(QObject::tr("Loading modules..."),
                        topRight, Qt::white);
    loadModules();

    splash->showMessage(QObject::tr("Establishing connections..."),
                        topRight, Qt::white);
    establishConnections();

    mainWin.show();
    splash->finish(&mainWin);
    delete splash;

    return app.exec();
}
```

We have now completed the Spreadsheet application's user interface. In the next chapter, we will complete the application by implementing the core spreadsheet functionality.

- *The Central Widget*
- *Subclassing QTableWidget*
- *Loading and Saving*
- *Implementing the Edit Menu*
- *Implementing the Other Menus*
- *Subclassing QTableWidgetItem*

4. Implementing Application Functionality

In the previous two chapters, we explained how to create the Spreadsheet application's user interface. In this chapter, we will complete the program by coding its underlying functionality. Among other things, we will see how to load and save files, how to store data in memory, how to implement clipboard operations, and how to add support for spreadsheet formulas to `QTableWidget`.

The Central Widget

The central area of a `QMainWindow` can be occupied by any kind of widget. Here's an overview of the possibilities:

1. **Use a standard Qt widget.**

   A standard widget such as `QTableWidget` or `QTextEdit` can be used as the central widget. In this case, the application's functionality, such as loading and saving files, must be implemented elsewhere (e.g., in a `QMainWindow` subclass).

2. **Use a custom widget.**

   Specialized applications often need to show data in a custom widget. For example, an icon editor program would have an `IconEditor` widget as its central widget. Chapter 5 explains how to write custom widgets in Qt.

3. **Use a plain QWidget with a layout manager.**

   Sometimes the application's central area is occupied by many widgets. This can be done by using a `QWidget` as the parent of all the other widgets, and using layout managers to size and position the child widgets.

4. **Use a splitter.**

   Another way of using multiple widgets together is to use a QSplitter. The QSplitter arranges its child widgets horizontally or vertically, with splitter handles to give some sizing control to the user. Splitters can contain all kinds of widgets, including other splitters.

5. **Use an MDI area.**

   If the application uses MDI, the central area is occupied by a QMdiArea widget, and each MDI window is a child of that widget.

Layouts, splitters, and MDI areas can be combined with standard Qt widgets or with custom widgets. Chapter 6 covers these classes in depth.

For the Spreadsheet application, a QTableWidget subclass is used as the central widget. The QTableWidget class already provides most of the spreadsheet capability we need, but it doesn't support clipboard operations and doesn't understand spreadsheet formulas such as "=A1+A2+A3". We will implement this missing functionality in the Spreadsheet class.

Subclassing QTableWidget

The Spreadsheet class is derived from QTableWidget, as Figure 4.1 shows. A QTableWidget is effectively a grid that represents a two-dimensional sparse array. It displays whichever cells the user scrolls to, within its specified dimensions. When the user enters some text into an empty cell, QTableWidget automatically creates a QTableWidgetItem to store the text.

QTableWidget is derived from QTableView, one of the model/view classes that we will look at more closely in Chapter 10. Another table, which has a lot more functionality out of the box, is QicsTable, available from http://www.ics.com/.

Let's start implementing Spreadsheet, beginning with the header file:

```
#ifndef SPREADSHEET_H
#define SPREADSHEET_H

#include <QTableWidget>

class Cell;
class SpreadsheetCompare;
```

The header starts with forward declarations for the Cell and SpreadsheetCompare classes.

The attributes of a QTableWidget cell, such as its text and its alignment, are stored in a QTableWidgetItem. Unlike QTableWidget, QTableWidgetItem isn't a widget class; it is a pure data class. The Cell class is derived from QTableWidgetItem and will be explained in this chapter's last section.

```
class Spreadsheet : public QTableWidget
{
```

```
    Q_OBJECT

public:
    Spreadsheet(QWidget *parent = 0);

    bool autoRecalculate() const { return autoRecalc; }
    QString currentLocation() const;
    QString currentFormula() const;
    QTableWidgetSelectionRange selectedRange() const;
    void clear();
    bool readFile(const QString &fileName);
    bool writeFile(const QString &fileName);
    void sort(const SpreadsheetCompare &compare);
```

The `autoRecalculate()` function is implemented inline since it just returns whether or not auto-recalculation is in force.

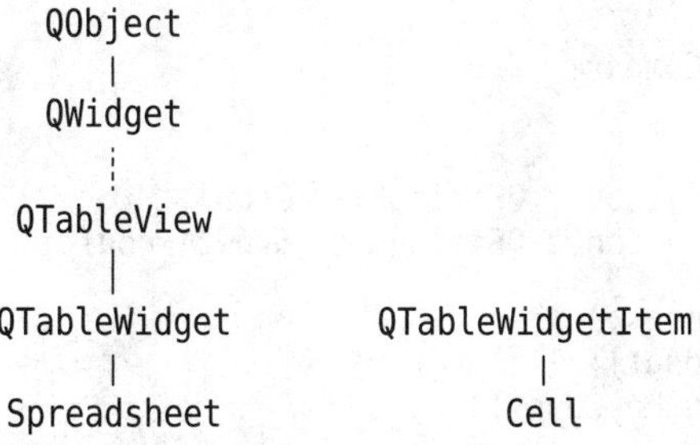

Figure 4.1. Inheritance trees for `Spreadsheet` and `Cell`

In Chapter 3, we relied on some public functions in `Spreadsheet` when we implemented `MainWindow`. For example, we called `clear()` from `MainWindow::newFile()` to reset the spreadsheet. We also used some functions inherited from `QTableWidget`, notably `setCurrentCell()` and `setShowGrid()`.

```
public slots:
    void cut();
    void copy();
    void paste();
    void del();
    void selectCurrentRow();
    void selectCurrentColumn();
    void recalculate();
    void setAutoRecalculate(bool recalc);
    void findNext(const QString &str, Qt::CaseSensitivity cs);
    void findPrevious(const QString &str, Qt::CaseSensitivity cs);

signals:
    void modified();
```

`Spreadsheet` provides many slots that implement actions from the Edit, Tools, and Options menus, and it provides one signal, `modified()`, to announce any change that has occurred.

```
private slots:
    void somethingChanged();
```

We define one private slot used internally by the `Spreadsheet` class.

```
private:
    enum { MagicNumber = 0x7F51C883, RowCount = 999, ColumnCount = 26 };

    Cell *cell(int row, int column) const;
    QString text(int row, int column) const;
    QString formula(int row, int column) const;
    void setFormula(int row, int column, const QString &formula);

    bool autoRecalc;
};
```

In the class's private section, we declare three constants, four functions, and one variable.

```
class SpreadsheetCompare
{
public:
    bool operator()(const QStringList &row1,
                    const QStringList &row2) const;

    enum { KeyCount = 3 };
    int keys[KeyCount];
    bool ascending[KeyCount];
};

#endif
```

The header file ends with the `SpreadsheetCompare` class definition. We will explain this when we review `Spreadsheet::sort()`.

We will now look at the implementation:

```
#include <QtGui>

#include "cell.h"
#include "spreadsheet.h"

Spreadsheet::Spreadsheet(QWidget *parent)
    : QTableWidget(parent)
{
    autoRecalc = true;

    setItemPrototype(new Cell);
    setSelectionMode(ContiguousSelection);

    connect(this, SIGNAL(itemChanged(QTableWidgetItem *)),
            this, SLOT(somethingChanged()));

    clear();
}
```

Normally, when the user enters some text on an empty cell, the `QTableWidget` will automatically create a `QTableWidgetItem` to hold the text. In our spreadsheet, we want `Cell` items to be created instead. This is achieved by the `setItemPrototype()` call in the constructor. Internally, `QTableWidget` clones the item passed as a prototype every time a new item is required.

Also in the constructor, we set the selection mode to `QAbstractItemView::ContiguousSelection` to allow a single rectangular selection. We connect the table widget's `itemChanged()` signal to the private `somethingChanged()` slot; this ensures that when the user edits a cell, the `somethingChanged()` slot is called. Finally, we call `clear()` to resize the table and to set the column headings.

```
void Spreadsheet::clear()
{
    setRowCount(0);
    setColumnCount(0);
    setRowCount(RowCount);
    setColumnCount(ColumnCount);

    for (int i = 0; i < ColumnCount; ++i) {
        QTableWidgetItem *item = new QTableWidgetItem;
        item->setText(QString(QChar('A' + i)));
        setHorizontalHeaderItem(i, item);
    }

    setCurrentCell(0, 0);
}
```

The `clear()` function is called from the `Spreadsheet` constructor to initialize the spreadsheet. It is also called from `MainWindow::newFile()`.

We could have used `QTableWidget::clear()` to clear all the items and any selections, but that would have left the headers at their current size. Instead, we resize the table down to 0×0. This clears the entire spreadsheet, including the headers. We then resize the table to `ColumnCount` × `RowCount` (26×999) and populate the horizontal header with `QTableWidgetItem`s containing the column names "A", "B", ..., "Z". We don't need to set the vertical header labels, because these default to "1", "2", ..., "999". At the end, we move the cell cursor to cell A1.

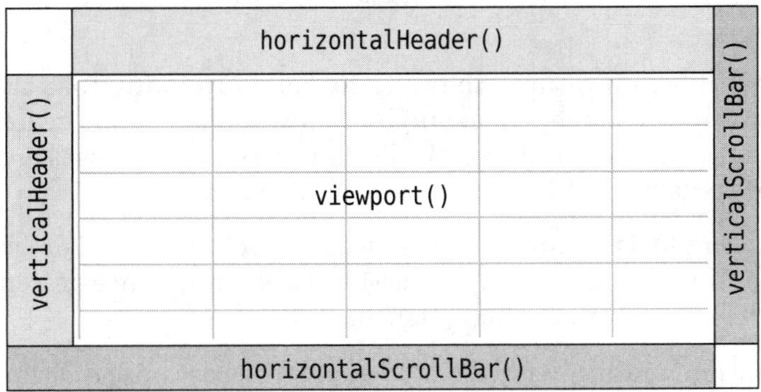

Figure 4.2. `QTableWidget`'s constituent widgets

A QTableWidget is composed of several child widgets. It has a horizontal QHeaderView at the top, a vertical QHeaderView on the left, and two QScrollBars. The area in the middle is occupied by a special widget called the *viewport*, on which QTableWidget draws the cells. The different child widgets are accessible through functions inherited from QTableView and QAbstractScrollArea (see Figure 4.2). QAbstractScrollArea provides a scrollable viewport and two scroll bars, which can be turned on and off. We cover the QScrollArea subclass in Chapter 6.

```
Cell *Spreadsheet::cell(int row, int column) const
{
    return static_cast<Cell *>(item(row, column));
}
```

The cell() private function returns the Cell object for a given row and column. It is almost the same as QTableWidget::item(), except that it returns a Cell pointer instead of a QTableWidgetItem pointer.

```
QString Spreadsheet::text(int row, int column) const
{
    Cell *c = cell(row, column);
    if (c) {
        return c->text();
    } else {
        return "";
    }
}
```

The text() private function returns the text for a given cell. If cell() returns a null pointer, the cell is empty, so we return an empty string.

```
QString Spreadsheet::formula(int row, int column) const
{
    Cell *c = cell(row, column);
    if (c) {
        return c->formula();
    } else {
        return "";
    }
}
```

The formula() function returns the cell's formula. In many cases, the formula and the text are the same; for example, the formula "Hello" evaluates to the string "Hello", so if the user types "Hello" into a cell and presses Enter, that cell will show the text "Hello". But there are a few exceptions:

- If the formula is a number, it is interpreted as such. For example, the formula "1.50" evaluates to the double value 1.5, which is rendered as a right-aligned "1.5" in the spreadsheet.
- If the formula starts with a single quote, the rest of the formula is interpreted as text. For example, the formula "'12345" evaluates to the string "12345".

Storing Data as Items

In the Spreadsheet application, every non-empty cell is stored in memory as an individual `QTableWidgetItem` object. Storing data as items is an approach that is also used by `QListWidget` and `QTreeWidget`, which operate on `QListWidgetItem`s and `QTreeWidgetItem`s.

Qt's item classes can be used out of the box as data holders. For example, a `QTableWidgetItem` already stores a few attributes, including a string, font, color, and icon, and a pointer back to the `QTableWidget`. The items can also hold data (`QVariant`s), including registered custom types, and by subclassing the item class we can provide additional functionality.

Older toolkits provide a `void` pointer in their item classes to store custom data. In Qt, the more natural approach is to use `setData()` with a `QVariant`, but if a `void` pointer is required, it can be trivially achieved by subclassing an item class and adding a `void` pointer member variable.

For more challenging data handling requirements, such as large data sets, complex data items, database integration, and multiple data views, Qt provides a set of model/view classes that separate the data from their visual representation. These are covered in Chapter 10.

- If the formula starts with an equals sign ('='), the formula is interpreted as an arithmetic formula. For example, if cell A1 contains "12" and cell A2 contains "6", the formula "=A1+A2" evaluates to 18.

The task of converting a formula into a value is performed by the `Cell` class. For the moment, the thing to bear in mind is that the text shown in the cell is the result of evaluating the formula, not the formula itself.

```
void Spreadsheet::setFormula(int row, int column,
                             const QString &formula)
{
    Cell *c = cell(row, column);
    if (!c) {
        c = new Cell;
        setItem(row, column, c);
    }
    c->setFormula(formula);
}
```

The `setFormula()` private function sets the formula for a given cell. If the cell already has a `Cell` object, we reuse it. Otherwise, we create a new `Cell` object and call `QTableWidget::setItem()` to insert it into the table. At the end, we call the cell's own `setFormula()` function, which will cause the cell to be repainted if it's shown on-screen. We don't need to worry about deleting the `Cell` object later on; `QTableWidget` takes ownership of the cell and will delete it automatically at the right time.

```
QString Spreadsheet::currentLocation() const
{
    return QChar('A' + currentColumn())
           + QString::number(currentRow() + 1);
}
```

The `currentLocation()` function returns the current cell's location in the usual spreadsheet format of column letter followed by row number. `MainWindow::updateStatusBar()` uses it to show the location in the status bar.

```
QString Spreadsheet::currentFormula() const
{
    return formula(currentRow(), currentColumn());
}
```

The `currentFormula()` function returns the current cell's formula. It is called from `MainWindow::updateStatusBar()`.

```
void Spreadsheet::somethingChanged()
{
    if (autoRecalc)
        recalculate();
    emit modified();
}
```

The `somethingChanged()` private slot recalculates the whole spreadsheet if "auto-recalculate" is enabled. It also emits the `modified()` signal.

Loading and Saving

We will now implement the loading and saving of Spreadsheet files using a custom binary format. We will do this using `QFile` and `QDataStream`, which together provide platform-independent binary I/O.

We will start with writing a Spreadsheet file:

```
bool Spreadsheet::writeFile(const QString &fileName)
{
    QFile file(fileName);
    if (!file.open(QIODevice::WriteOnly)) {
        QMessageBox::warning(this, tr("Spreadsheet"),
                             tr("Cannot write file %1:\n%2.")
                             .arg(file.fileName())
                             .arg(file.errorString()));
        return false;
    }

    QDataStream out(&file);
    out.setVersion(QDataStream::Qt_4_3);

    out << quint32(MagicNumber);

    QApplication::setOverrideCursor(Qt::WaitCursor);
    for (int row = 0; row < RowCount; ++row) {
```

```
        for (int column = 0; column < ColumnCount; ++column) {
            QString str = formula(row, column);
            if (!str.isEmpty())
                out << quint16(row) << quint16(column) << str;
        }
    }
    QApplication::restoreOverrideCursor();
    return true;
}
```

The `writeFile()` function is called from `MainWindow::saveFile()` to write the file to disk. It returns `true` on success, `false` on error.

We create a `QFile` object with the given file name and call `open()` to open the file for writing. We also create a `QDataStream` object that operates on the `QFile` and use it to write out the data.

Just before we write the data, we change the application's cursor to the standard wait cursor (usually an hourglass) and restore the normal cursor once all the data is written. At the end of the function, the file is automatically closed by `QFile`'s destructor.

`QDataStream` supports basic C++ types as well as many of Qt's types. The syntax is modeled after the Standard C++ `<iostream>` classes. For example,

```
out << x << y << z;
```

writes the variables `x`, `y`, and `z` to a stream, and

```
in >> x >> y >> z;
```

reads them from a stream. Because the C++ primitive integer types may have different sizes on different platforms, it is safest to cast these values to one of `qint8`, `quint8`, `qint16`, `quint16`, `qint32`, `quint32`, `qint64`, and `quint64`, which are guaranteed to be of the size they advertise (in bits).

The Spreadsheet application's file format is fairly simple. A Spreadsheet file starts with a 32-bit number that identifies the file format (`MagicNumber`, defined as `0x7F51C883` in `spreadsheet.h`, an arbitrary random number). Then comes a series of blocks, each containing a single cell's row, column, and formula. To save space, we don't write out empty cells. The format is shown in Figure 4.3.

Figure 4.3. The Spreadsheet file format

The precise binary representation of the data types is determined by `QDataStream`. For example, a `quint16` is stored as two bytes in big-endian order, and a `QString` as the string's length followed by the Unicode characters.

The binary representation of Qt types has evolved quite a lot since Qt 1.0. It is likely to continue evolving in future Qt releases to keep pace with the evolution of existing types and to allow for new Qt types. By default, QDataStream uses the most recent version of the binary format (version 9 in Qt 4.3), but it can be set to read older versions. To avoid any compatibility problems if the application is recompiled later using a newer Qt release, we explicitly tell QDataStream to use version 9 irrespective of the version of Qt we are compiling against. (QDataStream::Qt_4_3 is a convenience constant that equals 9.)

QDataStream is very versatile. It can be used on a QFile, and also on a QBuffer, a QProcess, a QTcpSocket, a QUdpSocket, or a QSslSocket. Qt also offers a QTextStream class that can be used instead of QDataStream for reading and writing text files. Chapter 12 explains these classes in depth, and also describes various approaches to handling different QDataStream versions.

```
bool Spreadsheet::readFile(const QString &fileName)
{
    QFile file(fileName);
    if (!file.open(QIODevice::ReadOnly)) {
        QMessageBox::warning(this, tr("Spreadsheet"),
                             tr("Cannot read file %1:\n%2.")
                             .arg(file.fileName())
                             .arg(file.errorString()));
        return false;
    }

    QDataStream in(&file);
    in.setVersion(QDataStream::Qt_4_3);

    quint32 magic;
    in >> magic;
    if (magic != MagicNumber) {
        QMessageBox::warning(this, tr("Spreadsheet"),
                             tr("The file is not a Spreadsheet file."));
        return false;
    }

    clear();

    quint16 row;
    quint16 column;
    QString str;

    QApplication::setOverrideCursor(Qt::WaitCursor);
    while (!in.atEnd()) {
        in >> row >> column >> str;
        setFormula(row, column, str);
    }
    QApplication::restoreOverrideCursor();
    return true;
}
```

The readFile() function is very similar to writeFile(). We use QFile to read in the file, but this time using the QIODevice::ReadOnly flag rather than QIODevice::WriteOnly. Then we set the QDataStream version to 9. The format for reading must always be the same as for writing.

If the file has the correct magic number at the beginning, we call `clear()` to blank out all the cells in the spreadsheet, and we read in the cell data. Since the file only contains the data for non-empty cells, and it is very unlikely that every cell in the spreadsheet will be set, we must ensure that all cells are cleared before reading.

Implementing the Edit Menu

We are now ready to implement the slots that correspond to the application's Edit menu. The menu is shown in Figure 4.4.

```
void Spreadsheet::cut()
{
    copy();
    del();
}
```

The `cut()` slot corresponds to Edit|Cut. The implementation is simple since Cut is the same as Copy followed by Delete.

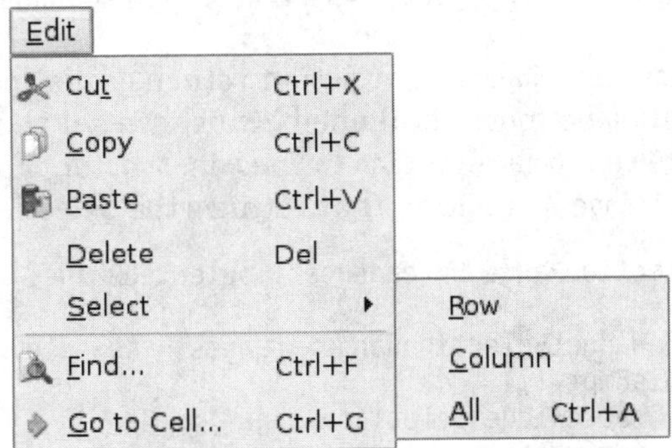

Figure 4.4. The Spreadsheet application's Edit menu

```
void Spreadsheet::copy()
{
    QTableWidgetSelectionRange range = selectedRange();
    QString str;

    for (int i = 0; i < range.rowCount(); ++i) {
        if (i > 0)
            str += "\n";
        for (int j = 0; j < range.columnCount(); ++j) {
            if (j > 0)
                str += "\t";
            str += formula(range.topRow() + i, range.leftColumn() + j);
        }
    }
    QApplication::clipboard()->setText(str);
}
```

The copy() slot corresponds to Edit|Copy. It iterates over the current selection (which is simply the current cell if there is no explicit selection). Each selected cell's formula is added to a QString, with rows separated by newline characters and columns separated by tab characters. This is illustrated in Figure 4.5.

The system clipboard is available in Qt through the QApplication::clipboard() static function. By calling QClipboard::setText(), we make the text available on the clipboard, both to this application and to other applications that support plain text. Our format with tab and newline characters as separators is understood by a variety of applications, including Microsoft Excel.

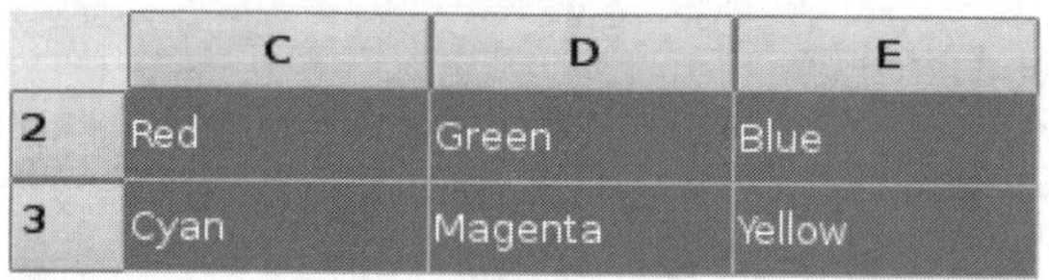

"Red **\t** Green **\t** Blue **\n** Cyan **\t** Magenta **\t** Yellow"

Figure 4.5. Copying a selection onto the clipboard

The QTableWidget::selectedRanges() function returns a list of selection ranges. We know there cannot be more than one because we set the selection mode to QAbstractItemView::ContiguousSelection in the constructor. For our convenience, we define a selectedRange() function that returns the selection range:

```
QTableWidgetSelectionRange Spreadsheet::selectedRange() const
{
    QList<QTableWidgetSelectionRange> ranges = selectedRanges();
    if (ranges.isEmpty())
        return QTableWidgetSelectionRange();
    return ranges.first();
}
```

If there is a selection at all, we simply return the first (and only) one. There should always be a selection since the ContiguousSelection mode treats the current cell as being selected. But to protect against the possibility of a bug in our program that makes no cell current, we handle this case.

```
void Spreadsheet::paste()
{
    QTableWidgetSelectionRange range = selectedRange();
    QString str = QApplication::clipboard()->text();
    QStringList rows = str.split('\n');
    int numRows = rows.count();
    int numColumns = rows.first().count('\t') + 1;

    if (range.rowCount() * range.columnCount() != 1
            && (range.rowCount() != numRows
                || range.columnCount() != numColumns)) {
```

```
        QMessageBox::information(this, tr("Spreadsheet"),
                tr("The information cannot be pasted because the copy "
                   "and paste areas aren't the same size."));
        return;
    }

    for (int i = 0; i < numRows; ++i) {
        QStringList columns = rows[i].split('\t');
        for (int j = 0; j < numColumns; ++j) {
            int row = range.topRow() + i;
            int column = range.leftColumn() + j;
            if (row < RowCount && column < ColumnCount)
                setFormula(row, column, columns[j]);
        }
    }
    somethingChanged();
}
```

The `paste()` slot corresponds to Edit|Paste. We fetch the text on the clipboard and call the static function `QString::split()` to break the string into a `QStringList`. Each row becomes one string in the list.

Next, we determine the dimensions of the copy area. The number of rows is the number of strings in the `QStringList`; the number of columns is the number of tab characters in the first row, plus 1. If only one cell is selected, we use that cell as the top-left corner of the paste area; otherwise, we use the current selection as the paste area.

To perform the paste, we iterate over the rows and split each of them into cells by using `QString::split()` again, but this time using tab as the separator. Figure 4.6 illustrates the steps.

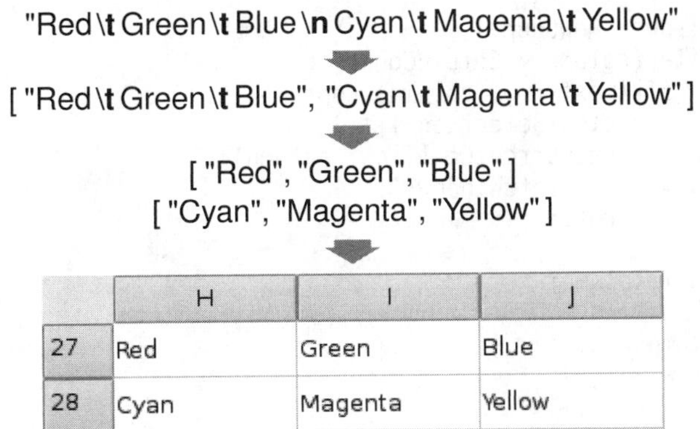

Figure 4.6. Pasting clipboard text into the spreadsheet

```
void Spreadsheet::del()
{
    QList<QTableWidgetItem *> items = selectedItems();
    if (!items.isEmpty()) {
        foreach (QTableWidgetItem *item, items)
```

```
            delete item;
        somethingChanged();
    }
}
```

The `del()` slot corresponds to Edit|Delete. If there are selected items, the function deletes them and calls `somethingChanged()`. It is sufficient to use `delete` on each `Cell` object in the selection to clear the cells. The `QTableWidget` notices when its `QTableWidgetItem`s are deleted and automatically repaints itself if any of the items were visible. If we call `cell()` with the location of a deleted cell, it will return a null pointer.

```
void Spreadsheet::selectCurrentRow()
{
    selectRow(currentRow());
}

void Spreadsheet::selectCurrentColumn()
{
    selectColumn(currentColumn());
}
```

The `selectCurrentRow()` and `selectCurrentColumn()` functions correspond to the Edit|Select|Row and Edit|Select|Column menu options. The implementations rely on `QTableWidget`'s `selectRow()` and `selectColumn()` functions. We do not need to implement the functionality behind Edit|Select|All, since that is provided by `QTableWidget`'s inherited function `QAbstractItemView::selectAll()`.

```
void Spreadsheet::findNext(const QString &str, Qt::CaseSensitivity cs)
{
    int row = currentRow();
    int column = currentColumn() + 1;

    while (row < RowCount) {
        while (column < ColumnCount) {
            if (text(row, column).contains(str, cs)) {
                clearSelection();
                setCurrentCell(row, column);
                activateWindow();
                return;
            }
            ++column;
        }
        column = 0;
        ++row;
    }
    QApplication::beep();
}
```

The `findNext()` slot iterates through the cells starting from the cell to the right of the cursor and moving right until the last column is reached, then continues from the first column in the row below, and so on until the text is found or until the very last cell is reached. For example, if the current cell is cell C24, we search D24, E24, ..., Z24, then A25, B25, C25, ..., Z25, and so on until Z999.

If we find a match, we clear the current selection, move the cell cursor to the cell that matched, and make the window that contains the Spreadsheet active. If no match is found, we make the application beep to indicate that the search finished unsuccessfully.

```
void Spreadsheet::findPrevious(const QString &str,
                               Qt::CaseSensitivity cs)
{
    int row = currentRow();
    int column = currentColumn() - 1;

    while (row >= 0) {
        while (column >= 0) {
            if (text(row, column).contains(str, cs)) {
                clearSelection();
                setCurrentCell(row, column);
                activateWindow();
                return;
            }
            --column;
        }
        column = ColumnCount - 1;
        --row;
    }
    QApplication::beep();
}
```

The findPrevious() slot is similar to findNext(), except that it iterates backward and stops at cell A1.

Implementing the Other Menus

We will now implement the slots for the Tools and Options menus. These menus are shown in Figure 4.7.

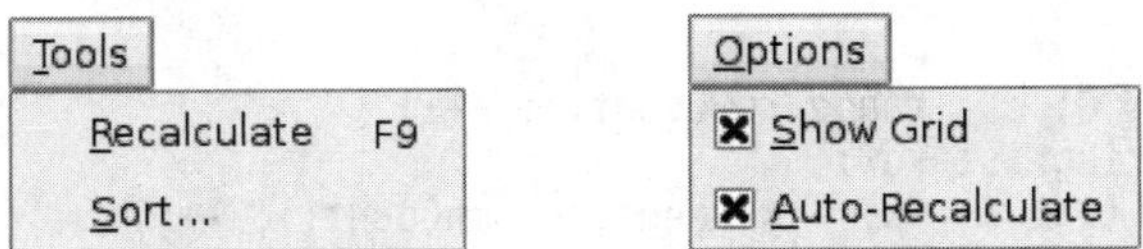

Figure 4.7. The Spreadsheet application's Tools and Options menus

```
void Spreadsheet::recalculate()
{
    for (int row = 0; row < RowCount; ++row) {
        for (int column = 0; column < ColumnCount; ++column) {
            if (cell(row, column))
                cell(row, column)->setDirty();
        }
    }
    viewport()->update();
}
```

The recalculate() slot corresponds to Tools|Recalculate. It is also called automatically by Spreadsheet when necessary.

We iterate over all the cells and call setDirty() on every cell to mark each one as requiring recalculation. The next time QTableWidget calls text() on a Cell to obtain the value to show in the spreadsheet, the value will be recalculated.

Then we call update() on the viewport to repaint the whole spreadsheet. The repaint code in QTableWidget then calls text() on each visible cell to obtain the value to display. Because we called setDirty() on every cell, the calls to text() will use a freshly calculated value. The calculation may require non-visible cells to be recalculated, cascading the calculation until every cell that needs to be recalculated to display the correct text in the viewport has been freshly calculated. The calculation is performed by the Cell class.

```
void Spreadsheet::setAutoRecalculate(bool recalc)
{
    autoRecalc = recalc;
    if (autoRecalc)
        recalculate();
}
```

The setAutoRecalculate() slot corresponds to Options|Auto-Recalculate. If the feature is being turned on, we recalculate the whole spreadsheet immediately to make sure that it's up-to-date; afterward, recalculate() is called automatically from somethingChanged().

We don't need to implement anything for Options|Show Grid because QTableWidget already has a setShowGrid() slot, which it inherits from QTableView. All that remains is Spreadsheet::sort(), which is called from MainWindow::sort():

```
void Spreadsheet::sort(const SpreadsheetCompare &compare)
{
    QList<QStringList> rows;
    QTableWidgetSelectionRange range = selectedRange();
    int i;

    for (i = 0; i < range.rowCount(); ++i) {
        QStringList row;
        for (int j = 0; j < range.columnCount(); ++j)
            row.append(formula(range.topRow() + i,
                               range.leftColumn() + j));
        rows.append(row);
    }

    qStableSort(rows.begin(), rows.end(), compare);

    for (i = 0; i < range.rowCount(); ++i) {
        for (int j = 0; j < range.columnCount(); ++j)
            setFormula(range.topRow() + i, range.leftColumn() + j,
                       rows[i][j]);
    }

    clearSelection();
```

```
        somethingChanged();
    }
```

Sorting operates on the current selection and reorders the rows according to the sort keys and sort orders stored in the `compare` object. We represent each row of data with a `QStringList` and store the selection as a list of rows. We use Qt's `qStableSort()` algorithm, and for simplicity sort by formula rather than by value. The process is illustrated by Figures 4.8 and 4.9. We cover Qt's standard algorithms and data structures in Chapter 11.

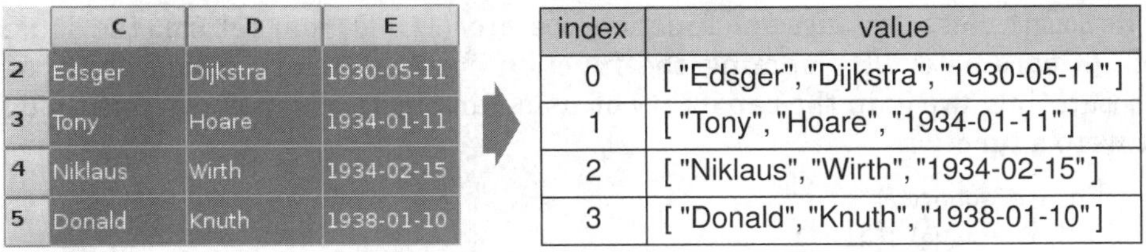

	C	D	E
2	Edsger	Dijkstra	1930-05-11
3	Tony	Hoare	1934-01-11
4	Niklaus	Wirth	1934-02-15
5	Donald	Knuth	1938-01-10

index	value
0	["Edsger", "Dijkstra", "1930-05-11"]
1	["Tony", "Hoare", "1934-01-11"]
2	["Niklaus", "Wirth", "1934-02-15"]
3	["Donald", "Knuth", "1938-01-10"]

Figure 4.8. Storing the selection as a list of rows

The `qStableSort()` function accepts a begin iterator, an end iterator, and a comparison function. The comparison function is a function that takes two arguments (two `QStringLists`) and that returns `true` if the first argument is "less than" the second argument, `false` otherwise. The `compare` object we pass as the comparison function isn't really a function, but it can be used as one, as we will see shortly.

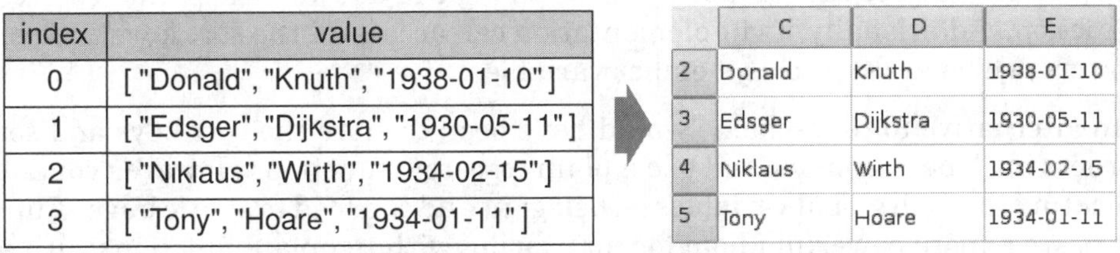

index	value
0	["Donald", "Knuth", "1938-01-10"]
1	["Edsger", "Dijkstra", "1930-05-11"]
2	["Niklaus", "Wirth", "1934-02-15"]
3	["Tony", "Hoare", "1934-01-11"]

	C	D	E
2	Donald	Knuth	1938-01-10
3	Edsger	Dijkstra	1930-05-11
4	Niklaus	Wirth	1934-02-15
5	Tony	Hoare	1934-01-11

Figure 4.9. Putting the data back into the table after sorting

After performing the `qStableSort()`, we move the data back into the table, clear the selection, and call `somethingChanged()`.

In `spreadsheet.h`, the `SpreadsheetCompare` class was defined like this:

```
class SpreadsheetCompare
{
public:
    bool operator()(const QStringList &row1,
                    const QStringList &row2) const;

    enum { KeyCount = 3 };
    int keys[KeyCount];
    bool ascending[KeyCount];
};
```

The `SpreadsheetCompare` class is special because it implements a `()` operator. This allows us to use the class as though it were a function. Such classes are called *function objects*, or *functors*. To understand how functors work, we will start with a simple example:

```
class Square
{
public:
    int operator()(int x) const { return x * x; }
}
```

The `Square` class provides one function, `operator()(int)`, that returns the square of its parameter. By naming the function `operator()(int)` rather than, say, `compute(int)`, we gain the capability of using an object of type `Square` as though it were a function:

```
Square square;
int y = square(5);
// y equals 25
```

Now let's see an example involving `SpreadsheetCompare`:

```
QStringList row1, row2;
SpreadsheetCompare compare;
...
if (compare(row1, row2)) {
    // row1 is less than row2
}
```

The `compare` object can be used just as though it had been a plain `compare()` function. Additionally, its implementation can access all the sort keys and sort orders, which are stored as member variables.

An alternative to this scheme would have been to store the sort keys and sort orders in global variables and use a plain `compare()` function. However, communicating through global variables is inelegant and can lead to subtle bugs. Functors are a more powerful idiom for interfacing with template functions such as `qStableSort()`.

Here is the implementation of the function that is used to compare two spreadsheet rows:

```
bool SpreadsheetCompare::operator()(const QStringList &row1,
                                    const QStringList &row2) const
{
    for (int i = 0; i < KeyCount; ++i) {
        int column = keys[i];
        if (column != -1) {
            if (row1[column] != row2[column]) {
                if (ascending[i]) {
                    return row1[column] < row2[column];
                } else {
                    return row1[column] > row2[column];
                }
```

```
            }
        }
    }
    return false;
}
```

The operator returns `true` if the first row is less than the second row; otherwise, it returns `false`. The `qStableSort()` function uses the result of this function to perform the sort.

The `SpreadsheetCompare` object's `keys` and `ascending` arrays are populated in the `MainWindow::sort()` function (shown in Chapter 2). Each key holds a column index, or -1 ("None").

We compare the corresponding cell entries in the two rows for each key in order. As soon as we find a difference, we return an appropriate `true` or `false` value. If all the comparisons turn out to be equal, we return `false`. The `qStableSort()` function uses the order before the sort to resolve tie situations; if `row1` preceded `row2` originally and neither compares as "less than" the other, `row1` will still precede `row2` in the result. This is what distinguishes `qStableSort()` from its unstable cousin `qSort()`.

We have now completed the `Spreadsheet` class. In the next section, we will review the `Cell` class. This class is used to hold cell formulas and provides a reimplementation of the `QTableWidgetItem::data()` function that `Spreadsheet` calls indirectly, through the `QTableWidgetItem::text()` function, to display the result of calculating a cell's formula.

Subclassing QTableWidgetItem

The `Cell` class is derived from `QTableWidgetItem`. The class is designed to work well with `Spreadsheet`, but it has no specific dependencies on that class and could in theory be used in any `QTableWidget`. Here's the header file:

```
#ifndef CELL_H
#define CELL_H

#include <QTableWidgetItem>

class Cell : public QTableWidgetItem
{
public:
    Cell();

    QTableWidgetItem *clone() const;
    void setData(int role, const QVariant &value);
    QVariant data(int role) const;
    void setFormula(const QString &formula);
    QString formula() const;
    void setDirty();

private:
    QVariant value() const;
```

```
    QVariant evalExpression(const QString &str, int &pos) const;
    QVariant evalTerm(const QString &str, int &pos) const;
    QVariant evalFactor(const QString &str, int &pos) const;

    mutable QVariant cachedValue;
    mutable bool cacheIsDirty;
};

#endif
```

The `Cell` class extends `QTableWidgetItem` by adding two private variables:

- `cachedValue` caches the cell's value as a `QVariant`.
- `cacheIsDirty` is `true` if the cached value isn't up-to-date.

We use `QVariant` because some cells have a `double` value, while others have a `QString` value.

The `cachedValue` and `cacheIsDirty` variables are declared with the C++ `mutable` keyword. This allows us to modify these variables in const functions. Alternatively, we could recalculate the value each time `text()` is called, but that would be needlessly inefficient.

Notice that there is no `Q_OBJECT` macro in the class definition. `Cell` is a plain C++ class, with no signals or slots. In fact, because `QTableWidgetItem` isn't derived from `QObject`, we cannot have signals and slots in `Cell` as it stands. Qt's item classes are not derived from `QObject` to keep their overhead to the barest minimum. If signals and slots are needed, they can be implemented in the widget that contains the items or, exceptionally, using multiple inheritance with `QObject`.

Here's the start of `cell.cpp`:

```
#include <QtGui>

#include "cell.h"

Cell::Cell()
{
    setDirty();
}
```

In the constructor, we only need to set the cache as dirty. There is no need to pass a parent; when the cell is inserted into a `QTableWidget` with `setItem()`, the `QTableWidget` will automatically take ownership of it.

Every `QTableWidgetItem` can hold some data, up to one `QVariant` for each data "role". The most commonly used roles are `Qt::EditRole` and `Qt::DisplayRole`. The edit role is used for data that is to be edited, and the display role is for data that is to be displayed. Often the data for both is the same, but in `Cell` the edit role corresponds to the cell's formula and the display role corresponds to the cell's value (the result of evaluating the formula).

```
QTableWidgetItem *Cell::clone() const
{
    return new Cell(*this);
}
```

The `clone()` function is called by `QTableWidget` when it needs to create a new cell—for example, when the user starts typing into an empty cell that has not been used before. The instance passed to `QTableWidget::setItemPrototype()` is the item that is cloned. Since member-wise copying is sufficient for `Cell`, we are relying on the default copy constructor automatically created by C++ to create new `Cell` instances in the `clone()` function.

```
void Cell::setFormula(const QString &formula)
{
    setData(Qt::EditRole, formula);
}
```

The `setFormula()` function sets the cell's formula. It is simply a convenience function for calling `setData()` with the edit role. It is called from `Spreadsheet::setFormula()`.

```
QString Cell::formula() const
{
    return data(Qt::EditRole).toString();
}
```

The `formula()` function is called from `Spreadsheet::formula()`. Like `setFormula()`, it is a convenience function, this time retrieving the item's `EditRole` data.

```
void Cell::setData(int role, const QVariant &value)
{
    QTableWidgetItem::setData(role, value);
    if (role == Qt::EditRole)
        setDirty();
}
```

If we have a new formula, we set `cacheIsDirty` to `true` to ensure that the cell is recalculated the next time `text()` is called.

There is no `text()` function defined in `Cell`, although we call `text()` on `Cell` instances in `Spreadsheet::text()`. The `text()` function is a convenience function provided by `QTableWidgetItem`; it is the equivalent of calling `data(Qt::DisplayRole).toString()`.

```
void Cell::setDirty()
{
    cacheIsDirty = true;
}
```

The `setDirty()` function is called to force a recalculation of the cell's value. It simply sets `cacheIsDirty` to `true`, meaning that `cachedValue` is no longer up-to-date. The recalculation isn't performed until it is necessary.

```
QVariant Cell::data(int role) const
{
    if (role == Qt::DisplayRole) {
        if (value().isValid()) {
            return value().toString();
        } else {
            return "####";
        }
    } else if (role == Qt::TextAlignmentRole) {
        if (value().type() == QVariant::String) {
            return int(Qt::AlignLeft | Qt::AlignVCenter);
        } else {
            return int(Qt::AlignRight | Qt::AlignVCenter);
        }
    } else {
        return QTableWidgetItem::data(role);
    }
}
```

The `data()` function is reimplemented from `QTableWidgetItem`. It returns the text that should be shown in the spreadsheet if called with `Qt::DisplayRole`, and the formula if called with `Qt::EditRole`. It returns a suitable alignment if called with `Qt::TextAlignmentRole`. In the `DisplayRole` case, it relies on `value()` to compute the cell's value. If the value is invalid (because the formula is wrong), we return "####".

The `Cell::value()` function used in `data()` returns a `QVariant`. A `QVariant` can store values of different types, such as `double` and `QString`, and provides functions to convert the variant to other types. For example, calling `toString()` on a variant that holds a `double` value produces a string representation of the `double`. A `QVariant` constructed using the default constructor is an "invalid" variant.

```
const QVariant Invalid;

QVariant Cell::value() const
{
    if (cacheIsDirty) {
        cacheIsDirty = false;

        QString formulaStr = formula();
        if (formulaStr.startsWith('\'')) {
            cachedValue = formulaStr.mid(1);
        } else if (formulaStr.startsWith('=')) {
            cachedValue = Invalid;
            QString expr = formulaStr.mid(1);
            expr.replace(" ", "");
            expr.append(QChar::Null);

            int pos = 0;
            cachedValue = evalExpression(expr, pos);
            if (expr[pos] != QChar::Null)
                cachedValue = Invalid;
        } else {
            bool ok;
            double d = formulaStr.toDouble(&ok);
```

```
            if (ok) {
                cachedValue = d;
            } else {
                cachedValue = formulaStr;
            }
        }
    }
    return cachedValue;
}
```

The `value()` private function returns the cell's value. If `cacheIsDirty` is `true`, we need to recalculate the value.

If the formula starts with a single quote (e.g., "'12345"), the single quote occupies position 0 and the value is the string from position 1 to the end.

If the formula starts with an equals sign ('='), we take the string from position 1 and remove any spaces it may contain. Then we call `evalExpression()` to compute the value of the expression. The `pos` argument is passed by reference; it indicates the position of the character where parsing should begin. After the call to `evalExpression()`, the character at position `pos` should be the `QChar::Null` character we appended, if it was successfully parsed. If the parse failed before the end, we set `cachedValue` to be `Invalid`.

If the formula doesn't begin with a single quote or an equals sign, we attempt to convert it to a floating-point value using `toDouble()`. If the conversion works, we set `cachedValue` to be the resulting number; otherwise, we set `cachedValue` to be the formula string. For example, a formula of "1.50" causes `toDouble()` to set `ok` to `true` and return 1.5, while a formula of "World Population" causes `toDouble()` to set `ok` to `false` and return 0.0.

By giving `toDouble()` a pointer to a `bool`, we are able to distinguish between the conversion of a string that represents the numeric value 0.0 and a conversion error (where 0.0 is also returned but the `bool` is set to `false`). Sometimes the returning of a zero value on conversion failure is exactly what we need, in which case we do not bother passing a pointer to a `bool`. For performance and portability reasons, Qt never uses C++ exceptions to report failure. This doesn't prevent you from using them in Qt programs if your compiler supports them.

The `value()` function is declared const. We had to declare `cachedValue` and `cacheIsValid` as mutable variables so that the compiler will allow us to modify them in const functions. It might be tempting to make `value()` non-const and remove the `mutable` keywords, but that would not compile because we call `value()` from `data()`, a const function.

We have now completed the Spreadsheet application, apart from parsing formulas. The rest of this section covers `evalExpression()` and the two helper functions `evalTerm()` and `evalFactor()`. The code is a bit complicated, but it is included here to make the application complete. Since the code is not related to GUI programming, you can safely skip it and continue reading from Chapter 5.

The evalExpression() function returns the value of a spreadsheet expression. An expression is defined as one or more terms separated by '+' or '–' operators. The terms themselves are defined as one or more factors separated by '*' or '/' operators. By breaking down expressions into terms and terms into factors, we ensure that the operators are applied with the correct precedence.

For example, "2*C5+D6" is an expression with "2*C5" as its first term and "D6" as its second term. The term "2*C5" has "2" as its first factor and "C5" as its second factor, and the term "D6" consists of the single factor "D6". A factor can be a number ("2"), a cell location ("C5"), or an expression in parentheses, optionally preceded by a unary minus.

The syntax of spreadsheet expressions is defined in Figure 4.10. For each symbol in the grammar (*Expression*, *Term*, and *Factor*), there is a corresponding member function that parses it and whose structure closely follows the grammar. Parsers written this way are called *recursive-descent parsers*.

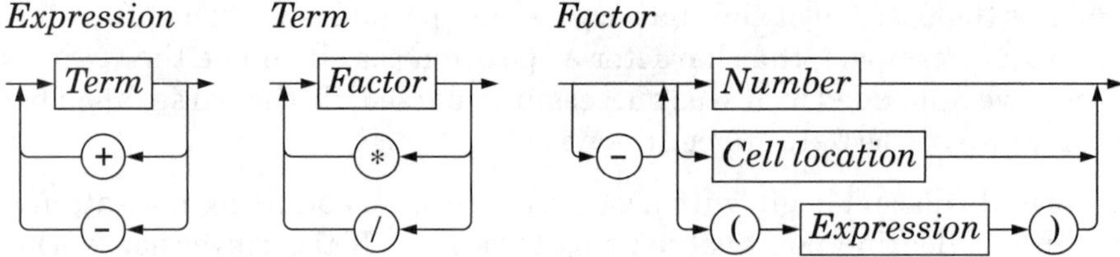

Figure 4.10. Syntax diagram for spreadsheet expressions

Let's start with evalExpression(), the function that parses an *Expression*:

```
QVariant Cell::evalExpression(const QString &str, int &pos) const
{
    QVariant result = evalTerm(str, pos);
    while (str[pos] != QChar::Null) {
        QChar op = str[pos];
        if (op != '+' && op != '-')
            return result;
        ++pos;

        QVariant term = evalTerm(str, pos);
        if (result.type() == QVariant::Double
                && term.type() == QVariant::Double) {
            if (op == '+') {
                result = result.toDouble() + term.toDouble();
            } else {
                result = result.toDouble() - term.toDouble();
            }
        } else {
            result = Invalid;
        }
    }
    return result;
}
```

First, we call `evalTerm()` to get the value of the first term. If the following character is '+' or '–', we continue by calling `evalTerm()` a second time; otherwise, the expression consists of a single term, and we return its value as the value of the whole expression. After we have the value of the first two terms, we compute the result of the operation, depending on the operator. If both terms evaluated to a `double`, we compute the result as a `double`; otherwise, we set the result to be `Invalid`.

We continue like this until there are no more terms. This works correctly because addition and subtraction are left-associative; that is, "1–2–3" means "(1–2)–3", not "1–(2–3)".

```
QVariant Cell::evalTerm(const QString &str, int &pos) const
{
    QVariant result = evalFactor(str, pos);
    while (str[pos] != QChar::Null) {
        QChar op = str[pos];
        if (op != '*' && op != '/')
            return result;
        ++pos;

        QVariant factor = evalFactor(str, pos);
        if (result.type() == QVariant::Double
                && factor.type() == QVariant::Double) {
            if (op == '*') {
                result = result.toDouble() * factor.toDouble();
            } else {
                if (factor.toDouble() == 0.0) {
                    result = Invalid;
                } else {
                    result = result.toDouble() / factor.toDouble();
                }
            }
        } else {
            result = Invalid;
        }
    }
    return result;
}
```

The `evalTerm()` function is very similar to `evalExpression()`, except that it deals with multiplication and division. The only subtlety in `evalTerm()` is that we must avoid division by zero, since it is an error on some processors. While it is generally inadvisable to test floating-point values for equality because of rounding errors, it is safe to test for equality against 0.0 to prevent division by zero.

```
QVariant Cell::evalFactor(const QString &str, int &pos) const
{
    QVariant result;
    bool negative = false;

    if (str[pos] == '-') {
        negative = true;
```

```
            ++pos;
        }

        if (str[pos] == '(') {
            ++pos;
            result = evalExpression(str, pos);
            if (str[pos] != ')')
                result = Invalid;
            ++pos;
        } else {
            QRegExp regExp("[A-Za-z][1-9][0-9]{0,2}");
            QString token;

            while (str[pos].isLetterOrNumber() || str[pos] == '.') {
                token += str[pos];
                ++pos;
            }

            if (regExp.exactMatch(token)) {
                int column = token[0].toUpper().unicode() - 'A';
                int row = token.mid(1).toInt() - 1;

                Cell *c = static_cast<Cell *>(
                                  tableWidget()->item(row, column));
                if (c) {
                    result = c->value();
                } else {
                    result = 0.0;
                }
            } else {
                bool ok;
                result = token.toDouble(&ok);
                if (!ok)
                    result = Invalid;
            }
        }

        if (negative) {
            if (result.type() == QVariant::Double) {
                result = -result.toDouble();
            } else {
                result = Invalid;
            }
        }
        return result;
    }
```

The `evalFactor()` function is a bit more complicated than `evalExpression()` and `evalTerm()`. We start by noting whether the factor is negated. We then see if it begins with an open parenthesis. If it does, we evaluate the contents of the parentheses as an expression by calling `evalExpression()`. When parsing a parenthesized expression, `evalExpression()` calls `evalTerm()`, which calls `evalFactor()`, which calls `evalExpression()` again. This is where recursion occurs in the parser.

If the factor isn't a nested expression, we extract the next token, which should be a cell location or a number. If the token matches the `QRegExp`, we take it to be a cell reference and we call `value()` on the cell at the given location. The cell could be anywhere in the spreadsheet, and it could have dependencies on other cells. The dependencies are not a problem; they will simply trigger more `value()` calls and (for "dirty" cells) more parsing until all the dependent cell values are calculated. If the token isn't a cell location, we take it to be a number.

What happens if cell A1 contains the formula "=A1"? Or if cell A1 contains "=A2" and cell A2 contains "=A1"? Although we have not written any special code to detect circular dependencies, the parser handles these cases gracefully by returning an invalid `QVariant`. This works because we set `cacheIsDirty` to `false` and `cachedValue` to `Invalid` in `value()` before we call `evalExpression()`. If `evalExpression()` recursively calls `value()` on the same cell, it returns `Invalid` immediately, and the whole expression then evaluates to `Invalid`.

We have now completed the formula parser. It would be straightforward to extend it to handle predefined spreadsheet functions, such as "sum()" and "avg()", by extending the grammatical definition of *Factor*. Another easy extension is to implement the '+' operator with string operands (as concatenation); this requires no changes to the grammar.

- *Customizing Qt Widgets*
- *Subclassing QWidget*
- *Integrating Custom Widgets with Qt Designer*
- *Double Buffering*

5. Creating Custom Widgets

This chapter explains how to develop custom widgets using Qt. Custom widgets can be created by subclassing an existing Qt widget or by subclassing QWidget directly. We will demonstrate both approaches, and we will also see how to integrate a custom widget with *Qt Designer* so that it can be used just like a built-in Qt widget. We will round off the chapter by presenting a custom widget that uses double buffering, a powerful technique for high-speed drawing.

Customizing Qt Widgets

In some cases, we find that a Qt widget requires more customization than is possible by setting its properties in *Qt Designer* or by calling its functions. A simple and direct solution is to subclass the relevant widget class and adapt it to suit our needs.

In this section, we will develop the hexadecimal spin box shown in Figure 5.1, to demonstrate how this works. QSpinBox supports only decimal integers, but by subclassing it's quite easy to make it accept and display hexadecimal values.

Figure 5.1. The HexSpinBox widget

```
#ifndef HEXSPINBOX_H
#define HEXSPINBOX_H

#include <QSpinBox>

class QRegExpValidator;

class HexSpinBox : public QSpinBox
{
    Q_OBJECT
```

```
public:
    HexSpinBox(QWidget *parent = 0);

protected:
    QValidator::State validate(QString &text, int &pos) const;
    int valueFromText(const QString &text) const;
    QString textFromValue(int value) const;

private:
    QRegExpValidator *validator;
};

#endif
```

The HexSpinBox inherits most of its functionality from QSpinBox. It provides a typical constructor and reimplements three virtual functions from QSpinBox.

```
#include <QtGui>

#include "hexspinbox.h"

HexSpinBox::HexSpinBox(QWidget *parent)
    : QSpinBox(parent)
{
    setRange(0, 255);
    validator = new QRegExpValidator(QRegExp("[0-9A-Fa-f]{1,8}"), this);
}
```

We set the default range to be from 0 to 255 (0x00 to 0xFF), which is more appropriate for a hexadecimal spin box than QSpinBox's default of 0 to 99.

The user can modify a spin box's current value either by clicking its up and down arrows or by typing a value into the spin box's line editor. In the latter case, we want to restrict the user's input to legitimate hexadecimal numbers. To achieve this, we use a QRegExpValidator that accepts between one and eight characters, all of which must be in the set {'0', …, '9', 'A', …, 'F', 'a', …, 'f'}.

```
QValidator::State HexSpinBox::validate(QString &text, int &pos) const
{
    return validator->validate(text, pos);
}
```

This function is called by QSpinBox to see if the text entered so far is valid. There are three possible results: Invalid (the text doesn't match the regular expression), Intermediate (the text is a plausible part of a valid value), and Acceptable (the text is valid). The QRegExpValidator has a suitable validate() function, so we simply return the result of calling it. In theory, we should return Invalid or Intermediate for values that lie outside the spin box's range, but QSpinBox is smart enough to detect that condition without any help.

```
QString HexSpinBox::textFromValue(int value) const
{
    return QString::number(value, 16).toUpper();
}
```

The `textFromValue()` function converts an integer value to a string. `QSpinBox` calls it to update the editor part of the spin box when the user presses the spin box's up or down arrows. We use the static function `QString::number()` with a second argument of 16 to convert the value to lowercase hexadecimal, and call `QString::toUpper()` on the result to make it uppercase.

```
int HexSpinBox::valueFromText(const QString &text) const
{
    bool ok;
    return text.toInt(&ok, 16);
}
```

The `valueFromText()` function performs the reverse conversion, from a string to an integer value. It is called by `QSpinBox` when the user types a value into the editor part of the spin box and presses Enter. We use the `QString::toInt()` function to attempt to convert the current text to an integer value, again using base 16. If the string is not valid hexadecimal, `ok` is set to `false` and `toInt()` returns 0. Here, we don't have to consider this possibility because the validator permits only valid hexadecimal strings to be entered. Instead of passing the address of a dummy variable (`ok`), we could pass a null pointer as the first argument to `toInt()`.

We have now finished the hexadecimal spin box. Customizing other Qt widgets follows the same pattern: Pick a suitable Qt widget, subclass it, and reimplement some virtual functions to change its behavior. If all we want to do is to customize an existing widget's look and feel, we can apply a style sheet or implement a custom style instead of subclassing the widget, as explained in Chapter 19.

Subclassing QWidget

Many custom widgets are simply a combination of existing widgets, whether they are built-in Qt widgets or other custom widgets such as `HexSpinBox`. Custom widgets that are built by composing existing widgets can usually be developed in *Qt Designer*:

- Create a new form using the "Widget" template.
- Add the necessary widgets to the form, and lay them out.
- Set up the signals and slots connections.
- If behavior beyond what can be achieved through signals and slots is required, write the necessary code in a class that is derived from both `QWidget` and the `uic`-generated class.

Naturally, combining existing widgets can also be done entirely in code. Whichever approach is taken, the resulting class is a `QWidget` subclass.

If the widget has no signals and slots of its own and doesn't reimplement any virtual functions, it is even possible to simply assemble the widget by combining existing widgets without a subclass. That's the approach we used in Chapter 1 to create the Age application, with a QWidget, a QSpinBox, and a QSlider. Even so, we could just as easily have subclassed QWidget and created the QSpinBox and QSlider in the subclass's constructor.

When none of Qt's widgets are suitable for the task at hand, and when there is no way to combine or adapt existing widgets to obtain the desired result, we can still create the widget we want. This is achieved by subclassing QWidget and reimplementing a few event handlers to paint the widget and to respond to mouse clicks. This approach gives us complete freedom to define and control both the appearance and the behavior of our widget. Qt's built-in widgets, such as QLabel, QPushButton, and QTableWidget, are implemented this way. If they didn't exist in Qt, it would still be possible to create them ourselves using the public functions provided by QWidget in a completely platform-independent manner.

To demonstrate how to write a custom widget using this approach, we will create the IconEditor widget shown in Figure 5.2. The IconEditor is a widget that could be used in an icon editing program.

In practice, before diving in and creating a custom widget, it is always worth checking whether the widget is already available, either as a Qt Solution (http://www.trolltech.com/products/qt/addon/solutions/catalog/4/) or from a commercial or non-commercial third party (http://www.trolltech.com/products/qt/3rdparty/), since this could save a lot of time and effort. In this case, we will assume that no suitable widget is available, and so we will create our own.

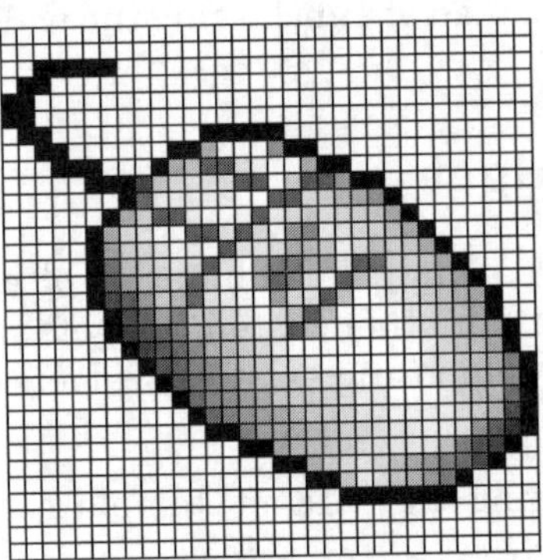

Figure 5.2. The IconEditor widget

Let's begin by reviewing the header file.

```
#ifndef ICONEDITOR_H
#define ICONEDITOR_H

#include <QColor>
#include <QImage>
#include <QWidget>

class IconEditor : public QWidget
```

```
{
    Q_OBJECT
    Q_PROPERTY(QColor penColor READ penColor WRITE setPenColor)
    Q_PROPERTY(QImage iconImage READ iconImage WRITE setIconImage)
    Q_PROPERTY(int zoomFactor READ zoomFactor WRITE setZoomFactor)

public:
    IconEditor(QWidget *parent = 0);

    void setPenColor(const QColor &newColor);
    QColor penColor() const { return curColor; }
    void setZoomFactor(int newZoom);
    int zoomFactor() const { return zoom; }
    void setIconImage(const QImage &newImage);
    QImage iconImage() const { return image; }
    QSize sizeHint() const;
```

The `IconEditor` class uses the `Q_PROPERTY()` macro to declare three custom properties: `penColor`, `iconImage`, and `zoomFactor`. Each property has a data type, a "read" function, and an optional "write" function. For example, the `penColor` property is of type `QColor` and can be read and written using the `penColor()` and `setPenColor()` functions.

When we make use of the widget in *Qt Designer*, custom properties appear in *Qt Designer*'s property editor below the properties inherited from `QWidget`. Properties may be of any type supported by `QVariant`. The `Q_OBJECT` macro is necessary for classes that define properties.

```
protected:
    void mousePressEvent(QMouseEvent *event);
    void mouseMoveEvent(QMouseEvent *event);
    void paintEvent(QPaintEvent *event);

private:
    void setImagePixel(const QPoint &pos, bool opaque);
    QRect pixelRect(int i, int j) const;

    QColor curColor;
    QImage image;
    int zoom;
};

#endif
```

`IconEditor` reimplements three protected functions from `QWidget` and has a few private functions and variables. The three private variables hold the values of the three properties.

The implementation file begins with the `IconEditor`'s constructor:

```
#include <QtGui>

#include "iconeditor.h"

IconEditor::IconEditor(QWidget *parent)
    : QWidget(parent)
```

```
{
    setAttribute(Qt::WA_StaticContents);
    setSizePolicy(QSizePolicy::Minimum, QSizePolicy::Minimum);

    curColor = Qt::black;
    zoom = 8;

    image = QImage(16, 16, QImage::Format_ARGB32);
    image.fill(qRgba(0, 0, 0, 0));
}
```

The constructor has some subtle aspects, such as the `Qt::WA_StaticContents` attribute and the `setSizePolicy()` call. We will discuss them shortly.

The pen color is set to black. The zoom factor is set to 8, meaning that each pixel in the icon will be rendered as an 8×8 square.

The icon data is stored in the `image` member variable and can be accessed through the `setIconImage()` and `iconImage()` functions. An icon editor program would typically call `setIconImage()` when the user opens an icon file and `iconImage()` to retrieve the icon when the user wants to save it. The `image` variable is of type `QImage`. We initialize it to 16×16 pixels and 32-bit ARGB format, a format that supports semi-transparency. We clear the image data by filling it with a transparent color.

The `QImage` class stores an image in a hardware-independent fashion. It can be set to use a 1-bit, 8-bit, or 32-bit depth. An image with 32-bit depth uses 8 bits for each of the red, green, and blue components of a pixel. The remaining 8 bits store the pixel's alpha component (opacity). For example, a pure red color's red, green, blue, and alpha components have the values 255, 0, 0, and 255. In Qt, this color can be specified as

```
QRgb red = qRgba(255, 0, 0, 255);
```

or, since the color is opaque, as

```
QRgb red = qRgb(255, 0, 0);
```

`QRgb` is simply a typedef for `unsigned int`, and `qRgb()` and `qRgba()` are inline functions that combine their arguments into one 32-bit ARGB integer value. It is also possible to write

```
QRgb red = 0xFFFF0000;
```

where the first `FF` corresponds to the alpha component and the second `FF` to the red component. In the `IconEditor` constructor, we fill the `QImage` with a transparent color by using 0 as the alpha component.

Qt provides two types for storing colors: `QRgb` and `QColor`. Whereas `QRgb` is only a typedef used in `QImage` to store 32-bit pixel data, `QColor` is a class with many useful functions and is widely used in Qt to store colors. In the `IconEditor` widget, we use `QRgb` only when dealing with the `QImage`; we use `QColor` for everything else, including the `penColor` property.

```
QSize IconEditor::sizeHint() const
{
    QSize size = zoom * image.size();
    if (zoom >= 3)
        size += QSize(1, 1);
    return size;
}
```

The `sizeHint()` function is reimplemented from `QWidget` and returns the ideal size of a widget. Here, we take the image size multiplied by the zoom factor, with one extra pixel in each direction to accommodate a grid if the zoom factor is 3 or more. (We don't show a grid if the zoom factor is 2 or 1, because then the grid would leave hardly any room for the icon's pixels.)

A widget's size hint is mostly useful in conjunction with layouts. Qt's layout managers try as much as possible to respect a widget's size hint when they lay out a form's child widgets. For `IconEditor` to be a good layout citizen, it must report a credible size hint.

In addition to the size hint, widgets have a size policy that tells the layout system whether they like to be stretched and shrunk. By calling `setSizePolicy()` in the constructor with `QSizePolicy::Minimum` as horizontal and vertical policies, we tell any layout manager that is responsible for this widget that the widget's size hint is really its minimum size. In other words, the widget can be stretched if required, but it should never shrink below the size hint. This can be overridden in *Qt Designer* by setting the widget's `sizePolicy` property. We explain the meaning of the various size policies in Chapter 6.

```
void IconEditor::setPenColor(const QColor &newColor)
{
    curColor = newColor;
}
```

The `setPenColor()` function sets the current pen color. The color will be used for newly drawn pixels.

```
void IconEditor::setIconImage(const QImage &newImage)
{
    if (newImage != image) {
        image = newImage.convertToFormat(QImage::Format_ARGB32);
        update();
        updateGeometry();
    }
}
```

The `setIconImage()` function sets the image to edit. We call `convertToFormat()` to make the image 32-bit with an alpha buffer, if it isn't already. Elsewhere in the code, we will assume that the image data is stored as 32-bit ARGB values.

After setting the `image` variable, we call `QWidget::update()` to schedule a repainting of the widget using the new image. Next, we call `QWidget::updateGeometry()` to tell any layout that contains the widget that the widget's size hint has changed. The layout will then automatically adapt to the new size hint.

```
void IconEditor::setZoomFactor(int newZoom)
{
    if (newZoom < 1)
        newZoom = 1;

    if (newZoom != zoom) {
        zoom = newZoom;
        update();
        updateGeometry();
    }
}
```

The `setZoomFactor()` function sets the zoom factor for the image. To prevent division by zero elsewhere, we correct any value below 1. Again, we call `update()` and `updateGeometry()` to repaint the widget and to notify any managing layout about the size hint change.

The `penColor()`, `iconImage()`, and `zoomFactor()` functions are implemented as inline functions in the header file.

We will now review the code for the `paintEvent()` function. This function is `IconEditor`'s most important function. It is called whenever the widget needs repainting. The default implementation in `QWidget` does nothing, leaving the widget blank.

Just like `closeEvent()`, which we met in Chapter 3, `paintEvent()` is an event handler. Qt has many other event handlers, each of which corresponds to a different type of event. Chapter 7 covers event processing in depth.

There are many situations when a paint event is generated and `paintEvent()` is called. For example:

- When a widget is shown for the first time, the system automatically generates a paint event to force the widget to paint itself.
- When a widget is resized, the system generates a paint event.
- If the widget is obscured by another window and then revealed again, a paint event is generated for the area that was hidden (unless the window system stored the area).

We can also force a paint event by calling `QWidget::update()` or `QWidget::repaint()`. The difference between these two functions is that `repaint()` forces an immediate repaint, whereas `update()` simply schedules a paint event for when Qt next processes events. (Both functions do nothing if the widget isn't visible on-screen.) If `update()` is called multiple times, Qt compresses the consecutive paint events into a single paint event to avoid flicker. In `IconEditor`, we always use `update()`.

Here's the code:

```
void IconEditor::paintEvent(QPaintEvent *event)
{
    QPainter painter(this);
```

```
        if (zoom >= 3) {
            painter.setPen(palette().foreground().color());
            for (int i = 0; i <= image.width(); ++i)
                painter.drawLine(zoom * i, 0,
                                 zoom * i, zoom * image.height());
            for (int j = 0; j <= image.height(); ++j)
                painter.drawLine(0, zoom * j,
                                 zoom * image.width(), zoom * j);
        }

        for (int i = 0; i < image.width(); ++i) {
            for (int j = 0; j < image.height(); ++j) {
                QRect rect = pixelRect(i, j);
                if (!event->region().intersect(rect).isEmpty()) {
                    QColor color = QColor::fromRgba(image.pixel(i, j));
                    if (color.alpha() < 255)
                        painter.fillRect(rect, Qt::white);
                    painter.fillRect(rect, color);
                }
            }
        }
    }
```

We start by constructing a `QPainter` object on the widget. If the zoom factor is 3 or more, we draw the horizontal and vertical lines that form the grid using the `QPainter::drawLine()` function.

A call to `QPainter::drawLine()` has the following syntax:

```
painter.drawLine(x1, y1, x2, y2);
```

where (*x1*, *y1*) is the position of one end of the line and (*x2*, *y2*) is the position of the other end. There is also an overloaded version of the function that takes two `QPoint`s instead of four `int`s.

The top-left pixel of a Qt widget is located at position (0, 0), and the bottom-right pixel is located at (`width()` − 1, `height()` − 1). This is similar to the conventional Cartesian coordinate system, but upside down, as Figure 5.3 illustrates. We can change `QPainter`'s coordinate system by using transformations, such as translation, scaling, rotation, and shearing. We cover these in Chapter 8.

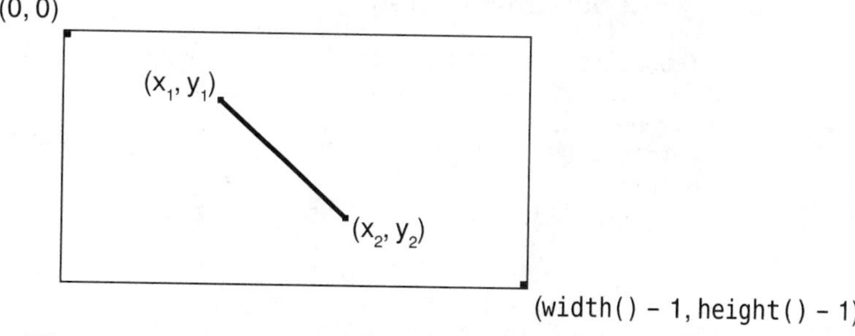

Figure 5.3. Drawing a line using `QPainter`

Before we call drawLine() on the QPainter, we set the line's color using setPen(). We could hard-code a color, such as black or gray, but a better approach is to use the widget's palette.

Every widget is equipped with a palette that specifies which colors should be used for what. For example, there is a palette entry for the background color of widgets (usually light gray) and one for the color of text on that background (usually black). By default, a widget's palette adopts the window system's color scheme. By using colors from the palette, we ensure that IconEditor respects the user's preferences.

A widget's palette consists of three color groups: active, inactive, and disabled. Which color group should be used depends on the widget's current state:

- The Active group is used for widgets in the currently active window.
- The Inactive group is used for widgets in the other windows.
- The Disabled group is used for disabled widgets in any window.

The QWidget::palette() function returns the widget's palette as a QPalette object. Color groups are specified as enums of type QPalette::ColorGroup.

When we want to get an appropriate brush or color for drawing, the correct approach is to use the current palette, obtained from QWidget::palette(), and the required role, for example, QPalette::foreground(). Each role function returns a brush, which is normally what we want, but if we just need the color we can extract it from the brush, as we did in the paintEvent(). By default, the brushes returned are those appropriate to the widget's state, so we do not need to specify a color group.

The paintEvent() function finishes by drawing the image itself. The call to IconEditor::pixelRect() returns a QRect that defines the region to repaint. (Figure 5.4 illustrates how a rectangle is drawn.) As an easy optimization, we don't redraw pixels that fall outside this region.

We call QPainter::fillRect() to draw a zoomed pixel. QPainter::fillRect() takes a QRect and a QBrush. By passing a QColor as the brush, we obtain a solid fill pattern. If the color isn't completely opaque (its alpha channel is less than 255), we draw a white background first.

```
QRect IconEditor::pixelRect(int i, int j) const
{
    if (zoom >= 3) {
        return QRect(zoom * i + 1, zoom * j + 1, zoom - 1, zoom - 1);
    } else {
        return QRect(zoom * i, zoom * j, zoom, zoom);
    }
}
```

The pixelRect() function returns a QRect suitable for QPainter::fillRect(). The i and j parameters are pixel coordinates in the QImage—not in the widget. If the zoom factor is 1, the two coordinate systems coincide exactly.

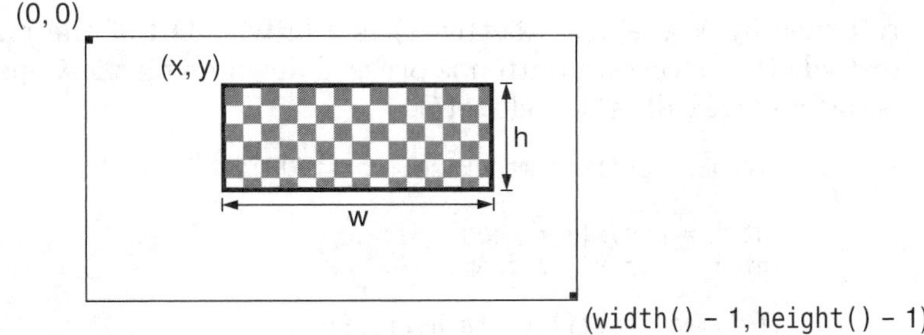

Figure 5.4. Drawing a rectangle using QPainter

The QRect constructor has the syntax QRect(*x*, *y*, *width*, *height*), where (*x*, *y*) is the position of the top-left corner of the rectangle and *width* × *height* is the size of the rectangle. If the zoom factor is 3 or more, we reduce the size of the rectangle by one pixel horizontally and vertically so that the fill does not draw over the grid lines.

```
void IconEditor::mousePressEvent(QMouseEvent *event)
{
    if (event->button() == Qt::LeftButton) {
        setImagePixel(event->pos(), true);
    } else if (event->button() == Qt::RightButton) {
        setImagePixel(event->pos(), false);
    }
}
```

When the user presses a mouse button, the system generates a "mouse press" event. By reimplementing QWidget::mousePressEvent(), we can respond to this event and set or clear the image pixel under the mouse cursor.

If the user pressed the left mouse button, we call the private function setImagePixel() with true as the second argument, telling it to set the pixel to the current pen color. If the user pressed the right mouse button, we also call setImagePixel(), but pass false to clear the pixel.

```
void IconEditor::mouseMoveEvent(QMouseEvent *event)
{
    if (event->buttons() & Qt::LeftButton) {
        setImagePixel(event->pos(), true);
    } else if (event->buttons() & Qt::RightButton) {
        setImagePixel(event->pos(), false);
    }
}
```

The mouseMoveEvent() handles "mouse move" events. By default, these events are generated only when the user is holding down a button. It is possible to change this behavior by calling QWidget::setMouseTracking(), but we don't need to do so for this example.

Just as pressing the left or right mouse button sets or clears a pixel, keeping it pressed and hovering over a pixel is also enough to set or clear a pixel. Since it's possible to hold more than one button pressed down at a time, the value returned by QMouseEvent::buttons() is a bitwise OR of the mouse buttons. We test whether a certain button is pressed down using the & operator, and if this is the case we call setImagePixel().

```
void IconEditor::setImagePixel(const QPoint &pos, bool opaque)
{
    int i = pos.x() / zoom;
    int j = pos.y() / zoom;

    if (image.rect().contains(i, j)) {
        if (opaque) {
            image.setPixel(i, j, penColor().rgba());
        } else {
            image.setPixel(i, j, qRgba(0, 0, 0, 0));
        }

        update(pixelRect(i, j));
    }
}
```

The setImagePixel() function is called from mousePressEvent() and mouseMoveEvent() to set or clear a pixel. The pos parameter is the position of the mouse on the widget.

The first step is to convert the mouse position from widget coordinates to image coordinates. This is done by dividing the x() and y() components of the mouse position by the zoom factor. Next, we check whether the point is within the correct range. The check is easily made using QImage::rect() and QRect::contains(); this effectively checks that i is between 0 and image.width() - 1 and that j is between 0 and image.height() - 1.

Depending on the opaque parameter, we set or clear the pixel in the image. Clearing a pixel is really setting it to be transparent. We must convert the pen QColor to a 32-bit ARGB value for the QImage::setPixel() call. At the end, we call update() with a QRect of the area that needs to be repainted.

Now that we have reviewed the member functions, we will return to the Qt::WA_StaticContents attribute that we used in the constructor. This attribute tells Qt that the widget's content doesn't change when the widget is resized and that the content stays rooted to the widget's top-left corner. Qt uses this information to avoid needlessly repainting areas that are already shown when resizing the widget. This is illustrated by Figure 5.5.

Normally, when a widget is resized, Qt generates a paint event for the widget's entire visible area. But if the widget is created with the Qt::WA_StaticContents attribute, the paint event's region is restricted to the pixels that were not previously shown. This implies that if the widget is resized to a smaller size, no paint event is generated at all.

The IconEditor widget is now complete. Using the information and examples from earlier chapters, we could write code that uses the IconEditor as a window in its own right, as a central widget in a QMainWindow, as a child widget inside a

Figure 5.5. Resizing a `Qt::WA_StaticContents` widget

layout, or as a child widget inside a `QScrollArea` (p. 152). In the next section, we will see how to integrate it with *Qt Designer*.

Integrating Custom Widgets with Qt Designer

Before we can use custom widgets in *Qt Designer*, we must make *Qt Designer* aware of them. There are two techniques for doing this: the "promotion" approach and the plugin approach.

The promotion approach is the quickest and easiest. It consists of choosing a built-in Qt widget that has a similar API to the one we want our custom widget to have and filling in *Qt Designer*'s custom widget dialog (shown in Figure 5.6) with some information about the widget. The custom widget can then be used in forms developed with *Qt Designer*, although it will be represented by the associated built-in Qt widget while the form is edited or previewed.

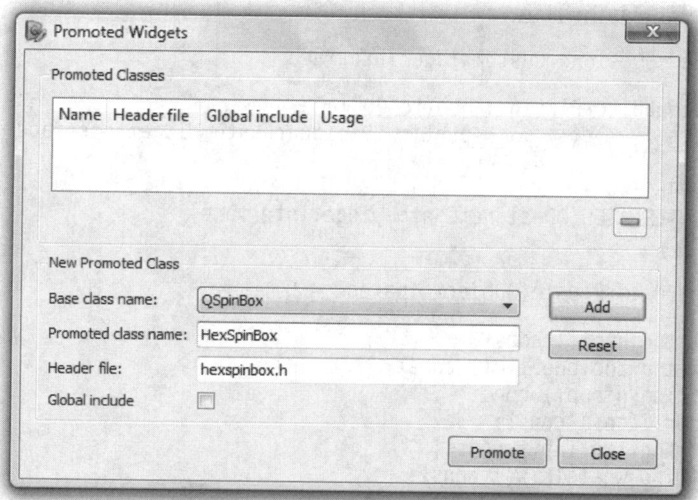

Figure 5.6. *Qt Designer*'s custom widget dialog

Here's how to insert a `HexSpinBox` widget into a form using this approach:

1. Create a `QSpinBox` by dragging it from *Qt Designer*'s widget box onto the form.

2. Right-click the spin box and choose Promote to Custom Widget from the context menu.
3. Fill in the dialog that pops up with “HexSpinBox” as the class name and “hexspinbox.h” as the header file.

Voilà! The code generated by uic will include hexspinbox.h instead of <QSpinBox> and instantiate a HexSpinBox. In *Qt Designer*, the HexSpinBox widget will be represented by a QSpinBox, allowing us to set all the properties of a QSpinBox (e.g., the range and the current value).

The drawbacks of the promotion approach are that properties that are specific to the custom widget aren't accessible in *Qt Designer* and that the widget isn't rendered as itself. Both these problems can be solved by using the plugin approach.

The plugin approach requires the creation of a plugin library that *Qt Designer* can load at run-time and use to create instances of the widget. *Qt Designer* then uses the real widget when editing the form and for previewing, and thanks to Qt's meta-object system, *Qt Designer* can dynamically obtain the list of its properties. To show how this works, we will integrate the IconEditor from the previous section as a plugin.

First, we must subclass QDesignerCustomWidgetInterface and reimplement some virtual functions. We will assume that the plugin source code is located in a directory called iconeditorplugin and that the IconEditor source code is located in a parallel directory called iconeditor.

Here's the class definition:

```
#include <QDesignerCustomWidgetInterface>

class IconEditorPlugin : public QObject,
                         public QDesignerCustomWidgetInterface
{
    Q_OBJECT
    Q_INTERFACES(QDesignerCustomWidgetInterface)

public:
    IconEditorPlugin(QObject *parent = 0);

    QString name() const;
    QString includeFile() const;
    QString group() const;
    QIcon icon() const;
    QString toolTip() const;
    QString whatsThis() const;
    bool isContainer() const;
    QWidget *createWidget(QWidget *parent);
};
```

The IconEditorPlugin subclass is a factory class that encapsulates the IconEditor widget. It is derived from both QObject and QDesignerCustomWidgetInterface and uses the Q_INTERFACES() macro to tell moc that the second base class is a plugin interface. *Qt Designer* uses the functions to create instances of the class and to obtain information about it.

```
IconEditorPlugin::IconEditorPlugin(QObject *parent)
    : QObject(parent)
{
}
```

The constructor is trivial.

```
QString IconEditorPlugin::name() const
{
    return "IconEditor";
}
```

The `name()` function returns the name of the widget provided by the plugin.

```
QString IconEditorPlugin::includeFile() const
{
    return "iconeditor.h";
}
```

The `includeFile()` function returns the name of the header file for the specified widget encapsulated by the plugin. The header file is included in the code generated by the `uic` tool.

```
QString IconEditorPlugin::group() const
{
    return tr("Image Manipulation Widgets");
}
```

The `group()` function returns the name of the widget box group to which this custom widget should belong. If the name isn't already in use, *Qt Designer* will create a new group for the widget.

```
QIcon IconEditorPlugin::icon() const
{
    return QIcon(":/images/iconeditor.png");
}
```

The `icon()` function returns the icon to use to represent the custom widget in *Qt Designer*'s widget box. Here, we assume that the `IconEditorPlugin` has an associated Qt resource file with a suitable entry for the icon editor image.

```
QString IconEditorPlugin::toolTip() const
{
    return tr("An icon editor widget");
}
```

The `toolTip()` function returns the tooltip to show when the mouse hovers over the custom widget in *Qt Designer*'s widget box.

```
QString IconEditorPlugin::whatsThis() const
{
```

```
    return tr("This widget is presented in Chapter 5 of <i>C++ GUI "
              "Programming with Qt 4</i> as an example of a custom Qt "
              "widget.");
}
```

The `whatsThis()` function returns the "What's This?" text for *Qt Designer* to display.

```
bool IconEditorPlugin::isContainer() const
{
    return false;
}
```

The `isContainer()` function returns `true` if the widget can contain other widgets; otherwise, it returns `false`. For example, `QFrame` is a widget that can contain other widgets. In general, any Qt widget can contain other widgets, but *Qt Designer* disallows this when `isContainer()` returns `false`.

```
QWidget *IconEditorPlugin::createWidget(QWidget *parent)
{
    return new IconEditor(parent);
}
```

Qt Designer calls the `createWidget()` function to create an instance of a widget class with the given parent.

```
Q_EXPORT_PLUGIN2(iconeditorplugin, IconEditorPlugin)
```

At the end of the source file that implements the plugin class, we must use the `Q_EXPORT_PLUGIN2()` macro to make the plugin available to *Qt Designer*. The first argument is the name we want to give the plugin; the second argument is the name of the class that implements it.

The `.pro` file for building the plugin looks like this:

```
TEMPLATE      = lib
CONFIG       += designer plugin release
HEADERS       = ../iconeditor/iconeditor.h \
                iconeditorplugin.h
SOURCES       = ../iconeditor/iconeditor.cpp \
                iconeditorplugin.cpp
RESOURCES     = iconeditorplugin.qrc
DESTDIR       = $$[QT_INSTALL_PLUGINS]/designer
```

The `qmake` build tool has some predefined variables built into it. One of them is `$$[QT_INSTALL_PLUGINS]`, which holds the path to the `plugins` directory inside the directory where Qt is installed. When you type `make` or `nmake` to build the plugin, it will automatically install itself in Qt's `plugins/designer` directory. Once the plugin is built, the `IconEditor` widget can be used in *Qt Designer* in the same way as any of Qt's built-in widgets.

If you want to integrate several custom widgets with *Qt Designer*, you can either create one plugin for each of them or combine them into a single plugin by deriving from `QDesignerCustomWidgetCollectionInterface`.

Double Buffering

Double buffering is a GUI programming technique that consists of rendering a widget to an off-screen pixmap and copying the pixmap onto the display. With earlier versions of Qt, this technique was frequently used to eliminate flicker and to provide a snappier user interface.

In Qt 4, `QWidget` handles this automatically, so we rarely need to worry about widgets flickering. Still, explicit double buffering remains beneficial if the widget's rendering is complex and is needed repeatedly. We can then store a pixmap permanently with the widget, always ready for the next paint event, and copy the pixmap to the widget whenever we receive a paint event. It is especially helpful when we want to make small modifications, such as drawing a rubber band, without recomputing the whole widget's rendering over and over.

We will round off this chapter by reviewing the `Plotter` custom widget shown in Figures 5.7 and 5.9. This widget uses double buffering and demonstrates some other aspects of Qt programming, including keyboard event handling, manual layout, and coordinate systems.

For a real application that needed a graphing or plotting widget, rather than creating a custom widget as we are doing here, we would most likely use one of the third party widgets that are available. For example, we might use GraphPak from `http://www.ics.com/`, KD Chart from `http://www.kdab.net/`, or Qwt from `http://qwt.sourceforge.net/`.

The `Plotter` widget displays one or more curves specified as vectors of coordinates. The user can draw a rubber band on the image, and the `Plotter` will zoom in on the area enclosed by the rubber band. The user draws the rubber band by clicking a point on the graph, dragging the mouse to another position with the left mouse button held down, and releasing the mouse button. Qt provides the `QRubberBand` class for drawing rubber bands, but here we draw it ourselves to have finer control over the look, and to demonstrate double buffering.

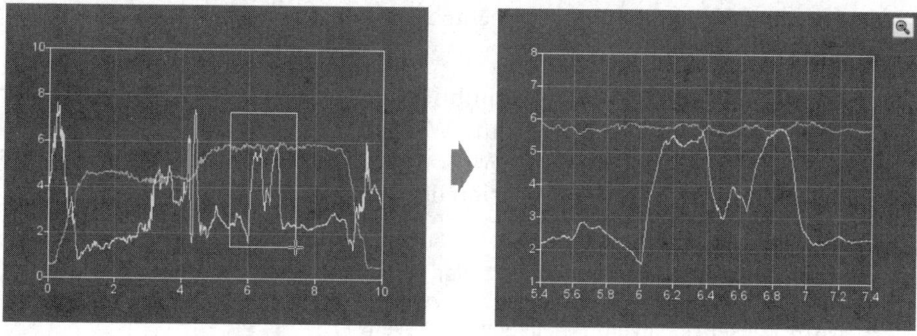

Figure 5.7. Zooming in on the `Plotter` widget

The user can zoom in repeatedly by drawing a rubber band multiple times, zooming out using the Zoom Out button and then zooming back in using the

Zoom In button. The Zoom In and Zoom Out buttons appear the first time they become available so that they don't clutter the display if the user doesn't zoom the graph.

The Plotter widget can hold the data for any number of curves. It also maintains a stack of PlotSettings objects, each of which corresponds to a particular zoom level.

Let's review the class, starting with plotter.h:

```
#ifndef PLOTTER_H
#define PLOTTER_H

#include <QMap>
#include <QPixmap>
#include <QVector>
#include <QWidget>

class QToolButton;
class PlotSettings;

class Plotter : public QWidget
{
    Q_OBJECT

public:
    Plotter(QWidget *parent = 0);

    void setPlotSettings(const PlotSettings &settings);
    void setCurveData(int id, const QVector<QPointF> &data);
    void clearCurve(int id);
    QSize minimumSizeHint() const;
    QSize sizeHint() const;

public slots:
    void zoomIn();
    void zoomOut();
```

We start by including the header files for the Qt classes that are used in the plotter's header file, and forward-declaring the classes that have pointers or references in the header.

In the Plotter class, we provide three public functions for setting up the plot, and two public slots for zooming in and out. We also reimplement minimumSizeHint() and sizeHint() from QWidget. We store a curve's points as a QVector<QPointF>, where QPointF is a floating-point version of QPoint.

```
protected:
    void paintEvent(QPaintEvent *event);
    void resizeEvent(QResizeEvent *event);
    void mousePressEvent(QMouseEvent *event);
    void mouseMoveEvent(QMouseEvent *event);
    void mouseReleaseEvent(QMouseEvent *event);
    void keyPressEvent(QKeyEvent *event);
    void wheelEvent(QWheelEvent *event);
```

In the protected section of the class, we declare all the QWidget event handlers that we want to reimplement.

```
private:
    void updateRubberBandRegion();
    void refreshPixmap();
    void drawGrid(QPainter *painter);
    void drawCurves(QPainter *painter);

    enum { Margin = 50 };

    QToolButton *zoomInButton;
    QToolButton *zoomOutButton;
    QMap<int, QVector<QPointF> > curveMap;
    QVector<PlotSettings> zoomStack;
    int curZoom;
    bool rubberBandIsShown;
    QRect rubberBandRect;
    QPixmap pixmap;
};
```

In the private section of the class, we declare a few functions for painting the widget, a constant, and several member variables. The Margin constant is used to provide some spacing around the graph.

Among the member variables is pixmap of type QPixmap. This variable holds a copy of the whole widget's rendering, identical to what is shown on-screen. The plot is always drawn onto this off-screen pixmap first; then the pixmap is copied onto the widget.

```
class PlotSettings
{
public:
    PlotSettings();

    void scroll(int dx, int dy);
    void adjust();
    double spanX() const { return maxX - minX; }
    double spanY() const { return maxY - minY; }

    double minX;
    double maxX;
    int numXTicks;
    double minY;
    double maxY;
    int numYTicks;

private:
    static void adjustAxis(double &min, double &max, int &numTicks);
};

#endif
```

The PlotSettings class specifies the range of the x- and y-axes and the number of ticks for these axes. Figure 5.8 shows the correspondence between a PlotSettings object and a Plotter widget.

By convention, numXTicks and numYTicks are off by one; if numXTicks is 5, Plotter will actually draw six tick marks on the x-axis. This simplifies the calculations later on.

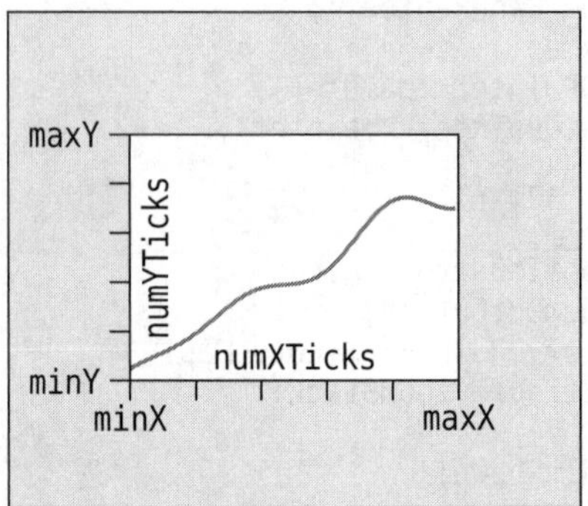

Figure 5.8. PlotSettings's member variables

Now let's review the implementation file:

```
Plotter::Plotter(QWidget *parent)
    : QWidget(parent)
{
    setBackgroundRole(QPalette::Dark);
    setAutoFillBackground(true);
    setSizePolicy(QSizePolicy::Expanding, QSizePolicy::Expanding);
    setFocusPolicy(Qt::StrongFocus);
    rubberBandIsShown = false;

    zoomInButton = new QToolButton(this);
    zoomInButton->setIcon(QIcon(":/images/zoomin.png"));
    zoomInButton->adjustSize();
    connect(zoomInButton, SIGNAL(clicked()), this, SLOT(zoomIn()));

    zoomOutButton = new QToolButton(this);
    zoomOutButton->setIcon(QIcon(":/images/zoomout.png"));
    zoomOutButton->adjustSize();
    connect(zoomOutButton, SIGNAL(clicked()), this, SLOT(zoomOut()));

    setPlotSettings(PlotSettings());
}
```

The setBackgroundRole() call tells QWidget to use the "dark" component of the palette as the color for erasing the widget, instead of the "window" component. This gives Qt a default color that it can use to fill any newly revealed pixels when the widget is resized to a larger size, before paintEvent() even has the chance to paint the new pixels. We also need to call setAutoFillBackground(true) to enable this mechanism. (By default, child widgets inherit the background from their parent widget.)

The setSizePolicy() call sets the widget's size policy to QSizePolicy::Expanding in both directions. This tells any layout manager that is responsible for the widget that the widget is especially willing to grow, but can also shrink. This setting is typical for widgets that can take up a lot of screen space. The default is `QSizePolicy::Preferred` in both directions, which means that the widget prefers to be the size of its size hint, but it can be shrunk to its minimum size hint or expanded indefinitely if necessary.

The `setFocusPolicy(Qt::StrongFocus)` call makes the widget accept focus by clicking or pressing Tab. When the `Plotter` has focus, it will receive events for key presses. The `Plotter` widget understands a few keys: + to zoom in; - to zoom out; and the arrow keys to scroll up, down, left, and right.

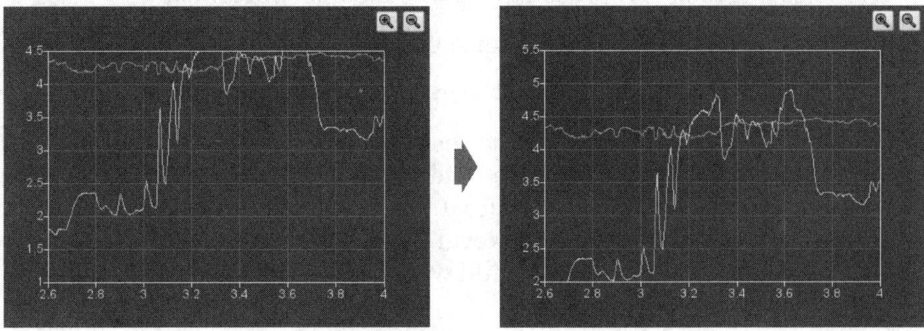

Figure 5.9. Scrolling the `Plotter` widget

Still in the constructor, we create two `QToolButtons`, each with an icon. These buttons allow the user to zoom in and out. The buttons' icons are stored in a resource file, so any application that uses the `Plotter` widget will need this entry in its `.pro` file:

```
RESOURCES = plotter.qrc
```

The resource file is similar to the one we have used for the Spreadsheet application:

```
<RCC>
<qresource>
    <file>images/zoomin.png</file>
    <file>images/zoomout.png</file>
</qresource>
</RCC>
```

The `adjustSize()` calls on the buttons set their sizes to be that of their size hints. The buttons are not put in a layout; instead, we will position them manually in the `Plotter`'s resize event. Since we are not using any layouts, we must specify the buttons' parent explicitly by passing `this` to the `QToolButton` constructor.

The call to `setPlotSettings()` at the end completes the initialization.

```
void Plotter::setPlotSettings(const PlotSettings &settings)
{
    zoomStack.clear();
```

```
        zoomStack.append(settings);
        curZoom = 0;
        zoomInButton->hide();
        zoomOutButton->hide();
        refreshPixmap();
    }
```

The setPlotSettings() function is used to specify the PlotSettings to use for displaying the plot. It is called by the Plotter constructor and can be called by users of the class. The plotter starts out at its default zoom level. Each time the user zooms in, a new PlotSettings instance is created and put onto the zoom stack. The zoom stack is represented by two member variables:

- zoomStack holds the different zoom settings as a QVector<PlotSettings>.
- curZoom holds the current PlotSettings's index in the zoomStack.

After the call to setPlotSettings(), the zoom stack contains only one entry, and the Zoom In and Zoom Out buttons are hidden. These buttons will not be shown until we call show() on them in the zoomIn() and zoomOut() slots. (Normally, it is sufficient to call show() on the top-level widget to show all the children. But when we explicitly call hide() on a child widget, it is hidden until we call show() on it.)

The call to refreshPixmap() is necessary to update the display. Usually, we would call update(), but here we do things slightly differently because we want to keep a QPixmap up-to-date at all times. After regenerating the pixmap, refreshPixmap() calls update() to copy the pixmap onto the widget.

```
    void Plotter::zoomOut()
    {
        if (curZoom > 0) {
            --curZoom;
            zoomOutButton->setEnabled(curZoom > 0);
            zoomInButton->setEnabled(true);
            zoomInButton->show();
            refreshPixmap();
        }
    }
```

The zoomOut() slot zooms out if the graph is zoomed in. It decrements the current zoom level and enables the Zoom Out button depending on whether the graph can be zoomed out any more or not. The Zoom In button is enabled and shown, and the display is updated with a call to refreshPixmap().

```
    void Plotter::zoomIn()
    {
        if (curZoom < zoomStack.count() - 1) {
            ++curZoom;
            zoomInButton->setEnabled(curZoom < zoomStack.count() - 1);
            zoomOutButton->setEnabled(true);
            zoomOutButton->show();
            refreshPixmap();
```

```
    }
}
```

If the user has previously zoomed in and then out again, the PlotSettings for the next zoom level will be in the zoom stack, and we can zoom in. (Otherwise, it is still possible to zoom in using a rubber band.)

The slot increments curZoom to move one level deeper into the zoom stack, sets the Zoom In button enabled or disabled depending on whether it's possible to zoom in any further, and enables and shows the Zoom Out button. Again, we call refreshPixmap() to make the plotter use the latest zoom settings.

```
void Plotter::setCurveData(int id, const QVector<QPointF> &data)
{
    curveMap[id] = data;
    refreshPixmap();
}
```

The setCurveData() function sets the curve data for a given curve ID. If a curve with the same ID already exists in curveMap, it is replaced with the new curve data; otherwise, the new curve is simply inserted. The curveMap member variable is of type QMap<int, QVector<QPointF> >.

```
void Plotter::clearCurve(int id)
{
    curveMap.remove(id);
    refreshPixmap();
}
```

The clearCurve() function removes the specified curve from the curve map.

```
QSize Plotter::minimumSizeHint() const
{
    return QSize(6 * Margin, 4 * Margin);
}
```

The minimumSizeHint() function is similar to sizeHint(). Just as sizeHint() specifies a widget's ideal size, minimumSizeHint() specifies a widget's ideal minimum size. A layout never resizes a widget below its minimum size hint.

The value we return is 300×200 (since Margin equals 50) to allow for the margin on all four sides and some space for the plot itself. Below that size, the plot would be too small to be useful.

```
QSize Plotter::sizeHint() const
{
    return QSize(12 * Margin, 8 * Margin);
}
```

In sizeHint(), we return an "ideal" size in proportion to the Margin constant and with the same pleasing 3:2 aspect ratio we used for the minimumSizeHint().

This finishes the review of the Plotter's public functions and slots. Now let's review the protected event handlers.

```
void Plotter::paintEvent(QPaintEvent * /* event */)
{
    QStylePainter painter(this);
    painter.drawPixmap(0, 0, pixmap);

    if (rubberBandIsShown) {
        painter.setPen(palette().light().color());
        painter.drawRect(rubberBandRect.normalized()
                                      .adjusted(0, 0, -1, -1));
    }

    if (hasFocus()) {
        QStyleOptionFocusRect option;
        option.initFrom(this);
        option.backgroundColor = palette().dark().color();
        painter.drawPrimitive(QStyle::PE_FrameFocusRect, option);
    }
}
```

Normally, `paintEvent()` is the place where we perform all the drawing. But here all the plot drawing is done beforehand in `refreshPixmap()`, so we can render the entire plot simply by copying the pixmap onto the widget at position (0, 0).

If the rubber band is visible, we draw it on top of the plot. We use the "light" component from the widget's current color group as the pen color to ensure good contrast with the "dark" background. Notice that we draw directly on the widget, leaving the off-screen pixmap untouched. Using `QRect::normalized()` ensures that the rubber band rectangle has positive width and height (swapping coordinates if necessary), and `adjusted()` reduces the size of the rectangle by one pixel to allow for its own 1-pixel-wide outline.

If the `Plotter` has focus, a focus rectangle is drawn using the widget style's `drawPrimitive()` function with `QStyle::PE_FrameFocusRect` as its first argument and a `QStyleOptionFocusRect` object as its second argument. The focus rectangle's drawing options are initialized based on the `Plotter` widget (by the `initFrom()` call). The background color must be specified explicitly.

When we want to paint using the current style, we can either call a `QStyle` function directly, for example,

```
style()->drawPrimitive(QStyle::PE_FrameFocusRect, &option, &painter,
                       this);
```

or use a `QStylePainter` instead of a normal `QPainter`, as we have done in `Plotter`, and paint more conveniently using that.

The `QWidget::style()` function returns the style that should be used to draw the widget. In Qt, a widget style is a subclass of `QStyle`. The built-in styles include `QWindowsStyle`, `QWindowsXPStyle`, `QWindowsVistaStyle`, `QMotifStyle`, `QCDEStyle`, `QMacStyle`, `QPlastiqueStyle`, and `QCleanlooksStyle`. Each style reimplements the virtual functions in `QStyle` to perform the drawing in the correct way for the platform the style is emulating. `QStylePainter`'s `drawPrimitive()` function calls the `QStyle` function of the same name, which can be used for drawing "primitive elements" such as panels, buttons, and focus rectangles. The widget style is usually the same for all widgets in an application (QApplication::style()), but it can be overridden on a per-widget basis using QWidget::setStyle().

By subclassing QStyle, it is possible to define a custom style. This can be done to give a distinctive look to an application or a suite of applications, as we will see in Chapter 19. While it is generally advisable to use the target platform's native look and feel, Qt offers a lot of flexibility if you want to be adventurous.

Qt's built-in widgets rely almost exclusively on QStyle to paint themselves. This is why they look like native widgets on all platforms supported by Qt. Custom widgets can be made style-aware either by using QStyle to paint themselves or by using built-in Qt widgets as child widgets. For Plotter, we use a combination of both approaches: The focus rectangle is drawn using QStyle (via a QStylePainter), and the Zoom In and Zoom Out buttons are built-in Qt widgets.

```
void Plotter::resizeEvent(QResizeEvent * /* event */)
{
    int x = width() - (zoomInButton->width()
                       + zoomOutButton->width() + 10);
    zoomInButton->move(x, 5);
    zoomOutButton->move(x + zoomInButton->width() + 5, 5);
    refreshPixmap();
}
```

Whenever the Plotter widget is resized, Qt generates a "resize" event. Here, we reimplement resizeEvent() to place the Zoom In and Zoom Out buttons at the top right of the Plotter widget.

We move the Zoom In button and the Zoom Out button to be side by side, separated by a 5-pixel gap and with a 5-pixel offset from the top and right edges of the parent widget.

If we wanted the buttons to stay rooted to the top-left corner, whose coordinates are (0, 0), we would simply have moved them there in the Plotter constructor. But we want to track the top-right corner, whose coordinates depend on the size of the widget. Because of this, it's necessary to reimplement resizeEvent() and to set the buttons' position there.

We didn't set any positions for the buttons in the Plotter constructor. This isn't a problem, since Qt always generates a resize event before a widget is shown for the first time.

An alternative to reimplementing resizeEvent() and laying out the child widgets manually would have been to use a layout manager (e.g., QGridLayout). Using a layout would have been a little more complicated and would have consumed more resources; on the other hand, it would gracefully handle right-to-left layouts, necessary for languages such as Arabic and Hebrew.

At the end, we call refreshPixmap() to redraw the pixmap at the new size.

```
void Plotter::mousePressEvent(QMouseEvent *event)
{
```

```
    QRect rect(Margin, Margin,
               width() - 2 * Margin, height() - 2 * Margin);

    if (event->button() == Qt::LeftButton) {
        if (rect.contains(event->pos())) {
            rubberBandIsShown = true;
            rubberBandRect.setTopLeft(event->pos());
            rubberBandRect.setBottomRight(event->pos());
            updateRubberBandRegion();
            setCursor(Qt::CrossCursor);
        }
    }
}
```

When the user presses the left mouse button, we start displaying a rubber band. This involves setting `rubberBandIsShown` to `true`, initializing the `rubberBandRect` member variable with the current mouse pointer position, scheduling a paint event to paint the rubber band, and changing the mouse cursor to have a crosshair shape.

The `rubberBandRect` variable is of type `QRect`. A `QRect` can be defined either as an (*x*, *y*, *width*, *height*) quadruple—where (*x*, *y*) is the position of the top-left corner and *width* × *height* is the size of the rectangle—or as a top-left and a bottom-right coordinate pair. Here, we have used the coordinate pair representation. We set the point where the user clicked as both the top-left corner and the bottom-right corner. Then we call `updateRubberBandRegion()` to force a repaint of the (tiny) area covered by the rubber band.

Qt provides two mechanisms for controlling the mouse cursor's shape:

- `QWidget::setCursor()` sets the cursor shape to use when the mouse hovers over a particular widget. If no cursor is set for a widget, the parent widget's cursor is used. The default for top-level widgets is an arrow cursor.
- `QApplication::setOverrideCursor()` sets the cursor shape for the entire application, overriding the cursors set by individual widgets until `restoreOverrideCursor()` is called.

In Chapter 4, we called `QApplication::setOverrideCursor()` with `Qt::WaitCursor` to change the application's cursor to the standard wait cursor.

```
void Plotter::mouseMoveEvent(QMouseEvent *event)
{
    if (rubberBandIsShown) {
        updateRubberBandRegion();
        rubberBandRect.setBottomRight(event->pos());
        updateRubberBandRegion();
    }
}
```

When the user moves the mouse cursor while holding down the left button, we first call `updateRubberBandRegion()` to schedule a paint event to repaint the area where the rubber band was, then we recompute `rubberBandRect` to account for the mouse move, and finally we call `updateRubberBandRegion()` a second time to repaint the area where the rubber band has moved to. This effectively erases the rubber band and redraws it at the new coordinates.

If the user moves the mouse upward or leftward, it's likely that `rubberBandRect`'s nominal bottom-right corner will end up above or to the left of its top-left corner. If this occurs, the `QRect` will have a negative width or height. We used `QRect::normalized()` in `paintEvent()` to ensure that the top-left and bottom-right coordinates are adjusted to obtain a nonnegative width and height.

```
void Plotter::mouseReleaseEvent(QMouseEvent *event)
{
    if ((event->button() == Qt::LeftButton) && rubberBandIsShown) {
        rubberBandIsShown = false;
        updateRubberBandRegion();
        unsetCursor();

        QRect rect = rubberBandRect.normalized();
        if (rect.width() < 4 || rect.height() < 4)
            return;
        rect.translate(-Margin, -Margin);

        PlotSettings prevSettings = zoomStack[curZoom];
        PlotSettings settings;
        double dx = prevSettings.spanX() / (width() - 2 * Margin);
        double dy = prevSettings.spanY() / (height() - 2 * Margin);
        settings.minX = prevSettings.minX + dx * rect.left();
        settings.maxX = prevSettings.minX + dx * rect.right();
        settings.minY = prevSettings.maxY - dy * rect.bottom();
        settings.maxY = prevSettings.maxY - dy * rect.top();
        settings.adjust();

        zoomStack.resize(curZoom + 1);
        zoomStack.append(settings);
        zoomIn();
    }
}
```

When the user releases the left mouse button, we erase the rubber band and restore the standard arrow cursor. If the rubber band is at least 4×4, we perform the zoom. If the rubber band is smaller than that, it's likely that the user clicked the widget by mistake or to give it focus, so we do nothing.

The code to perform the zoom is a bit complicated. This is because we deal with widget coordinates and plotter coordinates at the same time. Most of the work we perform here is to convert the `rubberBandRect` from widget coordinates to plotter coordinates. Once we have done the conversion, we call `PlotSettings::adjust()` to round the numbers and find a sensible number of ticks for each axis. Figures 5.10 and 5.11 illustrate the process.

Then we perform the zoom. The zoom is achieved by pushing the new `PlotSettings` that we have just calculated on top of the zoom stack and calling `zoomIn()` to do the job.

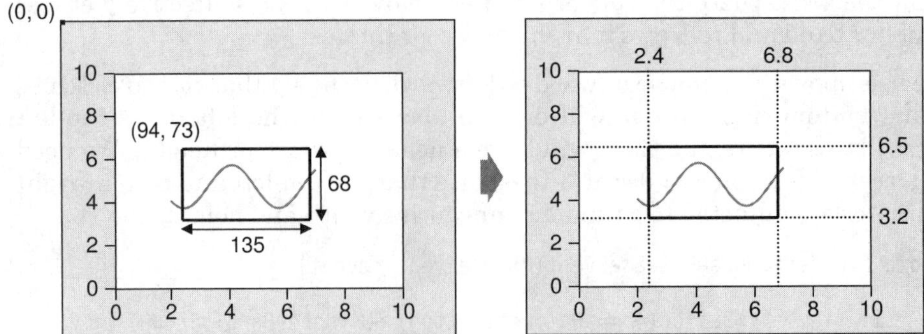

Figure 5.10. Converting the rubber band from widget to plotter coordinates

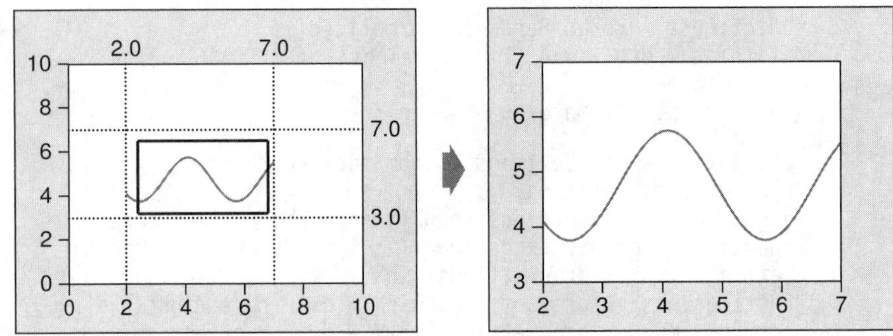

Figure 5.11. Adjusting plotter coordinates and zooming in on the rubber band

```
void Plotter::keyPressEvent(QKeyEvent *event)
{
    switch (event->key()) {
    case Qt::Key_Plus:
        zoomIn();
        break;
    case Qt::Key_Minus:
        zoomOut();
        break;
    case Qt::Key_Left:
        zoomStack[curZoom].scroll(-1, 0);
        refreshPixmap();
        break;
    case Qt::Key_Right:
        zoomStack[curZoom].scroll(+1, 0);
        refreshPixmap();
        break;
    case Qt::Key_Down:
        zoomStack[curZoom].scroll(0, -1);
        refreshPixmap();
        break;
    case Qt::Key_Up:
        zoomStack[curZoom].scroll(0, +1);
        refreshPixmap();
```

```
            break;
        default:
            QWidget::keyPressEvent(event);
        }
    }
```

When the user presses a key and the `Plotter` widget has focus, the `keyPressEvent()` function is called. We reimplement it here to respond to six keys: +, -, Up, Down, Left, and Right. If the user pressed a key that we are not handling, we call the base class implementation. For simplicity, we ignore the Shift, Ctrl, and Alt modifier keys, which are available through `QKeyEvent::modifiers()`.

```
void Plotter::wheelEvent(QWheelEvent *event)
{
    int numDegrees = event->delta() / 8;
    int numTicks = numDegrees / 15;

    if (event->orientation() == Qt::Horizontal) {
        zoomStack[curZoom].scroll(numTicks, 0);
    } else {
        zoomStack[curZoom].scroll(0, numTicks);
    }
    refreshPixmap();
}
```

Wheel events occur when a mouse wheel is turned. Most mice provide only a vertical wheel, but some also have a horizontal wheel. Qt supports both kinds of wheel. Wheel events go to the widget that has the focus. The `delta()` function returns the distance the wheel was rotated in eighths of a degree. Mice typically work in steps of 15 degrees. Here, we scroll by the requested number of ticks by modifying the topmost item on the zoom stack and update the display using `refreshPixmap()`.

The most common use of the mouse wheel is to scroll a scroll bar. When we use `QScrollArea` (covered in Chapter 6) to provide scroll bars, `QScrollArea` handles the mouse wheel events automatically, so we don't need to reimplement `wheelEvent()` ourselves.

This finishes the implementation of the event handlers. Now let's review the private functions.

```
void Plotter::updateRubberBandRegion()
{
    QRect rect = rubberBandRect.normalized();
    update(rect.left(), rect.top(), rect.width(), 1);
    update(rect.left(), rect.top(), 1, rect.height());
    update(rect.left(), rect.bottom(), rect.width(), 1);
    update(rect.right(), rect.top(), 1, rect.height());
}
```

The `updateRubberBand()` function is called from `mousePressEvent()`, `mouseMoveEvent()`, and `mouseReleaseEvent()` to erase or redraw the rubber band. It consists of four calls to `update()` that schedule a paint event for the four small rectangular areas that are covered by the rubber band (two vertical and two horizontal lines).

```
void Plotter::refreshPixmap()
{
    pixmap = QPixmap(size());
    pixmap.fill(this, 0, 0);

    QPainter painter(&pixmap);
    painter.initFrom(this);
    drawGrid(&painter);
    drawCurves(&painter);
    update();
}
```

The `refreshPixmap()` function redraws the plot onto the off-screen pixmap and updates the display. We resize the pixmap to have the same size as the widget and fill it with the widget's erase color. This color is the "dark" component of the palette, because of the call to `setBackgroundRole()` in the `Plotter` constructor. If the background is a non-solid brush, `QPixmap::fill()` needs to know the offset in the widget where the pixmap will end up to align the brush pattern correctly. Here, the pixmap corresponds to the entire widget, so we specify position (0, 0).

Then we create a `QPainter` to draw on the pixmap. The `initFrom()` call sets the painter's pen, background, and font to the same ones as the `Plotter` widget. Next, we call `drawGrid()` and `drawCurves()` to perform the drawing. At the end, we call `update()` to schedule a paint event for the whole widget. The pixmap is copied to the widget in the `paintEvent()` function (p. 128).

```
void Plotter::drawGrid(QPainter *painter)
{
    QRect rect(Margin, Margin,
               width() - 2 * Margin, height() - 2 * Margin);
    if (!rect.isValid())
        return;

    PlotSettings settings = zoomStack[curZoom];
    QPen quiteDark = palette().dark().color().light();
    QPen light = palette().light().color();

    for (int i = 0; i <= settings.numXTicks; ++i) {
        int x = rect.left() + (i * (rect.width() - 1)
                                 / settings.numXTicks);
        double label = settings.minX + (i * settings.spanX()
                                          / settings.numXTicks);
        painter->setPen(quiteDark);
        painter->drawLine(x, rect.top(), x, rect.bottom());
        painter->setPen(light);
        painter->drawLine(x, rect.bottom(), x, rect.bottom() + 5);
        painter->drawText(x - 50, rect.bottom() + 5, 100, 20,
                          Qt::AlignHCenter | Qt::AlignTop,
                          QString::number(label));
    }
```

```
        for (int j = 0; j <= settings.numYTicks; ++j) {
            int y = rect.bottom() - (j * (rect.height() - 1)
                                        / settings.numYTicks);
            double label = settings.minY + (j * settings.spanY()
                                               / settings.numYTicks);
            painter->setPen(quiteDark);
            painter->drawLine(rect.left(), y, rect.right(), y);
            painter->setPen(light);
            painter->drawLine(rect.left() - 5, y, rect.left(), y);
            painter->drawText(rect.left() - Margin, y - 10, Margin - 5, 20,
                              Qt::AlignRight | Qt::AlignVCenter,
                              QString::number(label));
        }
        painter->drawRect(rect.adjusted(0, 0, -1, -1));
    }
```

The `drawGrid()` function draws the grid behind the curves and the axes. The area on which we draw the grid is specified by `rect`. If the widget isn't large enough to accommodate the graph, we return immediately.

The first `for` loop draws the grid's vertical lines and the ticks along the *x*-axis. The second `for` loop draws the grid's horizontal lines and the ticks along the *y*-axis. At the end, we draw a rectangle along the margins. The `drawText()` function is used to draw the numbers corresponding to the tick marks on both axes.

The calls to `drawText()` have the following syntax:

```
painter->drawText(x, y, width, height, alignment, text);
```

where (*x*, *y*, *width*, *height*) define a rectangle, *alignment* the position of the text within that rectangle, and *text* the text to draw. In this example, we have calculated the rectangle in which to draw the text manually; a more adaptable alternative would involve calculating the text's bounding rectangle using `QFontMetrics`.

```
void Plotter::drawCurves(QPainter *painter)
{
    static const QColor colorForIds[6] = {
        Qt::red, Qt::green, Qt::blue, Qt::cyan, Qt::magenta, Qt::yellow
    };
    PlotSettings settings = zoomStack[curZoom];
    QRect rect(Margin, Margin,
               width() - 2 * Margin, height() - 2 * Margin);
    if (!rect.isValid())
        return;

    painter->setClipRect(rect.adjusted(+1, +1, -1, -1));

    QMapIterator<int, QVector<QPointF> > i(curveMap);
    while (i.hasNext()) {
        i.next();

        int id = i.key();
        QVector<QPointF> data = i.value();
        QPolygonF polyline(data.count());
```

```
        for (int j = 0; j < data.count(); ++j) {
            double dx = data[j].x() - settings.minX;
            double dy = data[j].y() - settings.minY;
            double x = rect.left() + (dx * (rect.width() - 1)
                                         / settings.spanX());
            double y = rect.bottom() - (dy * (rect.height() - 1)
                                           / settings.spanY());
            polyline[j] = QPointF(x, y);
        }
        painter->setPen(colorForIds[uint(id) % 6]);
        painter->drawPolyline(polyline);
    }
}
```

The `drawCurves()` function draws the curves on top of the grid. We start by calling `setClipRect()` to set the `QPainter`'s clip region to the rectangle that contains the curves (excluding the margins and the frame around the graph). `QPainter` will then ignore drawing operations on pixels outside the area.

Next, we iterate over all the curves using a Java-style iterator, and for each curve, we iterate over its constituent `QPointF`s. We call the iterator's `key()` function to retrieve the curve's ID, and its `value()` function to retrieve the corresponding curve data as a `QVector<QPointF>`. The inner `for` loop converts each `QPointF` from plotter coordinates to widget coordinates and stores them in the `polyline` variable.

Once we have converted all the points of a curve to widget coordinates, we set the pen color for the curve (using one of a set of predefined colors) and call `drawPolyline()` to draw a line that goes through all the curve's points.

This is the complete `Plotter` class. All that remains are a few functions in `PlotSettings`.

```
PlotSettings::PlotSettings()
{
    minX = 0.0;
    maxX = 10.0;
    numXTicks = 5;

    minY = 0.0;
    maxY = 10.0;
    numYTicks = 5;
}
```

The `PlotSettings` constructor initializes both axes to the range 0 to 10 with five tick marks.

```
void PlotSettings::scroll(int dx, int dy)
{
    double stepX = spanX() / numXTicks;
    minX += dx * stepX;
    maxX += dx * stepX;

    double stepY = spanY() / numYTicks;
    minY += dy * stepY;
```

```
        maxY += dy * stepY;
    }
```

The scroll() function increments (or decrements) minX, maxX, minY, and maxY by the interval between two ticks times a given number. This function is used to implement scrolling in Plotter::keyPressEvent().

```
    void PlotSettings::adjust()
    {
        adjustAxis(minX, maxX, numXTicks);
        adjustAxis(minY, maxY, numYTicks);
    }
```

The adjust() function is called from mouseReleaseEvent() to round the minX, maxX, minY, and maxY values to "nice" values and to determine the number of ticks appropriate for each axis. The private function adjustAxis() does its work one axis at a time.

```
    void PlotSettings::adjustAxis(double &min, double &max, int &numTicks)
    {
        const int MinTicks = 4;
        double grossStep = (max - min) / MinTicks;
        double step = std::pow(10.0, std::floor(std::log10(grossStep)));

        if (5 * step < grossStep) {
            step *= 5;
        } else if (2 * step < grossStep) {
            step *= 2;
        }

        numTicks = int(std::ceil(max / step) - std::floor(min / step));
        if (numTicks < MinTicks)
            numTicks = MinTicks;
        min = std::floor(min / step) * step;
        max = std::ceil(max / step) * step;
    }
```

The adjustAxis() function converts its min and max parameters into "nice" numbers and sets its numTicks parameter to the number of ticks it calculates to be appropriate for the given [min, max] range. Because adjustAxis() needs to modify the actual variables (minX, maxX, numXTicks, etc.) and not just copies, its parameters are non-const references.

Most of the code in adjustAxis() simply attempts to determine an appropriate value for the interval between two ticks (the "step"). To obtain nice numbers along the axis, we must select the step with care. For example, a step value of 3.8 would lead to an axis with multiples of 3.8, which is difficult for people to relate to. For axes labeled in decimal notation, "nice" step values are numbers of the form 10^n, $2 \cdot 10^n$, or $5 \cdot 10^n$.

We start by computing the "gross step", a kind of maximum for the step value. Then we find the corresponding number of the form 10^n that is smaller than or equal to the gross step. We do this by taking the decimal logarithm of the gross step, rounding that value down to a whole number, then raising 10 to the power of this rounded number. For example, if the gross step is 236, we compute log 236 = 2.37291...; then we round it down to 2 and obtain $10^2 = 100$ as the candidate step value of the form 10^n.

Once we have the first candidate step value, we can use it to calculate the other two candidates: $2 \cdot 10^n$ and $5 \cdot 10^n$. For the preceding example, the other two candidates are 200 and 500. The 500 candidate is larger than the gross step, so we can't use it. But 200 is smaller than 236, so we use 200 for the step size in this example.

It's fairly easy to calculate `numTicks`, `min`, and `max` from the step value. The new `min` value is obtained by rounding the original `min` down to the nearest multiple of the step, and the new `max` value is obtained by rounding up to the nearest multiple of the step. The new `numTicks` is the number of intervals between the rounded `min` and `max` values. For example, if `min` is 240 and `max` is 1 184 upon entering the function, the new range becomes [200, 1 200], with five tick marks.

This algorithm will give suboptimal results in some cases. A more sophisticated algorithm is described in Paul S. Heckbert's article "Nice Numbers for Graph Labels", published in *Graphics Gems* (Morgan Kaufmann, 1990).

This chapter brings us to the end of Part I of the book. It explained how to customize an existing Qt widget and how to build a widget from the ground up using `QWidget` as the base class. We already saw how to lay out child widgets using layout managers in Chapter 2, and we will explore the theme further in Chapter 6.

At this point, we know enough to write complete GUI applications using Qt. In Parts II and III, we will explore Qt in greater depth so that we can make full use of Qt's power.

Part II

Intermediate Qt

- *Laying Out Widgets on a Form*
- *Stacked Layouts*
- *Splitters*
- *Scrolling Areas*
- *Dock Windows and Toolbars*
- *Multiple Document Interface*

6. Layout Management

Every widget that is placed on a form must be given an appropriate size and position. Qt provides several classes that lay out widgets on a form: `QHBoxLayout`, `QVBoxLayout`, `QGridLayout`, and `QStackedLayout`. These classes are so convenient and easy to use that almost every Qt developer uses them, either directly in source code or through *Qt Designer*.

Another reason to use Qt's layout classes is that they ensure that forms adapt automatically to different fonts, languages, and platforms. If the user changes the system's font settings, the application's forms will respond immediately, resizing themselves if necessary. And if you translate the application's user interface to other languages, the layout classes take into consideration the widgets' translated contents to avoid text truncation.

Other classes that perform layout management include `QSplitter`, `QScrollArea`, `QMainWindow`, and `QMdiArea`. All of these classes provide a flexible layout that the user can manipulate. For example, `QSplitter` provides a splitter bar that the user can drag to resize widgets, and `QMdiArea` offers support for MDI (multiple document interface), a means of showing many documents simultaneously within an application's main window. Because they are often used as alternatives to the layout classes proper, we cover them in this chapter.

Laying Out Widgets on a Form

There are three basic ways of managing the layout of child widgets on a form: absolute positioning, manual layout, and layout managers. We will look at each of these approaches in turn, using the Find File dialog shown in Figure 6.1 as our example.

Absolute positioning is the crudest way of laying out widgets. It is achieved by assigning hard-coded sizes and positions to the form's child widgets and a fixed size to the form. Here's what the `FindFileDialog` constructor looks like using absolute positioning:

```
FindFileDialog::FindFileDialog(QWidget *parent)
    : QDialog(parent)
{
    ...
    namedLabel->setGeometry(9, 9, 50, 25);
    namedLineEdit->setGeometry(65, 9, 200, 25);
    lookInLabel->setGeometry(9, 40, 50, 25);
    lookInLineEdit->setGeometry(65, 40, 200, 25);
    subfoldersCheckBox->setGeometry(9, 71, 256, 23);
    tableWidget->setGeometry(9, 100, 256, 100);
    messageLabel->setGeometry(9, 206, 256, 25);
    findButton->setGeometry(271, 9, 85, 32);
    stopButton->setGeometry(271, 47, 85, 32);
    closeButton->setGeometry(271, 84, 85, 32);
    helpButton->setGeometry(271, 199, 85, 32);

    setWindowTitle(tr("Find Files or Folders"));
    setFixedSize(365, 240);
}
```

Absolute positioning has many disadvantages:

- The user cannot resize the window.
- Some text may be truncated if the user chooses an unusually large font or if the application is translated into another language.
- The widgets might have inappropriate sizes for some styles.
- The positions and sizes must be calculated manually. This is tedious and error-prone, and makes maintenance painful.

An alternative to absolute positioning is manual layout. With manual layout, the widgets are still given absolute positions, but their sizes are made proportional to the size of the window rather than being entirely hard-coded. This can

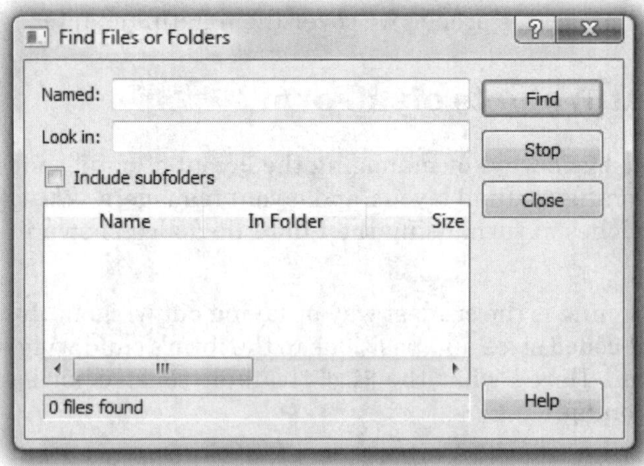

Figure 6.1. The Find File dialog

be achieved by reimplementing the form's `resizeEvent()` function to set its child widgets' geometries:

```
FindFileDialog::FindFileDialog(QWidget *parent)
    : QDialog(parent)
{
    ...
    setMinimumSize(265, 190);
    resize(365, 240);
}

void FindFileDialog::resizeEvent(QResizeEvent * /* event */)
{
    int extraWidth = width() - minimumWidth();
    int extraHeight = height() - minimumHeight();

    namedLabel->setGeometry(9, 9, 50, 25);
    namedLineEdit->setGeometry(65, 9, 100 + extraWidth, 25);
    lookInLabel->setGeometry(9, 40, 50, 25);
    lookInLineEdit->setGeometry(65, 40, 100 + extraWidth, 25);
    subfoldersCheckBox->setGeometry(9, 71, 156 + extraWidth, 23);

    tableWidget->setGeometry(9, 100, 156 + extraWidth,
                             50 + extraHeight);
    messageLabel->setGeometry(9, 156 + extraHeight, 156 + extraWidth,
                              25);
    findButton->setGeometry(171 + extraWidth, 9, 85, 32);
    stopButton->setGeometry(171 + extraWidth, 47, 85, 32);
    closeButton->setGeometry(171 + extraWidth, 84, 85, 32);
    helpButton->setGeometry(171 + extraWidth, 149 + extraHeight, 85,
                            32);
}
```

In the `FindFileDialog` constructor, we set the form's minimum size to 265×190 and the initial size to 365×240. In the `resizeEvent()` handler, we give any extra space to the widgets that we want to grow. This ensures that the form scales smoothly when the user resizes it.

Just like absolute positioning, manual layout requires a lot of hard-coded constants to be calculated by the programmer. Writing code like this is tiresome, especially if the design changes. And there is still the risk of text truncation. We can avoid this risk by taking account of the child widgets' size hints, but that would complicate the code even further.

The most convenient solution for laying out widgets on a form is to use Qt's layout managers. The layout managers provide sensible defaults for every type of widget and take into account each widget's size hint, which in turn typically depends on the widget's font, style, and contents. Layout managers also respect minimum and maximum sizes, and automatically adjust the layout in response to font changes, content changes, and window resizing. A resizable version of the Find File dialog is shown in Figure 6.2.

The three most important layout managers are `QHBoxLayout`, `QVBoxLayout`, and `QGridLayout`. These classes are derived from `QLayout`, which provides the basic

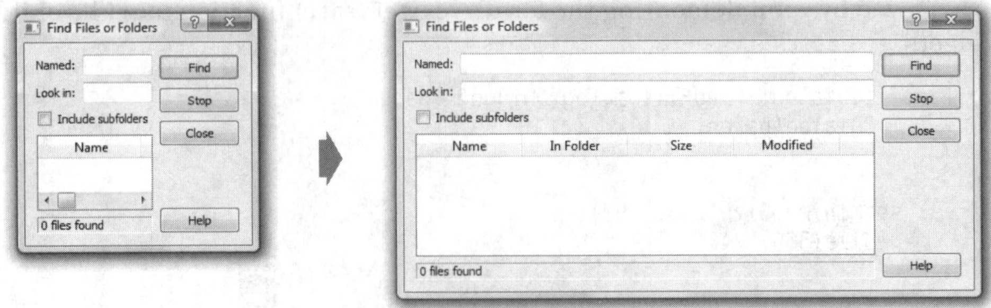

Figure 6.2. Resizing a resizable dialog

framework for layouts. All three classes are fully supported by *Qt Designer* and can also be used directly in code.

Here's the `FindFileDialog` code using layout managers:

```
FindFileDialog::FindFileDialog(QWidget *parent)
    : QDialog(parent)
{
    ...
    QGridLayout *leftLayout = new QGridLayout;
    leftLayout->addWidget(namedLabel, 0, 0);
    leftLayout->addWidget(namedLineEdit, 0, 1);
    leftLayout->addWidget(lookInLabel, 1, 0);
    leftLayout->addWidget(lookInLineEdit, 1, 1);
    leftLayout->addWidget(subfoldersCheckBox, 2, 0, 1, 2);
    leftLayout->addWidget(tableWidget, 3, 0, 1, 2);
    leftLayout->addWidget(messageLabel, 4, 0, 1, 2);

    QVBoxLayout *rightLayout = new QVBoxLayout;
    rightLayout->addWidget(findButton);
    rightLayout->addWidget(stopButton);
    rightLayout->addWidget(closeButton);
    rightLayout->addStretch();
    rightLayout->addWidget(helpButton);

    QHBoxLayout *mainLayout = new QHBoxLayout;
    mainLayout->addLayout(leftLayout);
    mainLayout->addLayout(rightLayout);
    setLayout(mainLayout);

    setWindowTitle(tr("Find Files or Folders"));
}
```

The layout is handled by one `QHBoxLayout`, one `QGridLayout`, and one `QVBoxLayout`. The `QGridLayout` on the left and the `QVBoxLayout` on the right are placed side by side by the outer `QHBoxLayout`. The margin around the dialog and the spacing between the child widgets are set to default values based on the current widget style; they can be changed using `QLayout::setContentsMargins()` and `QLayout::setSpacing()`.

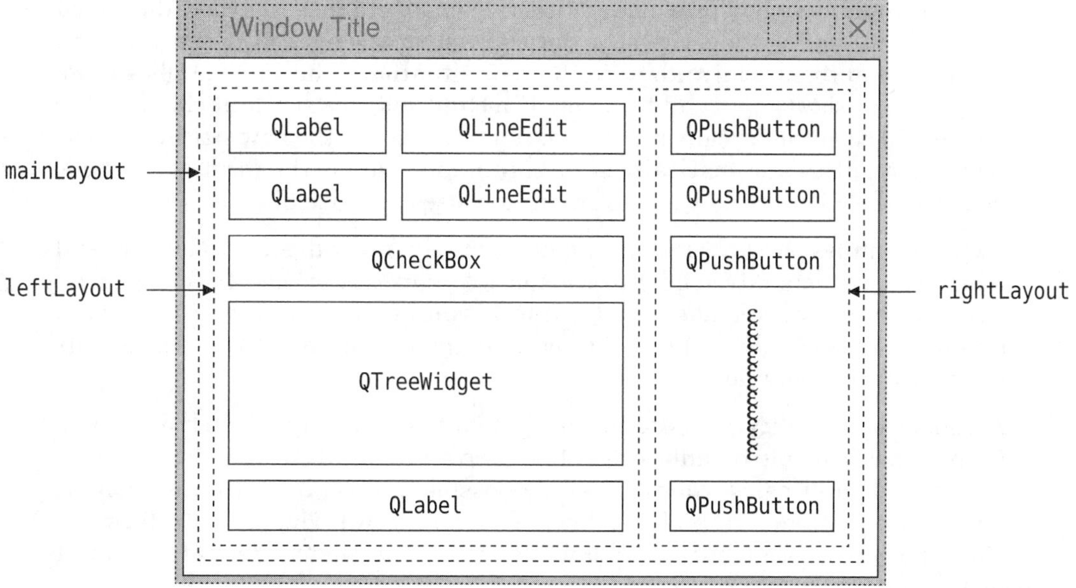

Figure 6.3. The Find File dialog's layout

The same dialog could be created visually in *Qt Designer* by placing the child widgets in their approximate positions; selecting those that need to be laid out together; and clicking Form|Lay Out Horizontally, Form|Lay Out Vertically, or Form|Lay Out in a Grid. We used this approach in Chapter 2 for creating the Spreadsheet application's Go to Cell and Sort dialogs.

Using `QHBoxLayout` and `QVBoxLayout` is fairly straightforward, but using `QGridLayout` is a bit more involved. `QGridLayout` works on a two-dimensional grid of cells. The `QLabel` in the top-left corner of the layout is at position (0, 0), and the corresponding `QLineEdit` is at position (0, 1). The `QCheckBox` spans two columns; it occupies the cells in positions (2, 0) and (2, 1). The `QTreeWidget` and the `QLabel` beneath it also span two columns. The calls to `QGridLayout::addWidget()` have the following syntax:

```
layout->addWidget(widget, row, column, rowSpan, columnSpan);
```

Here, *`widget`* is the child widget to insert into the layout, (*`row`*, *`column`*) is the top-left cell occupied by the widget, *`rowSpan`* is the number of rows occupied by the widget, and *`columnSpan`* is the number of columns occupied by the widget. If omitted, the *`rowSpan`* and *`columnSpan`* arguments default to 1.

The `addStretch()` call tells the vertical layout manager to consume space at that point in the layout. By adding a stretch item, we have told the layout manager to put any excess space between the Close button and the Help button. In *Qt Designer*, we can achieve the same effect by inserting a spacer. Spacers appear in *Qt Designer* as blue "springs".

Using layout managers provides additional benefits to those we have discussed so far. If we add a widget to a layout or remove a widget from a layout, the layout will automatically adapt to the new situation. The same applies if we call `hide()` or `show()` on a child widget. If a child widget's size hint changes, the layout will be automatically redone, taking into account the new size hint. Also, layout managers automatically set a minimum size for the form as a whole, based on the form's child widgets' minimum sizes and size hints.

In the examples presented so far, we have simply put widgets into layouts and used spacer items (stretches) to consume any excess space. In some cases, this isn't sufficient to make the layout look exactly the way we want. In these situations, we can adjust the layout by changing the size policies and size hints of the widgets being laid out.

A widget's size policy tells the layout system how it should stretch or shrink. Qt provides sensible default size policies for all its built-in widgets, but since no single default can account for every possible layout, it is still common for developers to change the size policies for one or two widgets on a form. A `QSizePolicy` has both a horizontal and a vertical component. Here are the most useful values:

- `Fixed` means that the widget cannot grow or shrink. The widget always stays at the size of its size hint.
- `Minimum` means that the widget's size hint is its minimum size. The widget cannot shrink below the size hint, but it can grow to fill available space if necessary.
- `Maximum` means that the widget's size hint is its maximum size. The widget can be shrunk to its minimum size hint.
- `Preferred` means that the widget's size hint is its preferred size, but that the widget can still shrink or grow if necessary.
- `Expanding` means that the widget can shrink or grow and that it is especially willing to grow.

Figure 6.4 summarizes the meaning of the different size policies, using a `QLabel` showing the text "Some Text" as an example.

In the figure, `Preferred` and `Expanding` are depicted the same way. So, what is the difference? When a form that contains both `Preferred` and `Expanding` widgets is resized, extra space is given to the `Expanding` widgets, while the `Preferred` widgets stay at their size hint.

There are two other size policies: `MinimumExpanding` and `Ignored`. The former was necessary in a few rare cases in older versions of Qt, but it isn't useful anymore; the preferred approach is to use `Expanding` and reimplement `minimumSizeHint()` appropriately. The latter is similar to `Expanding`, except that it ignores the widget's size hint and minimum size hint.

In addition to the size policy's horizontal and vertical components, the `QSize-Policy` class stores a horizontal and a vertical stretch factor. These stretch

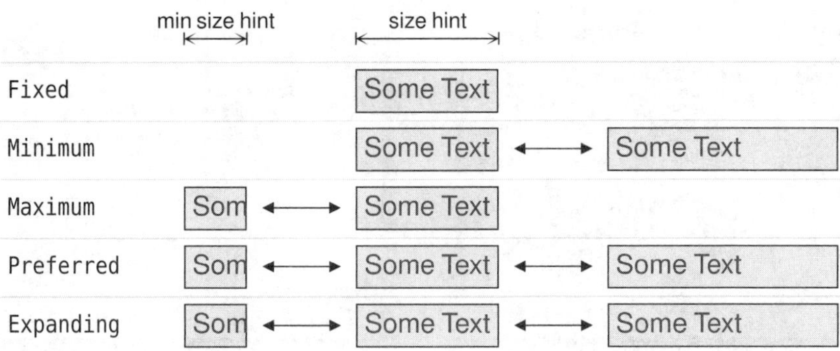

Figure 6.4. The meaning of the different size policies

factors can be used to indicate that different child widgets should grow at different rates when the form expands. For example, if we have a `QTreeWidget` above a `QTextEdit` and we want the `QTextEdit` to be twice as tall as the `QTreeWidget`, we can set the `QTextEdit`'s vertical stretch factor to 2 and the `QTreeWidget`'s vertical stretch factor to 1.

Yet another way of influencing a layout is to set a minimum size, a maximum size, or a fixed size on the child widgets. The layout manager will respect these constraints when laying out the widgets. And if this isn't sufficient, we can always derive from the child widget's class and reimplement `sizeHint()` to obtain the size hint we need.

Stacked Layouts

The `QStackedLayout` class lays out a set of child widgets, or "pages", and shows only one at a time, hiding the others from the user. The `QStackedLayout` itself is invisible and provides no intrinsic means for the user to change the page. The small arrows and the dark gray frame in Figure 6.5 are provided by *Qt Designer* to make the layout easier to design with. For convenience, Qt also includes `QStackedWidget`, which provides a `QWidget` with a built-in `QStackedLayout`.

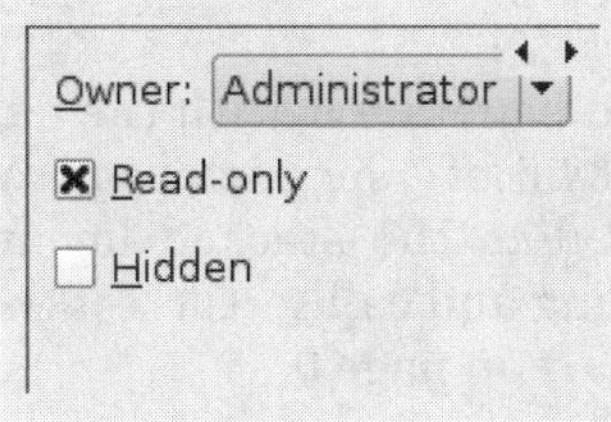

Figure 6.5. `QStackedLayout`

The pages are numbered from 0. To make a specific child widget visible, we can call `setCurrentIndex()` with a page number. The page number for a child widget is available using `indexOf()`.

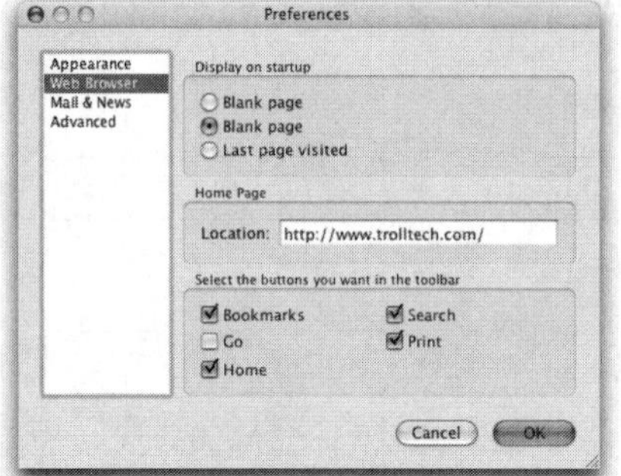

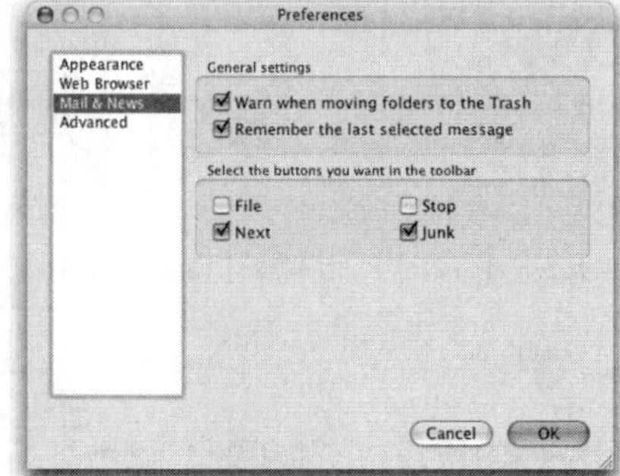

Figure 6.6. Two pages of the Preferences dialog

The Preferences dialog shown in Figure 6.6 is an example that uses `QStacked-Layout`. The dialog consists of a `QListWidget` on the left and a `QStackedLayout` on the right. Each item in the `QListWidget` corresponds to a different page in the `QStackedLayout`. Here's the relevant code from the dialog's constructor:

```
PreferenceDialog::PreferenceDialog(QWidget *parent)
    : QDialog(parent)
{
    ...
    listWidget = new QListWidget;
    listWidget->addItem(tr("Appearance"));
    listWidget->addItem(tr("Web Browser"));
    listWidget->addItem(tr("Mail & News"));
    listWidget->addItem(tr("Advanced"));

    stackedLayout = new QStackedLayout;
    stackedLayout->addWidget(appearancePage);
    stackedLayout->addWidget(webBrowserPage);
    stackedLayout->addWidget(mailAndNewsPage);
    stackedLayout->addWidget(advancedPage);
    connect(listWidget, SIGNAL(currentRowChanged(int)),
            stackedLayout, SLOT(setCurrentIndex(int)));
    ...
    listWidget->setCurrentRow(0);
}
```

We create a `QListWidget` and populate it with the page names. Then we create a `QStackedLayout` and call `addWidget()` for each page. We connect the list widget's `currentRowChanged(int)` signal to the stacked layout's `setCurrentIndex(int)` to implement the page switching and call `setCurrentRow()` on the list widget at the end of the constructor to start on page 0.

Forms such as this are also very easy to create using *Qt Designer*:

1. Create a new form based on one of the "Dialog" templates or on the "Widget" template.
2. Add a `QListWidget` and a `QStackedWidget` to the form.

3. Fill each page with child widgets and layouts.
   (To create a new page, right-click and choose Insert Page; to switch pages, click the tiny left or right arrow located at the top right of the `QStackedWidget`.)
4. Lay out the widgets side by side using a horizontal layout.
5. Connect the list widget's `currentRowChanged(int)` signal to the stacked widget's `setCurrentIndex(int)` slot.
6. Set the value of the list widget's `currentRow` property to 0.

Since we have implemented page switching using predefined signals and slots, the dialog will exhibit the correct behavior when previewed in *Qt Designer*.

For cases where the number of pages is small and likely to remain small, a simpler alternative to using a `QStackedWidget` and `QListWidget` is to use a `QTabWidget`.

Splitters

A `QSplitter` is a widget that contains other widgets. The widgets in a splitter are separated by splitter handles. Users can change the sizes of a splitter's child widgets by dragging the handles. Splitters can often be used as an alternative to layout managers, to give more control to the user.

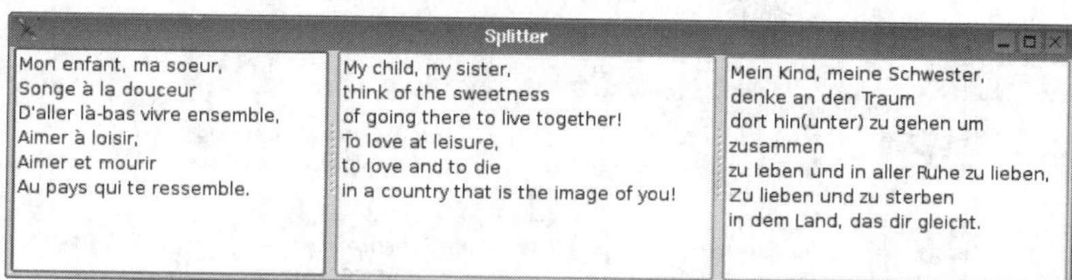

Figure 6.7. The Splitter application

The child widgets of a `QSplitter` are automatically placed side by side (or one below the other) in the order in which they are created, with splitter bars between adjacent widgets. Here's the code for creating the window depicted in Figure 6.7:

```
int main(int argc, char *argv[])
{
    QApplication app(argc, argv);

    QTextEdit *editor1 = new QTextEdit;
    QTextEdit *editor2 = new QTextEdit;
    QTextEdit *editor3 = new QTextEdit;

    QSplitter splitter(Qt::Horizontal);
    splitter.addWidget(editor1);
    splitter.addWidget(editor2);
    splitter.addWidget(editor3);
    ...
```

```
    splitter.show();
    return app.exec();
}
```

The example consists of three QTextEdits laid out horizontally by a QSplitter widget—this is shown schematically in Figure 6.8. Unlike layout managers, which simply lay out a form's child widgets and have no visual representation, QSplitter is derived from QWidget and can be used like any other widget.

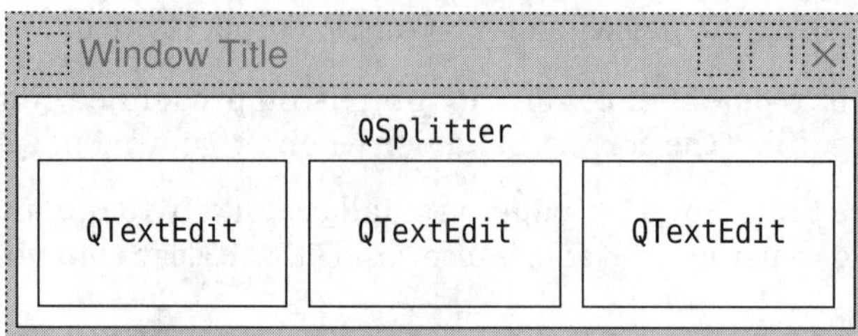

Figure 6.8. The Splitter application's widgets

Complex layouts can be achieved by nesting horizontal and vertical QSplitters. For example, the Mail Client application shown in Figure 6.9, consists of a horizontal QSplitter that contains a vertical QSplitter on its right side. The layout is shown schematically in Figure 6.10.

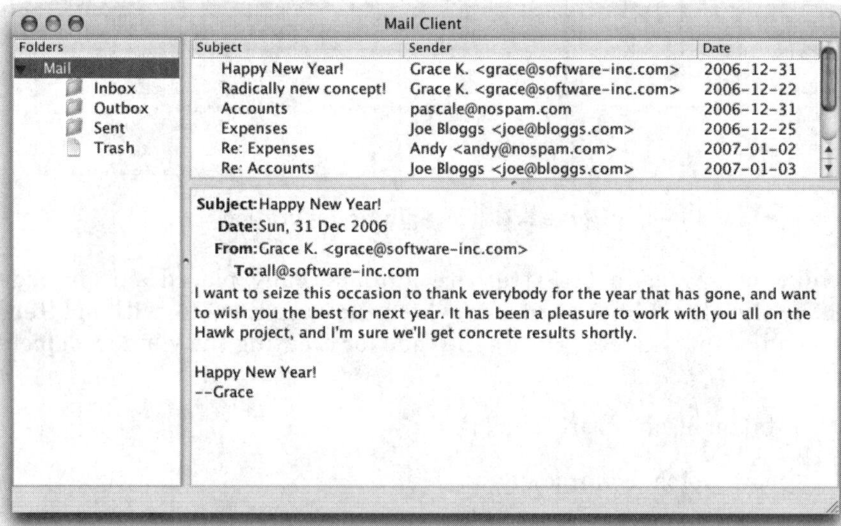

Figure 6.9. The Mail Client application

Here's the code in the constructor of the Mail Client application's QMainWindow subclass:

```
MailClient::MailClient()
{
```

```
    ...
    rightSplitter = new QSplitter(Qt::Vertical);
    rightSplitter->addWidget(messagesTreeWidget);
    rightSplitter->addWidget(textEdit);
    rightSplitter->setStretchFactor(1, 1);

    mainSplitter = new QSplitter(Qt::Horizontal);
    mainSplitter->addWidget(foldersTreeWidget);
    mainSplitter->addWidget(rightSplitter);
    mainSplitter->setStretchFactor(1, 1);
    setCentralWidget(mainSplitter);

    setWindowTitle(tr("Mail Client"));
    readSettings();
}
```

After creating the three widgets that we want to display, we create a vertical splitter, `rightSplitter`, and add the two widgets we want on the right. Then we create a horizontal splitter, `mainSplitter`, and add the widget we want it to display on the left and `rightSplitter` whose widgets we want shown on the right. We make `mainSplitter` the `QMainWindow`'s central widget.

When the user resizes a window, `QSplitter` normally distributes the space so that the relative sizes of the child widgets stay the same. In the Mail Client example, we don't want this behavior; instead, we want the `QTreeWidget` and the `QTableWidget` to keep their sizes and we want to give any extra space to the `QTextEdit`. This is achieved by the two `setStretchFactor()` calls. The first argument is the 0-based index of the splitter's child widget, and the second argument is the stretch factor we want to set; the default is 0.

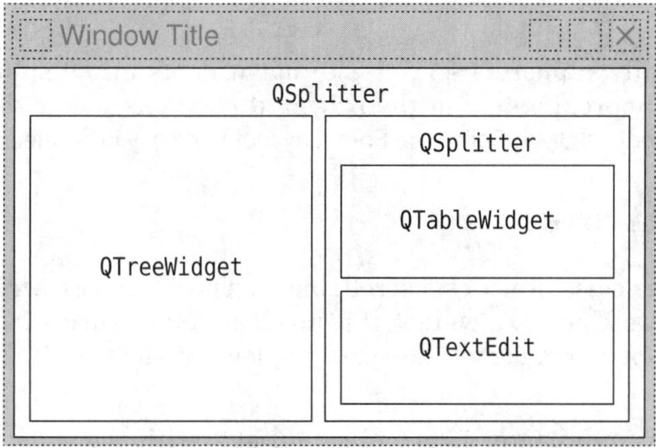

Figure 6.10. The Mail Client's splitter layout

The first `setStretchFactor()` call is on `rightSplitter`, and it sets the widget at position 1 (`textEdit`) to have a stretch factor of 1. The second `setStretchFactor()` call is on `mainSplitter`, and it sets the widget at position 1 (`rightSplitter`) to have a stretch factor of 1. This ensures that the `textEdit` will get any additional space that is available.

When the application is started, QSplitter gives the child widgets appropriate sizes based on their initial sizes (or based on their size hint if no initial size is specified). We can move the splitter handles programmatically by calling QSplitter::setSizes(). The QSplitter class also provides a means of saving and restoring its state the next time the application is run. Here's the writeSettings() function that saves the Mail Client's settings:

```
void MailClient::writeSettings()
{
    QSettings settings("Software Inc.", "Mail Client");

    settings.beginGroup("mainWindow");
    settings.setValue("geometry", saveGeometry());
    settings.setValue("mainSplitter", mainSplitter->saveState());
    settings.setValue("rightSplitter", rightSplitter->saveState());
    settings.endGroup();
}
```

Here's the corresponding readSettings() function:

```
void MailClient::readSettings()
{
    QSettings settings("Software Inc.", "Mail Client");

    settings.beginGroup("mainWindow");
    restoreGeometry(settings.value("geometry").toByteArray());
    mainSplitter->restoreState(
            settings.value("mainSplitter").toByteArray());
    rightSplitter->restoreState(
            settings.value("rightSplitter").toByteArray());
    settings.endGroup();
}
```

Qt Designer fully supports QSplitter. To put widgets into a splitter, place the child widgets approximately in their desired positions, select them, and click Form|Lay Out Horizontally in Splitter or Form|Lay Out Vertically in Splitter.

Scrolling Areas

The QScrollArea class provides a scrollable viewport and two scroll bars. If we want to add scroll bars to a widget, it is much simpler to use a QScrollArea than to instantiate our own QScrollBars and implement the scrolling functionality ourselves.

The way to use QScrollArea is to call setWidget() with the widget to which we want to add scroll bars. QScrollArea automatically reparents the widget to make it a child of the viewport (accessible through QScrollArea::viewport()) if it isn't already. For example, if we want scroll bars around the IconEditor widget we developed in Chapter 5 (as shown in Figure 6.11), we can write this:

```
int main(int argc, char *argv[])
{
    QApplication app(argc, argv);
```

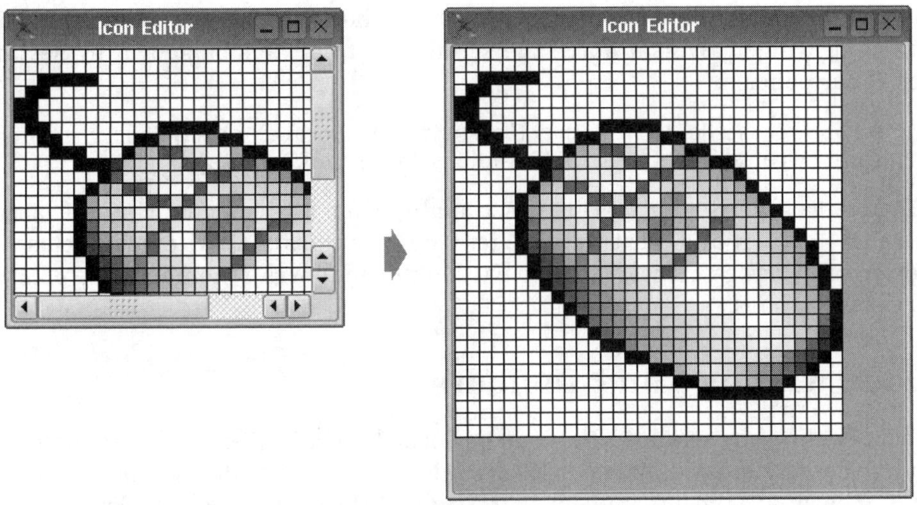

Figure 6.11. Resizing a QScrollArea

```
    IconEditor *iconEditor = new IconEditor;
    iconEditor->setIconImage(QImage(":/images/mouse.png"));

    QScrollArea scrollArea;
    scrollArea.setWidget(iconEditor);
    scrollArea.viewport()->setBackgroundRole(QPalette::Dark);
    scrollArea.viewport()->setAutoFillBackground(true);
    scrollArea.setWindowTitle(QObject::tr("Icon Editor"));

    scrollArea.show();
    return app.exec();
}
```

The QScrollArea (shown schematically in Figure 6.12) presents the widget at its current size or uses the size hint if the widget hasn't been resized yet. By calling setWidgetResizable(true), we can tell QScrollArea to automatically resize the widget to take advantage of any extra space beyond its size hint.

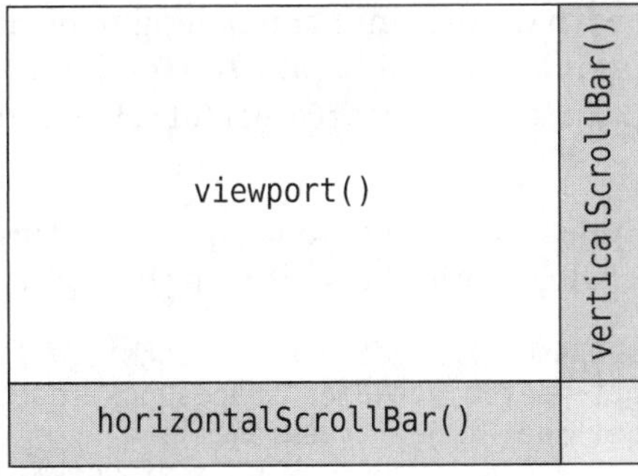

Figure 6.12. QScrollArea's constituent widgets

By default, the scroll bars are displayed only when the viewport is smaller than the child widget. We can force the scroll bars to always be shown by setting scroll bar policies:

```
scrollArea.setHorizontalScrollBarPolicy(Qt::ScrollBarAlwaysOn);
scrollArea.setVerticalScrollBarPolicy(Qt::ScrollBarAlwaysOn);
```

`QScrollArea` inherits much of its functionality from `QAbstractScrollArea`. Classes such as `QTextEdit` and `QAbstractItemView` (the base class of Qt's item view classes) derive from `QAbstractScrollArea`, so we don't need to wrap them in a `QScrollArea` to get scroll bars.

Dock Windows and Toolbars

Dock windows are windows that can be docked inside a `QMainWindow` or floated as independent windows. `QMainWindow` provides four dock window areas: one above, one below, one to the left, and one to the right of the central widget. Applications such as Microsoft Visual Studio and *Qt Linguist* make extensive use of dock windows to provide a very flexible user interface. In Qt, dock windows are instances of `QDockWidget`. Figure 6.13 shows a Qt application with toolbars and a dock window.

Every dock window has its own title bar, even when it is docked. Users can move dock windows from one dock area to another by dragging the title bar. They can also detach a dock window from an area and let the dock window float as an independent window by dragging the dock window outside of any dock area. Free-floating dock windows are always "on top" of their main window. Users can close a `QDockWidget` by clicking the close button in the window's title bar. Any combination of these features can be disabled by calling `QDockWidget::setFeatures()`.

In earlier versions of Qt, toolbars were treated like dock windows and shared the same dock areas. Starting with Qt 4, toolbars occupy their own areas around the central widget (as shown in Figure 6.14) and can't be undocked. If a floating toolbar is required, we can simply put it inside a `QDockWidget`.

The corners indicated with dotted lines can belong to either of their two adjoining dock areas. For example, we could make the top-left corner belong to the left dock area by calling `QMainWindow::setCorner(Qt::TopLeftCorner, Qt::LeftDockWidgetArea)`.

The following code snippet shows how to wrap an existing widget (in this case, a `QTreeWidget`) in a `QDockWidget` and insert it into the right dock area:

```
QDockWidget *shapesDockWidget = new QDockWidget(tr("Shapes"));
shapesDockWidget->setObjectName("shapesDockWidget");
shapesDockWidget->setWidget(treeWidget);
shapesDockWidget->setAllowedAreas(Qt::LeftDockWidgetArea
                                  | Qt::RightDockWidgetArea);
addDockWidget(Qt::RightDockWidgetArea, shapesDockWidget);
```

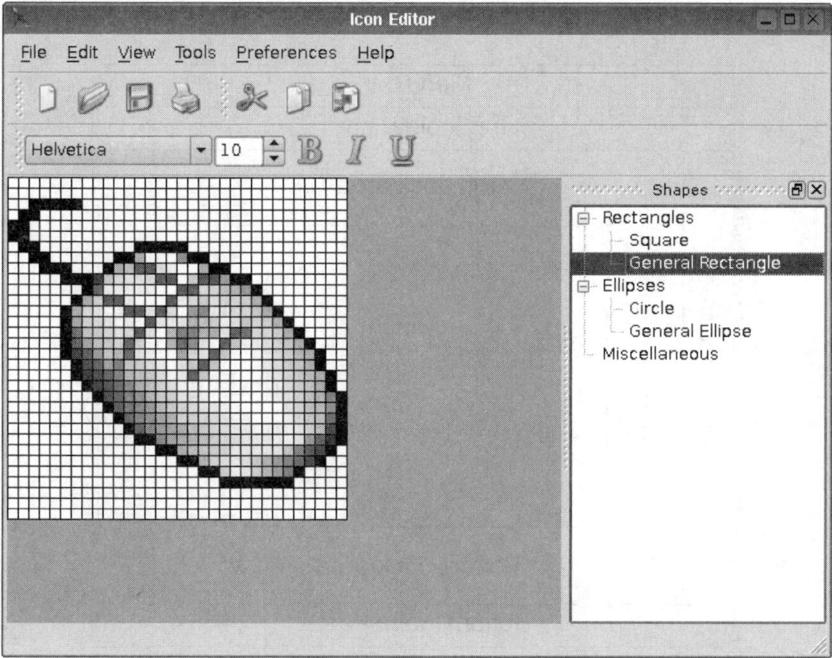

Figure 6.13. A QMainWindow with a dock window

The setAllowedAreas() call specifies constraints on which dock areas can accept the dock window. Here, we only allow the user to drag the dock window into the left and right dock areas, where there is enough vertical space for it to be displayed sensibly. If no allowed areas are explicitly set, the user can drag the dock window to any of the four areas.

Every QObject can be given an "object name". This name can be useful when debugging and is used by some test tools. Normally we do not bother to give widgets object names, but when we create dock windows and toolbars, doing so is necessary if we want to use QMainWindow::saveState() and QMainWindow::restoreState() to save and restore the dock window and toolbar geometries and states.

Here's how to create a toolbar containing a QComboBox, a QSpinBox, and a few QToolButtons from a QMainWindow subclass's constructor:

```
QToolBar *fontToolBar = new QToolBar(tr("Font"));
fontToolBar->setObjectName("fontToolBar");
fontToolBar->addWidget(familyComboBox);
fontToolBar->addWidget(sizeSpinBox);
fontToolBar->addAction(boldAction);
fontToolBar->addAction(italicAction);
fontToolBar->addAction(underlineAction);
fontToolBar->setAllowedAreas(Qt::TopToolBarArea
                             | Qt::BottomToolBarArea);
addToolBar(fontToolBar);
```

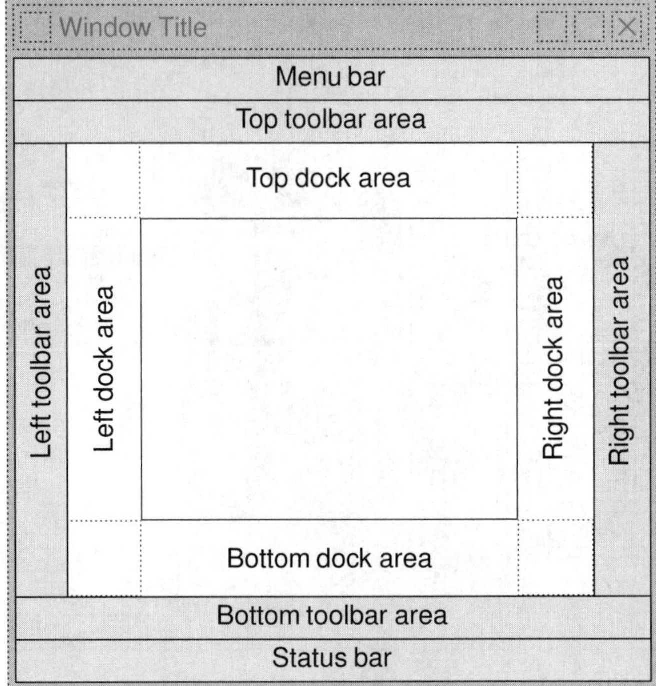

Figure 6.14. QMainWindow's dock and toolbar areas

If we want to save the position of all the dock windows and toolbars so that we can restore them the next time the application is run, we can write code that is similar to the code we used to save a QSplitter's state, using QMainWindow's saveState() and restoreState() functions:

```
void MainWindow::writeSettings()
{
    QSettings settings("Software Inc.", "Icon Editor");

    settings.beginGroup("mainWindow");
    settings.setValue("geometry", saveGeometry());
    settings.setValue("state", saveState());
    settings.endGroup();
}

void MainWindow::readSettings()
{
    QSettings settings("Software Inc.", "Icon Editor");

    settings.beginGroup("mainWindow");
    restoreGeometry(settings.value("geometry").toByteArray());
    restoreState(settings.value("state").toByteArray());
    settings.endGroup();
}
```

Finally, QMainWindow provides a context menu that lists all the dock windows and toolbars. This menu is shown in Figure 6.15. The user can close and restore dock windows and hide and restore toolbars using this menu.

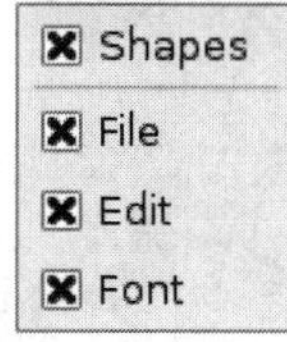

Figure 6.15. A QMainWindow context menu

Multiple Document Interface

Applications that provide multiple documents within the main window's central area are called multiple document interface applications, or MDI applications. In Qt, an MDI application is created by using the QMdiArea class as the central widget and by making each document window a QMdiArea subwindow.

It is conventional for MDI applications to provide a Window menu that includes some commands for managing both the windows and the list of windows. The active window is identified with a checkmark. The user can make any window active by clicking its entry in the Window menu.

In this section, we will develop the MDI Editor application shown in Figure 6.16 to demonstrate how to create an MDI application and how to implement its Window menu. All the application's menus are shown in Figure 6.17.

The application consists of two classes: MainWindow and Editor. The code is supplied with the book's examples, and since most of it is the same or similar to the Spreadsheet application from Part I, we will present only the MDI-relevant code.

Let's start with the MainWindow class.

```
MainWindow::MainWindow()
{
    mdiArea = new QMdiArea;
    setCentralWidget(mdiArea);
    connect(mdiArea, SIGNAL(subWindowActivated(QMdiSubWindow*)),
            this, SLOT(updateActions()));

    createActions();
    createMenus();
    createToolBars();
    createStatusBar();

    setWindowIcon(QPixmap(":/images/icon.png"));
    setWindowTitle(tr("MDI Editor"));
    QTimer::singleShot(0, this, SLOT(loadFiles()));
}
```

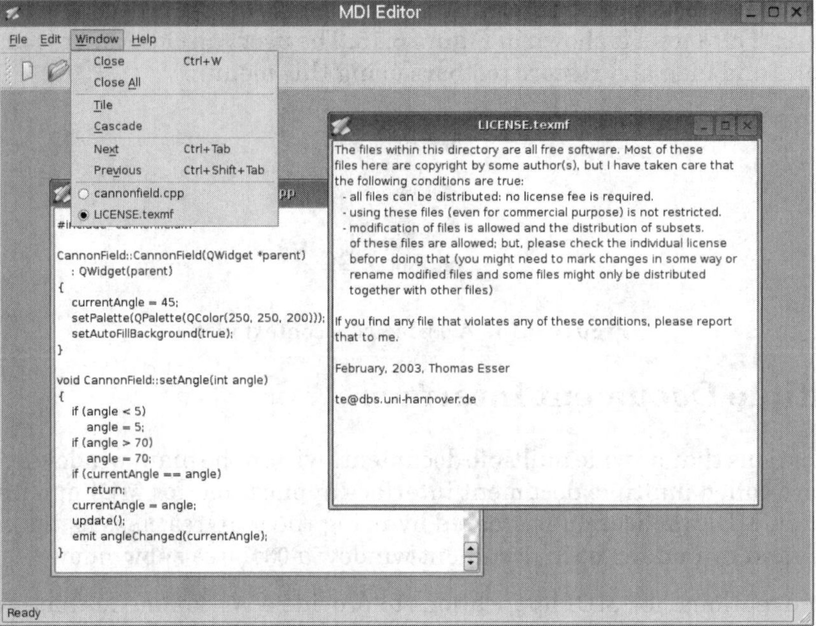

Figure 6.16. The MDI Editor application

In the MainWindow constructor, we create a QMdiArea widget and make it the central widget. We connect the QMdiArea's subWindowActivated() signal to the slot we will use to keep the window menu up-to-date, and where we ensure that actions are enabled or disabled depending on the application's state.

At the end of the constructor, we set a single-shot timer with a 0-millisecond interval to call the loadFiles() function. Such timers time out as soon as the event loop is idle. In practice, this means that the constructor will finish, and then after the main window has been shown, loadFiles() will be called. If we did not do this and there were a lot of large files to load, the constructor would not finish until all the files were loaded, and meanwhile, the user would not see anything on-screen and might think that the application had failed to start.

```
void MainWindow::loadFiles()
{
    QStringList args = QApplication::arguments();
    args.removeFirst();
    if (!args.isEmpty()) {
        foreach (QString arg, args)
            openFile(arg);
        mdiArea->cascadeSubWindows();
    } else {
        newFile();
    }
    mdiArea->activateNextSubWindow();
}
```

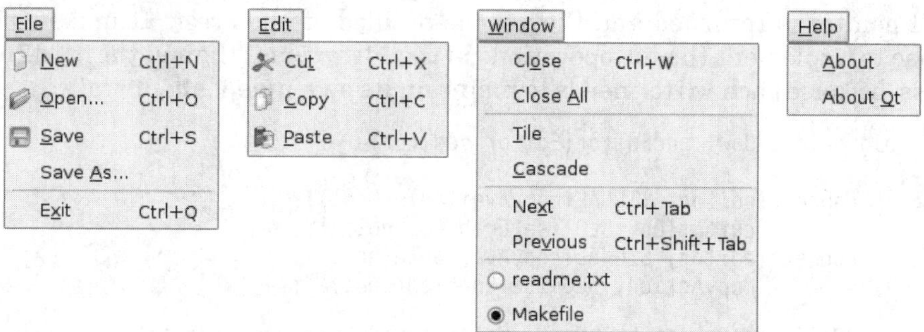

Figure 6.17. The MDI Editor application's menus

If the user started the application with one or more file names on the command line, this function attempts to load each file and at the end cascades the subwindows so that the user can easily see them. Qt-specific command-line options, such as `-style` and `-font`, are automatically removed from the argument list by the `QApplication` constructor. So, if we write

```
mdieditor -style motif readme.txt
```

on the command line, `QApplication::arguments()` returns a `QStringList` containing two items ("mdieditor" and "readme.txt"), and the MDI Editor application starts up with the document `readme.txt`.

If no file is specified on the command line, a single new empty editor subwindow is created so that the user can start typing straight away. The call to `activateNextSubWindow()` means that an editor window is given the focus, and ensures that the `updateActions()` function is called to update the Window menu and enable and disable actions according to the application's state.

```
void MainWindow::newFile()
{
    Editor *editor = new Editor;
    editor->newFile();
    addEditor(editor);
}
```

The `newFile()` slot corresponds to the File|New menu option. It creates an `Editor` widget and passes it on to the `addEditor()` private function.

```
void MainWindow::open()
{
    Editor *editor = Editor::open(this);
    if (editor)
    addEditor(editor);
}
```

The `open()` function corresponds to File|Open. It calls the static `Editor::open()` function, which pops up a file dialog. If the user chooses a file, a new `Editor` is created, the file's text is read in, and if the read is successful, a pointer to the `Editor` is returned. If the user cancels the file dialog, or if the reading fails, a null pointer is returned and the user is notified of the error. It makes more sense to implement the file operations in the Editor class than in the MainWindow class, because each Editor needs to maintain its own independent state.

```
void MainWindow::addEditor(Editor *editor)
{
    connect(editor, SIGNAL(copyAvailable(bool)),
            cutAction, SLOT(setEnabled(bool)));
    connect(editor, SIGNAL(copyAvailable(bool)),
            copyAction, SLOT(setEnabled(bool)));

    QMdiSubWindow *subWindow = mdiArea->addSubWindow(editor);
    windowMenu->addAction(editor->windowMenuAction());
    windowActionGroup->addAction(editor->windowMenuAction());
    subWindow->show();
}
```

The addEditor() private function is called from newFile() and open() to complete the initialization of a new Editor widget. It starts by establishing two signal–slot connections. These connections ensure that Edit|Cut and Edit|Copy are enabled or disabled depending on whether there is any selected text.

Because we are using MDI, it is possible that multiple Editor widgets will be in use. This is a concern since we are only interested in responding to the copyAvailable(bool) signal from the active Editor window, not from the others. But these signals can only ever be emitted by the active window, so this isn't a problem in practice.

The QMdiArea::addSubWindow() function creates a new QMdiSubWindow, puts the widget it is passed as a parameter inside the subwindow, and returns the subwindow. Next, we create a QAction representing the window to the Window menu. The action is provided by the Editor class, which we will cover in a moment. We also add the action to a QActionGroup object. The QActionGroup ensures that only one Window menu item is checked at a time. Finally, we call show() on the new QMdiSubWindow to make it visible.

```
void MainWindow::save()
{
    if (activeEditor())
        activeEditor()->save();
}
```

The save() slot calls Editor::save() on the active editor, if there is one. Again, the code that performs the real work is located in the Editor class.

```
Editor *MainWindow::activeEditor()
{
    QMdiSubWindow *subWindow = mdiArea->activeSubWindow();
    if (subWindow)
        return qobject_cast<Editor *>(subWindow->widget());
    return 0;
}
```

The activeEditor() private function returns the widget held inside the active subwindow as an Editor pointer, or a null pointer if there isn't an active subwindow.

```
void MainWindow::cut()
{
    if (activeEditor())
        activeEditor()->cut();
}
```

The cut() slot calls Editor::cut() on the active editor. We don't show the copy() and paste() slots because they follow the same pattern.

```
void MainWindow::updateActions()
{
    bool hasEditor = (activeEditor() != 0);
    bool hasSelection = activeEditor()
                        && activeEditor()->textCursor().hasSelection();

    saveAction->setEnabled(hasEditor);
    saveAsAction->setEnabled(hasEditor);
    cutAction->setEnabled(hasSelection);
    copyAction->setEnabled(hasSelection);
    pasteAction->setEnabled(hasEditor);
    closeAction->setEnabled(hasEditor);
    closeAllAction->setEnabled(hasEditor);
    tileAction->setEnabled(hasEditor);
    cascadeAction->setEnabled(hasEditor);
    nextAction->setEnabled(hasEditor);
    previousAction->setEnabled(hasEditor);
    separatorAction->setVisible(hasEditor);

    if (activeEditor())
        activeEditor()->windowMenuAction()->setChecked(true);
}
```

The subWindowActivated() signal is emitted every time a new subwindow becomes activated, and when the last subwindow is closed (in which case, its parameter is a null pointer). This signal is connected to the updateActions() slot.

Most menu options make sense only if there is an active window, so we disable them if there isn't one. At the end, we call setChecked() on the QAction representing the active window. Thanks to the QActionGroup, we don't need to explicitly uncheck the previously active window.

```
void MainWindow::createMenus()
{
    ...
    windowMenu = menuBar()->addMenu(tr("&Window"));
    windowMenu->addAction(closeAction);
    windowMenu->addAction(closeAllAction);
    windowMenu->addSeparator();
    windowMenu->addAction(tileAction);
    windowMenu->addAction(cascadeAction);
    windowMenu->addSeparator();
```

```
        windowMenu->addAction(nextAction);
        windowMenu->addAction(previousAction);
        windowMenu->addAction(separatorAction);
        ...
    }
```

The createMenus() private function populates the Window menu with actions. All the actions are typical of such menus and are easily implemented using QMdiArea's closeActiveSubWindow(), closeAllSubWindows(), tileSubWindows(), and cascadeSubWindows() slots. Every time the user opens a new window, it is added to the Window menu's list of actions. (This is done in the addEditor() function that we saw on page 160.) When the user closes an editor window, its action in the Window menu is deleted (since the action is owned by the editor window), and so the action is automatically removed from the Window menu.

```
void MainWindow::closeEvent(QCloseEvent *event)
{
    mdiArea->closeAllSubWindows();
    if (!mdiArea->subWindowList().isEmpty()) {
        event->ignore();
    } else {
        event->accept();
    }
}
```

The closeEvent() function is reimplemented to close all subwindows, causing each subwindow to receive a close event. If one of the subwindows "ignores" its close event (because the user canceled an "unsaved changes" message box), we ignore the close event for the MainWindow; otherwise, we accept it, resulting in Qt closing the entire application. If we didn't reimplement closeEvent() in MainWindow, the user would not be given the opportunity to save unsaved changes.

We have now finished our review of MainWindow, so we can move on to the Editor implementation. The Editor class represents one subwindow. It is derived from QTextEdit, which provides the text editing functionality. In a real-world application, if a code editing component is required, we might also consider using Scintilla, available for Qt as QScintilla from http://www.riverbankcomputing.co.uk/qscintilla/.

Just as any Qt widget can be used as a stand-alone window, any Qt widget can be put inside a QMdiSubWindow and used as a subwindow in an MDI area.

Here's the class definition:

```
class Editor : public QTextEdit
{
    Q_OBJECT

public:
    Editor(QWidget *parent = 0);

    void newFile();
    bool save();
    bool saveAs();
```

```
    QSize sizeHint() const;
    QAction *windowMenuAction() const { return action; }

    static Editor *open(QWidget *parent = 0);
    static Editor *openFile(const QString &fileName,
                            QWidget *parent = 0);

protected:
    void closeEvent(QCloseEvent *event);

private slots:
    void documentWasModified();

private:
    bool okToContinue();
    bool saveFile(const QString &fileName);
    void setCurrentFile(const QString &fileName);
    bool readFile(const QString &fileName);
    bool writeFile(const QString &fileName);
    QString strippedName(const QString &fullFileName);

    QString curFile;
    bool isUntitled;
    QAction *action;
};
```

Four of the private functions that were in the Spreadsheet application's `MainWindow` class (p. 59) are also present in the `Editor` class: `okToContinue()`, `saveFile()`, `setCurrentFile()`, and `strippedName()`.

```
Editor::Editor(QWidget *parent)
    : QTextEdit(parent)
{
    action = new QAction(this);
    action->setCheckable(true);
    connect(action, SIGNAL(triggered()), this, SLOT(show()));
    connect(action, SIGNAL(triggered()), this, SLOT(setFocus()));

    isUntitled = true;

    connect(document(), SIGNAL(contentsChanged()),
            this, SLOT(documentWasModified()));

    setWindowIcon(QPixmap(":/images/document.png"));
    setWindowTitle("[*]");
    setAttribute(Qt::WA_DeleteOnClose);
}
```

First, we create a `QAction` representing the editor in the application's Window menu and connect that action to the `show()` and `setFocus()` slots.

Since we allow users to create any number of editor windows, we must make some provision for naming them so that they can be distinguished before they have been saved for the first time. One common way of handling this is to allocate names that include a number (e.g., `document1.txt`). We use the `isUntitled` variable to distinguish between names supplied by the user and names we have created programmatically.

We connect the text document's contentsChanged() signal to the private documentWasModified() slot. This slot simply calls setWindowModified(true).

Finally, we set the Qt::WA_DeleteOnClose attribute to prevent memory leaks when the user closes an Editor window.

```
void Editor::newFile()
{
    static int documentNumber = 1;

    curFile = tr("document%1.txt").arg(documentNumber);
    setWindowTitle(curFile + "[*]");
    action->setText(curFile);
    isUntitled = true;
    ++documentNumber;
}
```

The newFile() function generates a name like document1.txt for the new document. The code belongs in newFile(), rather than the constructor, because we don't want to consume numbers when we call open() to open an existing document in a newly created Editor. Since documentNumber is declared static, it is shared across all Editor instances.

The "[*]" marker in the window title is a place marker for where we want the asterisk to appear when the file has unsaved changes on platforms other than Mac OS X. On Mac OS X, unsaved documents have a dot in their window's close button. We covered this place marker in Chapter 3 (p. 61).

In addition to creating new files, users often want to open existing files, picked from either a file dialog or a list such as a recently opened files list. Two static functions are provided to support these uses: open() for choosing a file name from the file system, and openFile() to create an Editor and to read into it the contents of a specified file.

```
Editor *Editor::open(QWidget *parent)
{
    QString fileName =
            QFileDialog::getOpenFileName(parent, tr("Open"), ".");
    if (fileName.isEmpty())
        return 0;

    return openFile(fileName, parent);
}
```

The static open() function pops up a file dialog through which the user can choose a file. If a file is chosen, openFile() is called to create an Editor and to read in the file's contents.

```
Editor *Editor::openFile(const QString &fileName, QWidget *parent)
{
    Editor *editor = new Editor(parent);
```

```
        if (editor->readFile(fileName)) {
            editor->setCurrentFile(fileName);
            return editor;
        } else {
            delete editor;
            return 0;
        }
    }
```

This static function begins by creating a new `Editor` widget, and then attempts to read in the specified file. If the read is successful, the `Editor` is returned; otherwise, the user is informed of the problem (in `readFile()`), the editor is deleted, and a null pointer is returned.

```
    bool Editor::save()
    {
        if (isUntitled) {
            return saveAs();
        } else {
            return saveFile(curFile);
        }
    }
```

The `save()` function uses the `isUntitled` variable to determine whether it should call `saveFile()` or `saveAs()`.

```
    void Editor::closeEvent(QCloseEvent *event)
    {
        if (okToContinue()) {
            event->accept();
        } else {
            event->ignore();
        }
    }
```

The `closeEvent()` function is reimplemented to allow the user to save unsaved changes. The logic is coded in the `okToContinue()` function, which pops up a message box that asks, "Do you want to save your changes?" If `okToContinue()` returns `true`, we accept the close event; otherwise, we "ignore" it and leave the window unaffected by it.

```
    void Editor::setCurrentFile(const QString &fileName)
    {
        curFile = fileName;
        isUntitled = false;
        action->setText(strippedName(curFile));
        document()->setModified(false);
        setWindowTitle(strippedName(curFile) + "[*]");
        setWindowModified(false);
    }
```

The `setCurrentFile()` function is called from `openFile()` and `saveFile()` to update the `curFile` and `isUntitled` variables, to set the window title and action text, and to set the document's "modified" flag to `false`. Whenever the user modifies the text in the editor, the underlying QTextDocument emits the contentsChanged() signal and sets its internal "modified" flag to true.

```
QSize Editor::sizeHint() const
{
    return QSize(72 * fontMetrics().width('x'),
                 25 * fontMetrics().lineSpacing());
}
```

Finally, the sizeHint() function returns a size based on the width of the letter 'x' and the height of a text line. QMdiArea uses the size hint to give an initial size to the window.

MDI is one way of handling multiple documents simultaneously. On Mac OS X, the preferred approach is to use multiple top-level windows. We covered this approach in the "Multiple Documents" section of Chapter 3.

- *Reimplementing Event Handlers*
- *Installing Event Filters*
- *Staying Responsive during Intensive Processing*

7. Event Processing

Events are generated by the window system or by Qt itself in response to various occurrences. When the user presses or releases a key or mouse button, a key or mouse event is generated; when a window is shown for the first time, a paint event is generated to tell the newly visible window that it needs to draw itself. Most events are generated in response to user actions, but some, such as timer events, are generated independently by the system.

When we program with Qt, we seldom need to think about events, because Qt widgets emit signals when something significant occurs. Events become useful when we write our own custom widgets or when we want to modify the behavior of existing Qt widgets.

Events should not be confused with signals. As a rule, signals are useful when *using* a widget, whereas events are useful when *implementing* a widget. For example, when we are using `QPushButton`, we are more interested in its `clicked()` signal than in the low-level mouse or key events that caused the signal to be emitted. But if we are implementing a class such as `QPushButton`, we need to write code to handle mouse and key events and emit the `clicked()` signal when necessary.

Reimplementing Event Handlers

In Qt, an event is an instance of a `QEvent` subclass. Qt handles more than a hundred types of events, each identified by an enum value. For example, `QEvent::type()` returns `QEvent::MouseButtonPress` for mouse press events.

Many event types require more information than can be stored in a plain `QEvent` object; for example, mouse press events need to store which mouse button triggered the event as well as where the mouse pointer was positioned when the event occurred. This additional information is stored in dedicated `QEvent` subclasses, such as `QMouseEvent`.

Events are notified to objects through their event() function, inherited from QObject. The event() implementation in QWidget forwards the most common types of events to specific event handlers, such as mousePressEvent(), keyPressEvent(), and paintEvent().

We have already seen many event handlers when implementing MainWindow, IconEditor, and Plotter in earlier chapters. Many other types of events are listed in the QEvent reference documentation, and it is also possible to create custom event types and to dispatch events ourselves. Here, we will review two common event types that deserve more explanation: key events and timer events.

Key events are handled by reimplementing keyPressEvent() and keyReleaseEvent(). The Plotter widget reimplements keyPressEvent(). Normally, we only need to reimplement keyPressEvent() since the only keys for which release is important are the modifier keys Ctrl, Shift, and Alt, and these can be checked for in a keyPressEvent() using QKeyEvent::modifiers(). For example, if we were implementing a CodeEditor widget, its stripped-down keyPressEvent() that distinguishes between Home and Ctrl+Home would look like this:

```
void CodeEditor::keyPressEvent(QKeyEvent *event)
{
    switch (event->key()) {
    case Qt::Key_Home:
        if (event->modifiers() & Qt::ControlModifier) {
            goToBeginningOfDocument();
        } else {
            goToBeginningOfLine();
        }
        break;
    case Qt::Key_End:
        ...
    default:
        QWidget::keyPressEvent(event);
    }
}
```

The Tab and Backtab (Shift+Tab) keys are special cases. QWidget::event() handles them before it calls keyPressEvent(), with the semantic of passing the focus to the next or previous widget in the focus chain. This behavior is usually what we want, but in a CodeEditor widget, we might prefer to make Tab indent a line. The event() reimplementation would then look like this:

```
bool CodeEditor::event(QEvent *event)
{
    if (event->type() == QEvent::KeyPress) {
        QKeyEvent *keyEvent = static_cast<QKeyEvent *>(event);
        if (keyEvent->key() == Qt::Key_Tab) {
            insertAtCurrentPosition('\t');
            return true;
        }
    }
    return QWidget::event(event);
}
```

If the event is a key press, we cast the QEvent object to a QKeyEvent and check which key was pressed. If the key is Tab, we do some processing and return true to tell Qt that we have handled the event. If we returned false, Qt would propagate the event to the parent widget.

A higher-level approach for implementing key bindings is to use a QAction. For example, if goToBeginningOfLine() and goToBeginningOfDocument() are public slots in the CodeEditor widget, and the CodeEditor is used as the central widget in a MainWindow class, we could add the key bindings with the following code:

```
MainWindow::MainWindow()
{
    editor = new CodeEditor;
    setCentralWidget(editor);

    goToBeginningOfLineAction =
            new QAction(tr("Go to Beginning of Line"), this);
    goToBeginningOfLineAction->setShortcut(tr("Home"));
    connect(goToBeginningOfLineAction, SIGNAL(activated()),
            editor, SLOT(goToBeginningOfLine()));

    goToBeginningOfDocumentAction =
            new QAction(tr("Go to Beginning of Document"), this);
    goToBeginningOfDocumentAction->setShortcut(tr("Ctrl+Home"));
    connect(goToBeginningOfDocumentAction, SIGNAL(activated()),
            editor, SLOT(goToBeginningOfDocument()));
    ...
}
```

This makes it easy to add the commands to a menu or a toolbar, as we saw in Chapter 3. If the commands don't appear in the user interface, the QAction objects could be replaced with a QShortcut object, the class used internally by QAction to support key bindings.

By default, key bindings set using QAction or QShortcut on a widget are enabled whenever the window that contains the widget is active. This can be changed using QAction::setShortcutContext() or QShortcut::setContext().

Another common type of event is the timer event. While most other event types occur as a result of a user action, timer events allow applications to perform processing at regular time intervals. Timer events can be used to implement blinking cursors and other animations, or simply to refresh the display.

To demonstrate timer events, we will implement the Ticker widget shown in Figure 7.1. This widget shows a text banner that scrolls left by one pixel every 30 milliseconds. If the widget is wider than the text, the text is repeated as often as necessary to fill the entire width of the widget.

say ++ How long it lasted was impossible to say ++ Ho

Figure 7.1. The Ticker widget

Here's the header file:

```
#ifndef TICKER_H
#define TICKER_H

#include <QWidget>

class Ticker : public QWidget
{
    Q_OBJECT
    Q_PROPERTY(QString text READ text WRITE setText)

public:
    Ticker(QWidget *parent = 0);

    void setText(const QString &newText);
    QString text() const { return myText; }
    QSize sizeHint() const;

protected:
    void paintEvent(QPaintEvent *event);
    void timerEvent(QTimerEvent *event);
    void showEvent(QShowEvent *event);
    void hideEvent(QHideEvent *event);

private:
    QString myText;
    int offset;
    int myTimerId;
};

#endif
```

We reimplement four event handlers in `Ticker`, three of which we have not seen before: `timerEvent()`, `showEvent()`, and `hideEvent()`.

Now let's review the implementation:

```
#include <QtGui>

#include "ticker.h"

Ticker::Ticker(QWidget *parent)
    : QWidget(parent)
{
    offset = 0;
    myTimerId = 0;
}
```

The constructor initializes the `offset` variable to 0. The x-coordinate at which the text is drawn is derived from the `offset` value. Timer IDs are always non-zero, so we use 0 to indicate that no timer has been started.

```
void Ticker::setText(const QString &newText)
{
    myText = newText;
    update();
```

```
        updateGeometry();
    }
```

The `setText()` function sets the text to display. It calls `update()` to request a repaint and `updateGeometry()` to notify any layout manager responsible for the `Ticker` widget about a size hint change.

```
QSize Ticker::sizeHint() const
{
    return fontMetrics().size(0, text());
}
```

The `sizeHint()` function returns the space needed by the text as the widget's ideal size. `QWidget::fontMetrics()` returns a `QFontMetrics` object that can be queried to obtain information relating to the widget's font. In this case, we ask for the size required by the given text. (The first argument to `QFontMetrics::size()` is a flag that isn't needed for simple strings, so we just pass 0.)

```
void Ticker::paintEvent(QPaintEvent * /* event */)
{
    QPainter painter(this);

    int textWidth = fontMetrics().width(text());
    if (textWidth < 1)
        return;
    int x = -offset;
    while (x < width()) {
        painter.drawText(x, 0, textWidth, height(),
                         Qt::AlignLeft | Qt::AlignVCenter, text());
        x += textWidth;
    }
}
```

The `paintEvent()` function draws the text using `QPainter::drawText()`. It uses `fontMetrics()` to ascertain how much horizontal space the text requires, and then draws the text as many times as necessary to fill the entire width of the widget, taking `offset` into account.

```
void Ticker::showEvent(QShowEvent * /* event */)
{
    myTimerId = startTimer(30);
}
```

The `showEvent()` function starts a timer. The call to `QObject::startTimer()` returns an ID number, which we can use later to identify the timer. `QObject` supports multiple independent timers, each with its own time interval. After the call to `startTimer()`, Qt will generate a timer event approximately every 30 milliseconds; the accuracy depends on the underlying operating system.

We could have called `startTimer()` in the `Ticker` constructor, but we save some resources by having Qt generate timer events only when the widget is actually visible.

```
void Ticker::timerEvent(QTimerEvent *event)
{
    if (event->timerId() == myTimerId) {
        ++offset;
        if (offset >= fontMetrics().width(text()))
            offset = 0;
        scroll(-1, 0);
    } else {
        QWidget::timerEvent(event);
    }
}
```

The system calls the `timerEvent()` function at intervals. It increments `offset` by 1 to simulate movement, wrapping at the width of the text. Then it scrolls the contents of the widget one pixel to the left using `QWidget::scroll()`. It would have been sufficient to call `update()` instead of `scroll()`, but `scroll()` is more efficient because it simply moves the existing pixels on-screen and generates a paint event only for the widget's newly revealed area (a 1-pixel-wide strip in this case).

If the timer event isn't for the timer we are interested in, we pass it on to the base class.

```
void Ticker::hideEvent(QHideEvent * /* event */)
{
    killTimer(myTimerId);
    myTimerId = 0;
}
```

The `hideEvent()` function calls `QObject::killTimer()` to stop the timer.

Timer events are low-level, and if we need multiple timers, it can become cumbersome to keep track of all the timer IDs. In such situations, it is usually easier to create a `QTimer` object for each timer. `QTimer` emits the `timeout()` signal at each time interval. `QTimer` also provides a convenient interface for single-shot timers (timers that time out just once), as we saw in Chapter 6 (p. 158).

Installing Event Filters

One really powerful feature of Qt's event model is that a `QObject` instance can be set to monitor the events of another `QObject` instance before the latter object even sees them.

Let's suppose that we have a `CustomerInfoDialog` widget composed of several `QLineEdit`s and that we want to use the Space key to move the focus to the next `QLineEdit`. This non-standard behavior might be appropriate for an in-house application whose users are trained in its use. A straightforward solution is to subclass `QLineEdit` and reimplement `keyPressEvent()` to call `focusNextChild()`, like this:

```
void MyLineEdit::keyPressEvent(QKeyEvent *event)
{
```

```
        if (event->key() == Qt::Key_Space) {
            focusNextChild();
        } else {
            QLineEdit::keyPressEvent(event);
        }
    }
```

This approach has one main disadvantage: If we use several different kinds of widgets in the form (e.g., QComboBoxes and QSpinBoxes), we must also subclass them to make them exhibit the same behavior. A better solution is to make CustomerInfoDialog monitor its child widgets' key press events and implement the required behavior in the monitoring code. This can be achieved using event filters. Setting up an event filter involves two steps:

1. Register the monitoring object with the target object by calling installEventFilter() on the target.
2. Handle the target object's events in the monitor's eventFilter() function.

A good place to register the monitoring object is in the constructor:

```
CustomerInfoDialog::CustomerInfoDialog(QWidget *parent)
    : QDialog(parent)
{
    ...
    firstNameEdit->installEventFilter(this);
    lastNameEdit->installEventFilter(this);
    cityEdit->installEventFilter(this);
    phoneNumberEdit->installEventFilter(this);
}
```

Once the event filter is registered, the events that are sent to the firstNameEdit, lastNameEdit, cityEdit, and phoneNumberEdit widgets are first sent to the CustomerInfoDialog's eventFilter() function before they are sent on to their intended destination.

Here's the eventFilter() function that receives the events:

```
bool CustomerInfoDialog::eventFilter(QObject *target, QEvent *event)
{
    if (target == firstNameEdit || target == lastNameEdit
            || target == cityEdit || target == phoneNumberEdit) {
        if (event->type() == QEvent::KeyPress) {
            QKeyEvent *keyEvent = static_cast<QKeyEvent *>(event);
            if (keyEvent->key() == Qt::Key_Space) {
                focusNextChild();
                return true;
            }
        }
    }
    return QDialog::eventFilter(target, event);
}
```

First, we check to see whether the target widget is one of the QLineEdits. If the event was a key press, we cast it to QKeyEvent and check which key was pressed.

If the pressed key was Space, we call focusNextChild() to pass focus on to the next widget in the focus chain, and we return true to tell Qt that we have handled the event. If we returned false, Qt would send the event to its intended target, resulting in a spurious space being inserted into the QLineEdit.

If the target widget isn't a QLineEdit, or if the event isn't a Space key press, we pass control to the base class's implementation of eventFilter(). The target widget could also be some widget that the base class, QDialog, is monitoring. (In Qt 4.3, this is not the case for QDialog. However, other Qt widget classes, such as QScrollArea, do monitor some of their child widgets for various reasons.)

Qt offers five levels at which events can be processed and filtered:

1. **We can reimplement a specific event handler.**

   Reimplementing event handlers such as mousePressEvent(), keyPressEvent(), and paintEvent() is by far the most common way to process events. We have already seen many examples of this.

2. **We can reimplement QObject::event().**

   By reimplementing the event() function, we can process events before they reach the specific event handlers. This approach is mostly needed to override the default meaning of the Tab key, as shown earlier (p. 168). This is also used to handle rare types of events for which no specific event handler exists (e.g., QEvent::HoverEnter). When we reimplement event(), we must call the base class's event() function for handling the cases we don't explicitly handle.

3. **We can install an event filter on a single QObject.**

   Once an object has been registered using installEventFilter(), all the events for the target object are first sent to the monitoring object's eventFilter() function. If multiple event filters are installed on the same object, the filters are activated in turn, from the most recently installed back to the first installed.

4. **We can install an event filter on the QApplication object.**

   Once an event filter has been registered for qApp (the unique QApplication object), every event for every object in the application is sent to the eventFilter() function before it is sent to any other event filter. This approach is mostly useful for debugging. It can also be used to handle mouse events sent to disabled widgets, which QApplication normally discards.

5. **We can subclass QApplication and reimplement notify().**

   Qt calls QApplication::notify() to send out an event. Reimplementing this function is the only way to get all the events, before any event filters get the opportunity to look at them. Event filters are generally more useful, because there can be any number of concurrent event filters, but only one notify() function.

Many event types, including mouse and key events, can be propagated. If the event has not been handled on the way to its target object or by the target object itself, the whole event processing process is repeated, but this time with the target object's parent as the new target. This continues, going from parent to parent, until either the event is handled or the top-level object is reached.

Figure 7.2 shows how a key press event is propagated from child to parent in a dialog. When the user presses a key, the event is first sent to the widget that has focus, in this case the bottom-right `QCheckBox`. If the `QCheckBox` doesn't handle the event, Qt sends it to the `QGroupBox`, and finally to the `QDialog` object.

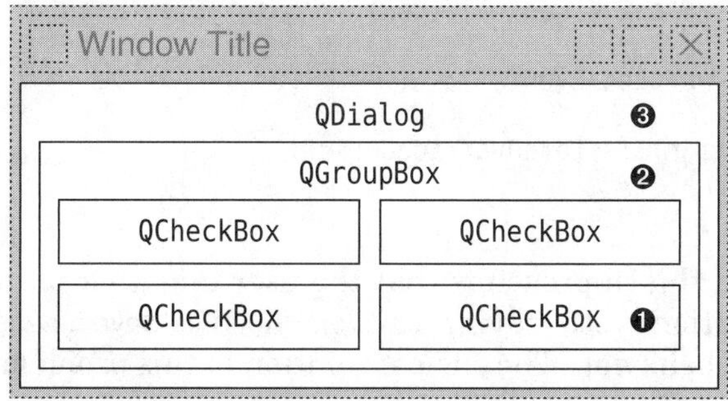

Figure 7.2. Event propagation in a dialog

Staying Responsive during Intensive Processing

When we call `QApplication::exec()`, we start Qt's event loop. Qt issues a few events on startup to show and paint the widgets. After that, the event loop is running, constantly checking to see whether any events have occurred and dispatching these events to `QObject`s in the application.

While one event is being processed, additional events may be generated and appended to Qt's event queue. If we spend too much time processing a particular event, the user interface will become unresponsive. For example, any events generated by the window system while the application is saving a file to disk will not be processed until the file is saved. During the save, the application will not respond to requests from the window system to repaint itself.

One solution is to use multiple threads: one thread for the application's user interface and another thread to perform file saving (or any other time-consuming operation). This way, the application's user interface will stay responsive while the file is being saved. We will see how to achieve this in Chapter 14.

A simpler solution is to make frequent calls to `QApplication::processEvents()` in the file saving code. This function tells Qt to process any pending events, and then returns control to the caller. In fact, `QApplication::exec()` is little more than a `while` loop around a `processEvents()` function call.

Here's an example of how we can keep the user interface responsive using processEvents(), based on the file saving code for Spreadsheet (p. 84):

```
bool Spreadsheet::writeFile(const QString &fileName)
{
    QFile file(fileName);
    ...
    QApplication::setOverrideCursor(Qt::WaitCursor);
    for (int row = 0; row < RowCount; ++row) {
        for (int column = 0; column < ColumnCount; ++column) {
            QString str = formula(row, column);
            if (!str.isEmpty())
                out << quint16(row) << quint16(column) << str;
        }
        qApp->processEvents();
    }
    QApplication::restoreOverrideCursor();
    return true;
}
```

One danger with this approach is that the user might close the main window while the application is still saving, or even click File|Save a second time, resulting in undefined behavior. The easiest solution to this problem is to replace

```
qApp->processEvents();
```

with

```
qApp->processEvents(QEventLoop::ExcludeUserInputEvents);
```

telling Qt to ignore mouse and key events.

Often, we want to show a QProgressDialog while a long-running operation is taking place. QProgressDialog has a progress bar that keeps the user informed about the application's progress. QProgressDialog also provides a Cancel button that allows the user to abort the operation. Here's the code for saving a Spreadsheet file using this approach:

```
bool Spreadsheet::writeFile(const QString &fileName)
{
    QFile file(fileName);
    ...
    QProgressDialog progress(this);
    progress.setLabelText(tr("Saving %1").arg(fileName));
    progress.setRange(0, RowCount);
    progress.setModal(true);

    for (int row = 0; row < RowCount; ++row) {
        progress.setValue(row);
        qApp->processEvents();
        if (progress.wasCanceled()) {
            file.remove();
            return false;
        }
```

```
        for (int column = 0; column < ColumnCount; ++column) {
            QString str = formula(row, column);
            if (!str.isEmpty())
                out << quint16(row) << quint16(column) << str;
        }
    }
    return true;
}
```

We create a QProgressDialog with NumRows as the total number of steps. Then, for each row, we call setValue() to update the progress bar. QProgressDialog automatically computes a percentage by dividing the current progress value by the total number of steps. We call QApplication::processEvents() to process any repaint events or any user clicks or key presses (e.g., to allow the user to click Cancel). If the user clicks Cancel, we abort the save and remove the file.

We don't call show() on the QProgressDialog because progress dialogs do that for themselves. If the operation turns out to be short, presumably because the file to save is small or because the machine is fast, QProgressDialog will detect this and will not show itself at all.

In addition to multithreading and using QProgressDialog, there is a completely different way of dealing with long-running operations: Instead of performing the processing when the user requests, we can defer the processing until the application is idle. This can work if the processing can be safely interrupted and resumed, since we cannot predict how long the application will be idle.

In Qt, this approach can be implemented by using a 0-millisecond timer. These timers time out whenever there are no pending events. Here's an example timerEvent() implementation that shows the idle processing approach:

```
void Spreadsheet::timerEvent(QTimerEvent *event)
{
    if (event->timerId() == myTimerId) {
        while (step < MaxStep && !qApp->hasPendingEvents()) {
            performStep(step);
            ++step;
        }
    } else {
        QTableWidget::timerEvent(event);
    }
}
```

If hasPendingEvents() returns true, we stop processing and give control back to Qt. The processing will resume when Qt has handled all its pending events.

```
        for (int column = 0; column < ColumnCount; ++column) {
            QString str = formula(row, column);
            if (!str.isEmpty())
                out << quint16(row) << quint16(column) << str;
        }
    }
    return true;
}
```

We create a QProgressDialog with NumRows as the total number of steps. Then, for each row, we call setValue() to update the progress bar. QProgressDialog automatically computes a percentage by dividing the current progress value by the total number of steps. We call QApplication::processEvents() to process any repaint events or any user clicks or key presses (e.g., to allow the user to click Cancel). If the user clicks Cancel, we abort the save and remove the file.

We don't call show() on the QProgressDialog because progress dialogs do that for themselves. If the operation turns out to be short, presumably because the file to save is small or because the machine is fast, QProgressDialog will detect this and will not show itself at all.

In addition to multithreading and using QProgressDialog, there is a completely different way of dealing with long-running operations: Instead of performing the processing when the user requests, we can defer the processing until the application is idle. This can work if the processing can be safely interrupted and resumed, since we cannot predict how long the application will be idle.

In Qt, this approach can be implemented by using a 0-millisecond timer. These timers time out whenever there are no pending events. Here's an example timerEvent() implementation that shows the idle processing approach:

```
void Spreadsheet::timerEvent(QTimerEvent *event)
{
    if (event->timerId() == myTimerId) {
        while (step < MaxStep && !qApp->hasPendingEvents()) {
            performStep(step);
            ++step;
        }
    } else {
        QTableWidget::timerEvent(event);
    }
}
```

If hasPendingEvents() returns true, we stop processing and give control back to Qt. The processing will resume when Qt has handled all its pending events.

- *Painting with QPainter*
- *Coordinate System Transformations*
- *High-Quality Rendering with QImage*
- *Item-Based Rendering with Graphics View*
- *Printing*

8. 2D Graphics

Qt's 2D graphics engine is based on the `QPainter` class. `QPainter` can draw geometric shapes (points, lines, rectangles, ellipses, arcs, chords, pie segments, polygons, and Bézier curves), as well as pixmaps, images, and text. Furthermore, `QPainter` supports advanced features such as antialiasing (for text and shape edges), alpha blending, gradient filling, and vector paths. `QPainter` also supports linear transformations, such as translation, rotation, shearing, and scaling.

`QPainter` can be used to draw on a "paint device", such as a `QWidget`, a `QPixmap`, a `QImage`, or a `QSvgGenerator`. `QPainter` can also be used in conjunction with `QPrinter` for printing and for generating PDF documents. This means that we can often use the same code to display data on-screen and to produce printed reports.

By reimplementing `QWidget::paintEvent()`, we can create custom widgets and exercise complete control over their appearance, as we saw in Chapter 5. For customizing the look and feel of predefined Qt widgets, we can also specify a style sheet or create a `QStyle` subclass; we cover both of these approaches in Chapter 19.

A common requirement is the need to display large numbers of lightweight arbitrarily shaped items that the user can interact with on a 2D canvas. Qt 4.2 introduced a completely new "graphics view" architecture centered on the `QGraphicsView`, `QGraphicsScene`, and `QGraphicsItem` classes. This architecture offers a high-level interface for doing item-based graphics, and supports standard user actions on items, including moving, selecting, and grouping. The items themselves are drawn using `QPainter` as usual and can be transformed individually. We cover this architecture later in the chapter.

An alternative to `QPainter` is to use OpenGL commands. OpenGL is a standard library for drawing 3D graphics. In Chapter 20, we will see how to use the *QtOpenGL* module, which makes it easy to integrate OpenGL code into Qt applications.

Painting with QPainter

To start painting to a paint device (typically a widget), we simply create a `QPainter` and pass a pointer to the device. For example:

```
void MyWidget::paintEvent(QPaintEvent *event)
{
    QPainter painter(this);
    ...
}
```

We can draw various shapes using `QPainter`'s `draw...()` functions. Figure 8.1 lists the most important ones. The way the drawing is performed is influenced by

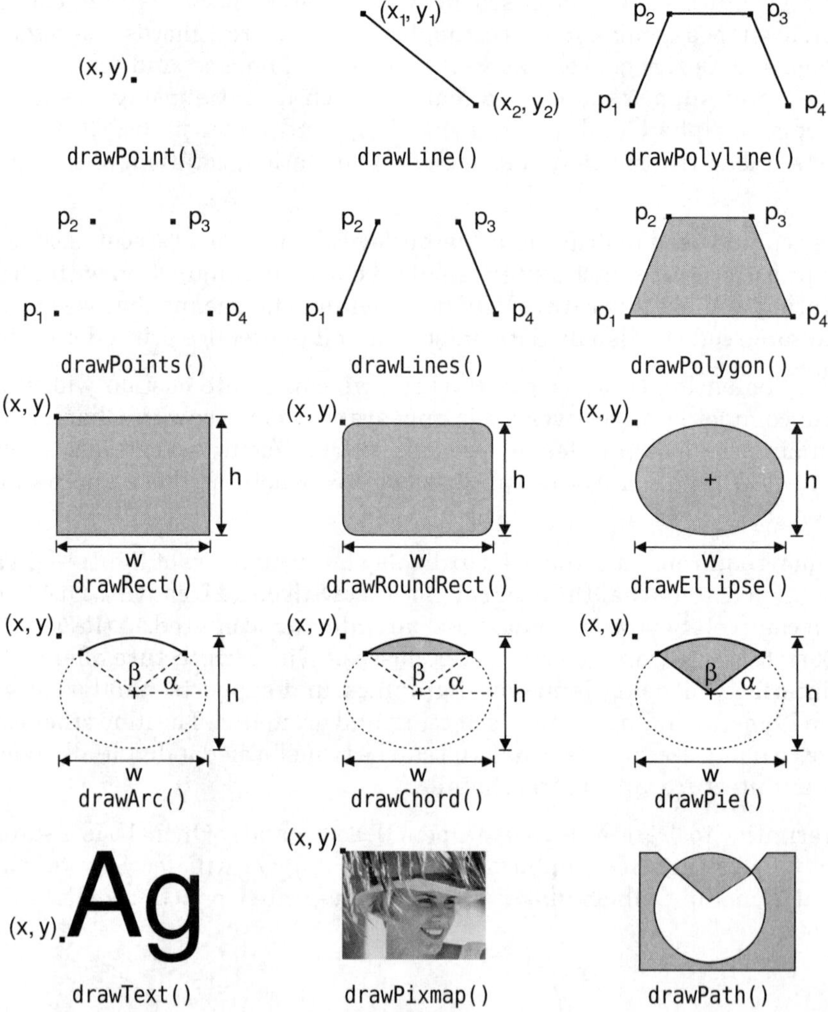

Figure 8.1. `QPainter`'s most frequently used `draw...()` functions

QPainter's settings. Some of these are adopted from the device, whereas others are initialized to default values. The three main painter settings are the pen, the brush, and the font:

- The *pen* is used for drawing lines and shape outlines. It consists of a color, a width, a line style, a cap style, and a join style. The pen styles are shown in Figures 8.2 and 8.3.
- The *brush* is the pattern used for filling geometric shapes. It normally consists of a color and a style, but it can also be a texture (a pixmap that is repeated infinitely) or a gradient. The brush styles are shown in Figure 8.4.
- The *font* is used for drawing text. A font has many attributes, including a family and a point size.

These settings can be modified at any time by calling setPen(), setBrush(), and setFont() with a QPen, QBrush, or QFont object.

Let's see a few examples in practice. Here's the code to draw the ellipse shown in Figure 8.5 (a):

```
QPainter painter(this);
painter.setRenderHint(QPainter::Antialiasing, true);
painter.setPen(QPen(Qt::black, 12, Qt::DashDotLine, Qt::RoundCap));
painter.setBrush(QBrush(Qt::green, Qt::SolidPattern));
painter.drawEllipse(80, 80, 400, 240);
```

The setRenderHint() call enables antialiasing, telling QPainter to use different color intensities on the edges to reduce the visual distortion that normally occurs when the edges of a shape are converted into pixels. The result is smoother edges on platforms and devices that support this feature.

Here's the code to draw the pie segment shown in Figure 8.5 (b):

```
QPainter painter(this);
painter.setRenderHint(QPainter::Antialiasing, true);
painter.setPen(QPen(Qt::black, 15, Qt::SolidLine, Qt::RoundCap,
                    Qt::MiterJoin));
painter.setBrush(QBrush(Qt::blue, Qt::DiagCrossPattern));
painter.drawPie(80, 80, 400, 240, 60 * 16, 270 * 16);
```

The last two arguments to drawPie() are expressed in sixteenths of a degree.

Here's the code to draw the cubic Bézier curve shown in Figure 8.5 (c):

```
QPainter painter(this);
painter.setRenderHint(QPainter::Antialiasing, true);

QPainterPath path;
path.moveTo(80, 320);
path.cubicTo(200, 80, 320, 80, 480, 320);

painter.setPen(QPen(Qt::black, 8));
painter.drawPath(path);
```

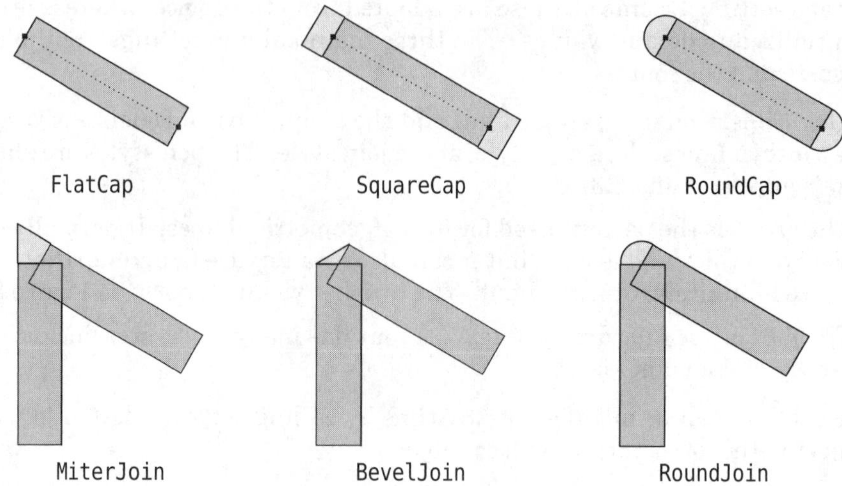

Figure 8.2. Cap and join styles

	Line width			
	1	2	3	4
SolidLine				
DashLine				
DotLine				
DashDotLine				
DashDotDotLine				
NoPen				

Figure 8.3. Line styles

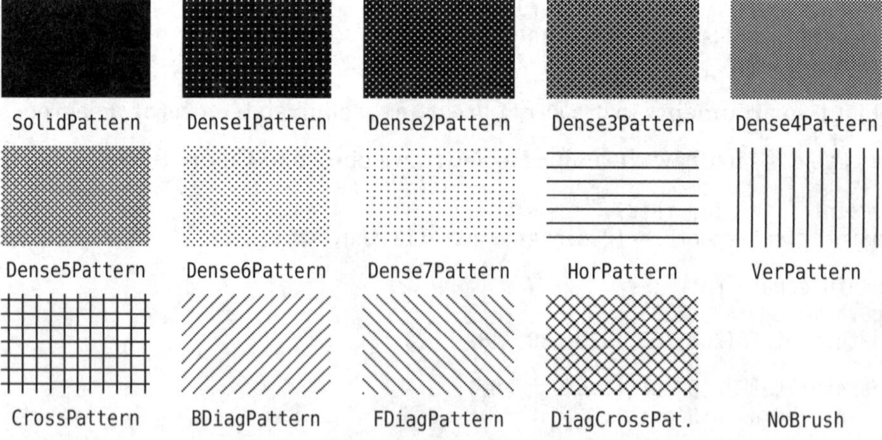

Figure 8.4. Predefined brush styles

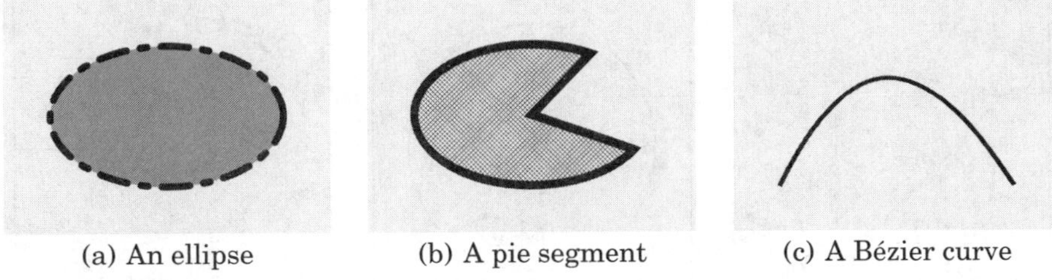

(a) An ellipse (b) A pie segment (c) A Bézier curve

Figure 8.5. Geometric shape examples

The `QPainterPath` class can specify arbitrary vector shapes by connecting basic graphical elements together: straight lines, ellipses, polygons, arcs, Bézier curves, and other painter paths. Painter paths are the ultimate drawing primitive in the sense that any shape or combination of shapes can be expressed as a painter path.

A path specifies an outline, and the area described by the outline can be filled using a brush. In the example in Figure 8.5 (c), we didn't set a brush, so only the outline is drawn.

These three examples use built-in brush patterns (`Qt::SolidPattern`, `Qt::DiagCrossPattern`, and `Qt::NoBrush`). In modern applications, gradient fills are a popular alternative to monochrome fill patterns. Gradients rely on color interpolation to obtain smooth transitions between two or more colors. They are frequently used to produce 3D effects; for example, the Plastique and Cleanlooks styles use gradients to render `QPushButton`s.

Qt supports three types of gradients: linear, conical, and radial. The Oven Timer example in the next section combines all three types of gradients in a single widget to make it look like the real thing.

- *Linear gradients* are defined by two control points and by a series of "color stops" on the line that connects these two points. For example, the linear gradient in Figure 8.6 is created using the following code:

  ```
  QLinearGradient gradient(50, 100, 300, 350);
  gradient.setColorAt(0.0, Qt::white);
  gradient.setColorAt(0.2, Qt::green);
  gradient.setColorAt(1.0, Qt::black);
  ```

  We specify three colors at three different positions between the two control points. Positions are specified as floating-point values between 0 and 1, where 0 corresponds to the first control point and 1 to the second control point. Colors between the specified stops are linearly interpolated.

- *Radial gradients* are defined by a center point (x_c, y_c), a radius r, and a focal point (x_f, y_f), in addition to the color stops. The center point and the radius specify a circle. The colors spread outward from the focal point, which can be the center point or any other point inside the circle.

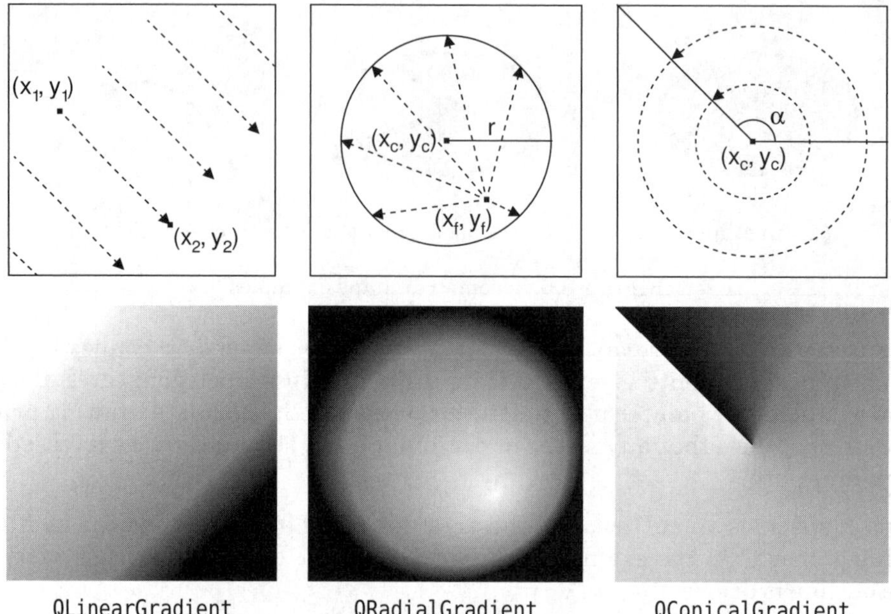

Figure 8.6. QPainter's gradient brushes

- *Conical gradients* are defined by a center point (x_c, y_c) and an angle α. The colors spread around the center point like the sweep of a watch's seconds hand.

So far, we have mentioned QPainter's pen, brush, and font settings. In addition to these, QPainter has other settings that influence the way shapes and text are drawn:

- The *background brush* is used to fill the background of geometric shapes (underneath the brush pattern), text, or bitmaps when the *background mode* is Qt::OpaqueMode (the default is Qt::TransparentMode).
- The *brush origin* is the starting point for brush patterns, normally the top-left corner of the widget.
- The *clip region* is the area of the device that can be painted. Painting outside the clip region has no effect.
- The *viewport*, *window*, and *world transform* determine how logical QPainter coordinates map to physical paint device coordinates. By default, these are set up so that the logical and physical coordinate systems coincide. We cover coordinate systems in the next section.
- The *composition mode* specifies how the newly drawn pixels should interact with the pixels already present on the paint device. The default is "source over", where drawn pixels are alpha-blended on top of existing pixels. This is supported only on certain devices and is covered later in this chapter.

At any time, we can save the current state of a painter on an internal stack by calling `save()` and restore it later on by calling `restore()`. This can be useful if we want to temporarily change some painter settings and then reset them to their previous values, as we will see in the next section.

Coordinate System Transformations

With `QPainter`'s default coordinate system, the point (0, 0) is located at the top-left corner of the paint device, *x*-coordinates increase rightward, and *y*-coordinates increase downward. Each pixel occupies an area of size 1×1 in the default coordinate system.

Conceptually, the center of a pixel lies on "half-pixel" coordinates. For example, the top-left pixel of a widget covers the area between points (0, 0) and (1, 1), and its center is located at (0.5, 0.5). If we tell `QPainter` to draw a pixel at, say, (100, 100), it will approximate the result by shifting the coordinate by +0.5 in both directions, resulting in the pixel centered at (100.5, 100.5) being drawn.

This distinction may seem rather academic at first, but it has important consequences in practice. First, the shifting by +0.5 occurs only if antialiasing is disabled (the default); if antialiasing is enabled and we try to draw a pixel at (100, 100) in black, `QPainter` will actually color the four pixels (99.5, 99.5), (99.5, 100.5), (100.5, 99.5), and (100.5, 100.5) light gray, to give the impression of a pixel lying exactly at the meeting point of the four pixels. If this effect is undesirable, we can avoid it by specifying half-pixel coordinates or by translating the `QPainter` by (+0.5, +0.5).

When drawing shapes such as lines, rectangles, and ellipses, similar rules apply. Figure 8.7 shows how the result of a `drawRect(2, 2, 6, 5)` call varies according to the pen's width, when antialiasing is off. In particular, it is important to notice that a 6×5 rectangle drawn with a pen width of 1 effectively covers an area of size 7×6. This is different from older toolkits, including earlier versions of Qt, but it is essential for making truly scalable, resolution-independent vector graphics possible. Figure 8.8 shows the result of `drawRect(2, 2, 6, 5)` when antialiasing is on, and Figure 8.9 shows what happens when we specify half-pixel coordinates.

Now that we understand the default coordinate system, we can take a closer look at how it can be changed using `QPainter`'s viewport, window, and world transform. (In this context, the term "window" does not refer to a window in the sense of a top-level widget, and the "viewport" has nothing to do with `QScrollArea`'s viewport.)

The viewport and the window are tightly bound. The viewport is an arbitrary rectangle specified in physical coordinates. The window specifies the same rectangle, but in logical coordinates. When we do the painting, we specify points in logical coordinates, and those coordinates are converted into physical coordinates in a linear algebraic manner, based on the current window–viewport settings.

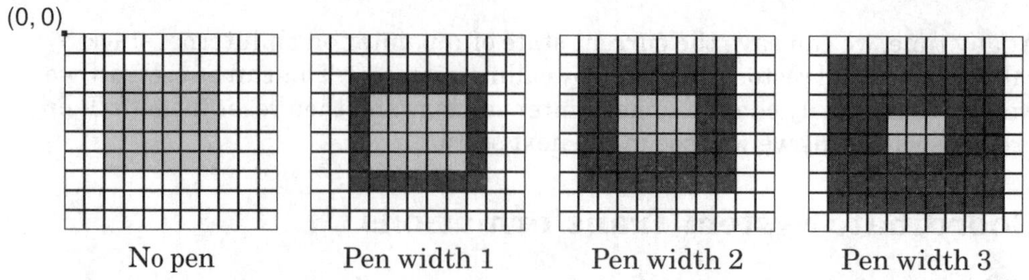

Figure 8.7. Result of `drawRect(2, 2, 6, 5)` with no antialiasing

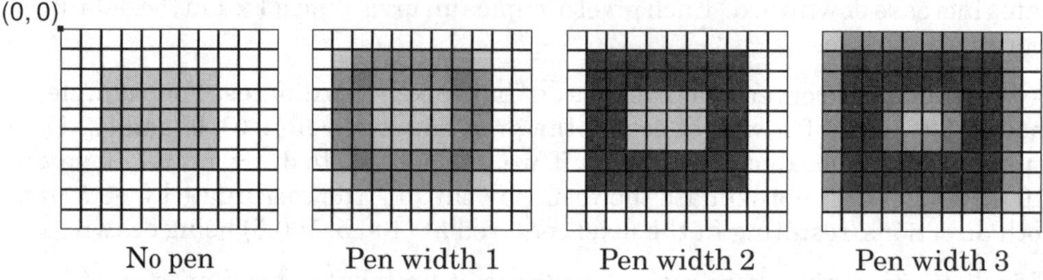

Figure 8.8. Result of `drawRect(2, 2, 6, 5)` with antialiasing

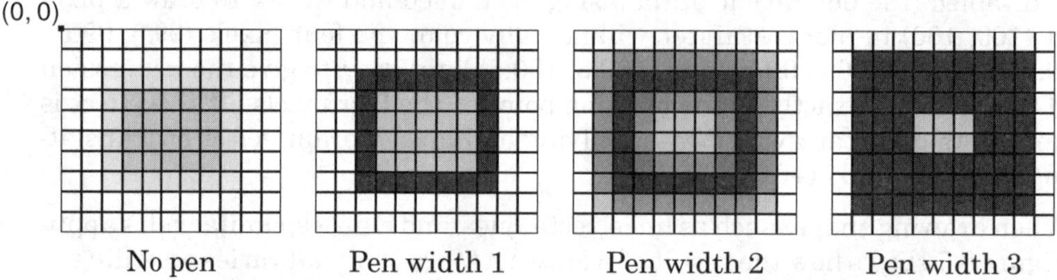

Figure 8.9. Result of `drawRect(2.5, 2.5, 6, 5)` with antialiasing

By default, the viewport and the window are set to the device's rectangle. For example, if the device is a 320 × 200 widget, both the viewport and the window are the same 320 × 200 rectangle with its top-left corner at position (0, 0). In this case, the logical and physical coordinate systems are the same.

The window–viewport mechanism is useful to make the drawing code independent of the size or resolution of the paint device. For example, if we want the logical coordinates to extend from (-50, -50) to (+50, +50), with (0, 0) in the middle, we can set the window as follows:

```
painter.setWindow(-50, -50, 100, 100);
```

The (-50, -50) pair specifies the origin, and the (100, 100) pair specifies the width and height. This means that the logical coordinates (-50, -50) now correspond to the physical coordinates (0, 0), and the logical coordinates (+50, +50) correspond to the physical coordinates (320, 200). This is illustrated in Figure 8.10. In this example, we didn't change the viewport.

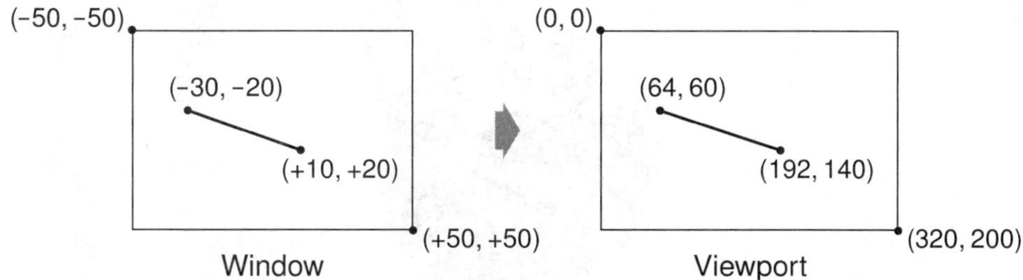

Figure 8.10. Converting logical coordinates into physical coordinates

Now comes the world transform. The world transform is a transformation matrix that is applied in addition to the window–viewport conversion. It allows us to translate, scale, rotate, or shear the items we are drawing. For example, if we wanted to draw text at a 45° angle, we would use this code:

```
QTransform transform;
transform.rotate(+45.0);
painter.setWorldTransform(transform);
painter.drawText(pos, tr("Sales"));
```

The logical coordinates we pass to `drawText()` are converted by the world transform, then mapped to physical coordinates using the window–viewport settings.

If we specify multiple transformations, they are applied in the order in which they are given. For example, if we want to use the point (50, 50) as the rotation's pivot point, we can do so by translating the window by (+50, +50), performing the rotation, and then translating the window back to its original position:

```
QTransform transform;
transform.translate(+50.0, +50.0);
transform.rotate(+45.0);
transform.translate(-50.0, -50.0);
painter.setWorldTransform(transform);
painter.drawText(pos, tr("Sales"));
```

A simpler way to specify transformations is to use `QPainter`'s `translate()`, `scale()`, `rotate()`, and `shear()` convenience functions:

```
painter.translate(-50.0, -50.0);
painter.rotate(+45.0);
painter.translate(+50.0, +50.0);
painter.drawText(pos, tr("Sales"));
```

If we want to use the same transformations repeatedly, it is more efficient to store them in a `QTransform` object and set the world transform on the painter whenever the transformations are needed.

To illustrate painter transformations, we will review the code of the `OvenTimer` widget shown in Figures 8.11 and 8.12. The `OvenTimer` widget is modeled after the kitchen timers that were used before it was common to have ovens with clocks built-in. The user can click a notch to set the duration. The wheel au-

Figure 8.11. The OvenTimer widget

tomatically turns counterclockwise until 0 is reached, at which point OvenTimer emits the timeout() signal.

```
class OvenTimer : public QWidget
{
    Q_OBJECT

public:
    OvenTimer(QWidget *parent = 0);

    void setDuration(int secs);
    int duration() const;
    void draw(QPainter *painter);

signals:
    void timeout();

protected:
    void paintEvent(QPaintEvent *event);
    void mousePressEvent(QMouseEvent *event);

private:
    QDateTime finishTime;
    QTimer *updateTimer;
    QTimer *finishTimer;
};
```

The OvenTimer class is derived from QWidget and reimplements two virtual functions: paintEvent() and mousePressEvent().

```
const double DegreesPerMinute = 7.0;
const double DegreesPerSecond = DegreesPerMinute / 60;
const int MaxMinutes = 45;
const int MaxSeconds = MaxMinutes * 60;
const int UpdateInterval = 5;
```

In oventimer.cpp, we start by defining a few constants that control the oven timer's look and feel.

```
OvenTimer::OvenTimer(QWidget *parent)
    : QWidget(parent)
{
    finishTime = QDateTime::currentDateTime();
```

```
        updateTimer = new QTimer(this);
        connect(updateTimer, SIGNAL(timeout()), this, SLOT(update()));

        finishTimer = new QTimer(this);
        finishTimer->setSingleShot(true);
        connect(finishTimer, SIGNAL(timeout()), this, SIGNAL(timeout()));
        connect(finishTimer, SIGNAL(timeout()), updateTimer, SLOT(stop()));

        QFont font;
        font.setPointSize(8);
        setFont(font);
    }
```

In the constructor, we create two `QTimer` objects: `updateTimer` is used to refresh the appearance of the widget every five seconds, and `finishTimer` emits the widget's `timeout()` signal when the oven timer reaches 0. The `finishTimer` needs to time out only once, so we call `setSingleShot(true)`; by default, timers fire repeatedly until they are stopped or destroyed. The last `connect()` call is an optimization to stop updating the widget when the timer is inactive.

At the end of the constructor, we set the point size of the font used for drawing the widget to 9 points. This is done to ensure that the numbers displayed on the timers have approximately the same size everywhere.

```
    void OvenTimer::setDuration(int secs)
    {
        secs = qBound(0, secs, MaxSeconds);

        finishTime = QDateTime::currentDateTime().addSecs(secs);

        if (secs > 0) {
            updateTimer->start(UpdateInterval * 1000);
            finishTimer->start(secs * 1000);
        } else {
            updateTimer->stop();
            finishTimer->stop();
        }
        update();
    }
```

The `setDuration()` function sets the duration of the oven timer to the given number of seconds. Using Qt's global `qBound()` function means that we can avoid writing code such as this:

```
    if (secs < 0) {
        secs = 0;
    } else if (secs > MaxSeconds) {
        secs = MaxSeconds;
    }
```

We compute the finish time by adding the duration to the current time (obtained from `QDateTime::currentDateTime()`) and store it in the `finishTime` private variable. At the end, we call `update()` to redraw the widget with the new duration.

The finishTime variable is of type QDateTime. Since the variable holds both a date and a time, we avoid a wrap-around bug when the current time is before midnight and the finish time is after midnight.

```
int OvenTimer::duration() const
{
    int secs = QDateTime::currentDateTime().secsTo(finishTime);
    if (secs < 0)
        secs = 0;
    return secs;
}
```

The duration() function returns the number of seconds left before the timer is due to finish. If the timer is inactive, we return 0.

```
void OvenTimer::mousePressEvent(QMouseEvent *event)
{
    QPointF point = event->pos() - rect().center();
    double theta = std::atan2(-point.x(), -point.y()) * 180.0 / M_PI;
    setDuration(duration() + int(theta / DegreesPerSecond));
    update();
}
```

If the user clicks the widget, we find the closest notch using a subtle but effective mathematical formula, and we use the result to set the new duration. Then we schedule a repaint. The notch that the user clicked will now be at the top and will move counterclockwise as time passes until 0 is reached.

```
void OvenTimer::paintEvent(QPaintEvent * /* event */)
{
    QPainter painter(this);
    painter.setRenderHint(QPainter::Antialiasing, true);

    int side = qMin(width(), height());

    painter.setViewport((width() - side) / 2, (height() - side) / 2,
                        side, side);
    painter.setWindow(-50, -50, 100, 100);

    draw(&painter);
}
```

In paintEvent(), we set the viewport to be the largest square area that fits inside the widget, and we set the window to be the rectangle (-50, -50, 100, 100), that is, the 100×100 rectangle extending from (-50, -50) to (+50, +50). The qMin() template function returns the lowest of its two arguments. Then we call the draw() function to actually perform the drawing.

If we had not set the viewport to be a square, the oven timer would be an ellipse when the widget is resized to a non-square rectangle. To avoid such deformations, we must set the viewport and the window to rectangles with the same aspect ratio.

Now let's look at the drawing code:

Figure 8.12. The `OvenTimer` widget at three different sizes

```
void OvenTimer::draw(QPainter *painter)
{
    static const int triangle[3][2] = {
        { -2, -49 }, { +2, -49 }, { 0, -47 }
    };
    QPen thickPen(palette().foreground(), 1.5);
    QPen thinPen(palette().foreground(), 0.5);
    QColor niceBlue(150, 150, 200);

    painter->setPen(thinPen);
    painter->setBrush(palette().foreground());
    painter->drawPolygon(QPolygon(3, &triangle[0][0]));
```

We start by drawing the tiny triangle that marks the 0 position at the top of the widget. The triangle is specified by three hard-coded coordinates, and we use `drawPolygon()` to render it.

What is so convenient about the window–viewport mechanism is that we can hard-code the coordinates we use in the draw commands and still get good resizing behavior.

```
    QConicalGradient coneGradient(0, 0, -90.0);
    coneGradient.setColorAt(0.0, Qt::darkGray);
    coneGradient.setColorAt(0.2, niceBlue);
    coneGradient.setColorAt(0.5, Qt::white);
    coneGradient.setColorAt(1.0, Qt::darkGray);

    painter->setBrush(coneGradient);
    painter->drawEllipse(-46, -46, 92, 92);
```

We draw the outer circle and fill it using a conical gradient. The gradient's center point is located at (0, 0), and the angle is –90°.

```
    QRadialGradient haloGradient(0, 0, 20, 0, 0);
    haloGradient.setColorAt(0.0, Qt::lightGray);
    haloGradient.setColorAt(0.8, Qt::darkGray);
    haloGradient.setColorAt(0.9, Qt::white);
```

```
    haloGradient.setColorAt(1.0, Qt::black);

    painter->setPen(Qt::NoPen);
    painter->setBrush(haloGradient);
    painter->drawEllipse(-20, -20, 40, 40);
```

We fill the inner circle using a radial gradient. The center point and the focal point of the gradient are located at (0, 0). The radius of the gradient is 20.

```
    QLinearGradient knobGradient(-7, -25, 7, -25);
    knobGradient.setColorAt(0.0, Qt::black);
    knobGradient.setColorAt(0.2, niceBlue);
    knobGradient.setColorAt(0.3, Qt::lightGray);
    knobGradient.setColorAt(0.8, Qt::white);
    knobGradient.setColorAt(1.0, Qt::black);

    painter->rotate(duration() * DegreesPerSecond);
    painter->setBrush(knobGradient);
    painter->setPen(thinPen);
    painter->drawRoundRect(-7, -25, 14, 50, 99, 49);

    for (int i = 0; i <= MaxMinutes; ++i) {
        if (i % 5 == 0) {
            painter->setPen(thickPen);
            painter->drawLine(0, -41, 0, -44);
            painter->drawText(-15, -41, 30, 30,
                              Qt::AlignHCenter | Qt::AlignTop,
                              QString::number(i));
        } else {
            painter->setPen(thinPen);
            painter->drawLine(0, -42, 0, -44);
        }
        painter->rotate(-DegreesPerMinute);
    }
}
```

We call `rotate()` to rotate the painter's coordinate system. In the old coordinate system, the 0-minute mark was on top; now, the 0-minute mark is moved to the place that is appropriate for the time left. We draw the rectangular knob handle after the rotation, since its orientation depends on the rotation angle.

In the `for` loop, we draw the tick marks along the outer circle's edge and the numbers for each multiple of five minutes. The text is drawn in an invisible rectangle underneath the tick mark. At the end of each iteration, we rotate the painter clockwise by 7°, which corresponds to one minute. The next time we draw a tick mark, it will be at a different position around the circle, even though the coordinates we pass to the `drawLine()` and `drawText()` calls are always the same.

The code in the `for` loop suffers from a minor flaw, which would quickly become apparent if we performed more iterations. Each time we call `rotate()`, we effectively multiply the current world transform with a rotation transform, producing a new world transform. The rounding errors associated with floating-point arithmetic gradually accumulate, resulting in an increasingly inaccurate world transform. Here's one way to rewrite the code to avoid this issue, using `save()` and `restore()` to save and reload the original transform for each iteration:

```
for (int i = 0; i <= MaxMinutes; ++i) {
    painter->save();
    painter->rotate(-i * DegreesPerMinute);

    if (i % 5 == 0) {
        painter->setPen(thickPen);
        painter->drawLine(0, -41, 0, -44);
        painter->drawText(-15, -41, 30, 30,
                          Qt::AlignHCenter | Qt::AlignTop,
                          QString::number(i));
    } else {
        painter->setPen(thinPen);
        painter->drawLine(0, -42, 0, -44);
    }
    painter->restore();
}
```

Another way of implementing an oven timer would have been to compute the (x, y) positions ourselves, using `sin()` and `cos()` to find the positions along the circle. But then we would still need to use a translation and a rotation to draw the text at an angle.

High-Quality Rendering with QImage

When drawing, we may be faced with a trade-off between speed and accuracy. For example, on X11 and Mac OS X, drawing on a `QWidget` or `QPixmap` relies on the platform's native paint engine. On X11, this ensures that communication with the X server is kept to a minimum; only paint commands are sent rather than actual image data. The main drawback of this approach is that Qt is limited by the platform's native support:

- On X11, features such as antialiasing and support for fractional coordinates are available only if the X Render extension is present on the X server.
- On Mac OS X, the native aliased graphics engine uses different algorithms for drawing polygons than X11 and Windows, with slightly different results.

When accuracy is more important than efficiency, we can draw to a `QImage` and copy the result onto the screen. This always uses Qt's own internal paint engine, giving identical results on all platforms. The only restriction is that the `QImage` on which we paint must be created with an argument of either `QImage::Format_RGB32` or `QImage::Format_ARGB32_Premultiplied`.

The premultiplied ARGB32 format is almost identical to the conventional ARGB32 format (`0x`*`AARRGGBB`*), the difference being that the red, green, and blue channels are "premultiplied" with the alpha channel. This means that the RGB values, which normally range from `0x00` to `0xFF`, are scaled from `0x00` to the alpha value. For example, a 50%-transparent blue color is represented as 0x7F0000FF in ARGB32 format, but 0x7F00007F in premultiplied ARGB32 format, and similarly a 75%-transparent dark green of 0x3F008000 in ARGB32 format would be 0x3F002000 in premultiplied ARGB32 format.

Let's suppose we want to use antialiasing for drawing a widget, and we want to obtain good results even on X11 systems with no X Render extension. The original paintEvent() handler, which relies on X Render for the antialiasing, might look like this:

```
void MyWidget::paintEvent(QPaintEvent *event)
{
    QPainter painter(this);
    painter.setRenderHint(QPainter::Antialiasing, true);
    draw(&painter);
}
```

Here's how to rewrite the widget's paintEvent() function to use Qt's platform-independent graphics engine:

```
void MyWidget::paintEvent(QPaintEvent *event)
{
    QImage image(size(), QImage::Format_ARGB32_Premultiplied);
    QPainter imagePainter(&image);
    imagePainter.initFrom(this);
    imagePainter.setRenderHint(QPainter::Antialiasing, true);
    imagePainter.eraseRect(rect());
    draw(&imagePainter);
    imagePainter.end();

    QPainter widgetPainter(this);
    widgetPainter.drawImage(0, 0, image);
}
```

We create a QImage of the same size as the widget in premultiplied ARGB32 format, and a QPainter to draw on the image. The initFrom() call initializes the painter's pen, background, and font based on the widget. We perform the drawing using the QPainter as usual, and at the end we reuse the QPainter object to copy the image onto the widget. This approach produces identical high-quality results on all platforms, with the exception of font rendering, which depends on the installed fonts.

One particularly powerful feature of Qt's graphics engine is its support for composition modes. These specify how a source and a destination pixel are merged together when drawing. This applies to all painting operations, including pen, brush, gradient, and image drawing.

The default composition mode is QImage::CompositionMode_SourceOver, meaning that the source pixel (the pixel we are drawing) is blended on top of the destination pixel (the existing pixel) in such a way that the alpha component of the source defines its translucency. Figure 8.13 shows the result of drawing a semi-transparent butterfly (the "source" image) on top of a checker pattern (the "destination" image) with the different modes.

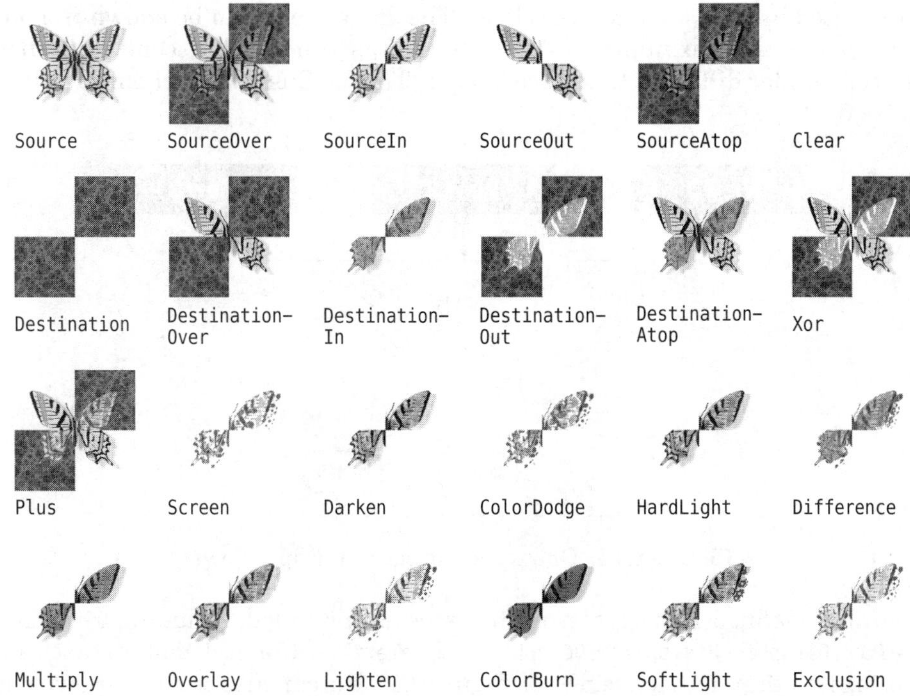

Figure 8.13. QPainter's composition modes

Composition modes are set using QPainter::setCompositionMode(). For example, here's how to create a QImage containing the XOR of the butterfly and the checker pattern:

```
QImage resultImage = checkerPatternImage;
QPainter painter(&resultImage);
painter.setCompositionMode(QPainter::CompositionMode_Xor);
painter.drawImage(0, 0, butterflyImage);
```

One issue to be aware of is that the QImage::CompositionMode_Xor operation also applies to the alpha channel. This means that if we XOR the color white (0xFFFFFFFF) with itself, we obtain a transparent color (0x00000000), not black (0xFF000000).

Item-Based Rendering with Graphics View

Drawing using QPainter is ideal for custom widgets and for drawing one or just a few items. For graphics in which we need to handle anything from a handful up to tens of thousands of items, and we want the user to be able to click, drag, and select items, Qt's graphics view classes provide the solution we need.

The graphics view architecture consists of a scene, represented by the QGraphicsScene class, and items in the scene, represented by QGraphicsItem subclasses. The scene (along with its item) is made visible to users by showing them in a view, represented by the QGraphicsView class. The same scene can be shown in more than one view—for example, to show different parts of a large scene, or to show the scene under different transformations. This is illustrated schematically in Figure 8.14.

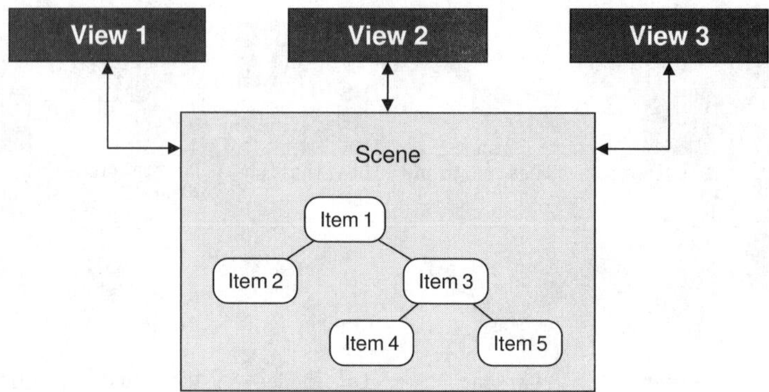

Figure 8.14. One scene can serve multiple views

Several predefined QGraphicsItem subclasses are provided, including QGraphics-LineItem, QGraphicsPixmapItem, QGraphicsSimpleTextItem (for styled plain text), and QGraphicsTextItem (for rich text); see Figure 8.15. We can also create our own custom QGraphicsItem subclasses, as we will see later in this section.*

A QGraphicsScene holds a collection of graphics items. A scene has three layers: a background layer, an item layer, and a foreground layer. The background and foreground are normally specified by QBrushes, but it is possible to reimplement drawBackground() or drawForeground() for complete control. If we want to use a pixmap as a background, we could simply create a texture QBrush based on that pixmap. The foreground brush could be set to a semi-transparent white to give a faded effect, or to be a cross pattern to provide a grid overlay.

The scene can tell us which items have collided, which are selected, and which are at a particular point or in a particular region. A scene's graphics items are either top-level (the scene is their parent) or children (their parent is another item). Any transformations applied to an item are automatically applied to its children.

The graphics view architecture provides two ways of grouping items. One is to simply make an item a child of another item. Another way is to use a QGraphics-ItemGroup. Adding an item to a group does not cause it to be transformed in any way; these groups are convenient for handling multiple items as though they were a single item.

A QGraphicsView is a widget that presents a scene, providing scroll bars if necessary and capable of applying transformations that affect how the scene

*Qt 4.4 is expected to support adding widgets to graphics scenes as though they were graphics items, including the ability to apply transformations to them.

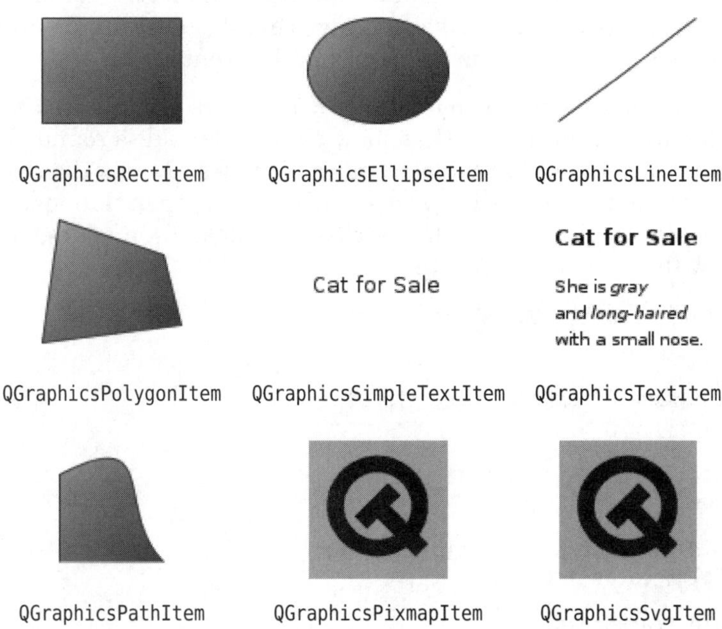

Figure 8.15. Graphics view items available in Qt 4.3

is rendered. This is useful to support zooming and rotating as aids for viewing the scene.

By default, `QGraphicsView` renders using Qt's built-in 2D paint engine, but it can be changed to use an OpenGL widget with a single `setViewport()` call after it has been constructed. It is also easy to print a scene, or parts of a scene, as we will discuss in the next section where we see several techniques for printing using Qt.

The architecture uses three different coordinate systems—viewport coordinates, scene coordinates, and item coordinates—with functions for mapping from one coordinate system to another. Viewport coordinates are coordinates inside the `QGraphicsView`'s viewport. Scene coordinates are logical coordinates that are used for positioning top-level items on the scene. Item coordinates are specific to each item and are centered about an item-local (0, 0) point; these remain unchanged when we move the item on the scene. In practice, we usually only care about the scene coordinates (for positioning top-level items) and item coordinates (for positioning child items and for drawing items). Drawing each item in terms of its own local coordinate system means that we do not have to worry about where an item is in the scene or what transformations have been applied to it.

The graphics view classes are straightforward to use and offer a great deal of functionality. To introduce some of what can be done with them, we will review two examples. The first example is a simple diagram editor, which will show

how to create items and how to handle user interaction. The second example is an annotated map program that shows how to handle large numbers of graphics objects and how to render them efficiently at different zoom levels.

The Diagram application shown in Figure 8.16 allows users to create nodes and links. Nodes are graphics items that show plain text inside a rounded rectangle, whereas links are lines that connect pairs of nodes. Nodes that are selected are shown with a dashed outline drawn with a thicker pen than usual. We will begin by looking at links, since they are the simplest, then nodes, and then we will see how they are used in context.

```
class Link : public QGraphicsLineItem
{
public:
    Link(Node *fromNode, Node *toNode);
    ~Link();

    Node *fromNode() const;
    Node *toNode() const;

    void setColor(const QColor &color);
    QColor color() const;

    void trackNodes();

private:
    Node *myFromNode;
    Node *myToNode;
};
```

The `Link` class is derived from `QGraphicsLineItem`, which represents a line in a `QGraphicsScene`. A link has three main attributes: the two nodes it connects and the color used to draw its line. We don't need a `QColor` member variable to store the color, for reasons that will become apparent shortly. `QGraphicsItem` is not

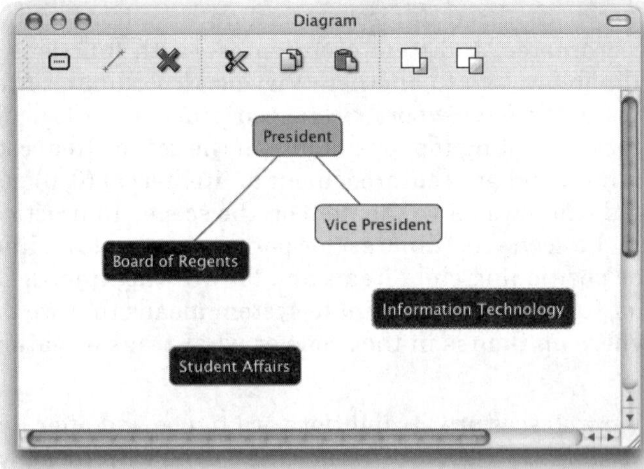

Figure 8.16. The Diagram application

a `QObject` subclass, but if we wanted to add signals and slots to `Link`, there is nothing to stop us from using multiple inheritance with `QObject`.

The `trackNodes()` function is used to update the line's endpoints, when the user drags a connected node into a different position.

```
Link::Link(Node *fromNode, Node *toNode)
{
    myFromNode = fromNode;
    myToNode = toNode;

    myFromNode->addLink(this);
    myToNode->addLink(this);

    setFlags(QGraphicsItem::ItemIsSelectable);
    setZValue(-1);

    setColor(Qt::darkRed);
    trackNodes();
}
```

When a link is constructed, it adds itself to the nodes it connects. Each node holds a set of links, and can have any number of connecting links. Graphics items have several flags, but in this case we only want links to be selectable so that the user can select and then delete them.

Every graphics item has an (x, y) position, and a z value that specifies how far forward or back it is in the scene. Since we are going to draw our lines from the center of one node to the center of another node, we give the line a negative z value so that it will always be drawn underneath the nodes it connects. As a result, links will appear as lines between the nearest edges of the nodes they connect.

At the end of the constructor, we set an initial line color and then set the line's endpoints by calling `trackNodes()`.

```
Link::~Link()
{
    myFromNode->removeLink(this);
    myToNode->removeLink(this);
}
```

When a link is destroyed, it removes itself from the nodes it is connecting.

```
void Link::setColor(const QColor &color)
{
    setPen(QPen(color, 1.0));
}
```

When the link's color is set, we simply change its pen, using the given color and a line width of 1. The `setPen()` function is inherited from `QGraphicsLineItem`. The `color()` getter simply returns the pen's color.

```
void Link::trackNodes()
{
```

```
    setLine(QLineF(myFromNode->pos(), myToNode->pos()));
}
```

The `QGraphicsItem::pos()` function returns the position of its graphics item relative to the scene (for top-level items) or to the parent item (for child items).

For the `Link` class, we can rely on its base class to handle the painting: `QGraphicsLineItem` draws a line (using `pen()`) between two points in the scene.

For the `Node` class, we will handle all the graphics ourselves. Another difference between nodes and links is that nodes are more interactive. We will begin by reviewing the `Node` declaration, breaking it into a few pieces since it is quite long.

```
class Node : public QGraphicsItem
{
    Q_DECLARE_TR_FUNCTIONS(Node)

public:
    Node();
```

For the `Node` class, we use `QGraphicsItem` as the base class. The `Q_DECLARE_TR_FUNCTIONS()` macro is used to add a `tr()` function to this class, even though it is not a `QObject` subclass. This is simply a convenience that allows us to use `tr()` rather than the static `QObject::tr()` or `QCoreApplication::translate()`.

```
    void setText(const QString &text);
    QString text() const;
    void setTextColor(const QColor &color);
    QColor textColor() const;
    void setOutlineColor(const QColor &color);
    QColor outlineColor() const;
    void setBackgroundColor(const QColor &color);
    QColor backgroundColor() const;
```

These functions are simply getters and setters for the private members. We provide control of the color of the text, the node's outline, and the node's background.

```
    void addLink(Link *link);
    void removeLink(Link *link);
```

As we saw earlier, these functions are called by the `Link` class to add or remove themselves from a node.

```
    QRectF boundingRect() const;
    QPainterPath shape() const;
    void paint(QPainter *painter,
               const QStyleOptionGraphicsItem *option, QWidget *widget);
```

When we create `QGraphicsItem` subclasses that we want to draw manually, we normally reimplement `boundingRect()` and `paint()`. If we don't reimplement `shape()`, the base class implementation will fall back on the `boundingRect()`. In this case, we have reimplemented `shape()` to return a more accurate shape that takes into account the node's rounded corners.

The graphics view architecture uses the bounding rectangle to determine whether an item needs to be drawn. This enables QGraphicsView to display arbitrarily large scenes very quickly, when only a fraction of the items are visible at any given time. The shape is used for determining whether a point is inside an item, or whether two items collide.

```
protected:
    void mouseDoubleClickEvent(QGraphicsSceneMouseEvent *event);
    QVariant itemChange(GraphicsItemChange change,
                        const QVariant &value);
```

In the Diagram application, we will provide a Properties dialog for editing a node's position, colors, and text. As an added convenience, we will let the user change the text by double-clicking the node.

If a node is moved, we must make sure that any associated links are updated accordingly. We reimplement the itemChange() handler to take care of this; it is called whenever the item's properties (including its position) change. The reason we don't use mouseMoveEvent() for this purpose is because it is not called when the node is moved programmatically.

```
private:
    QRectF outlineRect() const;
    int roundness(double size) const;

    QSet<Link *> myLinks;
    QString myText;
    QColor myTextColor;
    QColor myBackgroundColor;
    QColor myOutlineColor;
};
```

The outlineRect() private function returns the rectangle drawn by the Node, whereas roundness() returns an appropriate roundness coefficient based on the width or height of the rectangle.

Just as a Link keeps track of the nodes it connects, a Node keeps track of its links. When a node is deleted, all the links associated with the node are deleted as well.

We are now ready to look at Node's implementation, starting as usual with the constructor.

```
Node::Node()
{
    myTextColor = Qt::darkGreen;
    myOutlineColor = Qt::darkBlue;
    myBackgroundColor = Qt::white;

    setFlags(ItemIsMovable | ItemIsSelectable);
}
```

We initialize the colors, and make node items both movable and selectable. The z value will default to 0, and we leave the node's position in the scene to be set by the caller.

```
Node::~Node()
{
    foreach (Link *link, myLinks)
        delete link;
}
```

The destructor deletes all the node's links. Whenever a link is destroyed, it removes itself from the nodes it is connected to. We iterate over (a copy of) the set of links rather than use `qDeleteAll()` to avoid side effects, since the set of links is indirectly accessed by the `Link` destructor.

```
void Node::setText(const QString &text)
{
    prepareGeometryChange();
    myText = text;
    update();
}
```

Whenever we change a graphics item in a way that affects its appearance, we must call `update()` to schedule a repaint. And in cases such as this where the item's bounding rectangle might change (because the new text might be shorter or longer than the current text), we must call `prepareGeometryChange()` immediately before doing anything that will affect the item's bounding rectangle.

We will skip the `text()`, `textColor()`, `outlineColor()`, and `backgroundColor()` getters since they simply return their corresponding private member.

```
void Node::setTextColor(const QColor &color)
{
    myTextColor = color;
    update();
}
```

When we set the text's color, we must call `update()` to schedule a repaint so that the item is painted using the new color. We don't need to call `prepareGeometryChange()`, because the size of the item is not affected by a color change. We will omit the setters for the outline and background colors since they are structurally the same as this setter.

```
void Node::addLink(Link *link)
{
    myLinks.insert(link);
}

void Node::removeLink(Link *link)
{
    myLinks.remove(link);
}
```

Here we simply add or remove the given link to the node's set of links.

```
QRectF Node::outlineRect() const
{
    const int Padding = 8;
    QFontMetricsF metrics = qApp->font();
    QRectF rect = metrics.boundingRect(myText);
    rect.adjust(-Padding, -Padding, +Padding, +Padding);
    rect.translate(-rect.center());
    return rect;
}
```

We use this private function to calculate a rectangle that encompasses the node's text with an 8-pixel margin. The bounding rectangle returned by the font metrics function always has (0, 0) as its top-left corner. Since we want the text centered on the item's center point, we translate the rectangle so that its center is at (0, 0).

Although we think and calculate in terms of pixels, the unit is in a sense notional. The scene (or the parent item) may be scaled, rotated, sheared, or simply affected by antialiasing, so the actual number of pixels that appears on the screen may be different.

```
QRectF Node::boundingRect() const
{
    const int Margin = 1;
    return outlineRect().adjusted(-Margin, -Margin, +Margin, +Margin);
}
```

The `boundingRect()` function is called by `QGraphicsView` to determine whether the item needs to be drawn. We use the outline rectangle, but with a bit of additional margin, since the rectangle we return from this function must allow for at least half the width of the pen if an outline is going to be drawn.

```
QPainterPath Node::shape() const
{
    QRectF rect = outlineRect();

    QPainterPath path;
    path.addRoundRect(rect, roundness(rect.width()),
                      roundness(rect.height()));
    return path;
}
```

The `shape()` function is called by `QGraphicsView` for fine-grained collision detection. Often, we can omit it and leave the item to calculate the shape itself based on the bounding rectangle. Here we reimplement it to return a `QPainterPath` that represents a rounded rectangle. As a consequence, clicking the corner areas that fall outside the rounded rectangle but inside the bounding rectangle *won't* select the item.

When we create a rounded rectangle, we can pass optional arguments to specify the roundedness of the corners. We calculate suitable values using the `roundness()` private function.

```
void Node::paint(QPainter *painter,
                 const QStyleOptionGraphicsItem *option,
                 QWidget * /* widget */)
{
    QPen pen(myOutlineColor);
    if (option->state & QStyle::State_Selected) {
        pen.setStyle(Qt::DotLine);
        pen.setWidth(2);
    }
    painter->setPen(pen);
    painter->setBrush(myBackgroundColor);

    QRectF rect = outlineRect();
    painter->drawRoundRect(rect, roundness(rect.width()),
                           roundness(rect.height()));

    painter->setPen(myTextColor);
    painter->drawText(rect, Qt::AlignCenter, myText);
}
```

The `paint()` function is where we draw the item. If the item is selected, we change the pen's style to be a dotted line and make it thicker; otherwise, the default of a solid 1-pixel line is used. We also set the brush to use the background color.

Then we draw a rounded rectangle the same size as the outline rectangle, but using the rounding factors returned by the `roundness()` private function. Finally, we draw the text centered within the outline rectangle on top of the rounded rectangle.

The `option` parameter of type `QStyleOptionGraphicsItem` is an unusual class for Qt because it provides several public member variables. These include the current layout direction, font metrics, palette, rectangle, state (selected, "has focus", and many others), the transformation matrix, and the level of detail. Here we have checked the `state` member to see whether the node is selected.

```
QVariant Node::itemChange(GraphicsItemChange change,
                          const QVariant &value)
{
    if (change == ItemPositionHasChanged) {
        foreach (Link *link, myLinks)
            link->trackNodes();
    }
    return QGraphicsItem::itemChange(change, value);
}
```

Whenever the user drags a node, the `itemChange()` handler is called with `ItemPositionHasChanged` as the first argument. To ensure that the link lines are positioned correctly, we iterate over the node's set of links and tell each one to update its line's endpoints. At the end, we call the base class implementation to ensure that it also gets notified.

```
void Node::mouseDoubleClickEvent(QGraphicsSceneMouseEvent *event)
{
```

```
    QString text = QInputDialog::getText(event->widget(),
                            tr("Edit Text"), tr("Enter new text:"),
                            QLineEdit::Normal, myText);
    if (!text.isEmpty())
        setText(text);
}
```

If the user double-clicks the node, we pop up a dialog that shows the current text and allows them to change it. If the user clicks Cancel, an empty string is returned; therefore, we apply the change only if the string is non-empty. We will see how other node properties (such as the node's colors) can be changed shortly.

```
int Node::roundness(double size) const
{
    const int Diameter = 12;
    return 100 * Diameter / int(size);
}
```

The `roundness()` function returns appropriate rounding factors to ensure that the node's corners are quarter-circles with diameter 12. The rounding factors must be in the range 0 (square) to 99 (fully rounded).

We have now seen the implementation of two custom graphics item classes. Now it is time to see how they are actually used. The Diagram application is a standard main window application with menus and a toolbar. We won't look at all the details of the implementation, but instead concentrate on those relevant to the graphics view architecture. We will begin by looking at an extract from the `QMainWindow` subclass's definition.

```
class DiagramWindow : public QMainWindow
{
    Q_OBJECT

public:
    DiagramWindow();

private slots:
    void addNode();
    void addLink();
    void del();
    void cut();
    void copy();
    void paste();
    void bringToFront();
    void sendToBack();
    void properties();
    void updateActions();

private:
    typedef QPair<Node *, Node *> NodePair;

    void createActions();
    void createMenus();
    void createToolBars();
```

```
    void setZValue(int z);
    void setupNode(Node *node);
    Node *selectedNode() const;
    Link *selectedLink() const;
    NodePair selectedNodePair() const;

    QMenu *fileMenu;
    QMenu *editMenu;
    QToolBar *editToolBar;
    QAction *exitAction;
    ...
    QAction *propertiesAction;

    QGraphicsScene *scene;
    QGraphicsView *view;

    int minZ;
    int maxZ;
    int seqNumber;
};
```

The purpose of most of the private slots should be clear from their names. The `properties()` slot is used to pop up the Properties dialog if a node is selected, or a `QColorDialog` if a link is selected. The `updateActions()` slot is used to enable or disable actions depending on what items are selected.

```
DiagramWindow::DiagramWindow()
{
    scene = new QGraphicsScene(0, 0, 600, 500);

    view = new QGraphicsView;
    view->setScene(scene);
    view->setDragMode(QGraphicsView::RubberBandDrag);
    view->setRenderHints(QPainter::Antialiasing
                         | QPainter::TextAntialiasing);
    view->setContextMenuPolicy(Qt::ActionsContextMenu);
    setCentralWidget(view);

    minZ = 0;
    maxZ = 0;
    seqNumber = 0;

    createActions();
    createMenus();
    createToolBars();

    connect(scene, SIGNAL(selectionChanged()),
            this, SLOT(updateActions()));

    setWindowTitle(tr("Diagram"));
    updateActions();
}
```

We begin by creating a graphics scene, with an origin of (0, 0), a width of 600, and a height of 500. Then we create a graphics view to visualize the scene. In the next example, instead of using `QGraphicsView` directly, we will subclass it to customize its behavior.

Selectable items can be selected by clicking them. To select more than one item at a time, the user can click the items while pressing Ctrl. Setting the drag mode to `QGraphicsView::RubberBandDrag` means that the user can also select items by dragging a rubber band over them.

The `minZ` and `maxZ` numbers are used by the `sendToBack()` and `bringToFront()` functions. The sequence number is used to give a unique initial text to each node the user adds.

The signal–slot connection ensures that whenever the scene's selection changes, we enable or disable the application's actions so that only actions that make sense are available. We call `updateActions()` to set the actions' initial enabled states.

```
void DiagramWindow::addNode()
{
    Node *node = new Node;
    node->setText(tr("Node %1").arg(seqNumber + 1));
    setupNode(node);
}
```

When the user adds a new node, we create a new instance of the `Node` class, give it a default text, and then pass the node to `setupNode()` to position and select it. We use a separate function to finish adding a node because we will need this functionality again when implementing `paste()`.

```
void DiagramWindow::setupNode(Node *node)
{
    node->setPos(QPoint(80 + (100 * (seqNumber % 5)),
                        80 + (50 * ((seqNumber / 5) % 7))));
    scene->addItem(node);
    ++seqNumber;

    scene->clearSelection();
    node->setSelected(true);
    bringToFront();
}
```

This function positions a newly added or pasted node in the scene. The use of the sequence number ensures that new nodes are added in different positions rather than on top of each other. We clear the current selection and select just the newly added node. The `bringToFront()` call ensures that the new node is farther forward than any other node.

```
void DiagramWindow::bringToFront()
{
    ++maxZ;
    setZValue(maxZ);
}
```

```
void DiagramWindow::sendToBack()
{
    --minZ;
    setZValue(minZ);
}

void DiagramWindow::setZValue(int z)
{
    Node *node = selectedNode();
    if (node)
        node->setZValue(z);
}
```

The `bringToFront()` slot increments the `maxZ` value, and then sets the currently selected node's z value to `maxZ`. The `sendToBack()` slot uses `minZ` and has the opposite effect. Both are defined in terms of the `setZValue()` private function.

```
Node *DiagramWindow::selectedNode() const
{
    QList<QGraphicsItem *> items = scene->selectedItems();
    if (items.count() == 1) {
        return dynamic_cast<Node *>(items.first());
    } else {
        return 0;
    }
}
```

The list of all selected items in the scene is available by calling `QGraphicsScene::selectedItems()`. The `selectedNode()` function is designed to return a single node if just one node is selected, and a null pointer otherwise. If there is exactly one selected item, the cast will produce a `Node` pointer if the item is a `Node`, and a null pointer if the item is a `Link`.

There is also a `selectedLink()` function, which returns a pointer to the selected `Link` item if there is exactly one selected item and it is a link.

```
void DiagramWindow::addLink()
{
    NodePair nodes = selectedNodePair();
    if (nodes == NodePair())
        return;

    Link *link = new Link(nodes.first, nodes.second);
    scene->addItem(link);
}
```

The user can add a link if exactly two nodes are selected. If the `selectedNodePair()` function returns the two selected nodes, we create a new link. The link's constructor will make the link line's endpoints go from the center of the first node to the center of the second node.

```
DiagramWindow::NodePair DiagramWindow::selectedNodePair() const
{
    QList<QGraphicsItem *> items = scene->selectedItems();
    if (items.count() == 2) {
```

```
        Node *first = dynamic_cast<Node *>(items.first());
        Node *second = dynamic_cast<Node *>(items.last());
        if (first && second)
            return NodePair(first, second);
    }
    return NodePair();
}
```

This function is similar to the `selectedNode()` function we saw earlier. If there are exactly two selected items, and they are both nodes, the pair of them is returned; otherwise, a pair of null pointers is returned.

```
void DiagramWindow::del()
{
    QList<QGraphicsItem *> items = scene->selectedItems();
    QMutableListIterator<QGraphicsItem *> i(items);
    while (i.hasNext()) {
        Link *link = dynamic_cast<Link *>(i.next());
        if (link) {
            delete link;
            i.remove();
        }
    }

    qDeleteAll(items);
}
```

This slot deletes any selected items, whether they are nodes, links, or a mixture of both. When a node is deleted, its destructor deletes any links that are associated with it. To avoid double-deleting links, we delete the link items before deleting the nodes.

```
void DiagramWindow::properties()
{
    Node *node = selectedNode();
    Link *link = selectedLink();

    if (node) {
        PropertiesDialog dialog(node, this);
        dialog.exec();
    } else if (link) {
        QColor color = QColorDialog::getColor(link->color(), this);
        if (color.isValid())
            link->setColor(color);
    }
}
```

If the user triggers the Properties action and a node is selected, we invoke the Properties dialog. This dialog allows the user to change the node's text, position, and colors. Because `PropertiesDialog` operates directly on a `Node` pointer, we can simply execute it modally and leave it to take care of itself.

If a link is selected, we use Qt's built-in `QColorDialog::getColor()` static convenience function to pop up a color dialog. If the user chooses a color, we set that as the link's color.

If a node's properties or a link's color were changed, the changes are made through setter functions, and these call update() to ensure that the node or link is repainted with its new settings.

Users often want to cut, copy, and paste graphics items in this type of application, and one way to support this is to represent items textually, as we will see when we review the relevant code. We only handle nodes, because it would not make sense to copy or paste links, which only exist in relation to nodes.

```
void DiagramWindow::cut()
{
    Node *node = selectedNode();
    if (!node)
        return;

    copy();
    delete node;
}
```

The Cut action is a two-part process: Copy the selected item into the clipboard and delete the item. The copy is performed using the copy() slot associated with the Copy action, and the deletion uses C++'s standard delete operator, relying on the node's destructor to delete any links that are connected to the node and to remove the node from the scene.

```
void DiagramWindow::copy()
{
    Node *node = selectedNode();
    if (!node)
        return;

    QString str = QString("Node %1 %2 %3 %4")
                  .arg(node->textColor().name())
                  .arg(node->outlineColor().name())
                  .arg(node->backgroundColor().name())
                  .arg(node->text());
    QApplication::clipboard()->setText(str);
}
```

The QColor::name() function returns a QString that contains an HTML-style color string in "*#RRGGBB*" format, with each color component represented by a hexadecimal value in the range 0x00 to 0xFF (0 to 255). We write a string to the clipboard, which is a single line of text starting with the word "Node", then the node's three colors, and finally the node's text, with a space between each part. For example:

```
Node #aa0000 #000080 #ffffff Red herring
```

This text is decoded by the paste() function:

```
void DiagramWindow::paste()
{
    QString str = QApplication::clipboard()->text();
    QStringList parts = str.split(" ");
```

```
        if (parts.count() >= 5 && parts.first() == "Node") {
            Node *node = new Node;
            node->setText(QStringList(parts.mid(4)).join(" "));
            node->setTextColor(QColor(parts[1]));
            node->setOutlineColor(QColor(parts[2]));
            node->setBackgroundColor(QColor(parts[3]));
            setupNode(node);
        }
    }
```

We split the clipboard's text into a `QStringList`. Using the preceding example, this would give us the list ["Node", "#aa0000", "#000080", "#ffffff", "Red", "herring"]. To be a valid node, there must be at least five elements in the list: the word "Node", the three colors, and at least one word of text. If this is the case, we create a new node, setting its text to be the space-separated concatenation of the fifth and subsequent elements. We set the colors to be the second, third, and fourth elements, using the `QColor` constructor that accepts the names returned by `QColor::name()`.

For completeness, here is the `updateActions()` slot that is used to enable and disable the actions in the Edit menu and the context menu:

```
void DiagramWindow::updateActions()
{
    bool hasSelection = !scene->selectedItems().isEmpty();
    bool isNode = (selectedNode() != 0);
    bool isNodePair = (selectedNodePair() != NodePair());

    cutAction->setEnabled(isNode);
    copyAction->setEnabled(isNode);
    addLinkAction->setEnabled(isNodePair);
    deleteAction->setEnabled(hasSelection);
    bringToFrontAction->setEnabled(isNode);
    sendToBackAction->setEnabled(isNode);
    propertiesAction->setEnabled(isNode);

    foreach (QAction *action, view->actions())
        view->removeAction(action);

    foreach (QAction *action, editMenu->actions()) {
        if (action->isEnabled())
            view->addAction(action);
    }
}
```

We have now finished the review of the Diagram application and can turn our attention to the second graphics view example, Cityscape.

The Cityscape application shown in Figure 8.17 presents a fictitious map of the major buildings, blocks, and parks in a city, with the most important ones annotated with their names. It allows the user to scroll and zoom the map using the mouse and the keyboard. We will begin by showing the `Cityscape` class, which provides the application's main window.

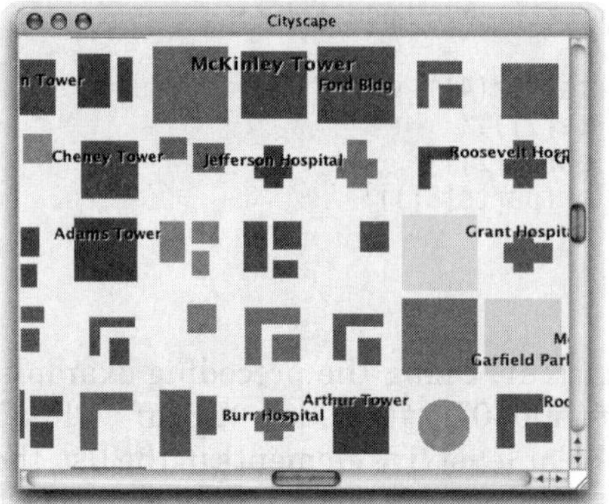

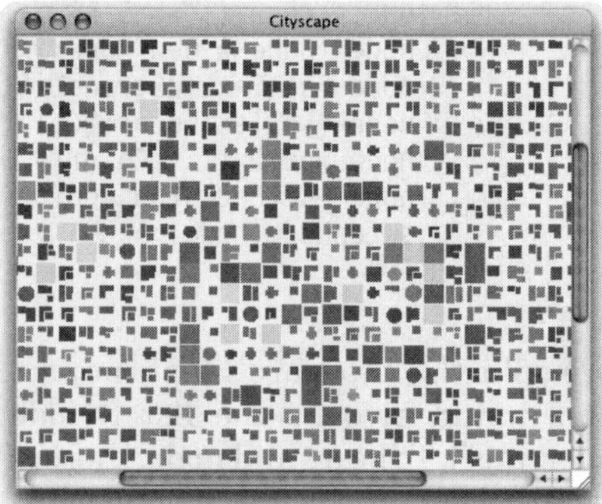

Figure 8.17. The Cityscape application at two different zoom levels

```
class Cityscape : public QMainWindow
{
    Q_OBJECT

public:
    Cityscape();

private:
    void generateCityBlocks();

    QGraphicsScene *scene;
    CityView *view;
};
```

The application has no menus or toolbars; it simply displays the annotated map using a `CityView` widget. The `CityView` class is derived from `QGraphicsView`.

```
Cityscape::Cityscape()
{
    scene = new QGraphicsScene(-22.25, -22.25, 1980, 1980);
    scene->setBackgroundBrush(QColor(255, 255, 238));
    generateCityBlocks();

    view = new CityView;
    view->setScene(scene);
    setCentralWidget(view);

    setWindowTitle(tr("Cityscape"));
}
```

The constructor creates a `QGraphicsScene` and calls `generateCityBlocks()` to generate a map. The map consists of about 2000 blocks and 200 annotations.

We will first look at the `CityBlock` graphics item subclass, then the `Annotation` graphics item subclass, and finally the `CityView` graphics view subclass.

```
class CityBlock : public QGraphicsItem
{
public:
```

```
    enum Kind { Park, SmallBuilding, Hospital, Hall, Building, Tower,
                LShapedBlock, LShapedBlockPlusSmallBlock, TwoBlocks,
                BlockPlusTwoSmallBlocks };

    CityBlock(Kind kind);

    QRectF boundingRect() const;
    void paint(QPainter *painter,
               const QStyleOptionGraphicsItem *option, QWidget *widget);

private:
    int kind;
    QColor color;
    QPainterPath shape;
};
```

A city block has a kind, a color, and a shape. Since the city blocks are not selectable, we have not bothered to reimplement the `shape()` function like we did for the `Node` class in the previous example.

```
CityBlock::CityBlock(Kind kind)
{
    this->kind = kind;

    int green = 96 + (std::rand() % 64);
    int red = 16 + green + (std::rand() % 64);
    int blue = 16 + (std::rand() % green);
    color = QColor(red, green, blue);

    if (kind == Park) {
        color = QColor(192 + (std::rand() % 32), 255,
                       192 + (std::rand() % 16));
        shape.addRect(boundingRect());
    } else if (kind == SmallBuilding) {
        ...
    } else if (kind == BlockPlusTwoSmallBlocks) {
        int w1 = (std::rand() % 10) + 8;
        int h1 = (std::rand() % 28) + 8;
        int w2 = (std::rand() % 10) + 8;
        int h2 = (std::rand() % 10) + 8;
        int w3 = (std::rand() % 6) + 8;
        int h3 = (std::rand() % 6) + 8;
        int y = (std::rand() % 4) - 16;
        shape.addRect(QRectF(-16, -16, w1, h1));
        shape.addRect(QRectF(-16 + w1 + 4, y, w2, h2));
        shape.addRect(QRectF(-16 + w1 + 4,
                             y + h2 + 4 + (std::rand() % 4), w3, h3));
    }
}
```

The constructor sets a random color and generates a suitable `QPainterPath` depending on what kind of block the node represents.

```
QRectF CityBlock::boundingRect() const
{
```

```
    return QRectF(-20, -20, 40, 40);
}
```

Each block occupies a 40×40 square, with its center at (0, 0).

```
void CityBlock::paint(QPainter *painter,
                      const QStyleOptionGraphicsItem *option,
                      QWidget * /* widget */)
{
    if (option->levelOfDetail < 4.0) {
        painter->fillPath(shape, color);
    } else {
        QLinearGradient gradient(QPoint(-20, -20), QPoint(+20, +20));
        int coeff = 105 + int(std::log(option->levelOfDetail - 4.0));
        gradient.setColorAt(0.0, color.lighter(coeff));
        gradient.setColorAt(1.0, color.darker(coeff));
        painter->fillPath(shape, gradient);
    }
}
```

In `paint()`, we draw the shape using the given `QPainter`. We distinguish two cases:

- If the zoom factor is less than 4.0, we use a solid color to fill the shape.
- If the zoom factor is 4.0 or more, we use a `QLinearGradient` to fill the shape to give a subtle lighting effect.

The `levelOfDetail` member of the `QStyleOptionGraphicsItem` class stores a floating-point value that tells us what the zoom factor is. A value of 1.0 means that the scene is being viewed at its natural size, a value of 0.5 means that the scene has been zoomed out to half its natural size, and a value of 2.5 means that the scene has been zoomed in to two and a half times its natural size. Using the "level of detail" information allows us to use faster drawing algorithms for scenes that are zoomed out too much to show any detail.

The `CityBlock` graphics item class works perfectly, but the fact that the items are scaled when the scene is zoomed raises the question of what happens to items that draw text. Normally, we don't want the text to scale with the scene. The graphics view architecture provide a general solution to this problem, through the `ItemIgnoresTransformations` flag. This is what we use in the `Annotation` class:

```
class Annotation : public QGraphicsItem
{
public:
    Annotation(const QString &text, bool major = false);

    void setText(const QString &text);
    QString text() const;

    QRectF boundingRect() const;
    void paint(QPainter *painter,
               const QStyleOptionGraphicsItem *option, QWidget *widget);

private:
```

```
        QFont font;
        QString str;
        bool major;
        double threshold;
        int y;
    };
```

The constructor takes a text and a `bool` flag, called `major`, that specifies whether the annotation is a major or a minor annotation. This will affect the size of the font.

```
    Annotation::Annotation(const QString &text, bool major)
    {
        font = qApp->font();
        font.setBold(true);
        if (major) {
            font.setPointSize(font.pointSize() + 2);
            font.setStretch(QFont::SemiExpanded);
        }

        if (major) {
            threshold = 0.01 * (40 + (std::rand() % 40));
        } else {
            threshold = 0.01 * (100 + (std::rand() % 100));
        }

        str = text;
        this->major = major;
        y = 20 - (std::rand() % 40);

        setZValue(1000);
        setFlag(ItemIgnoresTransformations, true);
    }
```

In the constructor, we begin by setting the font to be bigger and bolder if this is a major annotation, presumably one that refers to an important building or landmark. The threshold below which the annotation will not be shown is calculated pseudo-randomly, with a lower threshold for major annotations, so less important ones will disappear first as the scene is zoomed out.

The z value is set to 1000 to ensure that annotations are on top of everything else, and we use the `ItemIgnoresTransformations` flag to ensure that the annotation does not change size no matter how much the scene is zoomed.

```
    void Annotation::setText(const QString &text)
    {
        prepareGeometryChange();
        str = text;
        update();
    }
```

If the annotation's text is changed, it might be longer or shorter than before, so we must notify the graphics view architecture that the item's geometry may change.

```
QRectF Annotation::boundingRect() const
{
    QFontMetricsF metrics(font);
    QRectF rect = metrics.boundingRect(str);
    rect.moveCenter(QPointF(0, y));
    rect.adjust(-4, 0, +4, 0);
    return rect;
}
```

We get the font metrics for the annotation's font, and use them to calculate the text's bounding rectangle. We then move the rectangle's center point to the annotation's *y* offset, and make the rectangle slightly wider. The extra pixels on the left and right sides of the bounding rectangle will give the text some margin from the edges.

```
void Annotation::paint(QPainter *painter,
                       const QStyleOptionGraphicsItem *option,
                       QWidget * /* widget */)
{
    if (option->levelOfDetail <= threshold)
        return;

    painter->setFont(font);

    QRectF rect = boundingRect();

    int alpha = int(30 * std::log(option->levelOfDetail));
    if (alpha >= 32)
        painter->fillRect(rect, QColor(255, 255, 255, qMin(alpha, 63)));

    painter->setPen(Qt::white);
    painter->drawText(rect.translated(+1, +1), str,
                      QTextOption(Qt::AlignCenter));
    painter->setPen(Qt::blue);
    painter->drawText(rect, str, QTextOption(Qt::AlignCenter));
}
```

If the scene is zoomed out beyond the annotation's threshold, we don't paint the annotation at all. And if the scene is zoomed in sufficiently, we start by painting a semi-transparent white rectangle; this helps the text stand out when drawn on top of a dark block.

We draw the text twice, once in white and once in blue. The white text is offset by one pixel horizontally and vertically to create a shadow effect that makes the text easier to read.

Having seen how the blocks and annotations are done, we can now move on to the last aspect of the Cityscape application, the custom QGraphicsView subclass:

```
class CityView : public QGraphicsView
{
    Q_OBJECT

public:
    CityView(QWidget *parent = 0);
```

```
protected:
    void wheelEvent(QWheelEvent *event);
};
```

By default, the QGraphicsView class provides scroll bars that appear automatically when needed, but does not provide any means of zooming the scene it is being used to view. For this reason, we have created the tiny CityView subclass to provide the user with the ability to zoom in and out using the mouse wheel.

```
CityView::CityView(QWidget *parent)
    : QGraphicsView(parent)
{
    setDragMode(ScrollHandDrag);
}
```

Setting the drag mode is all that is required to support scrolling by dragging.

```
void CityView::wheelEvent(QWheelEvent *event)
{
    double numDegrees = -event->delta() / 8.0;
    double numSteps = numDegrees / 15.0;
    double factor = std::pow(1.125, numSteps);
    scale(factor, factor);
}
```

When the user rolls the mouse wheel, wheel events are generated; we simply have to calculate an appropriate scaling factor and call QGraphicsView::scale(). The mathematical formula is a bit tricky, but basically we scale the scene up or down by a factor of 1.125 for every mouse wheel step.

That completes our two graphics view examples. Qt's graphics view architecture is very rich, so bear in mind that it has a lot more to offer than we have had the space to cover. There is support for drag and drop, and graphics items can have tooltips and custom cursors. Animation effects can be achieved in a number of ways—for example, by associating QGraphicsItemAnimations with the items that we want to animate and performing the animation using a QTimeLine. It is also possible to achieve animation by creating custom graphics item subclasses that are derived from QObject (through multiple inheritance) and that reimplement QObject::timerEvent().

Printing

Printing in Qt is similar to drawing on a QWidget, QPixmap, or QImage. It consists of the following steps:

1. Create a QPrinter to serve as the paint device.
2. Pop up a QPrintDialog, allowing the user to choose a printer and to set a few options.
3. Create a QPainter to operate on the QPrinter.
4. Draw a page using the QPainter.

5. Call QPrinter::newPage() to advance to the next page.
6. Repeat steps 4 and 5 until all the pages are printed.

On Windows and Mac OS X, QPrinter uses the system's printer drivers. On Unix, it generates PostScript and sends it to lp or lpr (or to the program set using QPrinter::setPrintProgram()). QPrinter can also be used to generate PDF files by calling setOutputFormat(QPrinter::PdfFormat).*

Let's start with some simple examples that print on a single page. The first example, illustrated in Figure 8.18, prints a QImage:

```
void PrintWindow::printImage(const QImage &image)
{
    QPrintDialog printDialog(&printer, this);
    if (printDialog.exec()) {
        QPainter painter(&printer);
        QRect rect = painter.viewport();
        QSize size = image.size();
        size.scale(rect.size(), Qt::KeepAspectRatio);
        painter.setViewport(rect.x(), rect.y(),
                            size.width(), size.height());
        painter.setWindow(image.rect());
        painter.drawImage(0, 0, image);
    }
}
```

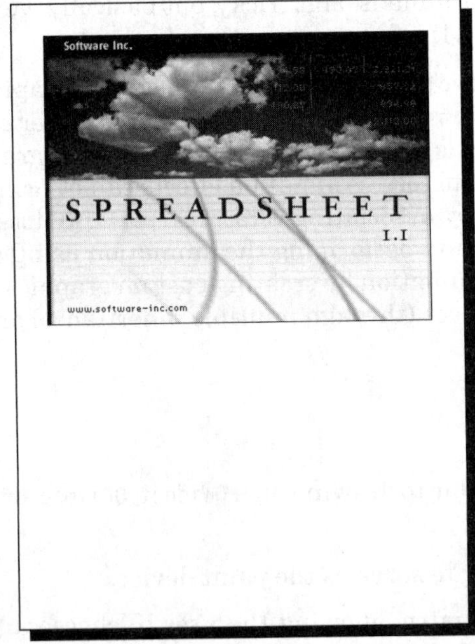

Figure 8.18. Printing a QImage

*Qt 4.4 is expected to introduce classes for showing print previews.

We assume that the `PrintWindow` class has a member variable called `printer` of type `QPrinter`. We could simply have created the `QPrinter` on the stack in `printImage()`, but then it would not remember the user's settings from one print run to another.

We create a `QPrintDialog` and call `exec()` to show it. It returns `true` if the user clicked the OK button; otherwise, it returns `false`. After the call to `exec()`, the `QPrinter` object is ready to use. (It is also possible to print without using a `QPrintDialog`, by directly calling `QPrinter` member functions to set things up.)

Next, we create a `QPainter` to draw on the `QPrinter`. We set the window to the image's rectangle and the viewport to a rectangle with the same aspect ratio, and we draw the image at position (0, 0).

By default, `QPainter`'s window is initialized so that the printer appears to have a similar resolution as the screen (usually somewhere between 72 and 100 dots per inch), making it easy to reuse widget painting code for printing. Here, it doesn't matter, because we set our own window.

In the example, we chose to print an image, but printing graphics view scenes is also very simple. To print the entire scene, we can call either `QGraphicsScene::render()` or `QGraphicsView::render()`, passing a `QPrinter` as the first parameter. If we want to print just part of the scene, we can use the `render()` functions' optional arguments to specify the target rectangle to paint on (where on the page the scene should be painted) and the source rectangle (what part of the scene should be painted).

Printing items that take up no more than a single page is simple, but many applications need to print multiple pages. For those, we need to paint one page at a time and call `newPage()` to advance to the next page. This raises the problem of determining how much information we can print on each page. There are two main approaches to handling multi-page documents with Qt:

- We can convert our data to HTML and render it using `QTextDocument`, Qt's rich text engine.
- We can perform the drawing and the page breaking by hand.

We will review both approaches in turn. As an example, we will print a flower guide: a list of flower names, each with a textual description. Each entry in the guide is stored as a string of the format "*name*: *description*", for example:

```
Miltonopsis santanae: A most dangerous orchid species.
```

Since each flower's data is represented by a single string, we can represent all the flowers in the guide using one `QStringList`. Here's the function that prints a flower guide using Qt's rich text engine:

```
void PrintWindow::printFlowerGuide(const QStringList &entries)
{
    QString html;

    foreach (QString entry, entries) {
```

```
        QStringList fields = entry.split(": ");
        QString title = Qt::escape(fields[0]);
        QString body = Qt::escape(fields[1]);
        html += "<table width=\"100%\" border=1 cellspacing=0>\n"
                "<tr><td bgcolor=\"lightgray\"><font size=\"+1\">"
                "<b><i>" + title + "</i></b></font>\n<tr><td>" + body
                + "\n</table>\n<br>\n";
    }
    printHtml(html);
}
```

The first step is to convert the `QStringList` into HTML. Each flower becomes an HTML table with two cells. We use `Qt::escape()` to replace the special characters '&', '<', and '>' with the corresponding HTML entities ("&", "<", and ">"). Then we call `printHtml()` to print the text.

```
void PrintWindow::printHtml(const QString &html)
{
    QPrintDialog printDialog(&printer, this);
    if (printDialog.exec()) {
        QTextDocument textDocument;
        textDocument.setHtml(html);
        textDocument.print(&printer);
    }
}
```

The `printHtml()` function pops up a `QPrintDialog` and takes care of printing an HTML document. It can be reused "as is" in any Qt application to print arbitrary HTML pages. The resulting pages are shown in Figure 8.19.

Converting a document to HTML and using `QTextDocument` to print it is by far the most convenient alternative for printing reports and other complex documents. In cases where we need more control, we can do the page layout and the drawing by hand. Let's now see how we can use this approach to print a flower guide. Here's the new `printFlowerGuide()` function:

```
void PrintWindow::printFlowerGuide(const QStringList &entries)
{
    QPrintDialog printDialog(&printer, this);
    if (printDialog.exec()) {
        QPainter painter(&printer);
        QList<QStringList> pages;

        paginate(&painter, &pages, entries);
        printPages(&painter, pages);
    }
}
```

After setting up the printer and constructing the painter, we call the `paginate()` helper function to determine which entry should appear on which page. The result of this is a list of `QStringList`s, with each `QStringList` holding the entries for one page. We pass on that result to `printPages()`.

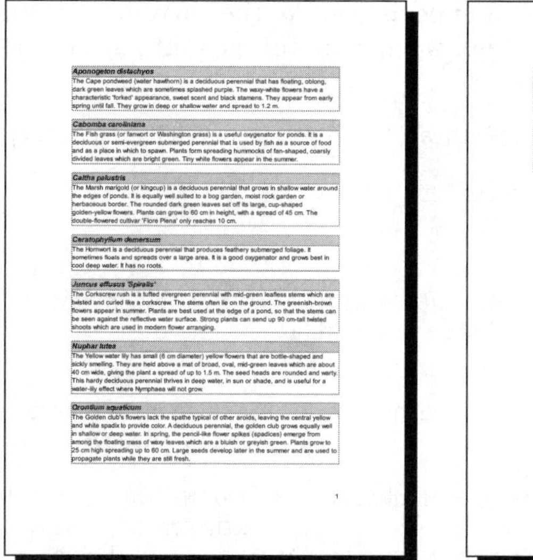

Aponogeton distachyos

The Cape pondweed (water hawthorn) is a deciduous perennial that has floating, oblong, dark green leaves which are sometimes splashed purple. The waxy-white flowers have a characteristic 'forked' appearance, sweet scent and black stamens. They appear from early spring until fall. They grow in deep or shallow water and spread to 1.2 m.

Cabomba caroliniana

The Fish grass (or fanwort or Washington grass) is a useful oxygenator for ponds. It is a deciduous or semi-evergreen submerged perennial that is used by fish as a source of food and as a place in which to spawn. Plants form spreading hummocks of fan-shaped, coarsly divided leaves which are bright green. Tiny white flowers appear in the summer.

Caltha palustris

The Marsh marigold (or kingcup) is a deciduous perennial that grows in shallow water around the edges of ponds. It is equally well suited to a bog garden, moist rock garden or herbaceous border. The rounded dark green leaves set off its large, cup-shaped golden-yellow flowers. Plants can grow to 60 cm in height, with a spread of 45 cm. The double-flowered cultivar 'Flore Plena' only reaches 10 cm.

Ceratophyllum demersum

The Hornwort is a deciduous perennial that produces feathery submerged foliage. It sometimes floats and spreads over a large area. It is a good oxygenator and grows best in cool deep water. It has no roots.

Juncus effusus 'Spiralis'

The Corkscrew rush is a tufted evergreen perennial with mid-green leafless stems which are twisted and curled like a corkscrew. The stems often lie on the ground. The greenish-brown flowers appear in summer. Plants are best used at the edge of a pond, so that the stems can be seen against the reflective water surface. Strong plants can send up 90 cm-tall twisted shoots which are used in modern flower arranging.

Nuphar lutea

The Yellow water lily has small (6 cm diameter) yellow flowers that are bottle-shaped and sickly smelling. They are held above a mat of broad, oval, mid-green leaves which are about 40 cm wide, giving the plant a spread of up to 1.5 m. The seed heads are rounded and warty. This hardy deciduous perennial thrives in deep water, in sun or shade, and is useful for a water-lily effect where Nymphaea will not grow.

Orontium aquaticum

The Golden club's flowers lack the spathe typical of other aroids, leaving the central yellow and white spadix to provide color. A deciduous perennial, the golden club grows equally well in shallow or deep water. In spring, the pencil-like flower spikes (spadices) emerge from among the floating mass of waxy leaves which are a bluish or greyish green. Plants grow to 25 cm high spreading up to 60 cm. Large seeds develop later in the summer and are used to propagate plants while they are still fresh.

1

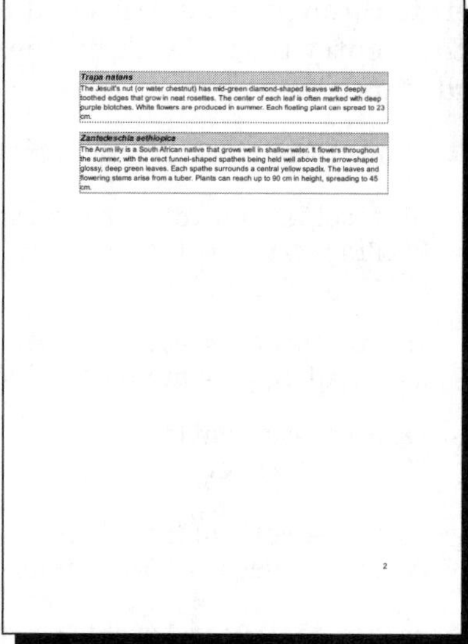

Trapa natans

The Jesuit's nut (or water chestnut) has mid-green diamond-shaped leaves with deeply toothed edges that grow in neat rosettes. The center of each leaf is often marked with deep purple blotches. White flowers are produced in summer. Each floating plant can spread to 23 cm.

Zantedeschia aethiopica

The Arum lily is a South African native that grows well in shallow water. It flowers throughout the summer, with the erect funnel-shaped spathes being held well above the arrow-shaped glossy, deep green leaves. Each spathe surrounds a central yellow spadix. The leaves and flowering stems arise from a tuber. Plants can reach up to 90 cm in height, spreading to 45 cm.

2

Figure 8.19. Printing a flower guide using `QTextDocument`

For example, let's suppose that the flower guide contains six entries, which we will refer to as $\mathcal{A}$, $\mathcal{B}$, $\mathcal{C}$, $\mathcal{D}$, $\mathcal{E}$, and $\mathcal{F}$. Now let's suppose that there is room for $\mathcal{A}$ and $\mathcal{B}$ on the first page; $\mathcal{C}$, $\mathcal{D}$, and $\mathcal{E}$ on the second page; and $\mathcal{F}$ on the third page. The `pages` list would then have the list [$\mathcal{A}$, $\mathcal{B}$] at index position 0, the list [$\mathcal{C}$, $\mathcal{D}$, $\mathcal{E}$] at index position 1, and the list [$\mathcal{F}$] at index position 2.

```
void PrintWindow::paginate(QPainter *painter, QList<QStringList> *pages,
                           const QStringList &entries)
{
    QStringList currentPage;
    int pageHeight = painter->window().height() - 2 * LargeGap;
    int y = 0;

    foreach (QString entry, entries) {
        int height = entryHeight(painter, entry);
        if (y + height > pageHeight && !currentPage.empty()) {
            pages->append(currentPage);
            currentPage.clear();
            y = 0;
        }
        currentPage.append(entry);
        y += height + MediumGap;
    }
    if (!currentPage.empty())
        pages->append(currentPage);
}
```

The `paginate()` function distributes the flower guide entries into pages. It relies on the `entryHeight()` function, which computes the height of one entry. It also takes into account the vertical gaps at the top and bottom of the page, of size `LargeGap`.

We iterate through the entries and append them to the current page until we come to an entry that doesn't fit; then we append the current page to the pages list and start a new page.

```
int PrintWindow::entryHeight(QPainter *painter, const QString &entry)
{
    QStringList fields = entry.split(": ");
    QString title = fields[0];
    QString body = fields[1];

    int textWidth = painter->window().width() - 2 * SmallGap;
    int maxHeight = painter->window().height();

    painter->setFont(titleFont);
    QRect titleRect = painter->boundingRect(0, 0, textWidth, maxHeight,
                                            Qt::TextWordWrap, title);
    painter->setFont(bodyFont);
    QRect bodyRect = painter->boundingRect(0, 0, textWidth, maxHeight,
                                           Qt::TextWordWrap, body);
    return titleRect.height() + bodyRect.height() + 4 * SmallGap;
}
```

The `entryHeight()` function uses `QPainter::boundingRect()` to compute the vertical space needed by one entry. Figure 8.20 shows the layout of a flower entry and the meaning of the `SmallGap` and `MediumGap` constants.

```
void PrintWindow::printPages(QPainter *painter,
                             const QList<QStringList> &pages)
{
    int firstPage = printer.fromPage() - 1;
    if (firstPage >= pages.size())
        return;
    if (firstPage == -1)
        firstPage = 0;

    int lastPage = printer.toPage() - 1;
    if (lastPage == -1 || lastPage >= pages.size())
        lastPage = pages.size() - 1;

    int numPages = lastPage - firstPage + 1;
```

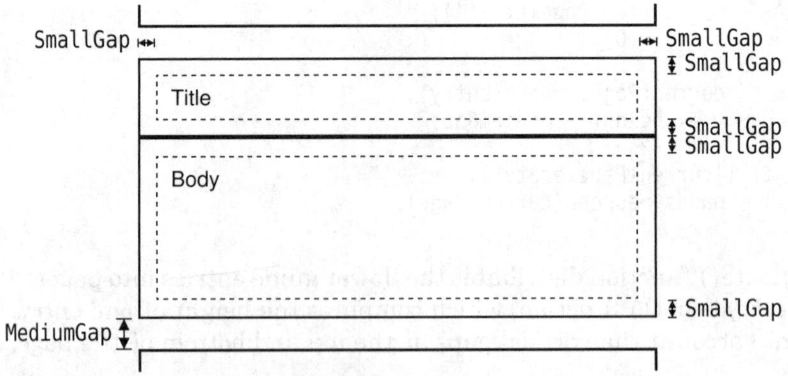

Figure 8.20. A flower entry's layout

```
        for (int i = 0; i < printer.numCopies(); ++i) {
            for (int j = 0; j < numPages; ++j) {
                if (i != 0 || j != 0)
                    printer.newPage();

                int index;
                if (printer.pageOrder() == QPrinter::FirstPageFirst) {
                    index = firstPage + j;
                } else {
                    index = lastPage - j;
                }
                printPage(painter, pages[index], index + 1);
            }
        }
    }
```

The `printPages()` function's role is to print each page using `printPage()` in the correct order and the correct number of times. The result it produces is shown in Figure 8.21. Using the `QPrintDialog`, the user might request several copies, specify a print range, or request the pages in reverse order. It is our responsibility to honor these options—or to disable them using `QPrintDialog::setEnabledOptions()`.

We start by determining the range to print. `QPrinter`'s `fromPage()` and `toPage()` functions return the page numbers selected by the user, or 0 if no range was chosen. We subtract 1 because our `pages` list is indexed from 0, and set `firstPage` and `lastPage` to cover the full range if the user didn't set any range.

Then we print each page. The outer `for` loop iterates as many times as necessary to produce the number of copies requested by the user. Most printer drivers support multiple copies, so for those, `QPrinter::numCopies()` always returns 1. If

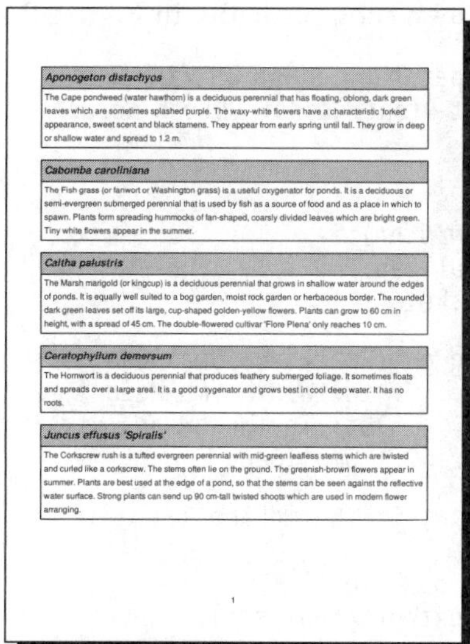

Aponogeton distachyos

The Cape pondweed (water hawthorn) is a deciduous perennial that has floating, oblong, dark green leaves which are sometimes splashed purple. The waxy-white flowers have a characteristic 'forked' appearance, sweet scent and black stamens. They appear from early spring until fall. They grow in deep or shallow water and spread to 1.2 m.

Cabomba caroliniana

The Fish grass (or fanwort or Washington grass) is a useful oxygenator for ponds. It is a deciduous or semi-evergreen submerged perennial that is used by fish as a source of food and as a place in which to spawn. Plants form spreading hummocks of fan-shaped, coarsly divided leaves which are bright green. Tiny white flowers appear in the summer.

Caltha palustris

The Marsh marigold (or kingcup) is a deciduous perennial that grows in shallow water around the edges of ponds. It is equally well suited to a bog garden, moist rock garden or herbaceous border. The rounded dark green leaves set off its large, cup-shaped golden-yellow flowers. Plants can grow to 60 cm in height, with a spread of 45 cm. The double-flowered cultivar 'Flore Plena' only reaches 10 cm.

Ceratophyllum demersum

The Hornwort is a deciduous perennial that produces feathery submerged foliage. It sometimes floats and spreads over a large area. It is a good oxygenator and grows best in cool deep water. It has no roots.

Juncus effusus 'Spiralis'

The Corkscrew rush is a tufted evergreen perennial with mid-green leafless stems which are twisted and curled like a corkscrew. The stems often lie on the ground. The greenish-brown flowers appear in summer. Plants are best used at the edge of a pond, so that the stems can be seen against the reflective water surface. Strong plants can send up 90 cm-tall twisted shoots which are used in modern flower arranging.

1

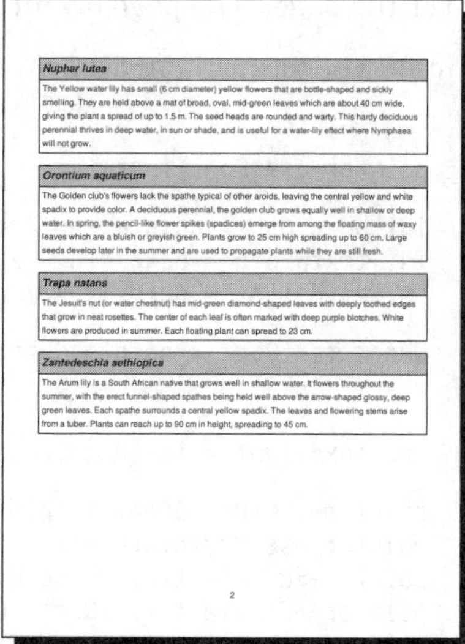

Nuphar lutea

The Yellow water lily has small (6 cm diameter) yellow flowers that are bottle-shaped and sickly smelling. They are held above a mat of broad, oval, mid-green leaves which are about 40 cm wide, giving the plant a spread of up to 1.5 m. The seed heads are rounded and warty. This hardy deciduous perennial thrives in deep water, in sun or shade, and is useful for a water-lily effect where Nymphaea will not grow.

Orontium aquaticum

The Golden club's flowers lack the spathe typical of other aroids, leaving the central yellow and white spadix to provide color. A deciduous perennial, the golden club grows equally well in shallow or deep water. In spring, the pencil-like flower spikes (spadices) emerge from among the floating mass of waxy leaves which are a bluish or greyish green. Plants grow to 25 cm high spreading up to 60 cm. Large seeds develop later in the summer and are used to propagate plants while they are still fresh.

Trapa natans

The Jesuit's nut (or water chestnut) has mid-green diamond-shaped leaves with deeply toothed edges that grow in neat rosettes. The center of each leaf is often marked with deep purple blotches. White flowers are produced in summer. Each floating plant can spread to 23 cm.

Zantedeschia aethiopica

The Arum lily is a South African native that grows well in shallow water. It flowers throughout the summer, with the erect funnel-shaped spathes being held well above the arrow-shaped glossy, deep green leaves. Each spathe surrounds a central yellow spadix. The leaves and flowering stems arise from a tuber. Plants can reach up to 90 cm in height, spreading to 45 cm.

2

Figure 8.21. Printing a flower guide using `QPainter`

the printer driver can't handle multiple copies, numCopies() returns the number of copies requested by the user, and the application is responsible for printing that number of copies. (In the QImage example earlier in this section, we ignored numCopies() for the sake of simplicity.)

The inner for loop iterates through the pages. If the page isn't the first page, we call newPage() to flush the old page and start painting on a fresh page. We call printPage() to paint each page.

```
void PrintWindow::printPage(QPainter *painter,
                            const QStringList &entries, int pageNumber)
{
    painter->save();
    painter->translate(0, LargeGap);
    foreach (QString entry, entries) {
        QStringList fields = entry.split(": ");
        QString title = fields[0];
        QString body = fields[1];
        printBox(painter, title, titleFont, Qt::lightGray);
        printBox(painter, body, bodyFont, Qt::white);
        painter->translate(0, MediumGap);
    }
    painter->restore();

    painter->setFont(footerFont);
    painter->drawText(painter->window(),
                      Qt::AlignHCenter | Qt::AlignBottom,
                      QString::number(pageNumber));
}
```

The printPage() function iterates through all the flower guide entries and prints them using two calls to printBox(): one for the title (the flower's name) and one for the body (its description). It also draws the page number centered at the bottom of the page. The page layout is shown schematically in Figure 8.22.

```
void PrintWindow::printBox(QPainter *painter, const QString &str,
                           const QFont &font, const QBrush &brush)
{
    painter->setFont(font);

    int boxWidth = painter->window().width();
    int textWidth = boxWidth - 2 * SmallGap;
    int maxHeight = painter->window().height();

    QRect textRect = painter->boundingRect(SmallGap, SmallGap,
                                           textWidth, maxHeight,
                                           Qt::TextWordWrap, str);
    int boxHeight = textRect.height() + 2 * SmallGap;

    painter->setPen(QPen(Qt::black, 2.0, Qt::SolidLine));
    painter->setBrush(brush);
    painter->drawRect(0, 0, boxWidth, boxHeight);
    painter->drawText(textRect, Qt::TextWordWrap, str);
    painter->translate(0, boxHeight);
}
```

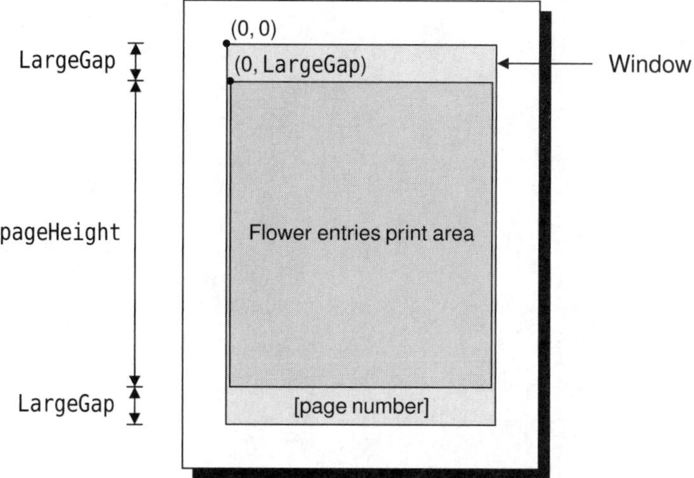

Figure 8.22. The flower guide's page layout

The `printBox()` function draws the outline of a box, then draws the text inside the box.

This completes our review of 2D graphics and printing. We will cover 3D graphics later, in Chapter 20.

- *Enabling Drag and Drop*
- *Supporting Custom Drag Types*
- *Clipboard Handling*

9. Drag and Drop

Drag and drop is a modern and intuitive way of transferring information within an application or between different applications. It is often provided in addition to clipboard support for moving and copying data.

In this chapter, we will see how to add drag and drop support to an application and how to handle custom formats. Then we will show how to reuse the drag and drop code to add clipboard support. This code reuse is possible because both mechanisms are based on `QMimeData`, a class that can provide data in several formats.

Enabling Drag and Drop

Drag and drop involves two distinct actions: dragging and dropping. Qt widgets can serve as drag sites, as drop sites, or as both.

Our first example shows how to make a Qt application accept a drag initiated by another application. The Qt application is a main window with a `QTextEdit` as its central widget. When the user drags a text file from the desktop or from a file explorer and drops it onto the application, the application loads the file into the `QTextEdit`.

Here's the definition of the example's `MainWindow` class:

```
class MainWindow : public QMainWindow
{
    Q_OBJECT

public:
    MainWindow();

protected:
    void dragEnterEvent(QDragEnterEvent *event);
    void dropEvent(QDropEvent *event);

private:
    bool readFile(const QString &fileName);
```

```
    QTextEdit *textEdit;
};
```

The MainWindow class reimplements dragEnterEvent() and dropEvent() from QWidget. Since the purpose of the example is to show drag and drop, much of the functionality we would expect to be in a main window class has been omitted.

```
MainWindow::MainWindow()
{
    textEdit = new QTextEdit;
    setCentralWidget(textEdit);

    textEdit->setAcceptDrops(false);
    setAcceptDrops(true);

    setWindowTitle(tr("Text Editor"));
}
```

In the constructor, we create a QTextEdit and set it as the central widget. By default, QTextEdit accepts textual drags from other applications, and if the user drops a file onto it, it will insert the file name into the text. Since drop events are propagated from child to parent, by disabling dropping on the QTextEdit and enabling it on the main window, we get the drop events for the whole window in MainWindow.

```
void MainWindow::dragEnterEvent(QDragEnterEvent *event)
{
    if (event->mimeData()->hasFormat("text/uri-list"))
        event->acceptProposedAction();
}
```

The dragEnterEvent() is called whenever the user drags an object onto a widget. If we call acceptProposedAction() on the event, we indicate that the user can drop the drag object on this widget. By default, the widget wouldn't accept the drag. Qt automatically changes the cursor to indicate to the user whether the widget is a legitimate drop site.

Here we want the user to be allowed to drag files, but nothing else. To do so, we check the MIME type of the drag. The MIME type text/uri-list is used to store a list of uniform resource identifiers (URIs), which can be file names, URLs (such as HTTP or FTP paths), or other global resource identifiers. Standard MIME types are defined by the Internet Assigned Numbers Authority (IANA). They consist of a type and a subtype separated by a slash. The clipboard and the drag and drop system use MIME types to identify different types of data. The official list of MIME types is available at http://www.iana.org/assignments/media-types/.

```
void MainWindow::dropEvent(QDropEvent *event)
{
    QList<QUrl> urls = event->mimeData()->urls();
    if (urls.isEmpty())
        return;

    QString fileName = urls.first().toLocalFile();
```

```
        if (fileName.isEmpty())
            return;

        if (readFile(fileName))
            setWindowTitle(tr("%1 - %2").arg(fileName)
                                        .arg(tr("Drag File")));
    }
```

The `dropEvent()` is called when the user drops an object onto the widget. We call `QMimeData::urls()` to obtain a list of `QUrl`s. Typically, users drag only one file at a time, but it is possible for them to drag multiple files by dragging a selection. If there is more than one URL, or if the URL is not a local file name, we return immediately.

`QWidget` also provides `dragMoveEvent()` and `dragLeaveEvent()`, but for most applications they don't need to be reimplemented.

The second example illustrates how to initiate a drag and accept a drop. We will create a `QListWidget` subclass that supports drag and drop, and use it as a component in the Project Chooser application shown in Figure 9.1.

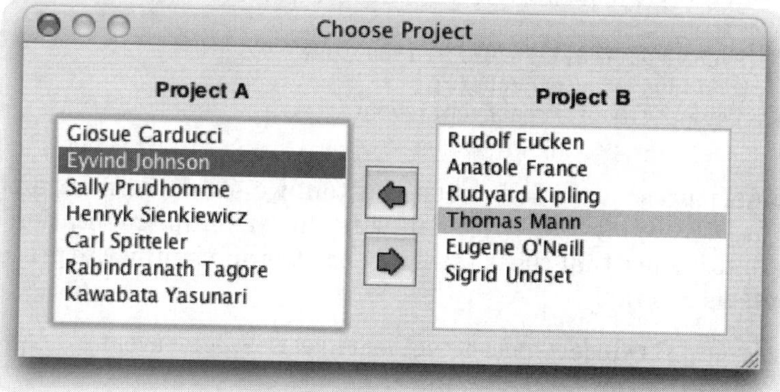

Figure 9.1. The Project Chooser application

The Project Chooser application presents the user with two list widgets, populated with names. Each list widget represents a project. The user can drag and drop the names in the list widgets to move a person from one project to another.

All of the drag and drop code is located in the `QListWidget` subclass. Here's the class definition:

```
class ProjectListWidget : public QListWidget
{
    Q_OBJECT

public:
    ProjectListWidget(QWidget *parent = 0);

protected:
    void mousePressEvent(QMouseEvent *event);
```

```
    void mouseMoveEvent(QMouseEvent *event);
    void dragEnterEvent(QDragEnterEvent *event);
    void dragMoveEvent(QDragMoveEvent *event);
    void dropEvent(QDropEvent *event);

private:
    void performDrag();

    QPoint startPos;
};
```

The ProjectListWidget class reimplements five event handlers declared in QWidget.

```
ProjectListWidget::ProjectListWidget(QWidget *parent)
    : QListWidget(parent)
{
    setAcceptDrops(true);
}
```

In the constructor, we enable drops on the list widget.

```
void ProjectListWidget::mousePressEvent(QMouseEvent *event)
{
    if (event->button() == Qt::LeftButton)
        startPos = event->pos();
    QListWidget::mousePressEvent(event);
}
```

When the user presses the left mouse button, we store the mouse position in the startPos private variable. We call QListWidget's implementation of mousePressEvent() to ensure that the QListWidget has the opportunity to process mouse press events as usual.

```
void ProjectListWidget::mouseMoveEvent(QMouseEvent *event)
{
    if (event->buttons() & Qt::LeftButton) {
        int distance = (event->pos() - startPos).manhattanLength();
        if (distance >= QApplication::startDragDistance())
            performDrag();
    }
    QListWidget::mouseMoveEvent(event);
}
```

When the user moves the mouse cursor while holding the left mouse button, we consider starting a drag. We compute the distance between the current mouse position and the position where the left mouse button was pressed—the "Manhattan length" is a quick-to-calculate approximation of the length of a vector from its origin. If the distance is greater than or equal to QApplication's recommended drag start distance (normally four pixels), we call the private function performDrag() to start dragging. This avoids initiating a drag just because the user's hand shakes.

```
void ProjectListWidget::performDrag()
{
```

```
        QListWidgetItem *item = currentItem();
        if (item) {
            QMimeData *mimeData = new QMimeData;
            mimeData->setText(item->text());

            QDrag *drag = new QDrag(this);
            drag->setMimeData(mimeData);
            drag->setPixmap(QPixmap(":/images/person.png"));
            if (drag->exec(Qt::MoveAction) == Qt::MoveAction)
                delete item;
        }
    }
```

In `performDrag()`, we create an object of type `QDrag` with `this` as its parent. The `QDrag` object stores the data in a `QMimeData` object. For this example, we provide the data as a `text/plain` string using `QMimeData::setText()`. `QMimeData` provides several functions for handling the most common types of drags (images, URLs, colors, etc.) and can handle arbitrary MIME types represented as `QByteArray`s. The call to `QDrag::setPixmap()` sets the icon that follows the cursor while the drag is taking place.

The `QDrag::exec()` call starts the dragging operation and blocks until the user drops or cancels the drag. It takes a combination of supported "drag actions" as argument (`Qt::CopyAction`, `Qt::MoveAction`, and `Qt::LinkAction`) and returns the drag action that was executed (or `Qt::IgnoreAction` if none was executed). Which action is executed depends on what the source widget allows, what the target supports, and which modifier keys are pressed when the drop occurs. After the `exec()` call, Qt takes ownership of the drag object and will delete it when it is no longer required.

```
void ProjectListWidget::dragEnterEvent(QDragEnterEvent *event)
{
    ProjectListWidget *source =
            qobject_cast<ProjectListWidget *>(event->source());
    if (source && source != this) {
        event->setDropAction(Qt::MoveAction);
        event->accept();
    }
}
```

The `ProjectListWidget` widget not only originates drags, but also accepts such drags if they come from another `ProjectListWidget` in the same application. `QDragEnterEvent::source()` returns a pointer to the widget that initiated the drag if that widget is part of the same application; otherwise, it returns a null pointer. We use `qobject_cast<T>()` to ensure that the drag comes from a `ProjectListWidget`. If all is correct, we tell Qt that we are ready to accept the action as a move action.

```
void ProjectListWidget::dragMoveEvent(QDragMoveEvent *event)
{
    ProjectListWidget *source =
            qobject_cast<ProjectListWidget *>(event->source());
    if (source && source != this) {
```

```
        event->setDropAction(Qt::MoveAction);
        event->accept();
    }
}
```

The code in dragMoveEvent() is identical to what we did in dragEnterEvent(). It is necessary because we need to override QListWidget's (actually, QAbstractItemView's) implementation of the function.

```
void ProjectListWidget::dropEvent(QDropEvent *event)
{
    ProjectListWidget *source =
            qobject_cast<ProjectListWidget *>(event->source());
    if (source && source != this) {
        addItem(event->mimeData()->text());
        event->setDropAction(Qt::MoveAction);
        event->accept();
    }
}
```

In dropEvent(), we retrieve the dragged text using QMimeData::text() and create an item with that text. We also need to accept the event as a "move action" to tell the source widget that it can now remove the original version of the dragged item.

Drag and drop is a powerful mechanism for transferring data between applications. But in some cases, it's possible to implement drag and drop without using Qt's drag and drop facilities. If all we want to do is to move data within one widget in one application, we can often simply reimplement mousePressEvent() and mouseReleaseEvent().

Supporting Custom Drag Types

In the examples so far, we have relied on QMimeData's support for common MIME types. Thus, we called QMimeData::setText() to create a text drag, and we used QMimeData:urls() to retrieve the contents of a text/uri-list drag. If we want to drag plain text, HTML text, images, URLs, or colors, we can use QMimeData without formality. But if we want to drag custom data, we must choose among the following alternatives:

1. We can provide arbitrary data as a QByteArray using QMimeData::setData() and extract it later using QMimeData::data().
2. We can subclass QMimeData and reimplement formats() and retrieveData() to handle our custom data types.
3. For drag and drop operations within a single application, we can subclass QMimeData and store the data using any data structure we want.

The first approach does not involve any subclassing, but does have some drawbacks: We need to convert our data structure to a QByteArray even if the drag is not ultimately accepted, and if we want to provide several MIME types to interact nicely with a wide range of applications, we need to store the data several times (once per MIME type). If the data is large, this can slow down the application needlessly. The second and third approaches can avoid or minimize these problems. They give us complete control and can be used together.

To show how these approaches work, we will show how to add drag and drop capabilities to a `QTableWidget`. The drag will support the following MIME types: `text/plain`, `text/html`, and `text/csv`. Using the first approach, starting a drag looks like this:

```
void MyTableWidget::mouseMoveEvent(QMouseEvent *event)
{
    if (event->buttons() & Qt::LeftButton) {
        int distance = (event->pos() - startPos).manhattanLength();
        if (distance >= QApplication::startDragDistance())
            performDrag();
    }
    QTableWidget::mouseMoveEvent(event);
}

void MyTableWidget::performDrag()
{
    QString plainText = selectionAsPlainText();
    if (plainText.isEmpty())
        return;

    QMimeData *mimeData = new QMimeData;
    mimeData->setText(plainText);
    mimeData->setHtml(toHtml(plainText));
    mimeData->setData("text/csv", toCsv(plainText).toUtf8());

    QDrag *drag = new QDrag(this);
    drag->setMimeData(mimeData);
    if (drag->exec(Qt::CopyAction | Qt::MoveAction) == Qt::MoveAction)
        deleteSelection();
}
```

The `performDrag()` private function is called from `mouseMoveEvent()` to start dragging a rectangular selection. We set the `text/plain` and `text/html` MIME types using `setText()` and `setHtml()`, and we set the `text/csv` type using `setData()`, which takes an arbitrary MIME type and a `QByteArray`. The code for the `selectionAsString()` is more or less the same as the `Spreadsheet::copy()` function from Chapter 4 (p. 87).

```
QString MyTableWidget::toCsv(const QString &plainText)
{
    QString result = plainText;
    result.replace("\\", "\\\\");
    result.replace("\"", "\\\"");
    result.replace("\t", "\", \"");
    result.replace("\n", "\"\n\"");
    result.prepend("\"");
    result.append("\"");
```

```
    return result;
}

QString MyTableWidget::toHtml(const QString &plainText)
{
    QString result = Qt::escape(plainText);
    result.replace("\t", "<td>");
    result.replace("\n", "\n<tr><td>");
    result.prepend("<table>\n<tr><td>");
    result.append("\n</table>");
    return result;
}
```

The `toCsv()` and `toHtml()` functions convert a "tabs and newlines" string into a CSV (comma-separated values) or an HTML string. For example, the data

```
Red     Green   Blue
Cyan    Yellow  Magenta
```

is converted to

```
"Red", "Green", "Blue"
"Cyan", "Yellow", "Magenta"
```

or to

```
<table>
<tr><td>Red<td>Green<td>Blue
<tr><td>Cyan<td>Yellow<td>Magenta
</table>
```

The conversion is performed in the simplest way possible, using `QString::replace()`. To escape HTML special characters, we use `Qt::escape()`.

```
void MyTableWidget::dropEvent(QDropEvent *event)
{
    if (event->mimeData()->hasFormat("text/csv")) {
        QByteArray csvData = event->mimeData()->data("text/csv");
        QString csvText = QString::fromUtf8(csvData);
        ...
        event->acceptProposedAction();
    } else if (event->mimeData()->hasFormat("text/plain")) {
        QString plainText = event->mimeData()->text();
        ...
        event->acceptProposedAction();
    }
}
```

Although we provide the data in three different formats, we accept only two of them in `dropEvent()`. If the user drags cells from a `QTableWidget` to an HTML editor, we want the cells to be converted into an HTML table. But if the user drags arbitrary HTML into a `QTableWidget`, we don't want to accept it.

To make this example work, we also need to call `setAcceptDrops(true)` and `setSelectionMode(ContiguousSelection)` in the `MyTableWidget` constructor.

We will now redo the example, but this time we will subclass QMimeData to postpone or avoid the (potentially expensive) conversions between QTableWidgetItems and QByteArray. Here's the definition of our subclass:

```
class TableMimeData : public QMimeData
{
    Q_OBJECT

public:
    TableMimeData(const QTableWidget *tableWidget,
                  const QTableWidgetSelectionRange &range);

    const QTableWidget *tableWidget() const { return myTableWidget; }
    QTableWidgetSelectionRange range() const { return myRange; }
    QStringList formats() const;

protected:
    QVariant retrieveData(const QString &format,
                          QVariant::Type preferredType) const;

private:
    static QString toHtml(const QString &plainText);
    static QString toCsv(const QString &plainText);

    QString text(int row, int column) const;
    QString rangeAsPlainText() const;

    const QTableWidget *myTableWidget;
    QTableWidgetSelectionRange myRange;
    QStringList myFormats;
};
```

Instead of storing actual data, we store a QTableWidgetSelectionRange that specifies which cells are being dragged and keep a pointer to the QTableWidget. The formats() and retrieveData() functions are reimplemented from QMimeData.

```
TableMimeData::TableMimeData(const QTableWidget *tableWidget,
                             const QTableWidgetSelectionRange &range)
{
    myTableWidget = tableWidget;
    myRange = range;
    myFormats << "text/csv" << "text/html" << "text/plain";
}
```

In the constructor, we initialize the private variables.

```
QStringList TableMimeData::formats() const
{
    return myFormats;
}
```

The formats() function returns a list of MIME types provided by the MIME data object. The precise order of the formats is usually irrelevant, but it's good practice to put the "best" formats first. Applications that support many formats will sometimes use the first one that matches.

```
QVariant TableMimeData::retrieveData(const QString &format,
                                     QVariant::Type preferredType) const
{
    if (format == "text/plain") {
        return rangeAsPlainText();
    } else if (format == "text/csv") {
        return toCsv(rangeAsPlainText());
    } else if (format == "text/html") {
        return toHtml(rangeAsPlainText());
    } else {
        return QMimeData::retrieveData(format, preferredType);
    }
}
```

The `retrieveData()` function returns the data for a given MIME type as a `QVariant`. The value of the `format` parameter is normally one of the strings returned by `formats()`, but we cannot assume that, since not all applications check the MIME type against `formats()`. The getter functions `text()`, `html()`, `urls()`, `imageData()`, `colorData()`, and `data()` provided by `QMimeData` are implemented in terms of `retrieveData()`.

The `preferredType` parameter gives us a hint about which type we should put in the `QVariant`. Here, we ignore it and trust `QMimeData` to convert the return value into the desired type, if necessary.

```
void MyTableWidget::dropEvent(QDropEvent *event)
{
    const TableMimeData *tableData =
            qobject_cast<const TableMimeData *>(event->mimeData());

    if (tableData) {
        const QTableWidget *otherTable = tableData->tableWidget();
        QTableWidgetSelectionRange otherRange = tableData->range();
        ...
        event->acceptProposedAction();
    } else if (event->mimeData()->hasFormat("text/csv")) {
        QByteArray csvData = event->mimeData()->data("text/csv");
        QString csvText = QString::fromUtf8(csvData);
        ...
        event->acceptProposedAction();
    } else if (event->mimeData()->hasFormat("text/plain")) {
        QString plainText = event->mimeData()->text();
        ...
        event->acceptProposedAction();
    }
    QTableWidget::mouseMoveEvent(event);
}
```

The `dropEvent()` function is similar to the one we had earlier in this section, but this time we optimize it by first checking whether we can safely cast the `QMimeData` object to a `TableMimeData`. If the `qobject_cast<T>()` works, this means the drag was originated by a `MyTableWidget` in the same application, and we can directly access the table data instead of going through QMimeData's API. If the cast fails, we extract the data the standard way.

In this example, we encoded the CSV text using the UTF-8 encoding. If we want to be certain of using the right encoding, we could use the charset parameter of the text/plain MIME type to specify an explicit encoding. Here are a few examples:

```
text/plain;charset=US-ASCII
text/plain;charset=ISO-8859-1
text/plain;charset=Shift_JIS
text/plain;charset=UTF-8
```

Clipboard Handling

Most applications make use of Qt's built-in clipboard handling in one way or another. For example, the QTextEdit class provides cut(), copy(), and paste() slots as well as keyboard shortcuts, so little or no additional code is required.

When writing our own classes, we can access the clipboard through QApplication::clipboard(), which returns a pointer to the application's QClipboard object. Handling the system clipboard is easy: Call setText(), setImage(), or setPixmap() to put data onto the clipboard, and call text(), image(), or pixmap() to retrieve data from the clipboard. We have already seen examples of clipboard use in the Spreadsheet application from Chapter 4.

For some applications, the built-in functionality might not be sufficient. For example, we might want to provide data that isn't just text or an image, or we might want to provide data in many different formats for maximum interoperability with other applications. The issue is very similar to what we encountered earlier with drag and drop, and the answer is also similar: We can subclass QMimeData and reimplement a few virtual functions.

If our application supports drag and drop through a custom QMimeData subclass, we can simply reuse the QMimeData subclass and put it on the clipboard using the setMimeData() function. To retrieve the data, we can call mimeData() on the clipboard.

On X11, it is usually possible to paste a selection by clicking the middle button of a three-button mouse. This is done using a separate "selection" clipboard. If you want your widgets to support this kind of clipboard as well as the standard one, you must pass QClipboard::Selection as an additional argument to the various clipboard calls. For example, here's how we would reimplement mouseReleaseEvent() in a text editor to support pasting using the middle mouse button:

```
void MyTextEditor::mouseReleaseEvent(QMouseEvent *event)
{
    QClipboard *clipboard = QApplication::clipboard();
    if (event->button() == Qt::MidButton
            && clipboard->supportsSelection()) {
        QString text = clipboard->text(QClipboard::Selection);
```

```
            pasteText(text);
        }
    }
```

On X11, the `supportsSelection()` function returns `true`. On other platforms, it returns `false`.

If we want to be notified whenever the clipboard's contents change, we can connect the `QClipboard::dataChanged()` signal to a custom slot.

- *Using the Item View Convenience Classes*
- *Using Predefined Models*
- *Implementing Custom Models*
- *Implementing Custom Delegates*

10. Item View Classes

Many applications let the user search, view, and edit individual items that belong to a data set. The data might be held in files or accessed from a database or a network server. The standard approach to dealing with data sets such as this is to use Qt's item view classes.

In earlier versions of Qt, the item view widgets were populated with the entire contents of a data set; the users would perform all their searches and edits on the data held in the widget, and at some point the changes would be written back to the data source. Although simple to understand and use, this approach doesn't scale very well to large data sets and doesn't lend itself to situations where we want to display the same data set in two or more different widgets.

The Smalltalk language popularized a flexible approach to visualizing large data sets: model–view–controller (MVC). In the MVC approach, the *model* represents the data set and is responsible for both fetching the data that is needed for viewing and saving back any changes. Each type of data set has its own model, but the API that the models provide to the views is uniform regardless of the underlying data set. The *view* presents the data to the user. With any large data set only a limited amount of data will be visible at any one time, so that is the only data that the view asks for. The *controller* mediates between the user and the view, converting user actions into requests to navigate or edit data, which the view then transmits to the model as necessary.

Qt provides a model/view architecture inspired by the MVC approach, as Figure 10.1 illustrates. In Qt, the model behaves the same as it does for classic MVC. But instead of a controller, Qt uses a slightly different abstraction: the *delegate*. The delegate is used to provide fine control over how items are rendered and edited. Qt provides a default delegate for every type of view. This is sufficient for most applications, so we usually don't need to care about it.

Using Qt's model/view architecture, we can use models that fetch only the data that is actually needed for display in the view, making it possible to handle very large data sets without compromising performance. And by registering a model with two or more views, we can give the user the opportunity to view and

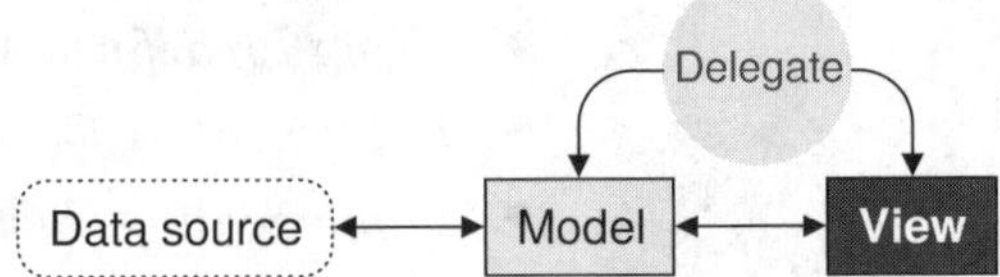

Figure 10.1. Qt's model/view architecture

interact with the data in different ways, with little overhead. Qt automatically keeps multiple views in sync, reflecting changes to one in all the others, as illustrated in Figure 10.2. An additional benefit of the model/view architecture is that if we decide to change how the underlying data set is stored, we just need to change the model; the views will continue to behave correctly.

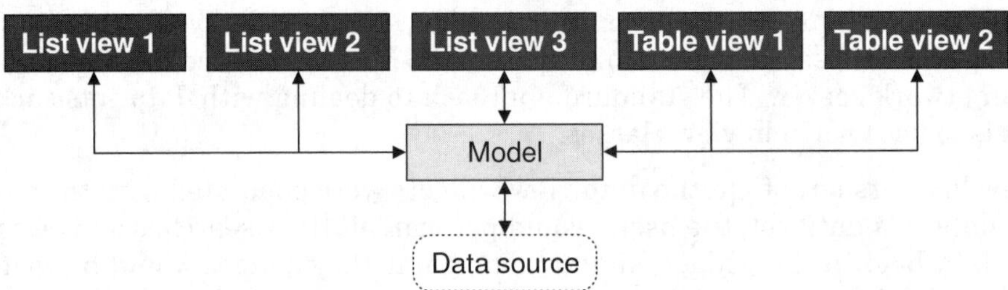

Figure 10.2. One model can serve multiple views

In many situations, we need to present only relatively small numbers of items to the user. In these common cases, we can use Qt's convenience item view classes (`QListWidget`, `QTableWidget`, and `QTreeWidget`) and populate them with items directly. These classes behave in a similar way to the item view classes provided by earlier versions of Qt. They store their data in "items" (e.g., a `QTableWidget` contains `QTableWidgetItem`s). Internally, the convenience classes use custom models that make the items visible to the views.

For large data sets, duplicating the data is often not an option. In these cases, we can use Qt's views (`QListView`, `QTableView`, and `QTreeView`) in conjunction with a data model, which can be a custom model or one of Qt's predefined models. For example, if the data set is held in a database, we can combine a `QTableView` with a `QSqlTableModel`.

Using the Item View Convenience Classes

Using Qt's item view convenience subclasses is usually simpler than defining a custom model and is appropriate when we don't need the benefits of separating the model and the view. We used this technique in Chapter 4 when we subclassed `QTableWidget` and `QTableWidgetItem` to implement spreadsheet functionality.

In this section, we will show how to use the convenience item view subclasses to display items. The first example shows a read-only `QListWidget` (Figure 10.3), the second example shows an editable QTableWidget (Figure 10.4), and the third example shows a read-only QTreeWidget (Figure 10.5).

We begin with a simple dialog that lets the user pick a flowchart symbol from a list. Each item consists of an icon, a text, and a unique ID.

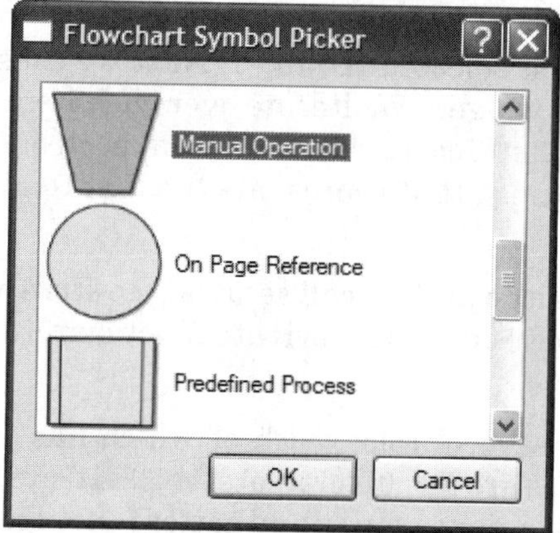

Figure 10.3. The Flowchart Symbol Picker application

Let's start with an extract from the dialog's header file:

```
class FlowChartSymbolPicker : public QDialog
{
    Q_OBJECT

public:
    FlowChartSymbolPicker(const QMap<int, QString> &symbolMap,
                          QWidget *parent = 0);

    int selectedId() const { return id; }
    void done(int result);
    ...
};
```

When we construct the dialog, we must pass it a QMap<int, QString>, and after it has executed we can retrieve the chosen ID (or −1 if the user didn't select any item) by calling selectedId().

```
FlowChartSymbolPicker::FlowChartSymbolPicker(
        const QMap<int, QString> &symbolMap, QWidget *parent)
    : QDialog(parent)
{
    id = -1;

    listWidget = new QListWidget;
    listWidget->setIconSize(QSize(60, 60));

    QMapIterator<int, QString> i(symbolMap);
    while (i.hasNext()) {
        i.next();
```

```
            QListWidgetItem *item = new QListWidgetItem(i.value(),
                                                        listWidget);
            item->setIcon(iconForSymbol(i.value()));
            item->setData(Qt::UserRole, i.key());
        }
        ...
    }
```

We initialize id (the last selected ID) to -1. Next we construct a QListWidget, a convenience item view widget. We iterate over each item in the flowchart symbol map and create a QListWidgetItem to represent each one. The QListWidgetItem constructor takes a QString that represents the text to display, followed by the parent QListWidget.

Then we set the item's icon and we call setData() to store our arbitrary ID in the QListWidgetItem. The iconForSymbol() private function returns a QIcon for a given symbol name.

QListWidgetItems have several roles, each of which has an associated QVariant. The most common roles are Qt::DisplayRole, Qt::EditRole, and Qt::IconRole, and for these there are convenience setter and getter functions (setText(), setIcon()), but there are several other roles. We can also define custom roles by specifying a numeric value of Qt::UserRole or higher. In our example, we use Qt::UserRole to store each item's ID.

The omitted part of the constructor is concerned with creating the buttons, laying out the widgets, and setting the window's title.

```
void FlowChartSymbolPicker::done(int result)
{
    id = -1;
    if (result == QDialog::Accepted) {
        QListWidgetItem *item = listWidget->currentItem();
        if (item)
            id = item->data(Qt::UserRole).toInt();
    }
    QDialog::done(result);
}
```

The done() function is reimplemented from QDialog. It is called when the user clicks OK or Cancel. If the user clicked OK, we retrieve the relevant item and extract the ID using the data() function. If we were interested in the item's text, we could retrieve it by calling item->data(Qt::DisplayRole).toString() or, more conveniently, item->text().

By default, QListWidget is read-only. If we wanted the user to edit the items, we could set the view's edit triggers using QAbstractItemView::setEditTriggers(); for example, a setting of QAbstractItemView::AnyKeyPressed means that the user can begin editing an item just by starting to type. Alternatively, we could provide an Edit button (and perhaps Add and Delete buttons) and use signal–slot connections so that we can handle the editing operations programmatically.

Now that we have seen how to use a convenience item view class for viewing and selecting data, we will look at an example in which we can edit data. Again we are using a dialog, this time one that presents a set of (x, y) coordinates that the user can edit.

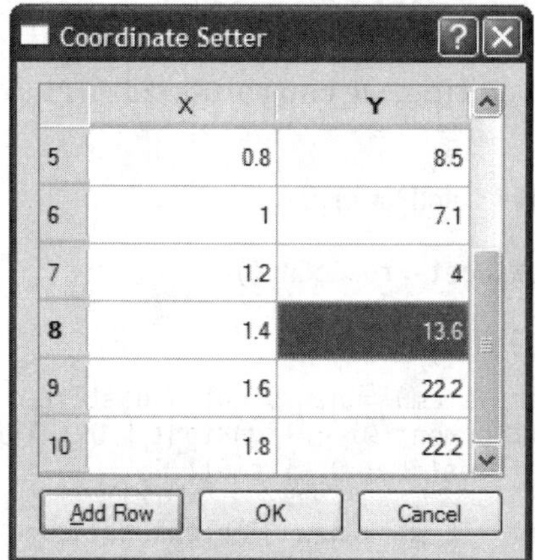

Figure 10.4. The Coordinate Setter application

As with the previous example, we will focus on the item view relevant code, starting with the constructor.

```
CoordinateSetter::CoordinateSetter(QList<QPointF> *coords,
                                   QWidget *parent)
    : QDialog(parent)
{
    coordinates = coords;

    tableWidget = new QTableWidget(0, 2);
    tableWidget->setHorizontalHeaderLabels(
            QStringList() << tr("X") << tr("Y"));

    for (int row = 0; row < coordinates->count(); ++row) {
        QPointF point = coordinates->at(row);
        addRow();
        tableWidget->item(row, 0)->setText(QString::number(point.x()));
        tableWidget->item(row, 1)->setText(QString::number(point.y()));
    }
    ...
}
```

The `QTableWidget` constructor takes the initial number of table rows and columns to display. Every item in a `QTableWidget` is represented by a `QTableWidgetItem`, including horizontal and vertical header items. The `setHorizontalHeaderLabels()` function sets the text for each horizontal table widget item to the corresponding text in the string list it is passed. By default, `QTableWidget` provides a vertical header with rows labeled from 1, which is exactly what we want, so we don't need to set the vertical header labels manually.

Once we have created the column labels, we iterate through the coordinate data that was passed in. For every (x, y) pair, we add a new row (using the private function addRow()) and set the text in each of the row's columns appropriately.

By default, QTableWidget allows editing. The user can edit any cell in the table by navigating to it and then either pressing F2 or simply by typing. All changes the user has made in the view will be automatically reflected into the QTableWidgetItems. To prevent editing, we can call setEditTriggers(QAbstractItemView::NoEditTriggers).

```
void CoordinateSetter::addRow()
{
    int row = tableWidget->rowCount();

    tableWidget->insertRow(row);

    QTableWidgetItem *item0 = new QTableWidgetItem;
    item0->setTextAlignment(Qt::AlignRight | Qt::AlignVCenter);
    tableWidget->setItem(row, 0, item0);

    QTableWidgetItem *item1 = new QTableWidgetItem;
    item1->setTextAlignment(Qt::AlignRight | Qt::AlignVCenter);
    tableWidget->setItem(row, 1, item1);

    tableWidget->setCurrentItem(item0);
}
```

The addRow() slot is invoked when the user clicks the Add Row button; it is also used in the constructor. We append a new row using QTableWidget::insertRow(). Then we create two QTableWidgetItems and add them to the table using QTableWidget::setItem(), which takes a row and a column in addition to the item. Finally, we set the current item so that the user can start editing the new row's first item.

```
void CoordinateSetter::done(int result)
{
    if (result == QDialog::Accepted) {
        coordinates->clear();
        for (int row = 0; row < tableWidget->rowCount(); ++row) {
            double x = tableWidget->item(row, 0)->text().toDouble();
            double y = tableWidget->item(row, 1)->text().toDouble();
            coordinates->append(QPointF(x, y));
        }
    }
    QDialog::done(result);
}
```

When the user clicks OK, we clear the coordinates that were passed in to the dialog, and create a new set based on the coordinates in the QTableWidget's items.

For our third and final example of Qt's convenience item view widgets, we will look at some snippets from an application that shows Qt application settings using a QTreeWidget. Read-only is the default for QTreeWidget.

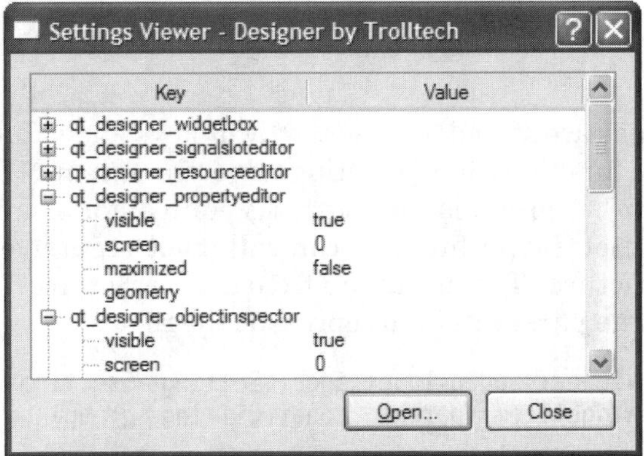

Figure 10.5. The Settings Viewer application

Here's an extract from the constructor:

```
SettingsViewer::SettingsViewer(QWidget *parent)
    : QDialog(parent)
{
    organization = "Trolltech";
    application = "Designer";

    treeWidget = new QTreeWidget;
    treeWidget->setColumnCount(2);
    treeWidget->setHeaderLabels(
            QStringList() << tr("Key") << tr("Value"));
    treeWidget->header()->setResizeMode(0, QHeaderView::Stretch);
    treeWidget->header()->setResizeMode(1, QHeaderView::Stretch);
    ...
    setWindowTitle(tr("Settings Viewer"));
    readSettings();
}
```

To access an application's settings, a `QSettings` object must be created with the organization's name and the application's name as parameters. We set default names ("Designer" by "Trolltech") and then construct a new `QTreeWidget`. The tree widget's header view governs the sizes of the tree's columns. We set both columns' resize mode to `Stretch`. This tells the header view to always make the columns fill the available space. In this mode, the columns cannot be resized by the user or programmatically. At the end of the constructor, we call the `readSettings()` function to populate the tree widget.

```
void SettingsViewer::readSettings()
{
    QSettings settings(organization, application);

    treeWidget->clear();
    addChildSettings(settings, 0, "");

    treeWidget->sortByColumn(0);
    treeWidget->setFocus();
```

```
    setWindowTitle(tr("Settings Viewer - %1 by %2")
                   .arg(application).arg(organization));
}
```

Application settings are stored in a hierarchy of keys and values. The addChildSettings() private function takes a settings object, a parent QTreeWidgetItem, and the current "group". A group is the QSettings equivalent of a file system directory. The addChildSettings() function can call itself recursively to traverse an arbitrary tree structure. The initial call from the readSettings() function passes a null pointer as the parent item to represent the root.

```
void SettingsViewer::addChildSettings(QSettings &settings,
        QTreeWidgetItem *parent, const QString &group)
{
    if (!parent)
        parent = treeWidget->invisibleRootItem();
    QTreeWidgetItem *item;

    settings.beginGroup(group);

    foreach (QString key, settings.childKeys()) {
        item = new QTreeWidgetItem(parent);
        item->setText(0, key);
        item->setText(1, settings.value(key).toString());
    }
    foreach (QString group, settings.childGroups()) {
        item = new QTreeWidgetItem(parent);
        item->setText(0, group);
        addChildSettings(settings, item, group);
    }
    settings.endGroup();
}
```

The addChildSettings() function is used to create all the QTreeWidgetItems. It iterates over all the keys at the current level in the settings hierarchy and creates one QTableWidgetItem per key. If a null pointer was passed as the parent item, we create the item as a child of QTreeWidget::invisibleRootItem(), making it a top-level item. The first column is set to the name of the key and the second column to the corresponding value.

Next, the function iterates over every group at the current level. For each group, a new QTreeWidgetItem is created with its first column set to the group's name. The function then calls itself recursively with the group item as the parent to populate the QTreeWidget with the group's child items.

The item view widgets shown in this section allow us to use a style of programming that is very similar to that used in earlier versions of Qt: reading an entire data set into an item view widget, using item objects to represent data elements, and (if the items are editable) writing back to the data source. In the following sections, we will go beyond this simple approach and take full advantage of Qt's model/view architecture.

Using Predefined Models

Qt provides several predefined models for use with the view classes:

QStringListModel	Stores a list of strings
QStandardItemModel	Stores arbitrary hierarchical data
QDirModel	Encapsulates the local file system
QSqlQueryModel	Encapsulates an SQL result set
QSqlTableModel	Encapsulates an SQL table
QSqlRelationalTableModel	Encapsulates an SQL table with foreign keys
QSortFilterProxyModel	Sorts and/or filters another model

In this section, we will look at how to use `QStringListModel`, `QDirModel`, and `QSortFilterProxyModel`. We cover the SQL models in Chapter 13.

Let's begin with a simple dialog that users can use to add, delete, and edit a `QStringList`, where each string represents a team leader. The dialog is shown in Figure 10.6.

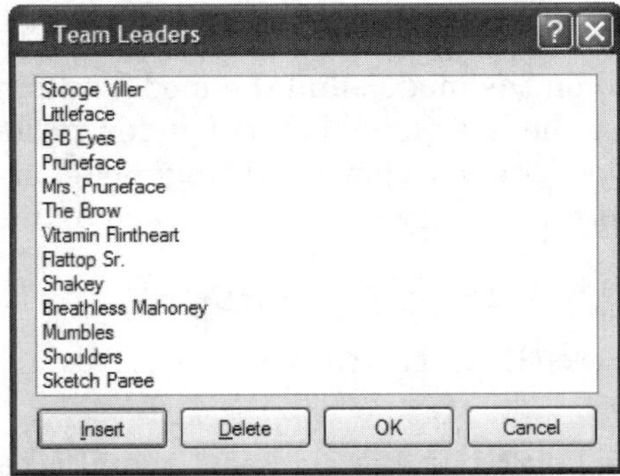

Figure 10.6. The Team Leaders application

Here's the relevant extract from the constructor:

```
TeamLeadersDialog::TeamLeadersDialog(const QStringList &leaders,
                                     QWidget *parent)
    : QDialog(parent)
{
    model = new QStringListModel(this);
    model->setStringList(leaders);

    listView = new QListView;
    listView->setModel(model);
    listView->setEditTriggers(QAbstractItemView::AnyKeyPressed
                              | QAbstractItemView::DoubleClicked);
    ...
}
```

We begin by creating and populating a QStringListModel. Next we create a QListView and set its model to the one we have just created. We also set some editing triggers to allow the user to edit a string simply by starting to type on it or by double-clicking it. By default, no editing triggers are set on a QListView, making the view effectively read-only.

```
void TeamLeadersDialog::insert()
{
    int row = listView->currentIndex().row();
    model->insertRows(row, 1);

    QModelIndex index = model->index(row);
    listView->setCurrentIndex(index);
    listView->edit(index);
}
```

When the user clicks the Insert button, the insert() slot is invoked. The slot begins by retrieving the row number for the list view's current item. Every data item in a model has a corresponding "model index", which is represented by a QModelIndex object. We will look at model indexes in detail in the next section, but for now it is sufficient to know that an index has three main components: a row, a column, and a pointer to the model to which it belongs. For a one-dimensional list model, the column is always 0.

Once we have the row number, we insert one new row at that position. The insertion is performed on the model, and the model automatically updates the list view. We then set the list view's current index to the blank row we just inserted. Finally, we set the list view to editing mode on the new row, just as though the user had pressed a key or double-clicked to initiate editing.

```
void TeamLeadersDialog::del()
{
    model->removeRows(listView->currentIndex().row(), 1);
}
```

In the constructor, the Delete button's clicked() signal is connected to the del() slot. Since we are just deleting the current row, we can call removeRows() with the current index position and a row count of 1. Just like with insertion, we rely on the model to update the view accordingly.

```
QStringList TeamLeadersDialog::leaders() const
{
    return model->stringList();
}
```

Finally, the leaders() function provides a means of reading back the edited strings when the dialog is closed.

TeamLeadersDialog could be made into a generic string list editing dialog simply by parameterizing its window title. Another generic dialog that is often required is one that presents a list of files or directories to the user. The next example, shown in Figure 10.7, uses the QDirModel class, which encapsulates the computer's file system and is capable of showing (and hiding) various file attributes. This model can apply a filter to restrict the kinds of file system entries that are shown and can order the entries in various ways.

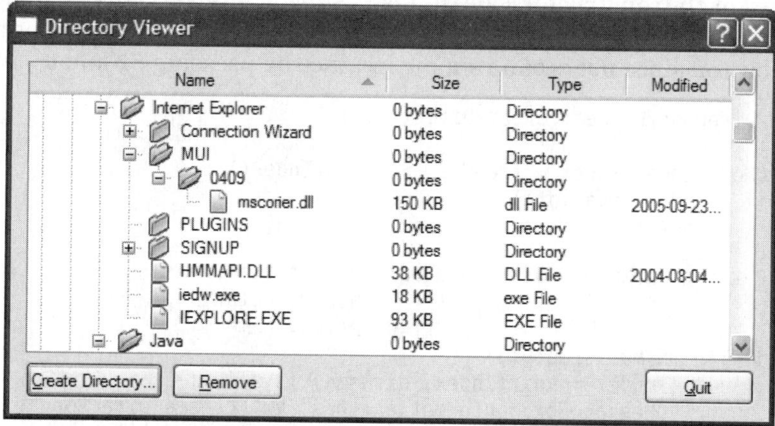

Figure 10.7. The Directory Viewer application

We will begin by looking at the creation and setting up of the model and the view in the Directory Viewer dialog's constructor.

```
DirectoryViewer::DirectoryViewer(QWidget *parent)
    : QDialog(parent)
{
    model = new QDirModel;
    model->setReadOnly(false);
    model->setSorting(QDir::DirsFirst | QDir::IgnoreCase | QDir::Name);

    treeView = new QTreeView;
    treeView->setModel(model);
    treeView->header()->setStretchLastSection(true);
    treeView->header()->setSortIndicator(0, Qt::AscendingOrder);
    treeView->header()->setSortIndicatorShown(true);
    treeView->header()->setClickable(true);

    QModelIndex index = model->index(QDir::currentPath());
    treeView->expand(index);
    treeView->scrollTo(index);
    treeView->resizeColumnToContents(0);
    ...
}
```

Once the model has been constructed, we make it editable and set various initial sort ordering attributes. We then create the `QTreeView` that will display the model's data. The `QTreeView`'s header can be used to provide user-controlled sorting. By making the header clickable, the user can sort by whichever column header they click, with repeated clicks alternating between ascending and descending orders. Once the tree view's header has been set up, we get the model index of the current directory and make sure that this directory is visible by expanding its parents if necessary using expand(), and scrolling to it using scrollTo(). Then we make sure that the first column is wide enough to show all its entries without using ellipses (...).

In the part of the constructor code that isn't shown here, we connected the Create Directory and Remove buttons to slots to perform these actions. We do not need a Rename button since users can rename in-place by pressing F2 and typing.

```
void DirectoryViewer::createDirectory()
{
    QModelIndex index = treeView->currentIndex();
    if (!index.isValid())
        return;

    QString dirName = QInputDialog::getText(this,
                              tr("Create Directory"),
                              tr("Directory name"));
    if (!dirName.isEmpty()) {
        if (!model->mkdir(index, dirName).isValid())
            QMessageBox::information(this, tr("Create Directory"),
                    tr("Failed to create the directory"));
    }
}
```

If the user enters a directory name in the input dialog, we attempt to create a directory with this name as a child of the current directory. The QDirModel::mkdir() function takes the parent directory's index and the name of the new directory, and returns the model index of the directory it created. If the operation fails, it returns an invalid model index.

```
void DirectoryViewer::remove()
{
    QModelIndex index = treeView->currentIndex();
    if (!index.isValid())
        return;

    bool ok;
    if (model->fileInfo(index).isDir()) {
        ok = model->rmdir(index);
    } else {
        ok = model->remove(index);
    }
    if (!ok)
        QMessageBox::information(this, tr("Remove"),
                tr("Failed to remove %1").arg(model->fileName(index)));
}
```

If the user clicks Remove, we attempt to remove the file or directory associated with the current item. We could use QDir to accomplish this, but QDirModel offers convenience functions that work on QModelIndexes.

The last example in this section, shown in Figure 10.8, demonstrates how to use QSortFilterProxyModel. Unlike the other predefined models, this model encapsulates an existing model and manipulates the data that passes between the underlying model and the view. In our example, the underlying model is a QStringListModel initialized with the list of color names recognized by Qt (obtained through QColor::colorNames()). The user can type a filter string in a QLineEdit and specify how this string is to be interpreted (as a regular expression, a wildcard pattern, or a fixed string) using a combobox.

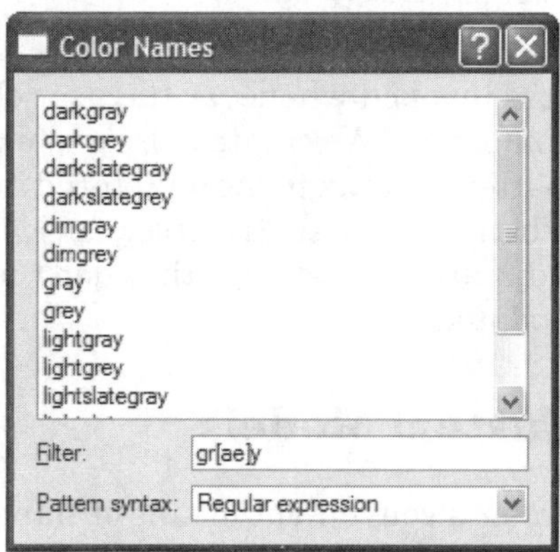

Figure 10.8. The Color Names application

Here's an extract from the ColorNamesDialog constructor:

```
ColorNamesDialog::ColorNamesDialog(QWidget *parent)
    : QDialog(parent)
{
    sourceModel = new QStringListModel(this);
    sourceModel->setStringList(QColor::colorNames());

    proxyModel = new QSortFilterProxyModel(this);
    proxyModel->setSourceModel(sourceModel);
    proxyModel->setFilterKeyColumn(0);

    listView = new QListView;
    listView->setModel(proxyModel);
    ...
    syntaxComboBox = new QComboBox;
    syntaxComboBox->addItem(tr("Regular expression"), QRegExp::RegExp);
    syntaxComboBox->addItem(tr("Wildcard"), QRegExp::Wildcard);
    syntaxComboBox->addItem(tr("Fixed string"), QRegExp::FixedString);
    ...
}
```

The QStringListModel is created and populated in the usual way. This is followed by the construction of the QSortFilterProxyModel. We pass the underlying model using setSourceModel() and tell the proxy to filter based on column 0 of the original model. The QComboBox::addItem() function accepts an optional "data" argument of type QVariant; we use this to store the QRegExp::PatternSyntax value that corresponds to each item's text.

```
void ColorNamesDialog::reapplyFilter()
{
    QRegExp::PatternSyntax syntax =
            QRegExp::PatternSyntax(syntaxComboBox->itemData(
                    syntaxComboBox->currentIndex()).toInt());
    QRegExp regExp(filterLineEdit->text(), Qt::CaseInsensitive, syntax);
    proxyModel->setFilterRegExp(regExp);
}
```

The `reapplyFilter()` slot is invoked whenever the user changes the filter string or the pattern syntax combobox. We create a `QRegExp` using the text in the line editor. Then we set its pattern syntax to the one stored in the syntax combobox's current item's data. When we call `setFilterRegExp()`, the new filter becomes active, meaning that it discards any strings that don't match the filter and the view is automatically updated.

Implementing Custom Models

Qt's predefined models offer a convenient means of handling and viewing data. However, some data sources cannot be used efficiently using the predefined models, and for these situations it is necessary to create custom models optimized for the underlying data source.

Before we embark on creating custom models, let's first review the key concepts used in Qt's model/view architecture. Every data element in a model has a model index and a set of attributes, called *roles*, that can take arbitrary values. We saw earlier in the chapter that the most commonly used roles are `Qt::DisplayRole` and `Qt::EditRole`. Other roles are used for supplementary data (e.g., `Qt::ToolTipRole`, `Qt::StatusTipRole`, and `Qt::WhatsThisRole`), and yet others for controlling basic display attributes (such as `Qt::FontRole`, `Qt::TextAlignmentRole`, `Qt::TextColorRole`, and `Qt::BackgroundColorRole`).

For a list model, the only relevant index component is the row number, accessible from `QModelIndex::row()`. For a table model, the relevant index components are the row and column numbers, accessible from `QModelIndex::row()` and `QModelIndex::column()`. For both list and table models, every item's parent is the root, which is represented by an invalid `QModelIndex`. The first two examples in this section show how to implement custom table models.

A tree model is similar to a table model, with the following differences. Like a table model, the parent of top-level items is the root (an invalid `QModelIndex`), but every other item's parent is some other item in the hierarchy. Parents are accessible from `QModelIndex::parent()`. Every item has its role data, and zero or more children, each an item in its own right. Since items can have other items as children, it is possible to represent recursive (tree-like) data structures, as the final example in this section will show. Figure 10.9 shows a schematic of the different models.

The first example in this section is a read-only table model that shows currency values in relation to each other. The application is shown in Figure 10.10.

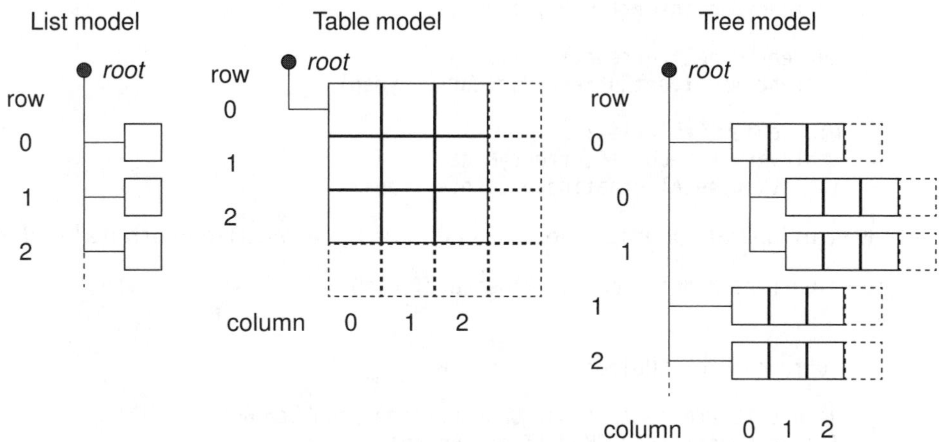

Figure 10.9. Schematic view of Qt's models

The application could be implemented using a simple table, but we want to use a custom model to take advantage of certain properties of the data to minimize storage. If we were to store the 162 currently traded currencies in a table, we would need to store $162 \times 162 = 26\,244$ values; with the custom `CurrencyModel` shown in this section, we need to store only 162 values (the value of each currency in relation to the U.S. dollar).

Currencies

	NOK	NZD	SEK	SGD	USD
NOK	1.0000	0.2254	1.1991	0.2592	0.1534
NZD	4.4363	1.0000	5.3195	1.1500	0.6804
SEK	0.8340	0.1880	1.0000	0.2162	0.1279
SGD	3.8578	0.8696	4.6258	1.0000	0.5917
USD	6.5200	1.4697	7.8180	1.6901	1.0000

Figure 10.10. The Currencies application

The `CurrencyModel` class will be used with a standard `QTableView`. The `CurrencyModel` is populated with a `QMap<QString,double>`; each key is a currency code and each value is the value of the currency in U.S. dollars. Here's a code snippet that shows how the map is populated and how the model is used:

```
QMap<QString, double> currencyMap;
currencyMap.insert("AUD", 1.3259);
currencyMap.insert("CHF", 1.2970);
...
currencyMap.insert("SGD", 1.6901);
```

```
    currencyMap.insert("USD", 1.0000);

    CurrencyModel currencyModel;
    currencyModel.setCurrencyMap(currencyMap);

    QTableView tableView;
    tableView.setModel(&currencyModel);
    tableView.setAlternatingRowColors(true);
```

Now we can look at the implementation of the model, starting with its header:

```
class CurrencyModel : public QAbstractTableModel
{
public:
    CurrencyModel(QObject *parent = 0);

    void setCurrencyMap(const QMap<QString, double> &map);
    int rowCount(const QModelIndex &parent) const;
    int columnCount(const QModelIndex &parent) const;
    QVariant data(const QModelIndex &index, int role) const;
    QVariant headerData(int section, Qt::Orientation orientation,
                        int role) const;

private:
    QString currencyAt(int offset) const;

    QMap<QString, double> currencyMap;
};
```

We have chosen to subclass QAbstractTableModel for our model since that most closely matches our data source. Qt provides several model base classes, including QAbstractListModel, QAbstractTableModel, and QAbstractItemModel; see Figure 10.11. The QAbstractItemModel class is used to support a wide variety of models, including those that are based on recursive data structures, while the QAbstractListModel and QAbstractTableModel classes are provided for convenience when using one-dimensional or two-dimensional data sets.

For a read-only table model, we must reimplement three functions: rowCount(), columnCount(), and data(). In this case, we have also reimplemented headerData(), and we provide a function to initialize the data (setCurrencyMap()).

```
CurrencyModel::CurrencyModel(QObject *parent)
    : QAbstractTableModel(parent)
{
}
```

We do not need to do anything in the constructor, except pass the parent parameter to the base class.

```
int CurrencyModel::rowCount(const QModelIndex & /* parent */) const
{
    return currencyMap.count();
}

int CurrencyModel::columnCount(const QModelIndex & /* parent */) const
{
```

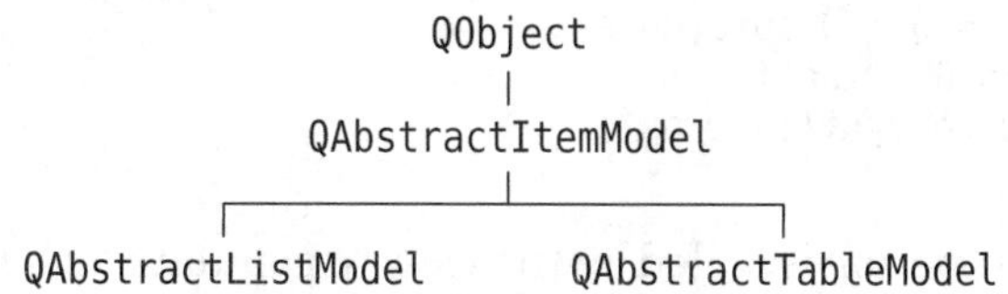

Figure 10.11. Inheritance tree for the abstract model classes

```
        return currencyMap.count();
    }
```

For this table model, the row and column counts are the number of currencies in the currency map. The `parent` parameter has no meaning for a table model; it is there because `rowCount()` and `columnCount()` are inherited from the more generic `QAbstractItemModel` base class, which supports hierarchies.

```
QVariant CurrencyModel::data(const QModelIndex &index, int role) const
{
    if (!index.isValid())
        return QVariant();

    if (role == Qt::TextAlignmentRole) {
        return int(Qt::AlignRight | Qt::AlignVCenter);
    } else if (role == Qt::DisplayRole) {
        QString rowCurrency = currencyAt(index.row());
        QString columnCurrency = currencyAt(index.column());

        if (currencyMap.value(rowCurrency) == 0.0)
            return "####";

        double amount = currencyMap.value(columnCurrency)
                        / currencyMap.value(rowCurrency);

        return QString("%1").arg(amount, 0, 'f', 4);
    }
    return QVariant();
}
```

The `data()` function returns the value of any of an item's roles. The item is specified as a `QModelIndex`. For a table model, the interesting components of a `QModelIndex` are its row and column number, available using `row()` and `column()`.

If the role is `Qt::TextAlignmentRole`, we return an alignment suitable for numbers. If the display role is `Qt::DisplayRole`, we look up the value for each currency and calculate the exchange rate.

We could return the calculated value as a `double`, but then we would have no control over how many decimal places were shown (unless we use a custom delegate). Instead, we return the value as a string, formatted as we want.

```
QVariant CurrencyModel::headerData(int section,
                                   Qt::Orientation /* orientation */,
                                   int role) const
{
```

```
    if (role != Qt::DisplayRole)
        return QVariant();
    return currencyAt(section);
}
```

The headerData() function is called by the view to populate its horizontal and vertical headers. The section parameter is the row or column number (depending on the orientation). Since the rows and columns have the same currency codes, we do not care about the orientation and simply return the code of the currency for the given section number.

```
void CurrencyModel::setCurrencyMap(const QMap<QString, double> &map)
{
    currencyMap = map;
    reset();
}
```

The caller can change the currency map using setCurrencyMap(). The QAbstractItemModel::reset() call tells any views that are using the model that all their data is invalid; this forces them to request fresh data for the items that are visible.

```
QString CurrencyModel::currencyAt(int offset) const
{
    return (currencyMap.begin() + offset).key();
}
```

The currencyAt() function returns the key (the currency code) at the given offset in the currency map. We use an STL-style iterator to find the item and call key() on it.

As we have just seen, it is not difficult to create read-only models, and depending on the nature of the underlying data, there are potential savings in memory and speed with a well-designed model. The next example, the Cities application shown in Figure 10.12, is also table-based, but this time all the data is entered by the user.

This application is used to store values indicating the distance between any two cities. Like the previous example, we could simply use a QTableWidget and store one item for every city pair. However, a custom model could be more efficient, because the distance from any city $\mathcal{A}$ to any different city $\mathcal{B}$ is the same whether traveling from $\mathcal{A}$ to $\mathcal{B}$ or from $\mathcal{B}$ to $\mathcal{A}$, so the items are mirrored along the main diagonal.

To see how a custom model compares with a simple table, let us assume that we have three cities, $\mathcal{A}$, $\mathcal{B}$, and $\mathcal{C}$. If we store a value for every combination, we would need to store nine values. A carefully designed model would require only the three items ($\mathcal{A}$, $\mathcal{B}$), ($\mathcal{A}$, $\mathcal{C}$), and ($\mathcal{B}$, $\mathcal{C}$).

Here's how we set up and use the model:

```
    QStringList cities;
    cities << "Arvika" << "Boden" << "Eskilstuna" << "Falun"
```

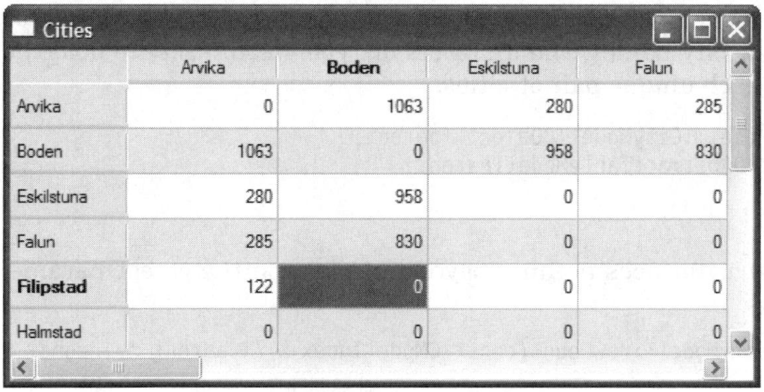

Figure 10.12. The Cities application

```
            << "Filipstad" << "Halmstad" << "Helsingborg" << "Karlstad"
            << "Kiruna" << "Kramfors" << "Motala" << "Sandviken"
            << "Skara" << "Stockholm" << "Sundsvall" << "Trelleborg";

    CityModel cityModel;
    cityModel.setCities(cities);

    QTableView tableView;
    tableView.setModel(&cityModel);
    tableView.setAlternatingRowColors(true);
```

We must reimplement the same functions as we did for the previous example. In addition, we must also reimplement `setData()` and `flags()` to make the model editable. Here is the class definition:

```
class CityModel : public QAbstractTableModel
{
    Q_OBJECT

public:
    CityModel(QObject *parent = 0);

    void setCities(const QStringList &cityNames);
    int rowCount(const QModelIndex &parent) const;
    int columnCount(const QModelIndex &parent) const;
    QVariant data(const QModelIndex &index, int role) const;
    bool setData(const QModelIndex &index, const QVariant &value,
                 int role);
    QVariant headerData(int section, Qt::Orientation orientation,
                        int role) const;
    Qt::ItemFlags flags(const QModelIndex &index) const;

private:
    int offsetOf(int row, int column) const;

    QStringList cities;
    QVector<int> distances;
};
```

For this model, we are using two data structures: cities of type QStringList to hold the city names, and distances of type QVector<int> to hold the distance between each unique pair of cities.

```
CityModel::CityModel(QObject *parent)
    : QAbstractTableModel(parent)
{
}
```

The constructor does nothing beyond passing on the parent parameter to the base class.

```
int CityModel::rowCount(const QModelIndex & /* parent */) const
{
    return cities.count();
}

int CityModel::columnCount(const QModelIndex & /* parent */) const
{
    return cities.count();
}
```

Since we have a square grid of cities, the number of rows and columns is the number of cities in our list.

```
QVariant CityModel::data(const QModelIndex &index, int role) const
{
    if (!index.isValid())
        return QVariant();

    if (role == Qt::TextAlignmentRole) {
        return int(Qt::AlignRight | Qt::AlignVCenter);
    } else if (role == Qt::DisplayRole) {
        if (index.row() == index.column())
            return 0;
        int offset = offsetOf(index.row(), index.column());
        return distances[offset];
    }
    return QVariant();
}
```

The data() function is similar to what we did in CurrencyModel. It returns 0 if the row and column are the same, because that corresponds to the case where the two cities are the same; otherwise, it finds the entry for the given row and column in the distances vector and returns the distance for that particular pair of cities.

```
QVariant CityModel::headerData(int section,
                               Qt::Orientation /* orientation */,
                               int role) const
{
    if (role == Qt::DisplayRole)
        return cities[section];
    return QVariant();
}
```

The headerData() function is simple because we have a square table with every row having an identical column header. We simply return the name of the city at the given offset in the cities string list.

```
bool CityModel::setData(const QModelIndex &index,
                        const QVariant &value, int role)
{
    if (index.isValid() && index.row() != index.column()
            && role == Qt::EditRole) {
        int offset = offsetOf(index.row(), index.column());
        distances[offset] = value.toInt();

        QModelIndex transposedIndex = createIndex(index.column(),
                                                  index.row());
        emit dataChanged(index, index);
        emit dataChanged(transposedIndex, transposedIndex);
        return true;
    }
    return false;
}
```

The setData() function is called when the user edits an item. Providing the model index is valid, the two cities are different, and the data element to modify is the Qt::EditRole, the function stores the value the user entered in the distances vector.

The createIndex() function is used to generate a model index. We need it to get the model index of the item on the other side of the main diagonal that corresponds with the item being set, since both items must show the same data. The createIndex() function takes the row before the column; here we invert the parameters to get the model index of the diagonally opposite item to the one specified by index.

We emit the dataChanged() signal with the model index of the item that was changed. This signal takes two model indexes because it is possible for a change to affect a rectangular region of more than one row and column, so the indexes passed are the index of the top-left and bottom-right items of those that have changed. We also emit the dataChanged() signal for the transposed index to ensure that the view will refresh the item. Finally, we return true or false to indicate whether the edit succeeded.

```
Qt::ItemFlags CityModel::flags(const QModelIndex &index) const
{
    Qt::ItemFlags flags = QAbstractItemModel::flags(index);
    if (index.row() != index.column())
        flags |= Qt::ItemIsEditable;
    return flags;
}
```

The model uses the flags() function to communicate what can be done with an item (e.g., whether it is editable). The default implementation from QAbstractTableModel returns Qt::ItemIsSelectable | Qt::ItemIsEnabled. We add the Qt::

`ItemIsEditable` flag for all items except those lying on the diagonals (which are always 0).

```
void CityModel::setCities(const QStringList &cityNames)
{
    cities = cityNames;
    distances.resize(cities.count() * (cities.count() - 1) / 2);
    distances.fill(0);
    reset();
}
```

If a new list of cities is given, we set the private `QStringList` to the new list, resize and clear the `distances` vector, and call `QAbstractItemModel::reset()` to notify any views that their visible items must be refetched.

```
int CityModel::offsetOf(int row, int column) const
{
    if (row < column)
        qSwap(row, column);
    return (row * (row - 1) / 2) + column;
}
```

The `offsetOf()` private function computes the index of a given city pair in the `distances` vector. For example, if we had cities $\mathcal{A}$, $\mathcal{B}$, $\mathcal{C}$, and $\mathcal{D}$, and the user updated row 3, column 1 ($\mathcal{B}$ to $\mathcal{D}$), the offset would be $3 \times (3 - 1)/2 + 1 = 4$. If the user had instead updated row 1, column 3 ($\mathcal{D}$ to $\mathcal{B}$), thanks to the `qSwap()` call, exactly the same calculation would be performed and an identical offset would be returned. Figure 10.13 illustrates the relationships between cities, distances, and the corresponding table model.

Cities

$\mathcal{A}$	$\mathcal{B}$	$\mathcal{C}$	$\mathcal{D}$

Distances

$\mathcal{A}\leftrightarrow\mathcal{B}$	$\mathcal{A}\leftrightarrow\mathcal{C}$	$\mathcal{A}\leftrightarrow\mathcal{D}$	$\mathcal{B}\leftrightarrow\mathcal{C}$	$\mathcal{B}\leftrightarrow\mathcal{D}$	$\mathcal{C}\leftrightarrow\mathcal{D}$

Table model

	$\mathcal{A}$	$\mathcal{B}$	$\mathcal{C}$	$\mathcal{D}$
$\mathcal{A}$	0	$\mathcal{A}\leftrightarrow\mathcal{B}$	$\mathcal{A}\leftrightarrow\mathcal{C}$	$\mathcal{A}\leftrightarrow\mathcal{D}$
$\mathcal{B}$	$\mathcal{A}\leftrightarrow\mathcal{B}$	0	$\mathcal{B}\leftrightarrow\mathcal{C}$	$\mathcal{B}\leftrightarrow\mathcal{D}$
$\mathcal{C}$	$\mathcal{A}\leftrightarrow\mathcal{C}$	$\mathcal{B}\leftrightarrow\mathcal{C}$	0	$\mathcal{C}\leftrightarrow\mathcal{D}$
$\mathcal{D}$	$\mathcal{A}\leftrightarrow\mathcal{D}$	$\mathcal{B}\leftrightarrow\mathcal{D}$	$\mathcal{C}\leftrightarrow\mathcal{D}$	0

Figure 10.13. The `cities` and `distances` data structures and the table model

The last example in this section is a model that shows the parse tree for a given Boolean expression. A Boolean expression is either a simple alphanumeric identifier, such as "bravo", a complex expression built from simpler expressions using the "&&", "||", or "!" operators, or a parenthesized expression. For example, "a || (b && !c)" is a Boolean expression.

The Boolean Parser application, shown in Figure 10.14, consists of four classes:

- `BooleanWindow` is a window that lets the user enter a Boolean expression and shows the corresponding parse tree.

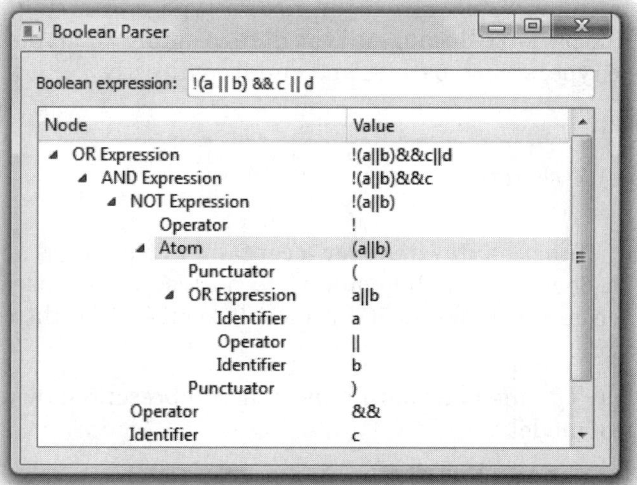

Figure 10.14. The Boolean Parser application

- `BooleanParser` generates a parse tree from a Boolean expression.
- `BooleanModel` is a tree model that encapsulates a parse tree.
- `Node` represents an item in a parse tree.

Let's start with the `Node` class:

```
class Node
{
public:
    enum Type { Root, OrExpression, AndExpression, NotExpression, Atom,
                Identifier, Operator, Punctuator };

    Node(Type type, const QString &str = "");
    ~Node();

    Type type;
    QString str;
    Node *parent;
    QList<Node *> children;
};
```

Every node has a type, a string (which may be empty), a parent (which may be null), and a list of child nodes (which may be empty).

```
Node::Node(Type type, const QString &str)
{
    this->type = type;
    this->str = str;
    parent = 0;
}
```

The constructor simply initializes the node's type and string, and sets the parent to null (no parent). Because all the data is public, code that uses Node can manipulate the type, string, parent, and children directly.

```
Node::~Node()
{
    qDeleteAll(children);
}
```

The qDeleteAll() function iterates over a container of pointers and calls delete on each one. It does not set the pointers to null, so if it is used outside of a destructor it is common to follow it with a call to clear() on the container that holds the pointers.

Now that we have defined our data items (each represented by a Node), we are ready to create a model:

```
class BooleanModel : public QAbstractItemModel
{
public:
    BooleanModel(QObject *parent = 0);
    ~BooleanModel();

    void setRootNode(Node *node);

    QModelIndex index(int row, int column,
                      const QModelIndex &parent) const;
    QModelIndex parent(const QModelIndex &child) const;

    int rowCount(const QModelIndex &parent) const;
    int columnCount(const QModelIndex &parent) const;
    QVariant data(const QModelIndex &index, int role) const;
    QVariant headerData(int section, Qt::Orientation orientation,
                        int role) const;

private:
    Node *nodeFromIndex(const QModelIndex &index) const;

    Node *rootNode;
};
```

This time we have used QAbstractItemModel as the base class rather than its convenience subclass QAbstractTableModel, because we want to create a hierarchical model. The essential functions that we must reimplement remain the same, except that we must also implement index() and parent(). To set the model's data, we have a setRootNode() function that must be called with a parse tree's root node.

```
BooleanModel::BooleanModel(QObject *parent)
    : QAbstractItemModel(parent)
{
    rootNode = 0;
}
```

In the model's constructor, we just need to set the root node to a safe null value and pass on the parent to the base class.

```
BooleanModel::~BooleanModel()
{
    delete rootNode;
}
```

In the destructor, we delete the root node. If the root node has children, each of these is deleted, and so on recursively, by the Node destructor.

```
void BooleanModel::setRootNode(Node *node)
{
    delete rootNode;
    rootNode = node;
    reset();
}
```

When a new root node is set, we begin by deleting any previous root node (and all of its children). Then we set the new root node and call reset() to notify any views that they must refetch the data for any visible items.

```
QModelIndex BooleanModel::index(int row, int column,
                                const QModelIndex &parent) const
{
    if (!rootNode || row < 0 || column < 0)
        return QModelIndex();
    Node *parentNode = nodeFromIndex(parent);
    Node *childNode = parentNode->children.value(row);
    if (!childNode)
        return QModelIndex();
    return createIndex(row, column, childNode);
}
```

The index() function is reimplemented from QAbstractItemModel. It is called whenever the model or the view needs to create a QModelIndex for a particular child item (or a top-level item if parent is an invalid QModelIndex). For table and list models, we don't need to reimplement this function, because QAbstractList-Model's and QAbstractTableModel's default implementations normally suffice.

In our index() implementation, if no parse tree is set, we return an invalid QModelIndex. Otherwise, we create a QModelIndex with the given row and column and with a Node * for the requested child. For hierarchical models, knowing the row and column of an item relative to its parent is not enough to uniquely identify it; we must also know *who* its parent is. To solve this, we can store a pointer to the internal node in the QModelIndex. QModelIndex gives us the option of storing a void * or an int in addition to the row and column numbers.

The Node * for the child is obtained through the parent node's children list. The parent node is extracted from the parent model index using the nodeFromIndex() private function:

```
Node *BooleanModel::nodeFromIndex(const QModelIndex &index) const
{
```

```
    if (index.isValid()) {
        return static_cast<Node *>(index.internalPointer());
    } else {
        return rootNode;
    }
}
```

The `nodeFromIndex()` function casts the given index's `void *` to a `Node *`, or returns the root node if the index is invalid, since an invalid model index is used to represent the root in a model.

```
int BooleanModel::rowCount(const QModelIndex &parent) const
{
    if (parent.column() > 0)
        return 0;
    Node *parentNode = nodeFromIndex(parent);
    if (!parentNode)
        return 0;
    return parentNode->children.count();
}
```

The number of rows for a given item is simply how many children it has.

```
int BooleanModel::columnCount(const QModelIndex & /* parent */) const
{
    return 2;
}
```

The number of columns is fixed at 2. The first column holds the node types; the second column holds the node values.

```
QModelIndex BooleanModel::parent(const QModelIndex &child) const
{
    Node *node = nodeFromIndex(child);
    if (!node)
        return QModelIndex();
    Node *parentNode = node->parent;
    if (!parentNode)
        return QModelIndex();
    Node *grandparentNode = parentNode->parent;
    if (!grandparentNode)
        return QModelIndex();

    int row = grandparentNode->children.indexOf(parentNode);
    return createIndex(row, 0, parentNode);
}
```

Retrieving the parent `QModelIndex` from a child is a bit more work than finding a parent's child. We can easily retrieve the parent node using `nodeFromIndex()` and going up using the `Node`'s parent pointer, but to obtain the row number (the position of the parent among its siblings), we need to go back to the grandparent and find the parent's index position in its parent's (i.e., the child's grandparent's) list of children.

```
QVariant BooleanModel::data(const QModelIndex &index, int role) const
{
```

```
    if (role != Qt::DisplayRole)
        return QVariant();

    Node *node = nodeFromIndex(index);
    if (!node)
        return QVariant();

    if (index.column() == 0) {
        switch (node->type) {
        case Node::Root:
             return tr("Root");
        case Node::OrExpression:
            return tr("OR Expression");
        case Node::AndExpression:
            return tr("AND Expression");
        case Node::NotExpression:
            return tr("NOT Expression");
        case Node::Atom:
            return tr("Atom");
        case Node::Identifier:
            return tr("Identifier");
        case Node::Operator:
            return tr("Operator");
        case Node::Punctuator:
            return tr("Punctuator");
        default:
            return tr("Unknown");
        }
    } else if (index.column() == 1) {
        return node->str;
    }
    return QVariant();
}
```

In `data()`, we retrieve the `Node` * for the requested item and we use it to access the underlying data. If the caller wants a value for any role except `Qt::DisplayRole` or if we cannot retrieve a `Node` for the given model index, we return an invalid `QVariant`. If the column is 0, we return the name of the node's type; if the column is 1, we return the node's value (its string).

```
QVariant BooleanModel::headerData(int section,
                                  Qt::Orientation orientation,
                                  int role) const
{
    if (orientation == Qt::Horizontal && role == Qt::DisplayRole) {
        if (section == 0) {
            return tr("Node");
        } else if (section == 1) {
            return tr("Value");
        }
    }
    return QVariant();
}
```

In our headerData() reimplementation, we return appropriate horizontal header labels. The QTreeView class, which is used to visualize hierarchical models, has no vertical header, so we ignore that possibility.

Now that we have covered the Node and BooleanModel classes, let's see how the root node is created when the user changes the text in the line editor:

```
void BooleanWindow::booleanExpressionChanged(const QString &expr)
{
    BooleanParser parser;
    Node *rootNode = parser.parse(expr);
    booleanModel->setRootNode(rootNode);
}
```

When the user changes the text in the application's line editor, the main window's booleanExpressionChanged() slot is called. In this slot, the user's text is parsed and the parser returns a pointer to the root node of the parse tree.

We have not shown the BooleanParser class because it is not relevant for GUI or model/view programming. The full source for this example is provided with the book's examples.

When implementing tree models such as BooleanModel, it can be quite easy to make mistakes, resulting in strange behavior of QTreeView. To help find and solve problems in custom data models, a ModelTest class is available from Trolltech Labs. The class performs a series of tests on the model to catch common errors. To use ModelTest, download it from http://labs.trolltech.com/page/Projects/Itemview/Modeltest and follow the instructions given in the README file.

In this section, we have seen how to create three different custom models. Many models are much simpler than those shown here, with one-to-one correspondences between items and model indexes. Further model/view examples are provided with Qt itself, along with extensive documentation.

Implementing Custom Delegates

Individual items in views are rendered and edited using delegates. In most cases, the default delegate supplied by a view is sufficient. If we want to have finer control over the rendering of items, we can often achieve what we want simply by using a custom model: In our data() reimplementation, we can handle the Qt::FontRole, Qt::TextAlignmentRole, Qt::TextColorRole, and Qt::BackgroundColorRole, and these are used by the default delegate. For example, in the Cities and Currencies examples shown earlier, we handled the Qt::TextAlignmentRole to get right-aligned numbers.

If we want even greater control, we can create our own delegate class and set it on the views that we want to make use of it. The Track Editor dialog shown in Figure 10.15 makes use of a custom delegate. It shows the titles of music tracks and their durations. The data held by the model will be simply QStrings (titles)

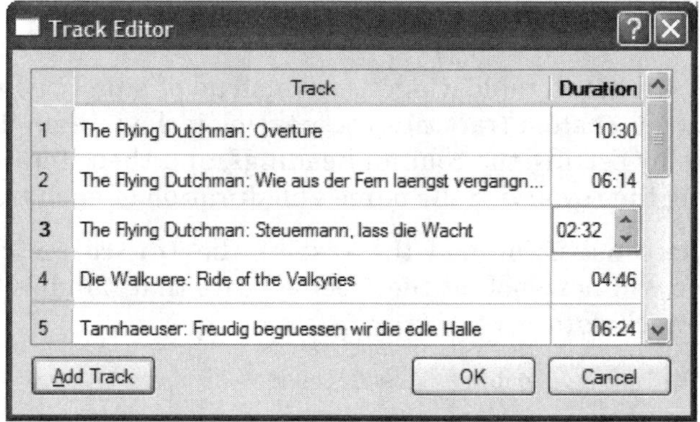

Figure 10.15. The Track Editor dialog

and `int`s (seconds), but the durations will be separated into minutes and seconds and will be editable using a `QTimeEdit`.

The Track Editor dialog uses a `QTableWidget`, a convenience item view subclass that operates on `QTableWidgetItem`s. The data is provided as a list of `Track`s:

```
class Track
{
public:
    Track(const QString &title = "", int duration = 0);

    QString title;
    int duration;
};
```

Here is an extract from the constructor that shows the creation and population of the table widget:

```
TrackEditor::TrackEditor(QList<Track> *tracks, QWidget *parent)
    : QDialog(parent)
{
    this->tracks = tracks;

    tableWidget = new QTableWidget(tracks->count(), 2);
    tableWidget->setItemDelegate(new TrackDelegate(1));
    tableWidget->setHorizontalHeaderLabels(
            QStringList() << tr("Track") << tr("Duration"));

    for (int row = 0; row < tracks->count(); ++row) {
        Track track = tracks->at(row);

        QTableWidgetItem *item0 = new QTableWidgetItem(track.title);
        tableWidget->setItem(row, 0, item0);

        QTableWidgetItem *item1
             = new QTableWidgetItem(QString::number(track.duration));
        item1->setTextAlignment(Qt::AlignRight);
        tableWidget->setItem(row, 1, item1);
    }
```

```
    ...
}
```

The constructor creates a table widget, and instead of simply using the default delegate, we set our custom TrackDelegate, passing it the column that holds time data. We begin by setting the column headings, and then iterate through the data, populating the rows with the name and duration of each track.

The rest of the constructor and the rest of the TrackEditor class holds no surprises, so we will now look at the TrackDelegate that handles the rendering and editing of track data.

```
class TrackDelegate : public QItemDelegate
{
    Q_OBJECT

public:
    TrackDelegate(int durationColumn, QObject *parent = 0);

    void paint(QPainter *painter, const QStyleOptionViewItem &option,
               const QModelIndex &index) const;
    QWidget *createEditor(QWidget *parent,
                          const QStyleOptionViewItem &option,
                          const QModelIndex &index) const;
    void setEditorData(QWidget *editor, const QModelIndex &index) const;
    void setModelData(QWidget *editor, QAbstractItemModel *model,
                      const QModelIndex &index) const;

private slots:
    void commitAndCloseEditor();

private:
    int durationColumn;
};
```

We use QItemDelegate as our base class so that we benefit from the default delegate implementation. We could also have used QAbstractItemDelegate if we had wanted to start from scratch.* To provide a delegate that can edit data, we must implement createEditor(), setEditorData(), and setModelData(). We also implement paint() to change the rendering of the duration column.

```
TrackDelegate::TrackDelegate(int durationColumn, QObject *parent)
    : QItemDelegate(parent)
{
    this->durationColumn = durationColumn;
}
```

The durationColumn parameter to the constructor tells the delegate which column holds the track duration.

```
void TrackDelegate::paint(QPainter *painter,
                          const QStyleOptionViewItem &option,
```

*Qt 4.4 is expected to introduce a QStyledItemDelegate class and use it as the default delegate. Unlike QItemDelegate, QStyledItemDelegate would rely on the current style to draw its items.

```
                                    const QModelIndex &index) const
{
    if (index.column() == durationColumn) {
        int secs = index.model()->data(index, Qt::DisplayRole).toInt();
        QString text = QString("%1:%2")
                       .arg(secs / 60, 2, 10, QChar('0'))
                       .arg(secs % 60, 2, 10, QChar('0'));

        QStyleOptionViewItem myOption = option;
        myOption.displayAlignment = Qt::AlignRight | Qt::AlignVCenter;

        drawDisplay(painter, myOption, myOption.rect, text);
        drawFocus(painter, myOption, myOption.rect);
    } else{
        QItemDelegate::paint(painter, option, index);
    }
}
```

Since we want to render the duration in the form "*minutes*:*seconds*", we have reimplemented the `paint()` function. The `arg()` calls take an integer to render as a string, how many characters the string should have, the base of the integer (10 for decimal), and the padding character.

To right-align the text, we copy the current style options and overwrite the default alignment. We then call `QItemDelegate::drawDisplay()` to draw the text, followed by `QItemDelegate::drawFocus()`, which will draw a focus rectangle if the item has focus and will do nothing otherwise. Using `drawDisplay()` is very convenient, especially when used with our own style options. We could also draw using the painter directly.

```
QWidget *TrackDelegate::createEditor(QWidget *parent,
        const QStyleOptionViewItem &option,
        const QModelIndex &index) const
{
    if (index.column() == durationColumn) {
        QTimeEdit *timeEdit = new QTimeEdit(parent);
        timeEdit->setDisplayFormat("mm:ss");
        connect(timeEdit, SIGNAL(editingFinished()),
                this, SLOT(commitAndCloseEditor()));
        return timeEdit;
    } else {
        return QItemDelegate::createEditor(parent, option, index);
    }
}
```

We only want to control the editing of track durations, leaving the editing of track names to the default delegate. We achieve this by checking for which column the delegate has been asked to provide an editor. If it's the duration column, we create a `QTimeEdit`, set the display format appropriately, and connect its `editingFinished()` signal to our `commitAndCloseEditor()` slot. For any other column, we pass on the edit handling to the default delegate.

```
void TrackDelegate::commitAndCloseEditor()
{
```

```
    QTimeEdit *editor = qobject_cast<QTimeEdit *>(sender());
    emit commitData(editor);
    emit closeEditor(editor);
}
```

If the user presses Enter or moves the focus out of the QTimeEdit (but not if they press Esc), the editingFinished() signal is emitted and the commitAndCloseEditor() slot is called. This slot emits the commitData() signal to inform the view that there is edited data to replace existing data. It also emits the closeEditor() signal to notify the view that this editor is no longer required, at which point the model will delete it. The editor is retrieved using QObject::sender(), which returns the object that emitted the signal that triggered the slot. If the user cancels (by pressing Esc), the view will simply delete the editor.

```
void TrackDelegate::setEditorData(QWidget *editor,
                                  const QModelIndex &index) const
{
    if (index.column() == durationColumn) {
        int secs = index.model()->data(index, Qt::DisplayRole).toInt();
        QTimeEdit *timeEdit = qobject_cast<QTimeEdit *>(editor);
        timeEdit->setTime(QTime(0, secs / 60, secs % 60));
    } else {
        QItemDelegate::setEditorData(editor, index);
    }
}
```

When the user initiates editing, the view calls createEditor() to create an editor, and then setEditorData() to initialize the editor with the item's current data. If the editor is for the duration column, we extract the track's duration in seconds and set the QTimeEdit's time to the corresponding number of minutes and seconds; otherwise, we let the default delegate handle the initialization.

```
void TrackDelegate::setModelData(QWidget *editor,
                                 QAbstractItemModel *model,
                                 const QModelIndex &index) const
{
    if (index.column() == durationColumn) {
        QTimeEdit *timeEdit = qobject_cast<QTimeEdit *>(editor);
        QTime time = timeEdit->time();
        int secs = (time.minute() * 60) + time.second();
        model->setData(index, secs);
    } else {
        QItemDelegate::setModelData(editor, model, index);
    }
}
```

If the user completes the edit (e.g., by left-clicking outside the editor widget, or by pressing Enter or Tab) rather than canceling it, the model must be updated with the editor's data. If the duration was edited, we extract the minutes and seconds from the QTimeEdit, and set the data to the corresponding number of seconds.

Although not necessary in this case, it is entirely possible to create a custom delegate that finely controls the editing and rendering of any item in a model. We have chosen to take control of a particular column, but since the `QModelIndex` is passed to all the `QItemDelegate` functions that we reimplement, we can take control by column, row, rectangular region, parent, or any combination of these, right down to individual items if required.

In this chapter, we presented a broad overview of Qt's model/view architecture. We showed how to use the view convenience subclasses, how to use Qt's predefined models, and how to create custom models and custom delegates. But the model/view architecture is so rich that we have not had the space to cover all the things it makes possible. For example, we could create a custom view that does not render its items as a list, table, or tree. This is done by the Chart example located in Qt's `examples/itemviews/chart` directory, which shows a custom view that renders model data in the form of a pie chart.

It is also possible to use multiple views to view the same model without any formality. Any edits made through one view will be automatically and immediately reflected in the other views. This kind of functionality is particularly useful for viewing large data sets where the user may wish to see sections of data that are logically far apart. The architecture also supports selections: Where two or more views are using the same model, each view can be set to have its own independent selections, or the selections can be shared across the views.

Qt's online documentation provides comprehensive coverage of item view programming and the classes that implement it. See `http://doc.trolltech.com/4.3/model-view.html` for a list of all the relevant classes, and `http://doc.trolltech.com/4.3/model-view-programming.html` for additional information and links to the relevant examples included with Qt.

- *Sequential Containers*
- *Associative Containers*
- *Generic Algorithms*
- *Strings, Byte Arrays, and Variants*

11. Container Classes

Container classes are general-purpose template classes that store items of a given type in memory. C++ already offers many containers as part of the Standard Template Library (STL), which is included in the Standard C++ library.

Qt provides its own container classes, so for Qt programs we can use both the Qt and the STL containers. The main advantages of the Qt containers are that they behave the same on all platforms and that they are implicitly shared. Implicit sharing, or "copy on write", is an optimization that makes it possible to pass entire containers as values without any significant performance cost. The Qt containers also feature easy-to-use iterator classes inspired by Java, they can be streamed using `QDataStream`, and they usually result in less code in the executable than the corresponding STL containers. Finally, on some hardware platforms supported by Qt/Embedded Linux, the Qt containers are the only ones available.

Qt offers both sequential containers such as `QVector<T>`, `QLinkedList<T>`, and `QList<T>`, and associative containers such as `QMap<K, T>` and `QHash<K, T>`. Conceptually, the sequential containers store items one after another, whereas the associative containers store key–value pairs.

Qt also provides generic algorithms that perform operations on arbitrary containers. For example, the `qSort()` algorithm sorts a sequential container, and `qBinaryFind()` performs a binary search on a sorted sequential container. These algorithms are similar to those offered by the STL.

If you are already familiar with the STL containers and have STL available on your target platforms, you might want to use them instead of, or in addition to, the Qt containers. For more information about the STL classes and functions, a good place to start is SGI's STL web site: `http://www.sgi.com/tech/stl/`.

In this chapter, we will also look at `QString`, `QByteArray`, and `QVariant`, since they have a lot in common with containers. `QString` is a 16-bit Unicode string used throughout Qt's API. `QByteArray` is an array of 8-bit `char`s useful for storing raw binary data. `QVariant` is a type that can store most C++ and Qt value types.

Sequential Containers

A QVector<T> is an array-like data structure that stores its items at adjacent positions in memory, as Figure 11.1 illustrates. What distinguishes a vector from a plain C++ array is that a vector knows its own size and can be resized. Appending extra items to the end of a vector is fairly efficient, whereas inserting items at the front or in the middle of a vector can be expensive.

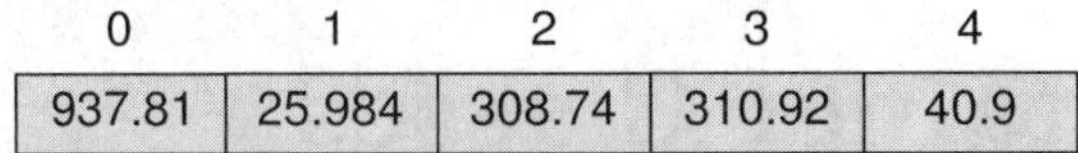

Figure 11.1. A vector of doubles

If we know in advance how many items we are going to need, we can give the vector an initial size when we define it and use the [] operator to assign a value to the items; otherwise, we must either resize the vector later on or append items. Here's an example where we specify the initial size:

```
QVector<double> vect(3);
vect[0] = 1.0;
vect[1] = 0.540302;
vect[2] = -0.416147;
```

Here's the same example, this time starting with an empty vector and using the append() function to append items at the end:

```
QVector<double> vect;
vect.append(1.0);
vect.append(0.540302);
vect.append(-0.416147);
```

We can also use the << operator instead of append():

```
vect << 1.0 << 0.540302 << -0.416147;
```

One way to iterate over the vector's items is to use [] and count():

```
double sum = 0.0;
for (int i = 0; i < vect.count(); ++i)
    sum += vect[i];
```

Vector entries that are created without being assigned an explicit value are initialized using the item class's default constructor. Basic types and pointer types are initialized to zero.

Inserting items at the beginning or in the middle of a QVector<T>, or removing items from these positions, can be inefficient for large vectors. For this reason, Qt also offers QLinkedList<T>, a data structure that stores its items at non-adjacent locations in memory, as illustrated by Figure 11.2. Unlike vectors, linked lists don't support random access, but they provide "constant time" insertions and removals.

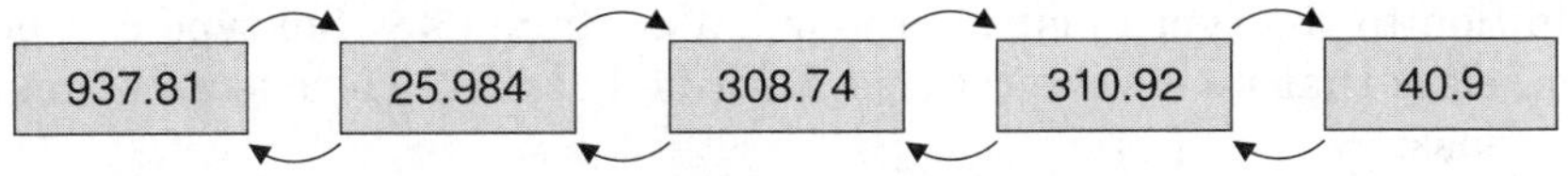

Figure 11.2. A linked list of doubles

Linked lists do not provide the [] operator, so iterators must be used to traverse their items. Iterators are also used to specify the position of items. For example, the following code inserts the string "Tote Hosen" between "Clash" and "Ramones":

```
QLinkedList<QString> list;
list.append("Clash");
list.append("Ramones");

QLinkedList<QString>::iterator i = list.find("Ramones");
list.insert(i, "Tote Hosen");
```

We will take a more detailed look at iterators later in this section.

The QList<T> sequential container is an "array-list" that combines the most important benefits of QVector<T> and QLinkedList<T> in a single class. It supports random access, and its interface is index-based like QVector's. Inserting or removing an item at either end of a QList<T> is very fast, and inserting in the middle is fast for lists with up to about one thousand items. Unless we want to perform insertions in the middle of huge lists or need the list's items to occupy consecutive addresses in memory, QList<T> is usually the most appropriate general-purpose container class to use.

The QStringList class is a subclass of QList<QString> that is widely used in Qt's API. In addition to the functions it inherits from its base class, it provides some extra functions that make the class more versatile for string handling. We discuss QStringList in the last section of this chapter (p. 290).

QStack<T> and QQueue<T> are two more examples of convenience subclasses. QStack<T> is a vector that provides push(), pop(), and top(). QQueue<T> is a list that provides enqueue(), dequeue(), and head().

For all the container classes seen so far, the value type T can be a basic type like int or double, a pointer type, or a class that has a default constructor (a constructor that takes no arguments), a copy constructor, and an assignment operator. Classes that qualify include QByteArray, QDateTime, QRegExp, QString, and QVariant. Qt classes that are derived from QObject do not qualify, because they lack a copy constructor and an assignment operator. This is no problem in practice, since we can simply store pointers to QObject types rather than the objects themselves.

The value type T can also be a container, in which case we must remember to separate consecutive angle brackets with spaces; otherwise, the compiler will choke on what it thinks is a >> operator. For example:

```
QList<QVector<double> > list;
```

In addition to the types just mentioned, a container's value type can be any custom class that meets the criteria described earlier. Here is an example of such a class:

```
class Movie
{
public:
    Movie(const QString &title = "", int duration = 0);

    void setTitle(const QString &title) { myTitle = title; }
    QString title() const { return myTitle; }
    void setDuration(int duration) { myDuration = duration; }
    QString duration() const { return myDuration; }

private:
    QString myTitle;
    int myDuration;
};
```

The class has a constructor that requires no arguments (although it can take up to two). It also has a copy constructor and an assignment operator, both implicitly provided by C++. For this class, a member-by-member copy is sufficient, so there is no need to implement our own copy constructor and assignment operator.

Qt provides two categories of iterators for traversing the items stored in a container: Java-style iterators and STL-style iterators. The Java-style iterators are easier to use, whereas the STL-style iterators can be combined with Qt's and STL's generic algorithms and are more powerful.

For each container class, there are two Java-style iterator types: a read-only iterator and a read-write iterator. Their valid positions are shown in Figure 11.3. The read-only iterator classes are `QVectorIterator<T>`, `QLinkedListIterator<T>`, and `QListIterator<T>`. The corresponding read-write iterators have `Mutable` in their name (e.g., `QMutableVectorIterator<T>`). In this discussion, we will concentrate on `QList`'s iterators; the iterators for linked lists and vectors have the same API.

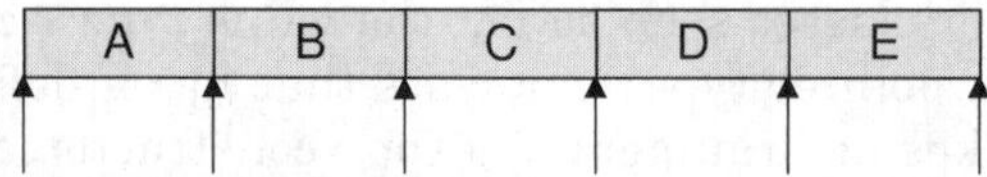

Figure 11.3. Valid positions for Java-style iterators

The first thing to keep in mind when using Java-style iterators is that they don't point directly at items. Instead, they can be located before the first item, after the last item, or between two items. A typical iteration loop looks like this:

```
QList<double> list;
...
QListIterator<double> i(list);
```

```
while (i.hasNext()) {
    do_something(i.next());
}
```

The iterator is initialized with the container to traverse. At this point, the iterator is located just before the first item. The call to `hasNext()` returns `true` if there is an item to the right of the iterator. The `next()` function returns the item to the right of the iterator and advances the iterator to the next valid position.

Iterating backward is similar, except that we must first call `toBack()` to position the iterator after the last item:

```
QListIterator<double> i(list);
i.toBack();
while (i.hasPrevious()) {
    do_something(i.previous());
}
```

The `hasPrevious()` function returns `true` if there is an item to the left of the iterator; `previous()` returns the item to the left of the iterator and moves the iterator back by one position. Another way to think about the `next()` and `previous()` iterators is that they return the item that the iterator has just jumped over, as Figure 11.4 illustrates.

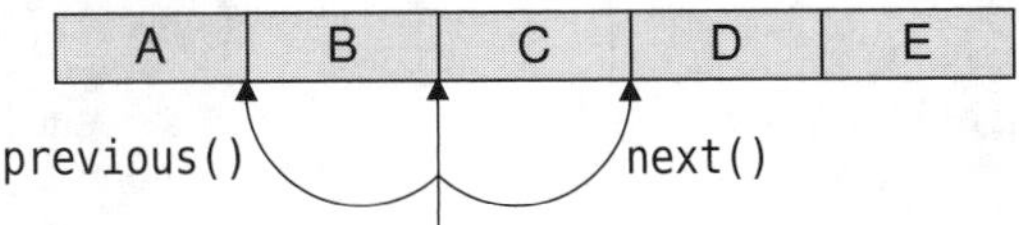

Figure 11.4. Effect of `previous()` and `next()` on a Java-style iterator

Mutable iterators provide functions to insert, modify, and remove items while iterating. The following loop removes all the negative numbers from a list:

```
QMutableListIterator<double> i(list);
while (i.hasNext()) {
    if (i.next() < 0.0)
        i.remove();
}
```

The `remove()` function always operates on the last item that was jumped over. It also works when iterating backward:

```
QMutableListIterator<double> i(list);
i.toBack();
while (i.hasPrevious()) {
    if (i.previous() < 0.0)
        i.remove();
}
```

Similarly, the mutable Java-style iterators provide a `setValue()` function that modifies the last item that was jumped over. Here's how we would replace negative numbers with their absolute value:

```
QMutableListIterator<double> i(list);
while (i.hasNext()) {
    int val = i.next();
    if (val < 0.0)
        i.setValue(-val);
}
```

It is also possible to insert an item at the current iterator position by calling `insert()`. The iterator is then advanced to point between the new item and the following item.

In addition to the Java-style iterators, every sequential container class `C<T>` has two STL-style iterator types: `C<T>::iterator` and `C<T>::const_iterator`. The difference between the two is that `const_iterator` doesn't let us modify the data.

A container's `begin()` function returns an STL-style iterator that refers to the first item in the container (e.g., `list[0]`), whereas `end()` returns an iterator to the "one past the last" item (e.g., `list[5]` for a list of size 5). Figure 11.5 shows the valid positions for STL-style iterators. If a container is empty, `begin()` equals `end()`. This can be used to see whether the container has any items, although it is usually more convenient to call `isEmpty()` for this purpose.

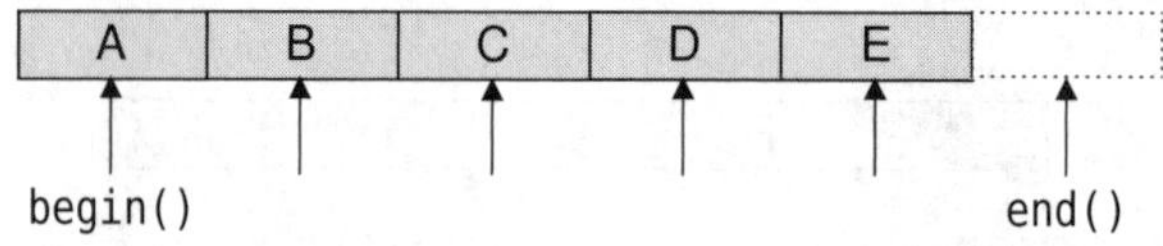

Figure 11.5. Valid positions for STL-style iterators

The STL-style iterator syntax is modeled after that of C++ pointers into an array. We can use the ++ and -- operators to move to the next or previous item, and the unary * operator to retrieve the current item. For `QVector<T>`, the `iterator` and `const_iterator` types are merely typedefs for `T *` and `const T *`. (This is possible because `QVector<T>` stores its items in consecutive memory locations.)

The following example replaces each value in a `QList<double>` with its absolute value:

```
QList<double>::iterator i = list.begin();
while (i != list.end()) {
    *i = qAbs(*i);
    ++i;
}
```

A few Qt functions return a container. If we want to iterate over the return value of a function using an STL-style iterator, we must take a copy of the container and iterate over the copy. For example, the following code is the correct way to iterate over the `QList<int>` returned by `QSplitter::sizes()`:

```
QList<int> list = splitter->sizes();
QList<int>::const_iterator i = list.begin();
```

```
while (i != list.end()) {
    do_something(*i);
    ++i;
}
```

The following code is wrong:

```
// WRONG
QList<int>::const_iterator i = splitter->sizes().begin();
while (i != splitter->sizes().end()) {
    do_something(*i);
    ++i;
}
```

This is because `QSplitter::sizes()` returns a new `QList<int>` by value every time it is called. If we don't store the return value, C++ automatically destroys it before we have even started iterating, leaving us with a dangling iterator. To make matters worse, each time the loop is run, `QSplitter::sizes()` must generate a new copy of the list because of the `splitter->sizes().end()` call. In summary: When using STL-style iterators, always iterate on a copy of a container returned by value.

With read-only Java-style iterators, we don't need to take a copy. The iterator takes a copy for us behind the scenes, ensuring that we always iterate over the data that the function first returned. For example:

```
QListIterator<int> i(splitter->sizes());
while (i.hasNext()) {
    do_something(i.next());
}
```

Copying a container like this sounds expensive, but it isn't, thanks to an optimization called *implicit sharing*. This means that copying a Qt container is about as fast as copying a single pointer. Only if one of the copies is changed is data actually copied—and this is all handled automatically behind the scenes. For this reason, implicit sharing is sometimes called "copy on write".

The beauty of implicit sharing is that it is an optimization that we don't need to think about; it simply works, without requiring any programmer intervention. At the same time, implicit sharing encourages a clean programming style where objects are returned by value. Consider the following function:

```
QVector<double> sineTable()
{
    QVector<double> vect(360);
    for (int i = 0; i < 360; ++i)
        vect[i] = std::sin(i / (2 * M_PI));
    return vect;
}
```

The call to the function looks like this:

```
QVector<double> table = sineTable();
```

STL, in comparison, encourages us to pass the vector as a non-const reference to avoid the copy that takes place when the function's return value is stored in a variable:

```
void sineTable(std::vector<double> &vect)
{
    vect.resize(360);
    for (int i = 0; i < 360; ++i)
        vect[i] = std::sin(i / (2 * M_PI));
}
```

The call then becomes more tedious to write and less clear to read:

```
std::vector<double> table;
sineTable(table);
```

Qt uses implicit sharing for all of its containers and for many other classes, including `QByteArray`, `QBrush`, `QFont`, `QImage`, `QPixmap`, and `QString`. This makes these classes very efficient to pass by value, both as function parameters and as return values.

Implicit sharing is a guarantee from Qt that the data won't be copied if we don't modify it. To get the best out of implicit sharing, we can adopt a couple of new programming habits. One habit is to use the `at()` function rather than the `[]` operator for read-only access on a (non-const) vector or list. Since Qt's containers cannot tell whether `[]` appears on the left side of an assignment or not, it assumes the worst and forces a deep copy to occur—whereas `at()` isn't allowed on the left side of an assignment.

A similar issue arises when we iterate over a container with STL-style iterators. Whenever we call `begin()` or `end()` on a non-const container, Qt forces a deep copy to occur if the data is shared. To prevent this inefficiency, the solution is to use `const_iterator`, `constBegin()`, and `constEnd()` whenever possible.

Qt provides one last method for iterating over items in a sequential container: the `foreach` loop. It looks like this:

```
QLinkedList<Movie> list;
...
foreach (Movie movie, list) {
    if (movie.title() == "Citizen Kane") {
        std::cout << "Found Citizen Kane" << std::endl;
        break;
    }
}
```

The `foreach` pseudo-keyword is implemented in terms of the standard `for` loop. At each iteration of the loop, the iteration variable (`movie`) is set to a new item, starting at the first item in the container and progressing forward. The `foreach` loop automatically takes a copy of the container when the loop is entered, and for this reason the loop is not affected if the container is modified during iteration.

How Implicit Sharing Works

Implicit sharing works automatically behind the scenes, so we don't have to do anything in our code to make this optimization happen. But since it's nice to know how things work, we will study an example and see what happens under the hood. The example uses QString, one of Qt's many implicitly shared classes.

```
QString str1 = "Humpty";
QString str2 = str1;
```

We set str1 to "Humpty" and str2 to be equal to str1. At this point, both QString objects point to the same internal data structure in memory. Along with the character data, the data structure holds a reference count that indicates how many QStrings point to the same data structure. Since both str1 and str2 point to the same data, the reference count is 2.

```
str2[0] = 'D';
```

When we modify str2, it first makes a deep copy of the data, to ensure that str1 and str2 point to different data structures, and it then applies the change to its own copy of the data. The reference count of str1's data ("Humpty") becomes 1, and the reference count of str2's data ("Dumpty") is set to 1. A reference count of 1 means that the data isn't shared.

```
str2.truncate(4);
```

If we modify str2 again, no copying takes place because the reference count of str2's data is 1. The truncate() function operates directly on str2's data, resulting in the string "Dump". The reference count stays at 1.

```
str1 = str2;
```

When we assign str2 to str1, the reference count for str1's data goes down to 0, which means that no QString is using the "Humpty" data anymore. The data is then freed from memory. Both QStrings point to "Dump", which now has a reference count of 2.

Data sharing is often disregarded as an option in multithreaded programs, because of race conditions in the reference counting. With Qt, this is not an issue. Internally, the container classes use assembly language instructions to perform atomic reference counting. This technology is available to Qt users through the QSharedData and QSharedDataPointer classes.

The break and continue loop statements are supported. If the body consists of a single statement, the braces are unnecessary. Just like a for statement, the iteration variable can be defined outside the loop, like this:

```
QLinkedList<Movie> list;
Movie movie;
...
```

```
foreach (movie, list) {
    if (movie.title() == "Citizen Kane") {
        std::cout << "Found Citizen Kane" << std::endl;
        break;
    }
}
```

Defining the iteration variable outside the loop is the only option for containers that hold data types that contain a comma (e.g., `QPair<QString, int>`).

Associative Containers

An associative container holds an arbitrary number of items of the same type, indexed by a key. Qt provides two main associative container classes: `QMap<K, T>` and `QHash<K, T>`.

A `QMap<K, T>` is a data structure that stores key–value pairs in ascending key order, as illustrated in Figure 11.6. This arrangement makes it possible to provide good lookup and insertion performance, and key-order iteration. Internally, `QMap<K, T>` is implemented as a skip-list.

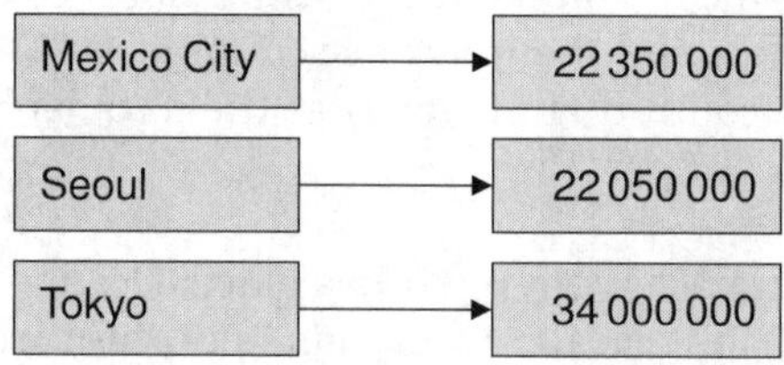

Figure 11.6. A map of `QString` to `int`

One simple way to insert items into a map is to call `insert()`:

```
QMap<QString, int> map;
map.insert("eins", 1);
map.insert("sieben", 7);
map.insert("dreiundzwanzig", 23);
```

Alternatively, we can simply assign a value to a given key as follows:

```
map["eins"] = 1;
map["sieben"] = 7;
map["dreiundzwanzig"] = 23;
```

The `[]` operator can be used for both insertion and retrieval. If `[]` is used to retrieve a value for a non-existent key in a non-const map, a new item will be created with the given key and an empty value. To avoid accidentally creating empty values, we can use the `value()` function to retrieve items instead of `[]`:

```
int val = map.value("dreiundzwanzig");
```

If the key doesn't exist, a default value is returned using the value type's default constructor, and no new item is created. For basic and pointer types, zero is returned. We can specify another default value as the second argument to `value()`, for example:

```
int seconds = map.value("delay", 30);
```

This is equivalent to

```
int seconds = 30;
if (map.contains("delay"))
    seconds = map.value("delay");
```

The `K` and `T` data types of a `QMap<K, T>` can be basic data types like `int` and `double`, pointer types, or classes that have a default constructor, a copy constructor, and an assignment operator. In addition, the `K` type must provide an `operator<()` since `QMap<K, T>` uses this operator to store the items in ascending key order.

`QMap<K, T>` has a couple of convenience functions, `keys()` and `values()`, that are especially useful when dealing with small data sets. They return `QList`s of a map's keys and values.

Maps are normally single-valued: If a new value is assigned to an existing key, the old value is replaced by the new value, ensuring that no two items share the same key. It is possible to have multiple key–value pairs with the same key by using the `insertMulti()` function or the `QMultiMap<K, T>` convenience subclass. `QMap<K, T>` has a `values(const K &)` overload that returns a `QList` of all the values for a given key. For example:

```
QMultiMap<int, QString> multiMap;
multiMap.insert(1, "one");
multiMap.insert(1, "eins");
multiMap.insert(1, "uno");

QList<QString> vals = multiMap.values(1);
```

A `QHash<K, T>` is a data structure that stores key–value pairs in a hash table. Its interface is almost identical to that of `QMap<K, T>`, but it has different requirements for the `K` template type and usually provides much faster lookups than `QMap<K, T>` can achieve. Another difference is that `QHash<K, T>` is unordered.

In addition to the standard requirements on any value type stored in a container, the `K` type of a `QHash<K, T>` needs to provide an `operator==()` and be supported by a global `qHash()` function that returns a hash value for a key. Qt already provides `qHash()` functions for integer types, pointer types, `QChar`, `QString`, and `QByteArray`.

`QHash<K, T>` automatically allocates a prime number of buckets for its internal hash table and resizes this as items are inserted or removed. It is also possible to fine-tune performance by calling `reserve()` to specify the number of items expected to be stored in the hash and `squeeze()` to shrink the hash table based on the current number of items. A common idiom is to call `reserve()` with the maximum number of items we expect, then insert the data, and finally call squeeze() to minimize memory usage if there were fewer items than expected.

Hashes are normally single-valued, but multiple values can be assigned to the same key using the insertMulti() function or the QMultiHash<K, T> convenience subclass.

Besides QHash<K, T>, Qt also provides a QCache<K, T> class that can be used to cache objects associated with a key, and a QSet<K> container that only stores keys. Internally, both rely on QHash<K, T> and both have the same requirements for the K type as QHash<K, T>.

The easiest way to iterate through all the key–value pairs stored in an associative container is to use a Java-style iterator. Because the iterators must give access to both a key and a value, the Java-style iterators for associative containers work slightly differently from their sequential counterparts. The main difference is that the next() and previous() functions return an object that represents a key–value pair, rather than simply a value. The key and value components are accessible from this object as key() and value(). For example:

```
QMap<QString, int> map;
...
int sum = 0;
QMapIterator<QString, int> i(map);
while (i.hasNext())
    sum += i.next().value();
```

If we need to access both the key and the value, we can simply ignore the return value of next() or previous() and use the iterator's key() and value() functions, which operate on the last item that was jumped over:

```
QMapIterator<QString, int> i(map);
while (i.hasNext()) {
    i.next();
    if (i.value() > largestValue) {
        largestKey = i.key();
        largestValue = i.value();
    }
}
```

Mutable iterators have a setValue() function that modifies the value associated with the current item:

```
QMutableMapIterator<QString, int> i(map);
while (i.hasNext()) {
    i.next();
    if (i.value() < 0.0)
        i.setValue(-i.value());
}
```

STL-style iterators also provide key() and value() functions. With the non-const iterator types, value() returns a non-const reference, allowing us to change the value as we iterate. Note that although these iterators are called "STL-style", they deviate significantly from the `std::map<K, T>` iterators, which are based on `std::pair<K, T>`.

The `foreach` loop also works on associative containers, but only on the value component of the key–value pairs. If we need both the key and the value components of the items, we can call the `keys()` and `values(const K &)` functions in nested `foreach` loops as follows:

```
QMultiMap<QString, int> map;
...
foreach (QString key, map.keys()) {
    foreach (int value, map.values(key)) {
        do_something(key, value);
    }
}
```

Generic Algorithms

The `<QtAlgorithms>` header declares a set of global template functions that implement basic algorithms on containers. Most of these functions operate on STL-style iterators.

The STL `<algorithm>` header provides a more complete set of generic algorithms. These algorithms can be used on Qt containers as well as STL containers. If STL implementations are available on all your platforms, there is probably no reason to avoid using the STL algorithms when Qt lacks an equivalent algorithm. Here, we will introduce the most important Qt algorithms.

The `qFind()` algorithm searches for a particular value in a container. It takes a "begin" and an "end" iterator and returns an iterator pointing to the first item that matches, or "end" if there is no match. In the following example, `i` is set to `list.begin() + 1`, whereas `j` is set to `list.end()`:

```
QStringList list;
list << "Emma" << "Karl" << "James" << "Mariette";

QStringList::iterator i = qFind(list.begin(), list.end(), "Karl");
QStringList::iterator j = qFind(list.begin(), list.end(), "Petra");
```

The `qBinaryFind()` algorithm performs a search just like `qFind()`, except that it assumes that the items are sorted in ascending order and uses fast binary searching rather than `qFind()`'s linear searching.

The `qFill()` algorithm populates a container with a particular value:

```
QLinkedList<int> list(10);
qFill(list.begin(), list.end(), 1009);
```

Like the other iterator-based algorithms, we can also use `qFill()` on a portion of the container by varying the arguments. The following code snippet initializes the first five items of a vector to 1009 and the last five items to 2013:

```
QVector<int> vect(10);
```

```
qFill(vect.begin(), vect.begin() + 5, 1009);
qFill(vect.end() - 5, vect.end(), 2013);
```

The `qCopy()` algorithm copies values from one container to another:

```
QVector<int> vect(list.count());
qCopy(list.begin(), list.end(), vect.begin());
```

`qCopy()` can also be used to copy values within the same container, as long as the source range and the target range don't overlap. In the next code snippet, we use it to overwrite the last two items of a list with the first two items:

```
qCopy(list.begin(), list.begin() + 2, list.end() - 2);
```

The `qSort()` algorithm sorts the container's items into ascending order:

```
qSort(list.begin(), list.end());
```

By default, `qSort()` uses the `<` operator to compare the items. To sort items in descending order, pass `qGreater<T>()` as the third argument (where `T` is the container's value type), as follows:

```
qSort(list.begin(), list.end(), qGreater<int>());
```

We can use the third parameter to define custom sort criteria. For example, here's a "less than" comparison function that compares `QString`s in a case-insensitive way:

```
bool insensitiveLessThan(const QString &str1, const QString &str2)
{
    return str1.toLower() < str2.toLower();
}
```

The call to `qSort()` then becomes

```
QStringList list;
...
qSort(list.begin(), list.end(), insensitiveLessThan);
```

The `qStableSort()` algorithm is similar to `qSort()`, except it guarantees that items that compare equal appear in the same order after the sort as before. This is useful if the sort criterion takes into account only parts of the value and the results are visible to the user. We used `qStableSort()` in Chapter 4 to implement sorting in the Spreadsheet application (p. 92).

The `qDeleteAll()` algorithm calls `delete` on every pointer stored in a container. It makes sense only on containers whose value type is a pointer type. After the call, the items are still present in the container as dangling pointers, so normally we should also call `clear()` on the container. For example:

```
qDeleteAll(list);
list.clear();
```

The `qSwap()` algorithm exchanges the value of two variables. For example:

```
int x1 = line.x1();
int x2 = line.x2();
if (x1 > x2)
    qSwap(x1, x2);
```

Finally, the `<QtGlobal>` header, which is included by every other Qt header, provides several useful definitions, including the `qAbs()` function, that returns the absolute value of its argument, and the `qMin()` and `qMax()` functions, that return the minimum or maximum of two values.

Strings, Byte Arrays, and Variants

`QString`, `QByteArray`, and `QVariant` are three classes that have many things in common with containers and that can be used as alternatives to containers in some contexts. Also, like the containers, these classes use implicit sharing as a memory and speed optimization.

We will start with `QString`. Every GUI program uses strings, not only for the user interface but often also as data structures. C++ natively provides two kinds of strings: traditional C-style '\0'-terminated character arrays and the `std::string` class. Unlike these, `QString` holds 16-bit Unicode values. Unicode contains ASCII and Latin-1 as a subset, with their usual numeric values. But since `QString` is 16-bit, it can represent thousands of other characters for writing most of the world's languages. See Chapter 18 for more information about Unicode.

When using `QString`, we don't need to worry about such arcane details as allocating enough memory or ensuring that the data is '\0'-terminated. Conceptually, `QString`s can be thought of as a vector of `QChar`s. A `QString` can embed '\0' characters. The `length()` function returns the size of the entire string, including embedded '\0' characters.

`QString` provides a binary + operator to concatenate two strings and a += operator to append one string to another. Because `QString` automatically preallocates memory at the end of the string data, building up a string by repeatedly appending characters is very fast. Here's an example that combines + and +=:

```
QString str = "User: ";
str += userName + "\n";
```

There is also a `QString::append()` function that does the same thing as the += operator:

```
str = "User: ";
str.append(userName);
str.append("\n");
```

A completely different way to combine strings is to use `QString`'s `sprintf()` function:

```
str.sprintf("%s %.1f%%", "perfect competition", 100.0);
```

This function supports the same format specifiers as the C++ library's `sprintf()` function. In the preceding example, `str` is assigned "perfect competition 100.0%".

Yet another way to build a string from other strings or from numbers is to use `arg()`:

```
str = QString("%1 %2 (%3s-%4s)")
      .arg("permissive").arg("society").arg(1950).arg(1970);
```

In this example, "%1" is replaced by "permissive", "%2" is replaced by "society", "%3" is replaced by "1950", and "%4" is replaced by "1970". The result is "permissive society (1950s-1970s)". There are `arg()` overloads to handle various data types. Some overloads have extra parameters for controlling the field width, the numerical base, or the floating-point precision. In general, `arg()` is a much better solution than `sprintf()`, because it is type-safe, fully supports Unicode, and allows translators to reorder the "%*n*" parameters.

`QString` can convert numbers into strings using the `QString::number()` static function:

```
str = QString::number(59.6);
```

Or using the `setNum()` function:

```
str.setNum(59.6);
```

The reverse conversion, from a string to a number, is achieved using `toInt()`, `toLongLong()`, `toDouble()`, and so on. For example:

```
bool ok;
double d = str.toDouble(&ok);
```

These functions accept an optional pointer to a `bool` variable and set the variable to `true` or `false` depending on the success of the conversion. If the conversion fails, these functions return zero.

Once we have a string, we often want to extract parts of it. The `mid()` function returns the substring starting at a given position (the first argument) and of up to a given length (the second argument). For example, the following code prints "pays" to the console:*

```
QString str = "polluter pays principle";
qDebug() << str.mid(9, 4);
```

If we omit the second argument, `mid()` returns the substring starting at the given position and ending at the end of the string. For example, the following code prints "pays principle" to the console:

```
QString str = "polluter pays principle";
qDebug() << str.mid(9);
```

---

*The convenient qDebug() << arg syntax used here requires the inclusion of the <QtDebug> header file, whereas the qDebug("...", arg) syntax is available in any file that includes at least one Qt header.

There are also `left()` and `right()` functions that perform a similar job. Both accept a number of characters, *n*, and return the first or last *n* characters of the string. For example, the following code prints "polluter principle" to the console:

```
QString str = "polluter pays principle";
qDebug() << str.left(8) << " " << str.right(9);
```

If we want to find out whether a string contains a particular character, substring, or regular expression, we can use one of QString's `indexOf()` functions:

```
QString str = "the middle bit";
int i = str.indexOf("middle");
```

This will set `i` to 4. The `indexOf()` function returns -1 on failure, and accepts an optional start position and case-sensitivity flag.

If we just want to check whether a string starts or ends with something, we can use the `startsWith()` and `endsWith()` functions:

```
if (url.startsWith("http:") && url.endsWith(".png"))
    ...
```

The preceding code is both simpler and faster than the following code:

```
if (url.left(5) == "http:" && url.right(4) == ".png")
    ...
```

String comparison with the == operator is case-sensitive. If we are comparing user-visible strings, `localeAwareCompare()` is usually the right choice, and if we want to make the comparisons case-insensitive, we can use `toUpper()` or `toLower()`. For example:

```
if (fileName.toLower() == "readme.txt")
    ...
```

If we want to replace a certain part of a string by another string, we can use `replace()`:

```
QString str = "a cloudy day";
str.replace(2, 6, "sunny");
```

The result is "a sunny day". The code can be rewritten to use `remove()` and `insert()`:

```
str.remove(2, 6);
str.insert(2, "sunny");
```

First, we remove six characters starting at position 2, resulting in the string "a day" (with two spaces), and then we insert "sunny" at position 2.

There are overloaded versions of `replace()` that replace all occurrences of their first argument with their second argument. For example, here's how to replace all occurrences of "&" with "&" in a string:

```
str.replace("&", "&amp;");
```

One very frequent need is to strip the whitespace (such as spaces, tabs, and newlines) from a string. `QString` has a function that eliminates whitespace from both ends of a string:

```
QString str = "   BOB \t THE  \nDOG \n";
qDebug() << str.trimmed();
```

String `str` can be depicted as

The string returned by `trimmed()` is

```
B O B   \t   T H E     \n D O G
```

When handling user input, we often also want to replace every sequence of one or more internal whitespace characters with single spaces, in addition to stripping whitespace from both ends. This is what the `simplified()` function does:

```
QString str = "   BOB \t THE  \nDOG \n";
qDebug() << str.simplified();
```

The string returned by `simplified()` is

```
B O B   T H E   D O G
```

A string can be split into a `QStringList` of substrings using `QString::split()`:

```
QString str = "polluter pays principle";
QStringList words = str.split(" ");
```

In the preceding example, we split the string "polluter pays principle" into three substrings: "polluter", "pays", and "principle". The `split()` function has an optional second argument that specifies whether empty substrings should be kept (the default) or discarded.

The items in a `QStringList` can be joined to form a single string using `join()`. The argument to `join()` is inserted between each pair of joined strings. For example, here's how to create a single string that is composed of all the strings contained in a `QStringList` sorted into alphabetical order and separated by newlines:

```
words.sort();
str = words.join("\n");
```

When dealing with strings, we often need to determine whether a string is empty or not. This is done by calling `isEmpty()` or by checking whether `length()` is 0.

The conversion from `const char *` strings to `QString` is automatic in most cases, for example:

```
str += " (1870)";
```

Here we add a const char * to a QString without formality. To explicitly convert a const char * to a QString, simply use a QString cast, or call fromAscii() or fromLatin1(). (See Chapter 18 for an explanation of handling literal strings in other encodings.)

To convert a QString to a const char *, use toAscii() or toLatin1(). These functions return a QByteArray, which can be converted into a const char * using QByteArray::data() or QByteArray::constData(). For example:

```
printf("User: %s\n", str.toAscii().data());
```

For convenience, Qt provides the qPrintable() macro that performs the same as the sequence toAscii().constData():

```
printf("User: %s\n", qPrintable(str));
```

When we call data() or constData() on a QByteArray, the returned string is owned by the QByteArray object. This means that we don't need to worry about memory leaks; Qt will reclaim the memory for us. On the other hand, we must be careful not to use the pointer for too long. If the QByteArray is not stored in a variable, it will be automatically deleted at the end of the statement.

The QByteArray class has a very similar API to QString. Functions such as left(), right(), mid(), toLower(), toUpper(), trimmed(), and simplified() exist in QByteArray with the same semantics as their QString counterparts. QByteArray is useful for storing raw binary data and 8-bit encoded text strings. In general, we recommend using QString for storing text rather than QByteArray because QString supports Unicode.

For convenience, QByteArray automatically ensures that the "one past the last" byte is always '\0', making it easy to pass a QByteArray to a function taking a const char *. QByteArray also supports embedded '\0' characters, allowing us to use it to store arbitrary binary data.

In some situations, we need to store data of different types in the same variable. One approach is to encode the data as a QByteArray or a QString. For example, a string could hold a textual value or a numeric value in string form. These approaches give complete flexibility, but do away with some of C++'s benefits, in particular type safety and efficiency. Qt provides a much cleaner way of handling variables that can hold different types: QVariant.

The QVariant class can hold values of many Qt types, including QBrush, QColor, QCursor, QDateTime, QFont, QKeySequence, QPalette, QPen, QPixmap, QPoint, QRect, QRegion, QSize, and QString, as well as basic C++ numeric types such as double and int. The QVariant class can also hold containers: QMap<QString, QVariant>, QStringList, and QList<QVariant>.

The item view classes, the database module, and QSettings use variants extensively, allowing us to read and write item data, database data, and user preferences for any QVariant-compatible type. We already saw an example of this in

Chapter 3, where we passed a QRect, a QStringList, and a couple of bools as variants to QSettings::setValue(), and retrieved them later as variants.

It is possible to create arbitrarily complex data structures using QVariant by nesting values of container types:

```
QMap<QString, QVariant> pearMap;
pearMap["Standard"] = 1.95;
pearMap["Organic"] = 2.25;

QMap<QString, QVariant> fruitMap;
fruitMap["Orange"] = 2.10;
fruitMap["Pineapple"] = 3.85;
fruitMap["Pear"] = pearMap;
```

Here we have created a map with string keys (product names) and values that are either floating-point numbers (prices) or maps. The top-level map contains three keys: "Orange", "Pear", and "Pineapple". The value associated with the "Pear" key is a map that contains two keys ("Standard" and "Organic"). When iterating over a map that holds variant values, we need to use type() to check the type that a variant holds so that we can respond appropriately.

Creating data structures like this can be very seductive since we can organize the data in any way we like. But the convenience of QVariant comes at the expense of efficiency and readability. As a rule, it is usually worth defining a proper C++ class to store our data whenever possible.

QVariant is used by Qt's meta-object system and is therefore part of the *QtCore* module. Nonetheless, when we link against the *QtGui* module, QVariant can store GUI-related types such as QColor, QFont, QIcon, QImage, and QPixmap:

```
QIcon icon("open.png");
QVariant variant = icon;
```

To retrieve the value of a GUI-related type from a QVariant, we can use the QVariant::value<T>() template member function as follows:

```
QIcon icon = variant.value<QIcon>();
```

The value<T>() function also works for converting between non-GUI data types and QVariant, but in practice we normally use the to...() conversion functions (e.g., toString()) for non-GUI types.

QVariant can also be used to store custom data types, assuming they provide a default constructor and a copy constructor. For this to work, we must first register the type using the Q_DECLARE_METATYPE() macro, typically in a header file below the class definition:

```
Q_DECLARE_METATYPE(BusinessCard)
```

This enables us to write code such as this:

```
BusinessCard businessCard;
QVariant variant = QVariant::fromValue(businessCard);
```

```
...
if (variant.canConvert<BusinessCard>()) {
    BusinessCard card = variant.value<BusinessCard>();
    ...
}
```

Because of a compiler limitation, these template member functions are not available for MSVC 6. If you need to use this compiler, use the qVariantFromValue(), qVariantValue<T>(), and qVariantCanConvert<T>() global functions instead.

If the custom data type has << and >> operators for writing to and reading from a QDataStream, we can register them using qRegisterMetaTypeStreamOperators<T>(). This makes it possible to store preferences of custom data types using QSettings, among other things. For example:

```
qRegisterMetaTypeStreamOperators<BusinessCard>("BusinessCard");
```

This chapter focused on the Qt containers, as well as on QString, QByteArray, and QVariant. In addition to these classes, Qt also provides a few other containers. One is QPair<T1, T2>, which simply stores two values and is similar to std::pair<T1, T2>. Another is QBitArray, which we will use in the first section of Chapter 21. Finally, there is QVarLengthArray<T, Prealloc>, a low-level alternative to QVector<T>. Because it preallocates memory on the stack and isn't implicitly shared, its overhead is less than that of QVector<T>, making it more appropriate for tight loops.

Qt's algorithms, including a few not covered here, such as qCopyBackward() and qEqual(), are described in Qt's documentation at http://doc.trolltech.com/4.3/qtalgorithms.html. And for more details of Qt's containers, including information on their time complexity and growth strategies, see http://doc.trolltech.com/4.3/containers.html.

- *Reading and Writing Binary Data*
- *Reading and Writing Text*
- *Traversing Directories*
- *Embedding Resources*
- *Inter-Process Communication*

12. Input/Output

The need to read from or write to files or other devices is common to almost every application. Qt provides excellent support for I/O through `QIODevice`, a powerful abstraction that encapsulates "devices" capable of reading and writing blocks of bytes. Qt includes the following `QIODevice` subclasses:

`QFile`	Accesses files in the local file system and in embedded resources
`QTemporaryFile`	Creates and accesses temporary files in the local file system
`QBuffer`	Reads data from or writes data to a `QByteArray`
`QProcess`	Runs external programs and handles inter-process communication
`QTcpSocket`	Transfers a stream of data over the network using TCP
`QUdpSocket`	Sends or receives UDP datagrams over the network
`QSslSocket`	Transfers an encrypted data stream over the network using SSL/TLS

`QProcess`, `QTcpSocket`, `QUdpSocket`, and `QSslSocket` are sequential devices, meaning that the data can be accessed only once, starting from the first byte and progressing serially to the last byte. `QFile`, `QTemporaryFile`, and `QBuffer` are random-access devices, so bytes can be read any number of times from any position; they provide the `QIODevice::seek()` function for repositioning the file pointer.

In addition to the device classes, Qt also provides two higher-level stream classes that we can use to read from, and write to, any I/O device: `QDataStream` for binary data and `QTextStream` for text. These classes take care of issues such as byte ordering and text encodings, ensuring that Qt applications running on different platforms or in different countries can read and write each other's files. This makes Qt's I/O classes much more convenient than the corresponding Standard C++ classes, which leave these issues to the application programmer.

`QFile` makes it easy to access individual files, whether they are in the file system or embedded in the application's executable as resources. For applications that need to identify whole sets of files to work on, Qt provides the `QDir` and

QFileInfo classes, which handle directories and provide information about the files inside them.

The QProcess class allows us to launch external programs and to communicate with them through their standard input, standard output, and standard error channels (cin, cout, and cerr). We can set the environment variables and working directory that the external application will use. By default, communication with the process is asynchronous (non-blocking), but it is also possible to block on certain operations.

Networking and reading and writing XML are such substantial topics that we cover separately in their own dedicated chapters (Chapter 15 and Chapter 16).

Reading and Writing Binary Data

The simplest way to load and save binary data with Qt is to instantiate a QFile, to open the file, and to access it through a QDataStream object. QDataStream provides a platform-independent storage format that supports basic C++ types such as int and double, and many Qt data types, including QByteArray, QFont, QImage, QPixmap, QString, and QVariant, as well as Qt container classes such as QList<T> and QMap<K, T>.

Here's how we would store an integer, a QImage, and a QMap<QString, QColor> in a file called facts.dat:

```
QImage image("philip.png");

QMap<QString, QColor> map;
map.insert("red", Qt::red);
map.insert("green", Qt::green);
map.insert("blue", Qt::blue);

QFile file("facts.dat");
if (!file.open(QIODevice::WriteOnly)) {
    std::cerr << "Cannot open file for writing: "
              << qPrintable(file.errorString()) << std::endl;
    return;
}

QDataStream out(&file);
out.setVersion(QDataStream::Qt_4_3);

out << quint32(0x12345678) << image << map;
```

If we cannot open the file, we inform the user and return. The qPrintable() macro returns a const char * for a QString. (Another approach would have been to use QString::toStdString(), which returns a std::string, for which <iostream> has a << overload.)

If the file is opened successfully, we create a QDataStream and set its version number. The version number is an integer that influences the way Qt data types are represented (basic C++ data types are always represented the same way). In

Qt 4.3, the most comprehensive format is version 9. We can either hard-code the constant 9 or use the `QDataStream::Qt_4_3` symbolic name.

To ensure that the number `0x12345678` is written as an unsigned 32-bit integer on all platforms, we cast it to `quint32`, a data type that is guaranteed to be exactly 32 bits. To ensure interoperability, `QDataStream` standardizes on big-endian by default; this can be changed by calling `setByteOrder()`.

We don't need to explicitly close the file, since this is done automatically when the `QFile` variable goes out of scope. If we want to verify that the data has actually been written, we can call `flush()` and check its return value (`true` on success).

The code to read back the data mirrors the code we used to write it:

```
quint32 n;
QImage image;
QMap<QString, QColor> map;

QFile file("facts.dat");
if (!file.open(QIODevice::ReadOnly)) {
    std::cerr << "Cannot open file for reading: "
              << qPrintable(file.errorString()) << std::endl;
    return;
}

QDataStream in(&file);
in.setVersion(QDataStream::Qt_4_3);

in >> n >> image >> map;
```

The `QDataStream` version we use for reading is the same as the one we used for writing. This must always be the case. By hard-coding the version number, we guarantee that the application can always read and write the data (assuming it is compiled with Qt 4.3 or any later Qt version).

`QDataStream` stores data in such a way that we can read it back seamlessly. For example, a `QByteArray` is represented as a 32-bit byte count followed by the bytes themselves. `QDataStream` can also be used to read and write raw bytes, without any byte count header, using `readRawBytes()` and `writeRawBytes()`.

Error handling when reading from a `QDataStream` is fairly easy. The stream has a `status()` value that can be `QDataStream::Ok`, `QDataStream::ReadPastEnd`, or `QDataStream::ReadCorruptData`. Once an error has occurred, the `>>` operator always reads zero or empty values. This means that we can often simply read an entire file without worrying about potential errors and check the `status()` value at the end to see if what we read was valid.

`QDataStream` handles a variety of C++ and Qt data types; the complete list is available at `http://doc.trolltech.com/4.3/datastreamformat.html`. We can also add support for our own custom types by overloading the `<<` and `>>` operators. Here's the definition of a custom data type that can be used with `QDataStream`:

```
class Painting
{
public:
    Painting() { myYear = 0; }
    Painting(const QString &title, const QString &artist, int year) {
        myTitle = title;
        myArtist = artist;
        myYear = year;
    }

    void setTitle(const QString &title) { myTitle = title; }
    QString title() const { return myTitle; }
    ...

private:
    QString myTitle;
    QString myArtist;
    int myYear;
};

QDataStream &operator<<(QDataStream &out, const Painting &painting);
QDataStream &operator>>(QDataStream &in, Painting &painting);
```

Here's how we would implement the << operator:

```
QDataStream &operator<<(QDataStream &out, const Painting &painting)
{
    out << painting.title() << painting.artist()
        << quint32(painting.year());
    return out;
}
```

To output a Painting, we simply output two QStrings and a quint32. At the end of the function, we return the stream. This is a common C++ idiom that allows us to use a chain of << operators with an output stream. For example:

```
out << painting1 << painting2 << painting3;
```

The implementation of operator>>() is similar to that of operator<<():

```
QDataStream &operator>>(QDataStream &in, Painting &painting)
{
    QString title;
    QString artist;
    quint32 year;

    in >> title >> artist >> year;
    painting = Painting(title, artist, year);
    return in;
}
```

There are several benefits to providing streaming operators for custom data types. One of them is that it allows us to stream containers that use the custom type. For example:

```
QList<Painting> paintings = ...;
```

```
out << paintings;
```

We can read in containers just as easily:

```
QList<Painting> paintings;
in >> paintings;
```

This would result in a compiler error if `Painting` didn't support << or >>. Another benefit of providing streaming operators for custom types is that we can store values of these types as `QVariant`s, which makes them more widely usable—for example, by `QSettings`. This works provided that we register the type using `qRegisterMetaTypeStreamOperators<T>()` beforehand, as explained in Chapter 11 (p. 292).

When we use `QDataStream`, Qt takes care of reading and writing each type, including containers with an arbitrary number of items. This relieves us from the need to structure what we write and from performing any kind of parsing on what we read. Our only obligation is to ensure that we read all the types in exactly the same order as we wrote them, leaving Qt to handle all the details.

`QDataStream` is useful both for our own custom application file formats and for standard binary formats. We can read and write standard binary formats using the streaming operators on basic types (such as `quint16` or `float`) or using `readRawBytes()` and `writeRawBytes()`. If the `QDataStream` is being used purely to read and write basic C++ data types, we don't even need to call `setVersion()`.

So far, we loaded and saved data with the stream's version hard-coded as `QDataStream::Qt_4_3`. This approach is simple and safe, but it does have one small drawback: We cannot take advantage of new or updated formats. For example, if a later version of Qt added a new attribute to `QFont` (in addition to its point size, family, etc.) and we hard-coded the version number to `Qt_4_3`, that attribute wouldn't be saved or loaded. There are two solutions. The first approach is to embed the `QDataStream` version number in the file:

```
QDataStream out(&file);
out << quint32(MagicNumber) << quint16(out.version());
```

(`MagicNumber` is a constant that uniquely identifies the file type.) This approach ensures that we always write the data using the most recent version of `QDataStream`, whatever that happens to be. When we come to read the file, we read the stream version:

```
quint32 magic;
quint16 streamVersion;

QDataStream in(&file);
in >> magic >> streamVersion;

if (magic != MagicNumber) {
    std::cerr << "File is not recognized by this application"
              << std::endl;
} else if (streamVersion > in.version()) {
    std::cerr << "File is from a more recent version of the "
```

```
                 << "application" << std::endl;
        return false;
    }

    in.setVersion(streamVersion);
```

We can read the data as long as the stream version is less than or equal to the version used by the application; otherwise, we report an error.

If the file format contains a version number of its own, we can use it to deduce the stream version number instead of storing it explicitly. For example, let's suppose that the file format is for version 1.3 of our application. We might then write the data as follows:

```
QDataStream out(&file);
out.setVersion(QDataStream::Qt_4_3);
out << quint32(MagicNumber) << quint16(0x0103);
```

When we read it back, we determine which QDataStream version to use based on the application's version number:

```
QDataStream in(&file);
in >> magic >> appVersion;

if (magic != MagicNumber) {
    std::cerr << "File is not recognized by this application"
              << std::endl;
    return false;
} else if (appVersion > 0x0103) {
    std::cerr << "File is from a more recent version of the "
              << "application" << std::endl;
    return false;
}

if (appVersion < 0x0103) {
    in.setVersion(QDataStream::Qt_3_0);
} else {
    in.setVersion(QDataStream::Qt_4_3);
}
```

In this example, we specify that any file saved with versions prior to 1.3 of the application uses data stream version 4 (`Qt_3_0`), and that files saved with version 1.3 of the application use data stream version 9 (`Qt_4_3`).

In summary, there are three policies for handling `QDataStream` versions: hard-coding the version number, explicitly writing and reading the version number, and using different hard-coded version numbers depending on the application's version. Any of these policies can be used to ensure that data written by an old version of an application can be read by a new version, even if the new version links against a more recent version of Qt. Once we have chosen a policy for handling `QDataStream` versions, reading and writing binary data using Qt is both simple and reliable.

If we want to read or write a file in one go, we can avoid using `QDataStream` and instead use `QIODevice`'s `write()` and `readAll()` functions. For example:

```
bool copyFile(const QString &source, const QString &dest)
{
    QFile sourceFile(source);
    if (!sourceFile.open(QIODevice::ReadOnly))
        return false;

    QFile destFile(dest);
    if (!destFile.open(QIODevice::WriteOnly))
        return false;

    destFile.write(sourceFile.readAll());

    return sourceFile.error() == QFile::NoError
           && destFile.error() == QFile::NoError;
}
```

In the line where `readAll()` is called, the entire contents of the input file are read into a `QByteArray`, which is then passed to the `write()` function to be written to the output file. Having all the data in a `QByteArray` requires more memory than reading item by item, but it offers some advantages. For example, we can then use `qCompress()` and `qUncompress()` to compress and uncompress the data. A less memory-hungry alternative to using `qCompress()` and `qUncompress()` is `QtIOCompressor` from Qt Solutions. A `QtIOCompressor` compresses the stream it writes and decompresses the stream it reads, without storing the entire file in memory.

There are other scenarios in which accessing `QIODevice` directly is more appropriate than using `QDataStream`. `QIODevice` provides a `peek()` function that returns the next data bytes without moving the device position as well as an `ungetChar()` function that "unreads" a byte. This works both for random-access devices (such as files) and for sequential devices (such as network sockets). There is also a `seek()` function that sets the device position, for devices that support random access.

Binary file formats provide the most versatile and most compact means of storing data, and `QDataStream` makes accessing binary data easy. In addition to the examples in this section, we already saw the use of `QDataStream` in Chapter 4 to read and write Spreadsheet files, and we will see it again in Chapter 21, where we use it to read and write Windows cursor files.

Reading and Writing Text

While binary file formats are typically more compact than text-based formats, they are not human-readable or human-editable. In cases where this is an issue, we can use text formats instead. Qt provides the `QTextStream` class for reading and writing plain text files and for files using other text formats, such as HTML, XML, and source code. We cover handling XML files separately in Chapter 16.

`QTextStream` takes care of converting between Unicode and the system's local encoding or any other encoding, and transparently handles the different line-ending conventions used by different operating systems ("\r\n" on Windows, "\n" on Unix and Mac OS X). `QTextStream` uses the 16-bit `QChar` type as its fundamental unit of data. In addition to characters and strings, `QTextStream` supports C++'s basic numeric types, which it converts to and from strings. For example, the following code writes "Thomas M. Disch: 334\n" to the file `sf-book.txt`:

```
QFile file("sf-book.txt");
if (!file.open(QIODevice::WriteOnly)) {
    std::cerr << "Cannot open file for writing: "
              << qPrintable(file.errorString()) << std::endl;
    return;
}

QTextStream out(&file);
out << "Thomas M. Disch: " << 334 << endl;
```

Writing text is very easy, but reading text can be challenging because textual data (unlike binary data written using `QDataStream`) is fundamentally ambiguous. Let's consider the following example:

```
out << "Denmark" << "Norway";
```

If `out` is a `QTextStream`, the data that actually gets written is the string "DenmarkNorway". We can't really expect the following code to read back the data correctly:

```
in >> str1 >> str2;
```

In fact, what happens is that `str1` gets the whole word "DenmarkNorway", and `str2` gets nothing. This problem doesn't occur with `QDataStream` because it stores the length of each string in front of the character data.

For complex file formats, a full-blown parser might be required. Such a parser might work by reading the data character by character using `>>` on a `QChar`, or line by line, using `QTextStream::readLine()`. At the end of this section, we present two small examples, one that reads an input file line by line, and another that reads it character by character. For parsers that work on an entire text, we could read the complete file in one go using `QTextStream::readAll()` if we are not concerned about memory usage, or if we know the file will be small.

By default, `QTextStream` uses the system's local encoding (e.g., ISO 8859-1 or ISO 8859-15 in America and much of Europe) for reading and writing. This can be changed using `setCodec()` as follows:

```
stream.setCodec("UTF-8");
```

The UTF-8 encoding used in the example is a popular ASCII-compatible encoding that can represent the entire Unicode character set. For more information about Unicode and `QTextStream`'s support for encodings, see Chapter 18.

`QTextStream` has various options modeled after those offered by `<iostream>`. These can be set by passing special objects, called *stream manipulators*, on the stream

`setIntegerBase(int)`	
`0`	Auto-detect based on prefix (when reading)
`2`	Binary
`8`	Octal
`10`	Decimal
`16`	Hexadecimal

`setNumberFlags(NumberFlags)`	
`ShowBase`	Show a prefix if the base is 2 ("0b"), 8 ("0"), or 16 ("0x")
`ForceSign`	Always show the sign in real numbers
`ForcePoint`	Always put the decimal separator in numbers
`UppercaseBase`	Use uppercase versions of base prefixes ("0B", "0X")
`UppercaseDigits`	Use uppercase letters in hexadecimal numbers

`setRealNumberNotation(RealNumberNotation)`	
`FixedNotation`	Fixed-point notation (e.g., "0.000123")
`ScientificNotation`	Scientific notation (e.g., "1.234568e-04")
`SmartNotation`	Fixed-point or scientific notation, whichever is most compact

`setRealNumberPrecision(int)`
Sets the maximum number of digits that should be generated (6 by default)

`setFieldWidth(int)`
Sets the minimum size of a field (0 by default)

`setFieldAlignment(FieldAlignment)`	
`AlignLeft`	Pad on the right side of the field
`AlignRight`	Pad on the left side of the field
`AlignCenter`	Pad on both sides of the field
`AlignAccountingStyle`	Pad between the sign and the number

`setPadChar(QChar)`
Sets the character used for padding fields (space by default)

Figure 12.1. Functions to set `QTextStream`'s options

to alter its state, or by calling the functions listed in Figure 12.1. The following example sets the `showbase`, `uppercasedigits`, and `hex` options before it outputs the integer 12 345 678, producing the text "0xBC614E":

```
out << showbase << uppercasedigits << hex << 12345678;
```

Options can also be set using member functions:

```
out.setNumberFlags(QTextStream::ShowBase
                   | QTextStream::UppercaseDigits);
out.setIntegerBase(16);
out << 12345678;
```

Like QDataStream, QTextStream operates on a QIODevice subclass, which can be a QFile, a QTemporaryFile, a QBuffer, a QProcess, a QTcpSocket, a QUdpSocket, or a QSslSocket. In addition, it can be used directly on a QString. For example:

```
QString str;
QTextStream(&str) << oct << 31 << " " << dec << 25 << endl;
```

This makes the contents of str "37 25\n", since the decimal number 31 is expressed as 37 in octal. In this case, we don't need to set an encoding on the stream, since QString is always Unicode.

Let's look at a simple example of a text-based file format. In the Spreadsheet application described in Part I, we used a binary format for storing Spreadsheet data. The data consisted of a sequence of (*row*, *column*, *formula*) triples, one for every non-empty cell. Writing the data as text is straightforward; here is an extract from a revised version of Spreadsheet::writeFile():

```
QTextStream out(&file);
for (int row = 0; row < RowCount; ++row) {
    for (int column = 0; column < ColumnCount; ++column) {
        QString str = formula(row, column);
        if (!str.isEmpty())
            out << row << " " << column << " " << str << endl;
    }
}
```

We have used a simple format, with each line representing one cell and with spaces between the row and the column and between the column and the formula. The formula can contain spaces, but we can assume that it contains no '\n' (which we use to terminate lines). Now let's look at the corresponding reading code:

```
QTextStream in(&file);
while (!in.atEnd()) {
    QString line = in.readLine();
    QStringList fields = line.split(' ');
    if (fields.size() >= 3) {
        int row = fields.takeFirst().toInt();
        int column = fields.takeFirst().toInt();
        setFormula(row, column, fields.join(' '));
    }
}
```

We read in the Spreadsheet data one line at a time. The readLine() function removes the trailing '\n'. QString::split() returns a string list, having split its string wherever the separator it is given appears. For example, the line "5 19 Total value" results in the four-item list ["5", "19", "Total", "value"].

If we have at least three fields, we are ready to extract the data. The `QStringList::takeFirst()` function removes the first item in a list and returns the removed item. We use it to extract the row and column numbers. We don't perform any error checking; if we read a non-integer row or column value, `QString::toInt()` will return 0. When we call `setFormula()`, we must concatenate the remaining fields back into a single string.

In our second `QTextStream` example, we will use a character by character approach to implement a program that reads in a text file and outputs the same text but with trailing spaces removed from lines and all tabs replaced by spaces. The `tidyFile()` function does the program's work:

```
void tidyFile(QIODevice *inDevice, QIODevice *outDevice)
{
    QTextStream in(inDevice);
    QTextStream out(outDevice);

    const int TabSize = 8;
    int endlCount = 0;
    int spaceCount = 0;
    int column = 0;
    QChar ch;

    while (!in.atEnd()) {
        in >> ch;

        if (ch == '\n') {
            ++endlCount;
            spaceCount = 0;
            column = 0;
        } else if (ch == '\t') {
            int size = TabSize - (column % TabSize);
            spaceCount += size;
            column += size;
        } else if (ch == ' ') {
            ++spaceCount;
            ++column;
        } else {
            while (endlCount > 0) {
                out << endl;
                --endlCount;
                column = 0;
            }
            while (spaceCount > 0) {
                out << ' ';
                --spaceCount;
                ++column;
            }
            out << ch;
            ++column;
        }
    }
    out << endl;
}
```

We create an input and an output QTextStream based on the QIODevices that are passed to the function. In addition to the current character, we maintain three state-tracking variables: one counting newlines, one counting spaces, and one marking the current column position in the current line (for converting the tabs to the correct number of spaces).

The parsing is done in a while loop that iterates over every character in the input file, one at a time. The code is a bit subtle in places. For example, although we set TabSize to 8, we replace tabs with precisely enough spaces to pad to the next tab boundary, rather than crudely replacing each tab with eight spaces. If we get a newline, tab, or space, we simply update the state data. Only when we get another kind of character do we produce any output, and before writing the character we write any pending newlines and spaces (to respect blank lines and to preserve indentation) and update the state.

```
int main()
{
    QFile inFile;
    QFile outFile;

    inFile.open(stdin, QFile::ReadOnly);
    outFile.open(stdout, QFile::WriteOnly);

    tidyFile(&inFile, &outFile);

    return 0;
}
```

For this example, we don't need a QApplication object, because we are only using Qt's tool classes. See http://doc.trolltech.com/4.3/tools.html for the list of all the tool classes. We have assumed that the program is used as a filter, for example:

```
tidy < cool.cpp > cooler.cpp
```

It would be easy to extend it to be able to handle file names given on the command line if they are given, and to filter cin to cout otherwise.

Since this is a console application, it has a slightly different .pro file from those we have seen for GUI applications:

```
TEMPLATE      = app
QT            = core
CONFIG       += console
CONFIG       -= app_bundle
SOURCES       = tidy.cpp
```

We only link against *QtCore* since we don't use any GUI functionality. Then we specify that we want to enable console output on Windows and that we don't want the application to live in a bundle on Mac OS X.

For reading and writing plain ASCII files or ISO 8859-1 (Latin-1) files, it is possible to use QIODevice's API directly instead of using a QTextStream. It is rarely wise to do this since most applications need support for other encodings at some point or other, and only `QTextStream` provides seamless support for these. If you still want to write text directly to a `QIODevice`, you must explicitly specify the `QIODevice::Text` flag to the `open()` function, for example:

```
file.open(QIODevice::WriteOnly | QIODevice::Text);
```

When writing, this flag tells `QIODevice` to convert '\n' characters into "\r\n" sequences on Windows. When reading, this flag tells the device to ignore '\r' characters on all platforms. We can then assume that the end of each line is signified with a '\n' newline character regardless of the line-ending convention used by the operating system.

Traversing Directories

The `QDir` class provides a platform-independent means of traversing directories and retrieving information about files. To see how `QDir` is used, we will write a small console application that calculates the space consumed by all the images in a particular directory and all its subdirectories to any depth.

The heart of the application is the `imageSpace()` function, which recursively computes the cumulative size of a given directory's images:

```
qlonglong imageSpace(const QString &path)
{
    QDir dir(path);
    qlonglong size = 0;

    QStringList filters;
    foreach (QByteArray format, QImageReader::supportedImageFormats())
        filters += "*." + format;

    foreach (QString file, dir.entryList(filters, QDir::Files))
        size += QFileInfo(dir, file).size();

    foreach (QString subDir, dir.entryList(QDir::Dirs
                                           | QDir::NoDotAndDotDot))
        size += imageSpace(path + QDir::separator() + subDir);

    return size;
}
```

We begin by creating a `QDir` object using the given path, which may be relative to the current directory or absolute. We pass the `entryList()` function two arguments. The first is a list of file name filters. These can contain '*' and '?' wildcard characters. In this example, we are filtering to include only file formats that `QImage` can read. The second argument specifies what kinds of entries we want (normal files, directories, drives, etc.).

We iterate over the list of files, accumulating their sizes. The `QFileInfo` class allows us to access a file's attributes, such as the file's size, permissions, owner, and timestamps.

The second entryList() call retrieves all the subdirectories in this directory. We iterate over them (excluding . and ..) and recursively call imageSpace() to ascertain their accumulated image sizes.

To create each subdirectory's path, we combine the current directory's path with the subdirectory name, separating them with a slash. QDir treats '/' as a directory separator on all platforms, in addition to recognizing '\' on Windows. When presenting paths to the user, we can call the static function QDir::toNativeSeparators() to convert slashes to the correct platform-specific separator.

Let's add a main() function to our small program:

```
int main(int argc, char *argv[])
{
    QCoreApplication app(argc, argv);
    QStringList args = QCoreApplication::arguments();

    QString path = QDir::currentPath();
    if (args.count() > 1)
        path = args[1];

    std::cout << "Space used by images in " << qPrintable(path)
              << " and its subdirectories is "
              << (imageSpace(path) / 1024) << " KB" << std::endl;

    return 0;
}
```

We use QDir::currentPath() to initialize the path to the current directory. Alternatively, we could have used QDir::homePath() to initialize it to the user's home directory. If the user has specified a path on the command line, we use that instead. Finally, we call our imageSpace() function to calculate how much space is consumed by images.

The QDir class provides other file- and directory-related functions, including entryInfoList() (which returns a list of QFileInfo objects), rename(), exists(), mkdir(), and rmdir(). The QFile class provides some static convenience functions, including remove() and exists(). And the QFileSystemWatcher class can notify us when a change occurs to a directory or to a file, by emitting directoryChanged() and fileChanged() signals.

Embedding Resources

So far in this chapter, we have talked about accessing data in external devices, but with Qt it is also possible to embed binary data or text inside the application's executable. This is achieved using Qt's resource system. In other chapters, we used resource files to embed images in the executable, but it is possible to embed any kind of file. Embedded files can be read using QFile just like normal files in the file system.

Resources are converted into C++ code by rcc, Qt's resource compiler. We can tell qmake to include special rules to run rcc by adding this line to the .pro file:

```
RESOURCES = myresourcefile.qrc
```

The `myresourcefile.qrc` file is an XML file that lists the files to embed in the executable.

Let's imagine that we are writing an application that keeps contact details. For the convenience of our users, we want to embed the international dialing codes in the executable. If the file is in the `datafiles` directory in the application's build directory, the resource file might look like this:

```
<RCC>
<qresource>
    <file>datafiles/phone-codes.dat</file>
</qresource>
</RCC>
```

From the application, resources are identified by the `:/` path prefix. In this example, the dialing codes file has the path `:/datafiles/phone-codes.dat` and can be read just like any other file using `QFile`.

Embedding data in the executable has the advantage that it cannot get lost and makes it possible to create truly stand-alone executables (if static linking is also used). Two disadvantages are that if the embedded data needs changing the whole executable must be replaced, and the size of the executable will be larger because it must accommodate the embedded data.

Qt's resource system provides more features than we presented in this example, including support for file name aliases and for localization. These facilities are documented at `http://doc.trolltech.com/4.3/resources.html`.

Inter-Process Communication

The `QProcess` class allows us to run external programs and to interact with them. The class works asynchronously, doing its work in the background so that the user interface remains responsive. `QProcess` emits signals to notify us when the external process has data or has finished.

We will review the code of a small application that provides a user interface for an external image conversion program. For this example, we rely on the ImageMagick `convert` program, which is freely available for all major platforms. Our user interface is shown in Figure 12.2.

The user interface was created in *Qt Designer*. The `.ui` file is with the examples that accompany this book. Here, we will focus on the subclass that is derived from the uic-generated `Ui::ConvertDialog` class, starting with the header:

```
#ifndef CONVERTDIALOG_H
#define CONVERTDIALOG_H

#include <QDialog>
#include <QProcess>
```

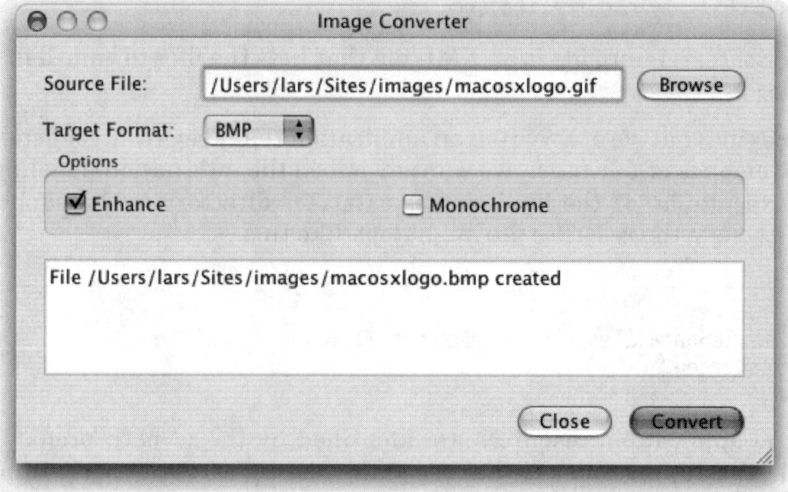

Figure 12.2. The Image Converter application

```
#include "ui_convertdialog.h"

class ConvertDialog : public QDialog, private Ui::ConvertDialog
{
    Q_OBJECT

public:
    ConvertDialog(QWidget *parent = 0);

private slots:
    void on_browseButton_clicked();
    void convertImage();
    void updateOutputTextEdit();
    void processFinished(int exitCode, QProcess::ExitStatus exitStatus);
    void processError(QProcess::ProcessError error);

private:
    QProcess process;
    QString targetFile;
};

#endif
```

The header follows the familiar pattern for subclasses of *Qt Designer* forms. One minor difference from some of the other examples we have seen is that here we have used private inheritance for the `Ui::ConvertDialog` class. This prevents access to the form's widgets from outside the form's functions. Thanks to *Qt Designer*'s automatic connection mechanism (p. 28), the `on_browseButton_clicked()` slot is automatically connected to the Browse button's `clicked()` signal.

```
ConvertDialog::ConvertDialog(QWidget *parent)
    : QDialog(parent)
{
```

```
    setupUi(this);

    QPushButton *convertButton =
            buttonBox->button(QDialogButtonBox::Ok);
    convertButton->setText(tr("&Convert"));
    convertButton->setEnabled(false);

    connect(convertButton, SIGNAL(clicked()),
            this, SLOT(convertImage()));
    connect(buttonBox, SIGNAL(rejected()), this, SLOT(reject()));
    connect(&process, SIGNAL(readyReadStandardError()),
            this, SLOT(updateOutputTextEdit()));
    connect(&process, SIGNAL(finished(int, QProcess::ExitStatus)),
            this, SLOT(processFinished(int, QProcess::ExitStatus)));
    connect(&process, SIGNAL(error(QProcess::ProcessError)),
            this, SLOT(processError(QProcess::ProcessError)));
}
```

The `setupUi()` call creates and lays out all the form's widgets, and establishes the signal–slot connection for the `on_browseButton_clicked()` slot. We get a pointer to the button box's OK button and give it more suitable text. We also disable it, since initially there is no image to convert, and we connect it to the `convertImage()` slot. Then we connect the button box's `rejected()` signal (emitted by the Close button) to the dialog's `reject()` slot. After that, we connect three signals from the `QProcess` object to three private slots. Whenever the external process has data on its `cerr`, we will handle it in `updateOutputTextEdit()`.

```
void ConvertDialog::on_browseButton_clicked()
{
    QString initialName = sourceFileEdit->text();
    if (initialName.isEmpty())
        initialName = QDir::homePath();
    QString fileName =
            QFileDialog::getOpenFileName(this, tr("Choose File"),
                                         initialName);
    fileName = QDir::toNativeSeparators(fileName);
    if (!fileName.isEmpty()) {
        sourceFileEdit->setText(fileName);
        buttonBox->button(QDialogButtonBox::Ok)->setEnabled(true);
    }
}
```

The Browse button's `clicked()` signal is automatically connected to the `on_browseButton_clicked()` slot by `setupUi()`. If the user has previously selected a file, we initialize the file dialog with that file's name; otherwise, we use the user's home directory.

```
void ConvertDialog::convertImage()
{
    QString sourceFile = sourceFileEdit->text();
    targetFile = QFileInfo(sourceFile).path() + QDir::separator()
                 + QFileInfo(sourceFile).baseName() + "."
                 + targetFormatComboBox->currentText().toLower();
    buttonBox->button(QDialogButtonBox::Ok)->setEnabled(false);
```

```
        outputTextEdit->clear();

        QStringList args;
        if (enhanceCheckBox->isChecked())
            args << "-enhance";
        if (monochromeCheckBox->isChecked())
            args << "-monochrome";
        args << sourceFile << targetFile;

        process.start("convert", args);
    }
```

When the user clicks the Convert button, we copy the source file's name and change the extension to match the target file format. We use the platform-specific directory separator ('/' or '\', available as `QDir::separator()`) instead of hard-coding slashes because the file name will be visible to the user.

We then disable the `Convert` button to avoid the user accidentally launching multiple conversions, and we clear the text editor that we use to show status information.

To initiate the external process, we call `QProcess::start()` with the name of the program we want to run (`convert`) and any arguments it requires. In this case, we pass the `-enhance` and `-monochrome` flags if the user checked the appropriate options, followed by the source and target file names. The `convert` program infers the required conversion from the file extensions.

```
    void ConvertDialog::updateOutputTextEdit()
    {
        QByteArray newData = process.readAllStandardError();
        QString text = outputTextEdit->toPlainText()
                       + QString::fromLocal8Bit(newData);
        outputTextEdit->setPlainText(text);
    }
```

Whenever the external process writes to `cerr`, the `updateOutputTextEdit()` slot is called. We read the error text and add it to the `QTextEdit`'s existing text.

```
    void ConvertDialog::processFinished(int exitCode,
                                        QProcess::ExitStatus exitStatus)
    {
        if (exitStatus == QProcess::CrashExit) {
            outputTextEdit->append(tr("Conversion program crashed"));
        } else if (exitCode != 0) {
            outputTextEdit->append(tr("Conversion failed"));
        } else {
            outputTextEdit->append(tr("File %1 created").arg(targetFile));
        }
        buttonBox->button(QDialogButtonBox::Ok)->setEnabled(true);
    }
```

When the process has finished, we let the user know the outcome and enable the Convert button.

```
    void ConvertDialog::processError(QProcess::ProcessError error)
```

```
{
    if (error == QProcess::FailedToStart) {
        outputTextEdit->append(tr("Conversion program not found"));
        buttonBox->button(QDialogButtonBox::Ok)->setEnabled(true);
    }
}
```

If the process cannot be started, `QProcess` emits `error()` instead of `finished()`. We report any error and enable the `Click` button.

In this example, we have performed the file conversions asynchronously—that is, we have told `QProcess` to run the `convert` program and to return control to the application immediately. This keeps the user interface responsive while the processing occurs in the background. But in some situations we need the external process to complete before we can go any further in our application, and in such cases we need `QProcess` to operate synchronously.

One common example where synchronous behavior is desirable is for applications that support plain text editing using the user's preferred text editor. This is straightforward to implement using `QProcess`. For example, let's assume that we have the plain text in a `QTextEdit`, and we provide an Edit button that the user can click, connected to an `edit()` slot.

```
void ExternalEditor::edit()
{
    QTemporaryFile outFile;
    if (!outFile.open())
        return;

    QString fileName = outFile.fileName();
    QTextStream out(&outFile);
    out << textEdit->toPlainText();
    outFile.close();

    QProcess::execute(editor, QStringList() << options << fileName);

    QFile inFile(fileName);
    if (!inFile.open(QIODevice::ReadOnly))
        return;

    QTextStream in(&inFile);
    textEdit->setPlainText(in.readAll());
}
```

We use `QTemporaryFile` to create an empty file with a unique name. We don't specify any arguments to `QTemporaryFile::open()` since it conveniently defaults to opening in read-write mode. We write the contents of the text editor to the temporary file, and then we close the file because some text editors cannot work on already open files.

The `QProcess::execute()` static function runs an external process and blocks until the process has finished. The `editor` argument is a `QString` holding the name of an editor executable (e.g., "gvim"). The `options` argument is a `QStringList` (containing one item, "-f", if we are using `gvim`).

After the user has closed the text editor, the process finishes and the `execute()` call returns. We then open the temporary file and read its contents into the `QTextEdit`. `QTemporaryFile` automatically deletes the temporary file when the object goes out of scope.

Signal–slot connections are not needed when `QProcess` is used synchronously. If finer control is required than provided by the static `execute()` function, we can use an alternative approach. This involves creating a `QProcess` object and calling `start()` on it, and then forcing it to block by calling `QProcess::waitForStarted()`, and if that is successful, calling `QProcess::waitForFinished()`. See the `QProcess` reference documentation for an example that uses this approach.

In this section, we used `QProcess` to give us access to preexisting functionality. Using applications that already exist can save development time and can insulate us from the details of issues that are of marginal interest to our main application's purpose. Another way to access preexisting functionality is to link against a library that provides it. But where no suitable library exists, wrapping a console application using `QProcess` can work well.

Another use of `QProcess` is to launch other GUI applications. However, if our aim is communication between applications rather than simply running one from another, we might be better off having them communicate directly, using Qt's networking classes or the ActiveQt extension on Windows. And if we want to launch the user's preferred web browser or email client, we can simply call `QDesktopServices::openUrl()`.

- *Connecting and Querying*
- *Viewing Tables*
- *Editing Records Using Forms*
- *Presenting Data in Tabular Forms*

13. Databases

The *QtSql* module provides a platform- and database-independent interface for accessing SQL databases. This interface is supported by a set of classes that use Qt's model/view architecture to provide database integration with the user interface. This chapter assumes familiarity with Qt's model/view classes, covered in Chapter 10.

A database connection is represented by a `QSqlDatabase` object. Qt uses drivers to communicate with the various database APIs. The Qt Desktop Edition includes the following drivers:

Driver	Database
QDB2	IBM DB2 version 7.1 and later
QIBASE	Borland InterBase
QMYSQL	MySQL
QOCI	Oracle (Oracle Call Interface)
QODBC	ODBC (includes Microsoft SQL Server)
QPSQL	PostgreSQL 7.3 and later
QSQLITE	SQLite version 3
QSQLITE2	SQLite version 2
QTDS	Sybase Adaptive Server

Due to license restrictions, not all of the drivers are provided with the Qt Open Source Edition. When configuring Qt, we can choose between including the SQL drivers inside Qt itself and building them as plugins. Qt is supplied with the SQLite database, a public domain in-process database.*

---

*SQL support must be enabled when Qt is built. For example, Qt can be compiled with support for SQLite built-in by passing the `-qt-sql-sqlite` command-line option to the `configure` script or by setting the appropriate option in the Qt installer.

For users who are comfortable with SQL syntax, the QSqlQuery class provides a means of directly executing arbitrary SQL statements and handling their results. For users who prefer a higher-level database interface that avoids SQL syntax, QSqlTableModel and QSqlRelationalTableModel provide suitable abstractions. These classes represent an SQL table in the same way as Qt's other model classes (covered in Chapter 10). They can be used stand-alone to traverse and edit data in code, or they can be attached to views through which end-users can view and edit the data themselves.

Qt also makes it straightforward to program the common database idioms, such as master–detail and drill-down, and to view database tables using forms or GUI tables, as the examples in this chapter will demonstrate.

Connecting and Querying

To execute SQL queries, we must first establish a connection with a database. Typically, database connections are set up in a separate function that we call at application startup. For example:

```
bool createConnection()
{
    QSqlDatabase db = QSqlDatabase::addDatabase("QMYSQL");
    db.setHostName("mozart.konkordia.edu");
    db.setDatabaseName("musicdb");
    db.setUserName("gbatstone");
    db.setPassword("T17aV44");
    if (!db.open()) {
        QMessageBox::critical(0, QObject::tr("Database Error"),
                              db.lastError().text());
        return false;
    }
    return true;
}
```

First, we call QSqlDatabase::addDatabase() to create a QSqlDatabase object. The first argument to addDatabase() specifies which database driver Qt must use to access the database. In this case, we use MySQL.

Next, we set the database host name, the database name, the user name, and the password, and we open the connection. If open() fails, we show an error message.

Typically, we would call createConnection() in main():

```
int main(int argc, char *argv[])
{
    QApplication app(argc, argv);
    if (!createConnection())
        return 1;
    ...
    return app.exec();
}
```

Once a connection is established, we can use `QSqlQuery` to execute any SQL statement that the underlying database supports. For example, here's how to execute a `SELECT` statement:

```
QSqlQuery query;
query.exec("SELECT title, year FROM cd WHERE year >= 1998");
```

After the `exec()` call, we can navigate through the query's result set:

```
while (query.next()) {
    QString title = query.value(0).toString();
    int year = query.value(1).toInt();
    std::cerr << qPrintable(title) << ": " << year << std::endl;
}
```

We call `next()` once to position the `QSqlQuery` on the *first* record of the result set. Subsequent calls to `next()` advance the record pointer by one record each time, until the end is reached, at which point `next()` returns `false`. If the result set is empty (or if the query failed), the first call to `next()` will return `false`.

The `value()` function returns the value of a field as a `QVariant`. The fields are numbered from 0 in the order given in the `SELECT` statement. The `QVariant` class can hold many C++ and Qt types, including `int` and `QString`. The different types of data that can be stored in a database are mapped into the corresponding C++ and Qt types and stored in `QVariant`s. For example, a `VARCHAR` is represented as a `QString` and a `DATETIME` as a `QDateTime`.

`QSqlQuery` provides some other functions to navigate through the result set: `first()`, `last()`, `previous()`, and `seek()`. These functions are convenient, but for some databases they can be slower and more memory-hungry than `next()`. For an easy optimization when operating on large data sets, we can call `QSqlQuery::setForwardOnly(true)` before calling `exec()`, and then only use `next()` for navigating through the result set.

Earlier we specified the SQL query as an argument to `QSqlQuery::exec()`, but we can also pass it directly to the constructor, which executes it immediately:

```
QSqlQuery query("SELECT title, year FROM cd WHERE year >= 1998");
```

We can check for an error by calling `isActive()` on the query:

```
if (!query.isActive())
    QMessageBox::warning(this, tr("Database Error"),
                         query.lastError().text());
```

If no error occurs, the query will become "active" and we can use `next()` to navigate through the result set.

Doing an `INSERT` is almost as easy as performing a `SELECT`:

```
QSqlQuery query("INSERT INTO cd (id, artistid, title, year) "
                "VALUES (203, 102, 'Living in America', 2002)");
```

After this, numRowsAffected() returns the number of rows that were affected by the SQL statement (or −1 on error).

If we need to insert a lot of records, or if we want to avoid converting values to strings (and escaping them correctly), we can use prepare() to specify a query that contains placeholders and then bind the values we want to insert. Qt supports both the Oracle-style and the ODBC-style syntax for placeholders for all databases, using native support where it is available and simulating it otherwise. Here's an example that uses the Oracle-style syntax with named placeholders:

```
QSqlQuery query;
query.prepare("INSERT INTO cd (id, artistid, title, year) "
              "VALUES (:id, :artistid, :title, :year)");
query.bindValue(":id", 203);
query.bindValue(":artistid", 102);
query.bindValue(":title", "Living in America");
query.bindValue(":year", 2002);
query.exec();
```

Here's the same example using ODBC-style positional placeholders:

```
QSqlQuery query;
query.prepare("INSERT INTO cd (id, artistid, title, year) "
              "VALUES (?, ?, ?, ?)");
query.addBindValue(203);
query.addBindValue(102);
query.addBindValue("Living in America");
query.addBindValue(2002);
query.exec();
```

After the call to exec(), we can call bindValue() or addBindValue() to bind new values, and then call exec() again to execute the query with the new values.

Placeholders are often used to specify binary data or strings that contain non-ASCII or non-Latin-1 characters. Behind the scenes, Qt uses Unicode with those databases that support Unicode, and for those that don't, Qt transparently converts strings to the appropriate encoding.

Qt supports SQL transactions on databases where they are available. To start a transaction, we call transaction() on the QSqlDatabase object that represents the database connection. To finish the transaction, we call either commit() or rollback(). For example, here's how we would look up a foreign key and execute an INSERT statement inside a transaction:

```
QSqlDatabase::database().transaction();
QSqlQuery query;
query.exec("SELECT id FROM artist WHERE name = 'Gluecifer'");
if (query.next()) {
    int artistId = query.value(0).toInt();
    query.exec("INSERT INTO cd (id, artistid, title, year) "
               "VALUES (201, " + QString::number(artistId)
               + ", 'Riding the Tiger', 1997)");
}
```

```
QSqlDatabase::database().commit();
```

The `QSqlDatabase::database()` function returns a `QSqlDatabase` object representing the connection we created in `createConnection()`. If a transaction cannot be started, `QSqlDatabase::transaction()` returns `false`. Some databases don't support transactions. For those, the `transaction()`, `commit()`, and `rollback()` functions do nothing. We can test whether a database supports transactions using `hasFeature()` on the `QSqlDriver` associated with the database:

```
QSqlDriver *driver = QSqlDatabase::database().driver();
if (driver->hasFeature(QSqlDriver::Transactions))
    ...
```

Several other database features can be tested for, including whether the database supports BLOBs (binary large objects), Unicode, and prepared queries.

It is also possible to access the low-level database driver handle and the low-level handle to a query's result set, using `QSqlDriver::handle()` and `QSqlResult::handle()`. However, both functions are dangerous unless you know exactly what you are doing and are very careful. See their documentation for examples and an explanation of the risks.

In the examples so far, we have assumed that the application is using a single database connection. If we want to create multiple connections, we can pass a name as a second argument to `addDatabase()`. For example:

```
QSqlDatabase db = QSqlDatabase::addDatabase("QPSQL", "OTHER");
db.setHostName("saturn.mcmanamy.edu");
db.setDatabaseName("starsdb");
db.setUserName("hilbert");
db.setPassword("ixtapa7");
```

We can then retrieve a pointer to the `QSqlDatabase` object by passing the name to `QSqlDatabase::database()`:

```
QSqlDatabase db = QSqlDatabase::database("OTHER");
```

To execute queries using the other connection, we pass the `QSqlDatabase` object to the `QSqlQuery` constructor:

```
QSqlQuery query(db);
query.exec("SELECT id FROM artist WHERE name = 'Mando Diao'");
```

Multiple connections are useful if we want to perform more than one transaction at a time, since each connection can handle only a single active transaction. When we use multiple database connections, we can still have one unnamed connection, and `QSqlQuery` will use that connection if none is specified.

In addition to `QSqlQuery`, Qt provides the `QSqlTableModel` class as a higher-level interface, allowing us to avoid using raw SQL for performing the most common SQL operations (`SELECT`, `INSERT`, `UPDATE`, and `DELETE`). The class can also be used stand-alone to manipulate a database without any GUI involvement, or it can be used as a data source for `QListView` or `QTableView`.

Here's an example that uses `QSqlTableModel` to perform a `SELECT`:

```
QSqlTableModel model;
model.setTable("cd");
model.setFilter("year >= 1998");
model.select();
```

This is equivalent to the query

```
SELECT * FROM cd WHERE year >= 1998
```

Navigating through the result set is done by retrieving a given record using `QSqlTableModel::record()` and by accessing individual fields using `value()`:

```
for (int i = 0; i < model.rowCount(); ++i) {
    QSqlRecord record = model.record(i);
    QString title = record.value("title").toString();
    int year = record.value("year").toInt();
    std::cerr << qPrintable(title) << ": " << year << std::endl;
}
```

The `QSqlRecord::value()` function takes either a field name or a field index. When operating on large data sets, it is recommended that fields are specified by their indexes. For example:

```
int titleIndex = model.record().indexOf("title");
int yearIndex = model.record().indexOf("year");
for (int i = 0; i < model.rowCount(); ++i) {
    QSqlRecord record = model.record(i);
    QString title = record.value(titleIndex).toString();
    int year = record.value(yearIndex).toInt();
    std::cerr << qPrintable(title) << ": " << year << std::endl;
}
```

To insert a record into a database table, we call `insertRow()` to create a new empty row (record), and we use `setData()` to set the values of each column (field):

```
QSqlTableModel model;
model.setTable("cd");
int row = 0;
model.insertRows(row, 1);
model.setData(model.index(row, 0), 113);
model.setData(model.index(row, 1), "Shanghai My Heart");
model.setData(model.index(row, 2), 224);
model.setData(model.index(row, 3), 2003);
model.submitAll();
```

After the call to `submitAll()`, the record might be moved to a different row position, depending on how the table is ordered. The `submitAll()` call will return `false` if the insertion failed.

An important difference between an SQL model and a standard model is that for an SQL model we must call `submitAll()` to have any changes written to the database.

To update a record, we must first position the `QSqlTableModel` on the record we want to modify (e.g., using `select()`). We then extract the record, update the fields we want to change, and write our changes back to the database:

```
QSqlTableModel model;
model.setTable("cd");
model.setFilter("id = 125");
model.select();
if (model.rowCount() == 1) {
    QSqlRecord record = model.record(0);
    record.setValue("title", "Melody A.M.");
    record.setValue("year", record.value("year").toInt() + 1);
    model.setRecord(0, record);
    model.submitAll();
}
```

If there is a record that matches the specified filter, we retrieve it using `QSqlTableModel::record()`. We apply our changes and overwrite the original record with our modified record.

It is also possible to perform an update using `setData()`, just as we would do for a non-SQL model. The model indexes that we retrieve are for a given row and column:

```
model.select();
if (model.rowCount() == 1) {
    model.setData(model.index(0, 1), "Melody A.M.");
    model.setData(model.index(0, 3),
                  model.data(model.index(0, 3)).toInt() + 1);
    model.submitAll();
}
```

Deleting a record is similar to updating:

```
model.setTable("cd");
model.setFilter("id = 125");
model.select();
if (model.rowCount() == 1) {
    model.removeRows(0, 1);
    model.submitAll();
}
```

The `removeRows()` call takes the row number of the first record to delete and the number of records to delete. The next example deletes all the records that match the filter:

```
model.setTable("cd");
model.setFilter("year < 1990");
model.select();
if (model.rowCount() > 0) {
    model.removeRows(0, model.rowCount());
```

```
        model.submitAll();
    }
```

The `QSqlQuery` and `QSqlTableModel` classes provide an interface between Qt and an SQL database. Using these classes, we can create forms that present data to users and that let them insert, update, and delete records.

For projects that use the SQL classes, we must add the line

```
    QT += sql
```

to their `.pro` file. This will ensure that the application is linked against the *QtSql* library.

Viewing Tables

In the preceding section, we saw how to interact with a database using `QSqlQuery` and `QSqlTableModel`. In this section, we will see how to present a `QSqlTableModel` in a `QTableView` widget.

The Scooters application, shown in Figure 13.1, presents a table of scooter models. The example is based on a single table, `scooter`, defined as follows:

```
    CREATE TABLE scooter (
        id INTEGER PRIMARY KEY AUTOINCREMENT,
        name VARCHAR(40) NOT NULL,
        maxspeed INTEGER NOT NULL,
        maxrange INTEGER NOT NULL,
        weight INTEGER NOT NULL,
        description VARCHAR(80) NOT NULL);
```

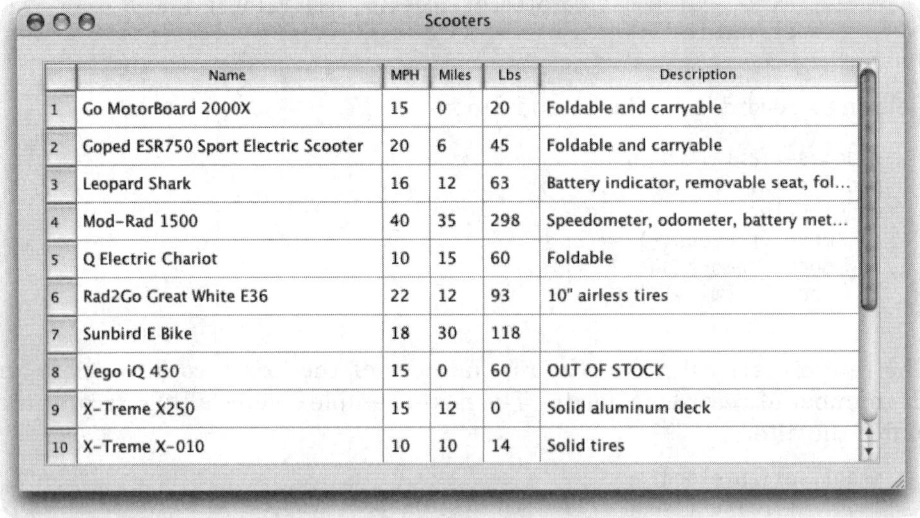

Scooters

	Name	MPH	Miles	Lbs	Description
1	Go MotorBoard 2000X	15	0	20	Foldable and carryable
2	Goped ESR750 Sport Electric Scooter	20	6	45	Foldable and carryable
3	Leopard Shark	16	12	63	Battery indicator, removable seat, fol...
4	Mod-Rad 1500	40	35	298	Speedometer, odometer, battery met...
5	Q Electric Chariot	10	15	60	Foldable
6	Rad2Go Great White E36	22	12	93	10" airless tires
7	Sunbird E Bike	18	30	118	
8	Vego iQ 450	15	0	60	OUT OF STOCK
9	X-Treme X250	15	12	0	Solid aluminum deck
10	X-Treme X-010	10	10	14	Solid tires

Figure 13.1. The Scooters application

The `id` field's values are generated automatically by the database, in this case by SQLite. Other databases may use a different syntax for this.

For ease of maintenance, we use an enum to give meaningful names to the column indexes:

```
enum {
    Scooter_Id = 0,
    Scooter_Name = 1,
    Scooter_MaxSpeed = 2,
    Scooter_MaxRange = 3,
    Scooter_Weight = 4,
    Scooter_Description = 5
};
```

Here is all the code that is necessary to set up a `QSqlTableModel` to display the `scooter` table:

```
    model = new QSqlTableModel(this);
    model->setTable("scooter");
    model->setSort(Scooter_Name, Qt::AscendingOrder);
    model->setHeaderData(Scooter_Name, Qt::Horizontal, tr("Name"));
    model->setHeaderData(Scooter_MaxSpeed, Qt::Horizontal, tr("MPH"));
    model->setHeaderData(Scooter_MaxRange, Qt::Horizontal, tr("Miles"));
    model->setHeaderData(Scooter_Weight, Qt::Horizontal, tr("Lbs"));
    model->setHeaderData(Scooter_Description, Qt::Horizontal,
                         tr("Description"));
    model->select();
```

Creating the model is similar to what we saw in the preceding section. One difference is that we have provided our own column titles. If we had not done so, the raw field names would have been used. We have also specified a sorting order using `setSort()`; behind the scenes, this is implemented by an `ORDER BY` clause.

Now that we have created the model and populated it with data using `select()`, we can create a view to present it:

```
    view = new QTableView;
    view->setModel(model);
    view->setSelectionMode(QAbstractItemView::SingleSelection);
    view->setSelectionBehavior(QAbstractItemView::SelectRows);
    view->setColumnHidden(Scooter_Id, true);
    view->resizeColumnsToContents();
    view->setEditTriggers(QAbstractItemView::NoEditTriggers);

    QHeaderView *header = view->horizontalHeader();
    header->setStretchLastSection(true);
```

In Chapter 10, we saw how to use `QTableView` to present data from a `QAbstractItemModel` in a table. Since `QSqlTableModel` is (indirectly) derived from `QAbstractItemModel`, it can readily be used as the data source of a `QTableView`. The `setModel()` call is all that is necessary to connect the view to the model. The rest of the code only customizes the table to make it more user-friendly.

The selection mode specifies what, if anything, the user can select; here we have made individual cells (fields) selectable. This selection is usually shown by a dotted outline around the selected cell. The selection behavior specifies how selections should work visually, in this case by entire rows. This selection is usually shown by using a different background color. We have chosen to hide the ID column because the IDs are not meaningful to the user. We have also set `NoEditTriggers` to make the table view read-only.

An alternative for presenting read-only tables is to use `QSqlTableModel`'s base class, `QSqlQueryModel`. This class provides the `setQuery()` function, so it is possible to set complex SQL queries to provide particular views of one or more tables—for example, using joins.

Unlike the Scooters database, most databases have lots of tables and foreign key relationships. Qt provides `QSqlRelationalTableModel`, a subclass of `QSqlTableModel` that can be used to display and edit tables with foreign keys. A `QSqlRelationalTableModel` is very similar to a `QSqlTableModel`, except that we can add `QSqlRelations` to the model, one for each foreign key. In many cases, a foreign key has an ID field and a name field; by using a `QSqlRelationalTableModel`, we can ensure that users can see and change the name field while behind the scenes the corresponding ID field is the one that is actually used. For this to work correctly, we must set a `QSqlRelationalDelegate` (or a custom subclass of our own) on the view that is being used to present the model.

We will show how to enable the presentation and changing of foreign keys in the next two sections, and we will give more coverage of `QTableViews` in the last section of this chapter.

Editing Records Using Forms

In this section, we will see how to create a dialog form that displays one record at a time. The dialog can be used to add, edit, and delete individual records, and to navigate through all the records in a table.

We will illustrate these concepts in the context of the Staff Manager application. The application keeps track of which department employees are in, where the departments are located, and some basic information about employees, such as their internal phone extension. The application uses the following three tables:

```
CREATE TABLE location (
    id INTEGER PRIMARY KEY AUTOINCREMENT,
    name VARCHAR(40) NOT NULL));

CREATE TABLE department (
    id INTEGER PRIMARY KEY AUTOINCREMENT,
    name VARCHAR(40) NOT NULL,
    locationid INTEGER NOT NULL,
    FOREIGN KEY (locationid) REFERENCES location));

CREATE TABLE employee (
```

```
    id INTEGER PRIMARY KEY AUTOINCREMENT,
    name VARCHAR(40) NOT NULL,
    departmentid INTEGER NOT NULL,
    extension INTEGER NOT NULL,
    email VARCHAR(40) NOT NULL,
    startdate DATE NOT NULL,
    FOREIGN KEY (departmentid) REFERENCES department));
```

The tables and their relationships are shown schematically in Figure 13.2. Each location can have any number of departments, and each department can have any number of employees. The syntax for specifying foreign keys is for SQLite 3 and may be different for other databases.

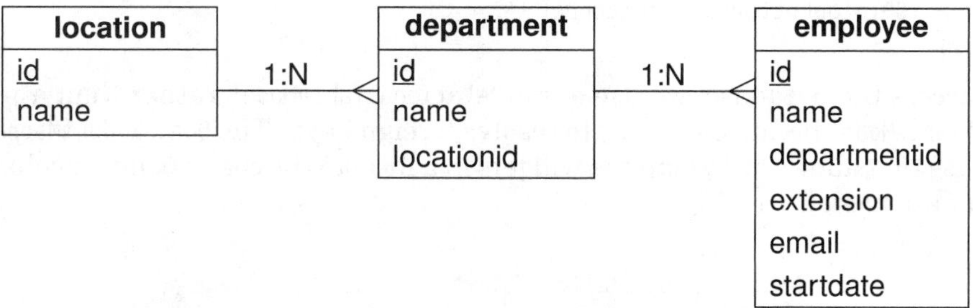

Figure 13.2. The Staff Manager application's tables

In this section, we will focus on `EmployeeForm`, the dialog for editing employees. In the next section, we will review `MainForm`, which provides a master–detail view of departments and employees.

The `EmployeeForm` class provides a drill-down from the main form's summary of employees to a particular employee's full details. When invoked, the form shows the specified employee if a valid employee ID is given, or the first employee otherwise. (The form is shown in Figure 13.3.) Users can navigate through the employees, edit or delete existing employees, and add new employees.

We have provided the following enum in `employeeform.h` to give meaningful names to the column indexes:

```
enum {
    Employee_Id = 0,
    Employee_Name = 1,
    Employee_DepartmentId = 2,
    Employee_Extension = 3,
    Employee_Email = 4,
    Employee_StartDate = 5
};
```

The rest of the header file defines the `EmployeeForm` class:

```
class EmployeeForm : public QDialog
{
    Q_OBJECT
```

```
public:
    EmployeeForm(int id, QWidget *parent = 0);

    void done(int result);

private slots:
    void addEmployee();
    void deleteEmployee();

private:
    QSqlRelationalTableModel *tableModel;
    QDataWidgetMapper *mapper;
    QLabel *nameLabel;
    ...
    QDialogButtonBox *buttonBox;
};
```

To access the database, we use a `QSqlRelationalTableModel` rather than a plain `QSqlTableModel` because we need to resolve foreign keys. The `QDataWidgetMapper` is a class that allows us to map the widgets in a form to the corresponding columns in a data model.

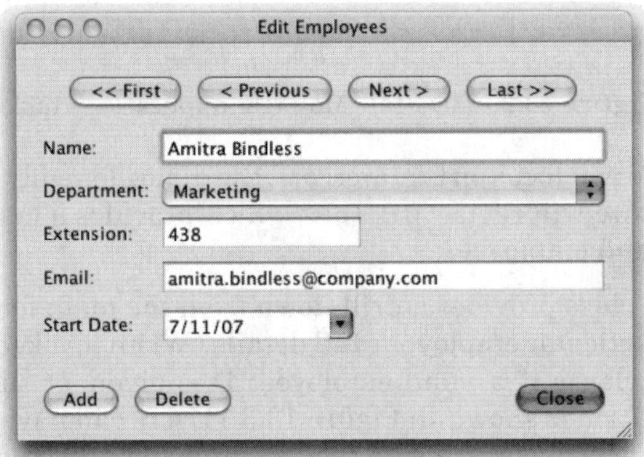

Figure 13.3. The Employee dialog

The form's constructor is quite long, so we will review it in parts, omitting the layout code since it isn't relevant.

```
EmployeeForm::EmployeeForm(int id, QWidget *parent)
    : QDialog(parent)
{
    nameEdit = new QLineEdit;

    nameLabel = new QLabel(tr("Na&me:"));
    nameLabel->setBuddy(nameEdit);

    departmentComboBox = new QComboBox;

    departmentLabel = new QLabel(tr("Depar&tment:"));
    departmentLabel->setBuddy(departmentComboBox);
```

```
    extensionLineEdit = new QLineEdit;
    extensionLineEdit->setValidator(new QIntValidator(0, 99999, this));

    extensionLabel = new QLabel(tr("E&xtension:"));
    extensionLabel->setBuddy(extensionLineEdit);

    emailEdit = new QLineEdit;

    emailLabel = new QLabel(tr("&Email:"));
    emailLabel->setBuddy(emailEdit);

    startDateEdit = new QDateEdit;
    startDateEdit->setCalendarPopup(true);
    QDate today = QDate::currentDate();
    startDateEdit->setDateRange(today.addDays(-90), today.addDays(90));

    startDateLabel = new QLabel(tr("&Start Date:"));
    startDateLabel->setBuddy(startDateEdit);
```

We begin by creating one editing widget for each field. We also create a label to put beside each editing widget to identify the corresponding field.

We use a `QIntValidator` to ensure that the Extension line editor will accept only valid extensions, in this case numbers in the range 0 to 99 999. We also set a date range for the Start Date editor, and set the editor to provide a pop-up calendar. We do not populate the combobox directly; later on we will give it a model from which it can populate itself.

```
    firstButton = new QPushButton(tr("<< &First"));
    previousButton = new QPushButton(tr("< &Previous"));
    nextButton = new QPushButton(tr("&Next >"));
    lastButton = new QPushButton(tr("&Last >>"));

    addButton = new QPushButton(tr("&Add"));
    deleteButton = new QPushButton(tr("&Delete"));
    closeButton = new QPushButton(tr("&Close"));

    buttonBox = new QDialogButtonBox;
    buttonBox->addButton(addButton, QDialogButtonBox::ActionRole);
    buttonBox->addButton(deleteButton, QDialogButtonBox::ActionRole);
    buttonBox->addButton(closeButton, QDialogButtonBox::AcceptRole);
```

We create the navigation buttons (<< First, < Previous, Next >, and Last >>), which are grouped together at the top of the dialog. Then we create the other buttons (Add, Delete, and Close) and put them inside a `QDialogButtonBox`, located at the bottom of the dialog. The code that creates the layouts is straightforward, so we won't review it.

At this point, we have set up the user interface's widgets, so now we can turn our attention to the underlying functionality.

```
    tableModel = new QSqlRelationalTableModel(this);
    tableModel->setTable("employee");
    tableModel->setRelation(Employee_DepartmentId,
                            QSqlRelation("department", "id", "name"));
    tableModel->setSort(Employee_Name, Qt::AscendingOrder);
```

```
tableModel->select();

QSqlTableModel *relationModel =
        tableModel->relationModel(Employee_DepartmentId);
departmentComboBox->setModel(relationModel);
departmentComboBox->setModelColumn(
        relationModel->fieldIndex("name"));
```

The model is constructed and set up in much the same way as the `QSqlTableModel` we saw earlier, but this time we use a `QSqlRelationalTableModel` and set up a foreign key relation. The `setRelation()` function takes the index of a foreign key field and a `QSqlRelation`. The `QSqlRelation` constructor takes a table name (the foreign key's table), the name of the foreign key field, and the name of the field to display to represent the foreign key field's value.

A `QComboBox` is like a `QListWidget` in that it has an internal model to hold its data items. We can replace that model with one of our own, and that is what we do here, giving it the relation model that is used by the `QSqlRelationalTableModel`. The relation has two columns, so we must specify which one the combobox should show. The relation model was created for us when we called `setRelation()`, so we do not know the index of the name column. For this reason, we use the `fieldIndex()` function with the field name to get the right index to make the combobox show the department names. Thanks to `QSqlRelationalTableModel`, the combobox will display department names rather than department IDs.

```
mapper = new QDataWidgetMapper(this);
mapper->setSubmitPolicy(QDataWidgetMapper::AutoSubmit);
mapper->setModel(tableModel);
mapper->setItemDelegate(new QSqlRelationalDelegate(this));
mapper->addMapping(nameEdit, Employee_Name);
mapper->addMapping(departmentComboBox, Employee_DepartmentId);
mapper->addMapping(extensionLineEdit, Employee_Extension);
mapper->addMapping(emailEdit, Employee_Email);
mapper->addMapping(startDateEdit, Employee_StartDate);
```

The `QDataWidgetMapper` reflects one database record's fields into the widgets it is mapped to, and reflects changes made in these widgets back to the database. We can either take responsibility for submitting (committing) changes ourselves, or tell the mapper to do it for us automatically; here we have chosen the automated option (`QDataWidgetMapper::AutoSubmit`).

The mapper must be given the model to work on, and in the case of a model that has foreign keys, we must also give it a `QSqlRelationalDelegate`. This delegate ensures that values from the `QSqlRelation`'s display column are shown to the user rather than raw IDs. The delegate also ensures that if the user initiates editing, the combobox shows display values, but the mapper actually writes the corresponding index value (the foreign key) back to the database.

In cases where foreign keys refer to tables with large numbers of records, it is probably best to create our own delegate and use it to present a "list of values" form with a search capability rather than relying on QSqlRelationalTableModel's default comboboxes.

Once the model and delegate are set, we add mappings between the form's widgets and the corresponding field indexes. The combobox is treated just like the other widgets since all the work of dealing with the foreign key is handled by the relation model we have already set on it.

```
    if (id != -1) {
        for (int row = 0; row < tableModel->rowCount(); ++row) {
            QSqlRecord record = tableModel->record(row);
            if (record.value(Employee_Id).toInt() == id) {
                mapper->setCurrentIndex(row);
                break;
            }
        }
    } else {
        mapper->toFirst();
    }
```

If the dialog was called with a valid employee ID, we look for the record with that ID and make it the mapper's current record. Otherwise, we simply navigate to the first record. In either case, the record's data will be reflected into the mapped widgets.

```
    connect(firstButton, SIGNAL(clicked()), mapper, SLOT(toFirst()));
    connect(previousButton, SIGNAL(clicked()),
            mapper, SLOT(toPrevious()));
    connect(nextButton, SIGNAL(clicked()), mapper, SLOT(toNext()));
    connect(lastButton, SIGNAL(clicked()), mapper, SLOT(toLast()));
    connect(addButton, SIGNAL(clicked()), this, SLOT(addEmployee()));
    connect(deleteButton, SIGNAL(clicked()),
            this, SLOT(deleteEmployee()));
    connect(closeButton, SIGNAL(clicked()), this, SLOT(accept()));
    ...
}
```

The navigation buttons are connected directly to the corresponding mapper slots. (If we were using the manual submit policy, we would need to implement our own slots, and in them we would submit the current record and then perform the navigation to avoid changes being lost.) The data widget mapper allows us to edit and to navigate. To add or delete records, we use the underlying model.

```
void EmployeeForm::addEmployee()
{
    int row = mapper->currentIndex();
    mapper->submit();
    tableModel->insertRow(row);
    mapper->setCurrentIndex(row);

    nameEdit->clear();
    extensionLineEdit->clear();
    startDateEdit->setDate(QDate::currentDate());
```

```
    nameEdit->setFocus();
}
```

The addEmployee() slot is invoked when the user clicks the Add button. We begin by retrieving the current row since this is lost after submitting. Then we call submit() to make sure no changes to the current record are lost. Although we have set the submit policy to QDataWidgetMapper::AutoSubmit, we must still manually submit. This is because the automatic submit is applied only when the user changes focus—to avoid the overhead of doing a database UPDATE every time the user inserts or deletes a character—and it is possible that the user has edited a field but not tabbed away from it when they click the Add button. Next, we insert a new blank row and make the mapper navigate to it. Finally, we initialize the widgets, and give the focus to the first widget ready for the user to begin typing.

```
void EmployeeForm::deleteEmployee()
{
    int row = mapper->currentIndex();
    tableModel->removeRow(row);
    mapper->submit();
    mapper->setCurrentIndex(qMin(row, tableModel->rowCount() - 1));
}
```

For deleting, we begin by noting the current row. Then we delete the row and submit the change. We must manually submit deletions since the automatic submit policy applies only to changes to records. At the end, we make the mapper's current index the row following the deleted row—or the last row if it was the last row that was deleted.

The QDataWidgetMapper class makes it easy to develop data-aware forms that display information from a data model. In the example, we used a QSqlRelationalTableModel as the underlying data model, but QDataWidgetMapper can be used with any data model, including non-SQL models. An alternative would have been to use QSqlQuery directly to fill in the form with data and to update the database. This approach requires more work, but it is also more flexible.

In the next section, we will review the rest of the Staff Manager application, including the code that uses the EmployeeForm class developed in this section.

Presenting Data in Tabular Forms

In many cases, it is simplest to present users with a tabular view of a data set. In this section, we will present the Staff Manager application's main form, which consists of two QTableViews in a master–detail relationship. (The form is shown in Figure 13.4.) The master view is a list of departments. The detail view is a list of employees in the current department. Both views use QSqlRelationalTableModels, since both of the database tables they are presenting have foreign key fields. The relevant CREATE TABLE statements are shown on page 324.

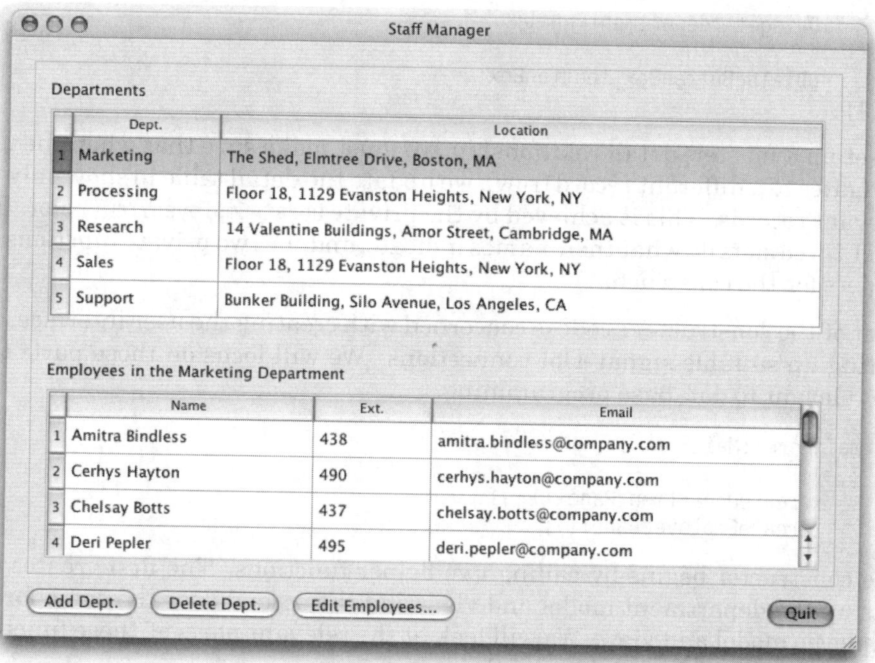

Figure 13.4. The Staff Manager application

As usual, we use an enum to give meaningful names to the column indexes:

```
enum {
    Department_Id = 0,
    Department_Name = 1,
    Department_LocationId = 2
};
```

We will begin by looking at the MainForm class definition in the header file:

```
class MainForm : public QWidget
{
    Q_OBJECT

public:
    MainForm();

private slots:
    void updateEmployeeView();
    void addDepartment();
    void deleteDepartment();
    void editEmployees();

private:
    void createDepartmentPanel();
    void createEmployeePanel();

    QSqlRelationalTableModel *departmentModel;
    QSqlRelationalTableModel *employeeModel;
```

```
    QWidget *departmentPanel;
    ...
    QDialogButtonBox *buttonBox;
};
```

To set up a master–detail relationship, we must make sure that when the user navigates to a different record (row), we update the detail table to show only the relevant records. This is achieved by the private `updateEmployeeView()` slot. The other three slots do what their names indicate, and the two private functions are helpers for the constructor.

Most of the constructor's code is concerned with creating the user interface, and setting up suitable signal–slot connections. We will focus on those parts that are relevant to database programming.

```
MainForm::MainForm()
{
    createDepartmentPanel();
    createEmployeePanel();
```

The constructor begins by calling two helper functions. The first creates and sets up the department model and view, and the second does the same for the employee model and view. We will look at the relevant parts of these functions after we have finished looking at the constructor.

The next part of the constructor sets up a splitter that contains the two table views, and also sets up the form's buttons. We will skip all this.

```
    ...
    connect(addButton, SIGNAL(clicked()), this, SLOT(addDepartment()));
    connect(deleteButton, SIGNAL(clicked()),
            this, SLOT(deleteDepartment()));
    connect(editButton, SIGNAL(clicked()), this, SLOT(editEmployees()));
    connect(quitButton, SIGNAL(clicked()), this, SLOT(close()));
    ...
    departmentView->setCurrentIndex(departmentModel->index(0, 0));
}
```

We connect the buttons to slots in the dialog, and we make sure that the first department is the current item.

Now that we have seen the constructor, we will look at the code in the `createDepartmentPanel()` helper function that sets up the department model and view:

```
void MainForm::createDepartmentPanel()
{
    departmentPanel = new QWidget;

    departmentModel = new QSqlRelationalTableModel(this);
    departmentModel->setTable("department");
    departmentModel->setRelation(Department_LocationId,
            QSqlRelation("location", "id", "name"));
    departmentModel->setSort(Department_Name, Qt::AscendingOrder);
```

```
    departmentModel->setHeaderData(Department_Name, Qt::Horizontal,
                                   tr("Dept."));
    departmentModel->setHeaderData(Department_LocationId,
                                   Qt::Horizontal, tr("Location"));
    departmentModel->select();

    departmentView = new QTableView;
    departmentView->setModel(departmentModel);
    departmentView->setItemDelegate(new QSqlRelationalDelegate(this));
    departmentView->setSelectionMode(
            QAbstractItemView::SingleSelection);
    departmentView->setSelectionBehavior(QAbstractItemView::SelectRows);
    departmentView->setColumnHidden(Department_Id, true);
    departmentView->resizeColumnsToContents();
    departmentView->horizontalHeader()->setStretchLastSection(true);

    departmentLabel = new QLabel(tr("Depar&tments"));
    departmentLabel->setBuddy(departmentView);

    connect(departmentView->selectionModel(),
            SIGNAL(currentRowChanged(const QModelIndex &,
                                     const QModelIndex &)),
            this, SLOT(updateEmployeeView()));
    ...
}
```

The code begins in a similar way to what we saw in the previous section when we set up a model for the `employee` table. The view is a standard `QTableView`, but because we have a foreign key, we must use a `QSqlRelationalDelegate` so that the foreign key's text appears in the view and can be changed by a combobox, instead of the raw ID.

We have chosen to hide the department's ID field since this is not meaningful to the user. We also stretch the last visible field, the department's address, to fill the horizontal space available.

The department view has its selection mode set to `QAbstractItemView::SingleSelection`, and its selection behavior set to `QAbstractItemView::SelectRows`. The mode setting means that users can navigate to individual cells in the table, and the behavior setting means that as the user navigates, entire rows are highlighted.

We connect the `currentRowChanged()` signal from the view's selection model to the `updateEmployeeView()` slot. This connection is what makes the master–detail relationship work, and ensures that the employee view always shows the employees for the highlighted department in the department view.

The code inside the `createEmployeePanel()` helper function is similar, but with some important differences:

```
void MainForm::createEmployeePanel()
{
    employeePanel = new QWidget;
```

```
    employeeModel = new QSqlRelationalTableModel(this);
    employeeModel->setTable("employee");
    employeeModel->setRelation(Employee_DepartmentId,
            QSqlRelation("department", "id", "name"));
    employeeModel->setSort(Employee_Name, Qt::AscendingOrder);
    employeeModel->setHeaderData(Employee_Name, Qt::Horizontal,
                                 tr("Name"));
    employeeModel->setHeaderData(Employee_Extension, Qt::Horizontal,
                                 tr("Ext."));
    employeeModel->setHeaderData(Employee_Email, Qt::Horizontal,
                                 tr("Email"));

    employeeView = new QTableView;
    employeeView->setModel(employeeModel);
    employeeView->setSelectionMode(QAbstractItemView::SingleSelection);
    employeeView->setSelectionBehavior(QAbstractItemView::SelectRows);
    employeeView->setEditTriggers(QAbstractItemView::NoEditTriggers);
    employeeView->horizontalHeader()->setStretchLastSection(true);
    employeeView->setColumnHidden(Employee_Id, true);
    employeeView->setColumnHidden(Employee_DepartmentId, true);
    employeeView->setColumnHidden(Employee_StartDate, true);

    employeeLabel = new QLabel(tr("E&mployees"));
    employeeLabel->setBuddy(employeeView);
    ...
}
```

The employee view's edit triggers are set to `QAbstractItemView::NoEditTriggers`, effectively making the view read-only. In this application, the user can add, edit, and delete employee records by clicking Edit Employees, which invokes the `EmployeeForm` developed in the previous section.

This time, we hide three columns, not just one. We hide the `id` column, because again that is not meaningful to the user. We also hide the `departmentid` column because the only employees shown at any one time are those that are in the currently selected department. Finally, we hide the `startdate` column because it is rarely relevant and can be accessed by clicking Edit Employees.

```
void MainForm::updateEmployeeView()
{
    QModelIndex index = departmentView->currentIndex();
    if (index.isValid()) {
        QSqlRecord record = departmentModel->record(index.row());
        int id = record.value("id").toInt();
        employeeModel->setFilter(QString("departmentid = %1").arg(id));
        employeeLabel->setText(tr("E&mployees in the %1 Department")
                               .arg(record.value("name").toString()));
    } else {
        employeeModel->setFilter("departmentid = -1");
        employeeLabel->setText(tr("E&mployees"));
    }
    employeeModel->select();
    employeeView->horizontalHeader()->setVisible(
            employeeModel->rowCount() > 0);
}
```

Whenever the current department changes (including at startup), this slot is called. If there is a valid current department, the function retrieves the department's ID and sets a filter on the employee model. This constrains the employees shown to those with a matching department ID foreign key. (A filter is just a WHERE clause without the WHERE keyword.) We also update the label that is shown above the employee table to show the name of the department the employees are in.

If there is no valid department (e.g., if the database is empty), we set the filter to match a non-existent department ID to ensure that no records match.

We then call select() on the model to apply the filter. This in turn will emit signals that the view will respond to by updating itself. Finally, we show or hide the employee table's column headers depending on whether or not any employees are shown.

```
void MainForm::addDepartment()
{
    int row = departmentModel->rowCount();
    departmentModel->insertRow(row);
    QModelIndex index = departmentModel->index(row, Department_Name);
    departmentView->setCurrentIndex(index);
    departmentView->edit(index);
}
```

If the user clicks the Add Dept. button, we insert a new row at the end of the department table, make this row the current row, and initiate editing of the department name column as though the user had pressed F2 or double-clicked it. If we needed to provide some default values, we would do so by calling setData() immediately after the insertRow() call.

We have not had to concern ourselves with creating unique keys for new records because we have used an auto-incrementing column to handle this for us. If this approach is not possible or not suitable, we can connect to the model's beforeInsert() signal. This is emitted after the user's edits, just before the insertion takes place in the database. This is the ideal time to put in IDs or to process the user's data. There are similar beforeDelete() and beforeUpdate() signals; these are useful for creating audit trails.

```
void MainForm::deleteDepartment()
{
    QModelIndex index = departmentView->currentIndex();
    if (!index.isValid())
        return;

    QSqlDatabase::database().transaction();
    QSqlRecord record = departmentModel->record(index.row());
    int id = record.value(Department_Id).toInt();
    int numEmployees = 0;

    QSqlQuery query(QString("SELECT COUNT(*) FROM employee "
                            "WHERE departmentid = %1").arg(id));
    if (query.next())
```

```
        numEmployees = query.value(0).toInt();
    if (numEmployees > 0) {
        int r = QMessageBox::warning(this, tr("Delete Department"),
                      tr("Delete %1 and all its employees?")
                      .arg(record.value(Department_Name).toString()),
                      QMessageBox::Yes | QMessageBox::No);
        if (r == QMessageBox::No) {
            QSqlDatabase::database().rollback();
            return;
        }

        query.exec(QString("DELETE FROM employee "
                           "WHERE departmentid = %1").arg(id));
    }

    departmentModel->removeRow(index.row());
    departmentModel->submitAll();
    QSqlDatabase::database().commit();

    updateEmployeeView();
    departmentView->setFocus();
}
```

If the user wants to delete a department, we let them do so without formality if the department has no employees. But if it has employees, we ask the user to confirm the deletion, and if they confirm, we do a cascading delete to ensure that the database's relational integrity is maintained. To achieve this, at least for databases such as SQLite 3 which don't enforce relational integrity for us, we must use a transaction.

Once the transaction has been initiated, we execute a query to find out how many employees are in the department. If there is at least one, we pop up a message box asking for confirmation. If the user says no, we roll back the transaction and return. Otherwise, we delete all the department's employees as well as the department itself, and we commit the transaction.

```
void MainForm::editEmployees()
{
    int employeeId = -1;
    QModelIndex index = employeeView->currentIndex();
    if (index.isValid()) {
        QSqlRecord record = employeeModel->record(index.row());
        employeeId = record.value(Employee_Id).toInt();
    }

    EmployeeForm form(employeeId, this);
    form.exec();
    updateEmployeeView();
}
```

The `editEmployees()` slot is invoked whenever the user clicks the Edit Employees button. We begin by assigning an invalid employee ID. Then we overwrite this with the current employee's ID if possible. Then we construct the `EmployeeForm` and show it modally. Finally, we call the `updateEmployeeView()` slot to make the main form's detail table view refresh itself since changes to employees may have occurred.

This chapter showed that Qt's model/view classes make viewing and editing data in SQL databases as easy as possible. In situations where we want to present records using a form view, we can use `QDataWidgetMapper` to map widgets in the user interface to the fields in a record in the database. Setting up master–detail relationships is quite easy, requiring just one signal–slot connection and the implementation of one simple slot. Drill-down is also straightforward, just requiring us to navigate to the selected record in the drilled-down form's constructor, or to go to the first record if no record is selected.

- *Creating Threads*
- *Synchronizing Threads*
- *Communicating with the Main Thread*
- *Using Qt's Classes in Secondary Threads*

14. Multithreading

Conventional GUI applications have one thread of execution and perform one operation at a time. If the user invokes a time-consuming operation from the user interface, the interface typically freezes while the operation is in progress. Chapter 7 presents some solutions to this problem. Multithreading is another solution.

In a multithreaded application, the GUI runs in its own thread and additional processing takes place in one or more other threads. This results in applications that have responsive GUIs even during intensive processing. When runnning on a single processor, multithreaded applications may run slower than a single-threaded equivalent due to the overhead of having multiple threads. But on multiprocessor systems, which are becoming increasingly common, multithreaded applications can execute several threads simultaneously on different processors, resulting in better overall performance.

In this chapter, we will start by showing how to subclass `QThread` and how to use `QMutex`, `QSemaphore`, and `QWaitCondition` to synchronize threads.* Then we will see how to communicate with the main thread from secondary threads while the event loop is running. Finally, we round off with a review of which Qt classes can be used in secondary threads and which cannot.

Multithreading is a large topic with many books devoted to the subject—for example, *Threads Primer: A Guide to Multithreaded Programming* by Bil Lewis and Daniel J. Berg (Prentice Hall, 1995) and *Multithreaded, Parallel, and Distributed Programming* by Gregory Andrews (Addison-Wesley, 2000). Here it is assumed that you already understand the fundamentals of multithreaded programming, so the focus is on explaining how to develop multithreaded Qt applications rather than on the subject of threading itself.

---

*Qt 4.4 is expected to provide a higher-level threading API, supplementing the threading classes described here, to make writing multithreaded applications less error-prone.

Creating Threads

Providing multiple threads in a Qt application is straightforward: We just subclass QThread and reimplement its run() function. To show how this works, we will start by reviewing the code for a very simple QThread subclass that repeatedly prints a given string on a console. The application's user interface is shown in Figure 14.1.

```
class Thread : public QThread
{
    Q_OBJECT

public:
    Thread();

    void setMessage(const QString &message);
    void stop();

protected:
    void run();

private:
    QString messageStr;
    volatile bool stopped;
};
```

The Thread class is derived from QThread and reimplements the run() function. It provides two additional functions: setMessage() and stop().

The stopped variable is declared volatile because it is accessed from different threads and we want to be sure that it is freshly read every time it is needed. If we omitted the volatile keyword, the compiler might optimize access to the variable, possibly leading to incorrect results.

```
Thread::Thread()
{
    stopped = false;
}
```

We set stopped to false in the constructor.

```
void Thread::run()
{
    while (!stopped)
        std::cerr << qPrintable(messageStr);
    stopped = false;
    std::cerr << std::endl;
}
```

The run() function is called to start executing the thread. As long as the stopped variable is false, the function keeps printing the given message to the console. The thread terminates when control leaves the run() function.

```
void Thread::stop()
{
```

```
        stopped = true;
    }
```

The stop() function sets the stopped variable to true, thereby telling run() to stop printing text to the console. This function can be called from any thread at any time. For the purposes of this example, we assume that assignment to a bool is an atomic operation. This is a reasonable assumption, considering that a bool can have only two states. We will see later in this section how to use QMutex to guarantee that assigning to a variable is an atomic operation.

QThread provides a terminate() function that terminates the execution of a thread while it is still running. Using terminate() is not recommended, since it can stop the thread at any point and does not give the thread any chance to clean up after itself. It is always safer to use a stopped variable and a stop() function as we did here.

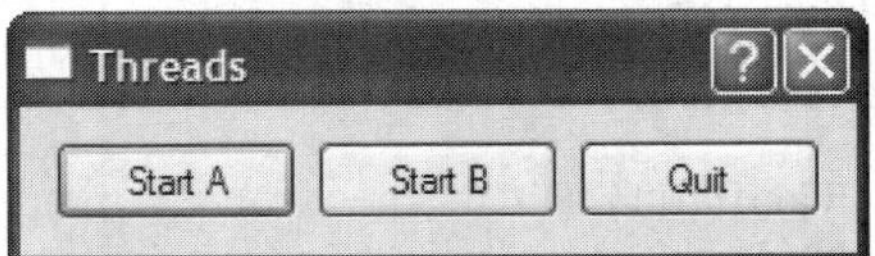

Figure 14.1. The Threads application

We will now see how to use the Thread class in a small Qt application that uses two threads, A and B, in addition to the main thread.

```
class ThreadDialog : public QDialog
{
    Q_OBJECT

public:
    ThreadDialog(QWidget *parent = 0);

protected:
    void closeEvent(QCloseEvent *event);

private slots:
    void startOrStopThreadA();
    void startOrStopThreadB();

private:
    Thread threadA;
    Thread threadB;
    QPushButton *threadAButton;
    QPushButton *threadBButton;
    QPushButton *quitButton;
};
```

The ThreadDialog class declares two variables of type Thread and some buttons to provide a basic user interface.

```
ThreadDialog::ThreadDialog(QWidget *parent)
    : QDialog(parent)
```

```
{
    threadA.setMessage("A");
    threadB.setMessage("B");

    threadAButton = new QPushButton(tr("Start A"));
    threadBButton = new QPushButton(tr("Start B"));
    quitButton = new QPushButton(tr("Quit"));
    quitButton->setDefault(true);

    connect(threadAButton, SIGNAL(clicked()),
            this, SLOT(startOrStopThreadA()));
    connect(threadBButton, SIGNAL(clicked()),
            this, SLOT(startOrStopThreadB()));
    ...
}
```

In the constructor, we call `setMessage()` to make the first thread repeatedly print 'A's and the second thread 'B's.

```
void ThreadDialog::startOrStopThreadA()
{
    if (threadA.isRunning()) {
        threadA.stop();
        threadAButton->setText(tr("Start A"));
    } else {
        threadA.start();
        threadAButton->setText(tr("Stop A"));
    }
}
```

When the user clicks the button for thread A, `startOrStopThreadA()` stops the thread if it was running and starts it otherwise. It also updates the button's text.

```
void ThreadDialog::startOrStopThreadB()
{
    if (threadB.isRunning()) {
        threadB.stop();
        threadBButton->setText(tr("Start B"));
    } else {
        threadB.start();
        threadBButton->setText(tr("Stop B"));
    }
}
```

The code for `startOrStopThreadB()` is structurally identical.

```
void ThreadDialog::closeEvent(QCloseEvent *event)
{
    threadA.stop();
    threadB.stop();
    threadA.wait();
    threadB.wait();
    event->accept();
}
```

If the user clicks Quit or closes the window, we stop any running threads and wait for them to finish (using `QThread::wait()`) before we call `QCloseEvent::accept()`. This ensures that the application exits in a clean state, although it doesn't really matter in this example.

If you run the application and click Start A, the console will be filled with 'A's. If you click Start B, it will now fill with alternating sequences of 'A's and 'B's. Click Stop A, and now it will print only 'B's.

Synchronizing Threads

A common requirement for multithreaded applications is that of synchronizing several threads. Qt provides the following synchronization classes: `QMutex`, `QReadWriteLock`, `QSemaphore`, and `QWaitCondition`.

The `QMutex` class provides a means of protecting a variable or a piece of code so that only one thread can access it at a time. The class provides a `lock()` function that locks the mutex. If the mutex is unlocked, the current thread seizes it immediately and locks it; otherwise, the current thread is blocked until the thread that holds the mutex unlocks it. Either way, when the call to `lock()` returns, the current thread holds the mutex until it calls `unlock()`. The `QMutex` class also provides a `tryLock()` function that returns immediately if the mutex is already locked.

For example, let's suppose that we wanted to protect the `stopped` variable of the `Thread` class from the preceding section with a `QMutex`. We would then add the following member variable to `Thread`:

```
private:
    ...
    QMutex mutex;
};
```

The `run()` function would change to this:

```
void Thread::run()
{
    forever {
        mutex.lock();
        if (stopped) {
            stopped = false;
            mutex.unlock();
            break;
        }
        mutex.unlock();

        std::cerr << qPrintable(messageStr);
    }
    std::cerr << std::endl;
}
```

The `stop()` function would become this:

```
void Thread::stop()
{
    mutex.lock();
    stopped = true;
    mutex.unlock();
}
```

Locking and unlocking a mutex in complex functions, or in functions that throw C++ exceptions, can be error-prone. Qt offers the `QMutexLocker` convenience class to simplify mutex handling. `QMutexLocker`'s constructor accepts a `QMutex` as argument and locks it. `QMutexLocker`'s destructor unlocks the mutex. For example, we could rewrite the earlier `run()` and `stop()` functions as follows:

```
void Thread::run()
{
    forever {
        {
            QMutexLocker locker(&mutex);
            if (stopped) {
                stopped = false;
                break;
            }
        }

        std::cerr << qPrintable(messageStr);
    }
    std::cerr << std::endl;
}

void Thread::stop()
{
    QMutexLocker locker(&mutex);
    stopped = true;
}
```

One issue with using mutexes is that only one thread can access the same variable at a time. In programs with lots of threads trying to read the same variable simultaneously (without modifying it), the mutex can be a serious performance bottleneck. In these cases, we can use `QReadWriteLock`, a synchronization class that allows simultaneous read-only access without compromising performance.

In the `Thread` class, it would make no sense to replace `QMutex` with `QReadWriteLock` to protect the `stopped` variable, because at most one thread might try to read the variable at any given time. A more appropriate example would involve one or many reader threads accessing some shared data and one or many writer threads modifying the data. For example:

```
MyData data;
QReadWriteLock lock;

void ReaderThread::run()
{
    ...
    lock.lockForRead();
```

```
        access_data_without_modifying_it(&data);
        lock.unlock();
        ...
    }

    void WriterThread::run()
    {
        ...
        lock.lockForWrite();
        modify_data(&data);
        lock.unlock();
        ...
    }
```

For convenience, we can use the QReadLocker and QWriteLocker classes to lock and unlock a QReadWriteLock.

QSemaphore is another generalization of mutexes, but unlike read-write locks, semaphores can be used to guard a certain number of identical resources. The following two code snippets show the correspondence between QSemaphore and QMutex:

```
QSemaphore semaphore(1);          |    QMutex mutex;
semaphore.acquire();              |    mutex.lock();
semaphore.release();              |    mutex.unlock();
```

By passing 1 to the constructor, we tell the semaphore that it controls a single resource. The advantage of using a semaphore is that we can pass numbers other than 1 to the constructor and then call acquire() multiple times to acquire many resources.

A typical application of semaphores is when transferring a certain amount of data (DataSize) between two threads using a shared circular buffer of a certain size (BufferSize):

```
const int DataSize = 100000;
const int BufferSize = 4096;
char buffer[BufferSize];
```

The producer thread writes data to the buffer until it reaches the end and then restarts from the beginning, overwriting existing data. The consumer thread reads the data as it is generated. Figure 14.2 illustrates this, assuming a tiny 16-byte buffer.

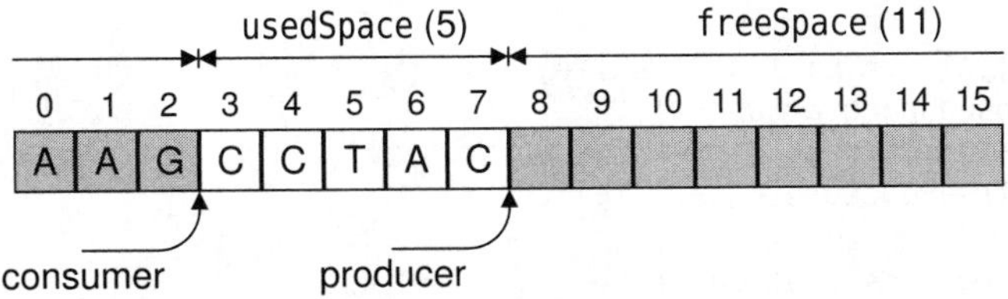

Figure 14.2. The producer–consumer model

The need for synchronization in the producer–consumer example is twofold: If the producer generates the data too fast, it will overwrite data that the consumer hasn't yet read; if the consumer reads the data too fast, it will pass the producer and read garbage.

A crude way to solve this problem is to have the producer fill the buffer, then wait until the consumer has read the entire buffer, and so on. However, on multiprocessor machines, this isn't as fast as letting the producer and consumer threads operate on different parts of the buffer at the same time.

One way to efficiently solve the problem involves two semaphores:

```
QSemaphore freeSpace(BufferSize);
QSemaphore usedSpace(0);
```

The `freeSpace` semaphore governs the part of the buffer that the producer can fill with data. The `usedSpace` semaphore governs the area that the consumer can read. These two areas are complementary. The `freeSpace` semaphore is initialized with `BufferSize` (4 096), meaning that it has that many resources that can be acquired. When the application starts, the reader thread will start acquiring "free" bytes and convert them into "used" bytes. The `usedSpace` semaphore is initialized with 0 to ensure that the consumer won't read garbage at startup.

For this example, each byte counts as one resource. In a real-world application, we would probably operate on larger units (e.g., 64 or 256 bytes at a time) to reduce the overhead associated with using semaphores.

```
void Producer::run()
{
    for (int i = 0; i < DataSize; ++i) {
        freeSpace.acquire();
        buffer[i % BufferSize] = "ACGT"[uint(std::rand()) % 4];
        usedSpace.release();
    }
}
```

In the producer, every iteration starts by acquiring one "free" byte. If the buffer is full of data that the consumer hasn't read yet, the call to `acquire()` will block until the consumer has started to consume the data. Once we have acquired the byte, we fill it with some random data ('A', 'C', 'G', or 'T') and release the byte as "used", so that the consumer thread can read it.

```
void Consumer::run()
{
    for (int i = 0; i < DataSize; ++i) {
        usedSpace.acquire();
        std::cerr << buffer[i % BufferSize];
        freeSpace.release();
    }
    std::cerr << std::endl;
}
```

In the consumer, we start by acquiring one "used" byte. If the buffer contains no data to read, the call to acquire() will block until the producer has produced some. Once we have acquired the byte, we print it and release the byte as "free", making it possible for the producer to fill it with data again.

```
int main()
{
    Producer producer;
    Consumer consumer;
    producer.start();
    consumer.start();
    producer.wait();
    consumer.wait();
    return 0;
}
```

Finally, in main(), we start the producer and consumer threads. Then the producer converts some "free" space into "used" space, and the consumer can convert it back to "free" space.

When we run the program, it writes a random sequence of 100 000 'A's, 'C's, 'G's, and 'T's to the console and terminates. To really understand what is going on, we can disable writing the output and instead write 'P' each time the producer generates a byte and 'c' each time the consumer reads a byte. And to make things as simple to follow as possible, we can use smaller values for DataSize and BufferSize.

For example, here's a possible run with a DataSize of 10 and a BufferSize of 4: "PcPcPcPcPcPcPcPcPcPc". In this case, the consumer reads the bytes as soon as the producer generates them; the two threads are executing at the same speed. Another possibility is that the producer fills the whole buffer before the consumer even starts reading it: "PPPPccccPPPPccccPPcc". There are many other possibilities. Semaphores give a lot of latitude to the system-specific thread scheduler, which can study the threads' behavior and choose an appropriate scheduling policy.

A different approach to the problem of synchronizing a producer and a consumer is to use QWaitCondition and QMutex. A QWaitCondition allows a thread to wake up other threads when some condition has been met. This allows for more precise control than is possible with mutexes alone. To show how it works, we will redo the producer–consumer example using wait conditions.

```
const int DataSize = 100000;
const int BufferSize = 4096;
char buffer[BufferSize];

QWaitCondition bufferIsNotFull;
QWaitCondition bufferIsNotEmpty;
QMutex mutex;
int usedSpace = 0;
```

In addition to the buffer, we declare two QWaitConditions, one QMutex, and one variable that stores how many bytes in the buffer are "used" bytes.

```
void Producer::run()
{
    for (int i = 0; i < DataSize; ++i) {
        mutex.lock();
        while (usedSpace == BufferSize)
            bufferIsNotFull.wait(&mutex);
        buffer[i % BufferSize] = "ACGT"[uint(std::rand()) % 4];
        ++usedSpace;
        bufferIsNotEmpty.wakeAll();
        mutex.unlock();
    }
}
```

In the producer, we start by checking whether the buffer is full. If it is, we wait on the "buffer is not full" condition. When that condition is met, we write one byte to the buffer, increment usedSpace, and wake any thread waiting for the "buffer is not empty" condition to turn true.

We use a mutex to protect all accesses to the usedSpace variable. The QWaitCondition::wait() function can take a locked mutex as its first argument, which it unlocks before blocking the current thread and then locks before returning.

For this example, we could have replaced the while loop

```
while (usedSpace == BufferSize)
    bufferIsNotFull.wait(&mutex);
```

with this if statement:

```
if (usedSpace == BufferSize) {
    mutex.unlock();
    bufferIsNotFull.wait();
    mutex.lock();
}
```

However, this would break as soon as we allow more than one producer thread, since another producer could seize the mutex immediately after the wait() call and make the "buffer is not full" condition false again.

```
void Consumer::run()
{
    for (int i = 0; i < DataSize; ++i) {
        mutex.lock();
        while (usedSpace == 0)
            bufferIsNotEmpty.wait(&mutex);
        std::cerr << buffer[i % BufferSize];
        --usedSpace;
        bufferIsNotFull.wakeAll();
        mutex.unlock();
    }
    std::cerr << std::endl;
}
```

The consumer does the exact opposite of the producer: It waits for the "buffer is not empty" condition and wakes up any thread waiting for the "buffer is not full" condition.

In all the examples so far, our threads have accessed the same global variables. But some multithreaded applications need to have a global variable hold different values in different threads. This is often called thread-local storage or thread-specific data. We can fake it using a map keyed on thread IDs (returned by QThread::currentThread()), but a nicer approach is to use the QThreadStorage<T> class.

A common use of QThreadStorage<T> is for caches. By having a separate cache in different threads, we avoid the overhead of locking, unlocking, and possibly waiting for a mutex. For example:

```
QThreadStorage<QHash<int, double> *> cache;

void insertIntoCache(int id, double value)
{
    if (!cache.hasLocalData())
        cache.setLocalData(new QHash<int, double>);
    cache.localData()->insert(id, value);
}

void removeFromCache(int id)
{
    if (cache.hasLocalData())
        cache.localData()->remove(id);
}
```

The cache variable holds one pointer to a QHash<int, double> per thread. (Because of problems with some compilers, the template type in QThreadStorage<T> must be a pointer type.) The first time we use the cache in a particular thread, hasLocalData() returns false and we create the QHash<int, double> object.

In addition to caching, QThreadStorage<T> can be used for global error-state variables (similar to errno) to ensure that modifications in one thread don't affect other threads.

Communicating with the Main Thread

When a Qt application starts, only one thread is running—the main thread. This is the only thread that is allowed to create the QApplication or QCoreApplication object and call exec() on it. After the call to exec(), this thread is either waiting for an event or processing an event.

The main thread can start new threads by creating objects of a QThread subclass, as we did in the previous section. If these new threads need to communicate among themselves, they can use shared variables together with mutexes, read-write locks, semaphores, or wait conditions. But none of these techniques can be used to communicate with the main thread, since they would lock the event loop and freeze the user interface.

The solution for communicating from a secondary thread to the main thread is to use signal–slot connections across threads. Normally, the signals and slots mechanism operates synchronously, meaning that the slots connected to a signal are invoked immediately when the signal is emitted, using a direct function call.

However, when we connect objects that "live" in different threads, the mechanism becomes asynchronous. (This behavior can be changed through an optional fifth parameter to `QObject::connect()`.) Behind the scenes, these connections are implemented by posting an event. The slot is then called by the event loop of the thread in which the receiver object exists. By default, a `QObject` exists in the thread in which it was created; this can be changed at any time by calling `QObject::moveToThread()`.

To illustrate how signal–slot connections across threads work, we will review the code of the Image Pro application, a basic image processing application that allows the user to rotate, resize, and change the color depth of an image. The application (shown in Figure 14.3), uses one secondary thread to perform operations on images without locking the event loop. This makes a significant difference when processing very large images. The secondary thread has a list of tasks, or "transactions", to accomplish and sends events to the main window to report progress.

```
ImageWindow::ImageWindow()
{
    imageLabel = new QLabel;
    imageLabel->setBackgroundRole(QPalette::Dark);
    imageLabel->setAutoFillBackground(true);
    imageLabel->setAlignment(Qt::AlignLeft | Qt::AlignTop);
    setCentralWidget(imageLabel);

    createActions();
    createMenus();

    statusBar()->showMessage(tr("Ready"), 2000);

    connect(&thread, SIGNAL(transactionStarted(const QString &)),
            statusBar(), SLOT(showMessage(const QString &)));
    connect(&thread, SIGNAL(allTransactionsDone()),
            this, SLOT(allTransactionsDone()));

    setCurrentFile("");
}
```

The interesting part of the `ImageWindow` constructor is the two signal–slot connections. Both of them involve signals emitted by the `TransactionThread` object, which we will cover in a moment.

```
void ImageWindow::flipHorizontally()
{
```

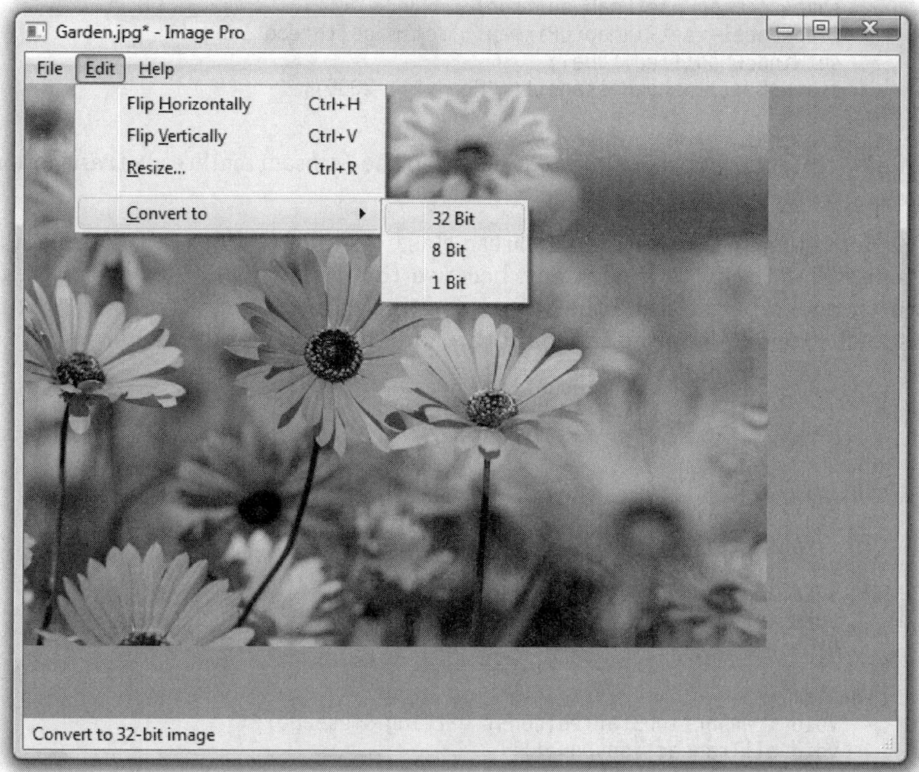

Figure 14.3. The Image Pro application

```
        addTransaction(new FlipTransaction(Qt::Horizontal));
    }
```

The `flipHorizontally()` slot creates a "flip" transaction and registers it using the private function `addTransaction()`. The `flipVertically()`, `resizeImage()`, `convertTo32Bit()`, `convertTo8Bit()`, and `convertTo1Bit()` functions are similar.

```
    void ImageWindow::addTransaction(Transaction *transact)
    {
        thread.addTransaction(transact);
        openAction->setEnabled(false);
        saveAction->setEnabled(false);
        saveAsAction->setEnabled(false);
    }
```

The `addTransaction()` function adds a transaction to the secondary thread's transaction queue and disables the Open, Save, and Save As actions while transactions are being processed.

```
    void ImageWindow::allTransactionsDone()
    {
        openAction->setEnabled(true);
        saveAction->setEnabled(true);
```

```
    saveAsAction->setEnabled(true);
    imageLabel->setPixmap(QPixmap::fromImage(thread.image()));
    setWindowModified(true);
    statusBar()->showMessage(tr("Ready"), 2000);
}
```

The `allTransactionsDone()` slot is called when the `TransactionThread`'s transaction queue becomes empty.

Now, let's turn to the `TransactionThread` class. Like most `QThread` subclasses, it is somewhat tricky to implement, because the `run()` function executes in its own thread, whereas the other functions (including the constructor and the destructor) are called from the main thread. The class definition follows:

```
class TransactionThread : public QThread
{
    Q_OBJECT

public:
    TransactionThread();
    ~TransactionThread();

    void addTransaction(Transaction *transact);
    void setImage(const QImage &image);
    QImage image();

signals:
    void transactionStarted(const QString &message);
    void allTransactionsDone();

protected:
    void run();

private:
    QImage currentImage;
    QQueue<Transaction *> transactions;
    QWaitCondition transactionAdded;
    QMutex mutex;
};
```

The `TransactionThread` class maintains a queue of transactions to process and executes them one after the other in the background. In the private section, we declare four member variables:

- `currentImage` holds the image onto which the transactions are applied.
- `transactions` is the queue of pending transactions.
- `transactionAdded` is a wait condition that is used to wake up the thread when a new transaction has been added to the queue.
- `mutex` is used to protect the `currentImage` and `transactions` member variables against concurrent access.

Here is the class's constructor:

```
TransactionThread::TransactionThread()
{
    start();
}
```

In the constructor, we simply call `QThread::start()` to launch the thread that will execute the transactions.

```
TransactionThread::~TransactionThread()
{
    {
        QMutexLocker locker(&mutex);
        while (!transactions.isEmpty())
            delete transactions.dequeue();
        transactions.enqueue(EndTransaction);
        transactionAdded.wakeOne();
    }

    wait();
}
```

In the destructor, we empty the transaction queue and add a special `EndTransaction` marker to the queue. Then we wake up the thread and wait for it to finish using `QThread::wait()`, before the base class's destructor is implicitly invoked. Failing to call `wait()` would most probably result in a crash when the thread tries to access the class's member variables.

The `QMutexLocker`'s destructor unlocks the mutex at the end of the inner block, just before the `wait()` call. It is important to unlock the mutex before calling `wait()`; otherwise, the program could end up in a deadlock situation, where the secondary thread waits forever for the mutex to be unlocked, and the main thread holds the mutex and waits for the secondary thread to finish before proceeding.

```
void TransactionThread::addTransaction(Transaction *transact)
{
    QMutexLocker locker(&mutex);
    transactions.enqueue(transact);
    transactionAdded.wakeOne();
}
```

The `addTransaction()` function adds a transaction to the transaction queue and wakes up the transaction thread if it isn't already running. All accesses to the `transactions` member variable are protected by a mutex, because the main thread might modify them through `addTransaction()` at the same time as the secondary thread is iterating over `transactions`.

```
void TransactionThread::setImage(const QImage &image)
{
    QMutexLocker locker(&mutex);
    currentImage = image;
}
```

```
QImage TransactionThread::image()
{
    QMutexLocker locker(&mutex);
    return currentImage;
}
```

The setImage() and image() functions allow the main thread to set the image on which the transactions should be performed, and to retrieve the resulting image once all the transactions are done.

```
void TransactionThread::run()
{
    Transaction *transact = 0;
    QImage oldImage;

    forever {
        {
            QMutexLocker locker(&mutex);

            if (transactions.isEmpty())
                transactionAdded.wait(&mutex);
            transact = transactions.dequeue();
            if (transact == EndTransaction)
                break;

            oldImage = currentImage;
        }

        emit transactionStarted(transact->message());
        QImage newImage = transact->apply(oldImage);
        delete transact;

        {
            QMutexLocker locker(&mutex);
            currentImage = newImage;
            if (transactions.isEmpty())
                emit allTransactionsDone();
        }
    }
}
```

The run() function goes through the transaction queue and executes each transaction in turn by calling apply() on them, until it reaches the EndTransaction marker. If the transaction queue is empty, the thread waits on the "transaction added" condition.

Just before we execute a transaction, we emit the transactionStarted() signal with a message to display in the application's status bar. When all the transactions have finished processing, we emit the allTransactionsDone() signal.

```
class Transaction
{
public:
    virtual ~Transaction() { }

    virtual QImage apply(const QImage &image) = 0;
```

```
    virtual QString message() = 0;
};
```

The `Transaction` class is an abstract base class for operations that the user can perform on an image. The virtual destructor is necessary because we need to delete instances of `Transaction` subclasses through a `Transaction` pointer. `Transaction` has three concrete subclasses: `FlipTransaction`, `ResizeTransaction`, and `ConvertDepthTransaction`. We will only review `FlipTransaction`; the other two classes are similar.

```
class FlipTransaction : public Transaction
{
public:
    FlipTransaction(Qt::Orientation orientation);

    QImage apply(const QImage &image);
    QString message();

private:
    Qt::Orientation orientation;
};
```

The `FlipTransaction` constructor takes one parameter that specifies the orientation of the flip (horizontal or vertical).

```
QImage FlipTransaction::apply(const QImage &image)
{
    return image.mirrored(orientation == Qt::Horizontal,
                          orientation == Qt::Vertical);
}
```

The `apply()` function calls `QImage::mirrored()` on the `QImage` it receives as a parameter and returns the resulting `QImage`.

```
QString FlipTransaction::message()
{
    if (orientation == Qt::Horizontal) {
        return QObject::tr("Flipping image horizontally...");
    } else {
        return QObject::tr("Flipping image vertically...");
    }
}
```

The `message()` function returns the message to display in the status bar while the operation is in progress. This function is called in `TransactionThread::run()` when emitting the `transactionStarted()` signal.

The Image Pro application shows how Qt's signals and slots mechanism makes it easy to communicate with the main thread from a secondary thread. Implementing the secondary thread is trickier, because we must protect our member variables using a mutex, and we must put the thread to sleep and wake it up appropriately using a wait condition. The two-part *Qt Quarterly* article series "Monitors and Wait Conditions in Qt", available online at `http://doc.trolltech.com/qq/qq21-monitors.html` and `http://doc.trolltech.com/qq/qq22-monitors2.html`, presents some more ideas on how to develop and test `QThread` subclasses that use mutexes and wait conditions for synchronization.

Using Qt's Classes in Secondary Threads

A function is said to be *thread-safe* when it can safely be called from different threads simultaneously. If two thread-safe functions are called concurrently from different threads on the same shared data, the result is always defined. By extension, a class is said to be thread-safe when all of its functions can be called from different threads simultaneously without interfering with each other, even when operating on the same object.

Qt's thread-safe classes include `QMutex`, `QMutexLocker`, `QReadWriteLock`, `QReadLocker`, `QWriteLocker`, `QSemaphore`, `QThreadStorage<T>`, and `QWaitCondition`. In addition, parts of the `QThread` API and several other functions are thread-safe, notably `QObject::connect()`, `QObject::disconnect()`, `QCoreApplication::postEvent()`, and `QCoreApplication::removePostedEvents()`.

Most of Qt's non-GUI classes meet a less stringent requirement: They are *reentrant*. A class is reentrant if different instances of the class can be used simultaneously in different threads. However, accessing the same reentrant object in multiple threads simultaneously is not safe, and such accesses should be protected with a mutex. Reentrant classes are marked as such in the Qt reference documentation. Typically, any C++ class that doesn't reference global or otherwise shared data is reentrant.

`QObject` is reentrant, but there are three constraints to keep in mind:

- **Child QObjects must be created in their parent's thread.**

  In particular, this means that the objects created in a secondary thread must never be created with the `QThread` object as their parent, because that object was created in another thread (either the main thread or a different secondary thread).

- **We must delete all QObjects created in a secondary thread before deleting the corresponding QThread object.**

  This can be done by creating the objects on the stack in `QThread::run()`.

- **QObjects must be deleted in the thread that created them.**

  If we need to delete a `QObject` that exists in a different thread, we must call the thread-safe `QObject::deleteLater()` function instead, which posts a "deferred delete" event.

Non-GUI `QObject` subclasses such as `QTimer`, `QProcess`, and the network classes are reentrant. We can use them in any thread, as long as the thread has an event loop. For secondary threads, the event loop is started by calling `QThread::exec()` or by convenience functions such as `QProcess::waitForFinished()` and `QAbstractSocket::waitForDisconnected()`.

Because of limitations inherited from the low-level libraries on which Qt's GUI support is built, `QWidget` and its subclasses are not reentrant. One consequence of this is that we cannot directly call functions on a widget from a secondary thread. If we want to, say, change the text of a `QLabel` from a secondary thread, we can emit a signal connected to `QLabel::setText()` or call `QMetaObject::invokeMethod()` from that thread. For example:

```
void MyThread::run()
{
    ...
    QMetaObject::invokeMethod(label, SLOT(setText(const QString &)),
                              Q_ARG(QString, "Hello"));
    ...
}
```

Many of Qt's non-GUI classes, including `QImage`, `QString`, and the container classes, use implicit sharing as an optimization technique. Although this optimization usually makes a class non-reentrant, in Qt this is not an issue because Qt uses atomic assembly language instructions to implement thread-safe reference counting, making Qt's implicitly shared classes reentrant.

Qt's *QtSql* module can also be used in multithreaded applications, but it has its own restrictions, which vary from database to database. For details, see `http://doc.trolltech.com/4.3/sql-driver.html`. For a complete list of multithreading caveats, see `http://doc.trolltech.com/4.3/threads.html`.

- *Writing FTP Clients*
- *Writing HTTP Clients*
- *Writing TCP Client–Server Applications*
- *Sending and Receiving UDP Datagrams*

15. Networking

Qt provides the `QFtp` and `QHttp` classes for working with FTP and HTTP. These protocols are easy to use for downloading and uploading files and, in the case of HTTP, for sending requests to web servers and retrieving the results.

Qt also provides the lower-level `QTcpSocket` and `QUdpSocket` classes, which implement the TCP and UDP transport protocols. TCP is a reliable connection-oriented protocol that operates in terms of data streams transmitted between network nodes, and UDP is an unreliable connectionless protocol based on discrete packets sent between network nodes. Both can be used to create network client and server applications. For servers, we also need the `QTcpServer` class to handle incoming TCP connections. Secure SSL/TLS connections can be established by using `QSslSocket` instead of `QTcpSocket`.

Writing FTP Clients

The `QFtp` class implements the client side of the FTP protocol in Qt. It offers various functions to perform the most common FTP operations and lets us execute arbitrary FTP commands.

The `QFtp` class works asynchronously. When we call a function such as `get()` or `put()`, it returns immediately and the data transfer occurs when control passes back to Qt's event loop. This ensures that the user interface remains responsive while FTP commands are executed.

We will start with an example that shows how to retrieve a single file using `get()`. The example is a console application called `ftpget` that downloads the remote file specified on the command line. Let's begin with the `main()` function:

```
int main(int argc, char *argv[])
{
    QCoreApplication app(argc, argv);
    QStringList args = QCoreApplication::arguments();

    if (args.count() != 2) {
```

```
        std::cerr << "Usage: ftpget url" << std::endl
                  << "Example:" << std::endl
                  << "    ftpget ftp://ftp.trolltech.com/mirrors"
                  << std::endl;
        return 1;
    }

    FtpGet getter;
    if (!getter.getFile(QUrl(args[1])))
        return 1;

    QObject::connect(&getter, SIGNAL(done()), &app, SLOT(quit()));

    return app.exec();
}
```

We create a QCoreApplication rather than its subclass QApplication to avoid linking in the *QtGui* library. The QCoreApplication::arguments() function returns the command-line arguments as a QStringList, with the first item being the name the program was invoked as, and any Qt-specific arguments such as -style removed. The heart of the main() function is the construction of the FtpGet object and the getFile() call. If the call succeeds, we let the event loop run until the download finishes.

All the work is done by the FtpGet subclass, which is defined as follows:

```
class FtpGet : public QObject
{
    Q_OBJECT

public:
    FtpGet(QObject *parent = 0);

    bool getFile(const QUrl &url);

signals:
    void done();

private slots:
    void ftpDone(bool error);

private:
    QFtp ftp;
    QFile file;
};
```

The class has a public function, getFile(), that retrieves the file specified by a URL. The QUrl class provides a high-level interface for extracting the different parts of a URL, such as the file name, path, protocol, and port.

FtpGet has a private slot, ftpDone(), that is called when the file transfer is completed, and a done() signal that it emits when the file has been downloaded. The class also has two private variables: the ftp variable, of type QFtp, which encapsulates the connection to an FTP server, and the file variable that is used for writing the downloaded file to disk.

```
FtpGet::FtpGet(QObject *parent)
    : QObject(parent)
{
    connect(&ftp, SIGNAL(done(bool)), this, SLOT(ftpDone(bool)));
}
```

In the constructor, we connect the `QFtp::done(bool)` signal to our `ftpDone(bool)` private slot. `QFtp` emits `done(bool)` when it has finished processing all requests. The `bool` parameter indicates whether an error occurred or not.

```
bool FtpGet::getFile(const QUrl &url)
{
    if (!url.isValid()) {
        std::cerr << "Error: Invalid URL" << std::endl;
        return false;
    }

    if (url.scheme() != "ftp") {
        std::cerr << "Error: URL must start with 'ftp:'" << std::endl;
        return false;
    }

    if (url.path().isEmpty()) {
        std::cerr << "Error: URL has no path" << std::endl;
        return false;
    }

    QString localFileName = QFileInfo(url.path()).fileName();
    if (localFileName.isEmpty())
        localFileName = "ftpget.out";

    file.setFileName(localFileName);
    if (!file.open(QIODevice::WriteOnly)) {
        std::cerr << "Error: Cannot write file "
                  << qPrintable(file.fileName()) << ": "
                  << qPrintable(file.errorString()) << std::endl;
        return false;
    }

    ftp.connectToHost(url.host(), url.port(21));
    ftp.login();
    ftp.get(url.path(), &file);
    ftp.close();
    return true;
}
```

The `getFile()` function begins by checking the URL that was passed in. If a problem is encountered, the function prints an error message to `cerr` and returns `false` to indicate that the download failed.

Instead of forcing the user to make up a local file name, we try to create a sensible name using the URL itself, with a fallback of `ftpget.out`. If we fail to open the file, we print an error message and return `false`.

Next, we execute a sequence of four FTP commands using our `QFtp` object. The `url.port(21)` call returns the port number specified in the URL, or port 21 if none is specified in the URL itself. Since no user name or password is given to the `login()` function, an anonymous login is attempted. The second argument to `get()` specifies the output I/O device.

The FTP commands are queued and executed in Qt's event loop. The completion of all the commands is indicated by `QFtp`'s `done(bool)` signal, which we connected to `ftpDone(bool)` in the constructor.

```
void FtpGet::ftpDone(bool error)
{
    if (error) {
        std::cerr << "Error: " << qPrintable(ftp.errorString())
                  << std::endl;
    } else {
        std::cerr << "File downloaded as "
                  << qPrintable(file.fileName()) << std::endl;
    }
    file.close();
    emit done();
}
```

Once the FTP commands have been executed, we close the file and emit our own `done()` signal. It may appear strange that we close the file here, rather than after the `ftp.close()` call at the end of the `getFile()` function, but remember that the FTP commands are executed asynchronously and may well be in progress after the `getFile()` function has returned. Only when the `QFtp` object's `done()` signal is emitted do we know that the download is finished and that it is safe to close the file.

`QFtp` provides several FTP commands, including `connectToHost()`, `login()`, `close()`, `list()`, `cd()`, `get()`, `put()`, `remove()`, `mkdir()`, `rmdir()`, and `rename()`. All of these functions schedule an FTP command and return an ID number that identifies the command. It is also possible to control the transfer mode (the default is passive) and the transfer type (the default is binary).

Arbitrary FTP commands can be executed using `rawCommand()`. For example, here's how to execute a `SITE CHMOD` command:

```
ftp.rawCommand("SITE CHMOD 755 fortune");
```

`QFtp` emits the `commandStarted(int)` signal when it starts executing a command, and it emits the `commandFinished(int, bool)` signal when the command is finished. The `int` parameter is the ID number that identifies the command. If we are interested in the fate of individual commands, we can store the ID numbers when we schedule the commands. Keeping track of the ID numbers allows us to provide detailed feedback to the user. For example:

```
bool FtpGet::getFile(const QUrl &url)
{
    ...
    connectId = ftp.connectToHost(url.host(), url.port(21));
    loginId = ftp.login();
    getId = ftp.get(url.path(), &file);
```

```
        closeId = ftp.close();
        return true;
    }

    void FtpGet::ftpCommandStarted(int id)
    {
        if (id == connectId) {
            std::cerr << "Connecting..." << std::endl;
        } else if (id == loginId) {
            std::cerr << "Logging in..." << std::endl;
        ...
    }
```

Another way to provide feedback is to connect to QFtp's stateChanged() signal, which is emitted whenever the connection enters a new state (QFtp::Connecting, QFtp::Connected, QFtp::LoggedIn, etc.).

In most applications, we are interested only in the fate of the sequence of commands as a whole rather than in particular commands. In such cases, we can simply connect to the done(bool) signal, which is emitted whenever the command queue becomes empty.

When an error occurs, QFtp automatically clears the command queue. This means that if the connection or the login fails, the commands that follow in the queue are never executed. If we schedule new commands after the error has occurred using the same QFtp object, these commands will be queued and executed.

In the application's .pro file, we need the following line to link against the *QtNetwork* library:

```
    QT += network
```

We will now review a more advanced example. The spider command-line program downloads all the files located in an FTP directory, recursively downloading from all the directory's subdirectories. The network logic is located in the Spider class:

```
    class Spider : public QObject
    {
        Q_OBJECT

    public:
        Spider(QObject *parent = 0);

        bool getDirectory(const QUrl &url);

    signals:
        void done();

    private slots:
        void ftpDone(bool error);
        void ftpListInfo(const QUrlInfo &urlInfo);

    private:
```

```
    void processNextDirectory();

    QFtp ftp;
    QList<QFile *> openedFiles;
    QString currentDir;
    QString currentLocalDir;
    QStringList pendingDirs;
};
```

The starting directory is specified as a `QUrl` and is set using the `getDirectory()` function.

```
Spider::Spider(QObject *parent)
    : QObject(parent)
{
    connect(&ftp, SIGNAL(done(bool)), this, SLOT(ftpDone(bool)));
    connect(&ftp, SIGNAL(listInfo(const QUrlInfo &)),
            this, SLOT(ftpListInfo(const QUrlInfo &)));
}
```

In the constructor, we establish two signal–slot connections. The `listInfo(const QUrlInfo &)` signal is emitted by `QFtp` when we request a directory listing (in `getDirectory()`) for each file that it retrieves. This signal is connected to a slot called `ftpListInfo()`, which downloads the file associated with the URL it is given.

```
bool Spider::getDirectory(const QUrl &url)
{
    if (!url.isValid()) {
        std::cerr << "Error: Invalid URL" << std::endl;
        return false;
    }

    if (url.scheme() != "ftp") {
        std::cerr << "Error: URL must start with 'ftp:'" << std::endl;
        return false;
    }

    ftp.connectToHost(url.host(), url.port(21));
    ftp.login();

    QString path = url.path();
    if (path.isEmpty())
        path = "/";

    pendingDirs.append(path);
    processNextDirectory();

    return true;
}
```

When the `getDirectory()` function is called, it begins by doing some sanity checks, and if all is well, it attempts to establish an FTP connection. It keeps track of the paths that it must process and calls `processNextDirectory()` to start downloading the root directory.

```
void Spider::processNextDirectory()
{
    if (!pendingDirs.isEmpty()) {
        currentDir = pendingDirs.takeFirst();
        currentLocalDir = "downloads/" + currentDir;
        QDir(".").mkpath(currentLocalDir);

        ftp.cd(currentDir);
        ftp.list();
    } else {
        emit done();
    }
}
```

The `processNextDirectory()` function takes the first remote directory out of the `pendingDirs` list and creates a corresponding directory in the local file system. It then tells the `QFtp` object to change to the taken directory and to list its files. For every file that `list()` processes, it emits a `listInfo()` signal that causes the `ftpListInfo()` slot to be called.

If there are no more directories to process, the function emits the `done()` signal to indicate that the downloading is complete.

```
void Spider::ftpListInfo(const QUrlInfo &urlInfo)
{
    if (urlInfo.isFile()) {
        if (urlInfo.isReadable()) {
            QFile *file = new QFile(currentLocalDir + "/"
                                    + urlInfo.name());

            if (!file->open(QIODevice::WriteOnly)) {
                std::cerr << "Warning: Cannot write file "
                          << qPrintable(QDir::toNativeSeparators(
                                        file->fileName()))
                          << ": " << qPrintable(file->errorString())
                          << std::endl;
                return;
            }

            ftp.get(urlInfo.name(), file);
            openedFiles.append(file);
        }
    } else if (urlInfo.isDir() && !urlInfo.isSymLink()) {
        pendingDirs.append(currentDir + "/" + urlInfo.name());
    }
}
```

The `ftpListInfo()` slot's `urlInfo` parameter provides detailed information about a remote file. If the file is a normal file (not a directory) and is readable, we call `get()` to download it. The `QFile` object used for downloading is allocated using `new` and a pointer to it is stored in the `openedFiles` list.

If the `QUrlInfo` holds the details of a remote directory that is not a symbolic link, we add this directory to the `pendingDirs` list. We skip symbolic links because they can easily lead to infinite recursion.

```
void Spider::ftpDone(bool error)
{
    if (error) {
        std::cerr << "Error: " << qPrintable(ftp.errorString())
                  << std::endl;
    } else {
        std::cout << "Downloaded " << qPrintable(currentDir) << " to "
                  << qPrintable(QDir::toNativeSeparators(
                                QDir(currentLocalDir).canonicalPath()));
    }

    qDeleteAll(openedFiles);
    openedFiles.clear();

    processNextDirectory();
}
```

The `ftpDone()` slot is called when all the FTP commands have finished or if an error occurred. We delete the `QFile` objects to prevent memory leaks and to close each file. Finally, we call `processNextDirectory()`. If there are any directories left, the whole process begins again with the next directory in the list; otherwise, the downloading stops and `done()` is emitted.

If there are no errors, the sequence of FTP commands and signals is as follows:

```
connectToHost(host, port)
login()

cd(directory_1)
list()
    emit listInfo(file_1_1)
        get(file_1_1)
    emit listInfo(file_1_2)
        get(file_1_2)
    ...
emit done()

...

cd(directory_N)
list()
    emit listInfo(file_N_1)
        get(file_N_1)
    emit listInfo(file_N_2)
        get(file_N_2)
    ...
emit done()
```

If a file is in fact a directory, it is added to the `pendingDirs` list, and when the last file of the current `list()` command has been downloaded, a new `cd()` command is issued, followed by a new `list()` command with the next pending directory, and the whole process begins again with the new directory. This is repeated, with new files being downloaded, and new directories added to the pendingDirs list, until every file has been downloaded from every directory, at which point the pendingDirs list will finally be empty.

If a network error occurs while downloading the fifth of, say, 20 files in a directory, the remaining files will not be downloaded. If we wanted to download as many files as possible, one solution would be to schedule the GET operations one at a time and to wait for the done(bool) signal before scheduling a new GET operation. In listInfo(), we would simply append the file name to a QStringList, instead of calling get() right away, and in done(bool) we would call get() on the next file to download in the QStringList. The sequence of execution would then look like this:

```
connectToHost(host, port)
login()

cd(directory_1)
list()
...
cd(directory_N)
list()
    emit listInfo(file_1_1)
    emit listInfo(file_1_2)
    ...
    emit listInfo(file_N_1)
    emit listInfo(file_N_2)
    ...
emit done()

get(file_1_1)
emit done()

get(file_1_2)
emit done()
...
get(file_N_1)
emit done()

get(file_N_2)
emit done()
...
```

Another solution would be to use one QFtp object per file. This would enable us to download the files in parallel, through separate FTP connections.

```
int main(int argc, char *argv[])
{
    QCoreApplication app(argc, argv);
    QStringList args = QCoreApplication::arguments();
```

```
    if (args.count() != 2) {
        std::cerr << "Usage: spider url" << std::endl
                  << "Example:" << std::endl
                  << "    spider ftp://ftp.trolltech.com/freebies/"
                  << "leafnode" << std::endl;
        return 1;
    }

    Spider spider;
    if (!spider.getDirectory(QUrl(args[1])))
        return 1;

    QObject::connect(&spider, SIGNAL(done()), &app, SLOT(quit()));

    return app.exec();
}
```

The `main()` function completes the program. If the user does not specify a URL on the command line, we give an error message and terminate the program.

In both FTP examples, the data retrieved using `get()` was written to a `QFile`. This need not be the case. If we wanted the data in memory, we could use a `QBuffer`, the `QIODevice` subclass that wraps a `QByteArray`. For example:

```
QBuffer *buffer = new QBuffer;
buffer->open(QIODevice::WriteOnly);
ftp.get(urlInfo.name(), buffer);
```

We could also omit the I/O device argument to `get()` or pass a null pointer. The `QFtp` class then emits a `readyRead()` signal every time new data is available, and the data can be read using `read()` or `readAll()`.

Writing HTTP Clients

The `QHttp` class implements the client side of the HTTP protocol in Qt. It provides various functions to perform the most common HTTP operations, including `get()` and `post()`, and provides a means of sending arbitrary HTTP requests. If you read the previous section about `QFtp`, you will find that there are many similarities between `QFtp` and `QHttp`.

The `QHttp` class works asynchronously. When we call a function such as `get()` or `post()`, the function returns immediately, and the data transfer occurs later, when control returns to Qt's event loop. This ensures that the application's user interface remains responsive while HTTP requests are being processed.

We will review a console application example called `httpget` that shows how to download a file using the HTTP protocol. It is very similar to the `ftpget` example from the previous section, in both functionality and implementation, so we will not show the header file.

```
HttpGet::HttpGet(QObject *parent)
    : QObject(parent)
{
```

```
    connect(&http, SIGNAL(done(bool)), this, SLOT(httpDone(bool)));
}
```

In the constructor, we connect the `QHttp` object's `done(bool)` signal to the private `httpDone(bool)` slot.

```
bool HttpGet::getFile(const QUrl &url)
{
    if (!url.isValid()) {
        std::cerr << "Error: Invalid URL" << std::endl;
        return false;
    }

    if (url.scheme() != "http") {
        std::cerr << "Error: URL must start with 'http:'" << std::endl;
        return false;
    }

    if (url.path().isEmpty()) {
        std::cerr << "Error: URL has no path" << std::endl;
        return false;
    }

    QString localFileName = QFileInfo(url.path()).fileName();
    if (localFileName.isEmpty())
        localFileName = "httpget.out";

    file.setFileName(localFileName);
    if (!file.open(QIODevice::WriteOnly)) {
        std::cerr << "Error: Cannot write file "
                  << qPrintable(file.fileName()) << ": "
                  << qPrintable(file.errorString()) << std::endl;
        return false;
    }

    http.setHost(url.host(), url.port(80));
    http.get(url.path(), &file);
    http.close();
    return true;
}
```

The `getFile()` function performs the same kind of error checks as the `FtpGet::getFile()` shown earlier and uses the same approach to giving the file a local name. When retrieving from web sites, no login is necessary, so we simply set the host and port (using the default HTTP port 80 if none is specified in the URL) and download the data into the file, since the second argument to `QHttp::get()` specifies the output I/O device.

The HTTP requests are queued and executed asynchronously in Qt's event loop. The completion of the requests is indicated by `QHttp`'s `done(bool)` signal, which we connected to `httpDone(bool)` in the constructor.

```
void HttpGet::httpDone(bool error)
{
    if (error) {
```

```
        std::cerr << "Error: " << qPrintable(http.errorString())
                  << std::endl;
    } else {
        std::cerr << "File downloaded as "
                  << qPrintable(file.fileName()) << std::endl;
    }
    file.close();
    emit done();
}
```

Once the HTTP requests are finished, we close the file, notifying the user if an error occurred.

The `main()` function is very similar to the one used by `ftpget`:

```
int main(int argc, char *argv[])
{
    QCoreApplication app(argc, argv);
    QStringList args = QCoreApplication::arguments();

    if (args.count() != 2) {
        std::cerr << "Usage: httpget url" << std::endl
                  << "Example:" << std::endl
                  << "    httpget http://doc.trolltech.com/index.html"
                  << std::endl;
        return 1;
    }

    HttpGet getter;
    if (!getter.getFile(QUrl(args[1])))
        return 1;

    QObject::connect(&getter, SIGNAL(done()), &app, SLOT(quit()));

    return app.exec();
}
```

The `QHttp` class provides many operations, including `setHost()`, `get()`, `post()`, and `head()`. If a site requires authentication, `setUser()` can be used to supply a user name and password. `QHttp` can use a socket supplied by the programmer rather than its own internal `QTcpSocket`. This makes it possible to use a secure `QSslSocket` to achieve HTTP over SSL or TLS.

To send a list of "*name* = *value*" pairs to a CGI script, we can use `post()`:

```
http.setHost("www.example.com");
http.post("/cgi/somescript.py", "x=200&y=320", &file);
```

We can pass the data either as an 8-bit string or by supplying an open `QIODevice`, such as a `QFile`. For more control, we can use the `request()` function, which accepts an arbitrary HTTP header and data. For example:

```
QHttpRequestHeader header("POST", "/search.html");
header.setValue("Host", "www.trolltech.com");
header.setContentType("application/x-www-form-urlencoded");
http.setHost("www.trolltech.com");
```

```
http.request(header, "qt-interest=on&search=opengl");
```

QHttp emits the requestStarted(int) signal when it starts executing a request, and it emits the requestFinished(int, bool) signal when the request has finished. The int parameter is an ID number that identifies a request. If we are interested in the fate of individual requests, we can store the ID numbers when we schedule the requests. Keeping track of the ID numbers allows us to provide detailed feedback to the user.

In most applications, we only want to know whether the entire sequence of requests completed successfully or not. This is easily achieved by connecting to the done(bool) signal, which is emitted when the request queue becomes empty.

When an error occurs, the request queue is automatically cleared. But if we schedule new requests after the error has occurred using the same QHttp object, these requests will be queued and sent as usual.

Like QFtp, QHttp provides a readyRead() signal as well as the read() and readAll() functions that we can use instead of specifying an I/O device.

Writing TCP Client–Server Applications

The QTcpSocket and QTcpServer classes can be used to implement TCP clients and servers. TCP is a transport protocol that forms the basis of most application-level Internet protocols, including FTP and HTTP, and that can also be used for custom protocols.

TCP is a stream-oriented protocol. For applications, the data appears to be a long stream, rather like a large flat file. The high-level protocols built on top of TCP are typically either line-oriented or block-oriented:

- Line-oriented protocols transfer data as lines of text, each terminated by a newline.
- Block-oriented protocols transfer data as binary data blocks. Each block consists of a size field followed by that much data.

QTcpSocket is indirectly derived from QIODevice (through QAbstractSocket), so it can be read from and written to using a QDataStream or a QTextStream. One notable difference when reading data from a network compared with reading from a file is that we must make sure that we have received enough data from the peer before we use the >> operator. Failing to do so may result in undefined behavior.

In this section, we will review the code of a client and a server that use a custom block-oriented protocol. The client, shown in Figure 15.1, is called Trip Planner and allows users to plan their next train trip. The server is called Trip Server and provides the trip information to the client. We will start by writing the Trip Planner client.

The Trip Planner provides a From field, a To field, a Date field, an Approximate Time field, and two radio buttons to select whether the approximate time is that of departure or arrival. When the user clicks Search, the application sends a request to the server, which responds with a list of train trips that match the user's criteria. The list is shown in a QTableWidget in the Trip Planner window. The very bottom of the window is occupied by a QLabel that shows the status of the last operation and a QProgressBar.

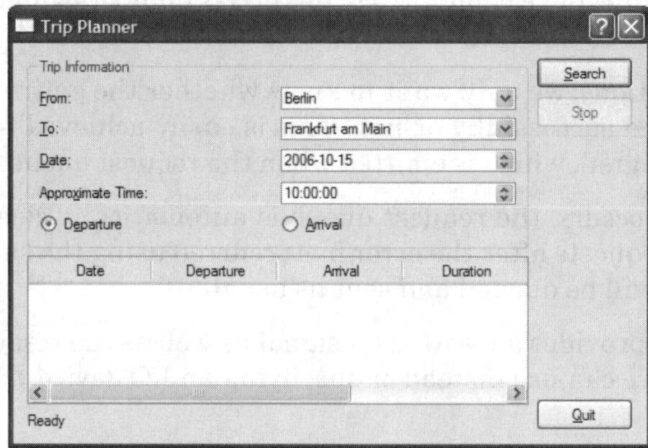

Figure 15.1. The Trip Planner application

The Trip Planner's user interface was created using *Qt Designer* in a file called tripplanner.ui. Here, we will focus on the source code of the QDialog subclass that implements the application's functionality:

```
#include "ui_tripplanner.h"

class QPushButton;

class TripPlanner : public QDialog, private Ui::TripPlanner
{
    Q_OBJECT

public:
    TripPlanner(QWidget *parent = 0);

private slots:
    void connectToServer();
    void sendRequest();
    void updateTableWidget();
    void stopSearch();
    void connectionClosedByServer();
    void error();

private:
    void closeConnection();

    QPushButton *searchButton;
    QPushButton *stopButton;
    QTcpSocket tcpSocket;
    quint16 nextBlockSize;
};
```

The TripPlanner class is derived from Ui::TripPlanner (which is generated by uic from tripplanner.ui) in addition to QDialog. The tcpSocket member variable encapsulates the TCP connection. The nextBlockSize variable is used when parsing the blocks received from the server.

```
TripPlanner::TripPlanner(QWidget *parent)
    : QDialog(parent)
{
    setupUi(this);

    searchButton = buttonBox->addButton(tr("&Search"),
                                        QDialogButtonBox::ActionRole);
    stopButton = buttonBox->addButton(tr("S&top"),
                                      QDialogButtonBox::ActionRole);
    stopButton->setEnabled(false);
    buttonBox->button(QDialogButtonBox::Close)->setText(tr("&Quit"));

    QDateTime dateTime = QDateTime::currentDateTime();
    dateEdit->setDate(dateTime.date());
    timeEdit->setTime(QTime(dateTime.time().hour(), 0));

    progressBar->hide();
    progressBar->setSizePolicy(QSizePolicy::Preferred,
                               QSizePolicy::Ignored);

    tableWidget->verticalHeader()->hide();
    tableWidget->setEditTriggers(QAbstractItemView::NoEditTriggers);

    connect(searchButton, SIGNAL(clicked()),
            this, SLOT(connectToServer()));
    connect(stopButton, SIGNAL(clicked()), this, SLOT(stopSearch()));
    connect(buttonBox, SIGNAL(rejected()), this, SLOT(reject()));

    connect(&tcpSocket, SIGNAL(connected()), this, SLOT(sendRequest()));
    connect(&tcpSocket, SIGNAL(disconnected()),
            this, SLOT(connectionClosedByServer()));
    connect(&tcpSocket, SIGNAL(readyRead()),
            this, SLOT(updateTableWidget()));
    connect(&tcpSocket, SIGNAL(error(QAbstractSocket::SocketError)),
            this, SLOT(error()));
}
```

In the constructor, we initialize the date and time editors based on the current date and time. We also hide the progress bar, because we want to show it only when a connection is active. In *Qt Designer*, the progress bar's minimum and maximum properties were both set to 0. This tells the QProgressBar to behave as a busy indicator instead of as a standard percentage-based progress bar.

Also in the constructor, we connect the QTcpSocket's connected(), disconnected(), readyRead(), and error(QAbstractSocket::SocketError) signals to private slots.

```
void TripPlanner::connectToServer()
{
    tcpSocket.connectToHost("tripserver.zugbahn.de", 6178);

    tableWidget->setRowCount(0);
```

```
        searchButton->setEnabled(false);
        stopButton->setEnabled(true);
        statusLabel->setText(tr("Connecting to server..."));
        progressBar->show();

        nextBlockSize = 0;
    }
```

The connectToServer() slot is executed when the user clicks Search to start a search. We call connectToHost() on the QTcpSocket object to connect to the server, which we assume is accessible at port 6178 on the fictitious host tripserver.zugbahn.de. (If you want to try the example on your own machine, replace the host name with QHostAddress::LocalHost.) The connectToHost() call is asynchronous; it always returns immediately. The connection is typically established later. The QTcpSocket object emits the connected() signal when the connection is up and running, or error(QAbstractSocket::SocketError) if the connection failed.

Next, we update the user interface, in particular making the progress bar visible.

Finally, we set the nextBlockSize variable to 0. This variable stores the length of the next block received from the server. We have chosen to use the value of 0 to mean that we don't yet know the size of the next block.

```
    void TripPlanner::sendRequest()
    {
        QByteArray block;
        QDataStream out(&block, QIODevice::WriteOnly);
        out.setVersion(QDataStream::Qt_4_3);
        out << quint16(0) << quint8('S') << fromComboBox->currentText()
            << toComboBox->currentText() << dateEdit->date()
            << timeEdit->time();

        if (departureRadioButton->isChecked()) {
            out << quint8('D');
        } else {
            out << quint8('A');
        }
        out.device()->seek(0);
        out << quint16(block.size() - sizeof(quint16));
        tcpSocket.write(block);

        statusLabel->setText(tr("Sending request..."));
    }
```

The sendRequest() slot is executed when the QTcpSocket object emits the connected() signal, indicating that a connection has been established. The slot's task is to generate a request to the server, with all the information entered by the user.

The request is a binary block with the following format:

`quint16`	Block size in bytes (excluding this field)
`quint8`	Request type (always 'S')
`QString`	Departure city
`QString`	Arrival city
`QDate`	Date of travel
`QTime`	Approximate time of travel
`quint8`	Time is for departure ('D') or arrival ('A')

We first write the data to a `QByteArray` called `block`. We can't write the data directly to the `QTcpSocket` because we won't know the size of the block, which must be sent first, until after we have put all the data into the block.

We initially write 0 as the block size, followed by the rest of the data. Then we call `seek(0)` on the I/O device (a `QBuffer` created by `QDataStream` behind the scenes) to move back to the beginning of the byte array, and overwrite the initial 0 with the size of the block's data. The size is calculated by taking the block's size and subtracting `sizeof(quint16)` (i.e., 2) to exclude the size field from the byte count. After that, we call `write()` on the `QTcpSocket` to send the block to the server.

```
void TripPlanner::updateTableWidget()
{
    QDataStream in(&tcpSocket);
    in.setVersion(QDataStream::Qt_4_3);

    forever {
        int row = tableWidget->rowCount();

        if (nextBlockSize == 0) {
            if (tcpSocket.bytesAvailable() < sizeof(quint16))
                break;
            in >> nextBlockSize;
        }

        if (nextBlockSize == 0xFFFF) {
            closeConnection();
            statusLabel->setText(tr("Found %1 trip(s)").arg(row));
            break;
        }

        if (tcpSocket.bytesAvailable() < nextBlockSize)
            break;

        QDate date;
        QTime departureTime;
        QTime arrivalTime;
        quint16 duration;
        quint8 changes;
        QString trainType;

        in >> date >> departureTime >> duration >> changes >> trainType;
        arrivalTime = departureTime.addSecs(duration * 60);
```

```
            tableWidget->setRowCount(row + 1);

            QStringList fields;
            fields << date.toString(Qt::LocalDate)
                   << departureTime.toString(tr("hh:mm"))
                   << arrivalTime.toString(tr("hh:mm"))
                   << tr("%1 hr %2 min").arg(duration / 60)
                                        .arg(duration % 60)
                   << QString::number(changes)
                   << trainType;
            for (int i = 0; i < fields.count(); ++i)
                tableWidget->setItem(row, i,
                                     new QTableWidgetItem(fields[i]));
            nextBlockSize = 0;
        }
    }
```

The `updateTableWidget()` slot is connected to the `QTcpSocket`'s `readyRead()` signal, which is emitted whenever the `QTcpSocket` has received new data from the server. The server sends us a list of possible train trips that match the user's criteria. Each matching trip is sent as a single block, and each block starts with a size. Figure 15.2 illustrates a stream of such blocks. The `forever` loop is necessary because we don't necessarily get one block of data from the server at a time.* We might have received an entire block, or just part of a block, or one and a half blocks, or even all of the blocks at once.

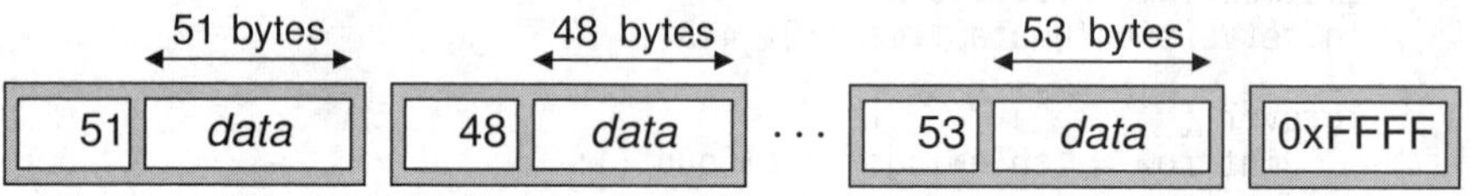

Figure 15.2. The Trip Server's blocks

So, how does the `forever` loop work? If the `nextBlockSize` variable is 0, this means that we have not read the size of the next block. We try to read it (assuming that at least 2 bytes are available for reading). The server uses a size value of `0xFFFF` to signify that there is no more data to receive, so if we read this value, we know that we have reached the end.

If the block size is not `0xFFFF`, we try to read in the next block. First, we check to see whether there are block size bytes available to read. If there are not, we stop there for now. The `readyRead()` signal will be emitted again when more data is available, and we will try again then.

Once we are sure that an entire block has arrived, we can safely use the >> operator on the `QDataStream` to extract the information related to a trip, and we create `QTableWidgetItem`s with that information. A block received from the server has the following format:

---

*The `forever` keyword is provided by Qt. It simply expands to `for (;;)`.

quint16	Block size in bytes (excluding this field)
QDate	Departure date
QTime	Departure time
quint16	Duration (in minutes)
quint8	Number of changes
QString	Train type

At the end, we reset the nextBlockSize variable to 0 to indicate that the next block's size is unknown and needs to be read.

```
void TripPlanner::closeConnection()
{
    tcpSocket.close();
    searchButton->setEnabled(true);
    stopButton->setEnabled(false);
    progressBar->hide();
}
```

The closeConnection() private function closes the connection to the TCP server and updates the user interface. It is called from updateTableWidget() when the 0xFFFF is read and from several other slots that we will cover shortly.

```
void TripPlanner::stopSearch()
{
    statusLabel->setText(tr("Search stopped"));
    closeConnection();
}
```

The stopSearch() slot is connected to the Stop button's clicked() signal. Essentially, it just calls closeConnection().

```
void TripPlanner::connectionClosedByServer()
{
    if (nextBlockSize != 0xFFFF)
        statusLabel->setText(tr("Error: Connection closed by server"));
    closeConnection();
}
```

The connectionClosedByServer() slot is connected to QTcpSocket's disconnected() signal. If the server closes the connection and we have not yet received the 0xFFFF end-of-data marker, we tell the user that an error occurred. We call closeConnection() as usual to update the user interface.

```
void TripPlanner::error()
{
    statusLabel->setText(tcpSocket.errorString());
    closeConnection();
}
```

The error() slot is connected to QTcpSocket's error(QAbstractSocket::SocketError) signal. We ignore the error code and instead use the QIODevice::errorString()

function, which returns a human-readable error message for the last error that occurred.

This is all for the TripPlanner class. The main() function for the Trip Planner application looks just as we would expect:

```
int main(int argc, char *argv[])
{
    QApplication app(argc, argv);
    TripPlanner tripPlanner;
    tripPlanner.show();
    return app.exec();
}
```

Now let's implement the server. The server consists of two classes: TripServer and ClientSocket. The TripServer class is derived from QTcpServer, a class that allows us to accept incoming TCP connections. ClientSocket reimplements QTcpSocket and handles a single connection. At any one time, there are as many ClientSocket objects in memory as there are clients being served.

```
class TripServer : public QTcpServer
{
    Q_OBJECT

public:
    TripServer(QObject *parent = 0);

private:
    void incomingConnection(int socketId);
};
```

The TripServer class reimplements the incomingConnection() function from QTcpServer. This function is called whenever a client attempts to connect to the port the server is listening to.

```
TripServer::TripServer(QObject *parent)
    : QTcpServer(parent)
{
}
```

The TripServer constructor is trivial.

```
void TripServer::incomingConnection(int socketId)
{
    ClientSocket *socket = new ClientSocket(this);
    socket->setSocketDescriptor(socketId);
}
```

In incomingConnection(), we create a ClientSocket object as a child of the TripServer object, and we set its socket descriptor to the number provided to us. The ClientSocket object will delete itself automatically when the connection is terminated.

```
class ClientSocket : public QTcpSocket
{
```

```
    Q_OBJECT

public:
    ClientSocket(QObject *parent = 0);

private slots:
    void readClient();

private:
    void generateRandomTrip(const QString &from, const QString &to,
                            const QDate &date, const QTime &time);

    quint16 nextBlockSize;
};
```

The ClientSocket class is derived from QTcpSocket and encapsulates the state of a single client.

```
ClientSocket::ClientSocket(QObject *parent)
    : QTcpSocket(parent)
{
    connect(this, SIGNAL(readyRead()), this, SLOT(readClient()));
    connect(this, SIGNAL(disconnected()), this, SLOT(deleteLater()));

    nextBlockSize = 0;
}
```

In the constructor, we establish the necessary signal–slot connections, and we set the nextBlockSize variable to 0, indicating that we do not yet know the size of the block sent by the client.

The disconnected() signal is connected to deleteLater(), a QObject-inherited function that deletes the object when control returns to Qt's event loop. This ensures that the ClientSocket object is deleted when the socket connection is closed.

```
void ClientSocket::readClient()
{
    QDataStream in(this);
    in.setVersion(QDataStream::Qt_4_3);

    if (nextBlockSize == 0) {
        if (bytesAvailable() < sizeof(quint16))
            return;
        in >> nextBlockSize;
    }
    if (bytesAvailable() < nextBlockSize)
        return;

    quint8 requestType;
    QString from;
    QString to;
    QDate date;
    QTime time;
    quint8 flag;

    in >> requestType;
    if (requestType == 'S') {
```

```
        in >> from >> to >> date >> time >> flag;

        std::srand(from.length() * 3600 + to.length() * 60
                   + time.hour());
        int numTrips = std::rand() % 8;
        for (int i = 0; i < numTrips; ++i)
            generateRandomTrip(from, to, date, time);

        QDataStream out(this);
        out << quint16(0xFFFF);
    }

    close();
}
```

The `readClient()` slot is connected to `QTcpSocket`'s `readyRead()` signal. If `nextBlockSize` is 0, we start by reading the block size; otherwise, we have already read it, and instead we check to see whether a whole block has arrived. Once an entire block is ready for reading, we read it in one go. We use the `QDataStream` directly on the `QTcpSocket` (the `this` object) and read the fields using the `>>` operator.

Once we have read the client's request, we are ready to generate a reply. If this were a real application, we would look up the information in a train schedule database and try to find matching train trips. But here we will be content with a function called `generateRandomTrip()` that will generate a random trip. We call the function a random number of times, and then we send `0xFFFF` to signify the end of the data. At the end, we close the connection.

```
void ClientSocket::generateRandomTrip(const QString & /* from */,
        const QString & /* to */, const QDate &date, const QTime &time)
{
    QByteArray block;
    QDataStream out(&block, QIODevice::WriteOnly);
    out.setVersion(QDataStream::Qt_4_3);
    quint16 duration = std::rand() % 200;
    out << quint16(0) << date << time << duration << quint8(1)
        << QString("InterCity");
    out.device()->seek(0);
    out << quint16(block.size() - sizeof(quint16));

    write(block);
}
```

The `generateRandomTrip()` function shows how to send a block of data over a TCP connection. This is very similar to what we did in the client in the `sendRequest()` function (p. 374). Once again, we write the block to a `QByteArray` so that we can determine its size before we send it using `write()`.

```
int main(int argc, char *argv[])
{
    QApplication app(argc, argv);
    TripServer server;
    if (!server.listen(QHostAddress::Any, 6178)) {
        std::cerr << "Failed to bind to port" << std::endl;
```

```
            return 1;
        }

        QPushButton quitButton(QObject::tr("&Quit"));
        quitButton.setWindowTitle(QObject::tr("Trip Server"));
        QObject::connect(&quitButton, SIGNAL(clicked()),
                         &app, SLOT(quit()));
        quitButton.show();
        return app.exec();
    }
```

In `main()`, we create a `TripServer` object and a `QPushButton` that enables the user to stop the server. We start the server by calling `QTcpSocket::listen()`, which takes the IP address and port number on which we want to accept connections. The special address 0.0.0.0 (`QHostAddress::Any`) signifies any IP interface present on the local host.

Using a `QPushButton` to represent the server is convenient during development. However, a deployed server would be expected to run without a GUI, as a Windows service or as a Unix daemon. Trolltech provides a commercial add-on for this purpose, called `QtService`.

This completes our client–server example. In this case, we used a block-oriented protocol that allows us to use `QDataStream` for reading and writing. If we wanted to use a line-oriented protocol, the simplest approach would be to use `QTcpSocket`'s `canReadLine()` and `readLine()` functions in a slot connected to the `readyRead()` signal:

```
QStringList lines;
while (tcpSocket.canReadLine())
    lines.append(tcpSocket.readLine());
```

We would then process each line that has been read. As for sending data, that can be done using a `QTextStream` on the `QTcpSocket`.

The server implementation that we have used doesn't scale very well when there are lots of connections. The problem is that while we are processing a request, we don't handle the other connections. A more scalable approach would be to start a new thread for each connection. The Threaded Fortune Server example located in Qt's `examples/network/threadedfortuneserver` directory illustrates how to do this.

Sending and Receiving UDP Datagrams

The `QUdpSocket` class can be used to send and receive UDP datagrams. UDP is an unreliable, datagram-oriented protocol. Some application-level protocols use UDP because it is more lightweight than TCP. With UDP, data is sent as packets (datagrams) from one host to another. There is no concept of connection, and if a UDP packet doesn't get delivered successfully, no error is reported to the sender.

We will see how to use UDP from a Qt application through the Weather Balloon and Weather Station example. The Weather Balloon application mimics a weather balloon that sends a UDP datagram (presumably using a wireless connection) containing the current atmospheric conditions every two seconds. The Weather Station application (shown in Figure 15.3), receives these datagrams and displays them on-screen. We will start by reviewing the code for the Weather Balloon.

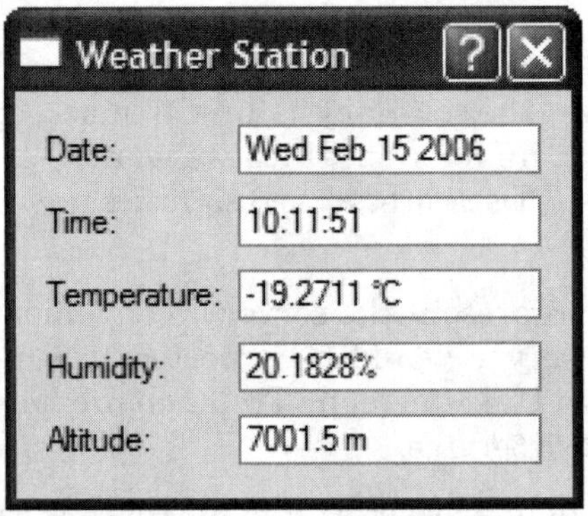

Figure 15.3. The Weather Station application

```
class WeatherBalloon : public QPushButton
{
    Q_OBJECT

public:
    WeatherBalloon(QWidget *parent = 0);

    double temperature() const;
    double humidity() const;
    double altitude() const;

private slots:
    void sendDatagram();

private:
    QUdpSocket udpSocket;
    QTimer timer;
};
```

The `WeatherBalloon` class is derived from `QPushButton`. It uses its `QUdpSocket` private variable for communicating with the Weather Station.

```
WeatherBalloon::WeatherBalloon(QWidget *parent)
    : QPushButton(tr("Quit"), parent)
{
    connect(this, SIGNAL(clicked()), this, SLOT(close()));
    connect(&timer, SIGNAL(timeout()), this, SLOT(sendDatagram()));

    timer.start(2 * 1000);
```

```
    setWindowTitle(tr("Weather Balloon"));
}
```

In the constructor, we start a `QTimer` to invoke `sendDatagram()` every 2 seconds.

```
void WeatherBalloon::sendDatagram()
{
    QByteArray datagram;
    QDataStream out(&datagram, QIODevice::WriteOnly);
    out.setVersion(QDataStream::Qt_4_3);
    out << QDateTime::currentDateTime() << temperature() << humidity()
        << altitude();

    udpSocket.writeDatagram(datagram, QHostAddress::LocalHost, 5824);
}
```

In `sendDatagram()`, we generate and send a datagram containing the current date, time, temperature, humidity, and altitude:

`QDateTime`	Date and time of measurement
`double`	Temperature (in °C)
`double`	Humidity (in %)
`double`	Altitude (in meters)

The datagram is sent using `QUdpSocket::writeDatagram()`. The second and third arguments to `writeDatagram()` are the IP address and the port number of the peer (the Weather Station). For this example, we assume that the Weather Station is running on the same machine as the Weather Balloon, so we use an IP address of 127.0.0.1 (`QHostAddress::LocalHost`), a special address that designates the local host.

Unlike `QTcpSocket::connectToHost()`, `QUdpSocket::writeDatagram()` does not accept host names, only host addresses. If we wanted to resolve a host name to its IP address here, we have two choices. If we are prepared to block while the lookup takes place, we can use the static `QHostInfo::fromName()` function. Otherwise, we can use the static `QHostInfo::lookupHost()` function, which returns immediately and calls the slot it is passed with a `QHostInfo` object containing the corresponding addresses when the lookup is complete.

```
int main(int argc, char *argv[])
{
    QApplication app(argc, argv);
    WeatherBalloon balloon;
    balloon.show();
    return app.exec();
}
```

The `main()` function simply creates a `WeatherBalloon` object, which serves both as a UDP peer and as a `QPushButton` on-screen. By clicking the `QPushButton`, the user can quit the application.

Now let's review the source code for the Weather Station client.

```
class WeatherStation : public QDialog
{
    Q_OBJECT

public:
    WeatherStation(QWidget *parent = 0);

private slots:
    void processPendingDatagrams();

private:
    QUdpSocket udpSocket;

    QLabel *dateLabel;
    QLabel *timeLabel;
    ...
    QLineEdit *altitudeLineEdit;
};
```

The `WeatherStation` class is derived from `QDialog`. It listens to a particular UDP port, parses any incoming datagrams (from the Weather Balloon), and displays their contents in five read-only `QLineEdit`s. The only private variable of interest here is `udpSocket` of type `QUdpSocket`, which we will use to receive datagrams.

```
WeatherStation::WeatherStation(QWidget *parent)
    : QDialog(parent)
{
    udpSocket.bind(5824);

    connect(&udpSocket, SIGNAL(readyRead()),
            this, SLOT(processPendingDatagrams()));
    ...
}
```

In the constructor, we start by binding the `QUdpSocket` to the port that the weather balloon is transmitting to. Since we have not specified a host address, the socket will accept datagrams sent to any IP address that belongs to the machine the Weather Station is running on. Then, we connect the socket's `readyRead()` signal to the private `processPendingDatagrams()` that extracts and displays the data.

```
void WeatherStation::processPendingDatagrams()
{
    QByteArray datagram;

    do {
        datagram.resize(udpSocket.pendingDatagramSize());
        udpSocket.readDatagram(datagram.data(), datagram.size());
    } while (udpSocket.hasPendingDatagrams());

    QDateTime dateTime;
    double temperature;
    double humidity;
    double altitude;
```

```
        QDataStream in(&datagram, QIODevice::ReadOnly);
        in.setVersion(QDataStream::Qt_4_3);
        in >> dateTime >> temperature >> humidity >> altitude;

        dateLineEdit->setText(dateTime.date().toString());
        timeLineEdit->setText(dateTime.time().toString());
        temperatureLineEdit->setText(tr("%1 °C").arg(temperature));
        humidityLineEdit->setText(tr("%1%").arg(humidity));
        altitudeLineEdit->setText(tr("%1 m").arg(altitude));
    }
```

The `processPendingDatagrams()` slot is called when a datagram has arrived. `QUdpSocket` queues the incoming datagrams and lets us access them one at a time. Normally, there should be only one datagram, but we can't exclude the possibility that the sender would send a few datagrams in a row before the `readyRead()` signal is emitted. In that case, we can ignore all the datagrams except the last one, since the earlier ones contain obsolete atmospheric conditions.

The `pendingDatagramSize()` function returns the size of the first pending datagram. From the application's point of view, datagrams are always sent and received as a single unit of data. This means that if any bytes are available, an entire datagram can be read. The `readDatagram()` call copies the contents of the first pending datagram into the specified `char *` buffer (truncating data if the buffer is too small) and advances to the next pending datagram. Once we have read all the datagrams, we decompose the last one (the one with the most recent atmospheric measurements) into its parts and populate the `QLineEdit`s with the new data.

```
    int main(int argc, char *argv[])
    {
        QApplication app(argc, argv);
        WeatherStation station;
        station.show();
        return app.exec();
    }
```

Finally, in `main()`, we create and show the `WeatherStation`.

We have now finished our UDP sender and receiver. The applications are as simple as possible, with the Weather Balloon sending datagrams and the Weather Station receiving them. In most real-world applications, both applications would need to both read and write on their socket. The `QUdpSocket::writeDatagram()` functions can be passed a host address and port number, so the `QUdpSocket` can read from the host and port it is bound to with `bind()`, and write to some other host and port.

- *Reading XML with QXmlStreamReader*
- *Reading XML with DOM*
- *Reading XML with SAX*
- *Writing XML*

16. XML

XML (eXtensible Markup Language) is a general-purpose text file format that is popular for data interchange and data storage. It was developed by the World Wide Web Consortium (W3C) as a lightweight alternative to SGML (Standard Generalized Markup Language). The syntax is similar to HTML, but XML is a metalanguage and as such does not mandate specific tags, attributes, or entities. The XML-compliant version of HTML is called XHTML.

For the popular SVG (Scalable Vector Graphics) XML format, the *QtSvg* module provides classes that can load and render SVG images. For rendering documents that use the MathML (Mathematical Markup Language) XML format, the `QtMmlWidget` from Qt Solutions can be used.

For general XML processing, Qt provides the *QtXml* module, which is the subject of this chapter.* The *QtXml* module offers three distinct APIs for reading XML documents:

- `QXmlStreamReader` is a fast parser for reading well-formed XML.
- DOM (Document Object Model) converts an XML document into a tree structure, which the application can then navigate.
- SAX (Simple API for XML) reports "parsing events" directly to the application through virtual functions.

The `QXmlStreamReader` class is the fastest and easiest to use and offers an API that is consistent with the rest of Qt. It is ideal for writing one-pass parsers. DOM's main benefit is that it lets us navigate a tree representation of the XML document in any order, allowing us to implement multi-pass parsing algorithms. Some applications even use the DOM tree as their primary data structure. SAX is provided mainly for historical reasons; using `QXmlStreamReader` usually leads to simpler and faster code.

For writing XML files, Qt also offers three options:

---

*Qt 4.4 is expected to include additional high-level classes for handling XML, providing support for XQuery and XPath, in a separate module called *QtXmlPatterns*.

- We can use a QXmlStreamWriter.
- We can represent the data as a DOM tree in memory and ask the tree to write itself to a file.
- We can generate the XML by hand.

Using QXmlStreamWriter is by far the easiest approach, and is more reliable than hand-generating XML. Using DOM to produce XML really makes sense only if a DOM tree is already used as the application's primary data structure. All three approaches to reading and writing XML are shown in this chapter.

Reading XML with QXmlStreamReader

Using QXmlStreamReader is the fastest and easiest way to read XML in Qt. Because the parser works incrementally, it is particularly useful for finding all occurrences of a given tag in an XML document, for reading very large files that may not fit in memory, and for populating custom data structures to reflect an XML document's contents.

The QXmlStreamReader parser works in terms of the tokens listed in Figure 16.1. Each time the readNext() function is called, the next token is read and becomes the current token. The current token's properties depend on the token's type and are accessible using the getter functions listed in the table.

Token Type	Example	Getter Functions
StartDocument	N/A	isStandaloneDocument()
EndDocument	N/A	isStandaloneDocument()
StartElement	<item>	namespaceUri(), name(), attributes(), namespaceDeclarations()
EndElement	</item>	namespaceUri(), name()
Characters	AT&T	text(), isWhitespace(), isCDATA()
Comment	<!-- fix -->	text()
DTD	<!DOCTYPE ...>	text(), notationDeclarations(), entityDeclarations()
EntityReference	™	name(), text()
ProcessingInstruction	<?alert?>	processingInstructionTarget(), processingInstructionData()
Invalid	>&<!	error(), errorString()

Figure 16.1. The QXmlStreamReader's tokens

Consider the following XML document:

```
<doc>
    <quote>Einmal ist keinmal</quote>
```

```
</doc>
```

If we parse this document, each `readNext()` call will produce a new token, with extra information available using getter functions:

```
StartDocument
StartElement (name() == "doc")
StartElement (name() == "quote")
Characters (text() == "Einmal ist keinmal")
EndElement (name() == "quote")
EndElement (name() == "doc")
EndDocument
```

After each `readNext()` call, we can test for the current token's type using `isStartElement()`, `isCharacters()`, and similar functions, or simply using `state()`.

We will review an example that shows how to use `QXmlStreamReader` to parse an ad hoc XML file format and render its contents in a `QTreeWidget`. The format we will parse is that of a book index, with index entries and sub-entries. Here's the book index file that is displayed in the `QTreeWidget` in Figure 16.2:

```
<?xml version="1.0"?>
<bookindex>
    <entry term="sidebearings">
        <page>10</page>
        <page>34-35</page>
        <page>307-308</page>
    </entry>
    <entry term="subtraction">
        <entry term="of pictures">
            <page>115</page>
            <page>244</page>
        </entry>
        <entry term="of vectors">
            <page>9</page>
        </entry>
    </entry>
</bookindex>
```

We will begin by looking at an extract from the application's `main()` function, to see how the XML reader is used in context, and then we will look at the reader's implementation.

```
int main(int argc, char *argv[])
{
    QApplication app(argc, argv);
    QStringList args = QApplication::arguments();
    ...
    QTreeWidget treeWidget;
    ...
    XmlStreamReader reader(&treeWidget);
    for (int i = 1; i < args.count(); ++i)
        reader.readFile(args[i]);
```

```
    return app.exec();
}
```

The application shown in Figure 16.2 begins by creating a QTreeWidget. It then creates an XmlStreamReader, passing it the tree widget and asking it to parse each file specified on the command line.

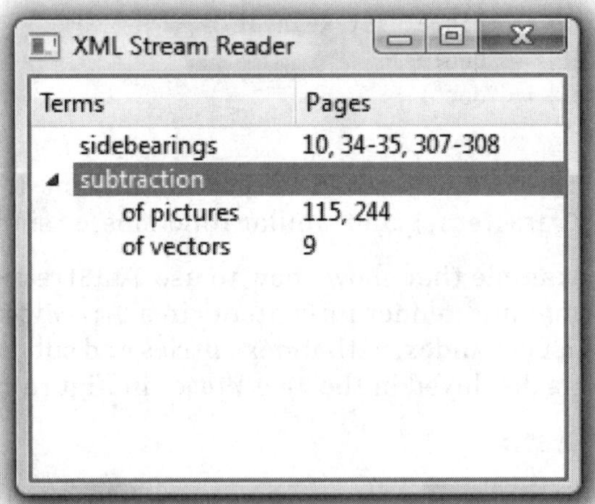

Figure 16.2. The XML Stream Reader application

```
class XmlStreamReader
{
public:
    XmlStreamReader(QTreeWidget *tree);

    bool readFile(const QString &fileName);

private:
    void readBookindexElement();
    void readEntryElement(QTreeWidgetItem *parent);
    void readPageElement(QTreeWidgetItem *parent);
    void skipUnknownElement();

    QTreeWidget *treeWidget;
    QXmlStreamReader reader;
};
```

The XmlStreamReader class provides two public functions: the constructor and parseFile(). The class uses a QXmlStreamReader instance to parse the XML file, and populates the QTreeWidget to reflect the XML data that is read. The parsing is done using recursive descent:

- readBookindexElement() parses a <bookindex>...</bookindex> element that contains zero or more <entry> elements.

- `readEntryElement()` parses an `<entry>...</entry>` element that contains zero or more `<page>` elements and zero or more `<entry>` elements nested to any depth.
- `readPageElement()` parses a `<page>...</page>` element.
- `skipUnknownElement()` skips an unrecognized element.

We will now look at the `XmlStreamReader` class's implementation, beginning with the constructor.

```
XmlStreamReader::XmlStreamReader(QTreeWidget *tree)
{
    treeWidget = tree;
}
```

The constructor is used only to establish which `QTreeWidget` the reader should use. All the action takes place in the `readFile()` function (called from `main()`), which we will look at in three parts.

```
bool XmlStreamReader::readFile(const QString &fileName)
{
    QFile file(fileName);
    if (!file.open(QFile::ReadOnly | QFile::Text)) {
        std::cerr << "Error: Cannot read file " << qPrintable(fileName)
                  << ": " << qPrintable(file.errorString())
                  << std::endl;
        return false;
    }

    reader.setDevice(&file);
```

The `readFile()` function begins by trying to open the file. If it fails, it outputs an error message and returns `false`. If the file is opened successfully, it is set as the `QXmlStreamReader`'s input device.

```
    reader.readNext();
    while (!reader.atEnd()) {
        if (reader.isStartElement()) {
            if (reader.name() == "bookindex") {
                readBookindexElement();
            } else {
                reader.raiseError(QObject::tr("Not a bookindex file"));
            }
        } else {
            reader.readNext();
        }
    }
```

The `QXmlStreamReader`'s `readNext()` function reads the next token from the input stream. If a token is successfully read and the end of the XML file has not been reached, the function enters the `while` loop. Because of the structure of the index files, we know that inside this loop there are just three possibilities: A `<bookindex>` start tag has just been read, another start tag has been read (in which case the file is not a book index), or some other token has been read.

If we have the correct start tag, we call `readBookindexElement()` to continue processing. Otherwise, we call `QXmlStreamReader::raiseError()` with an error message. The next time `atEnd()` is called (in the `while` loop condition), it will return `true`. This ensures that parsing stops as soon as possible after an error has been encountered. The error can be queried later by calling `error()` and `errorString()` on the `QFile`. An alternative would have been to return right away when we detect an error in the book index file. Using `raiseError()` is usually more convenient, because it lets us use the same error-reporting mechanism for low-level XML parsing errors, which are raised automatically when `QXmlStreamReader` runs into invalid XML, and for application-specific errors.

```
    file.close();
    if (reader.hasError()) {
        std::cerr << "Error: Failed to parse file "
                  << qPrintable(fileName) << ": "
                  << qPrintable(reader.errorString()) << std::endl;
        return false;
    } else if (file.error() != QFile::NoError) {
        std::cerr << "Error: Cannot read file " << qPrintable(fileName)
                  << ": " << qPrintable(file.errorString())
                  << std::endl;
        return false;
    }
    return true;
}
```

Once the processing has finished, the file is closed. If there was a parser error or a file error, the function outputs an error message and returns `false`; otherwise, it returns `true` to report a successful parse.

```
void XmlStreamReader::readBookindexElement()
{
    reader.readNext();
    while (!reader.atEnd()) {
        if (reader.isEndElement()) {
            reader.readNext();
            break;
        }

        if (reader.isStartElement()) {
            if (reader.name() == "entry") {
                readEntryElement(treeWidget->invisibleRootItem());
            } else {
                skipUnknownElement();
            }
        } else {
            reader.readNext();
        }
    }
}
```

The `readBookindexElement()` is responsible for reading the main part of the file. It starts by skipping the current token (which at this point can be only a `<bookindex>` start tag) and then loops over the input.

If an end tag is read, it can be only the `</bookindex>` tag, since otherwise, `QXmlStreamReader` would have reported an error (`UnexpectedElementError`). In that case, we skip the tag and break out of the loop. Otherwise, we should have a top-level index `<entry>` start tag. If this is the case, we call `readEntryElement()` to process the entry's data; if not, we call `skipUnknownElement()`. Using `skipUnknownElement()` rather than calling `raiseError()` means that if we extend the book index format in the future to include new tags, this reader will continue to work, since it will simply ignore the tags it does not recognize.

The `readEntryElement()` takes a `QTreeWidgetItem *` argument that identifies a parent item. We pass `QTreeWidget::invisibleRootItem()` as the parent to make the new items root items. In `readEntryElement()`, we will call `readEntryElement()` recursively, with a different parent.

```
void XmlStreamReader::readEntryElement(QTreeWidgetItem *parent)
{
    QTreeWidgetItem *item = new QTreeWidgetItem(parent);
    item->setText(0, reader.attributes().value("term").toString());

    reader.readNext();
    while (!reader.atEnd()) {
        if (reader.isEndElement()) {
            reader.readNext();
            break;
        }

        if (reader.isStartElement()) {
            if (reader.name() == "entry") {
                readEntryElement(item);
            } else if (reader.name() == "page") {
                readPageElement(item);
            } else {
                skipUnknownElement();
            }
        } else {
            reader.readNext();
        }
    }
}
```

The `readEntryElement()` function is called whenever an `<entry>` start tag is encountered. We want a tree widget item to be created for every index entry, so we create a new `QTreeWidgetItem`, and set its first column's text to be the entry's term attribute's text.

Once the entry has been added to the tree, the next token is read. If it is an end tag, we skip the tag and break out of the loop. If a start tag is encountered, it will be an `<entry>` tag (signifying a sub-entry), a `<page>` tag (a page number for this entry), or an unknown tag. If the start tag is a sub-entry, we call readEntry-Element() recursively. If the tag is a <page> tag, we call readPageElement().

```
void XmlStreamReader::readPageElement(QTreeWidgetItem *parent)
{
    QString page = reader.readElementText();
    if (reader.isEndElement())
        reader.readNext();

    QString allPages = parent->text(1);
    if (!allPages.isEmpty())
        allPages += ", ";
    allPages += page;
    parent->setText(1, allPages);
}
```

The readPageElement() function is called whenever we get a <page> tag. It is passed the tree item that corresponds to the entry to which the page text belongs. We begin by reading the text between the <page> and </page> tags. On success, the readElementText() function will leave the parser on the </page> tag, which we must skip.

The pages are stored in the tree widget item's second column. We begin by extracting the text that is already there. If the text is not empty, we append a comma to it, ready for the new page text. We then append the new text and update the column's text accordingly.

```
void XmlStreamReader::skipUnknownElement()
{
    reader.readNext();
    while (!reader.atEnd()) {
        if (reader.isEndElement()) {
            reader.readNext();
            break;
        }

        if (reader.isStartElement()) {
            skipUnknownElement();
        } else {
            reader.readNext();
        }
    }
}
```

Finally, when unknown tags are encountered, we keep reading until we get the unknown element's end tag, which we also skip. This means that we will skip over well-formed but unrecognized elements, and read as much of the recognizable data as possible from the XML file.

The example presented here could be used as the basis for similar XML recursive descent parsers. Nonetheless, sometimes implementing a parser like this can be tricky, if a readNext() call is missing or out of place. Some programmers address the problem by using assertions in their code. For example, at the beginning of readBookindexElement(), we could add the line

```
Q_ASSERT(reader.isStartElement() && reader.name() == "bookindex");
```

A similar assertion could be made in the `readEntryElement()` and `readPageElement()` functions. For `skipUnknownElement()`, we would simply assert that we have a start element.

A `QXmlStreamReader` can take input from any `QIODevice`, including `QFile`, `QBuffer`, `QProcess`, and `QTcpSocket`. Some input sources may not be able to provide the data that the parser needs when it needs it—for example, due to network latency. It is still possible to use `QXmlStreamReader` under such circumstances; more information on this is provided in the reference documentation for `QXmlStreamReader` under the heading "Incremental Parsing".

The `QXmlStreamReader` class used in this application is part of the *QtXml* library. To link against this library, we must add this line to the `.pro` file:

```
QT += xml
```

In the next two sections, we will see how to write the same application with DOM and SAX.

Reading XML with DOM

DOM is a standard API for parsing XML developed by the W3C. Qt provides a non-validating DOM Level 2 implementation for reading, manipulating, and writing XML documents.

DOM represents an XML file as a tree in memory. We can navigate through the DOM tree as much as we want, and we can modify the tree and save it back to disk as an XML file.

Let's consider the following XML document:

```
<doc>
    <quote>Scio me nihil scire</quote>
    <translation>I know that I know nothing</translation>
</doc>
```

It corresponds to the following DOM tree:

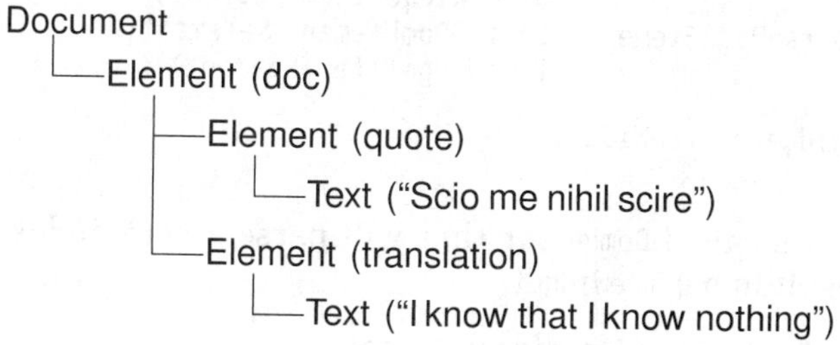

```
Document
 └─Element (doc)
      ├─Element (quote)
      │    └─Text ("Scio me nihil scire")
      └─Element (translation)
           └─Text ("I know that I know nothing")
```

The DOM tree contains nodes of different types. For example, an `Element` node corresponds to an opening tag and its matching closing tag. The material that falls between the tags appears as child nodes of the `Element` node. In Qt, the node types (like all other DOM-related classes) have a QDom prefix; thus, QDomElement represents an Element node, and QDomText represents a Text node.

Different types of nodes can have different kinds of child nodes. For example, an Element node can contain other Element nodes, as well as EntityReference, Text, CDATASection, ProcessingInstruction, and Comment nodes. Figure 16.3 shows which nodes can have which kinds of child nodes. The nodes shown in gray cannot have any child nodes of their own.

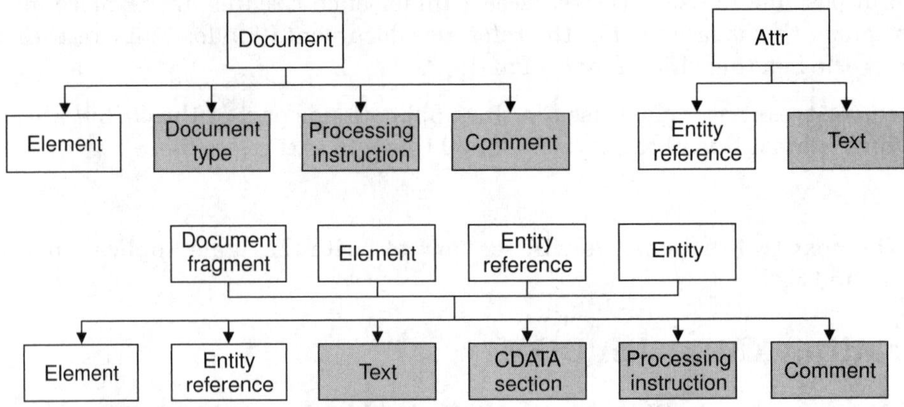

Figure 16.3. Parent–child relationships between DOM nodes

To illustrate how to use DOM for reading XML files, we will write a parser for the book index file format described in the preceding section (p. 389).

```
class DomParser
{
public:
    DomParser(QTreeWidget *tree);

    bool readFile(const QString &fileName);

private:
    void parseBookindexElement(const QDomElement &element);
    void parseEntryElement(const QDomElement &element,
                           QTreeWidgetItem *parent);
    void parsePageElement(const QDomElement &element,
                          QTreeWidgetItem *parent);

    QTreeWidget *treeWidget;
};
```

We define a class called DomParser that will parse a book index XML file and display the result in a QTreeWidget.

```
DomParser::DomParser(QTreeWidget *tree)
{
    treeWidget = tree;
}
```

In the constructor, we simply assign the given tree widget to the member variable. All the parsing is done inside the readFile() function.

```
bool DomParser::readFile(const QString &fileName)
{
    QFile file(fileName);
    if (!file.open(QFile::ReadOnly | QFile::Text)) {
        std::cerr << "Error: Cannot read file " << qPrintable(fileName)
                  << ": " << qPrintable(file.errorString())
                  << std::endl;
        return false;
    }

    QString errorStr;
    int errorLine;
    int errorColumn;

    QDomDocument doc;
    if (!doc.setContent(&file, false, &errorStr, &errorLine,
                        &errorColumn)) {
        std::cerr << "Error: Parse error at line " << errorLine << ", "
                  << "column " << errorColumn << ": "
                  << qPrintable(errorStr) << std::endl;
        return false;
    }

    QDomElement root = doc.documentElement();
    if (root.tagName() != "bookindex") {
        std::cerr << "Error: Not a bookindex file" << std::endl;
        return false;
    }

    parseBookindexElement(root);
    return true;
}
```

In readFile(), we begin by trying to open the file whose name was passed in. If an error occurs, we output an error message and return false to signify failure. Otherwise, we set up some variables to hold parse error information, should they be needed, and then create a QDomDocument. When we call setContent() on the DOM document, the entire XML document provided by the QIODevice is read and parsed. The setContent() function automatically opens the device if it isn't already open. The false argument to setContent() disables namespace processing; refer to the *QtXml* reference documentation for an introduction to XML namespaces and how to handle them in Qt.

If an error occurs, we output an error message and return false to indicate failure. If the parse is successful, we call documentElement() on the QDomDocument to obtain its single QDomElement child, and we check that it is a <bookindex> element. If we have a <bookindex>, we call parseBookindexElement() to parse it. As in the preceding section, the parsing is done using recursive descent.

```
void DomParser::parseBookindexElement(const QDomElement &element)
{
```

```
    QDomNode child = element.firstChild();
    while (!child.isNull()) {
        if (child.toElement().tagName() == "entry")
            parseEntryElement(child.toElement(),
                              treeWidget->invisibleRootItem());
        child = child.nextSibling();
    }
}
```

In parseBookindexElement(), we iterate over all the child nodes. We expect each node to be an <entry> element, and for each one that is, we call parseEntry() to parse it. We ignore unknown nodes, to allow for the book index format to be extended in the future without preventing old parsers from working. All <entry> nodes that are direct children of the <bookindex> node are top-level nodes in the tree widget we are populating to reflect the DOM tree, so when we want to parse each one we pass both the node element and the tree's invisible root item to be the widget tree item's parent.

The QDomNode class can store any type of node. If we want to process a node further, we must first convert it to the right data type. In this example, we only care about Element nodes, so we call toElement() on the QDomNode to convert it to a QDomElement and then call tagName() to retrieve the element's tag name. If the node is *not* of type Element, the toElement() function returns a null QDomElement object, with an empty tag name.

```
void DomParser::parseEntryElement(const QDomElement &element,
                                  QTreeWidgetItem *parent)
{
    QTreeWidgetItem *item = new QTreeWidgetItem(parent);
    item->setText(0, element.attribute("term"));

    QDomNode child = element.firstChild();
    while (!child.isNull()) {
        if (child.toElement().tagName() == "entry") {
            parseEntryElement(child.toElement(), item);
        } else if (child.toElement().tagName() == "page") {
            parsePageElement(child.toElement(), item);
        }
        child = child.nextSibling();
    }
}
```

In parseEntryElement(), we create a tree widget item. The parent item that is passed in is either the tree's invisible root item (if this is a top-level entry) or another entry (if this is a sub-entry). We call setText() to set the text shown in the item's first column to the value of the <entry> tag's term attribute.

Once we have initialized the QTreeWidgetItem, we iterate over the child nodes of the QDomElement node corresponding to the current <entry> tag. For each child element that is an <entry> tag, we call parseEntryElement() recursively with the current item as the second argument. Each child's QTreeWidgetItem will then be created with the current entry as its parent. If the child element is a <page>, we call parsePageElement().

```
void DomParser::parsePageElement(const QDomElement &element,
                                 QTreeWidgetItem *parent)
{
    QString page = element.text();
    QString allPages = parent->text(1);
    if (!allPages.isEmpty())
        allPages += ", ";
    allPages += page;
    parent->setText(1, allPages);
}
```

In parsePageElement(), we call text() on the element to obtain the text that occurs between the <page> and </page> tags; then we add the text to the comma-separated list of page numbers in the QTreeWidgetItem's second column. The QDomElement::text() function navigates through the element's child nodes and concatenates all the text stored in Text and CDATA nodes.

Let's now see how we can use the DomParser class to parse a file:

```
int main(int argc, char *argv[])
{
    QApplication app(argc, argv);
    QStringList args = QApplication::arguments();
    ...
    QTreeWidget treeWidget;
    ...
    DomParser parser(&treeWidget);
    for (int i = 1; i < args.count(); ++i)
        parser.readFile(args[i]);

    return app.exec();
}
```

We start by setting up a QTreeWidget. Then we create a DomParser. For each file listed on the command line, we call DomParser::readFile() to open and parse each file and populate the tree widget.

Like the previous example, we need the following line in the application's .pro file to link against the *QtXml* library:

```
QT += xml
```

As the example illustrates, navigating through a DOM tree is straightforward, although not quite as convenient as using QXmlStreamReader. Programmers who use DOM a lot often write their own higher-level wrapper functions to simplify commonly needed operations.

Reading XML with SAX

SAX is a public domain de facto standard API for reading XML documents. Qt's SAX classes are modeled after the SAX2 Java implementation, with some differences in naming to match the Qt conventions. Compared with DOM, SAX is more low-level and usually faster. But since the QXmlStreamReader class presented earlier in this chapter offers a more Qt-like API and is faster than the SAX parser, the main use of the SAX parser is for porting code that uses the SAX API into Qt. For more information about SAX, see http://www.saxproject.org/.

Qt provides a SAX-based non-validating XML parser called QXmlSimpleReader. This parser recognizes well-formed XML and supports XML namespaces. When the parser goes through the document, it calls virtual functions in registered handler classes to indicate parsing events. (These "parsing events" are unrelated to Qt events, such as key and mouse events.) For example, let's assume the parser is analyzing the following XML document:

```
<doc>
    <quote>Gnothi seauton</quote>
</doc>
```

The parser would call the following parsing event handlers:

```
startDocument()
startElement("doc")
startElement("quote")
characters("Gnothi seauton")
endElement("quote")
endElement("doc")
endDocument()
```

The preceding functions are all declared in QXmlContentHandler. For simplicity, we omitted some of the arguments to startElement() and endElement().

QXmlContentHandler is just one of many handler classes that can be used in conjunction with QXmlSimpleReader. The others are QXmlEntityResolver, QXmlDTDHandler, QXmlErrorHandler, QXmlDeclHandler, and QXmlLexicalHandler. These classes only declare pure virtual functions and give information about different kinds of parsing events. For most applications, QXmlContentHandler and QXmlErrorHandler are the only two that are needed. The class hierarchy we have used is shown in Figure 16.4.

For convenience, Qt also provides QXmlDefaultHandler, a class that is derived from all the handler classes and that provides trivial implementations for all the functions. This design, with many abstract handler classes and one trivial subclass, is unusual for Qt; it was adopted to closely follow the model Java implementation.

The most significant difference between using the SAX API and QXmlStreamReader or the DOM API is that the SAX API requires us to manually keep track

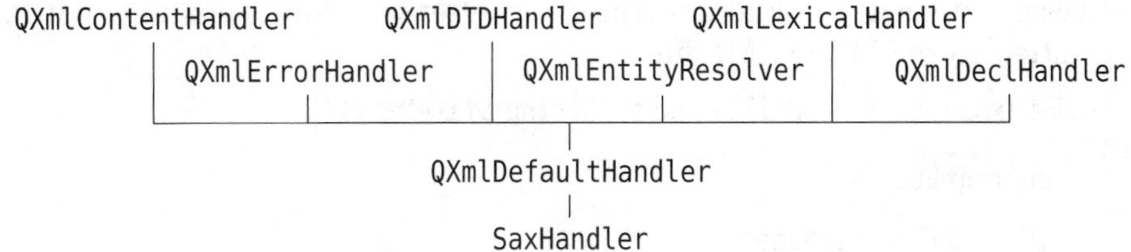

Figure 16.4. Inheritance tree for SaxHandler

of the parser's state using member variables, something that is not necessary in the other two approaches, which both allowed recursive descent.

To illustrate how to use SAX for reading XML files, we will write a parser for the book index file format described earlier in this chapter (p. 389). Here we will parse using a QXmlSimpleReader and a QXmlDefaultHandler subclass called SaxHandler.

The first step to implement the parser is to subclass QXmlDefaultHandler:

```
class SaxHandler : public QXmlDefaultHandler
{
public:
    SaxHandler(QTreeWidget *tree);

    bool readFile(const QString &fileName);

protected:
    bool startElement(const QString &namespaceURI,
                      const QString &localName,
                      const QString &qName,
                      const QXmlAttributes &attributes);
    bool endElement(const QString &namespaceURI,
                    const QString &localName,
                    const QString &qName);
    bool characters(const QString &str);
    bool fatalError(const QXmlParseException &exception);

private:
    QTreeWidget *treeWidget;
    QTreeWidgetItem *currentItem;
    QString currentText;
};
```

The SaxHandler class is derived from QXmlDefaultHandler and reimplements four functions: startElement(), endElement(), characters(), and fatalError(). The first three functions are declared in QXmlContentHandler; the last function is declared in QXmlErrorHandler.

```
SaxHandler::SaxHandler(QTreeWidget *tree)
{
    treeWidget = tree;
}
```

The SaxHandler constructor accepts the QTreeWidget we want to populate with the information stored in the XML file.

```
bool SaxHandler::readFile(const QString &fileName)
{
    currentItem = 0;

    QFile file(fileName);
    QXmlInputSource inputSource(&file);
    QXmlSimpleReader reader;
    reader.setContentHandler(this);
    reader.setErrorHandler(this);
    return reader.parse(inputSource);
}
```

This function is called when we have the name of a file to be parsed. We create a QFile object for the file and create a QXmlInputSource to read the file's contents. Then we create a QXmlSimpleReader to parse the file. We set the reader's content and error handlers to this class (SaxHandler), and then we call parse() on the reader to perform the parsing. In SaxHandler, we only reimplement functions from the QXmlContentHandler and QXmlErrorHandler classes; if we had implemented functions from other handler classes, we would also have needed to call the corresponding set*Xxx*Handler() functions.

Instead of passing a simple QFile object to the parse() function, we pass a QXmlInputSource. This class opens the file it is given, reads it (taking into account any character encoding specified in the <?xml?> declaration), and provides an interface through which the parser reads the file.

```
bool SaxHandler::startElement(const QString & /* namespaceURI */,
                              const QString & /* localName */,
                              const QString &qName,
                              const QXmlAttributes &attributes)
{
    if (qName == "entry") {
        currentItem = new QTreeWidgetItem(currentItem ?
                currentItem : treeWidget->invisibleRootItem());
        currentItem->setText(0, attributes.value("term"));
    } else if (qName == "page") {
        currentText.clear();
    }
    return true;
}
```

The startElement() function is called when the reader encounters a new opening tag. The third parameter is the tag's name (or more precisely, its "qualified name"). The fourth parameter is the list of attributes. In this example, we ignore the first and second parameters. They are useful for XML files that use XML's namespace mechanism, a subject that is discussed in detail in the reference documentation.

If the tag is <entry>, we create a new QTreeWidgetItem. If the tag is nested within another <entry> tag, the new tag defines a sub-entry in the index, and the new

QTreeWidgetItem is created as a child of the QTreeWidgetItem that represents the encompassing entry. Otherwise, we create the QTreeWidgetItem as a top-level item, using the tree widget's invisible root item as its parent. We call setText() to set the text shown in column 0 to the value of the <entry> tag's term attribute.

If the tag is <page>, we set the currentText variable to be an empty string. The variable serves as an accumulator for the text located between the <page> and </page> tags.

At the end, we return true to tell SAX to continue parsing the file. If we wanted to report unknown tags as errors, we would return false in those cases. We would then also reimplement errorString() from QXmlDefaultHandler to return an appropriate error message.

```
bool SaxHandler::characters(const QString &str)
{
    currentText += str;
    return true;
}
```

The characters() function is called to report character data in the XML document. We simply append the characters to the currentText variable.

```
bool SaxHandler::endElement(const QString & /* namespaceURI */,
                            const QString & /* localName */,
                            const QString &qName)
{
    if (qName == "entry") {
        currentItem = currentItem->parent();
    } else if (qName == "page") {
        if (currentItem) {
            QString allPages = currentItem->text(1);
            if (!allPages.isEmpty())
                allPages += ", ";
            allPages += currentText;
            currentItem->setText(1, allPages);
        }
    }
    return true;
}
```

The endElement() function is called when the reader encounters a closing tag. Just as with startElement(), the third parameter is the name of the tag.

If the tag is </entry>, we update the currentItem private variable to point to the current QTreeWidgetItem's parent. (For historical reasons, top-level items return 0 as their parent rather than the invisible root item.) This ensures that the currentItem variable is restored to the value it held before the corresponding <entry> tag was read.

If the tag is </page>, we add the specified page number or page range to the comma-separated list in the current item's text in column 1.

```
bool SaxHandler::fatalError(const QXmlParseException &exception)
{
    std::cerr << "Parse error at line " << exception.lineNumber()
              << ", " << "column " << exception.columnNumber() << ": "
              << qPrintable(exception.message()) << std::endl;
    return false;
}
```

The `fatalError()` function is called when the reader fails to parse the XML file. If this occurs, we simply print a message to the console, giving the line number, the column number, and the parser's error text.

This completes the implementation of `SaxHandler`. The `main()` function that uses it is almost identical to the one we reviewed in the previous section for `DomParser`, the difference being that we use a `SaxHandler` rather than a `DomParser`.

Writing XML

Most applications that can read XML files also need to write such files. There are three approaches for generating XML files from Qt applications:

- We can use a `QXmlStreamWriter`.
- We can build a DOM tree and call `save()` on it.
- We can generate XML by hand.

The choice between these approaches is mostly independent of whether we use `QXmlStreamReader`, DOM, or SAX for reading XML documents, although if the data is held in a DOM tree it often makes sense to save the tree directly.

Writing XML using the `QXmlStreamWriter` class is particularly easy since the class takes care of escaping special characters for us. If we wanted to output the book index data from a `QTreeWidget` using `QXmlStreamWriter`, we could do so using just two functions. The first function would take a file name and a `QTreeWidget *`, and would iterate over all the top-level items in the tree:

```
bool writeXml(const QString &fileName, QTreeWidget *treeWidget)
{
    QFile file(fileName);
    if (!file.open(QFile::WriteOnly | QFile::Text)) {
        std::cerr << "Error: Cannot write file "
                  << qPrintable(fileName) << ": "
                  << qPrintable(file.errorString()) << std::endl;
        return false;
    }

    QXmlStreamWriter xmlWriter(&file);
    xmlWriter.setAutoFormatting(true);
    xmlWriter.writeStartDocument();
    xmlWriter.writeStartElement("bookindex");
    for (int i = 0; i < treeWidget->topLevelItemCount(); ++i)
        writeIndexEntry(&xmlWriter, treeWidget->topLevelItem(i));
    xmlWriter.writeEndDocument();
```

```
        file.close();
        if (file.error()) {
            std::cerr << "Error: Cannot write file "
                      << qPrintable(fileName) << ": "
                      << qPrintable(file.errorString()) << std::endl;
            return false;
        }
        return true;
    }
```

If we switch on auto-formatting, the XML is output in a more human-friendly style, with indentation used to show the data's recursive structure. The `writeStartDocument()` function writes the XML header line

```
<?xml version="1.0" encoding="UTF-8"?>
```

The `writeStartElement()` function generates a new start tag with the given tag text. The `writeEndDocument()` function closes any open start tags. For each top-level item, we call `writeIndexEntry()`, passing it the `QXmlStreamWriter`, and the item to output. Here is the code for `writeIndexEntry()`:

```
void writeIndexEntry(QXmlStreamWriter *xmlWriter, QTreeWidgetItem *item)
{
    xmlWriter->writeStartElement("entry");
    xmlWriter->writeAttribute("term", item->text(0));
    QString pageString = item->text(1);
    if (!pageString.isEmpty()) {
        QStringList pages = pageString.split(", ");
        foreach (QString page, pages)
            xmlWriter->writeTextElement("page", page);
    }
    for (int i = 0; i < item->childCount(); ++i)
        writeIndexEntry(xmlWriter, item->child(i));
    xmlWriter->writeEndElement();
}
```

The function creates an `<entry>` element corresponding to the `QTreeWidgetItem` it receives as a parameter. The `writeAttribute()` function adds an attribute to the tag that has just been written; for example, it might turn `<entry>` into `<entry term="sidebearings">`. If there are page numbers, they are split on comma-spaces, and for each one, a separate `<page>...</page>` tag pair is written, with the page text in between. This is all achieved by calling `writeTextElement()` and passing it a tag name and the text to put between the start and end tags. In all cases, `QXmlStreamWriter` takes care of escaping XML special characters, so we never have to worry about this.

If the item has child items, we recursively call `writeIndexEntry()` on each of them. Finally, we call `writeEndElement()` to output `</entry>`.

Using `QXmlStreamWriter` to write XML is the easiest and safest approach, but if we already have the XML in a DOM tree, we can simply ask the tree to output the relevant XML by calling `save()` on the `QDomDocument` object. By default, `save()` uses UTF-8 as the encoding for the generated file. We can use another encoding by prepending an <?xml?> declaration such as

```
<?xml version="1.0" encoding="ISO-8859-1"?>
```

to the DOM tree. The following code snippet shows how to do this:

```
const int Indent = 4;

QDomDocument doc;
...
QTextStream out(&file);
QDomNode xmlNode = doc.createProcessingInstruction("xml",
                             "version=\"1.0\" encoding=\"ISO-8859-1\"");
doc.insertBefore(xmlNode, doc.firstChild());
doc.save(out, Indent);
```

Starting with Qt 4.3, an alternative is to set the encoding on the `QTextStream` using `setCodec()` and to pass `QDomNode::EncodingFromTextStream` as third parameter to `save()`.

Generating XML files by hand isn't much harder than using DOM. We can use `QTextStream` and write the strings as we would do with any other text file. The trickiest part is to escape special characters in text and attribute values. The `Qt::escape()` function escapes the characters '<', '>', and '&'. Here's some code that makes use of it:

```
QTextStream out(&file);
out.setCodec("UTF-8");
out << "<doc>\n"
    << "    <quote>" << Qt::escape(quoteText) << "</quote>\n"
    << "    <translation>" << Qt::escape(translationText)
    << "</translation>\n"
    << "</doc>\n";
```

When generating XML files like this, in addition to having to write the correct <?xml?> declaration and setting the right encoding, we must also remember to escape the text we write, and if we use attributes we must escape single or double quotes in their values. Using `QXmlStreamWriter` is much easier since it handles all of this for us.

- *Tooltips, Status Tips, and "What's This?" Help*
- *Using a Web Browser to Provide Online Help*
- *Using QTextBrowser as a Simple Help Engine*
- *Using Qt Assistant for Powerful Online Help*

17. Providing Online Help

Most applications provide their users with online help. Some help is short, such as tooltips, status tips, and "What's This?" help. Naturally, Qt supports all of these. Other help can be much more extensive, involving many pages of text. For this kind of help, you can use `QTextBrowser` as a simple online help browser, or you can invoke *Qt Assistant* or an HTML browser from your application.

Tooltips, Status Tips, and "What's This?" Help

A tooltip is a small piece of text that appears when the mouse hovers over a widget for a certain period of time. Tooltips are presented with black text on a yellow background. Their primary use is to provide textual descriptions of toolbar buttons.

We can add tooltips to arbitrary widgets in code using `QWidget::setToolTip()`. For example:

```
findButton->setToolTip(tr("Find next"));
```

To set the tooltip of a `QAction` that could be added to a menu or a toolbar, we can simply call `setToolTip()` on the action. For example:

```
newAction = new QAction(tr("&New"), this);
newAction->setToolTip(tr("New document"));
```

If we don't explicitly set a tooltip, `QAction` will automatically use the action text.

A status tip is also a short piece of descriptive text, usually a little longer than a tooltip. When the mouse hovers over a toolbar button or a menu option, a status tip appears in the status bar. Call `setStatusTip()` to add a status tip to an action or to a widget:

```
newAction->setStatusTip(tr("Create a new document"));
```

Figure 17.1 shows a tooltip and a status tip in an application.

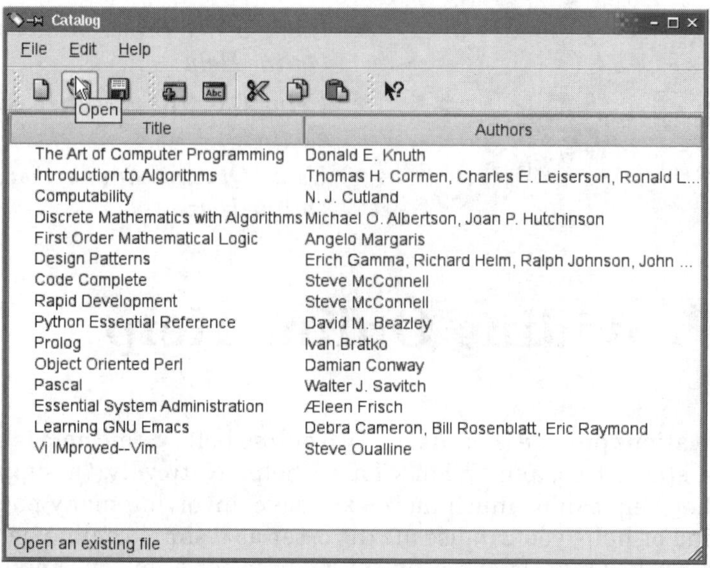

Figure 17.1. An application showing a tooltip and a status tip

In some situations, it is desirable to provide more information about a widget than tooltips or status tips can give. For example, we might want to provide a complex dialog with explanatory text about each field without forcing the user to invoke a separate help window. "What's This?" mode is an ideal solution for this. When a window is in "What's This?" mode, the cursor changes to **?** and the user can click on any user interface component to obtain its help text. To enter "What's This?" mode, the user can either click the ? button in the dialog's title bar (on Windows and KDE) or press Shift+F1.

Here is an example of "What's This?" text set on a dialog:

```
dialog->setWhatsThis(tr("<img src=\":/images/icon.png\">"
                        " The meaning of the Source field depends "
                        "on the Type field:"
                        "<ul>"
                        "<li><b>Books</b> have a Publisher"
                        "<li><b>Articles</b> have a Journal name with "
                        "volume and issue number"
                        "<li><b>Theses</b> have an Institution name "
                        "and a Department name"
                        "</ul>"));
```

We can use HTML tags to format "What's This?" text. In the example shown in Figure 17.2, we include an image (which is listed in the application's resource file), a bulleted list, and some text in bold. The tags and attributes that Qt supports are specified at http://doc.trolltech.com/4.3/richtext-html-subset.html.

When we set "What's This?" text on an action, the text will be shown when the user clicks the menu item or toolbar button or presses the shortcut key while

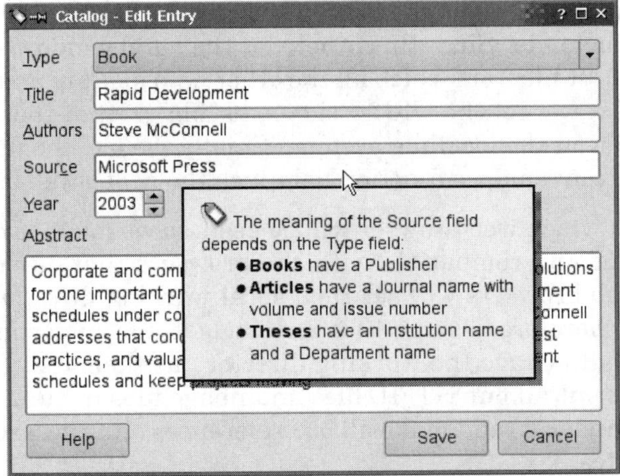

Figure 17.2. A dialog showing "What's This?" help text

in "What's This?" mode. When the user interface components of an application's main window provide "What's This?" text, it is customary to provide a What's This? option in the Help menu and a corresponding toolbar button. This can be done by creating a What's This? action with the static `QWhatsThis::createAction()` function and adding the action it returns to a Help menu and to a toolbar. The `QWhatsThis` class also provides static functions to programmatically enter and leave "What's This?" mode.

Using a Web Browser to Provide Online Help

Large applications may require more online help than tooltips, status tips, and "What's This?" help can reasonably show. A simple solution to this is to provide the help text in HTML format and launch the user's web browser at the appropriate page.

Applications that include a help browser typically have a Help entry in the main window's Help menu and a Help button in every dialog. In this section, we will show how to use the `QDesktopServices` class to provide the functionality for these buttons.

The application's main window will typically have a `help()` slot that is called when the user presses F1 or clicks the Help|Help menu option.

```
void MainWindow::help()
{
    QUrl url(directoryOf("doc").absoluteFilePath("index.html"));
    url.setScheme("file");
    QDesktopServices::openUrl(url);
}
```

In this example, we assume that our application's HTML help files are in a subdirectory called `doc`. The `QDir::absoluteFilePath()` function returns a `QString` with the full path to the given file name. We begin by creating a `QUrl` object with the path to the help file. Since this is help for the main window, we use our help system's `index.html` file from which all the other help files are accessible through hyperlinks. Next, we set the URL's scheme to "file" so that the file we have set will be looked for in the local file system. Finally, we use the desktop services' `openUrl()` static convenience function to launch the user's web browser.

We do not know which web browser will be used, so we must be careful to make our HTML valid and compatible with the browsers that our users might be using. Most web browsers will set their local working directory to the URL's path, and will therefore assume that any images and hyperlinks that do not have absolute paths have the working directory as their root. All this means is that we must put all our HTML files and image files in our `doc` directory (or subdirectories under it) and make all our references relative, except for links to external web sites.

```
QDir MainWindow::directoryOf(const QString &subdir)
{
    QDir dir(QApplication::applicationDirPath());
#if defined(Q_OS_WIN)
    if (dir.dirName().toLower() == "debug"
            || dir.dirName().toLower() == "release")
        dir.cdUp();
#elif defined(Q_OS_MAC)
    if (dir.dirName() == "MacOS") {
        dir.cdUp();
        dir.cdUp();
        dir.cdUp();
    }
#endif
    dir.cd(subdir);
    return dir;
}
```

The static `directoryOf()` function returns a `QDir` corresponding to the specified subdirectory relative to the application's directory. On Windows, the application's executable usually lives in a `debug` or `release` subdirectory, in which case we move one directory up; on Mac OS X, we take the bundle directory structure into account.

For dialogs, we will normally want to launch the web browser at a specific page from within our help system's pages, and perhaps at a specific point within the page. For example:

```
void EntryDialog::help()
{
    QUrl url(directoryOf("doc").absoluteFilePath("forms.html"));
    url.setScheme("file");
    url.setFragment("editing");
    QDesktopServices::openUrl(url);
}
```

This slot is called from inside a dialog when the user clicks the dialog's Help button. It is very similar to the previous example, except that we have chosen a different starting page. This particular page has help text for several different forms, with anchor references (e.g., `<a name="editing">`) in the HTML to indicate where each form's help text begins. To access a particular place within a page, we call `setFragment()` and pass the anchor we want the page scrolled to.

Providing help files in HTML format and making them available to users via their own web browser is simple and convenient. But web browsers cannot access the application's resources (such as icons), and they cannot easily be customized to suit the application. Also, if we jump to a particular page as we did for the `EntryDialog`, clicking the browser's Home or Back button will not have the desired effect.

Using QTextBrowser as a Simple Help Engine

Using the user's web browser to show online help is easy to do, but as we have noted, the approach does have a few drawbacks. We can eliminate these problems by providing our own help engine based on the `QTextBrowser` class.

In this section, we present the simple help browser shown in Figure 17.3 and explain how it can be used within an application. The window uses a `QTextBrowser` to display help pages that are marked up with an HTML-based syntax. `QTextBrowser` can handle a lot of HTML tags, so it is ideal for this purpose.

We begin with the class definition:

```
class HelpBrowser : public QWidget
{
    Q_OBJECT

public:
    HelpBrowser(const QString &path, const QString &page,
                QWidget *parent = 0);

    static void showPage(const QString &page);

private slots:
    void updateWindowTitle();

private:
    QTextBrowser *textBrowser;
    QPushButton *homeButton;
    QPushButton *backButton;
    QPushButton *closeButton;
};
```

The `HelpBrowser` provides a static function that can be called from anywhere in the application. This function creates a `HelpBrowser` window and shows the given page.

Here's the constructor:

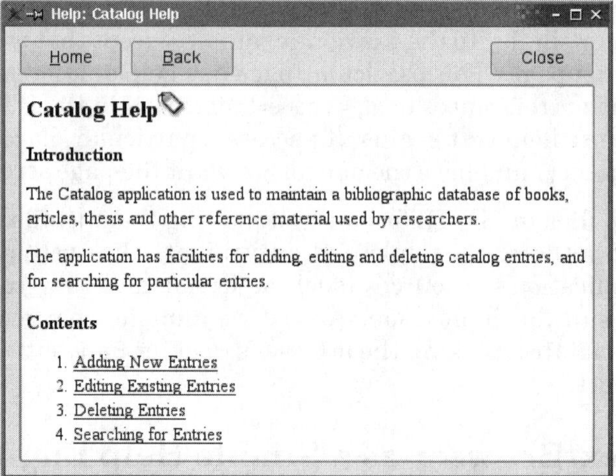

Figure 17.3. The `HelpBrowser` widget

```
HelpBrowser::HelpBrowser(const QString &path, const QString &page,
                         QWidget *parent)
    : QWidget(parent)
{
    setAttribute(Qt::WA_DeleteOnClose);
    setAttribute(Qt::WA_GroupLeader);

    textBrowser = new QTextBrowser;

    homeButton = new QPushButton(tr("&Home"));
    backButton = new QPushButton(tr("&Back"));
    closeButton = new QPushButton(tr("Close"));
    closeButton->setShortcut(tr("Esc"));

    QHBoxLayout *buttonLayout = new QHBoxLayout;
    buttonLayout->addWidget(homeButton);
    buttonLayout->addWidget(backButton);
    buttonLayout->addStretch();
    buttonLayout->addWidget(closeButton);

    QVBoxLayout *mainLayout = new QVBoxLayout;
    mainLayout->addLayout(buttonLayout);
    mainLayout->addWidget(textBrowser);
    setLayout(mainLayout);

    connect(homeButton, SIGNAL(clicked()), textBrowser, SLOT(home()));
    connect(backButton, SIGNAL(clicked()),
            textBrowser, SLOT(backward()));
    connect(closeButton, SIGNAL(clicked()), this, SLOT(close()));
    connect(textBrowser, SIGNAL(sourceChanged(const QUrl &)),
            this, SLOT(updateWindowTitle()));

    textBrowser->setSearchPaths(QStringList() << path << ":/images");
    textBrowser->setSource(page);
}
```

We set the Qt::WA_GroupLeader attribute because we want to pop up HelpBrowser windows from modal dialogs in addition to the main window. Modal dialogs normally prevent the user from interacting with any other window in the application. However, after requesting help, the user must obviously be allowed to interact with both the modal dialog and the help browser. Setting the Qt::WA_GroupLeader attribute makes this interaction possible.

We provide two search paths, the first a path in the file system that contains the application's documentation, and the second the location of the image resources. The HTML can include references to images in the file system in the normal way and references to image resources by using a path that begins with :/ (colon slash). The page parameter is the name of the documentation file, with an optional HTML anchor.

```
void HelpBrowser::updateWindowTitle()
{
    setWindowTitle(tr("Help: %1").arg(textBrowser->documentTitle()));
}
```

Whenever the source page changes, the updateWindowTitle() slot is called. The documentTitle() function returns the text specified in the page's <title> tag.

```
void HelpBrowser::showPage(const QString &page)
{
    QString path = directoryOf("doc").absolutePath();
    HelpBrowser *browser = new HelpBrowser(path, page);
    browser->resize(500, 400);
    browser->show();
}
```

In the showPage() static function, we create the HelpBrowser window and then show it. The window will be destroyed automatically when the user closes it, since we set the Qt::WA_DeleteOnClose attribute in the HelpBrowser constructor. For this example, we assume that the documentation is located in the application's doc directory. All the pages passed to the showPage() function will be taken from this subdirectory.

Now we are ready to invoke the help browser from the application. In the application's main window, we would create a Help action and connect it to a help() slot that could look like this:

```
void MainWindow::help()
{
    HelpBrowser::showPage("index.html");
}
```

This assumes that the main help file is called index.html. For dialogs, we would connect the Help button to a help() slot that might look like this:

```
void EntryDialog::help()
{
    HelpBrowser::showPage("forms.html#editing");
}
```

Here we look in a different help file, `forms.html`, and scroll the `QTextBrowser` to the `editing` anchor.

It is also possible to use Qt's resource system to embed the help files and their associated images directly into the executable. The only changes required to achieve this are to add entries to the application's `.qrc` file for each file we want embedded and to use the resource path (e.g., `:/doc/forms.html#editing`).

In this example, we used both approaches, embedding the icons (since they are also used by the application itself), but keeping our HTML files in the file system. This has the advantage that the help files can be updated independently of the application, and yet are guaranteed to be able to find the application's icons.

Using Qt Assistant for Powerful Online Help

Qt Assistant is a redistributable online help application supplied by Trolltech. Its main virtues are that it supports indexing and full text search and that it can handle documentation sets for multiple applications. To make use of *Qt Assistant*, we must incorporate the necessary code in our application, and we must make *Qt Assistant* aware of our documentation.*

Communication between a Qt application and *Qt Assistant* is handled by the `QAssistantClient` class, which is located in a separate library. To link this library with an application, we must add this line to the application's `.pro` file:

```
CONFIG += assistant
```

We will now review the code of a new `HelpBrowser` class that uses *Qt Assistant*.

```
class HelpBrowser
{
public:
    static void showPage(const QString &page);

private:
    static QDir directoryOf(const QString &subdir);

    static QAssistantClient *assistant;
};
```

Here's the new `showPage()` implementation:

```
QAssistantClient *HelpBrowser::assistant = 0;

void HelpBrowser::showPage(const QString &page)
{
    QString path = directoryOf("doc").absoluteFilePath(page);
    if (!assistant)
        assistant = new QAssistantClient("");
```

* Qt 4.4 is expected to feature a revamped help system, which will make it easier to integrate our documentation.

```
        assistant->showPage(path);
    }
```

The `QAssistantClient` constructor accepts a path string as its first argument, which it uses to locate the *Qt Assistant* executable. By passing an empty path, we signify that `QAssistantClient` should look for the executable in the `PATH` environment variable. `QAssistantClient` has a `showPage()` function that accepts a page name with an optional HTML anchor.

The next step is to prepare a table of contents and an index for the documentation. This is done by creating a *Qt Assistant* profile and writing a `.dcf` file that provides information about the documentation. All this is explained in *Qt Assistant*'s online documentation, so we will not duplicate that information here.

An alternative to using a web browser, `QTextBrowser`, or *Qt Assistant* is to use platform-specific approaches to providing online help. For Windows applications, it might be desirable to create Windows HTML Help files and to provide access to them using Microsoft Internet Explorer. You could use Qt's `QProcess` class or the ActiveQt framework for this. On Mac OS X, Apple Help provides similar functionality to *Qt Assistant*.

We have now reached the end of Part II. The chapters that follow in Part III cover more advanced and specialized features of Qt. The C++ and Qt code they present are no more difficult than the code we have presented in Part II, but some of the concepts and ideas may be more challenging in those areas that are new to you.

Part III

Advanced Qt

- *Working with Unicode*
- *Making Applications Translation-Aware*
- *Dynamic Language Switching*
- *Translating Applications*

18. Internationalization

In addition to the Latin alphabet used for English and for many European languages, Qt 4 also provides extensive support for the rest of the world's writing systems:

- Qt uses Unicode throughout the API and internally. No matter what language we use for the user interface, the application can support all users alike.
- Qt's text engine can handle all the major non-Latin writing systems, including Arabic, Chinese, Cyrillic, Hebrew, Japanese, Korean, Thai, and the Indic languages.
- Qt's layout engine supports right-to-left layouts for languages such as Arabic and Hebrew.
- Certain languages require special input methods for entering text. Editor widgets such as `QLineEdit` and `QTextEdit` work well with any input method installed on the user's system.

Often, it isn't enough to allow users to enter text in their native language; the entire user interface must be translated as well. Qt makes this easy: Simply wrap all user-visible strings with the `tr()` function (as we have done in earlier chapters) and use Qt's supporting tools to prepare translation files in the required languages. Qt provides a GUI tool called *Qt Linguist* for use by translators. *Qt Linguist* is complemented by two command-line programs, `lupdate` and `lrelease`, which are typically run by the application's developers.

For most applications, a translation file is loaded at startup, based on the user's locale settings. But in a few cases, it is also necessary for users to be able to switch languages at run-time. This is perfectly possible with Qt, although it does require a bit of extra work. And thanks to Qt's layout system, the various user interface components will automatically adjust to make room for the translated texts when they are longer than the original texts.

Working with Unicode

Unicode is a character encoding standard that supports most of the world's writing systems. The original idea behind Unicode is that by using 16 bits for storing characters instead of 8 bits, it would be possible to encode around 65 000 characters instead of only 256.* Unicode contains ASCII and ISO 8859-1 (Latin-1) as subsets at the same code positions. For example, the character 'A' has value `0x41` in ASCII, Latin-1, and Unicode, and the character 'Ñ' has value `0xD1` in both Latin-1 and Unicode.

Qt's `QString` class stores strings as Unicode. Each character in a `QString` is a 16-bit `QChar` rather than an 8-bit `char`. Here are two ways of setting the first character of a string to 'A':

```
str[0] = 'A';
str[0] = QChar(0x41);
```

If the source file is encoded in Latin-1, specifying Latin-1 characters is just as easy:

```
str[0] = 'Ñ';
```

And if the source file has another encoding, the numeric value works fine:

```
str[0] = QChar(0xD1);
```

We can specify any Unicode character by its numeric value. For example, here's how to specify the Greek capital letter sigma ('Σ') and the euro currency symbol ('€'):

```
str[0] = QChar(0x03A3);
str[0] = QChar(0x20AC);
```

The numeric values of all the characters supported by Unicode are listed at `http://www.unicode.org/standard/`. If you rarely need non-Latin-1 Unicode characters, looking up characters online is sufficient; but Qt provides more convenient ways of entering Unicode strings in a Qt program, as we will see later in this section.

Qt 4's text engine supports the following writing systems on all platforms: Arabic, Chinese, Cyrillic, Greek, Hebrew, Japanese, Korean, Lao, Latin, Thai, and Vietnamese. It also supports all the Unicode 4.1 scripts that don't require any special processing. In addition, the following writing systems are supported on X11 with Fontconfig and on recent versions of Windows: Bengali, Devanagari, Gujarati, Gurmukhi, Kannada, Khmer, Malayalam, Syriac, Tamil, Telugu, Thaana (Dhivehi), and Tibetan. Finally, Oriya is supported on X11, and Mongolian and Sinhala are supported on Windows XP. Assuming that the proper fonts are installed on the system, Qt can render text using any of these writing sys-

*Recent versions of the Unicode standard assign character values above 65 535. These characters can be represented using sequences of two 16-bit values called "surrogate pairs".

tems. And assuming that the proper input methods are installed, users will be able to enter text that uses these writing systems in their Qt applications.

Programming with `QChar` is slightly different from programming with `char`. To obtain the numeric value of a `QChar`, call `unicode()` on it. To obtain the ASCII or Latin-1 value of a `QChar` (as a `char`), call `toLatin1()`. For non-Latin-1 characters, `toLatin1()` returns '\0'.

If we know that all the strings in a program are ASCII, we can use standard `<cctype>` functions such as `isalpha()`, `isdigit()`, and `isspace()` on the return value of `toLatin1()`. However, it is generally better to use `QChar`'s member functions for performing these operations, since they will work for any Unicode character. The functions `QChar` provides include `isPrint()`, `isPunct()`, `isSpace()`, `isMark()`, `isLetter()`, `isNumber()`, `isLetterOrNumber()`, `isDigit()`, `isSymbol()`, `isLower()`, and `isUpper()`. For example, here's one way to test that a character is a digit or an uppercase letter:

```
if (ch.isDigit() || ch.isUpper())
    ...
```

The code snippet works for any alphabet that distinguishes between uppercase and lowercase, including Latin, Greek, and Cyrillic.

Once we have a Unicode string, we can use it anywhere in Qt's API where a `QString` is expected. It is then Qt's responsibility to display it properly and to convert it to the relevant encodings when talking to the operating system.

Special care is needed when we read and write text files. Text files can use a variety of encodings, and it is often impossible to guess a text file's encoding from its contents. By default, `QTextStream` uses the system's local 8-bit encoding (available as `QTextCodec::codecForLocale()`) for both reading and writing. For American and West European locales, this usually means Latin-1.

If we design our own file format and want to be able to read and write arbitrary Unicode characters, we can save the data as Unicode by calling

```
stream.setCodec("UTF-16");
stream.setGenerateByteOrderMark(true);
```

before we start writing to the `QTextStream`. The data will then be saved in UTF-16, a format that requires two bytes per character, and will be prefixed with a special 16-bit value (the Unicode byte order mark, `0xFFFE`) identifying that the file is in Unicode and whether the bytes are in little-endian or big-endian order. The UTF-16 format is identical to the memory representation of a `QString`, so reading and writing Unicode strings in UTF-16 can be very fast. On the other hand, there is an inherent overhead when saving pure ASCII data in UTF-16 format, since it stores two bytes for every character instead of just one.

Other encodings can be specified by calling `setCodec()` with an appropriate `QTextCodec`. A `QTextCodec` is an object that converts between Unicode and a given encoding. Qt uses `QTextCodec`s in a variety of contexts. Internally, they are used to support fonts, input methods, the clipboard, drag and drop, and file names. But they are also available to us when we write Qt applications.

When reading a text file, `QTextStream` detects UTF-16 automatically if the file starts with the byte order mark. This behavior can be turned off by calling `setAutoDetectUnicode(false)`. If the data is UTF-16 but can't be assumed to start with the byte order mark, it is best to call `setCodec()` with "UTF-16" before reading.

Another encoding that supports the whole of Unicode is UTF-8. Its main advantage over UTF-16 is that it is a superset of ASCII. Any character in the range `0x00` to `0x7F` is represented as a single byte. Other characters, including Latin-1 characters above `0x7F`, are represented by multi-byte sequences. For text that is mostly ASCII, UTF-8 takes up about half the space consumed by UTF-16. To use UTF-8 with `QTextStream`, call `setCodec()` with "UTF-8" as the codec name before reading and writing.

If we always want to read and write Latin-1 regardless of the user's locale, we can set the "ISO 8859-1" codec on the `QTextStream`. For example:

```
QTextStream in(&file);
in.setCodec("ISO 8859-1");
```

Some file formats specify their encoding in their header. The header is typically plain ASCII to ensure that it is read correctly no matter what encoding is used (assuming that it is a superset of ASCII). The XML file format is an interesting example of this. XML files are normally encoded as UTF-8 or UTF-16. The proper way to read them in is to call `setCodec()` with "UTF-8". If the format is UTF-16, `QTextStream` will automatically detect this and adjust itself. The `<?xml?>` header of an XML file sometimes contains an `encoding` argument, for example:

```
<?xml version="1.0" encoding="EUC-KR"?>
```

Since `QTextStream` doesn't allow us to change the encoding once it has started reading, the right way to respect an explicit encoding is to start reading the file afresh, using the correct codec (obtained from `QTextCodec::codecForName()`). In the case of XML, we can avoid having to handle the encoding ourselves by using Qt's XML classes, described in Chapter 16.

Another use of `QTextCodec`s is to specify the encoding of strings that occur in the source code. Let's consider, for example, a team of Japanese programmers who are writing an application targeted primarily at Japan's home market. These programmers are likely to write their source code in a text editor that uses an encoding such as EUC-JP or Shift-JIS. Such an editor allows them to type in Japanese characters seamlessly so that they can write code like this:

```
QPushButton *button = new QPushButton(tr("日諾"));
```

By default, Qt interprets arguments to `tr()` as Latin-1. To change this, call the `QTextCodec::setCodecForTr()` static function. For example:

```
QTextCodec::setCodecForTr(QTextCodec::codecForName("EUC-JP"));
```

This must be done before the first call to `tr()`. Typically, we would do this in `main()`, immediately after the `QCoreApplication` or `QApplication` object is created.

Other strings specified in the program will still be interpreted as Latin-1 strings. If the programmers want to enter Japanese characters in those as well, they can explicitly convert them to Unicode using a `QTextCodec`:

```
QString text = japaneseCodec->toUnicode("海鮮料理");
```

Alternatively, they can tell Qt to use a specific codec when converting between `const char *` and `QString` by calling `QTextCodec::setCodecForCStrings()`:

```
QTextCodec::setCodecForCStrings(QTextCodec::codecForName("EUC-JP"));
```

The techniques described above can be applied to any non-Latin-1 language, including Chinese, Greek, Korean, and Russian.

Here's a list of the encodings supported by Qt 4.3:

- Apple Roman
- Big5
- Big5-HKSCS
- EUC-JP
- EUC-KR
- GB18030-0
- IBM 850
- IBM 866
- IBM 874
- ISO 2022-JP
- ISO 8859-1
- ISO 8859-2
- ISO 8859-3
- ISO 8859-4
- ISO 8859-5
- ISO 8859-6
- ISO 8859-7
- ISO 8859-8
- ISO 8859-9
- ISO 8859-10
- ISO 8859-13
- ISO 8859-14
- ISO 8859-15
- ISO 8859-16
- Iscii-Bng
- Iscii-Dev
- Iscii-Gjr
- Iscii-Knd
- Iscii-Mlm
- Iscii-Ori
- Iscii-Pnj
- Iscii-Tlg
- Iscii-Tml
- JIS X 0201
- JIS X 0208
- KOI8-R
- KOI8-U
- MuleLao-1
- ROMAN8
- Shift-JIS
- TIS-620
- TSCII
- UTF-8
- UTF-16
- UTF-16BE
- UTF-16LE
- Windows-1250
- Windows-1251
- Windows-1252
- Windows-1253
- Windows-1254
- Windows-1255
- Windows-1256
- Windows-1257
- Windows-1258
- WINSAMI2

For all of these, `QTextCodec::codecForName()` will always return a valid pointer. Other encodings can be supported by subclassing `QTextCodec`.

Making Applications Translation-Aware

If we want to make our applications available in multiple languages, we must do two things:

- Make sure that every user-visible string goes through `tr()`.
- Load a translation (`.qm`) file at startup.

Neither of these is necessary for applications that will never be translated. However, using `tr()` requires almost no effort and leaves the door open for doing translations at a later date.

The `tr()` function is a static function defined in `QObject` and overridden in every subclass defined with the `Q_OBJECT` macro. When writing code inside a `QObject` subclass, we can call `tr()` without formality. A call to `tr()` returns a translation if one is available; otherwise, the original text is returned. Inside a non-`QObject` class, we can either write `QObject::tr()` with the class prefix or use the `Q_DECLARE_TR_FUNCTIONS()` macro to add `tr()` to the class, as we did in Chapter 8 (p. 200).

To prepare translation files, we must run Qt's `lupdate` tool. This tool extracts all the string literals that appear in `tr()` calls and produces translation files that contain all of these strings ready to be translated. The files can then be sent to a translator to have the translations added. This process is explained in the "Translating Applications" section later in this chapter.

A `tr()` call has the following general syntax:

```
Context::tr(sourceText, comment)
```

The *Context* part is the name of a `QObject` subclass defined with the `Q_OBJECT` macro. We don't need to specify it if we call `tr()` from a member function of the class in question. The *sourceText* part is the string literal that needs to be translated. The *comment* part is optional; it can be used to provide additional information to the translator.

Here are a few examples:

```
RockyWidget::RockyWidget(QWidget *parent)
    : QWidget(parent)
{
    QString str1 = tr("Letter");
    QString str2 = RockyWidget::tr("Letter");
    QString str3 = SnazzyDialog::tr("Letter");
    QString str4 = SnazzyDialog::tr("Letter", "US paper size");
}
```

The first two calls to `tr()` have "RockyWidget" as their context, and the last two calls have "SnazzyDialog". All four have "Letter" as their source text. The last call also has a comment to help the translator understand the meaning of the source text.

Strings in different contexts (classes) are translated independently of each other. Translators typically work on one context at a time, often with the application running and showing the widget or dialog being translated.

When we call `tr()` from a global function, we must specify the context explicitly. Any `QObject` subclass in the application can be used as the context. If none is appropriate, we can always use `QObject` itself. For example:

```
int main(int argc, char *argv[])
{
    QApplication app(argc, argv);
    ...
    QPushButton button(QObject::tr("Hello Qt!"));
```

```
    button.show();
    return app.exec();
}
```

In every example so far, the context has been a class name. This is convenient, because we can almost always omit it, but this doesn't have to be the case. The most general way of translating a string in Qt is to use the `QCoreApplication::translate()` function, which accepts up to three arguments: the context, the source text, and the optional comment. For example, here's another way to translate "Hello Qt!":

```
QCoreApplication::translate("Global Stuff", "Hello Qt!")
```

This time, we put the text in the "Global Stuff" context.

The `tr()` and `translate()` functions serve a dual purpose: They are markers that `lupdate` uses to find user-visible strings, and at the same time they are C++ functions that translate text. This has an impact on how we write code. For example, the following will not work:

```
// WRONG
const char *appName = "OpenDrawer 2D";
QString translated = tr(appName);
```

The problem here is that `lupdate` will not be able to extract the "OpenDrawer 2D" string literal, as it doesn't appear inside a `tr()` call. This means that the translator will not have the opportunity to translate the string. This issue often arises in conjunction with dynamic strings:

```
// WRONG
statusBar()->showMessage(tr("Host " + hostName + " found"));
```

Here, the string we pass to `tr()` varies depending on the value of `hostName`, so we can't reasonably expect `tr()` to translate it correctly.

The solution is to use `QString::arg()`:

```
statusBar()->showMessage(tr("Host %1 found").arg(hostName));
```

Notice how it works: The string literal "Host %1 found" is passed to `tr()`. Assuming that a French translation file is loaded, `tr()` would return something like "Hôte %1 trouvé". Then the "%1" parameter is replaced with the contents of the `hostName` variable.

Although it is generally inadvisable to call `tr()` on a variable, it can be made to work. We must use the `QT_TR_NOOP()` macro to mark the string literals for translation before we assign them to a variable. This is mostly useful for static arrays of strings. For example:

```
void OrderForm::init()
{
    static const char * const flowers[] = {
        QT_TR_NOOP("Medium Stem Pink Roses"),
        QT_TR_NOOP("One Dozen Boxed Roses"),
```

```
        QT_TR_NOOP("Calypso Orchid"),
        QT_TR_NOOP("Dried Red Rose Bouquet"),
        QT_TR_NOOP("Mixed Peonies Bouquet"),
        0
    };

    for (int i = 0; flowers[i]; ++i)
        comboBox->addItem(tr(flowers[i]));
}
```

The `QT_TR_NOOP()` macro simply returns its argument. But `lupdate` will extract all the strings wrapped in `QT_TR_NOOP()` so that they can be translated. When using the variable later on, we call `tr()` to perform the translation as usual. Even though we have passed `tr()` a variable, the translation will still work.

There is also a `QT_TRANSLATE_NOOP()` macro that works like `QT_TR_NOOP()` but also takes a context. This macro is useful when initializing variables outside of a class:

```
static const char * const flowers[] = {
    QT_TRANSLATE_NOOP("OrderForm", "Medium Stem Pink Roses"),
    QT_TRANSLATE_NOOP("OrderForm", "One Dozen Boxed Roses"),
    QT_TRANSLATE_NOOP("OrderForm", "Calypso Orchid"),
    QT_TRANSLATE_NOOP("OrderForm", "Dried Red Rose Bouquet"),
    QT_TRANSLATE_NOOP("OrderForm", "Mixed Peonies Bouquet"),
    0
};
```

The context argument must be the same as the context given to `tr()` or `translate()` later on.

When we start using `tr()` in an application, it's easy to forget to surround some user-visible strings with a `tr()` call, especially when we are just beginning to use it. These missing `tr()` calls are eventually discovered by the translator or, worse, by users of the translated application, when some strings appear in the original language. To avoid this problem, we can tell Qt to forbid implicit conversions from `const char *` to `QString`. We do this by defining the `QT_NO_CAST_FROM_ASCII` preprocessor symbol before including any Qt header. The easiest way to ensure that this symbol is set is to add the following line to the application's `.pro` file:

```
DEFINES += QT_NO_CAST_FROM_ASCII
```

This will force every string literal to require wrapping by `tr()` or by `QLatin1String()`, depending on whether it should be translated. Strings that are not suitably wrapped will produce a compile-time error, thereby compelling us to add the missing `tr()` or `QLatin1String()` wrapper.

Once we have wrapped every user-visible string by a `tr()` call, the only thing left to do to enable translation is to load a translation file. Typically, we would do this in the application's `main()` function. For example, here's how we would try to load a translation file depending on the user's locale:

```
int main(int argc, char *argv[])
{
    QApplication app(argc, argv);
    ...
    QTranslator appTranslator;
    appTranslator.load("myapp_" + QLocale::system().name(), qmPath);
    app.installTranslator(&appTranslator);
    ...
    return app.exec();
}
```

The `QLocale::system()` function returns a `QLocale` object that provides information about the user's locale. Conventionally, we use the locale's name as part of the `.qm` file name. Locale names can be more or less precise; for example, `fr` specifies a French-language locale, `fr_CA` specifies a French Canadian locale, and `fr_CA.ISO8859-15` specifies a French Canadian locale with ISO 8859-15 encoding (an encoding that supports '€', 'Œ', 'œ', and 'Ÿ').

Assuming that the locale is `fr_CA.ISO8859-15`, the `QTranslator::load()` function first tries to load the file `myapp_fr_CA.ISO8859-15.qm`. If this file does not exist, `load()` next tries `myapp_fr_CA.qm`, then `myapp_fr.qm`, and finally `myapp.qm`, before giving up. Normally, we would only provide `myapp_fr.qm`, containing a standard French translation, but if we need a different file for French-speaking Canada, we can also provide `myapp_fr_CA.qm` and it will be used for `fr_CA` locales.

The second argument to `QTranslator::load()` is the directory where we want `load()` to look for the translation file. In this case, we assume that the translation files are located in the directory given in the `qmPath` variable.

The Qt libraries contain a few strings that need to be translated. Trolltech provides French, German, and Simplified Chinese translations in Qt's `translations` directory. A few other languages are provided as well, but these are contributed by Qt users and are not officially supported. The Qt libraries' translation file should also be loaded:

```
QTranslator qtTranslator;
qtTranslator.load("qt_" + QLocale::system().name(), qmPath);
app.installTranslator(&qtTranslator);
```

A `QTranslator` object can hold only one translation file at a time, so we use a separate `QTranslator` for Qt's translation. Having just one file per translator is not a problem since we can install as many translators as we need. `QCoreApplication` will use all of them when searching for a translation.

Some languages, such as Arabic and Hebrew, are written right-to-left instead of left-to-right. In those languages, the whole layout of the application must be reversed, and this is done by calling `QApplication::setLayoutDirection(Qt::RightToLeft)`. The translation files for Qt contain a special marker called "LTR" that tells Qt whether the language is left-to-right or right-to-left, so we normally don't need to call `setLayoutDirection()` ourselves.

It may prove more convenient for our users if we supply our applications with the translation files embedded in the executable, using Qt's resource system. Not only does this reduce the number of files distributed as part of the product, but it also avoids the risk of translation files getting lost or deleted by accident. Assuming that the `.qm` files are located in a `translations` subdirectory in the source tree, we would then have a `myapp.qrc` file with the following contents:

```
<RCC>
<qresource>
    <file>translations/myapp_de.qm</file>
    <file>translations/myapp_fr.qm</file>
    <file>translations/myapp_zh.qm</file>
    <file>translations/qt_de.qm</file>
    <file>translations/qt_fr.qm</file>
    <file>translations/qt_zh.qm</file>
</qresource>
</RCC>
```

The `.pro` file would contain the following entry:

```
RESOURCES += myapp.qrc
```

Finally, in `main()`, we must specify `:/translations` as the path for the translation files. The leading colon indicates that the path refers to a resource as opposed to a file in the file system.

We have now covered all that is required to make an application able to operate using translations into other languages. But language and the direction of the writing system are not the only things that vary between countries and cultures. An internationalized program must also take into account the local date and time formats, monetary formats, numeric formats, and string collation order. Qt includes a `QLocale` class that provides localized numeric and date/time formats. To query other locale-specific information, we can use the standard C++ `setlocale()` and `localeconv()` functions.

Some Qt classes and functions adapt their behavior to the locale:

- `QString::localeAwareCompare()` compares two strings in a locale-dependent manner. It is useful for sorting user-visible items.
- The `toString()` function provided by `QDate`, `QTime`, and `QDateTime` returns a string in a local format when called with `Qt::LocalDate` as its argument.
- By default, the `QDateEdit` and `QDateTimeEdit` widgets present dates in the local format.

Finally, a translated application may need to use different icons in certain situations rather than the original icons. For example, the left and right arrows on a web browser's Back and Forward buttons should be swapped when dealing with a right-to-left language. We can do this as follows:

```
if (QApplication::isRightToLeft()) {
    backAction->setIcon(forwardIcon);
    forwardAction->setIcon(backIcon);
```

```
} else {
    backAction->setIcon(backIcon);
    forwardAction->setIcon(forwardIcon);
}
```

Icons that contain alphabetic characters very commonly need to be translated. For example, the letter 'I' on a toolbar button associated with a word processor's Italic option should be replaced by a 'C' in Spanish (Cursivo) and by a 'K' in Danish, Dutch, German, Norwegian, and Swedish (Kursiv). Here's a simple way to do it:

```
if (tr("Italic")[0] == 'C') {
    italicAction->setIcon(iconC);
} else if (tr("Italic")[0] == 'K') {
    italicAction->setIcon(iconK);
} else {
    italicAction->setIcon(iconI);
}
```

An alternative is to use the resource system's support for multiple locales. In the `.qrc` file, we can specify a locale for a resource using the `lang` attribute. For example:

```
<qresource>
    <file>italic.png</file>
</qresource>
<qresource lang="es">
    <file alias="italic.png">cursivo.png</file>
</qresource>
<qresource lang="sv">
    <file alias="italic.png">kursiv.png</file>
</qresource>
```

If the user's locale is `es` (Español), `:/italic.png` becomes a reference to the `cursivo.png` image. If the locale is `sv` (Svenska), the `kursiv.png` image is used. For other locales, `italic.png` is used.

Dynamic Language Switching

For most applications, detecting the user's preferred language in `main()` and loading the appropriate `.qm` files there is perfectly satisfactory. But there are some situations where users might need the ability to switch languages dynamically. An application that is used continuously by different people in shifts may need to change languages without having to be restarted. For example, applications used by call center operators, by simultaneous translators, and by computerized cash register operators often require this capability.

Making an application able to switch languages dynamically requires a little more work than loading a single translation at startup, but it is not difficult. Here is what must be done:

- Provide a means by which the user can switch language.

- For every widget or dialog, set all of its translatable strings in a separate function (often called `retranslateUi()`) and call this function when the language changes.

Let's review the relevant parts of a "call center" application's source code. The application provides a Language menu (shown in Figure 18.1), to allow the user to set the language at run-time. The default language is English.

Figure 18.1. A dynamic Language menu

Since we don't know which language the user will want to use when the application is started, we no longer load translations in the `main()` function. Instead, we will load them dynamically when they are needed, so all the code that we need to handle translations must go in the main window and dialog classes.

Let's have a look at the application's `QMainWindow` subclass.

```
MainWindow::MainWindow()
{
    journalView = new JournalView;
    setCentralWidget(journalView);

    qApp->installTranslator(&appTranslator);
    qApp->installTranslator(&qtTranslator);

    createActions();
    createMenus();

    retranslateUi();
}
```

In the constructor, we set the central widget to be a `JournalView`, a `QTableWidget` subclass. Then we install two `QTranslator` objects on the `QApplication`: The `appTranslator` object stores the current application's translation, and the `qtTranslator` object stores Qt's translation. At the end, we call the `createActions()` and `createMenus()` private functions to create the menu system, and we call `retranslateUi()` (also a private function) to set the user-visible strings for the first time.

```
void MainWindow::createActions()
{
    newAction = new QAction(this);
    newAction->setShortcut(QKeySequence::New);
```

```
    connect(newAction, SIGNAL(triggered()), this, SLOT(newFile()));
    ...
    exitAction = new QAction(this);
    connect(exitAction, SIGNAL(triggered()), this, SLOT(close()));
    ...
    aboutQtAction = new QAction(this);
    connect(aboutQtAction, SIGNAL(triggered()), qApp, SLOT(aboutQt()));
}
```

The `createActions()` function creates the `QAction` objects as usual, but without setting any of the texts. These will be done in `retranslateUi()`. For actions that have standardized shortcuts, we can set the shortcut here using the appropriate enum, and rely on Qt to translate as necessary. For actions that have custom shortcuts, such as the Exit action, we set the shortcut in the `retranslateUi()` function, along with the text.

```
void MainWindow::createMenus()
{
    fileMenu = new QMenu(this);
    fileMenu->addAction(newAction);
    fileMenu->addAction(openAction);
    fileMenu->addAction(saveAction);
    fileMenu->addAction(exitAction);

    editMenu = new QMenu(this);
    ...
    createLanguageMenu();

    helpMenu = new QMenu(this);
    helpMenu->addAction(aboutAction);
    helpMenu->addAction(aboutQtAction);

    menuBar()->addMenu(fileMenu);
    menuBar()->addMenu(editMenu);
    menuBar()->addMenu(reportsMenu);
    menuBar()->addMenu(languageMenu);
    menuBar()->addMenu(helpMenu);
}
```

The `createMenus()` function creates menus, but does not give them any titles. Again, this will be done in `retranslateUi()`.

In the middle of the function, we call `createLanguageMenu()` to fill the Language menu with the list of supported languages. We will review its source code in a moment. First, let's look at `retranslateUi()`:

```
void MainWindow::retranslateUi()
{
    newAction->setText(tr("&New"));
    newAction->setStatusTip(tr("Create a new journal"));
    ...
    exitAction->setText(tr("E&xit"));
    exitAction->setShortcut(tr("Ctrl+Q"));
    ...
    aboutQtAction->setText(tr("About &Qt"));
```

```
    aboutQtAction->setStatusTip(tr("Show the Qt library's About box"));

    fileMenu->setTitle(tr("&File"));
    editMenu->setTitle(tr("&Edit"));
    reportsMenu->setTitle(tr("&Reports"));
    languageMenu->setTitle(tr("&Language"));
    helpMenu->setTitle(tr("&Help"));

    setWindowTitle(tr("Call Center"));
}
```

The retranslateUi() function is where all the tr() calls for the MainWindow class occur. It is called at the end of the MainWindow constructor and every time a user changes the application's language using the Language menu.

We set each QAction's text and status tip, and the shortcuts for those actions that have non-standardized shortcuts. We also set each QMenu's title, as well as the window title.

The createMenus() function presented earlier called createLanguageMenu() to populate the Language menu with a list of languages:

```
void MainWindow::createLanguageMenu()
{
    languageMenu = new QMenu(this);

    languageActionGroup = new QActionGroup(this);
    connect(languageActionGroup, SIGNAL(triggered(QAction *)),
            this, SLOT(switchLanguage(QAction *)));

    QDir qmDir = directoryOf("translations");
    QStringList fileNames =
            qmDir.entryList(QStringList("callcenter_*.qm"));

    for (int i = 0; i < fileNames.size(); ++i) {
        QString locale = fileNames[i];
        locale.remove(0, locale.indexOf('_') + 1);
        locale.chop(3);

        QTranslator translator;
        translator.load(fileNames[i], qmDir.absolutePath());
        QString language = translator.translate("MainWindow",
                                                "English");

        QAction *action = new QAction(tr("&%1 %2")
                                      .arg(i + 1).arg(language), this);
        action->setCheckable(true);
        action->setData(locale);

        languageMenu->addAction(action);
        languageActionGroup->addAction(action);

        if (language == "English")
            action->setChecked(true);
    }
}
```

Instead of hard-coding the languages supported by the application, we create one menu entry for each .qm file located in the application's translations directory. The directoryOf() function is the same as the one we used in Chapter 17 (p. 410).

For simplicity, we assume that English also has a .qm file. An alternative would have been to call clear() on the QTranslator objects when the user chooses English.

One particular difficulty is to present a nice name for the language provided by each .qm file. Just showing "en" for "English" or "de" for "Deutsch", based on the name of the .qm file, looks crude and will confuse some users. The solution used in createLanguageMenu() is to check the translation of the string "English" in the "MainWindow" context. That string should be translated to "Deutsch" in a German translation, to "Français" in a French translation, and to "日本語" in a Japanese translation.

We create one checkable QAction for each language and store the locale name in the action's "data" item. We add them to a QActionGroup object to ensure that only one Language menu item is checked at a time. When the user chooses an action from the group, the QActionGroup emits the triggered(QAction *) signal, which is connected to switchLanguage().

```
void MainWindow::switchLanguage(QAction *action)
{
    QString locale = action->data().toString();
    QString qmPath = directoryOf("translations").absolutePath();

    appTranslator.load("callcenter_" + locale, qmPath);
    qtTranslator.load("qt_" + locale, qmPath);
    retranslateUi();
}
```

The switchLanguage() slot is called when the user chooses a language from the Language menu. We load the relevant translation files for the application and for Qt, and we call retranslateUi() to retranslate all the strings for the main window.

On Windows, an alternative to providing a Language menu is to respond to LocaleChange events, a type of event emitted by Qt when it detects a change in the environment's locale. The event type exists on all platforms supported by Qt, but is only actually generated on Windows, when the user changes the system's locale settings (in the Control Panel's Regional and Language Options section). To handle LocaleChange events, we can reimplement QWidget::changeEvent() as follows:

```
void MainWindow::changeEvent(QEvent *event)
{
    if (event->type() == QEvent::LocaleChange) {
        QString qmPath = directoryOf("translations").absolutePath();
        appTranslator.load("callcenter_"
                           + QLocale::system().name(), qmPath);
```

```
        qtTranslator.load("qt_" + QLocale::system().name(), qmPath);
        retranslateUi();
    }
    QMainWindow::changeEvent(event);
}
```

If the user switches locale while the application is being run, we attempt to load the correct translation files for the new locale and call `retranslateUi()` to update the user interface. In all cases, we pass the event to the base class's `changeEvent()` function, since the base class may also be interested in `LocaleChange` or other change events.

We have now finished our review of the `MainWindow` code. Next we will look at the code for one of the application's widget classes, the `JournalView` class, to see what changes are needed to make it support dynamic translation.

```
JournalView::JournalView(QWidget *parent)
    : QTableWidget(parent)
{
    ...
    retranslateUi();
}
```

The `JournalView` class is a `QTableWidget` subclass. At the end of the constructor, we call the private function `retranslateUi()` to set the widget's strings. This is similar to what we did for `MainWindow`.

```
void JournalView::changeEvent(QEvent *event)
{
    if (event->type() == QEvent::LanguageChange)
        retranslateUi();
    QTableWidget::changeEvent(event);
}
```

We also reimplement the `changeEvent()` function to call `retranslateUi()` on `LanguageChange` events. Qt generates a `LanguageChange` event when the contents of a `QTranslator` currently installed on `QCoreApplication` changes. In our application, this occurs when we call `load()` on `appTranslator` or `qtTranslator`, either from `MainWindow::switchLanguage()` or from `MainWindow::changeEvent()`.

`LanguageChange` events should not be confused with `LocaleChange` events. `LocaleChange` events are generated by the system and tell the application, "Maybe you should load a new translation." `LanguageChange` events are generated by Qt and tell the application's widgets, "Maybe you should retranslate all your strings."

When we implemented `MainWindow`, we didn't need to respond to `LanguageChange`. Instead, we simply called `retranslateUi()` whenever we called `load()` on a `QTranslator`.

```
void JournalView::retranslateUi()
{
    QStringList labels;
    labels << tr("Time") << tr("Priority") << tr("Phone Number")
           << tr("Subject");
```

```
        setHorizontalHeaderLabels(labels);
    }
```

The `retranslateUi()` function updates the column headers with newly translated texts, completing the translation-related code of a hand-written widget. For widgets and dialogs developed with *Qt Designer*, the `uic` tool automatically generates a function similar to our `retranslateUi()` function that is automatically called in response to `LanguageChange` events.

Translating Applications

Translating a Qt application that contains `tr()` calls is a three-step process:

1. Run `lupdate` to extract all the user-visible strings from the application's source code.
2. Translate the application using *Qt Linguist*.
3. Run `lrelease` to generate binary `.qm` files that the application can load using `QTranslator`.

Steps 1 and 3 are performed by application developers. Step 2 is handled by translators. This cycle can be repeated as often as necessary during the application's development and lifetime.

As an example, we will show how to translate the Spreadsheet application in Chapter 3. The application already contains `tr()` calls around every user-visible string.

First, we must modify the application's `.pro` file slightly to specify which languages we want to support. For example, if we want to support German and French in addition to English, we would add the following `TRANSLATIONS` entry to `spreadsheet.pro`:

```
TRANSLATIONS = spreadsheet_de.ts \
               spreadsheet_fr.ts
```

Here, we specify two translation files: one for German and one for French. These files will be created the first time we run `lupdate` and are updated every time we subsequently run `lupdate`.

These files normally have a `.ts` extension. They are in a straightforward XML format and are not as compact as the binary `.qm` files understood by `QTranslator`. It is `lrelease`'s job to convert human-readable `.ts` files into machine-efficient `.qm` files. For the curious, `.ts` stands for "translation source" and `.qm` for "Qt message" file.

Assuming that we are located in the directory that contains the Spreadsheet application's source code, we can run `lupdate` on `spreadsheet.pro` from the command line as follows:

```
lupdate -verbose spreadsheet.pro
```

The -verbose option tells lupdate to provide more feedback than usual. Here's the expected output:

```
Updating 'spreadsheet_de.ts'...
    Found 98 source texts (98 new and 0 already existing)
Updating 'spreadsheet_fr.ts'...
    Found 98 source texts (98 new and 0 already existing)
```

Every string that appears within a tr() call in the application's source code is stored in the .ts files, along with an empty translation. Strings that appear in the application's .ui files are also included.

The lupdate tool assumes by default that the arguments to tr() are Latin-1 strings. If this isn't the case, we must add a CODECFORTR entry to the .pro file. For example:

```
CODECFORTR = EUC-JP
```

This must be done in addition to calling QTextCodec::setCodecForTr() from the application's main() function.

Translations then need to be added to the spreadsheet_de.ts and spreadsheet_fr.ts files using *Qt Linguist*. (Figure 18.2 shows *Qt Linguist* in action.)

To run *Qt Linguist*, click Qt by Trolltech v4.x.y|Linguist in the Start menu on Windows, type linguist on the command line on Unix, or double-click Linguist in the Mac OS X Finder. To start adding translations to a .ts file, click File|Open and choose the file to translate.

The left-hand side of *Qt Linguist*'s main window shows a tree view. The top-level items are the contexts of the application being translated. For the Spreadsheet application, these are "FindDialog", "GoToCellDialog", "MainWindow", "SortDialog", and "Spreadsheet". Every context has zero or more child items. Each child item occupies three columns, the first showing a Done flag, the second showing a source text, and the third showing any translation. The top-right area shows the current source text and its translation; this is where translations are added and edited. The bottom-right area is a list of suggestions automatically provided by *Qt Linguist*.

Once we have a translated .ts file, we need to convert it to a binary .qm file for it to be usable by QTranslator. To do this from within *Qt Linguist*, click File|Release. Typically, we would start by translating only a few strings and run the application with the .qm file to make sure that everything works properly.

If we want to regenerate the .qm files for all .ts files, we can use the lrelease tool as follows:

```
lrelease -verbose spreadsheet.pro
```

Assuming that we translated 19 strings to French and clicked the Done flag for 17 of them, lrelease produces the following output:

```
Updating 'spreadsheet_de.qm'...
```

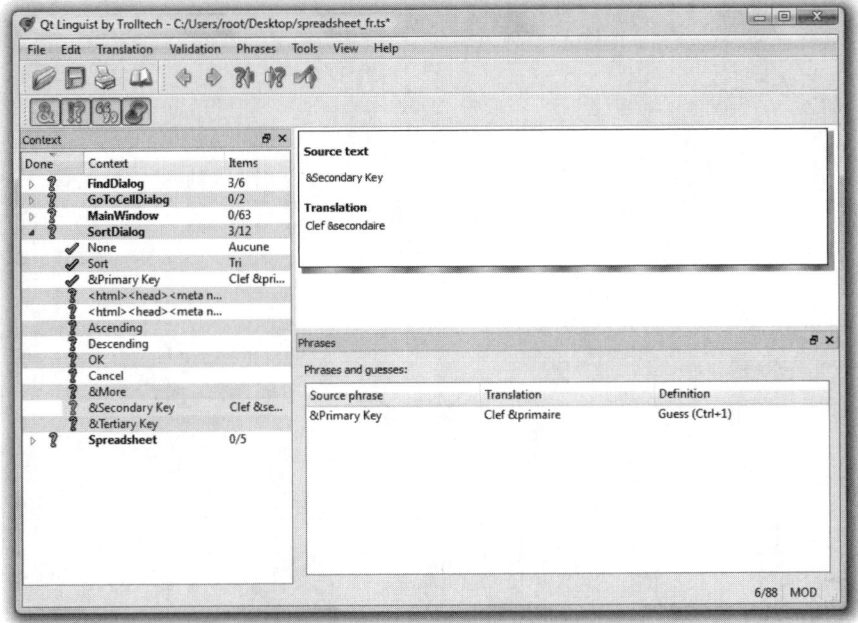

Figure 18.2. *Qt Linguist* in action

```
    Generated 0 translations (0 finished and 0 unfinished)
    Ignored 98 untranslated source texts
Updating 'spreadsheet_fr.qm'...
    Generated 19 translations (17 finished and 2 unfinished)
    Ignored 79 untranslated source texts
```

Untranslated strings are shown in the original languages when running the application. The Done flag is ignored by `lrelease`; it can be used by translators to identify which translations are finished and which ones must be revisited.

When we modify the source code of the application, the translation files may become out of date. The solution is to run `lupdate` again, provide translations for the new strings, and regenerate the `.qm` files. Some development teams find it useful to run `lupdate` frequently, whereas others prefer to wait until the application is almost ready to release.

The `lupdate` and *Qt Linguist* tools are quite smart. Translations that are no longer used are kept in the `.ts` files in case they are needed in later releases. When updating `.ts` files, `lupdate` uses an intelligent merging algorithm that can save translators considerable time with text that is the same or similar in different contexts.

For more information about *Qt Linguist*, `lupdate`, and `lrelease`, refer to the *Qt Linguist* manual at `http://doc.trolltech.com/4.3/linguist-manual.html`. The manual contains a full explanation of *Qt Linguist*'s user interface and a step-by-step tutorial for programmers.

- *Using Qt Style Sheets*
- *Subclassing QStyle*

19. Look and Feel Customization

In some circumstances, we might want to change the look and feel of Qt's built-in widgets. We may only want to do some minor customizations to tweak the aesthetics slightly, or we may wish to implement an entirely new style, to give our application or suite of applications a unique and distinctive appearance. In either case, there are three main approaches to redefining the look of Qt's built-in widgets:

- We can subclass the individual widget classes and reimplement their paint and mouse event handlers. This gives complete control but involves a lot of work. It also means that we must go through all of our code and *Qt Designer* forms and change all occurrences of Qt widget classes to use our subclasses.
- We can subclass `QStyle` or a predefined style such as `QWindowsStyle`. This approach is very powerful; it is used by Qt itself to provide a native look and feel on the different platforms it supports.
- Starting with Qt 4.2, we can use Qt style sheets, a mechanism inspired by HTML CSS (Cascading Style Sheets). Since style sheets are plain text files that are interpreted at run-time, no knowledge of programming is required to use them.

We have already covered the techniques required for the first approach, in Chapters 5 and 7, although our emphasis was on creating custom widgets. In this chapter, we will review the last two approaches. We will present two custom styles: the Candy style, specified as a style sheet, and the Bronze style, implemented as a `QStyle` subclass (see Figure 19.1). To keep the examples to a manageable size, both styles focus on a carefully chosen subset of Qt's widgets.

Using Qt Style Sheets

Qt style sheets are strongly inspired by CSS but adapted to work on widgets. A style sheet consists of style rules that affect the rendering of a widget. These rules are specified as plain text. Since style sheets are parsed at run-time, we can easily experiment with different designs by specifying a style sheet for a Qt application using the `-stylesheet` *`file.qss`* command-line option, by using *Qt Designer*'s style sheet editor, or by embedding a `QTextEdit` inside our application during development.

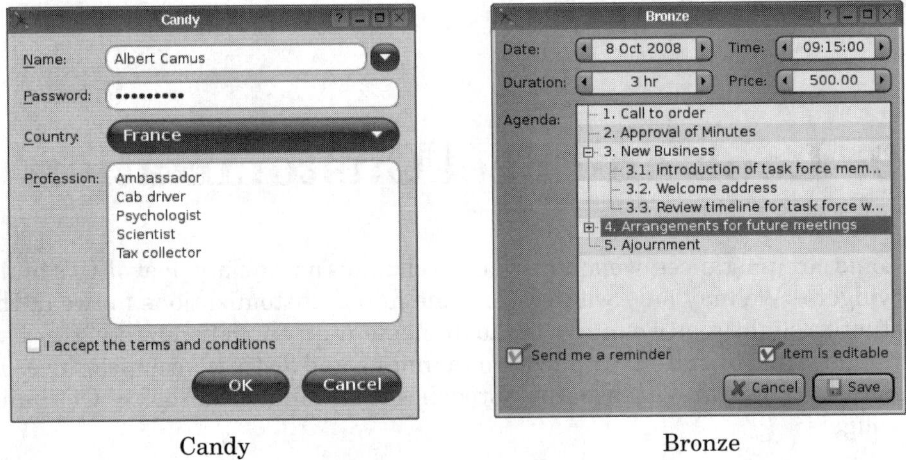

Candy Bronze

Figure 19.1. The custom styles presented in this chapter

Style sheets are applied on top of the currently active `QStyle` (e.g., `QWindowsVistaStyle` or `QPlastiqueStyle`).* Because creating style sheets doesn't involve any subclassing, they are ideal for minor customizations to existing widgets. For example, suppose we want to use yellow as the background color of all `QLineEdit`s in an application. This could be accomplished using the following style sheet:

```
QLineEdit {
    background-color: yellow;
}
```

In CSS-speak, `QLineEdit` is called a selector, `background-color` is an attribute, and `yellow` is a value.

For this kind of customization, using style sheets produces more reliable results than fiddling with the widget's palette. This is because a `QPalette`'s entries (`Base`, `Button`, `Highlight`, etc.) are used differently by different styles. For example, `QWindowsStyle` uses the `Base` palette entry to fill the background of a read-only combobox, whereas `QPlastiqueStyle` uses the `Button` entry for this purpose. Furthermore, certain styles use hard-coded images to render certain elements, bypassing the palette entirely. In contrast, style sheets guarantee that no matter which `QStyle` is active, the colors specified will be the ones used.

`QApplication::setStyleSheet()` sets a style sheet for the entire application:

*Style sheets are not supported for `QMacStyle` in Qt 4.3. It is expected that this will be addressed in a future release.

```
qApp->setStyleSheet("QLineEdit { background-color: yellow; }");
```

We can also set a style sheet on a widget and its children using `QWidget::setStyleSheet()`. For example:

```
dialog->setStyleSheet("QLineEdit { background-color: yellow; }");
```

If we set the style sheet directly on a `QLineEdit`, we can omit both the `QLineEdit` selector and the braces:

```
lineEdit->setStyleSheet("background-color: yellow;");
```

So far, we have set only a single property on a single class of widget. In practice, style rules are often combined. For example, the following rule sets the foreground and background colors of six widget classes and their subclasses:

```
QCheckBox, QComboBox, QLineEdit, QListView, QRadioButton, QSpinBox {
    color: #050505;
    background-color: yellow;
}
```

Colors can be specified by name, by an HTML-style string in *#RRGGBB* format, or by an RGB or RGBA value:

```
QLineEdit {
    color: rgb(0, 88, 152);
    background-color: rgba(97%, 80%, 9%, 50%);
}
```

When using color names, we can use any name that is recognized by the `QColor::setNamedColor()` function. For RGB, we must specify a red, a green, and a blue component, each on a scale of 0 to 255 or 0% to 100%. RGBA additionally lets us specify an alpha value as the fourth component of the color, which corresponds to the color's opacity. Instead of a uniform color, we can also specify a palette entry or a gradient:

```
QLineEdit {
    color: palette(Base);
    background-color: qlineargradient(x1: 0, y1: 0, x2: 1, y2: 1,
                                      stop: 0 white, stop: 0.4 gray,
                                      stop: 1 green);
}
```

The three types of gradients described in Chapter 8 (p. 184) are available as `qlineargradient()`, `qradialgradient()`, and `qconicalgradient()`. The syntax is explained in the style sheet reference documentation.

Using the `background-image` property, we can specify an image for the background:

```
QLineEdit {
    color: rgb(0, 88, 152);
    background-image: url(:/images/yellow-bg.png);
}
```

By default, the background image is rooted in the top-left corner of the widget (excluding any margin specified using margin) and is repeated horizontally and vertically to fill the entire widget. This can be configured using the background-position and background-repeat attributes. For example:

```
QLineEdit {
    background-image: url(:/images/yellow-bg.png);
    background-position: top right;
    background-repeat: repeat-y;
}
```

If we specify both a background image and a background color, the background color will shine through the semi-transparent areas of the image.

So far, all of the selectors we have used have been class names. There are several other selectors that we can use; they are listed in Figure 19.2. For example, if we want to use specific foreground colors for OK and Cancel buttons, we can write

```
QPushButton[text="OK"] {
    color: green;
}

QPushButton[text="Cancel"] {
    color: red;
}
```

This selector syntax works for any Qt property, although we must bear in mind that style sheets don't notice when a property changes behind their back. Selectors can also be combined in various ways; for example, to select all QPushButtons called "okButton" whose x and y properties are 0 and that are direct children of a QFrame called "frame", we can write

```
QFrame#frame > QPushButton[x="0"][y="0"]#okButton {
    ...
}
```

Selector	Example	Matched Widgets
Universal	*	Any widget
Type	QDial	Instances of a given class, including subclasses
Class	.QDial	Instances of a given class, excluding subclasses
ID	QDial#ageDial	Widgets with the given object name
Qt property	QDial[y="0"]	Widgets with certain properties set to given values
Child	QFrame > QDial	Widgets that are direct children of the given widgets
Descendant	QFrame QDial	Widgets that are descendants of the given widgets

Figure 19.2. Style sheet selectors

In an application that presents large forms with lots of line editors and comboboxes, such as those used by various bureaucracies, it is common to use a yellow background color for mandatory fields. Let's suppose that we want to apply this convention to our application. First, we would start with this style sheet:

```
*[mandatoryField="true"] {
    background-color: yellow;
}
```

Although there is no `mandatoryField` property defined anywhere in Qt, we can easily create one by calling `QObject::setProperty()`. Starting with Qt 4.2, setting the value of a non-existent property dynamically creates that property. For example:

```
nameLineEdit->setProperty("mandatoryField", true);
genderComboBox->setProperty("mandatoryField", true);
ageSpinBox->setProperty("mandatoryField", true);
```

Style sheets are not only useful for controlling colors. They also let us perform various adjustments to the size and position of widget elements. For example, the following rules can be used to increase the size of checkboxes and radio button indicators to 20×20 pixels, and ensure that there are 8 pixels between the indicator and the associated text:

```
QCheckBox::indicator, QRadioButton::indicator {
    width: 20px;
    height: 20px;
}

QCheckBox, QRadioButton {
    spacing: 8px;
}
```

Notice the selector syntax for the first rule. Had we written only `QCheckBox` instead of `QCheckBox::indicator`, we would have specified the dimensions of the entire widget instead of those of the indicator. The first rule is illustrated in Figure 19.3.

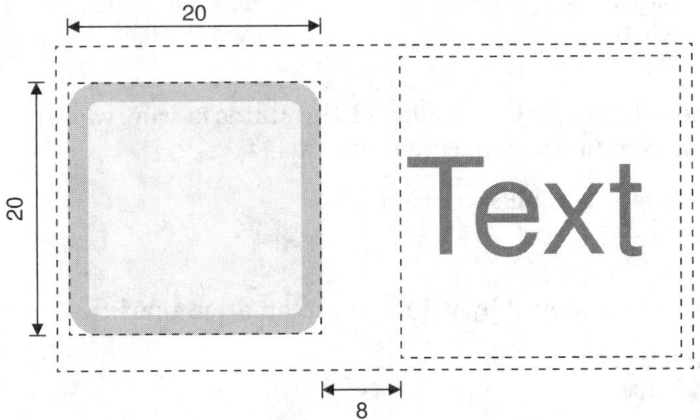

Figure 19.3. Setting a `QCheckBox`'s indicator size

Subcontrols such as `::indicator` can be styled in much the same way as widgets. Figure 19.4 lists some of the subcontrols supported by Qt.

Subcontrol	Description
`::indicator`	A checkbox, radio button, checkable menu item, or checkable group box's indicator
`::menu-indicator`	A push button's menu indicator
`::item`	A menu, menu bar, or status bar item
`::up-button`	A spin box or scroll bar's up button
`::down-button`	A spin box or scroll bar's down button
`::up-arrow`	A spin box, scroll bar, or header view's up arrow
`::down-arrow`	A spin box, scroll bar, header view, or combobox's down arrow
`::drop-down`	A combobox's drop-down arrow
`::title`	A group box's title

Figure 19.4. The most common customizable subcontrols

In addition to subcontrols, a style sheet can refer to specific widget states. For example, we may want to render the checkbox's text in white when the mouse hovers over it by specifying the `:hover` state:

```
QCheckBox:hover {
    color: white;
}
```

States are signified by using a single colon, whereas subcontrols are signified by using two colons. We can list several states one after another, each separated by a colon. In such cases, the rule will apply only when the widget is in *all* the specified states. For example, the following rule is applied only if the mouse is hovering over a checked checkbox:

```
QCheckBox:checked:hover {
    color: white;
}
```

If we want the rule to apply when *any* of the states is true, we can use multiple selectors, using commas to separate them:

```
QCheckBox:hover, QCheckBox:checked {
    color: white;
}
```

Logical negation is achieved by using an exclamation mark:

```
QCheckBox:!checked {
    color: blue;
}
```

States can be combined with subcontrols:

```
QComboBox::drop-down:hover {
    image: url(:/images/downarrow_bright.png);
}
```

Figure 19.5 lists the style sheet states that are available.

State	Description
`:disabled`	The widget is disabled
`:enabled`	The widget is enabled
`:focus`	The widget has input focus
`:hover`	The mouse is hovering over the widget
`:pressed`	The widget is being pressed using the mouse
`:checked`	The button is checked
`:unchecked`	The button is unchecked
`:indeterminate`	The button is partially checked
`:open`	The widget is in an open or expanded state
`:closed`	The widget is in a closed or collapsed state
`:on`	The widget is "on"
`:off`	The widget is "off"

Figure 19.5. Some of the widget states accessible to style sheets

Style sheets can also be used together with other techniques to perform more complex customizations. For example, suppose we want to position a tiny "erase" button inside a `QLineEdit`'s frame, to the right of the `QLineEdit`'s text. This involves creating an `EraseButton` class, and placing it on top of the `QLineEdit` (e.g., using layouts), but also reserving some space for the button, so that the typed-in text cannot collide with the erase button. Doing this by subclassing `QStyle` would be inconvenient, because we would have to subclass every style in Qt that might be used by the application (`QWindowsVistaStyle`, `QPlastiqueStyle`, etc.). Using style sheets, the following rule does the trick:

```
QLineEdit {
    padding: 0px 15px 0px 0px;
}
```

The `padding` property lets us specify the top, right, bottom, and left padding of the widget. The padding is inserted between the `QLineEdit`'s text and its frame. For convenience, CSS also defines `padding-top`, `padding-right`, `padding-bottom`, and `padding-left`, for when we want to set only one padding value. For example:

```
QLineEdit {
    padding-right: 15px;
}
```

Like most Qt widgets that are customizable using style sheets, QLineEdit supports the box model depicted in Figure 19.6. This model specifies four rectangles that affect the layout and rendering of a styled widget:

1. The *contents rectangle* is the innermost rectangle. This is where the actual contents of the widget (e.g., the text or image) is painted.
2. The *padding rectangle* encloses the contents rectangle. It takes into account any padding specified using the padding property.
3. The *border rectangle* encloses the padding rectangle. It reserves space for the border.
4. The *margin rectangle* is the outermost rectangle. It encloses the border rectangle and takes into account any specified margin.

For a plain widget with no padding, no border, and no margin, the four rectangles coincide exactly.

We will now present a style sheet that implements a custom style called Candy. Figure 19.7 shows a selection of Candy-styled widgets. The Candy style defines a custom look and feel for QLineEdits, QListViews, QPushButtons, and QComboBoxes, using the box model presented in Figure 19.6. We will present the style sheet piece by piece; the entire style sheet is available as qss/candy.qss in the Candy example's directory supplied with the book's examples.

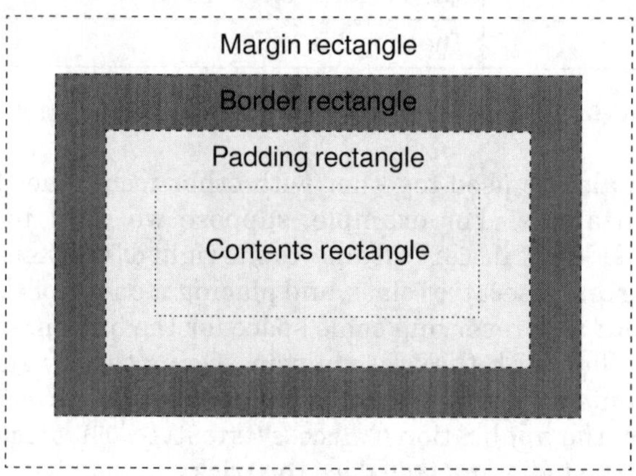

Figure 19.6. The CSS box model

The widgets are used in the dialog shown in Figure 19.1. The dialog itself has a background image set by the following rule:

```
QDialog {
    background-image: url(:/images/background.png);        [R1]
}
```

The following rule sets the color and font attributes for QLabels:

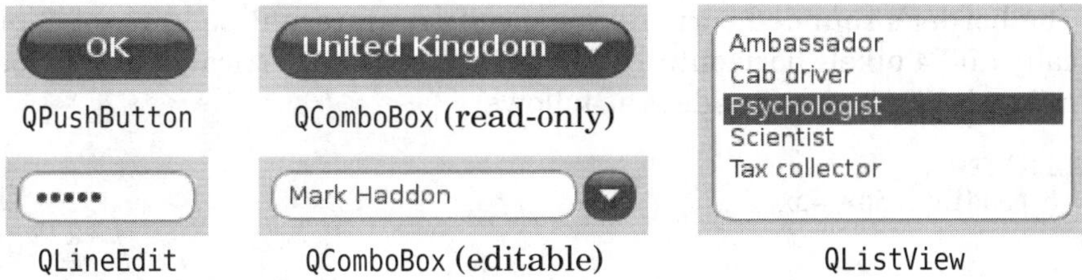

Figure 19.7. Widgets in the Candy style

```
QLabel {
    font: 9pt;
    color: rgb(0, 0, 127);                                [R2]
}
```

The next rule defines the look of the dialog's `QLineEdit` and of its `QListView`:

```
QLineEdit,
QListView {
    color: rgb(127, 0, 63);
    background-color: rgb(255, 255, 241);
    selection-color: white;
    selection-background-color: rgb(191, 31, 127);       [R3]
    border: 2px groove gray;
    border-radius: 10px;
    padding: 2px 4px;
}
```

To make the `QLineEdit` and `QListView` really stand out, we have specified custom foreground and background colors for normal and selected text. In addition, we have specified a gray 2-pixel-wide "grooved" border with the `border` attribute. Instead of using `border`, we could have set `border-width`, `border-style`, and `border-color` individually. We can round a border's corners by specifying a `border-radius`, and we have done so here using a radius of 10 pixels. Figure 19.8 provides a schematic representation of the effects of our changes to the widgets' border and padding attributes. To ensure that the widget's contents don't collide

Figure 19.8. Structure of a `QLineEdit`

with the border's rounded corners, we specify an internal padding of 2 pixels vertically and 4 pixels horizontally. For QListViews, the vertical padding doesn't look quite right, so we override it as follows:

```
QListView {
    padding: 5px 4px;                                        [R4]
}
```

When an attribute is set by several rules that have the same selector, the last rule is the one that is applied.

For styling QPushButtons, we will use a completely different approach. Instead of drawing the button using style sheet rules, we will use a ready-made image as the background. Also, to make the button scalable, the button background is defined using the CSS *border image* mechanism.

Unlike a background image specified using background-image, a border image is cut into a 3×3 grid, as shown in Figure 19.9. When filling the background of a widget, the four corners (cells $\mathcal{A}$, $\mathcal{C}$, $\mathcal{G}$, and $\mathcal{I}$ in the diagram) are taken as is, whereas the other five cells are stretched, or tiled, to fill the available space.

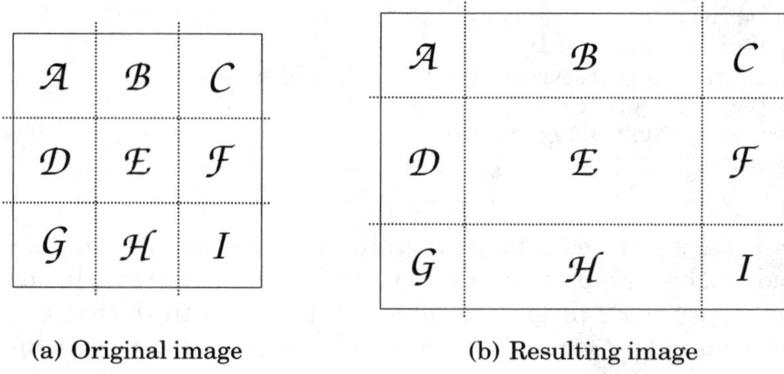

(a) Original image (b) Resulting image

Figure 19.9. Border image cuts

Border images are specified using the border-image property, which requires us to specify an image file name and the four "cuts" that define the nine cells. The cuts are defined as pixel distances from the top, right, bottom, and left edges. A border.png border image with cuts at 4, 8, 12, and 16 pixels from the top, right, bottom, and left edges would be specified as

```
border-image: url(border.png) 4 8 12 16;
```

When using a border image, we must also set the border-width attribute explicitly. Normally, border-width should correspond to where the cuts fall; otherwise, the corner cells will be stretched or shrunk to fit the border-width. For the border.png example, we would specify the border widths as follows:

```
border-width: 4px 8px 12px 16px;
```

Now that we know how the border image mechanism works, let us see how it is used for styling Candy QPushButtons. Here are the rules that define how push buttons are rendered in their normal state:

```
QPushButton {
    color: white;
    font: bold 10pt;
    border-image: url(:/images/button.png) 16;
    border-width: 16px;                                  [R5]
    padding: -16px 0px;
    min-height: 32px;
    min-width: 60px;
}
```

In the Candy style sheet, the four cuts for a QPushButton's border image are located at 16 pixels from the edges of a 34 × 34 pixel border image, as shown in Figure 19.10 (a). Because the four cuts are uniform, we only need to write "16" for the cuts and "16px" for the border width.

In the QPushButton example shown in Figure 19.10 (b), the border image cells corresponding to $\mathcal{D}$, $\mathcal{E}$, and $\mathcal{F}$ were dropped because the resized button was not tall enough to need them, and cells $\mathcal{B}$ and $\mathcal{H}$ were horizontally stretched to occupy the extra width.

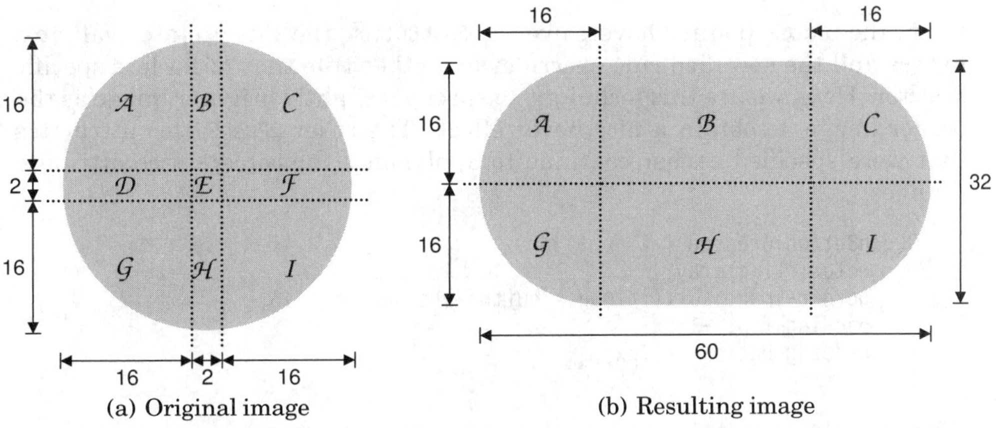

(a) Original image (b) Resulting image

Figure 19.10. Border image for QPushButton

The standard use of a border image is to provide a border around a widget, with the widget inside the border. But we have subverted the border image mechanism and used it to create the background of the widget itself. As a result, cell $\mathcal{E}$ has been dropped, and the padding rectangle has height 0. To make some room for the push button's text, we specify a vertical padding of −16 pixels. Figure 19.11 illustrates the situation. If we had used the border image mechanism to define an actual border, we probably wouldn't want the text to collide with it—but because we are using it to create a scalable background, we want the text to go on top of it rather than inside it.

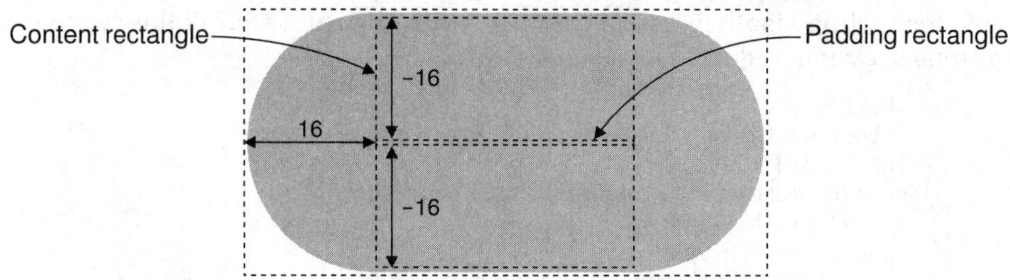

Figure 19.11. Structure of a `QPushButton`

Using `min-width` and `min-height`, we set the minimum size of the push button's contents. The values chosen here ensure that there is enough room for the border image corners and that an OK button is made a bit wider than necessary, to make it look better next to the Cancel button.

The preceding `QPushButton` rules apply to all push buttons. We will now define a few extra rules that apply only when buttons are in certain states.

```
QPushButton:hover {
    border-image: url(:/images/button-hover.png) 16;          [R6]
}
```

When the mouse pointer hovers over a `QPushButton`, the `:hover` state evaluates to `true` and the specified rule overrides any other rule that has a less specific selector. Here, we use this technique to specify a slightly brighter image as the border image, to obtain a nice hover effect. The other `QPushButton` attributes that were specified earlier continue to apply; only the `border-image` attribute changes.

```
QPushButton:pressed {
    color: lightgray;
    border-image: url(:/images/button-pressed.png) 16;        [R7]
    padding-top: -15px;
    padding-bottom: -17px;
}
```

When the user presses a push button, we change the foreground color to light gray, we use a darker border image, and we move the push button's text down one pixel by tweaking the padding.

Our final style rules will customize the appearance of `QComboBox`es. To show off the control and precision we can achieve using style sheets, we will distinguish between read-only and editable comboboxes, as Figure 19.12 shows. Read-only comboboxes are rendered as a `QPushButton` with a down arrow on the right, whereas editable comboboxes are made up of a `QLineEdit`-like component and of a small rounded button. It turns out that we can reuse most of the rules that we have already defined for `QLineEdit`s, `QListView`s, and `QPushButton`s.

- The rule that defines the look of a `QLineEdit` can be used to style editable comboboxes:

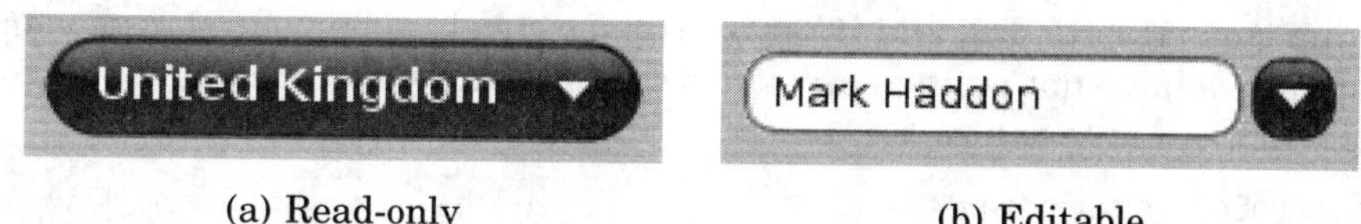

(a) Read-only (b) Editable

Figure 19.12. QComboBox in the Candy style

```
QComboBox:editable,
QLineEdit,
QListView {
    color: rgb(127, 0, 63);
    background-color: rgb(255, 255, 241);
    selection-color: white;                                   [R3′]
    selection-background-color: rgb(191, 31, 127);
    border: 2px groove gray;
    border-radius: 10px;
    padding: 2px 4px;
}
```

- The rules that define the look of a QPushButton in its normal state can be extended to apply to read-only comboboxes:

```
QComboBox:!editable,
QPushButton {
    color: white;
    font: bold 10pt;
    border-image: url(:/images/button.png) 16;                [R5′]
    border-width: 16px;
    padding: -16px 0px;
    min-height: 32px;
    min-width: 60px;
}
```

- Hovering over a read-only combobox or over the drop-down button of an editable combobox should change the background image, just like it already does for QPushButton:

```
QComboBox:!editable:hover,
QComboBox::drop-down:editable:hover,
QPushButton:hover {                                           [R6′]
    border-image: url(:/images/button-hover.png) 16;
}
```

- Pressing a read-only combobox is like pressing a QPushButton:

```
QComboBox:!editable:on,
QPushButton:pressed {
    color: lightgray;
    border-image: url(:/images/button-pressed.png) 16;        [R7′]
    padding-top: -15px;
    padding-bottom: -17px;
}
```

Reusing rules R3, R5, R6, and R7 saves time and helps keep our styling consistent. But we have not defined any rules that will draw the drop-down buttons, so we will create these now.

```
QComboBox::down-arrow {
    image: url(:/images/down-arrow.png);                    [R8]
}
```

We provide our own down arrow image so that it is a bit larger than the standard arrow.

```
QComboBox::down-arrow:on {
    top: 1px;                                               [R9]
}
```

If the combobox is open, the down arrow is moved down one pixel.

```
QComboBox * {
    font: 9pt;                                              [R10]
}
```

When the user clicks a combobox, it displays a list of items. Rule R10 ensures that the combobox's pop-up (or any other child widget) doesn't inherit the larger font size that applies to the combobox by rule R5′.

```
QComboBox::drop-down:!editable {
    subcontrol-origin: padding;
    subcontrol-position: center right;
    width: 11px;                                            [R11]
    height: 6px;
    background: none;
}
```

Using the `subcontrol-origin` and `subcontrol-position` attributes, we position the drop-down arrow vertically centered on the right-hand side of the padding rectangle used by read-only comboboxes. In addition, we also set its size to correspond to the size of the button's contents, the 11×6 pixel `down-arrow.png` image, and we disable its background because our drop-down button only consists of the drop-down arrow.

```
QComboBox:!editable {
    padding-right: 15px;                                    [R12]
}
```

For read-only comboboxes, we specify a right padding of 15 pixels to ensure that the text shown in the combobox doesn't overlap with the drop-down arrow. Figure 19.13 shows how these dimensions interact with each other.

For editable comboboxes, we need to configure the drop-down button so that it looks like a tiny `QPushButton`:

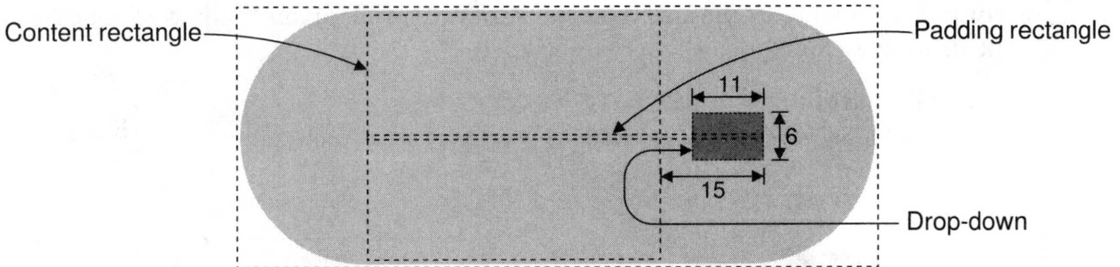

Figure 19.13. Structure of a read-only `QComboBox`

```
QComboBox::drop-down:editable {
    border-image: url(:/images/button.png) 16;
    border-width: 10px;
    subcontrol-origin: margin;                              [R13]
    subcontrol-position: center right;
    width: 7px;
    height: 6px;
}
```

We specify `button.png` as the border image. However, this time, we specify a border width of 10 pixels instead of 16, to scale the image down a bit, and specify a fixed size of the contents of 7 pixels horizontally and 6 pixels vertically. Figure 19.14 shows a schematic of what we have done.

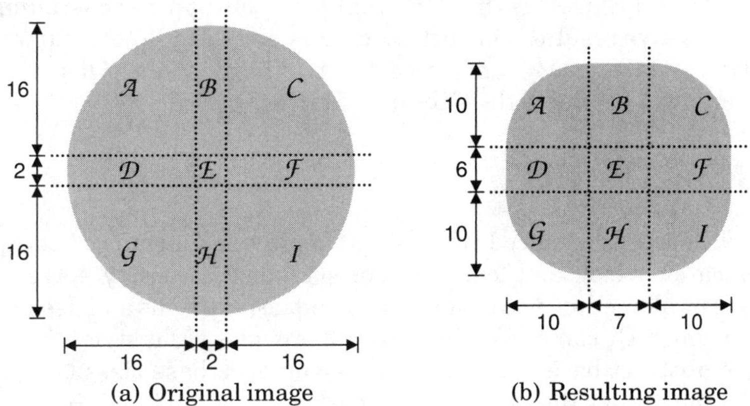

(a) Original image (b) Resulting image

Figure 19.14. The editable `QComboBox`'s drop-down button's border image

If the combobox is open, we use a different, darker image for the drop-down button:

```
QComboBox::drop-down:editable:open {
    border-image: url(:/images/button-pressed.png) 16;      [R14]
}
```

For editable comboboxes, we specify a right margin of 29 pixels to provide space for the drop-down button, as shown on Figure 19.15:

```
QComboBox:editable {
    margin-right: 29px;                                    [R15]
}
```

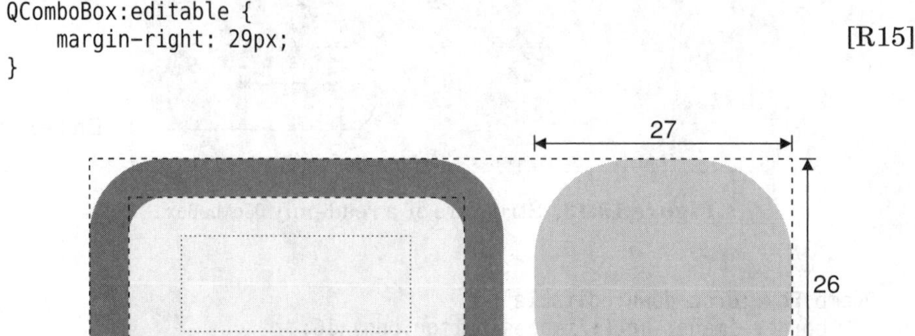

Figure 19.15. Structure of an editable QComboBox

We have now finished creating our Candy style sheet. The style sheet is about 100 lines long, and makes use of a few custom images. The result is a highly distinctive dialog.

Creating a custom style using style sheets can involve quite a lot of trial and error, especially for those who have not used CSS before. One of the main challenges with style sheets is that CSS conflict resolution and cascading don't always give intuitive results. For further details, see the online documentation at `http://doc.trolltech.com/4.3/stylesheet.html`. This describes Qt's style sheet support and provides links to the CSS specification.

Subclassing QStyle

The `QStyle` class was introduced with Qt 2.0 to provide a means of encapsulating an application's look and feel. Classes such as `QWindowsStyle`, `QMotifStyle`, and `QCDEStyle` implemented the look and feel for the platforms and desktop environments on which Qt ran at the time. Qt 4.3 provides eight styles, in addition to the `QStyle` abstract base class and the convenience base class `QCommonStyle`. Figure 19.16 shows how they relate to each other.

For Qt developers, the `QStyle` architecture makes it possible to develop a custom look and feel by subclassing `QStyle` or one of the existing styles. We can perform minor customizations on an existing style (e.g., `QWindowsStyle`), or we can develop an entire custom style from scratch.

The `QStyle` API consists of functions for drawing graphical elements (`drawPrimitive()`, `drawControl()`, `drawComplexControl()`, etc.) and for querying the style (`pixelMetrics()`, `styleHint()`, `hitTest()`, etc.). The `QStyle` member functions typically take a `QStyleOption` object that holds both general information about the

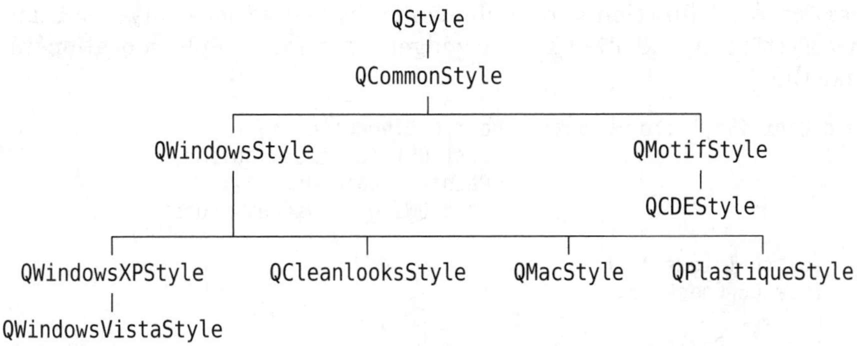

Figure 19.16. Inheritance tree for Qt's built-in styles

widget to be drawn (such as its palette) and widget-specific information (e.g., the text of a button). The functions also take an optional pointer to a `QWidget`, to cater to situations when the `QStyleOption` doesn't provide all the necessary information.

Suppose we want to create a `MyPushButton` class, which would look like a standard Qt push button but without deriving from `QPushButton`. (This example is rather contrived, but it will help us to clarify the relationship between widgets and styles.) In the `MyPushButton` paint event handler, we would set up a `QStyleOption` (actually, a `QStyleOptionButton`) and call `QStyle::drawControl()` as follows:

```
void MyPushButton::paintEvent(QPaintEvent * /* event */)
{
    QPainter painter(this);

    QStyleOptionButton option;
    option.initFrom(this);
    if (isFlat())
        option.features |= QStyleOptionButton::Flat;
    option.text = text();

    style()->drawControl(QStyle::CE_PushButton, &option, &painter,
                         this);
}
```

The `QStyleOption::initFrom()` function initializes the fundamental member variables that represent a widget, such as `rect`, `state` (enabled, focused, etc.), and `palette`. Member variables specific to `QStyleOptionButton` must be initialized manually. In the `MyPushButton` example, we initialize `features` and `text` and let `icon` and `iconSize` take their default values.

The `QWidget::style()` function returns the appropriate style for drawing the widget. The style is normally set for the entire application using `QApplication::setStyle()`, but it is also possible to override it for individual widgets using `QWidget::setStyle()`.

The drawControl() function is reimplemented by the various QStyle subclasses to draw QPushButton and other simple widgets. A typical implementation might look like this:

```
void QMotifStyle::drawControl(ControlElement element,
                              const QStyleOption *option,
                              QPainter *painter,
                              const QWidget *widget) const
{
    switch (element) {
    case CE_CheckBox:
        ...
    case CE_RadioButton:
        ...
    case CE_PushButton:
        if (const QStyleOptionButton *buttonOption =
                qstyleoption_cast<const QStyleOptionButton *>(option)) {
            // draw push button
        }
        break;
        ...
    }
}
```

The first parameter, element, indicates the type of widget to draw. If the type is CE_PushButton, the style attempts to cast the option parameter to QStyleOption-Button. If the cast is successful, it draws the push button described by QStyle-OptionButton. The cast from const QStyleOption * to const QStyleOptionButton * is performed using qstyleoption_cast<T>(), which returns a null pointer if option doesn't point to a QStyleOptionButton instance.

Instead of relying on the QStyleOption, a QStyle subclass may also query the widget directly:

```
case CE_PushButton:
    if (const QPushButton *button =
            qobject_cast<const QPushButton *>(widget)) {
        // draw push button
    }
    break;
```

The drawback with this version is that the style code is tied to QPushButton and thus cannot be used to render, say, a MyPushButton. For this reason, the built-in QStyle subclasses use the QStyleOption parameter whenever possible to obtain information about the widget to draw, and resort to using the QWidget parameter only if that is the only thing that will provide the required information.

In the rest of this section, we will review the code for the Bronze style shown in Figure 19.17. The Bronze style features round buttons with a gradient background, unconventional placement of spin box buttons, extravagant checkmarks, and a "brushed bronze" background. To implement this, it uses advanced 2D graphics features such as antialiasing, semi-transparency, linear gradients, and composition modes.

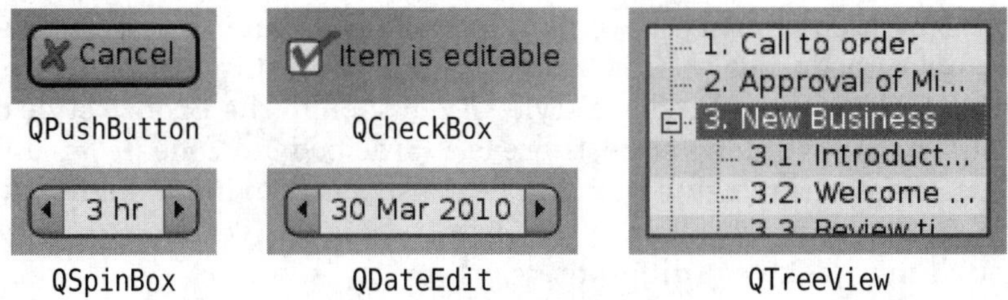

Figure 19.17. Widgets in the Bronze style

Here is the `BronzeStyle` class definition:

```
class BronzeStyle : public QWindowsStyle
{
    Q_OBJECT

public:
    BronzeStyle() {}

    void polish(QPalette &palette);
    void polish(QWidget *widget);
    void unpolish(QWidget *widget);
    int styleHint(StyleHint which, const QStyleOption *option,
                  const QWidget *widget = 0,
                  QStyleHintReturn *returnData = 0) const;
    int pixelMetric(PixelMetric which, const QStyleOption *option,
                    const QWidget *widget = 0) const;
    void drawPrimitive(PrimitiveElement which,
                       const QStyleOption *option, QPainter *painter,
                       const QWidget *widget = 0) const;
    void drawComplexControl(ComplexControl which,
                            const QStyleOptionComplex *option,
                            QPainter *painter,
                            const QWidget *widget = 0) const;
    QRect subControlRect(ComplexControl whichControl,
                         const QStyleOptionComplex *option,
                         SubControl whichSubControl,
                         const QWidget *widget = 0) const;

public slots:
    QIcon standardIconImplementation(StandardPixmap which,
                                     const QStyleOption *option,
                                     const QWidget *widget = 0) const;

private:
    void drawBronzeFrame(const QStyleOption *option,
                         QPainter *painter) const;
    void drawBronzeBevel(const QStyleOption *option,
                         QPainter *painter) const;
    void drawBronzeCheckBoxIndicator(const QStyleOption *option,
                                     QPainter *painter) const;
    void drawBronzeSpinBoxButton(SubControl which,
                                 const QStyleOptionComplex *option,
                                 QPainter *painter) const;
};
```

When creating a custom style, we usually base it on an existing style so that we don't have to do everything from scratch. For this example, we chose QWindowsStyle, the classic Windows style. Even though the Bronze style doesn't look much like the Windows style, there is a large body of code in QWindowsStyle and its base class QCommonStyle that can be reused as is to implement just about any style we can imagine. This is why QMacStyle is derived from QWindowsStyle even though they look very different.

BronzeStyle reimplements several public functions declared by QStyle. The polish() and unpolish() functions are called when the style is installed or uninstalled. They make it possible to tweak the widgets or the palette. The other public functions are either query functions (styleHint(), pixelMetric(), subControlRect()) or functions that draw a graphical element (drawPrimitive(), drawComplexControl()).

BronzeStyle also provides a public slot called standardIconImplementation(). This slot is discovered by Qt using introspection and is invoked when necessary as though it had been a virtual function. Qt sometimes uses this idiom to add functions that should have been virtual without breaking binary compatibility with earlier Qt 4 releases. It is expected that Qt 5 will replace the standardIconImplementation() slot with a standardIcon() virtual function.

The BronzeStyle class also declares a few private functions. These will be explained after we have covered the public functions.

```
void BronzeStyle::polish(QPalette &palette)
{
    QPixmap backgroundImage(":/images/background.png");
    QColor bronze(207, 155, 95);
    QColor veryLightBlue(239, 239, 247);
    QColor lightBlue(223, 223, 239);
    QColor darkBlue(95, 95, 191);

    palette = QPalette(bronze);
    palette.setBrush(QPalette::Window, backgroundImage);
    palette.setBrush(QPalette::BrightText, Qt::white);
    palette.setBrush(QPalette::Base, veryLightBlue);
    palette.setBrush(QPalette::AlternateBase, lightBlue);
    palette.setBrush(QPalette::Highlight, darkBlue);
    palette.setBrush(QPalette::Disabled, QPalette::Highlight,
                     Qt::darkGray);
}
```

One of the outstanding characteristics of the Bronze style is its color scheme. No matter what colors the user has set on their window system, the Bronze style has a bronze appearance. A custom style's color scheme can be set up in one of two ways: We can ignore the widget's QPalette and draw everything using our favorite colors (bronze, light bronze, dark bronze, etc.), or we can reimplement QStyle::polish(QPalette &) to adjust the application's or widget's palette and then use the palette. The second approach is more flexible because we can override the color scheme in a subclass (say, `SilverStyle`) by reimplementing `polish()`.

The concept of polishing is generalized to widgets. When a style is applied to a widget, `polish(QWidget *)` is called, allowing us to perform last-minute customizations:

```
void BronzeStyle::polish(QWidget *widget)
{
    if (qobject_cast<QAbstractButton *>(widget)
            || qobject_cast<QAbstractSpinBox *>(widget))
        widget->setAttribute(Qt::WA_Hover, true);
}
```

Here, we reimplement `polish(QWidget *)` to set the `Qt::WA_Hover` attribute on buttons and spin boxes. When this attribute is set, a paint event is generated when the mouse enters or leaves the area occupied by a widget. This gives us the opportunity to paint a widget differently depending on whether or not the mouse is hovering over it.

This function is called after the widget has been created and before it is shown for the first time, using the current style. It is then only ever called if the current style is dynamically changed.

```
void BronzeStyle::unpolish(QWidget *widget)
{
    if (qobject_cast<QAbstractButton *>(widget)
            || qobject_cast<QAbstractSpinBox *>(widget))
        widget->setAttribute(Qt::WA_Hover, false);
}
```

Just as `polish(QWidget *)` is called when a style is applied to a widget, `unpolish(QWidget *)` is called whenever the style is dynamically changed. The purpose of `unpolish()` is to undo the effects of the `polish()` so that the widget is in a state to be polished by the new style. Well-behaved styles try to undo what they did in their `polish()` function.

A common use of `polish(QWidget *)` is to install our style subclass as an event filter on a widget. This is necessary for some more advanced customizations; for example, `QWindowsVistaStyle` and `QMacStyle` use this technique to animate default buttons.

```
int BronzeStyle::styleHint(StyleHint which, const QStyleOption *option,
                           const QWidget *widget,
                           QStyleHintReturn *returnData) const
{
    switch (which) {
    case SH_DialogButtonLayout:
        return int(QDialogButtonBox::MacLayout);
    case SH_EtchDisabledText:
        return int(true);
    case SH_DialogButtonBox_ButtonsHaveIcons:
        return int(true);
    case SH_UnderlineShortcut:
```

```
        return int(false);
    default:
        return QWindowsStyle::styleHint(which, option, widget,
                                        returnData);
    }
}
```

The `styleHint()` function returns some hints about the look and feel provided by the style. For example, we return `MacLayout` for `SH_DialogButtonLayout` to signify that we want `QDialogButtonBox` to follow the Mac OS X guidelines, with OK to the right of Cancel. The return type of `styleHint()` is `int`. For the few style hints that cannot be represented as integers, `styleHint()` provides a pointer to a `QStyleHintReturn` object that can be used.

```
int BronzeStyle::pixelMetric(PixelMetric which,
                             const QStyleOption *option,
                             const QWidget *widget) const
{
    switch (which) {
    case PM_ButtonDefaultIndicator:
        return 0;
    case PM_IndicatorWidth:
    case PM_IndicatorHeight:
        return 16;
    case PM_CheckBoxLabelSpacing:
        return 8;
    case PM_DefaultFrameWidth:
        return 2;
    default:
        return QWindowsStyle::pixelMetric(which, option, widget);
    }
}
```

The `pixelMetric()` function returns a dimension in pixels that is used for a user interface element. By reimplementing this function, we affect both the drawing of the built-in Qt widgets and their size hints.

We return 0 for `PM_ButtonDefaultIndicator` because we don't want to reserve any extra spacing around default buttons (the default is 1 pixel in `QWindowsStyle`). For checkboxes, `PM_IndicatorWidth` and `PM_IndicatorHeight` control the size of the indicator (usually a small square), and `PM_CheckBoxLabelSpacing` controls the spacing between the checkbox indicator and the text to its right (see Figure 19.18). Finally, `PM_DefaultFrameWidth` defines the width of the line used around `QFrame`, `QPushButton`, `QSpinBox`, and many other widgets. For other `PM_`*`xxx`* values, we inherit the pixel metric value from the base class.

```
QIcon BronzeStyle::standardIconImplementation(StandardPixmap which,
        const QStyleOption *option, const QWidget *widget) const
{
    QImage image = QWindowsStyle::standardPixmap(which, option, widget)
                   .toImage();
    if (image.isNull())
        return QIcon();
```

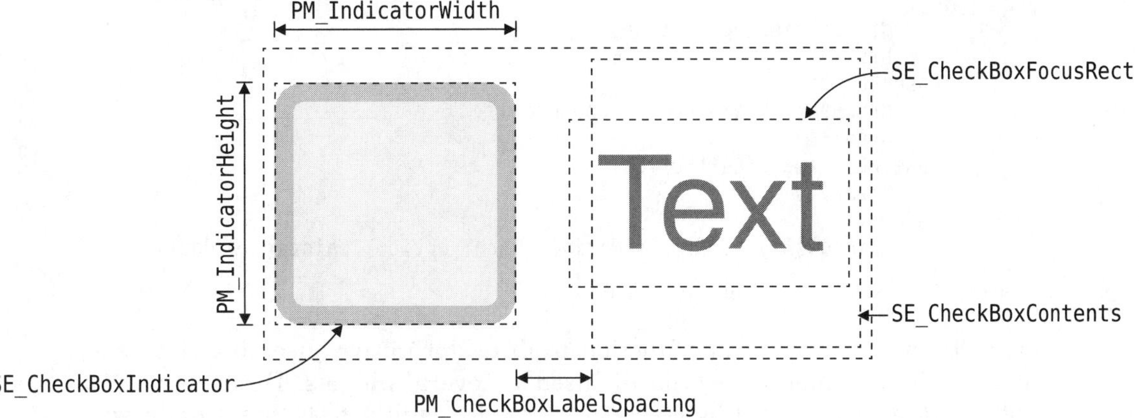

Figure 19.18. Structure of a `QCheckBox`

```
    QPalette palette;
    if (option) {
        palette = option->palette;
    } else if (widget) {
        palette = widget->palette();
    }

    QPainter painter(&image);
    painter.setOpacity(0.25);
    painter.setCompositionMode(QPainter::CompositionMode_SourceAtop);
    painter.fillRect(image.rect(), palette.highlight());
    painter.end();

    return QIcon(QPixmap::fromImage(image));
}
```

As explained earlier, Qt invokes the `standardIconImplementation()` slot to obtain the standard icons that should be used in user interfaces. We call the base class's `standardPixmap()` to obtain the icon and try to give it a slight blue tint, to make it blend in with the rest of the style. The tinting is achieved by drawing a 25% opaque blue color on top of the existing icon. By using the `SourceAtop` composition mode, we make sure that the existing transparent areas stay transparent, instead of becoming 25% blue and 75% transparent. We describe composition modes in the "High-Quality Rendering with QImage" section of Chapter 8 (p. 195).

```
void BronzeStyle::drawPrimitive(PrimitiveElement which,
                                const QStyleOption *option,
                                QPainter *painter,
                                const QWidget *widget) const
{
    switch (which) {
    case PE_IndicatorCheckBox:
        drawBronzeCheckBoxIndicator(option, painter);
        break;
    case PE_PanelButtonCommand:
```

```
            drawBronzeBevel(option, painter);
            break;
        case PE_Frame:
            drawBronzeFrame(option, painter);
            break;
        case PE_FrameDefaultButton:
            break;
        default:
            QWindowsStyle::drawPrimitive(which, option, painter, widget);
        }
    }
```

Qt calls the drawPrimitive() function to draw "primitive" user interface elements. These elements are typically used by several widgets. For example, PE_IndicatorCheckBox is used by QCheckBox, QGroupBox, and QItemDelegate to draw a checkbox indicator.

In the Bronze style, we reimplement drawPrimitive() to provide a custom look to checkbox indicators, push buttons, and frames. For example, Figure 19.19 shows the structure of a QPushButton which the Bronze style must handle. The drawBronzeCheckBoxIndicator(), drawBronzeBevel(), and drawBronzeFrame() functions are private functions that we will review later.

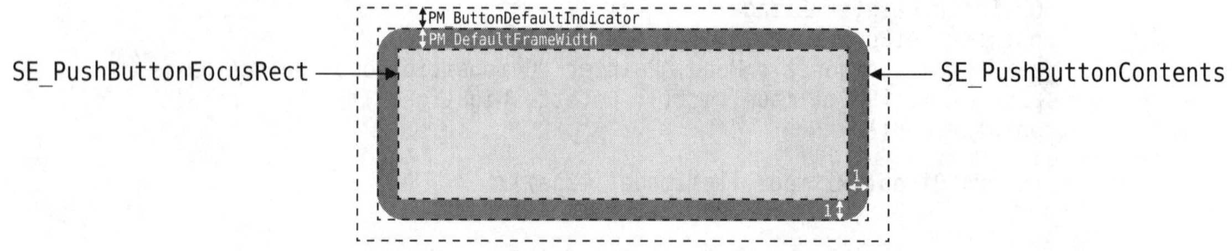

Figure 19.19. Structure of a QPushButton

For PE_FrameDefaultButton, we simply do nothing, because we don't want to draw an extra frame around default buttons. For all other primitive elements, we simply forward the call to the base class.

```
void BronzeStyle::drawComplexControl(ComplexControl which,
                                     const QStyleOptionComplex *option,
                                     QPainter *painter,
                                     const QWidget *widget) const
{
    if (which == CC_SpinBox) {
        drawBronzeSpinBoxButton(SC_SpinBoxDown, option, painter);
        drawBronzeSpinBoxButton(SC_SpinBoxUp, option, painter);

        QRect rect = subControlRect(CC_SpinBox, option,
                                    SC_SpinBoxEditField)
                     .adjusted(-1, 0, +1, 0);
        painter->setPen(QPen(option->palette.mid(), 1.0));
        painter->drawLine(rect.topLeft(), rect.bottomLeft());
        painter->drawLine(rect.topRight(), rect.bottomRight());
```

```
        } else {
            return QWindowsStyle::drawComplexControl(which, option, painter,
                                                     widget);
        }
    }
```

Qt calls the `drawComplexControl()` function to draw widgets that consist of multiple subcontrols—notably `QSpinBox`. Since we want to give a radically new look to `QSpinBox`, we reimplement `drawComplexControl()` and handle the `CC_SpinBox` case.

To draw a `QSpinBox` we must draw the up and down buttons and the frame around the entire spin box. (The structure of a `QSpinBox` is shown in Figure 19.20.) Since the code required for drawing an up button is almost identical to that for drawing a down button, we have factored it out into the `drawBronzeSpinBoxButton()` private function. The function also draws the frame around the entire spin box.

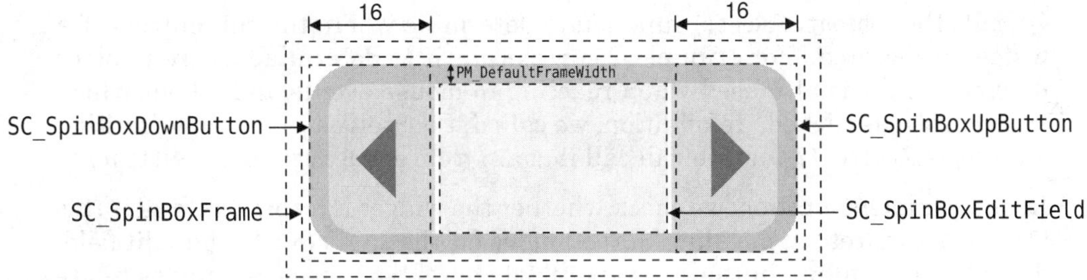

Figure 19.20. Structure of a `QSpinBox`

`QSpinBox` uses a `QLineEdit` to represent the editable part of the widget, so we don't need to draw that part of the widget. However, to cleanly separate the `QLineEdit` and the spin box buttons, we draw two light brown vertical lines at the edge of the `QLineEdit`. The `QLineEdit`'s geometry is obtained by calling `subControlRect()` with `SC_SpinBoxEditField` as the third argument.

```
    QRect BronzeStyle::subControlRect(ComplexControl whichControl,
                                      const QStyleOptionComplex *option,
                                      SubControl whichSubControl,
                                      const QWidget *widget) const
    {
        if (whichControl == CC_SpinBox) {
            int frameWidth = pixelMetric(PM_DefaultFrameWidth, option,
                                         widget);
            int buttonWidth = 16;

            switch (whichSubControl) {
            case SC_SpinBoxFrame:
                return option->rect;
            case SC_SpinBoxEditField:
                return option->rect.adjusted(+buttonWidth, +frameWidth,
                                             -buttonWidth, -frameWidth);
            case SC_SpinBoxDown:
                return visualRect(option->direction, option->rect,
```

```
                                  QRect(option->rect.x(), option->rect.y(),
                                        buttonWidth,
                                        option->rect.height()));
        case SC_SpinBoxUp:
            return visualRect(option->direction, option->rect,
                              QRect(option->rect.right() - buttonWidth,
                                    option->rect.y(),
                                    buttonWidth,
                                    option->rect.height()));
        default:
            return QRect();
        }
    } else {
        return QWindowsStyle::subControlRect(whichControl, option,
                                             whichSubControl, widget);
    }
}
```

Qt calls the `subControlRect()` function to determine where the subcontrols of a widget are located. For example, `QSpinBox` calls it to determine where to place its `QLineEdit`. It is also used when reacting to mouse events, to find out which subcontrol was clicked. In addition, we called it ourselves when implementing `drawComplexControl()`, and we will call it again from `drawBronzeSpinBoxButton()`.

In our reimplementation, we check whether the widget is a spin box, and if this is the case, we return meaningful rectangles for the spin box's frame, edit field, down button, and up button. Figure 19.20 shows how these rectangles relate to each other. For the other widgets, including `QPushButton`, we rely on the base class's implementation.

The rectangles we return for `SC_SpinBoxDown` and `SC_SpinBoxUp` are passed through `QStyle::visualRect()`. Calls to `visualRect()` have the following syntax:

```
visualRect(direction, outerRect, logicalRect)
```

If the *direction* is `Qt::LeftToRight`, then *logicalRect* is returned unchanged; otherwise, *logicalRect* is flipped with respect to *outerRect*. This ensures that graphical elements are mirrored in right-to-left mode, which is used for languages such as Arabic and Hebrew. For symmetric elements such as `SC_SpinBoxFrame` and `SC_SpinBoxEditField`, flipping would have no effect, so we don't bother calling `visualRect()`. To test a style in right-to-left mode, we can simply pass the `-reverse` command-line option to an application that uses the style. Figure 19.21 shows the Bronze style in right-to-left mode.

This completes our review of the public functions reimplemented from `QWindowsStyle`. The next four functions are private drawing functions.

```
void BronzeStyle::drawBronzeFrame(const QStyleOption *option,
                                  QPainter *painter) const
{
    painter->save();
    painter->setRenderHint(QPainter::Antialiasing, true);
    painter->setPen(QPen(option->palette.foreground(), 1.0));
```

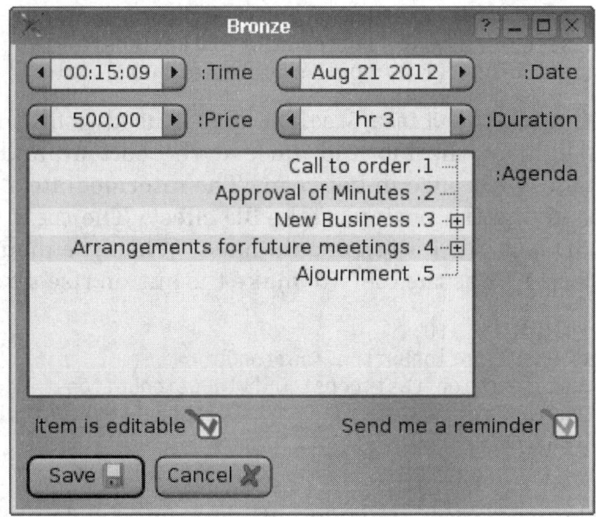

Figure 19.21. The Bronze style in right-to-left mode

```
        painter->drawRect(option->rect.adjusted(+1, +1, -1, -1));
        painter->restore();
    }
```

The `drawBronzeFrame()` function was called from `drawPrimitive()` to draw a `PE_Frame` primitive element. This is used to draw the frame around a `QFrame` (or a subclass, such as `QTreeView`) when the frame shape is `QFrame::StyledPanel`. (The other frame shapes, such as `Box`, `Panel`, and `VLine`, are drawn directly by `QFrame` without going through the style.)

The frame we draw is an antialiased 1-pixel-wide outline around the widget, using the palette's foreground brush (available through the `QStyleOption`'s `palette` member variable). Since the rectangle is antialiased and is located on an integer coordinate, the resulting effect is a blurred 2-pixel-wide outline, which is precisely what we want for the Bronze style.

To ensure that we leave the `QPainter` in the same state as we got it, we call `save()` before we call `setRenderHint()` and `setPen()`, and call `restore()` at the end. This is necessary because Qt optimizes drawing by reusing the same `QPainter` to draw several graphical elements.

The next function we will study is `drawBronzeBevel()`, which draws the background of a `QPushButton`:

```
    void BronzeStyle::drawBronzeBevel(const QStyleOption *option,
                                      QPainter *painter) const
    {
        QColor buttonColor = option->palette.button().color();
        int coeff = (option->state & State_MouseOver) ? 115 : 105;

        QLinearGradient gradient(0, 0, 0, option->rect.height());
        gradient.setColorAt(0.0, option->palette.light().color());
```

```
    gradient.setColorAt(0.2, buttonColor.lighter(coeff));
    gradient.setColorAt(0.8, buttonColor.darker(coeff));
    gradient.setColorAt(1.0, option->palette.dark().color());
```

We start by setting up the QLinearGradient that is used to fill the background. The gradient is light at the top and dark at the bottom, and goes through intermediate shades of bronze in between. The intermediate steps at 0.2 and 0.8 contribute to giving the button a fake 3D effect. The coeff factor controls how much of a 3D look the button should have. When the mouse hovers over the button, we use 115% as the coeff to make the button rise up slightly.

```
    double penWidth = 1.0;
    if (const QStyleOptionButton *buttonOpt =
            qstyleoption_cast<const QStyleOptionButton *>(option)) {
        if (buttonOpt->features & QStyleOptionButton::DefaultButton)
            penWidth = 2.0;
    }
```

The Bronze style uses a 2-pixel-wide outline around default buttons and a 1-pixel-wide outline otherwise. To find out whether the push button is a default button, we cast option to a const QStyleOptionButton * and check its features member variable.

```
    QRect roundRect = option->rect.adjusted(+1, +1, -1, -1);
    if (!roundRect.isValid())
        return;

    int diameter = 12;
    int cx = 100 * diameter / roundRect.width();
    int cy = 100 * diameter / roundRect.height();
```

We define some more variables that will be used below to draw the button. The cx and cy coefficients specify how rounded we want the push button corners to be. They are computed in terms of diameter, which specifies the rounded corners' desired diameters.

```
    painter->save();
    painter->setPen(Qt::NoPen);
    painter->setBrush(gradient);
    painter->drawRoundRect(roundRect, cx, cy);

    if (option->state & (State_On | State_Sunken)) {
        QColor slightlyOpaqueBlack(0, 0, 0, 63);
        painter->setBrush(slightlyOpaqueBlack);
        painter->drawRoundRect(roundRect, cx, cy);
    }

    painter->setRenderHint(QPainter::Antialiasing, true);
    painter->setPen(QPen(option->palette.foreground(), penWidth));
    painter->setBrush(Qt::NoBrush);
    painter->drawRoundRect(roundRect, cx, cy);
    painter->restore();
}
```

Finally, we perform the drawing. We start by drawing the background using the QLinearGradient that we defined earlier in the function. If the button is currently pressed (or is a toggle button in its "on" state), we draw a 75% transparent black color on top of it to make it a bit darker.

Once we have drawn the background, we turn on antialiasing to obtain smooth rounded corners, we set an appropriate pen, we clear the brush, and we draw the outline.

```
void BronzeStyle::drawBronzeSpinBoxButton(SubControl which,
        const QStyleOptionComplex *option, QPainter *painter) const
{
    PrimitiveElement arrow = PE_IndicatorArrowLeft;
    QRect buttonRect = option->rect;
    if ((which == SC_SpinBoxUp)
            != (option->direction == Qt::RightToLeft)) {
        arrow = PE_IndicatorArrowRight;
        buttonRect.translate(buttonRect.width() / 2, 0);
    }
    buttonRect.setWidth((buttonRect.width() + 1) / 2);

    QStyleOption buttonOpt(*option);

    painter->save();
    painter->setClipRect(buttonRect, Qt::IntersectClip);
    if (!(option->activeSubControls & which))
        buttonOpt.state &= ~(State_MouseOver | State_On | State_Sunken);
    drawBronzeBevel(&buttonOpt, painter);

    QStyleOption arrowOpt(buttonOpt);
    arrowOpt.rect = subControlRect(CC_SpinBox, option, which)
                    .adjusted(+3, +3, -3, -3);
    if (arrowOpt.rect.isValid())
        drawPrimitive(arrow, &arrowOpt, painter);
    painter->restore();
}
```

The drawBronzeSpinBoxButton() function draws the up or down button of a spin box, depending on whether which is SC_SpinBoxDown or SC_SpinBoxUp. We start by setting up the arrow to draw on the button (a left or a right arrow) and the rectangle in which we draw the button.

If which is SC_SpinBoxDown (or which is SC_SpinBoxUp and the layout direction is right-to-left), we use a left arrow (PE_IndicatorArrowLeft) and we draw the button in the left half of the spin box's rectangle; otherwise, we use a right arrow and we draw the button in the right half.

To draw the button, we call drawBronzeBevel() with a QStyleOption that correctly reflects the state of the spin box button we want to draw. For example, if the mouse is hovering over the spin box but not over the spin box button corresponding to which, we clear the State_MouseOver, State_On, and State_Sunken flags from the QStyleOption's state. This is necessary to ensure that the two spin box buttons behave independently of each other.

Before we perform any drawing, we call `setClipRect()` to set the clipping rectangle on the `QPainter`. This is because we want to draw only the left or right half of a button bevel, not the entire button bevel.

Finally, at the end, we draw the arrow by calling `drawPrimitive()`. The `QStyleOption` used to draw the arrow is set up with a rectangle that corresponds to the spin box button's rectangle (`SC_SpinBoxUp` or `SC_SpinBoxDown`) but is a bit smaller, to obtain a smaller arrow.

```
void BronzeStyle::drawBronzeCheckBoxIndicator(
        const QStyleOption *option, QPainter *painter) const
{
    painter->save();
    painter->setRenderHint(QPainter::Antialiasing, true);

    if (option->state & State_MouseOver) {
        painter->setBrush(option->palette.alternateBase());
    } else {
        painter->setBrush(option->palette.base());
    }
    painter->drawRoundRect(option->rect.adjusted(+1, +1, -1, -1));

    if (option->state & (State_On | State_NoChange)) {
        QPixmap pixmap;
        if (!(option->state & State_Enabled)) {
            pixmap.load(":/images/checkmark-disabled.png");
        } else if (option->state & State_NoChange) {
            pixmap.load(":/images/checkmark-partial.png");
        } else {
            pixmap.load(":/images/checkmark.png");
        }

        QRect pixmapRect = pixmap.rect()
                                .translated(option->rect.topLeft())
                                .translated(+2, -6);
        QRect painterRect = visualRect(option->direction, option->rect,
                                       pixmapRect);
        if (option->direction == Qt::RightToLeft) {
            painter->scale(-1.0, +1.0);
            painterRect.moveLeft(-painterRect.right() - 1);
        }
        painter->drawPixmap(painterRect, pixmap);
    }
    painter->restore();
}
```

Although the `drawBronzeCheckBoxIndicator()` code might look complex at first sight, drawing a checkbox indicator is actually quite simple: We draw a rectangle using `drawRoundRect()`, and we draw the checkmark using `drawPixmap()`. The complications arise because we want to use a different background color when the mouse hovers over the checkbox indicator, because we distinguish between normal checkmarks, disabled checkmarks, and partial checkmarks (for tri-state checkboxes), and because we flip the checkmark in right-to-left mode (by flipping the `QPainter`'s coordinate system).

QStyleOption Versioning

The information that QStyle needs to draw a widget is passed around using QStyleOption and its subclasses (QStyleOptionButton, QStyleOptionComboBox, QStyleOptionFrame, etc.). For performance reasons, the data is stored in public member variables.

To ensure binary compatibility across all Qt 4 versions, Trolltech cannot add new member variables to these classes until Qt 5. To allow enhancements in future Qt 4.*x* releases, QStyleOption has a version variable that can be used to distinguish between different versions of the same class. When new data members are needed, Trolltech adds them to a subclass identified by the same type but with a different version. For example, Qt 4.1 introduced QStyleOptionFrameV2, which is derived from QStyleOptionFrame but also provides a features member variable that the style can query. The QStyleOptionFrameV2 subclass is of type SO_Frame, but its version is 2 instead of 1.

In a QStyle subclass, we can use QStyleOptionFrame as usual, and if we want to access the features variable, which is defined only in version 2 of the class, we can write code such as this:

```
if (const QStyleOptionFrame *frameOption =
            qstyleoption_cast<const QStyleOptionFrame *>(option)) {
    QStyleOptionFrameV2 frameOptionV2(*frameOption);

    int lineWidth = frameOptionV2.lineWidth;
    bool flat = (frameOptionV2.features & QStyleOptionFrameV2::Flat);
    ...
}
```

The QStyleOptionFrameV2 copy constructor accepts both version 1 and version 2 instances of the class. If a version 1 object is supplied, the copy constructor will initialize the features field with a default value of None; otherwise, it will copy the features field from frameOption object.

Another way to achieve the same effect, but without performing a copy, is to use qstyleoption_cast<T>() to distinguish between different versions:

```
if (const QStyleOptionFrame *frameOption =
        qstyleoption_cast<const QStyleOptionFrame *>(option)) {
    int lineWidth = frameOption.lineWidth;
    bool flat = false;

    if (const QStyleOptionFrame *frameOptionV2 =
            qstyleoption_cast<const QStyleOptionFrameV2 *>(option))
        flat = (frameOptionV2.features & QStyleOptionFrameV2::Flat);
    ...
}
```

In Qt 5, the features variable will most probably be moved to QStyleOptionFrame, because Qt does not maintain binary compatibility between major releases.

We have now completed the implementation of our Bronze `QStyle` subclass. In the screenshots shown in Figure 19.17, a `QDateEdit` and a `QTreeWidget` are shown, both of which use the Bronze style even though we have not written any code specifically for them. This is because `QDateEdit`, `QDoubleSpinBox`, and some other widgets are all "spin boxes", and so make use of the Bronze style code for rendering themselves; similarly, `QTreeWidget` and all other widget classes that are derived from `QFrame` get the custom look defined by the Bronze style.

The Bronze style presented in this section can easily be used in an application, by linking it in and calling

```
QApplication::setStyle(new BronzeStyle);
```

in the application's `main()` function. Widgets that aren't handled explicitly by the Bronze style will have a classic Windows look. Custom styles can also be compiled as plugins and used afterwards in *Qt Designer* to preview forms using that style. In Chapter 21, we will show how to make the Bronze style available as a Qt plugin.

Although the style developed here is only about 300 lines of code, be aware that developing a fully functional custom style is a major undertaking that typically requires 3000 to 5000 lines of C++ code. For this reason, it is often easier and more convenient to use Qt style sheets whenever possible, or to use a hybrid approach, combining style sheets and a custom `QStyle`. If you plan to create a custom `QStyle`, implementing styles and style-aware widgets is covered in depth in the document `http://doc.trolltech.com/4.3/style-reference.html`.

- *Drawing Using OpenGL*
- *Combining OpenGL and QPainter*
- *Doing Overlays Using Framebuffer Objects*

20. 3D Graphics

OpenGL is a standard API for rendering 3D graphics. Qt applications can draw 3D graphics by using the *QtOpenGL* module, which relies on the system's OpenGL library. The module provides the `QGLWidget` class, which we can subclass to develop our own widgets that draw themselves using OpenGL commands. For many 3D applications, this is sufficient. The first section of this chapter presents a simple application that uses this technique to draw a tetrahedron and lets the user interact with it using the mouse.

Starting with Qt 4, it is possible to use a `QPainter` on a `QGLWidget` as though it were a normal `QWidget`. One huge benefit of this is that we get the high performance of OpenGL for most drawing operations, such as transformations and pixmap drawing. Another benefit of using `QPainter` is that we can use its higher-level API for 2D graphics, and combine it with OpenGL calls to perform 3D graphics. In the chapter's second section, we will show how to combine 2D and 3D drawing in the same widget using a mixture of `QPainter` and OpenGL commands.

Using `QGLWidget`, we can draw 3D scenes on the screen, using OpenGL as the back-end. To render to a hardware-accelerated off-screen surface, we can use the *pbuffer* and *framebuffer object* extensions, which are available through the `QGLPixelBuffer` and `QGLFramebufferObject` classes. In the third section of the chapter, we will show how to use a framebuffer object to implement overlays.

This chapter assumes that you are familiar with OpenGL. If OpenGL is new to you, a good place to start learning it is `http://www.opengl.org/`.

Drawing Using OpenGL

Drawing graphics with OpenGL from a Qt application is straightforward: We must subclass `QGLWidget`, reimplement a few virtual functions, and link the application against the *QtOpenGL* and OpenGL libraries. Because `QGLWidget` is derived from `QWidget`, most of what we already know still applies. The main difference is that we use standard OpenGL functions to perform the drawing instead of `QPainter`.

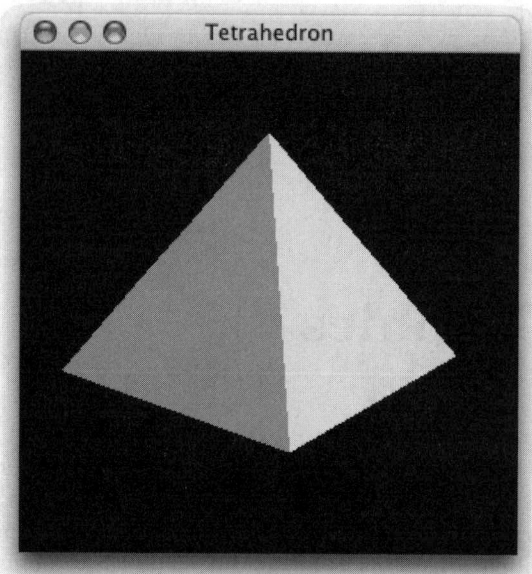

Figure 20.1. The Tetrahedron application

To show how this works, we will review the code of the Tetrahedron application shown in Figure 20.1. The application presents a 3D tetrahedron, or four-sided die, with each face drawn using a different color. The user can rotate the tetrahedron by pressing a mouse button and dragging. The user can set the color of a face by double-clicking it and choosing a color from the `QColorDialog` that pops up.

```
class Tetrahedron : public QGLWidget
{
    Q_OBJECT

public:
    Tetrahedron(QWidget *parent = 0);

protected:
    void initializeGL();
    void resizeGL(int width, int height);
    void paintGL();
    void mousePressEvent(QMouseEvent *event);
    void mouseMoveEvent(QMouseEvent *event);
    void mouseDoubleClickEvent(QMouseEvent *event);

private:
    void draw();
    int faceAtPosition(const QPoint &pos);

    GLfloat rotationX;
    GLfloat rotationY;
    GLfloat rotationZ;
    QColor faceColors[4];
```

```
    QPoint lastPos;
};
```

The Tetrahedron class is derived from QGLWidget. The initializeGL(), resizeGL(), and paintGL() functions are reimplemented from QGLWidget. The mouse event handlers are reimplemented from QWidget as usual.

```
Tetrahedron::Tetrahedron(QWidget *parent)
    : QGLWidget(parent)
{
    setFormat(QGLFormat(QGL::DoubleBuffer | QGL::DepthBuffer));

    rotationX = -21.0;
    rotationY = -57.0;
    rotationZ = 0.0;
    faceColors[0] = Qt::red;
    faceColors[1] = Qt::green;
    faceColors[2] = Qt::blue;
    faceColors[3] = Qt::yellow;
}
```

In the constructor, we call QGLWidget::setFormat() to specify the OpenGL display context, and we initialize the class's private variables.

```
void Tetrahedron::initializeGL()
{
    qglClearColor(Qt::black);
    glShadeModel(GL_FLAT);
    glEnable(GL_DEPTH_TEST);
    glEnable(GL_CULL_FACE);
}
```

The initializeGL() function is called just once, before paintGL() is called. This is the place where we can set up the OpenGL rendering context, define display lists, and perform other initializations.

All the code is standard OpenGL, except for the call to QGLWidget's qglClearColor() function. If we wanted to stick to standard OpenGL, we would call glClearColor() in RGBA mode and glClearIndex() in color index mode instead.

```
void Tetrahedron::resizeGL(int width, int height)
{
    glViewport(0, 0, width, height);
    glMatrixMode(GL_PROJECTION);
    glLoadIdentity();
    GLfloat x = GLfloat(width) / height;
    glFrustum(-x, +x, -1.0, +1.0, 4.0, 15.0);
    glMatrixMode(GL_MODELVIEW);
}
```

The resizeGL() function is called before paintGL() is called the first time, but after initializeGL() is called. It is also called whenever the widget is resized. This is the place where we can set up the OpenGL viewport, projection, and any other settings that depend on the widget's size.

```
void Tetrahedron::paintGL()
{
    glClear(GL_COLOR_BUFFER_BIT | GL_DEPTH_BUFFER_BIT);
    draw();
}
```

The paintGL() function is called whenever the widget needs to be repainted. This is similar to QWidget::paintEvent(), but instead of QPainter functions we use OpenGL functions. The actual drawing is performed by the private function draw().

```
void Tetrahedron::draw()
{
    static const GLfloat P1[3] = { 0.0, -1.0, +2.0 };
    static const GLfloat P2[3] = { +1.73205081, -1.0, -1.0 };
    static const GLfloat P3[3] = { -1.73205081, -1.0, -1.0 };
    static const GLfloat P4[3] = { 0.0, +2.0, 0.0 };

    static const GLfloat * const coords[4][3] = {
        { P1, P2, P3 }, { P1, P3, P4 }, { P1, P4, P2 }, { P2, P4, P3 }
    };

    glMatrixMode(GL_MODELVIEW);
    glLoadIdentity();
    glTranslatef(0.0, 0.0, -10.0);
    glRotatef(rotationX, 1.0, 0.0, 0.0);
    glRotatef(rotationY, 0.0, 1.0, 0.0);
    glRotatef(rotationZ, 0.0, 0.0, 1.0);

    for (int i = 0; i < 4; ++i) {
        glLoadName(i);
        glBegin(GL_TRIANGLES);
        qglColor(faceColors[i]);
        for (int j = 0; j < 3; ++j) {
            glVertex3f(coords[i][j][0], coords[i][j][1],
                       coords[i][j][2]);
        }
        glEnd();
    }
}
```

In draw(), we draw the tetrahedron, taking into account the x, y, and z rotations and the colors stored in the faceColors array. Everything is standard OpenGL, except for the qglColor() call. We could have used one of the OpenGL functions glColor3d() or glIndex() instead, depending on the mode.

```
void Tetrahedron::mousePressEvent(QMouseEvent *event)
{
    lastPos = event->pos();
}

void Tetrahedron::mouseMoveEvent(QMouseEvent *event)
{
    GLfloat dx = GLfloat(event->x() - lastPos.x()) / width();
    GLfloat dy = GLfloat(event->y() - lastPos.y()) / height();
```

```
    if (event->buttons() & Qt::LeftButton) {
        rotationX += 180 * dy;
        rotationY += 180 * dx;
        updateGL();
    } else if (event->buttons() & Qt::RightButton) {
        rotationX += 180 * dy;
        rotationZ += 180 * dx;
        updateGL();
    }
    lastPos = event->pos();
}
```

The `mousePressEvent()` and `mouseMoveEvent()` functions are reimplemented from `QWidget` to allow the user to rotate the view by clicking and dragging. The left mouse button allows the user to rotate around the x- and y-axes, the right mouse button around the x- and z-axes.

After modifying the `rotationX` variable, and either the `rotationY` or the `rotationZ` variable, we call `updateGL()` to redraw the scene.

```
void Tetrahedron::mouseDoubleClickEvent(QMouseEvent *event)
{
    int face = faceAtPosition(event->pos());
    if (face != -1) {
        QColor color = QColorDialog::getColor(faceColors[face], this);
        if (color.isValid()) {
            faceColors[face] = color;
            updateGL();
        }
    }
}
```

The `mouseDoubleClickEvent()` is reimplemented from `QWidget` to allow the user to set the color of a tetrahedron face by double-clicking it. We call the private function `faceAtPosition()` to determine which face, if any, is located under the cursor. If a face was double-clicked, we call `QColorDialog::getColor()` to obtain a new color for that face. Then we update the `faceColors` array with the new color, and we call `updateGL()` to redraw the scene.

```
int Tetrahedron::faceAtPosition(const QPoint &pos)
{
    const int MaxSize = 512;
    GLuint buffer[MaxSize];
    GLint viewport[4];

    makeCurrent();

    glGetIntegerv(GL_VIEWPORT, viewport);
    glSelectBuffer(MaxSize, buffer);
    glRenderMode(GL_SELECT);

    glInitNames();
    glPushName(0);

    glMatrixMode(GL_PROJECTION);
```

```
        glPushMatrix();
        glLoadIdentity();
        gluPickMatrix(GLdouble(pos.x()), GLdouble(viewport[3] - pos.y()),
                      5.0, 5.0, viewport);
        GLfloat x = GLfloat(width()) / height();
        glFrustum(-x, x, -1.0, 1.0, 4.0, 15.0);
        draw();
        glMatrixMode(GL_PROJECTION);
        glPopMatrix();

        if (!glRenderMode(GL_RENDER))
            return -1;
        return buffer[3];
    }
```

The `faceAtPosition()` function returns the number of the face at a certain position on the widget, or −1 if there is no face at that position. The code for determining this in OpenGL is a bit complicated. Essentially, we render the scene in `GL_SELECT` mode to take advantage of OpenGL's picking capabilities and then retrieve the face number (its "name") from the OpenGL hit record. The code is all standard OpenGL code, except for the `QGLWidget::makeCurrent()` call at the beginning, which is necessary to ensure that we use the correct OpenGL context. (`QGLWidget` does this automatically before it calls `initializeGL()`, `resizeGL()`, or `paintGL()`, so we don't need this call anywhere else in the `Tetrahedron` implementation.)

Here's the application's `main()` function:

```
int main(int argc, char *argv[])
{
    QApplication app(argc, argv);

    if (!QGLFormat::hasOpenGL()) {
        std::cerr << "This system has no OpenGL support" << std::endl;
        return 1;
    }

    Tetrahedron tetrahedron;
    tetrahedron.setWindowTitle(QObject::tr("Tetrahedron"));
    tetrahedron.resize(300, 300);
    tetrahedron.show();

    return app.exec();
}
```

If the user's system doesn't support OpenGL, we print an error message to the console and return immediately.

To link the application against the *QtOpenGL* module and the system's OpenGL library, the `.pro` file needs this entry:

```
QT += opengl
```

That completes the Tetrahedron application.

Combining OpenGL and QPainter

In the preceding section, we saw how to use OpenGL commands to draw a 3D scene on a `QGLWidget`. It is also possible to use `QPainter` to draw 2D graphics on a `QGLWidget`. The Vowel Cube example we will look at in this section combines OpenGL calls and `QPainter`, showing how to get the best of both worlds. It also demonstrates the use of the `QGLWidget::renderText()` function, which lets us draw untransformed textual annotations on top of a 3D scene. The application is shown in Figure 20.2.

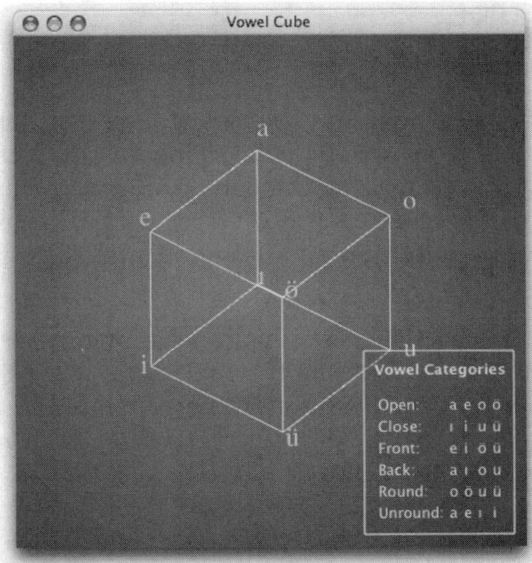

Figure 20.2. The Vowel Cube application

Vowel Cube shows a window with the eight vowels of the Turkish language as a cube—an image frequently seen in Turkish grammars and linguistics books. In the foreground, a legend lists the vowel categories and which vowels belong in which category. The cube makes this information more visual; for example, front vowels are shown in the front of the cube, and back vowels are at the back. For the background, we use a radial gradient.

```
class VowelCube : public QGLWidget
{
    Q_OBJECT

public:
    VowelCube(QWidget *parent = 0);
    ~VowelCube();

protected:
    void paintEvent(QPaintEvent *event);
    void mousePressEvent(QMouseEvent *event);
    void mouseMoveEvent(QMouseEvent *event);
    void wheelEvent(QWheelEvent *event);
```

```
private:
    void createGradient();
    void createGLObject();
    void drawBackground(QPainter *painter);
    void drawCube();
    void drawLegend(QPainter *painter);

    GLuint glObject;
    QRadialGradient gradient;
    GLfloat rotationX;
    GLfloat rotationY;
    GLfloat rotationZ;
    GLfloat scaling;
    QPoint lastPos;
};
```

The VowelCube class is derived from QGLWidget. It uses QPainter to draw the background gradient, then it draws the cube using OpenGL calls, then it draws the eight vowels at the corners of the cube using renderText(), and finally it draws the legend using QPainter and QTextDocument. The user can rotate the cube by pressing a mouse button and dragging, and zoom in or out using the mouse wheel.

Unlike in the preceding section's Tetrahedron example, where we reimplemented the high-level QGLWidget functions initializeGL(), resizeGL(), and paintGL(), this time we reimplement the traditional QWidget handlers. This gives us more control over how we update the OpenGL framebuffer.

Here's the VowelCube constructor:

```
VowelCube::VowelCube(QWidget *parent)
    : QGLWidget(parent)
{
    setFormat(QGLFormat(QGL::SampleBuffers));

    rotationX = -38.0;
    rotationY = -58.0;
    rotationZ = 0.0;
    scaling = 1.0;

    createGradient();
    createGLObject();
}
```

In the constructor, we start by calling QGLWidget::setFormat() to specify an OpenGL display context that supports antialiasing. Then we initialize the class's private variables. At the end, we call createGradient() to set up the QRadialGradient used to fill the background, and createGLObject() to create the OpenGL cube object. By doing all of this in the constructor, we obtain snappier results later on, when we need to redraw the scene.

```
void VowelCube::createGradient()
{
    gradient.setCoordinateMode(QGradient::ObjectBoundingMode);
```

```
        gradient.setCenter(0.45, 0.50);
        gradient.setFocalPoint(0.40, 0.45);
        gradient.setColorAt(0.0, QColor(105, 146, 182));
        gradient.setColorAt(0.4, QColor(81, 113, 150));
        gradient.setColorAt(0.8, QColor(16, 56, 121));
    }
```

In `createGradient()`, we simply set up the `QRadialGradient` to use different shades of blue. The call to `setCoordinateMode()` ensures that the coordinates specified for the center and focal points are adjusted to the size of the widget. The positions are specified as floating-point values between 0 and 1, where 0 corresponds to the focal point and 1 corresponds to the outline of the circle defined by the gradient.

```
    void VowelCube::createGLObject()
    {
        makeCurrent();

        glShadeModel(GL_FLAT);

        glObject = glGenLists(1);
        glNewList(glObject, GL_COMPILE);
        qglColor(QColor(255, 239, 191));
        glLineWidth(1.0);

        glBegin(GL_LINES);
        glVertex3f(+1.0, +1.0, -1.0);
        ...
        glVertex3f(-1.0, +1.0, +1.0);
        glEnd();

        glEndList();
    }
```

The `createGLObject()` creates an OpenGL list that stores the drawing of the lines that represent the vowel cube. The code is all standard OpenGL code, except for the `QGLWidget::makeCurrent()` call at the beginning, which ensures that we use the correct OpenGL context.

```
    VowelCube::~VowelCube()
    {
        makeCurrent();
        glDeleteLists(glObject, 1);
    }
```

In the destructor, we call `glDeleteLists()` to delete the OpenGL cube object that we created in the constructor. Again, we must call `makeCurrent()`.

```
    void VowelCube::paintEvent(QPaintEvent * /* event */)
    {
        QPainter painter(this);
        drawBackground(&painter);
        drawCube();
        drawLegend(&painter);
    }
```

In the paintEvent(), we set up a QPainter as we would normally do for a plain QWidget; then we draw the background, the cube, and the legend.

```
void VowelCube::drawBackground(QPainter *painter)
{
    painter->setPen(Qt::NoPen);
    painter->setBrush(gradient);
    painter->drawRect(rect());
}
```

Drawing the background is simply a matter of calling drawRect() with an appropriate brush.

The drawCube() function is the heart of the custom widget. We'll review it in two parts:

```
void VowelCube::drawCube()
{
    glPushAttrib(GL_ALL_ATTRIB_BITS);

    glMatrixMode(GL_PROJECTION);
    glPushMatrix();
    glLoadIdentity();
    GLfloat x = 3.0 * GLfloat(width()) / height();
    glOrtho(-x, +x, -3.0, +3.0, 4.0, 15.0);

    glMatrixMode(GL_MODELVIEW);
    glPushMatrix();
    glLoadIdentity();
    glTranslatef(0.0, 0.0, -10.0);
    glScalef(scaling, scaling, scaling);

    glRotatef(rotationX, 1.0, 0.0, 0.0);
    glRotatef(rotationY, 0.0, 1.0, 0.0);
    glRotatef(rotationZ, 0.0, 0.0, 1.0);

    glEnable(GL_MULTISAMPLE);
```

Because we have some OpenGL code between two pieces of code that use QPainter, we must be careful—specifically, we must save the OpenGL state that we change in the function and restore it after we are done. So we save the OpenGL attributes, the projection matrix, and the model view matrix before we change them. At the end, we set the GL_MULTISAMPLE option to enable antialiasing.

```
    glCallList(glObject);

    setFont(QFont("Times", 24));
    qglColor(QColor(255, 223, 127));

    renderText(+1.1, +1.1, +1.1, QChar('a'));
    renderText(-1.1, +1.1, +1.1, QChar('e'));
    renderText(+1.1, +1.1, -1.1, QChar('o'));
    renderText(-1.1, +1.1, -1.1, QChar(0x00F6));
    renderText(+1.1, -1.1, +1.1, QChar(0x0131));
    renderText(-1.1, -1.1, +1.1, QChar('i'));
```

```
        renderText(+1.1, -1.1, -1.1, QChar('u'));
        renderText(-1.1, -1.1, -1.1, QChar(0x00FC));

        glMatrixMode(GL_MODELVIEW);
        glPopMatrix();

        glMatrixMode(GL_PROJECTION);
        glPopMatrix();

        glPopAttrib();
    }
```

Next, we call `glCallList()` to draw the cube object. Then we set the font and color, and call `QGLWidget::renderText()` to draw the vowels at the corners of the cube. The Turkish vowels that fall outside the ASCII character range are specified using their Unicode value.

The `renderText()` function takes an (x, y, z) coordinate triple to position the text in model view coordinates. The text itself is not transformed.

```
    void VowelCube::drawLegend(QPainter *painter)
    {
        const int Margin = 11;
        const int Padding = 6;

        QTextDocument textDocument;
        textDocument.setDefaultStyleSheet("* { color: #FFEFEF }");
        textDocument.setHtml("<h4 align=\"center\">Vowel Categories</h4>"
                             "<p align=\"center\"><table width=\"100%\">"
                             "<tr><td>Open:<td>a<td>e<td>o<td>&ouml;"
                             ...
                             "</table>");
        textDocument.setTextWidth(textDocument.size().width());

        QRect rect(QPoint(0, 0), textDocument.size().toSize()
                                 + QSize(2 * Padding, 2 * Padding));
        painter->translate(width() - rect.width() - Margin,
                           height() - rect.height() - Margin);
        painter->setPen(QColor(255, 239, 239));
        painter->setBrush(QColor(255, 0, 0, 31));
        painter->drawRect(rect);

        painter->translate(Padding, Padding);
        textDocument.drawContents(painter);
    }
```

In `drawLegend()`, we set up a `QTextDocument` object with some HTML text that lists the Turkish vowel categories and vowels, and we render it on top of a semi-transparent blue rectangle.

The `VowelCube` widget also reimplements `mousePressEvent()`, `mouseMoveEvent()`, and `wheelEvent()`, but there is nothing special about these. Like in a standard Qt custom widget, we call `update()` whenever we want to schedule a repaint. For example, here is the code for `wheelEvent()`:

```
void VowelCube::wheelEvent(QWheelEvent *event)
{
    double numDegrees = -event->delta() / 8.0;
    double numSteps = numDegrees / 15.0;
    scaling *= std::pow(1.125, numSteps);
    update();
}
```

This completes our review of the example. In the `VowelCube`'s `paintEvent()` handler reimplementation, we used the following general pattern:

1. Create a `QPainter`.
2. Use the `QPainter` to draw the background.
3. Save the OpenGL state.
4. Draw the scene using OpenGL operations.
5. Restore the OpenGL state.
6. Use the `QPainter` to draw the foreground.
7. Destroy the `QPainter`.

There are other possibilities. For example, if we don't draw a background, we could do this:

1. Draw the scene using OpenGL operations.
2. Create a `QPainter`.
3. Use the `QPainter` to draw the foreground.
4. Destroy the `QPainter`.

This corresponds to the following code:

```
void VowelCube::paintEvent(QPaintEvent * /* event */)
{
    drawCube();
    drawLegend();
}

void VowelCube::drawCube()
{
    ...
}

void VowelCube::drawLegend()
{
    QPainter painter(this);
    ...
}
```

Notice that this time, we create the `QPainter` object locally in `drawLegend()`. The main advantage of this approach is that we don't need to save and restore the OpenGL state. However, out of the box, this won't work, because `QPainter` automatically clears the background before it starts painting, overwriting the

OpenGL scene. To prevent that, we must call `setAutoFillBackground(false)` in the widget's constructor.

Another interesting pattern occurs if we draw a background and a cube, but no foreground:

1. Create a `QPainter`.
2. Use the `QPainter` to draw the background.
3. Destroy the `QPainter`.
4. Draw the scene using OpenGL operations.

Again, we can avoid saving and restoring the OpenGL state. However, this won't work as is, because `QPainter` automatically calls `QGLWidget::swapBuffers()` in its destructor to make the result of drawing visible, and any OpenGL calls that occur after the `QPainter` destructor will go to the off-screen buffer and won't show up on-screen. To prevent that, we must call `setAutoBufferSwap(false)` in the widget's constructor and call `swapBuffer()` at the end of `paintEvent()`. For example:

```
void VowelCube::paintEvent(QPaintEvent * /* event */)
{
    drawBackground();
    drawCube();
    swapBuffers();
}

void VowelCube::drawBackground()
{
    QPainter painter(this);
    ...
}

void VowelCube::drawCube()
{
    ...
}
```

In summary, the most general approach is to create a `QPainter` in `paintEvent()` and to save and restore the state whenever we perform raw OpenGL operations. It is possible to avoid some state saving, provided we keep in mind the following points:

- `QPainter`'s constructor (or `QPainter::begin()`) automatically calls `glClear()` unless we called `setAutoFillBackground(false)` on the widget beforehand.
- `QPainter`'s destructor (or `QPainter::end()`) automatically calls `QGLWidget::swapBuffers()` to swap the visible buffer and the off-screen buffer unless we call `setAutoBufferSwap(false)` on the widget beforehand.
- While `QPainter` is active, we can interleave raw OpenGL commands, as long as we save the OpenGL state before issuing raw OpenGL commands and restore the OpenGL state afterward.

With these points it mind, combining OpenGL and `QPainter` is straightforward and gives us the best of `QPainter`'s and OpenGL's graphics capabilities.

Doing Overlays Using Framebuffer Objects

Often, we need to draw simple annotations on top of a complex 3D scene. If the scene is very complex, it may take several seconds to render it. To avoid rendering the scene repeatedly, whenever an annotation changes we could use X11 overlays or the built-in OpenGL support for overlays.

More recently, the availability of pbuffers and framebuffer objects has provided a more convenient and more flexible idiom for doing overlays. The basic idea is that we render the 3D scene onto an off-screen surface, which we bind to a texture. The texture is mapped onto the screen by drawing a rectangle, and the annotations are drawn on top. When the annotations change, we need to redraw only the rectangle and the annotations. Conceptually, this is very similar to what we did in Chapter 5 for the 2D `Plotter` widget.

To illustrate this technique, we will review the code of the Teapots application shown in Figure 20.3. The application consists of a single OpenGL window that shows an array of teapots and that lets the user draw a rubber band on top by clicking and dragging the mouse. The teapots do not move or change in any way, except when the window is resized. The implementation relies on a framebuffer object to store the teapot scene. A similar effect could be implemented using a pbuffer by substituting `QGLPixelBuffer` for `QGLFramebufferObject`.

```
class Teapots : public QGLWidget
{
    Q_OBJECT

public:
    Teapots(QWidget *parent = 0);
    ~Teapots();

protected:
    void initializeGL();
    void resizeGL(int width, int height);
    void paintGL();
    void mousePressEvent(QMouseEvent *event);
    void mouseMoveEvent(QMouseEvent *event);
    void mouseReleaseEvent(QMouseEvent *event);

private:
    void createGLTeapotObject();
    void drawTeapot(GLfloat x, GLfloat y, GLfloat ambientR,
                    GLfloat ambientG, GLfloat ambientB,
                    GLfloat diffuseR, GLfloat diffuseG,
                    GLfloat diffuseB, GLfloat specularR,
                    GLfloat specularG, GLfloat specularB,
                    GLfloat shininess);
    void drawTeapots();
```

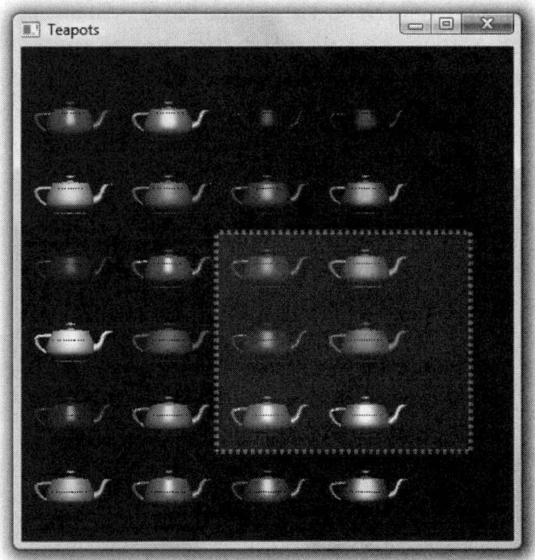

Figure 20.3. The Teapots application

```
    QGLFramebufferObject *fbObject;
    GLuint glTeapotObject;
    QPoint rubberBandCorner1;
    QPoint rubberBandCorner2;
    bool rubberBandIsShown;
};
```

The Teapots class is derived from QGLWidget and reimplements the high-level OpenGL handlers initializeGL(), resizeGL(), and paintGL(). It also reimplements mousePressEvent(), mouseMoveEvent(), and mouseReleaseEvent() to let the user draw a rubber band.

The private functions take care of creating the teapot object and of drawing teapots. The code is rather complex and is based on the teapots example in *OpenGL Programming Guide* by Jackie Neider, Tom Davis, and Mason Woo (Addison-Wesley, 1993). Since it is not directly relevant to our purposes, we will not present it here.

The private variables store the framebuffer object, the teapot object, the rubber band's corners, and whether the rubber band is visible.

```
Teapots::Teapots(QWidget *parent)
    : QGLWidget(parent)
{
    rubberBandIsShown = false;

    makeCurrent();
    fbObject = new QGLFramebufferObject(1024, 1024,
                                        QGLFramebufferObject::Depth);
    createGLTeapotObject();
}
```

The Teapots constructor initializes the rubberBandIsShown private variable, creates the framebuffer object, and creates the teapot object. We will skip the createGLTeapotObject() function since it is rather long and contains no Qt-relevant code.

```
Teapots::~Teapots()
{
    makeCurrent();
    delete fbObject;
    glDeleteLists(glTeapotObject, 1);
}
```

In the destructor, we release the resources associated with the framebuffer object and the teapot.

```
void Teapots::initializeGL()
{
    static const GLfloat ambient[] = { 0.0, 0.0, 0.0, 1.0 };
    static const GLfloat diffuse[] = { 1.0, 1.0, 1.0, 1.0 };
    static const GLfloat position[] = { 0.0, 3.0, 3.0, 0.0 };
    static const GLfloat lmodelAmbient[] = { 0.2, 0.2, 0.2, 1.0 };
    static const GLfloat localView[] = { 0.0 };

    glLightfv(GL_LIGHT0, GL_AMBIENT, ambient);
    glLightfv(GL_LIGHT0, GL_DIFFUSE, diffuse);
    glLightfv(GL_LIGHT0, GL_POSITION, position);
    glLightModelfv(GL_LIGHT_MODEL_AMBIENT, lmodelAmbient);
    glLightModelfv(GL_LIGHT_MODEL_LOCAL_VIEWER, localView);

    glFrontFace(GL_CW);
    glEnable(GL_LIGHTING);
    glEnable(GL_LIGHT0);
    glEnable(GL_AUTO_NORMAL);
    glEnable(GL_NORMALIZE);
    glEnable(GL_DEPTH_TEST);
    glDepthFunc(GL_LESS);
}
```

The initializeGL() function is reimplemented to set up the lighting model and to turn on various OpenGL features. The code is taken directly from the teapots example described in the *OpenGL Programming Guide* referred to earlier.

```
void Teapots::resizeGL(int width, int height)
{
    fbObject->bind();

    glDisable(GL_TEXTURE_2D);
    glEnable(GL_LIGHTING);
    glEnable(GL_DEPTH_TEST);

    glViewport(0, 0, width, height);
    glMatrixMode(GL_PROJECTION);
    glLoadIdentity();
    if (width <= height) {
        glOrtho(0.0, 20.0, 0.0, 20.0 * GLfloat(height) / GLfloat(width),
                -10.0, 10.0);
```

```
        } else {
            glOrtho(0.0, 20.0 * GLfloat(width) / GLfloat(height), 0.0, 20.0,
                    -10.0, 10.0);
        }
        glMatrixMode(GL_MODELVIEW);
        drawTeapots();

        fbObject->release();
    }
```

The `resizeGL()` function is reimplemented to redraw the teapot scene whenever the `Teapot` widget is resized. To render the teapots onto the framebuffer object, we call `QGLFramebufferObject::bind()` at the beginning of the function. Then, we set up some OpenGL features and the projection and model view matrices. The call to `drawTeapots()` near the end draws the teapots onto the framebuffer object. Finally, the call to `release()` unbinds the framebuffer object, ensuring that subsequent OpenGL drawing operations don't go to our framebuffer object.

```
    void Teapots::paintGL()
    {
        glDisable(GL_LIGHTING);
        glViewport(0, 0, width(), height());
        glMatrixMode(GL_PROJECTION);
        glLoadIdentity();
        glMatrixMode(GL_MODELVIEW);
        glLoadIdentity();
        glDisable(GL_DEPTH_TEST);

        glClear(GL_COLOR_BUFFER_BIT);
        glEnable(GL_TEXTURE_2D);
        glBindTexture(GL_TEXTURE_2D, fbObject->texture());
        glColor3f(1.0, 1.0, 1.0);
        GLfloat s = width() / GLfloat(fbObject->size().width());
        GLfloat t = height() / GLfloat(fbObject->size().height());

        glBegin(GL_QUADS);
        glTexCoord2f(0.0, 0.0);
        glVertex2f(-1.0, -1.0);
        glTexCoord2f(s, 0.0);
        glVertex2f(1.0, -1.0);
        glTexCoord2f(s, t);
        glVertex2f(1.0, 1.0);
        glTexCoord2f(0.0, t);
        glVertex2f(-1.0, 1.0);
        glEnd();
```

In `paintGL()`, we start by resetting the projection and model view matrices. Then we bind the framebuffer object to a texture, and draw a rectangle with the texture to cover the entire widget.

```
        if (rubberBandIsShown) {
            glMatrixMode(GL_PROJECTION);
            glOrtho(0, width(), height(), 0, 0, 100);
            glMatrixMode(GL_MODELVIEW);
```

```
        glDisable(GL_TEXTURE_2D);
        glEnable(GL_BLEND);
        glBlendFunc(GL_SRC_ALPHA, GL_ONE_MINUS_SRC_ALPHA);
        glLineWidth(4.0);
        glColor4f(1.0, 1.0, 1.0, 0.2);
        glRecti(rubberBandCorner1.x(), rubberBandCorner1.y(),
                rubberBandCorner2.x(), rubberBandCorner2.y());
        glColor4f(1.0, 1.0, 0.0, 0.5);
        glLineStipple(3, 0xAAAA);
        glEnable(GL_LINE_STIPPLE);

        glBegin(GL_LINE_LOOP);
        glVertex2i(rubberBandCorner1.x(), rubberBandCorner1.y());
        glVertex2i(rubberBandCorner2.x(), rubberBandCorner1.y());
        glVertex2i(rubberBandCorner2.x(), rubberBandCorner2.y());
        glVertex2i(rubberBandCorner1.x(), rubberBandCorner2.y());
        glEnd();

        glLineWidth(1.0);
        glDisable(GL_LINE_STIPPLE);
        glDisable(GL_BLEND);
    }
}
```

If the rubber band is currently shown, we draw it on top of the rectangle. The code is standard OpenGL.

```
void Teapots::mousePressEvent(QMouseEvent *event)
{
    rubberBandCorner1 = event->pos();
    rubberBandCorner2 = event->pos();
    rubberBandIsShown = true;
}

void Teapots::mouseMoveEvent(QMouseEvent *event)
{
    if (rubberBandIsShown) {
        rubberBandCorner2 = event->pos();
        updateGL();
    }
}

void Teapots::mouseReleaseEvent(QMouseEvent * /* event */)
{
    if (rubberBandIsShown) {
        rubberBandIsShown = false;
        updateGL();
    }
}
```

The mouse event handlers update the `rubberBandCorner1`, `rubberBandCorner2`, and `rubberBandIsShown` variables that represent the rubber band and call `updateGL()` to schedule a repaint of the scene. Repainting the scene is very quick, because `paintGL()` only draws a textured rectangle and a rubber band on top of it. The scene is rendered anew only when the user resizes the window, in `resizeGL()`.

Here's the application's `main()` function:

```
int main(int argc, char *argv[])
{
    QApplication app(argc, argv);

    if (!QGLFormat::hasOpenGL()) {
        std::cerr << "This system has no OpenGL support" << std::endl;
        return 1;
    }

    if (!QGLFramebufferObject::hasOpenGLFramebufferObjects()) {
        std::cerr << "This system has no framebuffer object support"
                  << std::endl;
        return 1;
    }

    Teapots teapots;
    teapots.setWindowTitle(QObject::tr("Teapots"));
    teapots.resize(400, 400);
    teapots.show();

    return app.exec();
}
```

The function gives an error message and terminates with an error code if the system has no OpenGL support, or if it has no framebuffer object support.

The Teapots example gives us a taste of how we can bind an off-screen surface to a texture and draw onto that surface using OpenGL commands. Many variations are possible; for example, we could use a `QPainter` instead of OpenGL commands to draw on a `QGLFramebufferObject` or `QGLPixelBuffer`. This provides a way to render transformed text in an OpenGL scene. Another common idiom is to use a framebuffer object to render a scene and then call `toImage()` on the result to produce a `QImage`. The examples included with Qt show many of these idioms in action, both for framebuffer objects and for pbuffers.

- *Extending Qt with Plugins*
- *Making Applications Plugin-Aware*
- *Writing Application Plugins*

21. Creating Plugins

Dynamic libraries (also called shared libraries or DLLs) are independent modules that are stored in a separate file on disk and can be accessed by multiple applications. Programs usually specify which dynamic libraries they need at link time, in which case the libraries are automatically loaded when the application starts. This approach usually involves adding the library and possibly its include path to the application's `.pro` file and including the relevant headers in the source files. For example:

```
LIBS        += -ldb_cxx
INCLUDEPATH += /usr/local/BerkeleyDB.4.2/include
```

The alternative is to dynamically load the library when it is required, and then resolve the symbols that we want to use from it. Qt provides the `QLibrary` class to achieve this in a platform-independent manner. Given the stem of a library's name, `QLibrary` searches the platform's standard locations for the library, looking for an appropriate file. For example, given the name `mimetype`, it will look for `mimetype.dll` on Windows, `mimetype.so` on Linux, and `mimetype.dylib` on Mac OS X.

Modern GUI applications can often be extended by the use of plugins. A plugin is a dynamic library that implements a particular interface to provide optional extra functionality. For example, in Chapter 5, we created a plugin to integrate a custom widget with *Qt Designer* (p. 117).

Qt recognizes its own set of plugin interfaces for various domains, including image formats, database drivers, widget styles, text encodings, and accessibility. This chapter's first section explains how to extend Qt with Qt plugins.

It is also possible to create application-specific plugins for particular Qt applications. Qt makes writing such plugins easy through its plugin framework, which adds crash safety and convenience to `QLibrary`. In the last two sections of this chapter, we show how to make an application support plugins and how to create a custom plugin for an application.

Extending Qt with Plugins

Qt can be extended with a variety of plugin types, the most common being database drivers, image formats, styles, and text codecs. For each type of plugin, we normally need at least two classes: a plugin wrapper class that implements the generic plugin API functions, and one or more handler classes that each implement the API for a particular type of plugin. The handlers are accessed through the wrapper class. These classes are shown in Figure 21.1.

Plugin Class	Handler Base Class
QAccessibleBridgePlugin	QAccessibleBridge
QAccessiblePlugin	QAccessibleInterface
QDecorationPlugin*	QDecoration*
QFontEnginePlugin	QAbstractFontEngine
QIconEnginePluginV2	QIconEngineV2
QImageIOPlugin	QImageIOHandler
QInputContextPlugin	QInputContext
QKbdDriverPlugin*	QWSKeyboardHandler*
QMouseDriverPlugin*	QWSMouseHandler*
QPictureFormatPlugin	N/A
QScreenDriverPlugin*	QScreen*
QScriptExtensionPlugin	N/A
QSqlDriverPlugin	QSqlDriver
QStylePlugin	QStyle
QTextCodecPlugin	QTextCodec

Figure 21.1. Qt plugin and handler classes

To demonstrate how to extend Qt with plugins, we will implement two plugins in this section. The first is a very simple `QStyle` plugin for the Bronze style we developed in Chapter 19. The second is a plugin that can read monochrome Windows cursor files.

Creating a `QStyle` plugin is very easy, provided we have already developed the style itself. All we need are three files: a `.pro` file that is rather different from the ones we have seen before, and small `.h` and `.cpp` files to provide a `QStylePlugin` subclass that acts as a wrapper for the style. We will begin with the `.h` file:

```
class BronzeStylePlugin : public QStylePlugin
{
```

*Available only in Qt/Embedded Linux.

```
public:
    QStringList keys() const;
    QStyle *create(const QString &key);
};
```

All plugins at least provide a `keys()` function and a `create()` function. The `keys()` function returns a list of the objects that the plugin can create. For style plugins, the keys are case-insensitive, so "mystyle" and "MyStyle" are treated the same. The `create()` function returns an object given a key; the key must be the same as one of those in the list returned by `keys()`.

The `.cpp` file is almost as small and simple as the `.h` file.

```
QStringList BronzeStylePlugin::keys() const
{
    return QStringList() << "Bronze";
}
```

The `keys()` function returns a list of styles provided by the plugin. Here, we offer only one style, called "Bronze".

```
QStyle *BronzeStylePlugin::create(const QString &key)
{
    if (key.toLower() == "bronze")
        return new BronzeStyle;
    return 0;
}
```

If the key is "Bronze" (regardless of case), we create a `BronzeStyle` object and return it.

At the end of the `.cpp` file, we must add the following macro to export the style properly:

```
Q_EXPORT_PLUGIN2(bronzestyleplugin, BronzeStylePlugin)
```

The first argument to `Q_EXPORT_PLUGIN2()` is the base name of the target library, excluding any extension, prefix, or version number. By default, `qmake` uses the name of the current directory as the base name; this can be overriden using the `TARGET` entry in the `.pro` file. The second argument to `Q_EXPORT_PLUGIN2()` is the plugin's class name.

The `.pro` file is different for plugins than for applications, so we will finish by looking at the Bronze style's `.pro` file:

```
TEMPLATE      = lib
CONFIG       += plugin
HEADERS       = ../bronze/bronzestyle.h \
                bronzestyleplugin.h
SOURCES       = ../bronze/bronzestyle.cpp \
                bronzestyleplugin.cpp
RESOURCES     = ../bronze/bronze.qrc
DESTDIR       = $$[QT_INSTALL_PLUGINS]/styles
```

By default, .pro files use the app template, but here we must specify the lib template because a plugin is a library, not a stand-alone application. The CONFIG line is used to tell Qt that the library is not just a plain library, but a plugin library. The DESTDIR specifies the directory where the plugin should go. All Qt plugins must go in the appropriate plugins subdirectory where Qt was installed; this path is built into qmake and available from the $$[QT_INSTALL_PLUGINS] variable. Since our plugin provides a new style, we put it in Qt's plugins/styles directory. The list of directory names and plugin types is available at http://doc.trolltech.com/4.3/plugins-howto.html.

Plugins built for Qt in release mode and debug mode are different, so if both versions of Qt are installed, it is wise to specify which one to use in the .pro file—for example, by adding the line

```
CONFIG += release
```

Once the Bronze style plugin is built, it is ready for use. Applications can use the style by specifying it in code. For example:

```
QApplication::setStyle("Bronze");
```

We can also use the style without changing the application's source code at all, simply by running the application with the -style option. For example:

```
./spreadsheet -style bronze
```

When *Qt Designer* is run, it automatically looks for plugins. If it finds a style plugin, it will offer the option to preview using the style in its Form|Preview in submenu.

Applications that use Qt plugins must be deployed with the plugins they are intended to use. Qt plugins must be placed in specific subdirectories (e.g., plugins/styles for custom styles). Qt applications search for plugins in the plugins directory in the directory where the application's executable resides. If we want to deploy Qt plugins in a different directory, the plugins search path can be augmented by calling QCoreApplication::addLibraryPath() at startup or by setting the QT_PLUGIN_PATH environment variable before launching the application.

Now that we have seen a very simple plugin, we will tackle one that is a bit more challenging: an image format plugin for Windows cursor (.cur) files. (The format is shown in Figure 21.2.) Windows cursor files can hold several images of the same cursor at different sizes. Once the cursor plugin is built and installed, Qt will be able to read .cur files and access individual cursors (e.g., through QImage, QImageReader, or QMovie), and will be able to write the cursors out in any of Qt's other image file formats, such as BMP, JPEG, and PNG.

New image format plugin wrappers must subclass QImageIOPlugin and reimplement a few virtual functions:

```
class CursorPlugin : public QImageIOPlugin
{
public:
```

```
    QStringList keys() const;
    Capabilities capabilities(QIODevice *device,
                              const QByteArray &format) const;
    QImageIOHandler *create(QIODevice *device,
                            const QByteArray &format) const;
};
```

The `keys()` function returns a list of the image formats the plugin supports. The `format` parameter of the `capabilities()` and `create()` functions can be assumed to have a value from that list.

```
QStringList CursorPlugin::keys() const
{
    return QStringList() << "cur";
}
```

Our plugin supports only one image format, so it returns a list with just one name. Ideally, the name should be the file extension used by the format. When dealing with formats with several extensions (such as `.jpg` and `.jpeg` for JPEG), we can return a list with several entries for the same format, one for each extension.

```
QImageIOPlugin::Capabilities
CursorPlugin::capabilities(QIODevice *device,
                           const QByteArray &format) const
{
    if (format == "cur")
        return CanRead;

    if (format.isEmpty()) {
        CursorHandler handler;
        handler.setDevice(device);
        if (handler.canRead())
            return CanRead;
    }

    return 0;
}
```

The `capabilities()` function returns what the image handler is capable of doing with the given image format. There are three capabilities (`CanRead`, `CanWrite`, and `CanReadIncremental`), and the return value is a bitwise OR of those that apply.

If the format is "cur", our implementation returns `CanRead`. If no format is given, we create a cursor handler and check whether it is capable of reading the data from the given device. The `canRead()` function only peeks at the data, seeing whether it recognizes the file, without changing the file pointer. A capability of 0 means that the file cannot be read or written by this handler.

```
QImageIOHandler *CursorPlugin::create(QIODevice *device,
                                      const QByteArray &format) const
{
    CursorHandler *handler = new CursorHandler;
    handler->setDevice(device);
    handler->setFormat(format);
```

```
        return handler;
    }
```

When a cursor file is opened (e.g., by `QImageReader`), the plugin wrapper's `create()` function will be called with the device pointer and with "cur" as the format. We create a `CursorHandler` instance and set it up with the specified device and format. The caller takes ownership of the handler and will delete it when it is no longer required. If multiple files are to be read, a fresh handler will be created for each one.

```
Q_EXPORT_PLUGIN2(cursorplugin, CursorPlugin)
```

At the end of the `.cpp` file, we use the `Q_EXPORT_PLUGIN2()` macro to ensure that Qt recognizes the plugin. The first parameter is an arbitrary name that we want to give to the plugin. The second parameter is the plugin class name.

Subclassing `QImageIOPlugin` is straightforward. The real work of the plugin is done in the handler. Image format handlers must subclass `QImageIOHandler` and reimplement some or all of its public functions. Let's start with the header:

```
class CursorHandler : public QImageIOHandler
{
public:
    CursorHandler();

    bool canRead() const;
    bool read(QImage *image);
    bool jumpToNextImage();
    int currentImageNumber() const;
    int imageCount() const;

private:
    enum State { BeforeHeader, BeforeImage, AfterLastImage, Error };

    void readHeaderIfNecessary() const;
    QBitArray readBitmap(int width, int height, QDataStream &in) const;
    void enterErrorState() const;

    mutable State state;
    mutable int currentImageNo;
    mutable int numImages;
};
```

The signatures of all the public functions are fixed. We have omitted several functions that we don't need to reimplement for a read-only handler, in particular `write()`. The member variables are declared with the `mutable` keyword because they are modified inside const functions.

```
CursorHandler::CursorHandler()
{
    state = BeforeHeader;
    currentImageNo = 0;
    numImages = 0;
}
```

When the handler is constructed, we begin by setting its state. We set the current cursor image number to the first cursor, but since we set `numImages` to 0 it is clear that we have no images yet.

```
bool CursorHandler::canRead() const
{
    if (state == BeforeHeader) {
        return device()->peek(4) == QByteArray("\0\0\2\0", 4);
    } else {
        return state != Error;
    }
}
```

The `canRead()` function can be called at any time to determine whether the image handler can read more data from the device. If the function is called before we have read any data, while we are still in the `BeforeHeader` state, we check for the particular signature that identifies Windows cursor files. The `QIODevice::peek()` call reads the first four bytes *without* changing the device's file pointer. If `canRead()` is called later on, we return `true` unless an error has occurred.

```
int CursorHandler::currentImageNumber() const
{
    return currentImageNo;
}
```

This trivial function returns the number of the cursor at which the device file pointer is positioned.

Once the handler is constructed, it is possible for the user to call any of its public functions, in any order. This is a potential problem since we must assume that we can only read serially, so we need to read the file header once before doing anything else. We solve the problem by calling the `readHeaderIfNecessary()` function in those functions that depend on the header having been read.

```
int CursorHandler::imageCount() const
{
    readHeaderIfNecessary();
    return numImages;
}
```

This function returns the number of images in the file. For a valid file where no reading errors have occurred, it will return a count of at least 1.

The next function is quite involved, so we will review it in pieces:

```
bool CursorHandler::read(QImage *image)
{
    readHeaderIfNecessary();

    if (state != BeforeImage)
        return false;
```

The `read()` function reads the data for whichever image begins at the current device pointer position. If the file's header is read successfully, or after an image

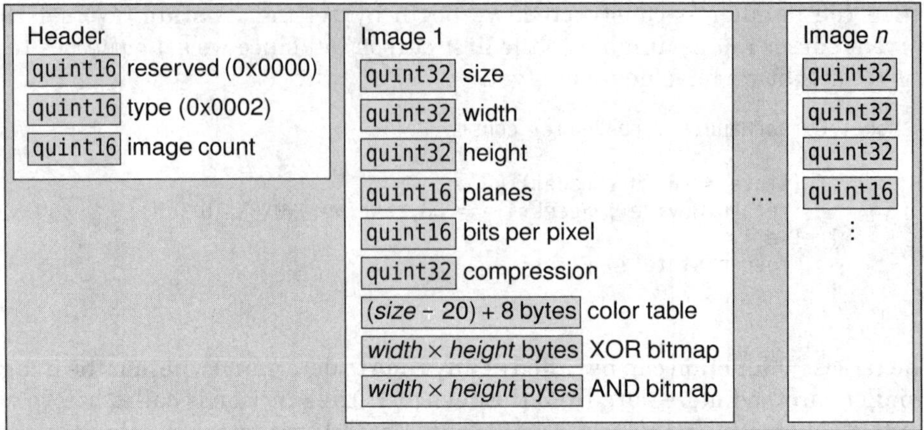

Figure 21.2. The .cur file format

has been read and the device pointer is at the start of another image, we can read the next image.

```
quint32 size;
quint32 width;
quint32 height;
quint16 numPlanes;
quint16 bitsPerPixel;
quint32 compression;

QDataStream in(device());
in.setByteOrder(QDataStream::LittleEndian);
in >> size;
if (size != 40) {
    enterErrorState();
    return false;
}
in >> width >> height >> numPlanes >> bitsPerPixel >> compression;
height /= 2;

if (numPlanes != 1 || bitsPerPixel != 1 || compression != 0) {
    enterErrorState();
    return false;
}

in.skipRawData((size - 20) + 8);
```

We create a QDataStream to read the device. We must set the byte order to match that specified by the .cur file format specification. There is no need to set a QDataStream version number since the format of integers and floating-point numbers does not vary between data stream versions. Next, we read in various items of cursor header data, and we skip the irrelevant parts of the header and the 8-byte color table using QDataStream::skipRawData().

We must account for all the format's idiosyncrasies—for example, halving the height because the `.cur` format gives a height that is twice as high as the actual image's height. The `bitsPerPixel` and `compression` values are always 1 and 0 in a monochrome `.cur` file. If we have any problems, we call `enterErrorState()` and return `false`.

```
    QBitArray xorBitmap = readBitmap(width, height, in);
    QBitArray andBitmap = readBitmap(width, height, in);

    if (in.status() != QDataStream::Ok) {
        enterErrorState();
        return false;
    }
```

The next items in the file are two bitmaps, one an XOR mask and the other an AND mask. We read these into `QBitArray`s rather than into `QBitmap`s. A `QBitmap` is a class designed to be drawn on and painted on-screen, but what we need here is a plain array of bits.

When we are done with reading the file, we check the `QDataStream`'s status. This works because if a `QDataStream` enters an error state, it stays in that state and can only return zeros. For example, if reading fails on the first bit array, the attempt to read the second will result in an empty `QBitArray`.

```
    *image = QImage(width, height, QImage::Format_ARGB32);

    for (int i = 0; i < int(height); ++i) {
        for (int j = 0; j < int(width); ++j) {
            QRgb color;
            int bit = (i * width) + j;

            if (andBitmap.testBit(bit)) {
                if (xorBitmap.testBit(bit)) {
                    color = 0x7F7F7F7F;
                } else {
                    color = 0x00FFFFFF;
                }
            } else {
                if (xorBitmap.testBit(bit)) {
                    color = 0xFFFFFFFF;
                } else {
                    color = 0xFF000000;
                }
            }
            image->setPixel(j, i, color);
        }
    }
```

We construct a new `QImage` of the correct size and assign it to `*image`. Then we iterate over every pixel in the XOR and AND bit arrays and convert them into 32-bit ARGB color specifications. The AND and XOR bit arrays are used as shown in the following table to obtain the color of each cursor pixel:

AND	XOR	Result
1	1	Inverted background pixel
1	0	Transparent pixel
0	1	White pixel
0	0	Black pixel

Black, white, and transparent pixels are no problem, but there is no way to obtain an inverted background pixel using an ARGB color specification without knowing the color of the original background pixel. As a substitute, we use a semi-transparent gray color (`0x7F7F7F7F`).

```
    ++currentImageNo;
    if (currentImageNo == numImages)
        state = AfterLastImage;
    return true;
}
```

Once we have finished reading the image, we update the current image number and update the state if we have reached the last image. At that point, the device will be positioned at the next image or at the end of the file.

```
bool CursorHandler::jumpToNextImage()
{
    QImage image;
    return read(&image);
}
```

The `jumpToNextImage()` function is used to skip an image. For simplicity, we simply call `read()` and ignore the resulting `QImage`. A more efficient implementation would use the information stored in the `.cur` file header to skip directly to the appropriate offset in the file.

```
void CursorHandler::readHeaderIfNecessary() const
{
    if (state != BeforeHeader)
        return;

    quint16 reserved;
    quint16 type;
    quint16 count;

    QDataStream in(device());
    in.setByteOrder(QDataStream::LittleEndian);

    in >> reserved >> type >> count;
    in.skipRawData(16 * count);

    if (in.status() != QDataStream::Ok || reserved != 0
            || type != 2 || count == 0) {
        enterErrorState();
        return;
    }
```

```
        state = BeforeImage;
        currentImageNo = 0;
        numImages = int(count);
    }
```

The `readHeaderIfNecessary()` private function is called from `imageCount()` and `read()`. If the file's header has already been read, the state is not `BeforeHeader` and we return immediately. Otherwise, we open a data stream on the device, read in some generic data (including the number of cursors in the file), and set the state to `BeforeImage`. At the end, the device's file pointer is positioned before the first image.

```
void CursorHandler::enterErrorState() const
{
    state = Error;
    currentImageNo = 0;
    numImages = 0;
}
```

If an error occurs, we assume that there are no valid images and set the state to `Error`. Once in the `Error` state, the handler's state cannot change.

```
QBitArray CursorHandler::readBitmap(int width, int height,
                                    QDataStream &in) const
{
    QBitArray bitmap(width * height);
    quint32 word = 0;
    quint8 byte;

    for (int i = 0; i < height; ++i) {
        for (int j = 0; j < width; ++j) {
            if ((j % 32) == 0) {
                word = 0;
                for (int k = 0; k < 4; ++k) {
                    in >> byte;
                    word = (word << 8) | byte;
                }
            }

            bitmap.setBit(((height - i - 1) * width) + j,
                          word & 0x80000000);
            word <<= 1;
        }
    }
    return bitmap;
}
```

The `readBitmap()` function is used to read a cursor's AND and XOR masks. These masks have two unusual features. First, they store the rows from bottom to top, instead of the more common top-to-bottom approach. Second, the endianness of the data appears to be reversed from that used everywhere else in `.cur` files. In view of this, we must invert the *y*-coordinate in the `setBit()` call, and we read in the mask values one byte at a time, bit-shifting and masking to extract their correct values.

To build the plugin, we must use a `.pro` file that is very similar to the one we used for the Bronze style plugin shown earlier (p. 493):

```
TEMPLATE      = lib
CONFIG       += plugin
HEADERS       = cursorhandler.h \
                cursorplugin.h
SOURCES       = cursorhandler.cpp \
                cursorplugin.cpp
DESTDIR       = $$[QT_INSTALL_PLUGINS]/imageformats
```

This completes the Windows cursor plugin. Plugins for other image formats would follow the same pattern, although some might implement more of the `QImageIOHandler` API, in particular the functions used for writing images. Plugins of other kinds follow the pattern of having a plugin wrapper that exports one or several handlers that provide the underlying functionality.

Making Applications Plugin-Aware

An application plugin is a dynamic library that implements one or more *interfaces.* An interface is a class that consists exclusively of pure virtual functions. The communication between the application and the plugins is done through the interface's virtual table. In this section, we will focus on how to use a plugin in a Qt application through its interfaces, and in the next section we will show how to implement a plugin.

To provide a concrete example, we will create the simple Text Art application shown in Figure 21.3. The text effects are provided by plugins; the application retrieves the list of text effects provided by each plugin and iterates over them to show each one as an item in a `QListWidget`.

The Text Art application defines one interface:

```
class TextArtInterface
{
public:
    virtual ~TextArtInterface() { }

    virtual QStringList effects() const = 0;
    virtual QPixmap applyEffect(const QString &effect,
                                const QString &text,
                                const QFont &font, const QSize &size,
                                const QPen &pen,
                                const QBrush &brush) = 0;
};

Q_DECLARE_INTERFACE(TextArtInterface,
                    "com.software-inc.TextArt.TextArtInterface/1.0")
```

An interface class normally declares a virtual destructor, a virtual function that returns a `QStringList`, and one or more other virtual functions. The destructor is there primarily to silence the compiler, which might otherwise complain about

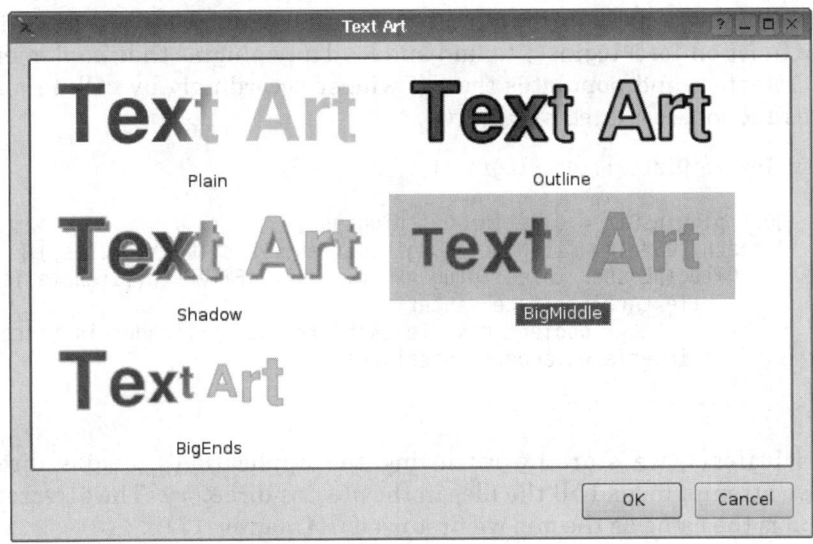

Figure 21.3. The Text Art application

the lack of a virtual destructor in a class that has virtual functions. In this example, the `effects()` function returns a list of the text effects the plugin can provide. We can think of this list as a list of keys. Every time we call one of the other functions, we pass one of these keys as first argument, making it possible to implement multiple effects in one plugin.

At the end, we use the `Q_DECLARE_INTERFACE()` macro to associate an identifier to the interface. The identifier normally has four components: an inverted domain name specifying the creator of the interface, the name of the application, the name of the interface, and a version number. Whenever we alter the interface (e.g., by adding a virtual function or changing the signature of an existing function), we must remember to increase the version number; otherwise, the application might crash trying to access an outdated plugin.

The application is implemented in a class called `TextArtDialog`. We will show only the code that is relevant to making it plugin-aware. Let's start with the constructor:

```
TextArtDialog::TextArtDialog(const QString &text, QWidget *parent)
    : QDialog(parent)
{
    listWidget = new QListWidget;
    listWidget->setViewMode(QListWidget::IconMode);
    listWidget->setMovement(QListWidget::Static);
    listWidget->setIconSize(QSize(260, 80));
    ...
    loadPlugins();
    populateListWidget(text);
    ...
}
```

The constructor creates a QListWidget to list the available effects. It calls the private function loadPlugins() to find and load any plugins that implement the TextArtInterface and populates the list widget accordingly by calling another private function, populateListWidget().

```
void TextArtDialog::loadPlugins()
{
    QDir pluginsDir = directoryOf("plugins");
    foreach (QString fileName, pluginsDir.entryList(QDir::Files)) {
        QPluginLoader loader(pluginsDir.absoluteFilePath(fileName));
        if (TextArtInterface *interface =
                    qobject_cast<TextArtInterface *>(loader.instance()))
            interfaces.append(interface);
    }
}
```

In loadPlugins(), we start by retrieving the application's plugins directory. Then we attempt to load all the files in the plugins directory. The directoryOf() function is the same as the one we first used in Chapter 17 (p. 410).

If the file we try to load is a Qt plugin that uses the same version of Qt as the application, QPluginLoader::instance() will return a QObject * that points to a Qt plugin. We use qobject_cast<T>() to check whether the plugin implements the TextArtInterface. Each time the cast is successful, we add the interface to the TextArtDialog's list of interfaces (of type QList<TextArtInterface *>).

Some applications may want to load two or more different interfaces. In such cases, the code for obtaining the interfaces would look more like this:

```
QObject *plugin = loader.instance();
if (TextArtInterface *i = qobject_cast<TextArtInterface *>(plugin))
    textArtInterfaces.append(i);
if (BorderArtInterface *i = qobject_cast<BorderArtInterface *>(plugin))
    borderArtInterfaces.append(i);
if (TextureInterface *i = qobject_cast<TextureInterface *>(plugin))
    textureInterfaces.append(i);
```

The same plugin may successfully cast to more than one interface pointer if it uses multiple inheritance.

```
void TextArtDialog::populateListWidget(const QString &text)
{
    QFont font("Helvetica", iconSize.height(), QFont::Bold);
    QSize iconSize = listWidget->iconSize();
    QPen pen(QColor("darkseagreen"));

    QLinearGradient gradient(0, 0, iconSize.width() / 2,
                             iconSize.height() / 2);
    gradient.setColorAt(0.0, QColor("darkolivegreen"));
    gradient.setColorAt(0.8, QColor("darkgreen"));
    gradient.setColorAt(1.0, QColor("lightgreen"));

    foreach (TextArtInterface *interface, interfaces) {
        foreach (QString effect, interface->effects()) {
```

```
            QListWidgetItem *item = new QListWidgetItem(effect,
                                                        listWidget);
            QPixmap pixmap = interface->applyEffect(effect, text, font,
                                                    iconSize, pen,
                                                    gradient);
            item->setData(Qt::DecorationRole, pixmap);
        }
    }
    listWidget->setCurrentRow(0);
}
```

The populateListWidget() function begins by creating some variables to pass to the applyEffect() function, in particular a font, a pen, and a linear gradient. It then iterates over every TextArtInterface that was found by loadPlugins(). For each effect provided by each interface, a new QListWidgetItem is created with its text set to the name of the effect, and with a QPixmap created using applyEffect().

In this section, we have seen how to load plugins by calling loadPlugins() in the constructor, and how to make use of them in populateListWidget(). The code copes gracefully whether there are no plugins providing TextArtInterfaces, just one, or more than one. Furthermore, additional plugins could be added later: Every time the application starts up, it loads whatever plugins it finds that provide the interfaces it wants. This makes it easy to extend the application's functionality without changing the application itself.

Writing Application Plugins

An application plugin is a subclass of QObject and of the interfaces it wants to provide. The examples that accompany this book includes two plugins for the Text Art application presented in the preceding section, to show that the application correctly handles multiple plugins.

Here, we will review the code for only one of them, the Basic Effects plugin. We will assume that the plugin's source code is located in a directory called basiceffectsplugin and that the Text Art application is located in a parallel directory called textart. Here's the declaration of the plugin class:

```
class BasicEffectsPlugin : public QObject, public TextArtInterface
{
    Q_OBJECT
    Q_INTERFACES(TextArtInterface)

public:
    QStringList effects() const;
    QPixmap applyEffect(const QString &effect, const QString &text,
                        const QFont &font, const QSize &size,
                        const QPen &pen, const QBrush &brush);
};
```

The plugin implements only one interface, `TextArtInterface`. In addition to `Q_OBJECT`, we must use the `Q_INTERFACES()` macro for each interface that is subclassed to ensure smooth cooperation between `moc` and `qobject_cast<T>()`.

```
QStringList BasicEffectsPlugin::effects() const
{
    return QStringList() << "Plain" << "Outline" << "Shadow";
}
```

The `effects()` function returns a list of text effects supported by the plugin. This plugin supports three effects, so we just return a list containing the name of each one.

The `applyEffect()` function provides the plugin's functionality and is slightly involved, so we will review it in pieces.

```
QPixmap BasicEffectsPlugin::applyEffect(const QString &effect,
        const QString &text, const QFont &font, const QSize &size,
        const QPen &pen, const QBrush &brush)
{
    QFont myFont = font;
    QFontMetrics metrics(myFont);
    while ((metrics.width(text) > size.width()
            || metrics.height() > size.height())
           && myFont.pointSize() > 9) {
        myFont.setPointSize(myFont.pointSize() - 1);
        metrics = QFontMetrics(myFont);
    }
```

We want to ensure that the given text will fit in the specified size, if possible. For this reason, we use the font's metrics to see whether the text is too large to fit, and if it is, we enter a loop where we reduce the point size until we find a size that will fit, or until we reach 9 points, our fixed minimum size.

```
    QPixmap pixmap(size);

    QPainter painter(&pixmap);
    painter.setFont(myFont);
    painter.setPen(pen);
    painter.setBrush(brush);
    painter.setRenderHint(QPainter::Antialiasing, true);
    painter.setRenderHint(QPainter::TextAntialiasing, true);
    painter.setRenderHint(QPainter::SmoothPixmapTransform, true);
    painter.eraseRect(pixmap.rect());
```

We create a pixmap of the required size and a painter to paint onto the pixmap. We also set some render hints to ensure the smoothest possible results. The call to `eraseRect()` clears the pixmap with the background color.

```
    if (effect == "Plain") {
        painter.setPen(Qt::NoPen);
    } else if (effect == "Outline") {
        QPen pen(Qt::black);
        pen.setWidthF(2.5);
```

```
            painter.setPen(pen);
        } else if (effect == "Shadow") {
            QPainterPath path;
            painter.setBrush(Qt::darkGray);
            path.addText(((size.width() - metrics.width(text)) / 2) + 3,
                         (size.height() - metrics.descent()) + 3, myFont,
                         text);
            painter.drawPath(path);
            painter.setBrush(brush);
        }
```

For the "Plain" effect, no outline is required. For the "Outline" effect, we ignore the original pen and create our own black pen with a 2.5-pixel width. For the "Shadow" effect, we need to draw the shadow first so that the text can be painted on top of it.

```
        QPainterPath path;
        path.addText((size.width() - metrics.width(text)) / 2,
                     size.height() - metrics.descent(), myFont, text);
        painter.drawPath(path);

        return pixmap;
    }
```

We now have the pen and brushes set appropriately for each text effect, and in the "Shadow" effect case we have drawn the shadow. We are now ready to render the text. The text is horizontally centered and drawn far enough above the bottom of the pixmap to allow room for descenders.

```
    Q_EXPORT_PLUGIN2(basiceffectsplugin, BasicEffectsPlugin)
```

At the end of the .cpp file, we use the Q_EXPORT_PLUGIN2() macro to make the plugin available to Qt.

The .pro file is similar to the one we used for the Bronze style plugin earlier in this chapter (p. 493):

```
    TEMPLATE      = lib
    CONFIG       += plugin
    HEADERS       = ../textart/textartinterface.h \
                    basiceffectsplugin.h
    SOURCES       = basiceffectsplugin.cpp
    DESTDIR       = ../textart/plugins
```

If this chapter has whetted your appetite for application plugins, you might like to study the more advanced Plug & Paint example provided with Qt. The application supports three different interfaces and includes a useful Plugin Information dialog that lists the plugins and interfaces that are available to the application.

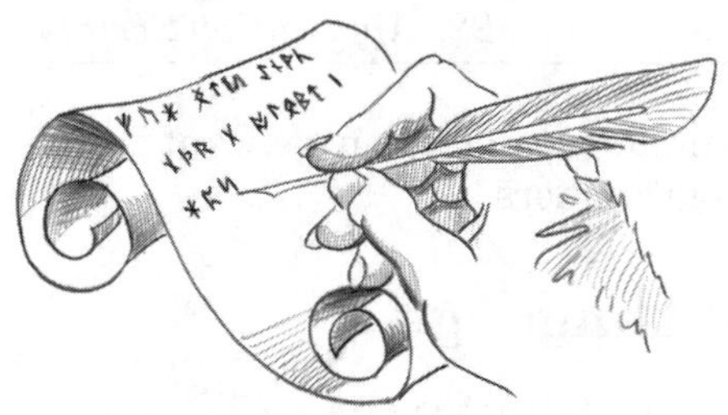

- *Overview of the ECMAScript Language*
- *Extending Qt Applications with Scripts*
- *Implementing GUI Extensions Using Scripts*
- *Automating Tasks through Scripting*

22. Application Scripting

Scripts are programs written in an interpreted language that extend the facilities of an existing system. Some scripts are run as stand-alone applications, whereas others execute embedded in applications. Starting with version 4.3, Qt includes *QtScript*, a module that can be used to make Qt applications scriptable using ECMAScript, the standardized version of JavaScript. This module is a complete rewrite of the earlier Trolltech product Qt Script for Applications (QSA) and provides full support for ECMAScript Edition 3.

ECMAScript is the official name of the language standardized by Ecma International. It forms the basis of JavaScript (Mozilla), JScript (Microsoft), and ActionScript (Adobe). Although the language's syntax is superficially similar to C++ and Java, the underlying concepts are radically different and set it apart from most other object-oriented programming languages. In the first section of this chapter, we will quickly review the ECMAScript language and show how to run ECMAScript code using Qt. If you already know JavaScript or any other ECMAScript-based language, you can probably just skim this section.

In the second section, we will see how to add scripting support to a Qt application. This makes it possible for users to add their own functionality in addition to what the application already provides. This approach is also frequently used to make it easier to support users; technical support staff can supply bug fixes and workarounds in the form of scripts.

In the third section, we will show how to develop GUI front-ends by combining ECMAScript code and forms created using *Qt Designer*. This technique is appealing to developers who dislike the "compile, link, run" cycle associated with C++ development and prefer the scripting approach. It also enables users with JavaScript experience to design fully functional GUI interfaces without having to learn C++.

Finally, in the last section, we will show how to develop scripts that rely on C++ components as part of their processing. This can be done with arbitrary C++ and C++/Qt components, which don't need to have been designed with scriptability in mind. This approach is especially useful when several programs need to be written using the same basic components, or when we want to make C++ functionality available to non-C++ programmers.

Overview of the ECMAScript Language

This section presents a brief introduction to the ECMAScript language so that you can understand the code snippets presented in the rest of the chapter and can start writing your own scripts. The Mozilla Foundation's web site hosts a more complete tutorial at `http://developer.mozilla.org/en/docs/Core_JavaScript_1.5_Guide`, and David Flanagan's *JavaScript: The Definitive Guide* (O'Reilly, 2006) is recommended both as a tutorial and as a reference manual. The official ECMAScript specification is available online at `http://www.ecma-international.org/publications/standards/Ecma-262.htm`.

The basic ECMAScript control structures—`if` statements, `for` loops, and `while` loops—are the same as in C++ and Java. ECMAScript also provides more or less the same assignment, relational, and arithmetic operators. ECMAScript strings support concatenation with + and appending with +=.

To get a feel for the ECMAScript syntax, we will start by studying the following program, which prints a list of all the prime numbers less than 1000:

```
const MAX = 1000;
var isPrime = new Array(MAX);

for (var i = 2; i < MAX; ++i)
    isPrime[i] = true;

for (var i = 2; i < MAX; ++i) {
    if (isPrime[i]) {
        for (var j = i; i * j < MAX; ++j)
            isPrime[i * j] = false;
    }
}

for (var i = 2; i < MAX; ++i) {
    if (isPrime[i])
        print(i);
}
```

From a C++ programmer's perspective, probably the most striking feature of ECMAScript is that variables are not explicitly typed; the `var` keyword is all that is required to declare a variable. Read-only variables are declared with `const` instead of `var`. Another noteworthy feature of the preceding program is that there is no `main()` function. Instead, code that is located outside any function is executed immediately, starting from the top of the file and working down to the bottom.

Unlike in C++, semicolons at the end of statements are generally optional in ECMAScript. Using sophisticated rules, the interpreter can insert most missing semicolons itself. Despite this, typing semicolons ourselves is recommended, to avoid unpleasant surprises.

To run the above program, we can use the `qscript` interpreter located in Qt's `examples/script/qscript` directory. If the interpreter is called with a file name as a command-line argument, the file is taken to be ECMAScript and is executed; otherwise, an interactive session begins.

If we don't provide an initial value when declaring a variable with `var`, the default value is `undefined`, a special value of type `Undefined`. We can later assign any value of any type to the variable using the assignment operator (`=`). Consider the following examples:

```
var x;
typeof x;              // returns "undefined"

x = null;
typeof x;              // returns "null"

x = true;
typeof x;              // returns "boolean"

x = 5;
typeof x;              // returns "number"

x = "Hello";
typeof x;              // returns "string"
```

The `typeof` operator returns a lowercase string representation of the data type associated with the value stored in a variable. ECMAScript defines five primitive data types: `Undefined`, `Null`, `Boolean`, `Number`, and `String`. The `Undefined` and `Null` types are special types for the `undefined` and `null` constants, respectively. The `Boolean` type consists of two values, `true` and `false`. The `Number` type stores floating-point numbers. The `String` type stores Unicode strings.

Variables can also store objects and functions, corresponding to the data types `Object` and `Function`. For example:

```
x = new Array(10);
typeof x;              // returns "object"

x = print;
typeof x;              // returns "function"
```

Like Java, ECMAScript distinguishes between primitive data types and object types. Primitive data types behave like C++ value types, such as `int` and `QString`. These are created without the `new` operator and are copied by value. In contrast, object types must be created using the `new` operator, and variables of these types store only a reference (a pointer) to the object. When allocating objects with `new`, we do not need to worry about releasing their memory, since the garbage collector does this automatically.

If we assign a value to a variable without declaring it first using the `var` keyword, the variable will be created as a global variable. And if we try to read the value of a variable that doesn't exist, we get a ReferenceError exception. We can catch the exception using a try ... catch statement, as follows:

```
try {
    print(y);
} catch (e) {
    print(e.name + ": " + e.message);
}
```

If the variable y does not exist, the message "ReferenceError: y is not defined" is printed on the console.

If undefined variables can cause havoc in our programs, so can variables that are defined but that hold the undefined constant—the default value if no initializer is provided when declaring a variable using var. To test for undefined, we can use the strict comparison operators === or !==. For example:

```
var x;
...
var y = 0;
if (x !== undefined)
    y = x;
```

The familiar == and != comparison operators are also available in ECMAScript, but unlike === and !==, they sometimes return true when the compared values have different types. For example, 24 == "24" and null == undefined return true, whereas 24 === "24" and null === undefined return false.

We will now review a more complex program that illustrates how to define our own functions in ECMAScript:

```
function square(x)
{
    return x * x;
}

function sumOfSquares(array)
{
    var result = 0;
    for (var i = 0; i < array.length; ++i)
        result += square(array[i]);
    return result;
}

var array = new Array(100);
for (var i = 0; i < array.length; ++i)
    array[i] = (i * 257) % 101;

print(sumOfSquares(array));
```

Functions are defined using the function keyword. In keeping with ECMAScript's dynamic nature, the parameters are declared with no type, and the function has no explicit return type.

By looking at the code, we can guess that `square()` should be called with a `Number` and that `sumOfSquares()` should be called with an `Array` object, but this doesn't have to be the case. For example, `square("7")` will return 49, because ECMAScript's multiplication operator will convert strings to numbers in a numeric context. Similarly, the `sumOfSquare()` function will work not only for `Array` objects but also for other objects that have a similar interface.

In general, ECMAScript applies the *duck typing* principle: "If it walks like a duck and quacks like a duck, it must be a duck." This stands in contrast to the strong typing used by C++ and Java, where parameter types must be declared and arguments must match the declared types.

In the preceding example, `sumOfSquares()` was hard-coded to apply `square()` on each element of the array. We can make it more flexible by letting it accept a unary function as the second argument and renaming it `sum()`:

```
function sum(array, unaryFunc)
{
    var result = 0;
    for (var i = 0; i < array.length; ++i)
        result += unaryFunc(array[i]);
    return result;
}

var array = new Array(100);
for (var i = 0; i < array.length; ++i)
    array[i] = (i * 257) % 101;

print(sum(array, square));
```

The call `sum(array, square)` is equivalent to `sumOfSquares(array)`. Instead of defining a `square()` function, we can also pass an anonymous function to `sum()`:

```
print(sum(array, function(x) { return x * x; }));
```

And instead of defining an `array` variable, we can pass an array literal:

```
print(sum([4, 8, 11, 15], function(x) { return x * x; }));
```

ECMAScript lets us supply more arguments to a function than there are parameters declared. The extra arguments are accessible through the `arguments` array. Consider the following example:

```
function sum(unaryFunc)
{
    var result = 0;
    for (var i = 1; i < arguments.length; ++i)
        result += unaryFunc(arguments[i]);
    return result;
}

print(sum(square, 1, 2, 3, 4, 5, 6));
```

Here, the `sum()` function is defined to take a variable number of arguments. The first argument is the function that we want to apply. The other arguments are the numbers that we want to sum. When iterating over the `arguments` array, we must skip the item at index position 0 because it corresponds to `unaryFunc`, the unary function. We could also omit the `unaryFunc` parameter from the parameter list and extract it from the `arguments` array:

```
function sum()
{
    var unaryFunc = arguments[0];
    var result = 0;
    for (var i = 1; i < arguments.length; ++i)
        result += unaryFunc(arguments[i]);
    return result;
}
```

The `arguments` array can be used to overload the behavior of functions based on the types of the arguments or on their number. For example, suppose that we want to let `sum()` take an optional unary argument followed by a list of numbers, allowing us to invoke it as follows:

```
print(sum(1, 2, 3, 4, 5, 6));
print(sum(square, 1, 2, 3, 4, 5, 6));
```

Here's how we can implement `sum()` to support this:

```
function sum()
{
    var unaryFunc = function(x) { return x; };
    var i = 0;

    if (typeof arguments[0] == "function") {
        unaryFunc = arguments[0];
        i = 1;
    }

    var result = 0;
    while (i < arguments.length)
        result += unaryFunc(arguments[i++]);
    return result;
}
```

If we supply a function as the first argument, that function is applied to each number before it is added to the sum; otherwise, we use the identity function `function(x) { return x; }`.

For C++ programmers, arguably the most difficult aspect of ECMAScript is its object model. ECMAScript is an *object-based* object-oriented language, setting it apart from C++, C#, Java, Simula, and Smalltalk, which are all class-based. Instead of a class concept, ECMAScript provides us with lower-level mechanisms that let us achieve the same results.

The first mechanism that lets us implement classes in ECMAScript is that of a constructor. A *constructor* is a function that can be invoked using the `new` operator. For example, here is a constructor for a `Shape` object:

```
function Shape(x, y) {
    this.x = x;
    this.y = y;
}
```

The `Shape` constructor has two parameters and initializes the new object's `x` and `y` properties (member variables) based on the values passed to the constructor. The `this` keyword refers to the object being created. In ECMAScript, an object is essentially a collection of properties; properties can be added, removed, or modified at any time. A property is created the first time it is set, so when we assign to `this.x` and `this.y` in the constructor, the `x` and `y` properties are created as a result.

A common mistake for C++ and Java developers is to forget the `this` keyword when accessing object properties. In the preceding example, this would have been unlikely, because a statement such as `x = x` would have looked very suspicious, but in other examples this would have led to the creation of spurious global variables.

To instantiate a `Shape` object, we use the `new` operator as follows:

```
var shape = new Shape(10, 20);
```

If we use the `typeof` operator on the `shape` variable, we obtain `Object`, not `Shape`, as the data type. If we want to determine whether an object has been created using the `Shape` constructor, we can use the `instanceof` operator:

```
var array = new Array(100);
array instanceof Shape;                // returns false

var shape = new Shape(10, 20);
shape instanceof Shape;                // returns true
```

ECMAScript lets any function serve as a constructor. However, if the function doesn't perform any modifications to the `this` object, it doesn't make much sense to invoke it as a constructor. Conversely, a constructor can be invoked as a plain function, but again this rarely makes sense.

In addition to the primitive data types, ECMAScript provides built-in constructors that let us instantiate fundamental object types, notably `Array`, `Date`, and `RegExp`. Other constructors correspond to the primitive data types, allowing us to create objects that store primitive values. The `valueOf()` member function lets us retrieve the primitive value stored in the object. For example:

```
var boolObj = new Boolean(true);
typeof boolObj;                        // returns "object"

var boolVal = boolObj.valueOf();
typeof boolVal;                        // returns "boolean"
```

Figure 22.1 lists the built-in global constants, functions, and objects provided by ECMAScript. In the next section, we will see how to supplement this built-in functionality with additional, application-specific components written in C++.

We have seen how to define a constructor in ECMAScript and how to add member variables to the constructed object. Normally, we also want to define member functions. Because functions are treated as first-class citizens in ECMAScript, this turns out to be surprisingly easy. Here's a new version of the `Shape` constructor, this time with two member functions, `manhattanPos()` and `translate()`:

```
function Shape(x, y) {
    this.x = x;
    this.y = y;

    this.manhattanPos = function() {
        return Math.abs(this.x) + Math.abs(this.y);
    };
    this.translate = function(dx, dy) {
        this.x += dx;
        this.y += dy;
    };
}
```

We can then invoke the member functions using the `.` (dot) operator:

```
var shape = new Shape(10, 20);
shape.translate(100, 100);
print(shape.x + ", " + shape.y + " (" + shape.manhattanPos() + ")");
```

With this approach, each `Shape` instance has its own `manhattanPos` and `translate` properties. Since these properties should be identical for all `Shape` instances, it is desirable to store them only once rather than in every instance. ECMAScript lets us achieve this by using a prototype. A *prototype* is an object that serves as a fallback for other objects, providing an initial set of properties. One advantage of this approach is that it is possible to change the prototype object at any time and the changes are immediately reflected in all objects that were created with that prototype.

Consider the following example:

```
function Shape(x, y) {
    this.x = x;
    this.y = y;
}

Shape.prototype.manhattanPos = function() {
    return Math.abs(this.x) + Math.abs(this.y);
};

Shape.prototype.translate = function(dx, dy) {
    this.x += dx;
    this.y += dy;
};
```

Constants	
`NaN`	IEEE 754 Not-a-Number (NaN) value
`Infinity`	Positive infinity ($+\infty$)
`undefined`	Default value for uninitialized variables
Functions	
`print(x)`*	Prints a value on the console
`eval(str)`	Executes an ECMAScript program
`parseInt(str, base)`	Converts a string to an integer value
`parseFloat(str)`	Converts a string to a floating-point value
`isNaN(n)`	Returns `true` if `n` is NaN
`isFinite(n)`	Returns `true` if `n` is a number other than NaN, $+\infty$, or $-\infty$
`decodeURI(str)`	Converts an 8-bit-encoded URI to Unicode
`decodeURIComponent(str)`	Converts an 8-bit-encoded URI component to Unicode
`encodeURI(str)`	Converts a Unicode URI to an 8-bit-encoded URI
`encodeURIComponent(str)`	Converts a Unicode URI component to 8-bit-encoded
Classes (Constructors)	
`Object`	Provides functionality common to all objects
`Function`	Encapsulates an ECMAScript function
`Array`	Represents a resizable vector of items
`String`	Stores a Unicode string
`Boolean`	Stores a Boolean value (`true` or `false`)
`Number`	Stores a floating-point number
`Date`	Stores a date and time
`RegExp`	Provides regular expression pattern matching
`Error`	Base type for error types
`EvalError`	Raised when using `eval()` wrongly
`RangeError`	Raised when a numeric value is outside the legal range
`ReferenceError`	Raised when trying to access an undefined variable
`SyntaxError`	Raised when a syntax error is detected by `eval()`
`TypeError`	Raised when an argument has the wrong type
`URIError`	Raised when URI parsing fails
Object	
`Math`	Provides mathematical constants and functions

Figure 22.1. Built-in properties of the global object

*Not specified by the ECMAScript standard.

In this version of Shape, we create the manhattanPos and translate properties outside the constructor, as properties of the Shape.prototype object. When we instantiate a Shape, the newly created object keeps an internal pointer back to Shape.prototype. Whenever we retrieve the value of a property that doesn't exist in our Shape object, the property is looked up in the prototype as a fallback. Thus, the Shape prototype is the ideal place to put member functions, which should be shared by all Shape instances.

It might be tempting to put all sorts of properties that we want to share between Shape instances in the prototype, similar to C++'s static member variables or Java's class variables. This idiom works for read-only properties (including member functions) because the prototype acts as a fallback when we retrieve the value of a property. However, it doesn't work as expected when we try to assign a new value to the shared variable; instead, a fresh variable is created directly in the Shape object, shadowing any property of the same name in the prototype. This asymmetry between read and write access to a variable is a frequent source of confusion for novice ECMAScript programmers.

In class-based languages such as C++ and Java, we can use class inheritance to create specialized object types. For example, we would define a Shape class and then derive Triangle, Square, and Circle from Shape. In ECMAScript, a similar effect can be achieved using prototypes. The following example shows how to define Circle objects that are also Shape instances:

```
function Shape(x, y) {
    this.x = x;
    this.y = y;
}

Shape.prototype.area = function() { return 0; };

function Circle(x, y, radius) {
    Shape.call(this, x, y);
    this.radius = radius;
}

Circle.prototype = new Shape;
Circle.prototype.area = function() {
    return Math.PI * this.radius * this.radius;
};
```

We start by defining a Shape constructor and associate an area() function with it, which always returns 0. Then we define a Circle constructor, which calls the "base class" constructor using the call() function defined for all function objects (including constructors), and we add a radius property. Outside the constructor, we set the Circle's prototype to be a Shape object, and we override Shape's area() function with a Circle-specific implementation. This corresponds to the following C++ code:

```
class Shape
{
public:
```

```
    Shape(double x, double y) {
        this->x = x;
        this->y = y;
    }

    virtual double area() const { return 0; }

    double x;
    double y;
};

class Circle : public Shape
{
public:
    Circle(double x, double y, double radius)
        : Shape(x, y)
    {
        this->radius = radius;
    }

    double area() const { return M_PI * radius * radius; }

    double radius;
};
```

The `instanceof` operator walks through the prototype chain to determine which constructors have been invoked. As a consequence, instances of a subclass are also considered to be instances of the base class:

```
var circle = new Circle(0, 0, 50);
circle instanceof Circle;          // returns true
circle instanceof Shape;           // returns true
circle instanceof Object;          // returns true
circle instanceof Array;           // returns false
```

This concludes our short introduction to ECMAScript. In the following sections, we will show how to use this language in conjunction with C++/Qt applications to provide more flexibility and customizability to end-users or simply to speed up the development process.

Extending Qt Applications with Scripts

Using the *QtScript* module, we can write C++ applications that can execute ECMAScript. Scripts can be used to extend application functionality without requiring the application itself to be rebuilt and redeployed. We can limit the scripts to a hard-coded set of ECMAScript files that are provided as part of the application and that can be replaced with new versions independently of new releases of the application, or we can make the application able to use arbitrary ECMAScript files.

Executing a script from a C++ application typically involves the following steps:

1. Load the script into a `QString`.

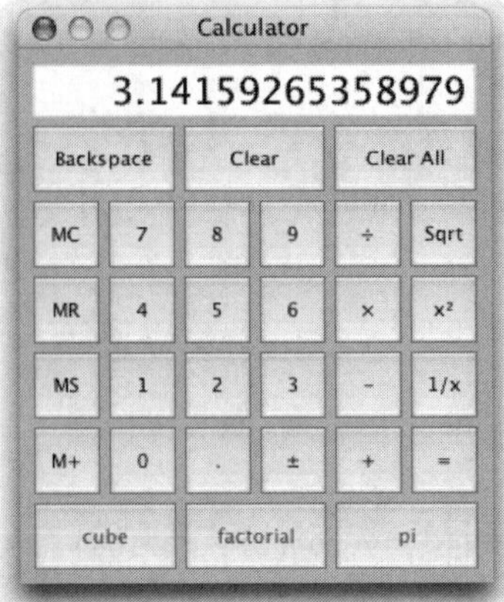

Figure 22.2. The Calculator application

2. Create a `QScriptEngine` object and set it up to expose application-specific functionality.
3. Execute the script.

To illustrate this, we will study the Calculator application shown in Figure 22.2. The Calculator application lets the user provide custom buttons by implementing their functionality in scripts. When the application starts up, it traverses the `scripts` subdirectory, looking for script files, and creates calculator buttons associated with these scripts. By default, Calculator includes the following scripts:

- `cube.js` computes the cube of the current value (x^3).
- `factorial.js` computes the factorial of the current value ($x!$).
- `pi.js` overwrites the current value with an approximation of π.

Most of the Calculator application's code is the same kind of C++/Qt code that we have seen throughout the book. Here, we will review only those parts of the code that are relevant to scripting, starting with the `createCustomButtons()` private function, which is called from the `Calculator` constructor:

```
void Calculator::createCustomButtons()
{
    QDir scriptsDir = directoryOf("scripts");
    QStringList fileNames = scriptsDir.entryList(QStringList("*.js"),
                                                 QDir::Files);
    foreach (QString fileName, fileNames) {
        QString text = fileName;
        text.chop(3);
        QToolButton *button = createButton(text,
                                  SLOT(customButtonClicked()));
        button->setStyleSheet("color: rgb(31, 63, 127)");
        button->setProperty("scriptFileName",
                            scriptsDir.absoluteFilePath(fileName));
```

```
            customButtons.append(button);
        }
    }
```

The `createCustomButtons()` function uses a `QDir` object to traverse the application's `scripts` subdirectory, looking for files with a `.js` extension. It uses the same `directoryOf()` function we used in Chapter 17 (p. 410).

For each `.js` file, we create a `QToolButton` by calling the private `createButton()` function. This function also connects the new button's `clicked()` signal to the `customButtonClicked()` slot. Then we set the button's style sheet to make the foreground text blue, to distinguish the custom buttons from the built-in buttons.

The call to `QObject::setProperty()` dynamically creates a new `scriptFileName` property for each `QToolButton`. We use this property in the `customButtonClicked()` slot to determine which script should be executed.

Finally, we add the new button to the `customButtons` list. The `Calculator` constructor uses this list to add the custom buttons to the window's grid layout.

For this application, we have chosen to traverse the `scripts` directory just once, at application startup. An alternative would be to use a `QFileSystemWatcher` to monitor the `scripts` directory, and update the calculator whenever the directory's content changes, allowing the user to add new scripts and remove existing scripts without having to restart the application.

```
void Calculator::customButtonClicked()
{
    QToolButton *clickedButton = qobject_cast<QToolButton *>(sender());
    QFile file(clickedButton->property("scriptFileName").toString());
    if (!file.open(QIODevice::ReadOnly)) {
        abortOperation();
        return;
    }

    QTextStream in(&file);
    in.setCodec("UTF-8");
    QString script = in.readAll();
    file.close();

    QScriptEngine interpreter;
    QScriptValue operand(&interpreter, display->text().toDouble());
    interpreter.globalObject().setProperty("x", operand);
    QScriptValue result = interpreter.evaluate(script);
    if (!result.isNumber()) {
        abortOperation();
        return;
    }

    setDisplayValue(result.toNumber());
    waitingForOperand = true;
}
```

In the `customButtonClicked()` slot, we first call `QObject::sender()` to determine which button was clicked. Then we extract the `scriptFileName` property to retrieve the name of the `.js` file associated with the button. Next, we load the file's contents into a string called `script`.

The ECMAScript standard requires that interpreters support Unicode, but it does not mandate any particular encoding to use for storing scripts on disk. We have chosen to assume that our `.js` files use UTF-8, a superset of plain ASCII.

Once we have the script in a `QString`, we create a `QScriptEngine` to execute it. A `QScriptEngine` instance represents an ECMAScript interpreter and holds a current state. We can have any number of `QScriptEngine`s at the same time for different purposes, each with its own state.

Before we can run the script, we must make it possible for the script to retrieve the current value displayed by the calculator. The approach we have chosen here is to create an ECMAScript global variable called `x`—or, more precisely, we have added a dynamic property called `x` to the interpreter's global object. From script code, this property is available directly as `x`.

The value we set for `x` must be of type `QScriptValue`. Conceptually, a `QScriptValue` is similar to `QVariant` in that it can store many data types, except that it is tailored to store ECMAScript data types.

Finally, we run the script using `QScriptEngine::evaluate()`. The result is the value returned by the script, or an exception object if an error occurred. (In the next section, we will see how to report errors to the user in a message box.) A script's return value is the value explicitly returned by a `return` call; if `return` is omitted, the return value is the result of the last expression evaluated in the script. Once we have the return value, we check whether it is a number, and if it is, we display it.

For this example, we evaluate a script every time the user presses its corresponding button. Since this step involves loading and parsing the entire script, it is often preferable to use a different approach, where the script doesn't directly perform an operation, but rather returns a function or an object that can be used later on. We will use this alternative approach in the next section.

To link against the *QtScript* library, we must add this line to the application's `.pro` file:

```
QT += script
```

The example scripts are quite simple. Here's the one-line `pi.js`:

```
return 3.14159265358979323846;
```

Notice that we ignore the calculator's `x` value. The `cube.js` script is also a one-liner, but it does make use of the `x` value:

```
return x * x * x;
```

The `factorial.js` script defines a function and calls it:

```
function factorial(n)
{
    if (n <= 1) {
        return 1;
    } else {
        return n * factorial(n - 1);
    }
}

return factorial(Math.floor(x));
```

The standard factorial function only operates on integers, so we have used the `Math.floor()` function to convert `x` to an integer.

We have now seen the fundamentals of the *QtScript* module: the `QScriptEngine`, which represents an interpreter with its current state, and `QScriptValue`, which stores an ECMAScript value.

In the Calculator example, there was very little interaction between the scripts and the application: The scripts take only one parameter from the application and return a single value. In the following sections, we will see more advanced integration strategies and show how to report exceptions to the user.

Implementing GUI Extensions Using Scripts

Providing scripts to compute values, as we did in the preceding section, is useful but limited. Often, we want to access some of the application's widgets and other components directly from the script. We might also want to provide additional dialogs by combining ECMAScript files with *Qt Designer* `.ui` files. Using these techniques, it is possible to develop applications mostly in ECMAScript, which is appealing to some programmers.

In this section, we will look at the HTML Editor application shown in Figure 22.3. This application is a plain text editor that highlights HTML tags using a `QSyntaxHighlighter`. What makes the application special is that it provides a Scripts menu that is populated with extensions provided as `.js` scripts, along with corresponding `.ui` dialogs, in the application's `scripts` subdirectory. The dialogs let the user parameterize the operation they want performed.

We have provided two extensions: a Statistics dialog and a Reformat Text dialog, both shown in Figure 22.4. The Statistics dialog is purely informative. It counts the number of characters, words, and lines in a document and presents the totals to the user in a modal dialog. The Reformat Text dialog is more sophisticated. It is a modeless dialog, which means that the user can continue to interact with the application's main window while the dialog is shown. The dialog can be used to reindent the text, to wrap long lines, and to standardize the case used for tags. All these operations are implemented in ECMAScript.

The heart of the application is the `HtmlWindow` class, a `QMainWindow` subclass that uses a `QTextEdit` as its central widget. Here, we will review only those parts of the code that are relevant to application scripting.

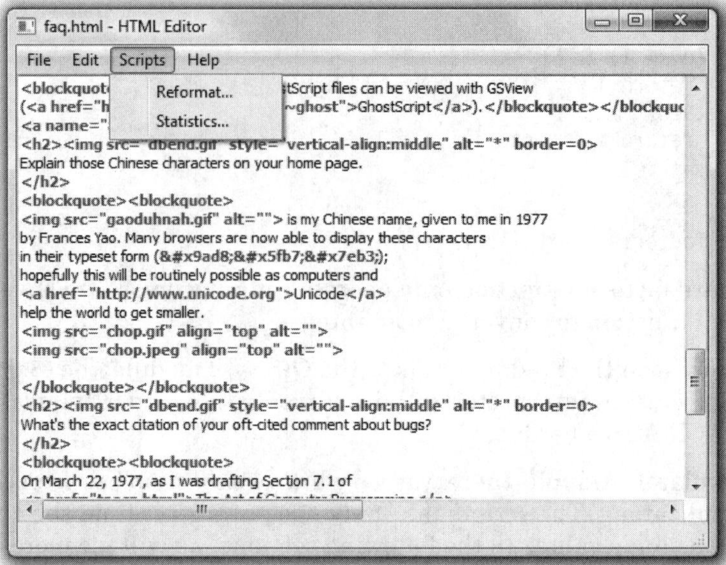

Figure 22.3. The HTML Editor application

When the application starts up, we must populate the Scripts menu with actions corresponding to the `.js` and `.ui` files found in the `scripts` subdirectory. This is quite similar to what we did in the Calculator application's `createCustomButtons()` function in the preceding section:

```
void HtmlWindow::createScriptsMenu()
{
    scriptsMenu = menuBar()->addMenu(tr("&Scripts"));

    QDir scriptsDir = directoryOf("scripts");
    QStringList jsFileNames = scriptsDir.entryList(QStringList("*.js"),
                                                   QDir::Files);
    foreach (QString jsFileName, jsFileNames)
        createScriptAction(scriptsDir.absoluteFilePath(jsFileName));

    scriptsMenu->setEnabled(!scriptsMenu->isEmpty());
}
```

For each script, we call the `createScriptAction()` function to create an action and add it to the Scripts menu. If no scripts are found, we disable the menu.

The `createScriptAction()` function performs the following steps:

1. Load and evaluate the script, storing the resulting object in a variable.
2. Construct a dialog from the `.ui` file using `QUiLoader`.
3. Make the dialog accessible to the script.
4. Expose application-specific functionality to the script.
5. Create a `QAction` to make the script accessible to the user.

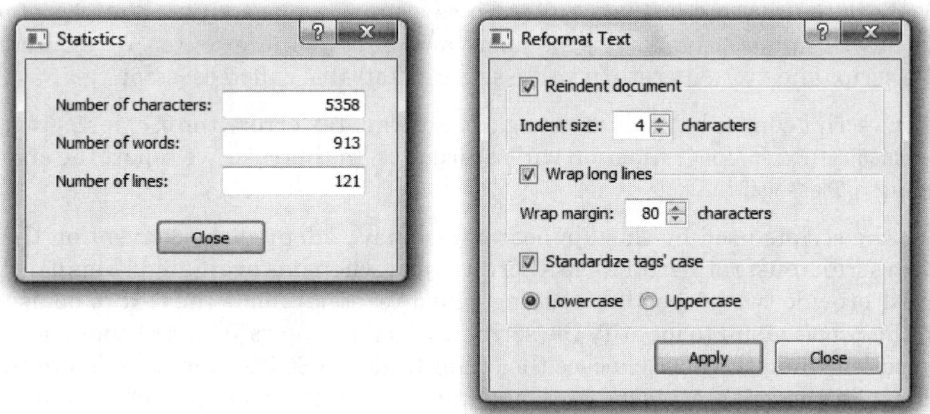

Figure 22.4. The Statistics and Reformat Text dialogs

The function has to do a lot of work and is quite long, so we will review it in parts.

```
bool HtmlWindow::createScriptAction(const QString &jsFileName)
{
    QFile jsFile(jsFileName);
    if (!jsFile.open(QIODevice::ReadOnly)) {
        QMessageBox::warning(this, tr("HTML Editor"),
                             tr("Cannot read file %1:\n%2.")
                             .arg(strippedName(jsFileName))
                             .arg(jsFile.errorString()));
        return false;
    }

    QTextStream in(&jsFile);
    in.setCodec("UTF-8");
    QString script = in.readAll();
    jsFile.close();

    QScriptValue qsScript = interpreter.evaluate(script);
    if (interpreter.hasUncaughtException()) {
        QMessageBox messageBox(this);
        messageBox.setIcon(QMessageBox::Warning);
        messageBox.setWindowTitle(tr("HTML Editor"));
        messageBox.setText(tr("An error occurred while executing the "
                              "script %1.")
                           .arg(strippedName(jsFileName)));
        messageBox.setInformativeText(
                tr("%1.").arg(interpreter.uncaughtException()
                              .toString()));
        messageBox.setDetailedText(
                interpreter.uncaughtExceptionBacktrace().join("\n"));
        messageBox.exec();
        return false;
    }
```

We begin by reading in the .js file. Since we need to use only one interpreter, we have a single QScriptEngine member variable called interpreter. We evaluate the script and store its return value as a QScriptValue called qsScript.

If the script cannot be evaluated (e.g., due to a syntax error), the QScriptEngine::hasUncaughtException() function will return true. In this case, we report the error using a QMessageBox.

For the scripts used by this application, we have adopted the convention that each script must return an ECMAScript Object when it is evaluated. This Object must provide two properties: a string called text that holds the text to be used in the Scripts menu to identify the script, and a function called run() that should be called when the user chooses the script from the Scripts menu. We store the Object in the qsScript variable. The main benefit of this approach is that we need to read and parse the scripts only once, at startup.

```
QString uiFileName = jsFileName;
uiFileName.chop(3);
uiFileName += ".ui";

QFile uiFile(uiFileName);
if (!uiFile.open(QIODevice::ReadOnly)) {
    QMessageBox::warning(this, tr("HTML Editor"),
                         tr("Cannot read file %1:\n%2.")
                         .arg(strippedName(uiFileName))
                         .arg(uiFile.errorString()));
    return false;
}

QUiLoader loader;
QWidget *dialog = loader.load(&uiFile, this);
uiFile.close();
if (!dialog) {
    QMessageBox::warning(this, tr("HTML Editor"),
                         tr("Error loading %1.")
                         .arg(strippedName(uiFileName)));
    return false;
}
```

Another convention we have adopted is that each script must have a corresponding .ui file to provide the script with a GUI dialog. The .ui file must have the same base name as the script.

We attempt to read the .ui file and to dynamically create a QWidget that contains all the widgets, layouts, and connections specified in the .ui file. The widget's parent is given as the second argument to the load() call. If an error occurs, we warn the user and return.

```
QScriptValue qsDialog = interpreter.newQObject(dialog);
qsScript.setProperty("dialog", qsDialog);

QScriptValue qsTextEdit = interpreter.newQObject(textEdit);
qsScript.setProperty("textEdit", qsTextEdit);
```

```
        QAction *action = new QAction(this);
        action->setText(qsScript.property("text").toString());
        action->setData(QVariant::fromValue(qsScript));
        connect(action, SIGNAL(triggered()),
                this, SLOT(scriptActionTriggered()));

        scriptsMenu->addAction(action);

        return true;
    }
```

Once we have successfully read the script and its user interface file, we are almost ready to add the script to the Scripts menu. But first, there are a few details that we must attend to. We want the `run()` function of our script to have access to the dialog we just created. In addition, the script should be allowed to access the `QTextEdit` that contains the HTML document being edited.

We begin by adding the dialog to the interpreter as a `QObject *`. In response, the interpreter returns the `Object` that it uses to represent the dialog. We store this in `qsDialog`. We add the `qsDialog` object to the `qsScript` object as a new property called `dialog`. This means that the script can access the dialog, including its widgets, through the newly created `dialog` property. We use the same technique to provide the script with access to the application's `QTextEdit`.

Finally, we create a new `QAction` to represent the script in the GUI. We set the action's text to `qsScript`'s `text` property, and the action's "data" item to `qsScript` itself. Lastly, we connect the action's `triggered()` signal to a custom `scriptActionTriggered()` slot, and add the action to the Scripts menu.

```
    void HtmlWindow::scriptActionTriggered()
    {
        QAction *action = qobject_cast<QAction *>(sender());
        QScriptValue qsScript = action->data().value<QScriptValue>();
        qsScript.property("run").call(qsScript);
    }
```

When this slot is called, we begin by finding out which `QAction` was triggered. Then we extract the action's user data using `QVariant::value<T>()` to cast it to a `QScriptValue`, which we store in `qsScript`. Then we invoke `qsScript`'s `run()` function, passing `qsScript` as a parameter; this will make `qsScript` the `this` object inside the `run()` function.*

`QAction`'s "data" item mechanism is based on `QVariant`. The `QScriptValue` type is not one of the data types that `QVariant` recognizes. Fortunately, Qt provides a mechanism for extending the types that `QVariant` can handle. At the beginning of `htmlwindow.cpp`, after the `#include`s, we have the following line:

```
    Q_DECLARE_METATYPE(QScriptValue)
```

*Qt 4.4 is expected to provide a `qScriptConnect()` function that will allow us to establish C++-to-script connections. Using this function, we could then connect the `QAction`'s `triggered()` signal directly to the `qsScript`'s `run()` function as follows:

```
    qScriptConnect(action, SIGNAL(triggered()), qsScript, qsScript.property("run"));
```

This line should appear after the custom data type it refers to has been declared, and can be done only for data types that have a default constructor and a copy constructor.

Now that we have seen how to load a script and a user interface file, and how to provide an action that the user can trigger to run the script, we are ready to look at the scripts themselves. We will begin with the Statistics script since it is the easiest and shortest, reviewing it in parts.

```
var obj = new Object;

obj.text = "&Statistics...";
```

We begin by creating a new `Object`. This is the object we will add properties to and that we will return to the interpreter. The first property we set is the `text` property, with the text that we want to appear in the Scripts menu.

```
obj.run = function() {
    var text = this.textEdit.plainText;
    this.dialog.frame.charCountLineEdit.text = text.length;
    this.dialog.frame.wordCountLineEdit.text = this.wordCount(text);
    this.dialog.frame.lineCountLineEdit.text = this.lineCount(text);
    this.dialog.exec();
};
```

The second property we create is the `run()` function. The function reads the text from the dialog's `QTextEdit`, populates the dialog's widgets with the results of the calculations, and finishes by modally showing the dialog.

This function can work only if the `Object` variable, `obj`, has suitable `textEdit` and `dialog` properties, which is why we needed to add them at the end of the `createScriptAction()` function. The dialog itself must have a `frame` object (in this case a `QFrame`, but the type does not matter), with three child widgets—`charCountLineEdit`, `wordCountLineEdit`, and `lineCountLineEdit`, each with a writable `text` property. Instead of `this.dialog.frame.`*xxx*`CountLineEdit`, we could also write `findChild("`*xxx*`CountLineEdit")`, which performs a recursive search and is therefore more robust if we choose to change the dialog's design.

```
obj.wordCount = function(text) {
    var regExp = new RegExp("\\w+", "g");
    var count = 0;
    while (regExp.exec(text))
        ++count;
    return count;
};

obj.lineCount = function(text) {
    var count = 0;
    var pos = 0;
    while ((pos = text.indexOf("\n", pos)) != -1) {
        ++count;
        ++pos;
    }
    return count + 1;
```

```
};

return obj;
```

The `wordCount()` and `lineCount()` functions have no external dependencies and work purely in terms of the `String` passed in to them. Note that the `wordCount()` function uses the ECMAScript `RegExp` class, not Qt's `QRegExp` class. At the end of the script file, the `return` statement ensures that the `Object` with the `text` and `run()` function properties is returned to the interpreter, ready to be used.

The Reformat script follows a similar pattern to the Statistics script. We will look at it next.

```
var obj = new Object;

obj.initialized = false;

obj.text = "&Reformat...";

obj.run = function() {
    if (!this.initialized) {
        this.dialog.applyButton.clicked.connect(this, this.apply);
        this.dialog.closeButton.clicked.connect(this, this.dialog.close);
        this.initialized = true;
    }
    this.dialog.show();
};

obj.apply = function() {
    var text = this.textEdit.plainText;

    this.textEdit.readOnly = true;
    this.dialog.applyButton.enabled = false;

    if (this.dialog.indentGroupBox.checked) {
        var size = this.dialog.indentGroupBox.indentSizeSpinBox.value;
        text = this.reindented(text, size);
    }
    if (this.dialog.wrapGroupBox.checked) {
        var margin = this.dialog.wrapGroupBox.wrapMarginSpinBox.value;
        text = this.wrapped(text, margin);
    }
    if (this.dialog.caseGroupBox.checked) {
        var lowercase = this.dialog.caseGroupBox.lowercaseRadio.checked;
        text = this.fixedTagCase(text, lowercase);
    }

    this.textEdit.plainText = text;
    this.textEdit.readOnly = false;
    this.dialog.applyButton.enabled = true;
};

obj.reindented = function(text, size) {
    ...
};
```

```
obj.wrapped = function(text, margin) {
    ...
};
obj.fixedTagCase = function(text, lowercase) {
    ...
};
return obj;
```

We use the same pattern as before, creating a featureless `Object`, adding properties to it, and returning it to the interpreter. In addition to the `text` and `run()` properties, we add an `initialized` property. The first time `run()` is called, `initialized` is `false`, so we set up the signal–slot connections that link button clicks in the dialog to functions defined in the script.

The same kinds of assumptions apply here as applied to the Statistics script. We assume that there is a suitable `dialog` property and that it has buttons called `applyButton` and `closeButton`. The `apply()` function interacts with the dialog's widgets, in particular with the Apply button (to disable and enable it) and with the group boxes, checkboxes, and spin boxes. It also interacts with the main window's `QTextEdit` from where it gets the text to work on, and to which it gives the text that results from the reformatting.

We omitted the code for the `reindented()`, `wrapped()`, and `fixedTagCase()` functions used internally by the script, since the actual computations are not relevant to understanding how to make Qt applications scriptable.

We have now completed our technical review of how to use scripts within C++/Qt applications, including ones that have their own dialogs. In applications such as HTML Editor, where the scripts interact with application objects, we must also consider licensing issues. For open source applications, there are no constraints beyond those imposed by the requirements of the open source license itself. For commercial applications, the story is slightly more complicated. Those who write scripts for commercial applications, including an application's end-users, are free to do so if their scripts use only built-in ECMAScript classes and application-specific APIs, or if they use the Qt API to perform minor extensions or modifications to existing components. But any script writer whose scripts implement core GUI functionality must have a commercial Qt license. Commercial Qt users should contact their Trolltech sales representative if they have licensing questions.

Automating Tasks through Scripting

Sometimes we use GUI applications to manipulate data sets in the same way each time. If the manipulation consists of invoking many menu options, or interacting with a dialog, not only does it become tedious but there is a risk that on some occasions we may miss steps, or transpose the order of a couple of steps—and perhaps not realize that a mistake has been made. One way to make things easier for users is to allow them to write scripts to perform sequences of actions automatically.

In this section, we will present a GUI application that offers a command-line option, `-script`, that lets the user specify a script to execute. The application will then start up, execute the script, and terminate, with no GUI appearing at all.

The application we will use to illustrate this technique is called Gas Pump. It reads in lists of transactions recorded by a trucker gas station's pumps and presents the data in a tabular format, as shown in Figure 22.5.

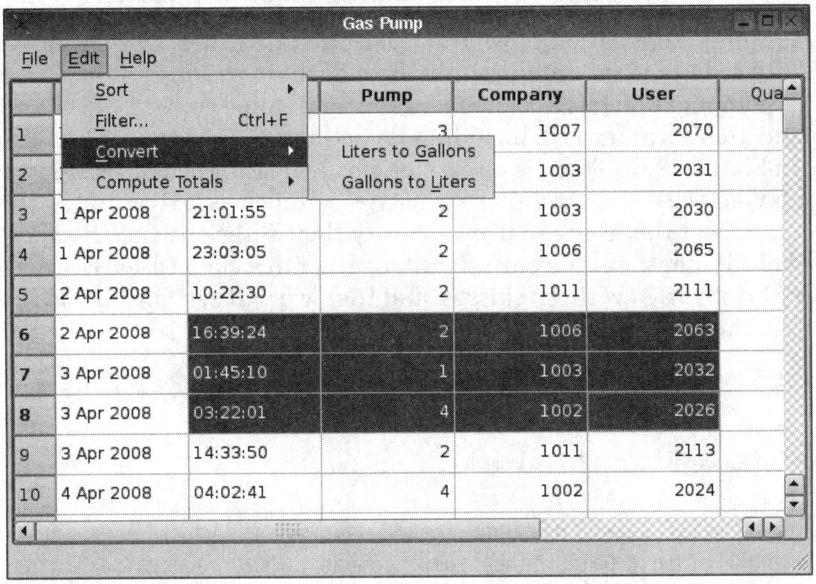

Figure 22.5. The Gas Pump application

Each transaction is recorded by date and time, and by the pump, the quantity taken, the company ID and user ID of the trucker, and the transaction's status. The Gas Pump application can be used to manipulate the data in quite sophisticated ways, sorting it, filtering it, computing totals, and converting between liters and gallons.

The Gas Pump application supports transaction data in two formats: "Pump 2000", a plain text format with extension `.p20`, and "XML Gas Pump", an XML format with extension `.gpx`. The application can load and save in both formats, so it can be used to convert between them, simply by loading in one format and saving in the other.

The application is supplied with four standard scripts:

- `onlyok.js` removes all transactions whose status is not "OK".
- `p20togpx.js` converts a Pump 2000 file to the XML Gas Pump file format.

- tohtml.js produces reports in HTML format.
- toliters.js converts the units from gallons to liters.

The scripts are invoked using the -script command-line option followed by the name of the script, and then the name of the files to operate on. For example:

```
gaspump -script scripts/toliters.js data/2008q2.p20
```

Here, we run the toliters.js script from the scripts subdirectory on the 2008q2.p20 Pump 2000 data file from the data subdirectory. The script converts all the quantity values from gallons to liters, changing the file in-place.

The Gas Pump application is written just like any other C++/Qt application. In fact, its code is very similar to the Spreadsheet example from Chapters 3 and 4. The application has a QMainWindow subclass called PumpWindow that provides the application's framework, including its actions and menus. (The menus are shown in Figure 22.6.) There is also a custom QTableWidget called PumpSpreadsheet for displaying the data. And there is a QDialog subclass, FilterDialog shown in Figure 22.7, that the user can use to specify their filter options. Because there are a lot of filter options, they are stored together in a class called PumpFilter. We will very briefly review these classes, and then we will see how to add scripting support to the application.

```
class PumpSpreadsheet : public QTableWidget
{
    Q_OBJECT
    Q_ENUMS(FileFormat Column)

public:
    enum FileFormat { Pump2000, GasPumpXml };
    enum Column { Date, Time, Pump, Company, User, Quantity, Status,
                  ColumnCount };

    PumpSpreadsheet(QWidget *parent = 0);

public slots:
    void clearData();
    bool addData(const QString &fileName, FileFormat format);
    bool saveData(const QString &fileName, FileFormat format);
    void sortByColumn(Column column,
                      Qt::SortOrder order = Qt::AscendingOrder);
    void applyFilter(const PumpFilter &filter);
    void convertUnits(double factor);
    void computeTotals(Column column);
    void setText(int row, int column, const QString &text);
    QString text(int row, int column) const;

private:
    ...
};
```

The PumpSpreadsheet holds the data and provides the functions (which we have made into slots) that the user can use to manipulate the data. The slots are

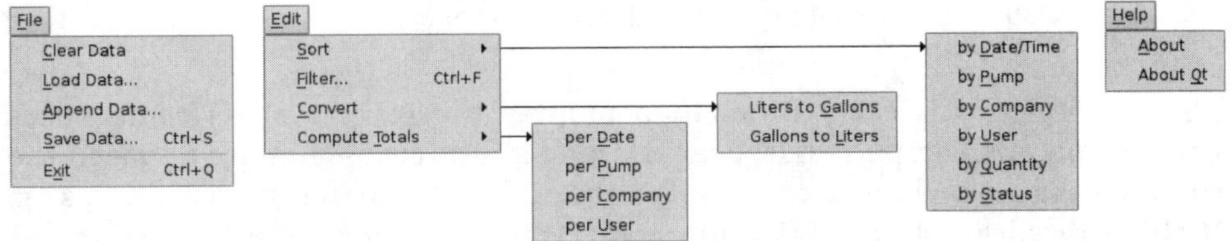

Figure 22.6. The Gas Pump application's menus

accessible through the user interface, and will also be available for scripting. The `Q_ENUMS()` macro is used to generate meta-information about the `FileFormat` and `Column` enum types; we will come back to this shortly.

The `QMainWindow` subclass, `PumpWindow`, has a `loadData()` function that makes use of some `PumpSpreadsheet` slots:

```
void PumpWindow::loadData()
{
    QString fileName = QFileDialog::getOpenFileName(this,
                               tr("Open Data File"), ".",
                               fileFilters);
    if (!fileName.isEmpty()) {
        spreadsheet->clearData();
        spreadsheet->addData(fileName, fileFormat(fileName));
    }
}
```

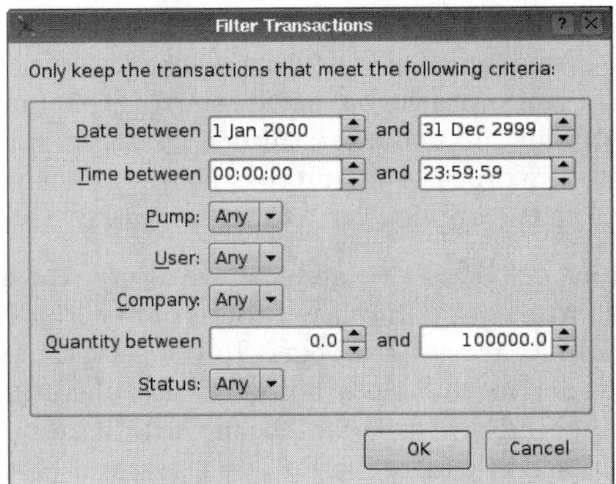

Figure 22.7. The Filter dialog

The `PumpSpreadsheet` is stored in the `PumpWindow` as a member variable called `spreadsheet`. The `PumpWindow`'s `filter()` slot is less typical:

```
void PumpWindow::filter()
{
    FilterDialog dialog(this);
    dialog.initFromSpreadsheet(spreadsheet);
    if (dialog.exec())
```

```
        spreadsheet->applyFilter(dialog.filter());
}
```

The `initFromSpreadsheet()` function populates the `FilterDialog`'s comboboxes with the pumps, company IDs, user IDs, and status codes that are in use in the current data set. When `exec()` is called, the dialog shown in Figure 22.7 pops up. If the user clicks OK, the `FilterDialog`'s `filter()` function returns a `PumpFilter` object that we pass on to `PumpSpreadsheet::applyFilter()`.

```
class PumpFilter
{
public:
    PumpFilter();

    QDate fromDate;
    QDate toDate;
    QTime fromTime;
    QTime toTime;
    QString pump;
    QString company;
    QString user;
    double fromQuantity;
    double toQuantity;
    QString status;
};
```

The purpose of `PumpFilter` is to make it easier to pass around filter options as a group rather than having ten separate parameters.

So far, all we have seen has been unsurprising. The only barely noticeable differences are that we have made all the `PumpSpreadsheet` functions that we want scriptable into public slots, and we have used the `Q_ENUMS()` macro. To make Gas Pump scriptable, we must do two more things. First, we must change `main.cpp` to add the command-line processing and to execute the script if one is specified. Second, we must make the application's functionality available to scripts.

The *QtScript* module provides two general ways of exposing C++ classes to scripts. The easiest way is to define the functionality in a `QObject` class and to expose one or more instances of that class to the script, using `QScriptEngine::newQObject()`. The properties and slots defined by the class (and optionally by its ancestors) are then available to scripts. The more difficult but also more flexible approach is to write a C++ prototype for the class and possibly a constructor function, for classes that need to be instantiated from the script using the `new` operator. The Gas Pump example illustrates both approaches.

Before we study the infrastructure used to run scripts, let us look at one of the scripts that is supplied with Gas Pump. Here is the complete `onlyok.js` script:

```
if (args.length == 0)
    throw Error("No files specified on the command line");

for (var i = 0; i < args.length; ++i) {
    spreadsheet.clearData();
```

```
        if (!spreadsheet.addData(args[i], PumpSpreadsheet.Pump2000))
            throw Error("Error loading Pump 2000 data");

        var filter = new PumpFilter;
        filter.status = "OK";

        spreadsheet.applyFilter(filter);
        if (!spreadsheet.saveData(args[i], PumpSpreadsheet.Pump2000))
            throw Error("Error saving Pump 2000 data");

        print("Removed erroneous transactions from " + args[i]);
    }
```

This script relies on two global variables: `args` and `spreadsheet`. The `args` variable returns the command-line arguments supplied after the `-script` option. The `spreadsheet` variable is a reference to a `PumpSpreadsheet` object that we can use to perform various operations (file format conversion, unit conversion, filtering, etc.). The script also calls some slots on the `PumpSpreadsheet` object, instantiates and initializes `PumpFilter` objects, and uses the `PumpSpreadsheet::FileFormat` enum.

We begin with a simple sanity check, and then for each file name listed on the command line we clear the global `spreadsheet` object and attempt to load in the file's data. We assume that the files are all in Pump 2000 (`.p20`) format. For each successfully loaded file, we create a new `PumpFilter` object. We set the filter's `status` property and then call the `PumpSpreadsheet`'s `applyFilter()` function (which is accessible because we made it a slot). Finally, we save the updated spreadsheet data back to the original file, and output a message to the user.

The other three scripts have a similar structure; they are included with the book's source code.

To support scripts such as the `onlyok.js` script, we need to perform the following steps in the Gas Pump application:

1. Detect the `-script` command-line option.
2. Load the specified script file.
3. Expose a `PumpSpreadsheet` instance to the interpreter.
4. Expose the command-line arguments to the interpreter.
5. Expose the `FileFormat` and `Column` enums to the interpreter.
6. Wrap the `PumpFilter` class so that its member variables can be accessed from the script.
7. Make it possible to instantiate `PumpFilter` objects from the script.
8. Execute the script.

The relevant code is located in `main.cpp`, `scripting.cpp`, and `scripting.h`. Let's begin with `main.cpp`:

```
int main(int argc, char *argv[])
```

```
{
    QApplication app(argc, argv);
    QStringList args = QApplication::arguments();
    if (args.count() >= 3 && args[1] == "-script") {
        runScript(args[2], args.mid(3));
        return 0;
    } else if (args.count() == 1) {
        PumpWindow window;
        window.show();
        window.resize(600, 400);
        return app.exec();
    } else {
        std::cerr << "Usage: gaspump [-script myscript.js <arguments>]"
                  << std::endl;
        return 1;
    }
}
```

The command-line arguments are accessible through the `QApplication::arguments()` function, which returns a `QStringList`. The first item in the list is the application's name. If there are at least three arguments and the second argument is `-script`, we assume that the third argument is a script name. In this case, we call `runScript()` with the script's name as its first argument and the rest of the string list as its second parameter. Once the script has been run, the application terminates immediately.

If there is just one argument, the application's name, we create and show a `PumpWindow`, and start off the application's event loop in the conventional way.

The application's scripting support is provided by `scripting.h` and `scripting.cpp`. These files define the `runScript()` function, the `pumpFilterConstructor()` support function, and the `PumpFilterPrototype` supporting class. The supporting function and class are specific to the Gas Pump application, but we will still review them since they illustrate some general points about making applications scriptable.

We will review the `runScript()` function in several parts, since it contains several subtle details.

```
bool runScript(const QString &fileName, const QStringList &args)
{
    QFile file(fileName);
    if (!file.open(QIODevice::ReadOnly)) {
        std::cerr << "Error: Cannot read file " << qPrintable(fileName)
                  << ": " << qPrintable(file.errorString())
                  << std::endl;
        return false;
    }

    QTextStream in(&file);
    in.setCodec("UTF-8");
    QString script = in.readAll();
    file.close();
```

We start by reading the script into a `QString`.

```
QScriptEngine interpreter;

PumpSpreadsheet spreadsheet;
QScriptValue qsSpreadsheet = interpreter.newQObject(&spreadsheet);
interpreter.globalObject().setProperty("spreadsheet",
                                       qsSpreadsheet);
```

Once we have the script in a QString, we create a QScriptEngine and a PumpSpreadsheet instance. We then create a QScriptValue to refer to the PumpSpreadsheet instance, and set this as a global property of the interpreter, making it accessible inside scripts as the spreadsheet global variable. All the PumpSpreadsheet's slots and properties are available through the spreadsheet variable to any script that cares to use them.

```
QScriptValue qsArgs = qScriptValueFromSequence(&interpreter, args);
interpreter.globalObject().setProperty("args", qsArgs);
```

The (possibly empty) args list of type QStringList that is passed to the runScript() function contains the command-line arguments the user wants to pass to the script. To make these arguments accessible to scripts, we must, as always, create a QScriptValue to represent them. To convert a sequential container such as QList<T> or QVector<T> to a QScriptValue, we can use the global qScriptValueFromSequence() function provided by the *QtScript* module. We make the arguments available to scripts as a global variable called args.

```
QScriptValue qsMetaObject =
        interpreter.newQMetaObject(spreadsheet.metaObject());
interpreter.globalObject().setProperty("PumpSpreadsheet",
                                       qsMetaObject);
```

In pumpspreadsheet.h, we defined the FileFormat and Column enums. In addition we also included a Q_ENUMS() declaration that specified these enums. It is rare to use Q_ENUMS() in general Qt programming; its main use is when we are creating custom widgets that we want to make accessible to *Qt Designer*. But it is also useful in a scripting context, since we can make the enums available to scripts by registering the meta-object of the class that contains them.

By adding the PumpSpreadsheet's meta-object as the PumpSpreadsheet global variable, the FileFormat and Column enums are made accessible to scripts. Script writers can refer to enum values by typing, say, PumpSpreadsheet.Pump2000.

```
PumpFilterPrototype filterProto;
QScriptValue qsFilterProto = interpreter.newQObject(&filterProto);
interpreter.setDefaultPrototype(qMetaTypeId<PumpFilter>(),
                                qsFilterProto);
```

Because ECMAScript uses prototypes rather than classes in the C++ sense, if we want to make a custom C++ class available for scripting, we must take a rather round-about approach. In the Gas Pump example, we want to make the PumpFilter class scriptable.

One approach would be to change the class itself and have it use Qt's meta-object system to export its data members as Qt properties. For the Gas Pump example, we have chosen to keep the original application intact and create a wrapper class, PumpFilterPrototype, that can hold and provide access to a PumpFilter, to show how it's done.

The call to setDefaultPrototype() shown earlier tells the interpreter to use a PumpFilterPrototype instance as the implicit prototype for all PumpFilter objects. This prototype is derived from QObject and provides Qt properties for accessing the PumpFilter data members.

```
    QScriptValue qsFilterCtor =
            interpreter.newFunction(pumpFilterConstructor,
                                    qsFilterProto);
    interpreter.globalObject().setProperty("PumpFilter", qsFilterCtor);
```

We register a constructor for PumpFilter so that script writers can instantiate PumpFilter. Behind the scenes, accesses to PumpFilter instances are mediated through PumpFilterPrototype.

The preliminaries are now complete. We have read the script into a QString, and we have set up the script environment, providing two global variables, spreadsheet and args. We have also made the PumpSpreadsheet meta-object available and provided wrapped access to PumpFilter instances. Now we are ready to execute the script.

```
    interpreter.evaluate(script);
    if (interpreter.hasUncaughtException()) {
        std::cerr << "Uncaught exception at line "
                  << interpreter.uncaughtExceptionLineNumber() << ": "
                  << qPrintable(interpreter.uncaughtException()
                                .toString())
                  << std::endl << "Backtrace: "
                  << qPrintable(interpreter.uncaughtExceptionBacktrace()
                                .join(", "))
                  << std::endl;
        return false;
    }

    return true;
}
```

As usual, we call evaluate() to run the script. If there are syntax errors or other problems, we output suitable error information.

Now we will look at the tiny supporting function, pumpFilterConstructor(), and at the longer (but simple) supporting class, PumpFilterPrototype.

```
QScriptValue pumpFilterConstructor(QScriptContext * /* context */,
                                   QScriptEngine *interpreter)
{
    return interpreter->toScriptValue(PumpFilter());
}
```

The constructor function is invoked whenever the script creates a new object using the ECMAScript syntax new PumpFilter. The arguments passed to the constructor are accessible using the `context` parameter. We simply ignore them here and create a default `PumpFilter` object, wrapped in a `QScriptValue`. The `toScriptValue<T>()` function is a template function that converts its argument of type `T` to a `QScriptValue`. The type `T` (in our case, `PumpFilter`) must be registered using `Q_DECLARE_METATYPE()`:

```
Q_DECLARE_METATYPE(PumpFilter)
```

Here's the prototype class's definition:

```
class PumpFilterPrototype : public QObject, public QScriptable
{
    Q_OBJECT
    Q_PROPERTY(QDate fromDate READ fromDate WRITE setFromDate)
    Q_PROPERTY(QDate toDate READ toDate WRITE setToDate)
    ...
    Q_PROPERTY(QString status READ status WRITE setStatus)

public:
    PumpFilterPrototype(QObject *parent = 0);

    void setFromDate(const QDate &date);
    QDate fromDate() const;
    void setToDate(const QDate &date);
    QDate toDate() const;
    ...
    void setStatus(const QString &status);
    QString status() const;

private:
    PumpFilter *wrappedFilter() const;
};
```

The prototype class is derived from both `QObject` and `QScriptable`. We have used `Q_PROPERTY()` for every getter/setter accessor pair. Normally, we bother using `Q_PROPERTY()` only to make properties available to custom widget classes that we want to integrate with *Qt Designer*, but they are also useful in the context of scripting. When we want to make functions available for scripting, we can make them either public slots or properties.

All the accessors are similar, so we will just show one typical example pair:

```
void PumpFilterPrototype::setFromDate(const QDate &date)
{
    wrappedFilter()->fromDate = date;
}

QDate PumpFilterPrototype::fromDate() const
{
    return wrappedFilter()->fromDate;
}
```

And here's the `wrappedFilter()` private function:

```
PumpFilter *PumpFilterPrototype::wrappedFilter() const
```

```
{
    return qscriptvalue_cast<PumpFilter *>(thisObject());
}
```

The `QScriptable::thisObject()` function returns the `this` object associated with the interpreter's currently executing function. It is returned as a `QScriptValue`, and we cast it to the C++/Qt type it represents, in this case a `PumpFilter *`. The cast will work only if we register `PumpFilter *` using `Q_DECLARE_METATYPE()`:

```
Q_DECLARE_METATYPE(PumpFilter *)
```

Finally, here's the `PumpFilterPrototype` constructor:

```
PumpFilterPrototype::PumpFilterPrototype(QObject *parent)
    : QObject(parent)
{
}
```

In this example, we don't let script writers instantiate their own `PumpSpreadsheet` objects; instead, we provide a global singleton object, `spreadsheet`, that they can use. To allow script writers to instantiate `PumpSpreadsheets` for themselves, we would need to register a `pumpSpreadsheetConstructor()` function, like we did for `PumpFilter`.

In the Gas Pump example, it was sufficient to provide scripts with access to the application's widgets (e.g., to `PumpSpreadsheet`) and to the application's custom data classes such as `PumpFilter`. Although not necessary for the Gas Pump example, it is sometimes also useful to make functions in C++ available to scripts. For example, here is a simple function defined in C++ that can be made accessible to a script:

```
QScriptValue square(QScriptContext *context, QScriptEngine *interpreter)
{
    double x = context->argument(0).toNumber();
    return QScriptValue(interpreter, x * x);
}
```

The signature for this and other functions intended for script use is always

```
QScriptValue myFunc(QScriptContext *context, QScriptEngine *interpreter)
```

The function's arguments are accessible through the `QScriptContext::argument()` function. The return value is a `QScriptValue`, and we create this with the `QScriptEngine` that was passed in as its first argument.

The next example is more elaborate:

```
QScriptValue sum(QScriptContext *context, QScriptEngine *interpreter)
{
    QScriptValue unaryFunc;
    int i = 0;

    if (context->argument(0).isFunction()) {
        unaryFunc = context->argument(0);
        i = 1;
```

```
        }

        double result = 0.0;
        while (i < context->argumentCount()) {
            QScriptValue qsArg = context->argument(i);
            if (unaryFunc.isValid()) {
                QScriptValueList qsArgList;
                qsArgList << qsArg;
                qsArg = unaryFunc.call(QScriptValue(), qsArgList);
            }
            result += qsArg.toNumber();
            ++i;
        }
        return QScriptValue(interpreter, result);
    }
```

The `sum()` function can be called in two different ways. The simple way is to call it with numbers as arguments. In this case, `unaryFunc` will be an invalid `QScriptValue`, and the action performed will be simply to sum the given numbers and return the result. The subtler way is to call the function with an ECMAScript function as the first argument, followed by any number of numeric arguments. In this case, the given function is called for each number, and the sum of the results of these calls is accumulated and returned. We saw this same function written in ECMAScript in the first section of this chapter (p. 514). Using C++ rather than ECMAScript to implement low-level functionality can sometimes lead to significant performance gains.

Before we can call C++ functions from a script, we must make them available to the interpreter using `newFunction()` and `setProperty()`:

```
QScriptValue qsSquare = interpreter.newFunction(square);
interpreter.globalObject().setProperty("square", qsSquare);

QScriptValue qsSum = interpreter.newFunction(sum);
interpreter.globalObject().setProperty("sum", qsSum);
```

We have made both `square()` and `sum()` available as global functions to the interpreter. Now we can use them in scripts, as the following snippet shows:

```
interpreter.evaluate("print(sum(1, 2, 3, 4, 5, 6));");
interpreter.evaluate("print(sum(square, 1, 2, 3, 4, 5, 6));");
```

This concludes our coverage of making Qt applications scriptable using the *QtScript* module. The module is provided with extensive documentation including a broad overview, and detailed descriptions of the classes it provides, including `QScriptContext`, `QScriptEngine`, `QScriptValue`, and `QScriptable`, all of which are worth reading.

- *Interfacing with Native APIs*
- *Using ActiveX on Windows*
- *Handling X11 Session Management*

23. Platform-Specific Features

In this chapter, we will review some of the platform-specific options available to Qt programmers. We begin by looking at how to access native APIs such as the Win32 API on Windows, Carbon on Mac OS X, and Xlib on X11. We then move on to explore the ActiveQt extension, showing how to use ActiveX controls within Qt/Windows applications and how to create applications that act as ActiveX servers. In the last section, we explain how to make Qt applications cooperate with the session manager under X11.

In addition to the features presented here, Trolltech offers several platform-specific Qt Solutions, including the Qt/Motif and Qt/MFC migration frameworks to ease the migration of Motif/Xt and MFC applications to Qt. A similar extension for Tcl/Tk applications is provided by *froglogic*, and a Microsoft Windows resource converter is available from Klarälvdalens Datakonsult. See the following web pages for details:

- `http://www.trolltech.com/products/qt/addon/solutions/catalog/4/`
- `http://www.froglogic.com/tq/`
- `http://www.kdab.net/knut/`

For embedded development, Trolltech offers the Qtopia application platform, which we cover in Chapter 24.

Some Qt functionality that might have been expected to be platform-specific is available in a platform-independent manner. For example, there is a Qt Solution for creating services (daemons) on Windows, Unix, and Mac OS X.

Interfacing with Native APIs

Qt's comprehensive API caters for most needs on all platforms, but in some circumstances, we may want to use the underlying platform-specific APIs. In this section, we will show how to use the native APIs for the different platforms supported by Qt to accomplish particular tasks.

On every platform, QWidget provides a winId() function that returns the window ID or handle. QWidget also provides a static function called find() that returns the QWidget with a particular window ID. We can pass this ID to native API functions to achieve platform-specific effects. For example, the following code uses winId() to move the title bar of a tool window to the left using native Mac OS X (Carbon) functions (see Figure 23.1):

```
#ifdef Q_WS_MAC
    ChangeWindowAttributes(HIViewGetWindow(HIViewRef(toolWin.winId())),
                           kWindowSideTitlebarAttribute,
                           kWindowNoAttributes);
#endif
```

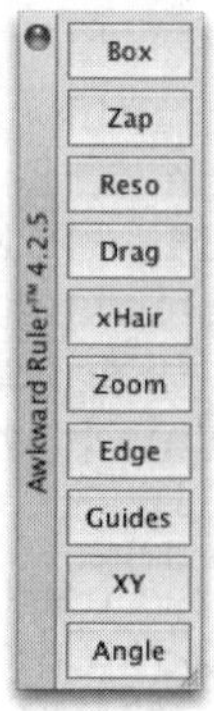

Figure 23.1. A Mac OS X tool window with the title bar on the side

On X11, here's how we would modify a window property:

```
#ifdef Q_WS_X11
    Atom atom = XInternAtom(QX11Info::display(), "MY_PROPERTY", False);
    long data = 1;
    XChangeProperty(QX11Info::display(), window->winId(), atom, atom,
                    32, PropModeReplace,
                    reinterpret_cast<uchar *>(&data), 1);
#endif
```

The #ifdef and #endif directives around the platform-specific code ensure that the application will still compile on other platforms.

For a Windows-only application, here's an example of how we can use GDI calls to draw on a Qt widget:

```
void GdiControl::paintEvent(QPaintEvent * /* event */)
{
    RECT rect;
    GetClientRect(winId(), &rect);
    HDC hdc = GetDC(winId());

    FillRect(hdc, &rect, HBRUSH(COLOR_WINDOW + 1));
    SetTextAlign(hdc, TA_CENTER | TA_BASELINE);
    TextOutW(hdc, width() / 2, height() / 2, text.utf16(), text.size());
```

```
    ReleaseDC(winId(), hdc);
}
```

For this to work, we must also reimplement `QPaintDevice::paintEngine()` to return a null pointer and set the `Qt::WA_PaintOnScreen` attribute in the widget's constructor.

The next example shows how to combine `QPainter` and GDI calls in a paint event handler using `QPaintEngine`'s `getDC()` and `releaseDC()` functions:

```
void MyWidget::paintEvent(QPaintEvent * /* event */)
{
    QPainter painter(this);
    painter.fillRect(rect().adjusted(20, 20, -20, -20), Qt::red);
#ifdef Q_WS_WIN
    HDC hdc = painter.paintEngine()->getDC();
    Rectangle(hdc, 40, 40, width() - 40, height() - 40);
    painter.paintEngine()->releaseDC();
#endif
}
```

Mixing `QPainter` and GDI calls like this can sometimes lead to strange results, especially when `QPainter` calls occur after GDI calls, because `QPainter` makes some assumptions about the state of the underlying drawing layer.

Qt defines one of the following four window system symbols: `Q_WS_WIN`, `Q_WS_X11`, `Q_WS_MAC`, or `Q_WS_QWS` (Qtopia). We must include at least one Qt header before we can use them in applications. Qt also provides preprocessor symbols to identify the operating system:

- `Q_OS_AIX`
- `Q_OS_BSD4`
- `Q_OS_BSDI`
- `Q_OS_CYGWIN`
- `Q_OS_DGUX`
- `Q_OS_DYNIX`
- `Q_OS_FREEBSD`
- `Q_OS_HPUX`
- `Q_OS_HURD`
- `Q_OS_IRIX`
- `Q_OS_LINUX`
- `Q_OS_LYNX`
- `Q_OS_MAC`
- `Q_OS_NETBSD`
- `Q_OS_OPENBSD`
- `Q_OS_OS2EMX`
- `Q_OS_OSF`
- `Q_OS_QNX6`
- `Q_OS_QNX`
- `Q_OS_RELIANT`
- `Q_OS_SCO`
- `Q_OS_SOLARIS`
- `Q_OS_ULTRIX`
- `Q_OS_UNIXWARE`
- `Q_OS_WIN32`
- `Q_OS_WIN64`

We can assume that at most one of these will be defined. For convenience, Qt also defines `Q_OS_WIN` when either Win32 or Win64 is detected, and `Q_OS_UNIX` when any Unix-based operating system (including Linux and Mac OS X) is detected. At run-time, we can check `QSysInfo::WindowsVersion` or `QSysInfo::MacintoshVersion` to distinguish between different versions of Windows (2000, ME, etc.) or Mac OS X (10.2, 10.3, etc.).

In addition to the operating system and window system macros, there is also a set of compiler macros. For example, `Q_CC_MSVC` is defined if the compiler is Microsoft Visual C++. These can be useful for working around compiler bugs.

Several of Qt's GUI-related classes provide platform-specific functions that return low-level handles to the underlying object. These are listed in Figure 23.2.

Mac OS X	
ATSFontFormatRef	QFont::handle()
CGImageRef	QPixmap::macCGHandle()
GWorldPtr	QPixmap::macQDAlphaHandle()
GWorldPtr	QPixmap::macQDHandle()
RgnHandle	QRegion::handle()
HIViewRef	QWidget::winId()
Windows	
HCURSOR	QCursor::handle()
HDC	QPaintEngine::getDC()
HDC	QPrintEngine::getPrinterDC()
HFONT	QFont::handle()
HPALETTE	QColormap::hPal()
HRGN	QRegion::handle()
HWND	QWidget::winId()
X11	
Cursor	QCursor::handle()
Font	QFont::handle()
Picture	QPixmap::x11PictureHandle()
Picture	QWidget::x11PictureHandle()
Pixmap	QPixmap::handle()
QX11Info	QPixmap::x11Info()
QX11Info	QWidget::x11Info()
Region	QRegion::handle()
Screen	QCursor::x11Screen()
SmcConn	QSessionManager::handle()
Window	QWidget::handle()
Window	QWidget::winId()

Figure 23.2. Platform-specific functions to access low-level handles

On X11, `QPixmap::x11Info()` and `QWidget::x11Info()` return a `QX11Info` object that provides various pointers or handles, such as `display()`, `screen()`, `colormap()`, and `visual()`. We can use these to set up an X11 graphics context on a `QPixmap` or `QWidget`, for example.

Qt applications that need to interface with other toolkits or libraries frequently need to access the low-level events (XEvents on X11, MSGs on Windows, EventRef on Mac OS X, QWSEvents on QWS) before they are converted into QEvents. We can do this by subclassing QApplication and reimplementing the relevant platform-specific event filter, one of x11EventFilter(), winEventFilter(), macEventFilter(), and qwsEventFilter(). Alternatively, we can access the platform-specific events that are sent to a given QWidget by reimplementing one of x11Event(), winEvent(), macEvent(), and qwsEvent(). This can be useful for handling certain types of events that Qt normally ignores, such as joystick events.

For more information about platform-specific issues, including how to deploy Qt applications on different platforms, see http://doc.trolltech.com/4.3/winsystem.html.

Using ActiveX on Windows

Microsoft's ActiveX technology allows applications to incorporate user interface components provided by other applications or libraries. It is built on Microsoft COM and defines one set of interfaces for applications that use components and another set of interfaces for applications and libraries that provide components.

The Qt/Windows Desktop Edition provides the ActiveQt framework to seamlessly combine ActiveX and Qt. ActiveQt consists of two modules:

- The *QAxContainer* module allows us to use COM objects and to embed ActiveX controls in Qt applications.
- The *QAxServer* module allows us to export custom COM objects and ActiveX controls written using Qt.

Our first example will embed the Windows Media Player in a Qt application using the *QAxContainer* module (see Figure 23.3). The Qt application adds an Open button, a Play/Pause button, a Stop button, and a slider to the Windows Media Player ActiveX control.

The application's main window is of type PlayerWindow:

```
class PlayerWindow : public QWidget
{
    Q_OBJECT
    Q_ENUMS(ReadyStateConstants)

public:
    enum PlayStateConstants { Stopped = 0, Paused = 1, Playing = 2 };
    enum ReadyStateConstants { Uninitialized = 0, Loading = 1,
                               Interactive = 3, Complete = 4 };

    PlayerWindow();

protected:
    void timerEvent(QTimerEvent *event);
```

Figure 23.3. The Media Player application

```
private slots:
    void onPlayStateChange(int oldState, int newState);
    void onReadyStateChange(ReadyStateConstants readyState);
    void onPositionChange(double oldPos, double newPos);
    void sliderValueChanged(int newValue);
    void openFile();

private:
    QAxWidget *wmp;
    QToolButton *openButton;
    QToolButton *playPauseButton;
    QToolButton *stopButton;
    QSlider *seekSlider;
    QString fileFilters;
    int updateTimer;
};
```

The `PlayerWindow` class is derived from `QWidget`. The `Q_ENUMS()` macro (just below `Q_OBJECT`) is necessary to tell `moc` that the `ReadyStateConstants` type used in the `onReadyStateChange()` slot is an enum type. In the private section, we declare a `QAxWidget *` member variable.

```
PlayerWindow::PlayerWindow()
{
    wmp = new QAxWidget;
    wmp->setControl("{22D6F312-B0F6-11D0-94AB-0080C74C7E95}");
```

In the constructor, we start by creating a `QAxWidget` object to encapsulate the Windows Media Player ActiveX control. The *QAxContainer* module consists of three classes: `QAxObject` encapsulates a COM object, `QAxWidget` encapsulates an ActiveX control, and `QAxBase` implements the core COM functionality for `QAxObject` and `QAxWidget`. The relationships between these classes are illustrated in Figure 23.4.

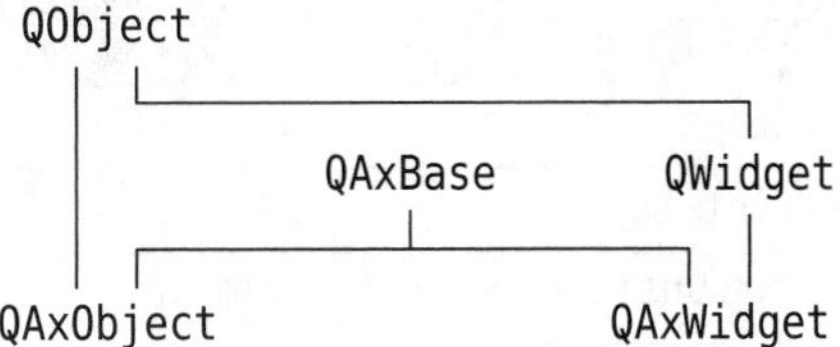

Figure 23.4. Inheritance tree for the *QAxContainer* module

We call setControl() on the QAxWidget with the class ID of the Windows Media Player 6.4 control. This will create an instance of the required component. From then on, all the properties, events, and methods of the ActiveX control are available as Qt properties, signals, and slots through the QAxWidget object.

The COM data types are automatically converted into the corresponding Qt types, as summarized in Figure 23.5. For example, an in-parameter of type VARIANT_BOOL becomes a bool, and an out-parameter of type VARIANT_BOOL becomes a bool &. If the resulting type is a Qt class (QString, QDateTime, etc.), the in-parameter is a const reference (e.g., const QString &).

To obtain the list of the properties, signals, and slots available in a QAxObject or QAxWidget with their Qt data types, call QAxBase::generateDocumentation() or use Qt's dumpdoc command-line tool, located in Qt's tools\activeqt\dumpdoc directory.

Let's continue with the PlayerWindow constructor:

```
    wmp->setProperty("ShowControls", false);
    wmp->setSizePolicy(QSizePolicy::Expanding, QSizePolicy::Expanding);
    connect(wmp, SIGNAL(PlayStateChange(int, int)),
            this, SLOT(onPlayStateChange(int, int)));
    connect(wmp, SIGNAL(ReadyStateChange(ReadyStateConstants)),
            this, SLOT(onReadyStateChange(ReadyStateConstants)));
    connect(wmp, SIGNAL(PositionChange(double, double)),
            this, SLOT(onPositionChange(double, double)));
```

After calling QAxWidget::setControl(), we call QObject::setProperty() to set the ShowControls property of the Windows Media Player to false, since we provide our own buttons to manipulate the component. QObject::setProperty() can be used both for COM properties and for normal Qt properties. Its second parameter is of type QVariant.

Next, we call setSizePolicy() to make the ActiveX control take all the available space in the layout, and we connect three ActiveX events from the COM component to three slots.

```
    ...
    stopButton = new QToolButton;
    stopButton->setText(tr("&Stop"));
    stopButton->setEnabled(false);
    connect(stopButton, SIGNAL(clicked()), wmp, SLOT(Stop()));
    ...
}
```

COM Types	Qt Types
VARIANT_BOOL	bool
char, short, int, long	int
unsigned char, unsigned short, unsigned int, unsigned long	uint
float, double	double
CY	qlonglong, qulonglong
BSTR	QString
DATE	QDateTime, QDate, QTime
OLE_COLOR	QColor
SAFEARRAY(VARIANT)	QList<QVariant>
SAFEARRAY(BSTR)	QStringList
SAFEARRAY(BYTE)	QByteArray
VARIANT	QVariant
IFontDisp *	QFont
IPictureDisp *	QPixmap
User defined type	QRect, QSize, QPoint

Figure 23.5. Relationship between COM types and Qt types

The rest of the `PlayerWindow` constructor follows the usual pattern, except that we connect some Qt signals to slots provided by the COM object (`Play()`, `Pause()`, and `Stop()`). Since the buttons are similar, we have shown only the Stop button's implementation here.

Let's leave the constructor and look at the `timerEvent()` function:

```
void PlayerWindow::timerEvent(QTimerEvent *event)
{
    if (event->timerId() == updateTimer) {
        double curPos = wmp->property("CurrentPosition").toDouble();
        onPositionChange(-1, curPos);
    } else {
        QWidget::timerEvent(event);
    }
}
```

The `timerEvent()` function is called at regular intervals while a media clip is playing. We use it to advance the slider. This is done by calling `property()` on the ActiveX control to obtain the value of the `CurrentPosition` property as a `QVariant` and calling `toDouble()` to convert it to a `double`. We then call `onPositionChange()` to perform the update.

We will not review the rest of the code because most of it isn't directly relevant to ActiveX and doesn't show anything that we haven't covered already. The code is included with the book's examples.

In the .pro file, we need this entry to link with the *QAxContainer* module:

```
CONFIG += qaxcontainer
```

One frequent need when dealing with COM objects is to be able to call a COM method directly (as opposed to connecting it to a Qt signal). The easiest way to do this is to invoke `QAxBase::dynamicCall()` with the name and signature of the method as the first parameter and the arguments to the method as additional parameters. For example:

```
wmp->dynamicCall("TitlePlay(uint)", 6);
```

The `dynamicCall()` function takes up to eight parameters of type `QVariant` and returns a `QVariant`. If we need to pass an `IDispatch *` or an `IUnknown *` this way, we can encapsulate the component in a `QAxObject` and call `asVariant()` on it to convert it to a `QVariant`. If we need to call a COM method that returns an `IDispatch *` or an `IUnknown *`, or if we need to access a COM property of one of those types, we can use `querySubObject()` instead:

```
QAxObject *session = outlook.querySubObject("Session");
QAxObject *defaultContacts =
        session->querySubObject("GetDefaultFolder(OlDefaultFolders)",
                                "olFolderContacts");
```

If we want to call methods that have unsupported data types in their parameter list, we can use `QAxBase::queryInterface()` to retrieve the COM interface and call the method directly. As usual with COM, we must call `Release()` when we have finished using the interface. If we often need to call such methods, we can subclass `QAxObject` or `QAxWidget` and provide member functions that encapsulate the COM interface calls. Be aware that `QAxObject` and `QAxWidget` subclasses cannot define their own properties, signals, or slots.

We will now review the *QAxServer* module. This module enables us to turn a standard Qt program into an ActiveX server. The server can be either a shared library or a stand-alone application. Servers built as shared libraries are often called *in-process servers*; stand-alone applications are called *out-of-process servers*.

Our first *QAxServer* example is an in-process server that provides a widget that shows a ball bouncing left and right. We will also see how to embed the widget in Internet Explorer.

Here's the beginning of the class definition of the `AxBouncer` widget:

```
class AxBouncer : public QWidget, public QAxBindable
{
    Q_OBJECT
    Q_ENUMS(SpeedValue)
    Q_PROPERTY(QColor color READ color WRITE setColor)
```

```
    Q_PROPERTY(SpeedValue speed READ speed WRITE setSpeed)
    Q_PROPERTY(int radius READ radius WRITE setRadius)
    Q_PROPERTY(bool running READ isRunning)
```

AxBouncer, shown in Figure 23.6, is derived from both QWidget and QAxBindable. The QAxBindable class provides an interface between the widget and an ActiveX client. Any QWidget can be exported as an ActiveX control, but by subclassing QAxBindable we can notify the client when a property's value changes, and we can implement COM interfaces to supplement those already implemented by *QAxServer*.

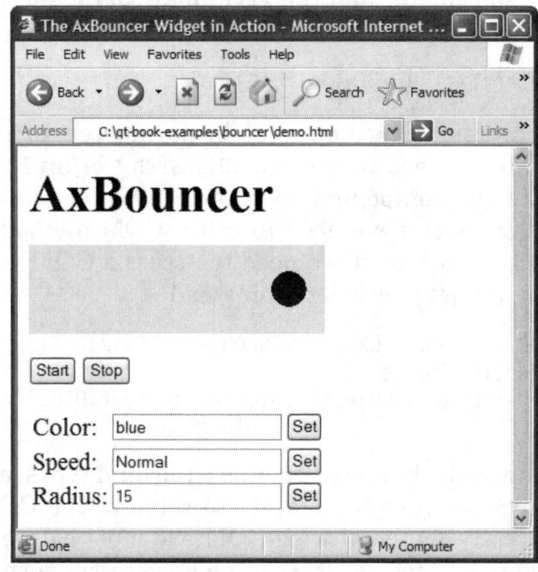

Figure 23.6. The AxBouncer widget in Internet Explorer

When doing multiple inheritance involving a QObject-derived class, we must always put the QObject-derived class first so that moc can pick it up.

We declare three read-write properties and one read-only property. The Q_ENUMS() macro is necessary to tell moc that the SpeedValue type is an enum type. The enum is declared in the public section of the class:

```
public:
    enum SpeedValue { Slow, Normal, Fast };

    AxBouncer(QWidget *parent = 0);

    void setSpeed(SpeedValue newSpeed);
    SpeedValue speed() const { return ballSpeed; }
    void setRadius(int newRadius);
    int radius() const { return ballRadius; }
    void setColor(const QColor &newColor);
    QColor color() const { return ballColor; }
    bool isRunning() const { return myTimerId != 0; }
```

```
    QSize sizeHint() const;
    QAxAggregated *createAggregate();

public slots:
    void start();
    void stop();

signals:
    void bouncing();
```

The AxBouncer constructor is a standard constructor for a widget, with a parent parameter. The QAXFACTORY_DEFAULT() macro, which we will use to export the component, expects a constructor with this signature.

The createAggregate() function is reimplemented from QAxBindable. We will explain it in a moment.

```
protected:
    void paintEvent(QPaintEvent *event);
    void timerEvent(QTimerEvent *event);

private:
    int intervalInMilliseconds() const;

    QColor ballColor;
    SpeedValue ballSpeed;
    int ballRadius;
    int myTimerId;
    int x;
    int delta;
};
```

The protected and private sections of the class are the same as those we would have if this was a standard Qt widget.

```
AxBouncer::AxBouncer(QWidget *parent)
    : QWidget(parent)
{
    ballColor = Qt::blue;
    ballSpeed = Normal;
    ballRadius = 15;
    myTimerId = 0;
    x = 20;
    delta = 2;
}
```

The AxBouncer constructor initializes the class's private variables.

```
void AxBouncer::setColor(const QColor &newColor)
{
    if (newColor != ballColor && requestPropertyChange("color")) {
        ballColor = newColor;
        update();
        propertyChanged("color");
    }
}
```

The setColor() function sets the value of the color property. It calls update() to repaint the widget.

The unusual part is the requestPropertyChange() and propertyChanged() calls. These functions are inherited from QAxBindable and should ideally be called whenever we change a property. The requestPropertyChange() asks the client's permission to change a property, and returns true if the client allows the change. The propertyChanged() function notifies the client that the property has been changed.

The setSpeed() and setRadius() setters also follow this pattern, and so do the start() and stop() slots, since they change the value of the running property.

One interesting AxBouncer member function is left:

```
QAxAggregated *AxBouncer::createAggregate()
{
    return new ObjectSafetyImpl;
}
```

The createAggregate() function is reimplemented from QAxBindable. It allows us to implement COM interfaces that the *QAxServer* module doesn't already implement or to bypass *QAxServer*'s default COM interfaces. Here, we do it to provide the IObjectSafety interface, which Internet Explorer uses to access a component's safety options. This is the standard trick to get rid of Internet Explorer's infamous "Object not safe for scripting" error message.

Here's the definition of the class that implements the IObjectSafety interface:

```
class ObjectSafetyImpl : public QAxAggregated, public IObjectSafety
{
public:
    long queryInterface(const QUuid &iid, void **iface);

    QAXAGG_IUNKNOWN

    HRESULT WINAPI GetInterfaceSafetyOptions(REFIID riid,
            DWORD *pdwSupportedOptions, DWORD *pdwEnabledOptions);
    HRESULT WINAPI SetInterfaceSafetyOptions(REFIID riid,
            DWORD pdwSupportedOptions, DWORD pdwEnabledOptions);
};
```

The ObjectSafetyImpl class is derived from both QAxAggregated and IObjectSafety. The QAxAggregated class is an abstract base class for implementations of additional COM interfaces. The COM object that the QAxAggregated extends is accessible through controllingUnknown(). The *QAxServer* module creates this COM object behind the scenes.

The QAXAGG_IUNKNOWN macro provides standard implementations of QueryInterface(), AddRef(), and Release(). These implementations simply call the same functions on the controlling COM object.

```
long ObjectSafetyImpl::queryInterface(const QUuid &iid, void **iface)
{
```

```
        *iface = 0;
        if (iid == IID_IObjectSafety) {
            *iface = static_cast<IObjectSafety *>(this);
        } else {
            return E_NOINTERFACE;
        }
        AddRef();
        return S_OK;
    }
```

The `queryInterface()` function is a pure virtual function of `QAxAggregated`. It is called by the controlling COM object to give access to the interfaces provided by the `QAxAggregated` subclass. We must return `E_NOINTERFACE` for interfaces that we don't implement and for `IUnknown`.

```
HRESULT WINAPI ObjectSafetyImpl::GetInterfaceSafetyOptions(
        REFIID /* riid */, DWORD *pdwSupportedOptions,
        DWORD *pdwEnabledOptions)
{
    *pdwSupportedOptions = INTERFACESAFE_FOR_UNTRUSTED_DATA
                           | INTERFACESAFE_FOR_UNTRUSTED_CALLER;
    *pdwEnabledOptions = *pdwSupportedOptions;
    return S_OK;
}

HRESULT WINAPI ObjectSafetyImpl::SetInterfaceSafetyOptions(
        REFIID /* riid */, DWORD /* pdwSupportedOptions */,
        DWORD /* pdwEnabledOptions */)
{
    return S_OK;
}
```

The `GetInterfaceSafetyOptions()` and `SetInterfaceSafetyOptions()` functions are declared in `IObjectSafety`. We implement them to tell the world that our object is safe for scripting.

Let's now review `main.cpp`:

```
#include <QAxFactory>

#include "axbouncer.h"

QAXFACTORY_DEFAULT(AxBouncer,
                   "{5e2461aa-a3e8-4f7a-8b04-307459a4c08c}",
                   "{533af11f-4899-43de-8b7f-2ddf588d1015}",
                   "{772c14a5-a840-4023-b79d-19549ece0cd9}",
                   "{dbce1e56-70dd-4f74-85e0-95c65d86254d}",
                   "{3f3db5e0-78ff-4e35-8a5d-3d3b96c83e09}")
```

The `QAXFACTORY_DEFAULT()` macro exports an ActiveX control. We can use it for ActiveX servers that export only one control. The next example in this section will show how to export many ActiveX controls.

The first argument to `QAXFACTORY_DEFAULT()` is the name of the Qt class to export. This is also the name under which the control is exported. The other five arguments are the class ID, the interface ID, the event interface ID, the type library ID, and the application ID. We can use standard tools such as guidgen or uuidgen to generate these identifiers. Because the server is a library, we don't need a main() function.

Here's the .pro file for our in-process ActiveX server:

```
TEMPLATE      = lib
CONFIG       += dll qaxserver
HEADERS       = axbouncer.h \
                objectsafetyimpl.h
SOURCES       = axbouncer.cpp \
                main.cpp \
                objectsafetyimpl.cpp
RC_FILE       = qaxserver.rc
DEF_FILE      = qaxserver.def
```

The qaxserver.rc and qaxserver.def files referred to in the .pro file are standard files that can be copied from Qt's src\activeqt\control directory.

The makefile or Visual C++ project file generated by qmake contains rules to register the server in the Windows registry. To register the server on end-user machines, we can use the regsvr32 tool available on all Windows systems.

We can then include the Bouncer component in an HTML page using the <object> tag:

```
<object id="AxBouncer"
        classid="clsid:5e2461aa-a3e8-4f7a-8b04-307459a4c08c">
<b>The ActiveX control is not available. Make sure you have built and
registered the component server.</b>
</object>
```

We can create buttons that invoke slots:

```
<input type="button" value="Start" onClick="AxBouncer.start()">
<input type="button" value="Stop" onClick="AxBouncer.stop()">
```

We can manipulate the widget using JavaScript or VBScript just like any other ActiveX control. See the demo.html file included with the book's examples for a rudimentary page that uses the ActiveX server.

Our last example is a scriptable Address Book application. The application can serve as a standard Qt/Windows application or an out-of-process ActiveX server. The latter possibility allows us to script the application using, say, Visual Basic.

```
class AddressBook : public QMainWindow
{
    Q_OBJECT
    Q_PROPERTY(int count READ count)
    Q_CLASSINFO("ClassID", "{588141ef-110d-4beb-95ab-ee6a478b576d}")
    Q_CLASSINFO("InterfaceID", "{718780ec-b30c-4d88-83b3-79b3d9e78502}")
    Q_CLASSINFO("ToSuperClass", "AddressBook")
```

```
public:
    AddressBook(QWidget *parent = 0);
    ~AddressBook();

    int count() const;

public slots:
    ABItem *createEntry(const QString &contact);
    ABItem *findEntry(const QString &contact) const;
    ABItem *entryAt(int index) const;

private slots:
    void addEntry();
    void editEntry();
    void deleteEntry();

private:
    void createActions();
    void createMenus();

    QTreeWidget *treeWidget;
    QMenu *fileMenu;
    QMenu *editMenu;
    QAction *exitAction;
    QAction *addEntryAction;
    QAction *editEntryAction;
    QAction *deleteEntryAction;
};
```

The `AddressBook` widget is the application's main window. The widget's property and its public slots will be available for scripting. The `Q_CLASSINFO()` macro is used to specify the class and interface IDs associated with the class. These were generated using a tool such as `guid` or `uuid`.

In the previous example, we specified the class and interface IDs when we exported the `QAxBouncer` class using the `QAXFACTORY_DEFAULT()` macro. In this example, we want to export several classes, so we cannot use `QAXFACTORY_DEFAULT()`. Two options are available to us:

- We can subclass `QAxFactory`, reimplement its virtual functions to provide information about the types we want to export, and use the `QAXFACTORY_EXPORT()` macro to register the factory.
- We can use the `QAXFACTORY_BEGIN()`, `QAXFACTORY_END()`, `QAXCLASS()`, and `QAXTYPE()` macros to declare and register the factory. This approach requires us to specify the class and interface IDs using `Q_CLASSINFO()`.

Back to the `AddressBook` class definition: The third occurrence of `Q_CLASSINFO()` may seem a bit mysterious. By default, ActiveX controls expose not only their own properties, signals, and slots to clients, but also those of their ancestors up to `QWidget`. The `ToSuperClass` attribute lets us specify the highest ancestor in the inheritance tree that we want to expose. Here, we specify the class name of the component (`AddressBook`) as the highest ancestor to export, meaning that properties, signals, and slots inherited from AddressBook's own ancestors will not be exported.

```
class ABItem : public QObject, public QTreeWidgetItem
{
    Q_OBJECT
    Q_PROPERTY(QString contact READ contact WRITE setContact)
    Q_PROPERTY(QString address READ address WRITE setAddress)
    Q_PROPERTY(QString phoneNumber READ phoneNumber
               WRITE setPhoneNumber)
    Q_CLASSINFO("ClassID", "{bc82730e-5f39-4e5c-96be-461c2cd0d282}")
    Q_CLASSINFO("InterfaceID", "{c8bc1656-870e-48a9-9937-fbe1ceff8b2e}")
    Q_CLASSINFO("ToSuperClass", "ABItem")

public:
    ABItem(QTreeWidget *treeWidget);

    void setContact(const QString &contact);
    QString contact() const { return text(0); }
    void setAddress(const QString &address);
    QString address() const { return text(1); }
    void setPhoneNumber(const QString &number);
    QString phoneNumber() const { return text(2); }

public slots:
    void remove();
};
```

The ABItem class represents one entry in the address book. It is derived from QTreeWidgetItem so that it can be shown in a QTreeWidget and from QObject so that it can be exported as a COM object.

```
int main(int argc, char *argv[])
{
    QApplication app(argc, argv);
    if (!QAxFactory::isServer()) {
        AddressBook addressBook;
        addressBook.show();
        return app.exec();
    }
    return app.exec();
}
```

In main(), we check whether the application is being run stand-alone or as a server. The -activex command-line option is recognized by QApplication and makes the application run as a server. If the application isn't run as a server, we create the main widget and show it as we would normally do in any stand-alone Qt application.

In addition to -activex, ActiveX servers understand the following command-line options:

- -regserver registers the server in the system registry.
- -unregserver unregisters the server from the system registry.

- `-dumpidl` *`file.idl`* writes the server's IDL to the specified file.

When the application is run as a server, we must export the `AddressBook` and `ABItem` classes as COM components:

```
QAXFACTORY_BEGIN("{2b2b6f3e-86cf-4c49-9df5-80483b47f17b}",
                 "{8e827b25-148b-4307-ba7d-23f275244818}")
QAXCLASS(AddressBook)
QAXTYPE(ABItem)
QAXFACTORY_END()
```

The preceding macros export a factory for creating COM objects. Since we want to export two types of COM objects, we cannot simply use `QAXFACTORY_DEFAULT()` as we did in the previous example.

The first argument to `QAXFACTORY_BEGIN()` is the type library ID; the second argument is the application ID. Between `QAXFACTORY_BEGIN()` and `QAXFACTORY_END()`, we specify all the classes that can be instantiated and all the data types that we want to make accessible as COM objects.

This is the `.pro` file for our out-of-process ActiveX server:

```
TEMPLATE      = app
CONFIG       += qaxserver
HEADERS       = abitem.h \
                addressbook.h \
                editdialog.h
SOURCES       = abitem.cpp \
                addressbook.cpp \
                editdialog.cpp \
                main.cpp
FORMS         = editdialog.ui
RC_FILE       = qaxserver.rc
```

The `qaxserver.rc` file referred to in the `.pro` file is a standard file that can be copied from Qt's `src\activeqt\control` directory.

Look in the example's `vb` directory for a Visual Basic project that uses the Address Book server.

This completes our overview of the ActiveQt framework. The Qt distribution includes additional examples, and the documentation contains information about how to build the *QAxContainer* and *QAxServer* modules and how to solve common interoperability issues.

Handling X11 Session Management

When we log out on X11, some window managers ask us whether we want to save the session. If we say yes, the applications that were running are automatically restarted the next time we log in, with the same screen positions and, ideally, with the same state as they had when we logged out. An example of this is shown in Figure 23.7.

The X11-specific component that takes care of saving and restoring the session is called the *session manager*. To make a Qt/X11 application aware of the session manager, we must reimplement `QApplication::saveState()` and save the application's state there.

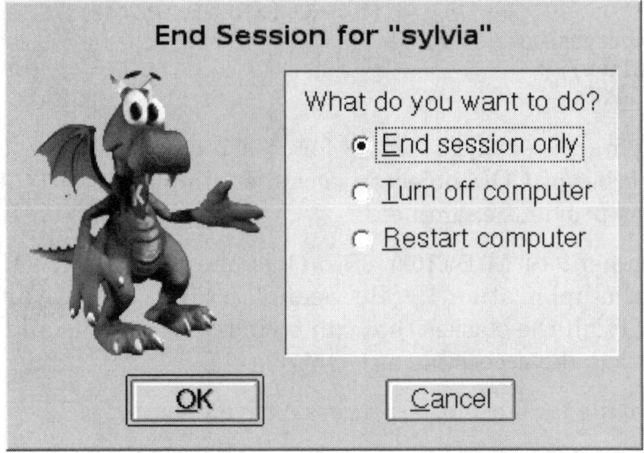

Figure 23.7. Logging out on KDE

Microsoft Windows and some Unix systems offer a different mechanism called hibernation. When the user puts the computer into hibernation, the operating system simply dumps the computer's memory onto disk and reloads it when it wakes up. Applications do not need to do anything or even be aware that this happens.

When the user initiates a shutdown, we can take control just before the shutdown occurs by reimplementing `QApplication::commitData()`. This allows us to save any unsaved data and to interact with the user if required. This part of session management is supported on both X11 and Windows.

We will explore session management by going through the code of the session-aware Tic-Tac-Toe application shown in Figure 23.8. First, let's look at the `main()` function:

```
int main(int argc, char *argv[])
{
    Application app(argc, argv);
    TicTacToe toe;
    toe.setObjectName("toe");
    app.setTicTacToe(&toe);
    toe.show();
    return app.exec();
}
```

We create an `Application` object. The `Application` class is derived from `QApplication` and reimplements both `commitData()` and `saveState()` to support session management.

Next, we create a `TicTacToe` widget, make the `Application` object aware of it, and show it. We have called the `TicTacToe` widget "toe". We must give unique object names to top-level widgets if we want the session manager to restore the windows' sizes and positions.

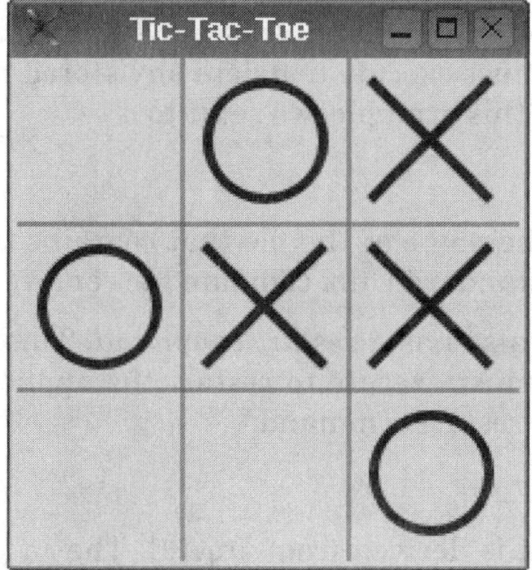

Figure 23.8. The Tic-Tac-Toe application

Here's the definition of the `Application` class:

```
class Application : public QApplication
{
    Q_OBJECT

public:
    Application(int &argc, char *argv[]);

    void setTicTacToe(TicTacToe *toe);
    void saveState(QSessionManager &sessionManager);
    void commitData(QSessionManager &sessionManager);

private:
    TicTacToe *ticTacToe;
};
```

The `Application` class keeps a pointer to the `TicTacToe` widget as a private variable.

```
void Application::saveState(QSessionManager &sessionManager)
{
    QString fileName = ticTacToe->saveState();

    QStringList discardCommand;
    discardCommand << "rm" << fileName;
    sessionManager.setDiscardCommand(discardCommand);
}
```

On X11, the `saveState()` function is called when the session manager wants the application to save its state. The function is available on other platforms as well, but it is never called. The `QSessionManager` parameter allows us to communicate with the session manager.

We start by asking the `TicTacToe` widget to save its state to a file. Then we set the session manager's discard command. A *discard command* is a command that the session manager must execute to delete any stored information regarding the current state. For this example, we set it to

```
rm sessionfile
```

where *sessionfile* is the name of the file that contains the saved state for the session, and `rm` is the standard Unix command to remove files.

The session manager also has a *restart command*. This is the command that the session manager must execute to restart the application. By default, Qt provides the following restart command:

```
appname -session id_key
```

The first part, *appname*, is derived from `argv[0]`. The *id* part is the session ID provided by the session manager; it is guaranteed to be unique among different applications and among different runs of the same application. The *key* part is added to uniquely identify the time at which the state was saved. For various reasons, the session manager can call `saveState()` multiple times during the same session, and the different states must be distinguished.

Because of limitations in existing session managers, we must ensure that the application's directory is in the `PATH` environment variable if we want the application to restart correctly. In particular, if you want to try out the Tic-Tac-Toe example for yourself, you must install it in, say, `/usr/local/bin` and invoke it as `tictactoe`.

For simple applications, including Tic-Tac-Toe, we could save the state as an additional command-line argument to the restart command. For example:

```
tictactoe -state OX-XO-X-O
```

This would save us from storing the data in a file and providing a discard command to remove the file.

```
void Application::commitData(QSessionManager &sessionManager)
{
    if (ticTacToe->gameInProgress()
            && sessionManager.allowsInteraction()) {
        int r = QMessageBox::warning(ticTacToe, tr("Tic-Tac-Toe"),
                        tr("The game hasn't finished.\n"
                           "Do you really want to quit?"),
                        QMessageBox::Yes | QMessageBox::No);
        if (r == QMessageBox::Yes) {
            sessionManager.release();
        } else {
```

```
                sessionManager.cancel();
            }
        }
    }
```

The `commitData()` function is called when the user logs out. We can reimplement it to pop up a message box warning the user about potential data loss. The default implementation closes all top-level widgets, which results in the same behavior as when the user closes the windows one after another by clicking the close button in their title bars. In Chapter 3, we saw how to reimplement `closeEvent()` to catch this and pop up a message box.

For the purposes of this example, we reimplement `commitData()` and pop up a message box asking the user to confirm the logout if a game is in progress and if the session manager allows us to interact with the user (see Figure 23.9). If the user clicks Yes, we call `release()` to tell the session manager to continue logging out; if the user clicks No, we call `cancel()` to cancel the logout.

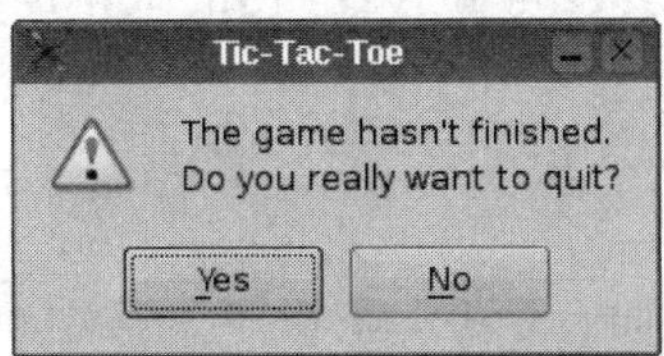

Figure 23.9. "Do you really want to quit?"

Now let's look at the `TicTacToe` class:

```
class TicTacToe : public QWidget
{
    Q_OBJECT

public:
    TicTacToe(QWidget *parent = 0);

    bool gameInProgress() const;
    QString saveState() const;
    QSize sizeHint() const;

protected:
    void paintEvent(QPaintEvent *event);
    void mousePressEvent(QMouseEvent *event);

private:
    enum { Empty = '-', Cross = 'X', Nought = 'O' };

    void clearBoard();
    void restoreState();
    QString sessionFileName() const;
    QRect cellRect(int row, int column) const;
    int cellWidth() const { return width() / 3; }
    int cellHeight() const { return height() / 3; }
    bool threeInARow(int row1, int col1, int row3, int col3) const;
```

```
    char board[3][3];
    int turnNumber;
};
```

The TicTacToe class is derived from QWidget and reimplements sizeHint(), paintEvent(), and mousePressEvent(). It also provides the gameInProgress() and saveState() functions that we used in our Application class.

```
TicTacToe::TicTacToe(QWidget *parent)
    : QWidget(parent)
{
    clearBoard();
    if (qApp->isSessionRestored())
        restoreState();

    setWindowTitle(tr("Tic-Tac-Toe"));
}
```

In the constructor, we clear the board, and if the application was invoked with the -session option, we call the private function restoreState() to reload the old session.

```
void TicTacToe::clearBoard()
{
    for (int row = 0; row < 3; ++row) {
        for (int column = 0; column < 3; ++column) {
            board[row][column] = Empty;
        }
    }
    turnNumber = 0;
}
```

In clearBoard(), we clear all the cells and set turnNumber to 0.

```
QString TicTacToe::saveState() const
{
    QFile file(sessionFileName());
    if (file.open(QIODevice::WriteOnly)) {
        QTextStream out(&file);
        for (int row = 0; row < 3; ++row) {
            for (int column = 0; column < 3; ++column)
                out << board[row][column];
        }
    }
    return file.fileName();
}
```

In saveState(), we write the state of the board to disk. The format is straightforward, with 'X' for crosses, 'O' for noughts, and '–' for empty cells.

```
QString TicTacToe::sessionFileName() const
{
    return QDir::homePath() + "/.tictactoe_" + qApp->sessionId() + "_"
           + qApp->sessionKey();
}
```

The `sessionFileName()` private function returns the file name for the current session ID and session key. This function is used for both `saveState()` and `restoreState()`. The file name is derived from the session ID and session key.

```
void TicTacToe::restoreState()
{
    QFile file(sessionFileName());
    if (file.open(QIODevice::ReadOnly)) {
        QTextStream in(&file);
        for (int row = 0; row < 3; ++row) {
            for (int column = 0; column < 3; ++column) {
                in >> board[row][column];
                if (board[row][column] != Empty)
                    ++turnNumber;
            }
        }
    }
    update();
}
```

In `restoreState()`, we load the file that corresponds to the restored session and fill the board with that information. We deduce the value of `turnNumber` from the number of X's and O's on the board.

In the `TicTacToe` constructor, we called `restoreState()` if `QApplication::isSessionRestored()` returned `true`. In that case, `sessionId()` and `sessionKey()` return the same values as when the application's state was saved, and so `sessionFileName()` returns the file name for that session.

Testing and debugging session management can be frustrating, because we need to log in and out all the time. One way to avoid this is to use the standard `xsm` utility provided with X11. The first time we invoke `xsm`, it pops up a session manager window and a terminal. The applications we start from that terminal will all use `xsm` as their session manager instead of the usual, system-wide session manager. We can then use `xsm`'s window to end, restart, or discard a session, and see whether our application behaves as it should. For details about how to do this, see `http://doc.trolltech.com/4.3/session.html`.

- *Getting Started with Qt/Embedded Linux*
- *Customizing Qt/Embedded Linux*
- *Integrating Qt Applications with Qtopia*
- *Using Qtopia APIs*

24. Embedded Programming

Developing software to run on mobile devices such as PDAs and mobile phones can be very challenging because embedded systems generally have slower processors, less permanent storage (flash memory or hard disk), less memory, and smaller displays than desktop computers.

Qt/Embedded Linux (also called Qtopia Core) is an edition of Qt optimized for embedded Linux. Qt/Embedded Linux provides the same API and tools as the desktop versions of Qt (Qt/Windows, Qt/X11, and Qt/Mac), and adds the classes and tools necessary for embedded programming. Through dual licensing, it is available for both open source and commercial development.

Qt/Embedded Linux can run on any hardware that runs Linux—including Intel x86, MIPS, ARM, StrongARM, Motorola/Freescale 68000, and PowerPC architectures.* Unlike Qt/X11, it does not need the X Window System; instead, it implements its own window system, QWS, enabling significant storage and memory savings. To reduce its memory footprint even more, Qt/Embedded Linux can be recompiled to exclude unused features. If the applications and components used on a device are known in advance, they can be compiled together into a single executable that links statically against the Qt/Embedded Linux libraries.

Qt/Embedded Linux also benefits from various features that are also part of the desktop versions of Qt, including the extensive use of implicit data sharing ("copy on write") as a memory-saving technique, support for custom widget styles through `QStyle`, and a layout system that adapts to make the best use of the available screen space.

Qt/Embedded Linux forms the basis of Trolltech's embedded offering, which also includes Qtopia Platform, Qtopia PDA, and Qtopia Phone. These provide classes and applications designed specifically for portable devices and can be integrated with several third-party Java virtual machines.

---

*Starting with version 4.4, Qt is expected to run on Windows CE as well.

Getting Started with Qt/Embedded Linux

Qt/Embedded Linux applications can be developed on any platform equipped with an appropriate tool chain. The most common option is to build a GNU C++ cross-compiler on a Unix system. This process is simplified by a script and a set of patches provided by Dan Kegel at http://kegel.com/crosstool/. For this chapter, we have used the Qtopia Open Source Edition version 4.2 available from http://www.trolltech.com/products/qtopia/opensource/. This edition is suitable only for Linux and includes its own copy of Qt/Embedded Linux 4.2, along with additional tools to support Qtopia programming on a desktop PC.

Qt/Embedded Linux's configuration system supports cross-compiling, through the configure script's -embedded and -xplatform options. For example, to build for the ARM architecture we would type

```
./configure -embedded arm -xplatform qws/linux-arm-g++
```

We can create custom configurations by adding new files to Qt's mkspecs/qws directory.

Qt/Embedded Linux draws directly to the Linux framebuffer (the memory area associated with the video display). The virtual framebuffer shown in Figure 24.1 is an X11 application that simulates, pixel for pixel, the actual framebuffer. To access the framebuffer, you might need to grant write permissions to the /dev/fb0 device.

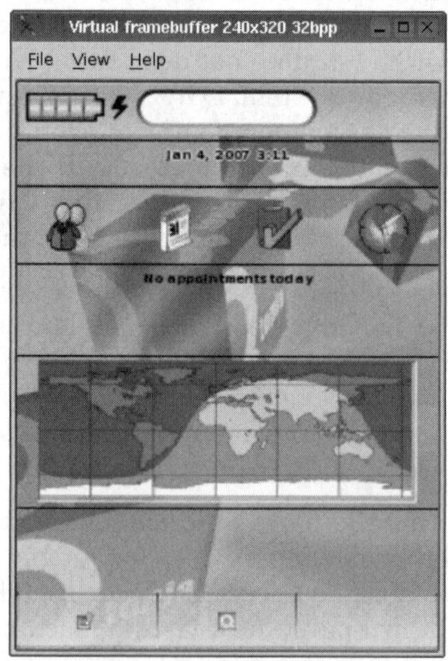

Figure 24.1. Qt/Embedded Linux running in a virtual framebuffer

To run Qt/Embedded Linux applications, we must first start one process to act as a GUI server. The server is responsible for allocating screen regions to clients and for generating mouse and keyboard events. Any Qt/Embedded Linux application can become a server by specifying `-qws` on its command line or by passing `QApplication::GuiServer` as the third parameter to the `QApplication` constructor.

Client applications communicate with the Qt/Embedded Linux server using shared memory and Unix pipes. Behind the scenes, the clients draw themselves into the Linux framebuffer and are responsible for painting their own window decorations.

Clients can communicate with each other using QCOP—the Qt Communication Protocol. A client can listen on a named channel by creating a `QCopChannel` object and connecting to its `received()` signal. For example:

```
QCopChannel *channel = new QCopChannel("System", this);
connect(channel, SIGNAL(received(const QString &, const QByteArray &)),
        this, SLOT(received(const QString &, const QByteArray &)));
```

A QCOP message consists of a name and an optional `QByteArray`. The static `QCopChannel::send()` function broadcasts a message on a channel. For example:

```
QByteArray data;
QDataStream out(&data, QIODevice::WriteOnly);
out << QDateTime::currentDateTime();

QCopChannel::send("System", "clockSkew(QDateTime)", data);
```

The preceding example illustrates a common idiom: We encode the data using `QDataStream`, and we mangle the data format in the message name as though it were a C++ function to ensure that receiver interprets the `QByteArray` correctly.

Various environment variables affect Qt/Embedded Linux applications. The most important ones are `QWS_MOUSE_PROTO` and `QWS_KEYBOARD`, which specify the mouse device and the keyboard type. See `http://doc.trolltech.com/4.2/qtopiacore-envvars.html` for a complete list of environment variables.

If we use Unix as our development platform, we can test the application using the Qt virtual framebuffer (`qvfb`), an X11 application that simulates the actual framebuffer. This accelerates the development cycle considerably. To enable virtual buffer support in Qt/Embedded Linux, pass the `-qvfb` option to the `configure` script. Be aware that this option is not intended for production use. The virtual framebuffer application is located in `tools/qvfb` and can be invoked as follows:

```
qvfb -width 320 -height 480 -depth 32
```

An alternative to using the X11-specific virtual framebuffer is to use VNC (Virtual Network Computing) to run the applications remotely. To enable VNC support in Qt/Embedded Linux, pass the `-qt-gfx-vnc` option to `configure`. Then launch your Qt/Embedded Linux applications with the `-display VNC:0` command-line option and run a VNC client pointing at the host on which your applications are running. The display size and bit depth can be specified by setting the `QWS_SIZE` and `QWS_DEPTH` environment variables on the host that runs the Qt/Embedded Linux applications (e.g., `QWS_SIZE=320x480` and `QWS_DEPTH=32`).

Customizing Qt/Embedded Linux

When installing Qt/Embedded Linux, we can specify features we want to leave out to reduce its memory footprint. Qt/Embedded Linux includes more than one hundred configurable features, each of which is associated with a preprocessor symbol. For example, `QT_NO_FILEDIALOG` excludes `QFileDialog` from the *QtGui* library, and `QT_NO_I18N` leaves out all support for internationalization. The features are listed in `src/corelib/global/qfeatures.txt`.

Qt/Embedded Linux provides five example configurations (`minimum`, `small`, `medium`, `large`, and `dist`) that are stored in `src/corelib/global/qconfig-`*`xxx`*`.h` files. These configurations can be specified using the `configure` script's `-qconfig` *`xxx`* option, for example:

```
./configure -qconfig small
```

To create custom configurations, we can manually provide a `qconfig-`*`xxx`*`.h` file and use it as though it were a standard configuration. Alternatively, we can use the `qconfig` graphical tool, located in Qt's `tools` subdirectory.

Qt/Embedded Linux provides the following classes for interfacing with input and output devices and for customizing the look and feel of the window system:

Class	Base Class for
`QScreen`	Screen drivers
`QScreenDriverPlugin`	Screen driver plugins
`QWSMouseHandler`	Mouse drivers
`QMouseDriverPlugin`	Mouse driver plugins
`QWSKeyboardHandler`	Keyboard drivers
`QKbdDriverPlugin`	Keyboard driver plugins
`QWSInputMethod`	Input methods
`QDecoration`	Window decoration styles
`QDecorationPlugin`	Window decoration style plugins

To obtain the list of predefined drivers, input methods, and window decoration styles, run the `configure` script with the `-help` option.

The screen driver can be specified using the `-display` command-line option when starting the Qt/Embedded Linux server, as seen in the previous section, or by setting the `QWS_DISPLAY` environment variable. The mouse driver and the associated device can be specified using the `QWS_MOUSE_PROTO` environment variable, whose value must have the syntax *type*:*device*, where *type* is one of the supported drivers and *device* is the path to the device (e.g., `QWS_MOUSE_PROTO=IntelliMouse:/dev/mouse`). Keyboards are handled similarly through the `QWS_KEYBOARD` environment variable. Input methods and window decorations are set programmatically in the server using `QWSServer::setCurrentInputMethod()` and `QApplication::qwsSetDecoration()`.

Window decoration styles can be set independently of the widget style, which is encapsulated by a `QStyle` subclass. For example, it is entirely possible to set Windows as the window decoration style and Plastique as the widget style. If desired, decorations can be set on a per-window basis.

The `QWSServer` class provides various functions for customizing the window system. Applications that run as Qt/Embedded Linux servers can access the unique `QWSServer` instance through the `QWSServer::instance()` static function.

Qt/Embedded Linux supports the following font formats: TrueType (TTF), PostScript Type 1, Bitmap Distribution Format (BDF), and Qt Pre-rendered Fonts (QPF).

Because QPF is a raster format, it is designed to be faster and more compact than vector formats such as TTF and Type 1 if we need it only at one or two different sizes. The `makeqpf` tool can be used to pre-render a TTF or a Type 1 file and save the result in QPF format. An alternative is to run our applications with the `-savefonts` command-line option.

Integrating Qt Applications with Qtopia

Since Qt/Embedded Linux offers the same API as the desktop editions of Qt, any standard Qt application can be recompiled to run on Qt/Embedded Linux. However, in practice, it is usually wise to create dedicated applications that account for the smaller screens, limited (or non-existent) keyboards, and resource limits that are typical of the small devices that run Qt/Embedded Linux. Furthermore, Qtopia provides additional libraries with features specific to mobile devices that we might want to use in our Qt/Embedded Linux applications.

Before we can start writing applications that make use of the Qtopia APIs, we must build and install the Qtopia SDK, including its own separate copy of Qt/Embedded Linux. Here we are assuming the use of the Qtopia Open Source Edition version 4.2, which includes almost everything in the Qtopia Phone Edition.

Building Qtopia is different from standard Unix practice, because Qtopia should not be built inside its source directory. For example, if we download the package `qtopia-opensource-src-4.2.4.tar.gz` to our `$HOME/downloads` directory, we would prepare to build Qtopia as follows:

```
cd $HOME/downloads
gunzip qtopia-opensource-src-4.2.4.tar.gz
```

```
tar xvf qtopia-opensource-src-4.2.4.tar
```

Now we must make a directory in which Qtopia will be built, for example:

```
cd $HOME
mkdir qtopia
```

For convenience, the documentation recommends setting up the `QPEDIR` environment variable. For example:

```
export QPEDIR=$HOME/qtopia
```

Here we have assumed the use of the Bash shell. Now we are ready to build Qtopia:

```
cd $QPEDIR
$HOME/downloads/qtopia-opensource-src-4.2.4/configure
make
make install
```

We haven't specified any options to `configure`, but you might wish to. Run `configure -help` to see what options are available.

After installation, all the Qtopia files will be in `$QPEDIR/image`, and all the files created by the user as a result of interacting with Qtopia will be in `$QPEDIR/home`. In Qtopia-speak, an "image" is a Qtopia file system that resides on a desktop computer and is used by the Qtopia environment when it is run in the virtual framebuffer.

Qtopia provides its own comprehensive documentation set, and it is well worth becoming familiar with it since Qtopia offers many classes that are not available (or relevant to) the desktop editions of Qt. The starting point is `$QPEDIR/doc/html/index.html`.

Once building and installing are complete, we can do an initial test by running `$QPEDIR/scripts/runqtopia`. This script launches the virtual framebuffer with a special skin and `qpe`, the Qtopia environment that contains the Qtopia application stack. It is possible to start the virtual framebuffer and the Qtopia environment separately, but then we have to start them in the correct order. If we inadvertently start `qpe` first, Qtopia will write to the X11 framebuffer, which at best will corrupt the screen. The `runqtopia` script can be executed with `-help` to see the list of command-line options it supports. These include `-skin`, with a list of skins to choose from.

The virtual framebuffer has a context menu that can be popped up by right-clicking anywhere except the Qtopia area. The menu lets us adjust the display and terminate Qtopia.

Now that we have Qtopia running in a virtual framebuffer, we can build one of the supplied example applications, just to see how the process works. Then, we will create a very simple application from scratch.

Change directory to `$QPEDIR/examples/application`. Qtopia has its own version of `qmake` called `qtopiamake`, located in `$QPEDIR/bin`. Run this to create a makefile, and then run `make`. This will create an executable called `example`. Now run `make install`; this will copy `example` (and some other files) into Qtopia's `image` directory. Now, if we terminate Qtopia and then start it again, using `runqtopia`, our new "Example" application will be available. To run the example, click the 'Q' button that is in the middle at the bottom of the Qtopia area, then click the Packages icon (the "boxes" icon, just above the pointing hand), and then click "Example" (see Figure 24.3).

We will finish this section by creating a small but useful Qtopia application from scratch, since there are a few details that we must be aware of. The application is called Unit Converter and is shown in Figure 24.2. It only uses the Qt API and therefore has few surprises. In the next section, we will create a more complex example that uses some of the Qtopia-specific APIs.

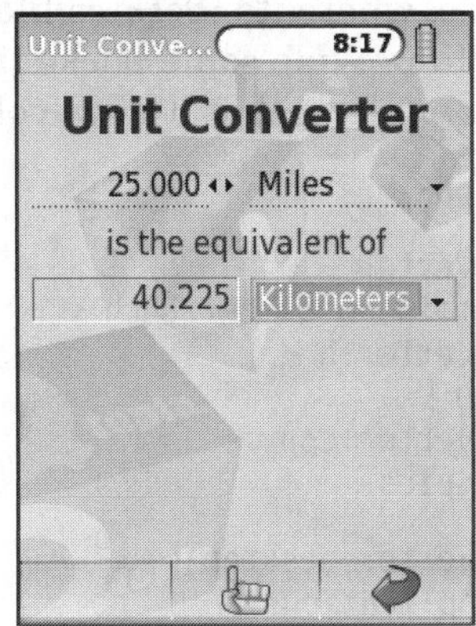

Figure 24.2. The Unit Converter application

The Unit Converter application will be made from three files: `main.cpp`, `unitconverter.h`, and `unitconverter.cpp`. Create a new directory called `unitconverter`, then `cd` into it and create the `.cpp` and `.h` files as empty files. Now run

```
qtopiamake -project
```

to produce a `.pro` file. The file will look something like this:

```
qtopia_project(qtopia app)

TARGET        = unitconverter
CONFIG       += qtopia_main no_quicklaunch
HEADERS      += unitconverter.h
SOURCES      += main.cpp \
                unitconverter.cpp
pkg.domain    = none
```

Even if we wrote the code, built the executable, and installed it, it would not appear in Qtopia's list of applications. To achieve that, we must specify where

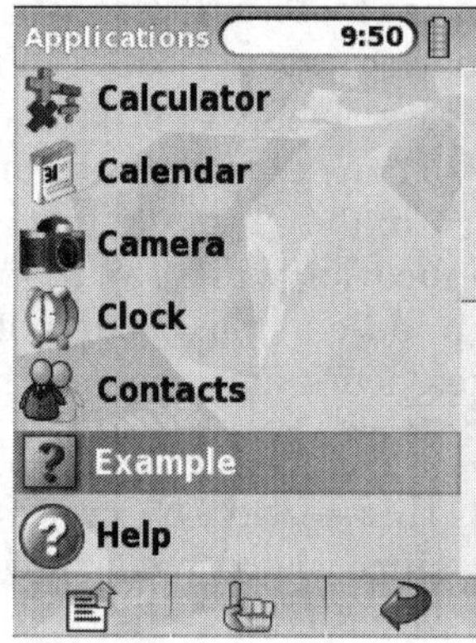

Figure 24.3. Locating the Example Application

the application's pictures are, where its `.desktop` file is, and where that should go. It is also good practice to provide some packaging information. For these reasons, we hand-edit the `.pro` file so that it now looks like this:

```
qtopia_project(qtopia app)

TARGET          = unitconverter
CONFIG         += qtopia_main no_quicklaunch
HEADERS        += unitconverter.h
SOURCES        += main.cpp \
                  unitconverter.cpp
INSTALLS       += desktop pics

desktop.files = unitconverter.desktop
desktop.path  = /apps/Applications
desktop.hint  = desktop

pics.files    = pics/*
pics.path     = /pics/unitconverter
pics.hint     = pics

pkg.name      = unitconverter
pkg.desc      = A program to convert between various units of measurement
pkg.version   = 1.0.0
pkg.domain    = window
```

The `.pro` file now contains an `INSTALLS` entry that says that the application's `.desktop` file and pictures must be installed in addition to the executable when we run `make install`.

By convention, pictures are stored in a `pics` subdirectory, and the `pics.`*`xxx`* entries in the `.pro` file specify where the source pictures are located and where they should be installed. The `desktop.`*`xxx`* entries specify the name of the application's `.desktop` file and where it should be installed. Installing it in `/apps/Applications` ensures that it appears in the list of applications shown when the user clicks the Packages icon. When the application is run on a desktop machine, absolute paths such as /apps/Applications and /pics/expenses are actually relative to Qtopia's image directory (with apps being replaced by bin).

The unitconverter.desktop file provides some basic information about the application. For our purposes, it is used to ensure that the application shows up in the list of applications. This is the complete file:

```
[Desktop Entry]
Comment[]=A program to convert between various units of measurement
Exec=unitconverter
Icon=unitconverter/Example
Type=Application
Name[]=Unit Converter
```

The information we have provided is only a subset of what can be specified. For example, we can provide information about translations. Notice that the icon has no file extension, such as .png; we leave the Qtopia resource system to find and show the appropriate picture.

So far, we have seen a special and manually edited .pro file and a .desktop file. We must do just one more Qtopia-specific thing, and then we can write unitconverter.h and unitconverter.cpp using standard Qt in the standard way. For Qtopia, we must follow a particular idiom to hook into the rest of the environment; the complete main.cpp is reduced to just these lines:

```
#include <QtopiaApplication>

#include "unitconverter.h"

QTOPIA_ADD_APPLICATION("UnitConverter", UnitConverter)
QTOPIA_MAIN
```

The name of the main window's class, included from unitconverter.h, is UnitConverter. Used in conjunction with qtopiamake and the unitconverter.h and unitconverter.cpp files, we can produce a Qtopia application that will run in the Qtopia environment. The main() function is defined by the QTOPIA_MAIN macro.

Since the application, apart from main.cpp, uses only standard Qt classes, it could also be compiled and run as a normal Qt application. To do this, we would need to use the standard qmake and change main.cpp to this:

```
#include <QApplication>

#include "unitconverter.h"

int main(int argc, char *argv[])
{
    QApplication app(argc, argv);
    UnitConverter converter;
    converter.show();
    return app.exec();
}
```

In addition, we would have to comment out the qtopia_project() line in the .pro file.

For applications that need only Qt/Embedded Linux, it is often more convenient to develop them as standard Qt applications, perhaps with an explicit `resize()` of the main window to the dimensions of a phone or PDA, and turn them into Qtopia applications when they are ready for alpha testing. Alternatively, we could have two different `main.cpp` files, perhaps `main_desktop.cpp` and `main_qtopia.cpp`, and two `.pro` files.

Most of the code for the Unit Converter application is similar to that in the other Qt examples shown throughout the book, so we will not review it here.

To test the application, we must run `make`, then `make install`, and then `runqtopia`. Once Qtopia is running in the virtual framebuffer, we can click the 'Q' button, then the Packages icon, then "Unit Converter". After this, we can exercise the application by changing the amount and by selecting different units in the comboboxes.

Creating Qtopia applications is not very different from creating conventional Qt applications, apart from some initial setup differences (the special `.pro` file and the `.desktop` file) and using `qtopiamake` instead of `qmake`. Testing embedded applications is reasonably easy since they can be built, installed, and then run from within the virtual framebuffer. As for the applications themselves, although they can simply be conventional Qt applications, in practice it is usually better to write specifically with the limitations of the embedded environment in mind and to use the Qtopia-specific APIs to ensure that they integrate well with the rest of the Qtopia application stack.

Using Qtopia APIs

Qtopia PDA Edition and Qtopia Phone Edition provide sets of applications that are relevant to mobile device users. Most of these applications have their functionality abstracted out into libraries, or make use of edition-specific libraries. These libraries can be used in our own Qtopia applications, giving us access to device services such as alarms, email, phone dialing, SMS, voice recording, and many others.

If we want to access device-specific features from our applications, we have many options:

- We can use Qt/Embedded Linux and write our own code for interacting with the device.
- We can take an existing Qtopia application and modify it to have the functionality we want.
- We can write using the additional APIs, for example, the Qtopia Phone API or the Qtopia PIM (Personal Information Manager) application's library.

In this section, we will take the last of these approaches. We will write a small application that records simple information about expenses. It makes use of the Qtopia PIM application's data to pop up a list of contacts, and then sends an expense report to the selected contact as an SMS message. It also demonstrates how to use Qtopia's support for the multi-function "soft keys" found on most mobile phones.

As Figure 24.4 shows, the application will end up in the application packages list, just like the example application we built in the previous section. As before, we will begin by looking at the `.pro` file, then the `.desktop` file, and finally the application's source files. Here's `expenses.pro`:

```
qtopia_project(qtopia app)
depends(libraries/qtopiapim)

CONFIG       += qtopia_main no_quicklaunch
HEADERS      += expense.h \
                expensedialog.h \
                expensewindow.h
SOURCES      += expense.cpp \
                expensedialog.cpp \
                expensewindow.cpp \
                main.cpp
INSTALLS     += desktop pics

desktop.files = expenses.desktop
desktop.path  = /apps/Applications
desktop.hint  = desktop

pics.files    = pics/*
pics.path     = /pics/expenses
pics.hint     = pics

pkg.name      = expenses
pkg.desc      = A program to record and SMS expenses
pkg.version   = 1.0.0
pkg.domain    = window
```

The `qtopia_project()` line is the same as before. Since this application relies on the Qtopia PIM library, we use a `depends()` directive to specify the library. If we want to use multiple libraries, we can do so by separating them with commas. The rest of the `.pro` file is similar to what we saw in the Unit Converter example, only this time we have a few more source files because the application is more elaborate.

The `expenses.desktop` file is very similar to the one we saw before:

```
[Desktop Entry]
Comment[]=A program to record and SMS expenses
Exec=expenses
Icon=expenses/expenses
Type=Application
Name[]=Expenses
```

The same is true of `main.cpp`:

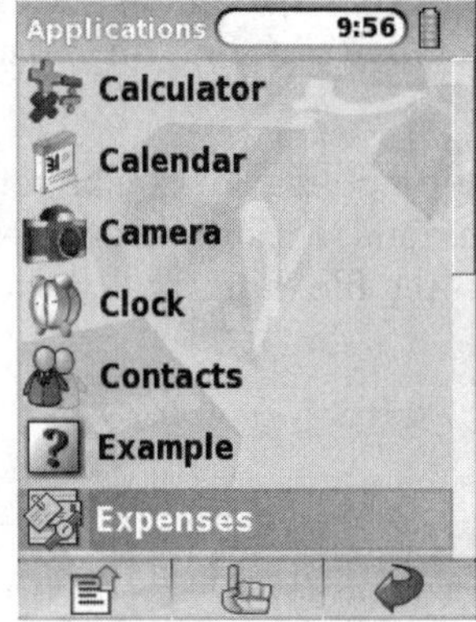

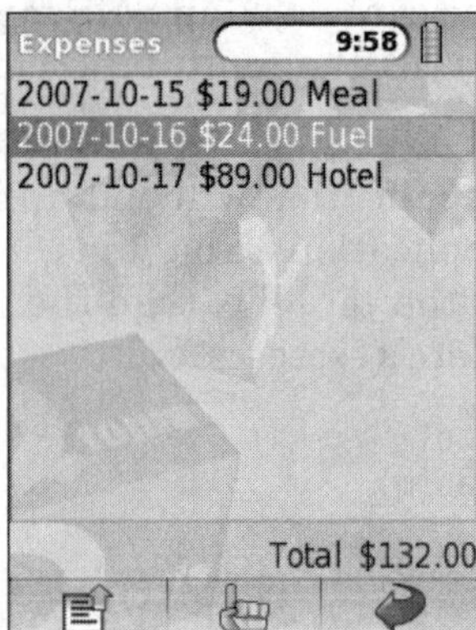

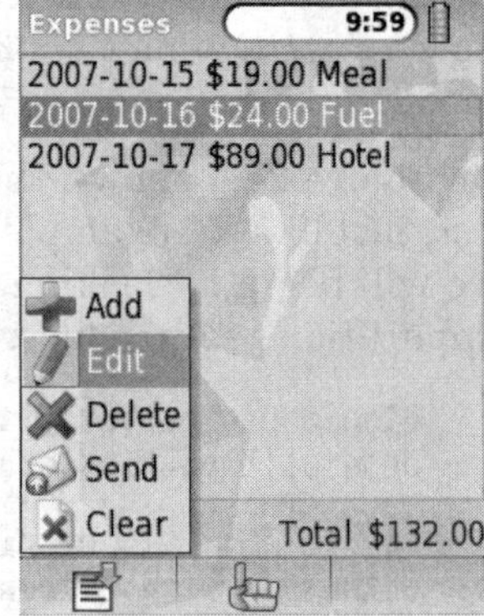

Figure 24.4. Locating and running the Expenses application

```
#include <QtopiaApplication>

#include "expensewindow.h"

QTOPIA_ADD_APPLICATION("Expenses", ExpenseWindow)
QTOPIA_MAIN
```

We will now look at the Expenses application's header files and those parts of the source files that are Qtopia-specific or particularly relevant, starting with the `Expense` class:

```
class Expense
{
public:
    Expense();
    Expense(const QDate &date, const QString &desc, qreal amount);

    bool isNull() const;
    void setDate(const QDate &date);
    QDate date() const;
    void setDescription(const QString &desc);
    QString description() const;
    void setAmount(qreal amount);
    qreal amount() const;

private:
    QDate myDate;
    QString myDesc;
    qreal myAmount;
};
```

This simple class holds a date, a description, and an amount. We won't review the `expense.cpp` file since none of its code is Qtopia-specific and it is very simple.

```
class ExpenseWindow : public QMainWindow
{
    Q_OBJECT
```

```
public:
    ExpenseWindow(QWidget *parent = 0, Qt::WFlags flags = 0);

protected:
    void closeEvent(QCloseEvent *event);

private slots:
    void add();
    void edit();
    void del();
    void send();
    void clear();

private:
    void createActions();
    void createMenuOrToolBar();
    void loadData();
    void showData();
    ...
    QList<Expense> expenses;
};
```

The `ExpenseWindow` is the application's main form. It provides functions for the user to add, edit, and delete individual expense items, to send an SMS message with all of them listed, and to clear them. The expenses are held as values in a `QList<Expense>`.

The constructor creates a `QListWidget` and two `QLabels`. One label shows the text "Total", and the other the sum of the expenses. The actions are created by the `createActions()` function, and the menu or toolbar is created by the `createMenuOrToolBar()` function. Both functions are called from the constructor. Any preexisting expenses are loaded at the end of the constructor by calling the `loadData()` function. We will skip the constructor itself, and instead just review the functions that it calls.

```
void ExpenseWindow::createActions()
{
    addAction = new QAction(tr("Add"), this);
    addAction->setIcon(QIcon(":icon/add"));
    connect(addAction, SIGNAL(triggered()), this, SLOT(add()));
    ...
    clearAction = new QAction(tr("Clear"), this);
    clearAction->setIcon(QIcon(":icon/clear"));
    connect(clearAction, SIGNAL(triggered()), this, SLOT(clear()));
}
```

The `createActions()` function creates the Add, Edit, Delete, Send, and Clear actions. Although it is possible to use Qt resource (`.qrc`) files, when programming Qtopia applications the standard practice for icons is to store them in a `pics` subdirectory that gets copied on to the device (thanks to the `.pro` file's `INSTALLS` line). These can then be shared among several applications, and Qtopia optimizes access to them using a special database.

Everywhere Qt or Qtopia expects a file name, we can supply a Qtopia resource name instead. These are identified by a leading colon in the file name, followed by a word specifying the kind of resource. In this case, we specify that we want icons and give a file name, for example, `:icon/add`, omitting the file extension. Qtopia will look for a suitable icon in a number of standard locations, starting with the application's `pics` directory. See `http://doc.trolltech.com/qtopia4.2/qtopia-resource-system.html` for all the details.

```
void ExpenseWindow::createMenuOrToolBar()
{
#ifdef QTOPIA_PHONE
    QMenu *menuOrToolBar = QSoftMenuBar::menuFor(listWidget);
#else
    QToolBar *menuOrToolBar = new QToolBar;
    addToolBar(menuOrToolBar);
#endif

    menuOrToolBar->addAction(addAction);
    menuOrToolBar->addAction(editAction);
    menuOrToolBar->addAction(deleteAction);
    menuOrToolBar->addAction(sendAction);
    menuOrToolBar->addAction(clearAction);
}
```

Some phones have "soft keys", that is, multi-function keys whose actions are application- or context-specific. The `QSoftMenuBar` class takes advantage of soft keys where they are available, and provides a popup menu when they are not. For PDAs, we would normally have a toolbar rather than a popup menu. The `#ifdef` directive ensures that the actions are added to a soft menu if the target is a phone and to a toolbar if the target is a PDA.

Users will expect to be able to close the application without being forced to explicitly save their data. They will also expect the data to be restored when they restart the application at a later time. This is easily taken care of by calling `loadData()` in the constructor, and saving the data in the application's `closeEvent()`. Qtopia offers many choices for data storage, including saving to a table in a SQLite database or saving to a file. Since the expense data is so small, we will save it using `QSettings`. We will look at how it is saved, and then at how it is loaded.

```
void ExpenseWindow::closeEvent(QCloseEvent *event)
{
    QByteArray data;

    QDataStream out(&data, QIODevice::WriteOnly);
    out.setVersion(QDataStream::Qt_4_2);

    foreach (Expense expense, expenses) {
        out << expense.date() << expense.description()
            << expense.amount();
    }

    QSettings settings("BookSoft Ltd", "Expenses");
```

```
        settings.setValue("data", data);

        event->accept();
    }
```

We create a single `QByteArray` and write all the data to it. Then we save the byte array as a single value under the key `data`, before accepting the close event to allow the application to terminate.

```
    void ExpenseWindow::loadData()
    {
        QSettings settings("BookSoft Ltd", "Expenses");
        QByteArray data = settings.value("data").toByteArray();
        if (data.isEmpty())
            return;

        expenses.clear();
        QDataStream in(&data, QIODevice::ReadOnly);
        in.setVersion(QDataStream::Qt_4_2);

        while (!in.atEnd()) {
            QDate date;
            QString desc;
            qreal amount;

            in >> date >> desc >> amount;
            expenses.append(Expense(date, desc, amount));
        }
        showData();
    }
```

If data exists from a previous session, we clear the existing data and then read in each new expense item. The `showData()` function clears the list widget, then iterates over the expenses, adding a new list item for each expense, and finishes by updating the total amount label.

Once the application is running, the user can add, edit, or delete expense items, send them all in an SMS message, or clear them all.

For deleting, we check to see whether there is a valid current row in the list widget, and then we use a standard `QMessageBox::warning()` static convenience function to ask the user to confirm the deletion. If the user chooses to clear all their expenses, again we use a message box. All of this is standard Qt programming. Qtopia takes care of making the message box display and integrate properly in the Qtopia environment.

If the user chooses the Add option to add a new expense item, the `add()` slot is called:

```
    void ExpenseWindow::add()
    {
        ExpenseDialog dialog(Expense(), this);
        if (QtopiaApplication::execDialog(&dialog)) {
            expenses.append(dialog.expense());
            showData();
```

```
        }
    }
```

This slot creates an ExpenseDialog, a class we will look at shortly, but instead of calling the dialog's QDialog::exec() function, we call QtopiaApplication::execDialog(), passing the dialog as the argument. Calling exec() is perfectly valid and does work, but using execDialog() ensures that the dialog is sized and positioned appropriately for a small device, maximizing it if necessary.

The edit() slot is similar. If the edit() function is called, it checks that there is a valid current row in the list widget, and if there is, it passes the expense that corresponds to that row as the first parameter to the ExpenseDialog's constructor. If the user accepts the edit, the original expense's details are overwritten with the edited details.

The last ExpenseWindow function that we will cover is send(), but before that, we will discuss the ExpenseDialog class:

```
class ExpenseDialog : public QDialog
{
    Q_OBJECT

public:
    ExpenseDialog(const Expense &expense, QWidget *parent = 0);

    Expense expense() const { return currentExpense; }

public slots:
    void accept();

private:
    void createActions();
    void createMenuOrToolBar();

    Expense currentExpense;
    ...
};
```

One aspect that is immediately apparent is that we have functions for creating actions and a menu or toolbar just like in ExpenseWindow. We will not be creating QPushButtons or a QDialogButtonBox, but instead will create a toolbar or a QSoftMenuBar since these provide much better integration with the Qtopia environment than creating buttons. The code is very similar to what we did for the application's main window:

```
void ExpenseDialog::createActions()
{
    okAction = new QAction(tr("OK"), this);
    okAction->setIcon(QIcon(":icon/ok"));
    connect(okAction, SIGNAL(triggered()), this, SLOT(accept()));

    cancelAction = new QAction(tr("Cancel"), this);
    cancelAction->setIcon(QIcon(":icon/cancel"));
    connect(cancelAction, SIGNAL(triggered()), this, SLOT(reject()));
}
```

```
void ExpenseDialog::createMenuOrToolBar()
{
#ifdef QTOPIA_PHONE
    QMenu *menuOrToolBar = QSoftMenuBar::menuFor(this);
#else
    QToolBar *menuOrToolBar = new QToolBar;
    menuOrToolBar->setMovable(false);
    addToolBar(menuOrToolBar);
#endif

    menuOrToolBar->addAction(okAction);
    menuOrToolBar->addAction(cancelAction);
}
```

If the user accepts the dialog, we set the date, description, and amount attributes of the current expense, and leave the caller to retrieve this using the dialog's `expense()` function.

If the user chooses the Send action, the `send()` function is called. This function prompts the user to choose a contact to send the expenses to, prepares the text of a message to send, and then sends the message using the SMS protocol (see Figure 24.5).

```
void ExpenseWindow::send()
{
    QContactSelector dialog(false, this);
    dialog.setModel(new QContactModel);
    QtopiaApplication::execDialog(&dialog);
    if (!dialog.contactSelected())
        return;
```

The `QContactSelector` dialog and the `QContactModel` model/view class are both provided by the PIM library. `QContactModel` accesses the user's centralized contacts database. If there are more than a few contacts, `QtopiaApplication::execDialog()` will pop up the `QContactSelector` dialog maximized. If the user does not choose a contact, the `contactSelected()` function returns a null contact (which evaluates to `false`), in which case we do nothing. Otherwise, we prepare and then send the expenses:

```
    QTemporaryFile file;
    file.setAutoRemove(false);
    if (!file.open()) {
        QMessageBox::warning(this, tr("Expenses"),
                             tr("Failed to send expenses: %1.")
                             .arg(file.errorString()));
        return;
    }

    QString fileName = file.fileName();
    qreal total = 0.00;

    QTextStream out(&file);
    out.setCodec("UTF-8");

    out << tr("Expenses\n");
```

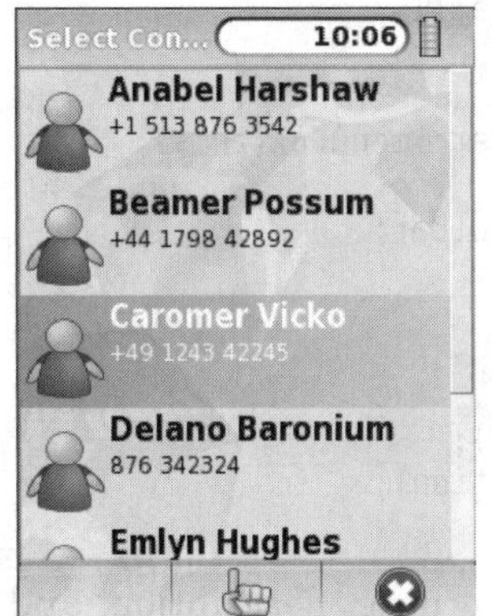

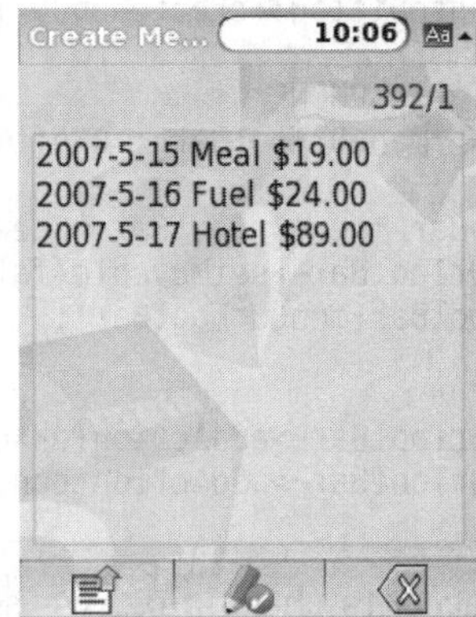

Figure 24.5. Choosing a contact and sending an SMS message

```
    foreach (Expense expense, expenses) {
        out << tr("%1 $%2 %3\n")
               .arg(expense.date().toString(Qt::ISODate))
               .arg(expense.amount(), 0, 'f', 2)
               .arg(expense.description());
        total += expense.amount();
    }
    out << tr("Total $%1\n").arg(total, 0, 'f', 2);
    file.close();
```

To send an SMS message, we will need to pass the name of a file that contains the SMS message. Here, we write the expenses data to a temporary file using `QTextStream`. Normally, `QTemporaryFile` removes the file as soon as we call `close()`, but we switch off this behavior because the file must be available until the SMS has been sent, at which point Qtopia will automatically remove it.

The `total` variable is declared with type `qreal`. This type is a typedef for `float` or `double`, depending on the architecture. For example, on ARM, it is defined as a `float` for performance reasons. Throughout Qt's API (notably in `QPainter`), `qreal` is used rather than `double`.

```
    QContact contact = dialog.selectedContact();
    QtopiaServiceRequest request("SMS",
                                 "writeSms(QString,QString,QString)");
    request << QString("%1 %2").arg(contact.firstName())
                               .arg(contact.lastName())
            << contact.defaultPhoneNumber() << fileName;
    request.send();
}
```

Qtopia implements the SMS protocol as a service rather than as a library. To send an SMS, we create a `QtopiaServiceRequest` object, giving it the name of the service, "SMS", and the name of the function we want to use with the arguments listed in parentheses: "writeSms(QString,QString,QString)". Under the hood, `QtopiaServiceRequest` uses QCOP to communicate with the process that provides the "SMS" service.

We populate the request with the recipient's name and phone number, and the name of the file we created, and we call `send()` to send the message. When `send()` is executed, a Create Message dialog is popped up by the Qtopia system with the body of the message filled in from the file. The user can change the text, and then either send or cancel the SMS. The Expenses application can only be properly tested using an actual or simulated device that provides the SMS service.

As this example illustrates, embedded programming means that we must consider how we can use and interoperate with the services and Qtopia-specific APIs that are available. And it requires us to think very differently about user interface design to account for the small screens and limited input facilities that small devices have to offer. From a programmer's point of view, writing applications for Qtopia is no different than for desktop platforms, except that we must familiarize ourselves with the additional tools, libraries, and services that are available with Qtopia.

Appendixes

- *A Note on Licensing*
- *Installing Qt / Windows*
- *Installing Qt / Mac*
- *Installing Qt / X11*

Obtaining and Installing Qt

This appendix explains how to obtain and install a GPL edition of Qt onto your system. Editions are available for Windows, Mac OS X, and X11 (for Linux and most versions of Unix). The pre-built binaries for Windows and Mac OS X include SQLite, a public domain in-process database, together with a SQLite driver. The versions built from source can include SQLite at your option. To begin, download the latest version of Qt from `http://www.trolltech.com/download/`. If you plan to develop commercial software, you will need to buy a commercial edition, and when you get it you should follow the installation instructions that are provided.

Trolltech also provides Qt/Embedded Linux for building applications for Linux-based embedded devices such as PDAs and mobile phones. If you are interested in creating embedded applications, you can obtain Qt/Embedded Linux from Trolltech's download web page.

The example applications used in this book are available from the book's web site, `http://www.informit.com/title/0132354160`. In addition, Qt provides many small example applications located in the `examples` subdirectory.

A Note on Licensing

Qt is available in two forms: open source and commercial. The open source editions are available free of charge; the commercial editions can be purchased for a fee.

If you want to distribute the applications that you create with an open source edition of Qt, you must comply with the specific terms and conditions laid down in the licenses for the software you use to create the applications. For open source editions, the terms and conditions include the requirement to use the GNU General Public License (GPL). Open licenses such as the GPL give the applications' users certain rights, including the right to view and modify the source and to distribute the applications (on the same terms). If you want to distribute your applications without source code (to keep your code private) or if you want to apply your own commercial license conditions to your applications, you must buy commercial editions of the software you use to create the applications. The commercial editions of the software allow you to sell and distribute your applications on your own terms.

The full legal texts of the licenses are included with the GPL versions of Qt for Windows, Mac OS X, and X11, along with information on how to obtain commercial versions.

Installing Qt/Windows

At the time of this writing, the Windows installer was called `qt-win-opensource-4.3.2-mingw.exe`. The version number will probably be different by the time you read this, but the process should be the same. Download the file and run it to begin the installation process.

When the installer reaches the MinGW page, if you already have the MinGW C++ compiler, you must specify the directory where it is located; otherwise, check the checkbox and have the installer install MinGW for you. The GPL version of Qt will not work with Visual C++, so if you do not have MinGW already installed, you will need to install it. Qt's standard examples are automatically installed, along with the documentation.

If you choose to install the MinGW compiler, there may be a small delay between the completion of the MinGW installation and the start of the Qt installation.

After installation, you will have a new folder in the Start menu called Qt by Trolltech v4.3.2 (OpenSource). This folder has shortcuts to *Qt Assistant* and *Qt Designer*, and also one called Qt 4.3.2 Command Prompt that starts a console window. When you start this window it will set the environment variables for compiling Qt programs with MinGW. In this window, you can run `qmake` and `make` to build Qt applications.

Installing Qt/Mac

Before Qt can be installed on Mac OS X, Apple's Xcode Tools must already be installed. The CD (or DVD) containing these tools is usually supplied with Mac OS X; they can also be downloaded from the Apple Developer Connection, `http://developer.apple.com/`.

If you have Mac OS X 10.4 and Xcode Tools $2.x$ (with GCC $4.0.x$) or later, you can use the installer described shortly. If you have an earlier version of Mac OS X, or an older version of GCC, you will need to install the source package manually. This package is called `qt-mac-opensource-4.3.2.tar.gz` and is available from Trolltech's web site. If you install this package, follow the instructions in the next section for installing Qt on X11.

To use the installer, download `qt-mac-opensource-4.3.2.dmg`. (This version was correct at the time of this writing, but it will probably be different by the time you read this.) Double-click the .dmg file, and then double-click the package called Qt.mpkg. This will launch the installer, which will install Qt in /Developer, along with its documentation and the standard examples.

To run commands such as qmake and make, you will need to use a terminal window, for example, Terminal.app in /Applications/Utilities. It is also possible to generate Xcode projects using qmake. For example, to generate an Xcode project for the hello example, start a console such as Terminal.app, change to your examples/chap01/hello directory, and enter the following command:

```
qmake -spec macx-xcode hello.pro
```

Installing Qt/X11

Download the file qt-x11-opensource-src-4.3.2.tar.gz from Trolltech's web site. (This version was correct at the time of this writing, but it will probably be different by the time you read this.) To install Qt in its default location on X11, you will need to be root. If you do not have root access, use configure's -prefix option to specify a directory to which you have permission to write.

1. Change directory to the directory where you downloaded the archive file. For example:

   ```
   cd /tmp
   ```

2. Unpack the archive file:

   ```
   gunzip qt-x11-opensource-src-4.3.2.tar.gz
   tar xvf qt-x11-opensource-src-4.3.2.tar
   ```

   This will create the directory /tmp/qt-x11-opensource-src-4.3.2. Qt requires GNU tar; on some systems it is called gtar.

3. Execute the configure tool with your preferred options to build the Qt library and the tools supplied with it:

   ```
   cd /tmp/qt-x11-opensource-src-4.3.2
   ./configure
   ```

   You can run ./configure -help to get a list of configuration options.

4. To build Qt, type

   ```
   make
   ```

   This will create the library and compile all the demos, examples, and tools. On some systems, make is called gmake.

5. To install Qt, type

   ```
   su -c "make install"
   ```

and enter the root password. (On some systems, the command is `sudo make install`.) This will install Qt into `/usr/local/Trolltech/Qt-4.3.2`. You can change the destination by using the `-prefix` option with `configure`, and if you have write access to the destination you can simply type:

```
make install
```

6. Set up certain environment variables for Qt.

   If your shell is `bash`, `ksh`, `zsh`, or `sh`, add the following two lines to your `.profile` file:

   ```
   PATH=/usr/local/Trolltech/Qt-4.3.2/bin:$PATH
   export PATH
   ```

   If your shell is `csh` or `tcsh`, add the following line to your `.login` file:

   ```
   setenv PATH /usr/local/Trolltech/Qt-4.3.2/bin:$PATH
   ```

   If you used `-prefix` with `configure`, use the path you specified instead of the default path shown here.

   If you are using a compiler that does not support `rpath`, you must also extend the `LD_LIBRARY_PATH` environment variable to include `/usr/local/Trolltech/Qt-4.3.2/lib`. This is not necessary on Linux with GCC.

Qt comes with a demo application, `qtdemo`, that shows off many of the library's features. It serves as a nice starting point to see what Qt can do. To see Qt's documentation, either visit `http://doc.trolltech.com/` or run *Qt Assistant*, Qt's help application, invoked by typing `assistant` in a console window.

- *Using qmake*
- *Using Third-Party Build Tools*

Building Qt Applications

Building Qt applications is greatly simplified by the use of a build tool. Three options are open to us: We can use the qmake tool supplied with Qt, we can use a third-party build tool, or we can use an integrated development environment (IDE).

The qmake tool generates a platform-specific makefile from a platform-neutral .pro file. The tool has the necessary logic to invoke Qt's code-generating tools (moc, uic, and rcc) built-in. We have used qmake for all the examples in the book, in most cases using relatively simple .pro files. In fact, qmake provides a rich range of features including the ability to create makefiles that recursively invoke other makefiles and to switch certain features on or off depending on the target platform. In the first section of this appendix, we will review qmake and introduce some of its more advanced features.

In theory, any third-party build tool can be used for Qt development, but it is much easier to use one that is already Qt-aware. We will look at some of the Qt-aware build tools in the second section.

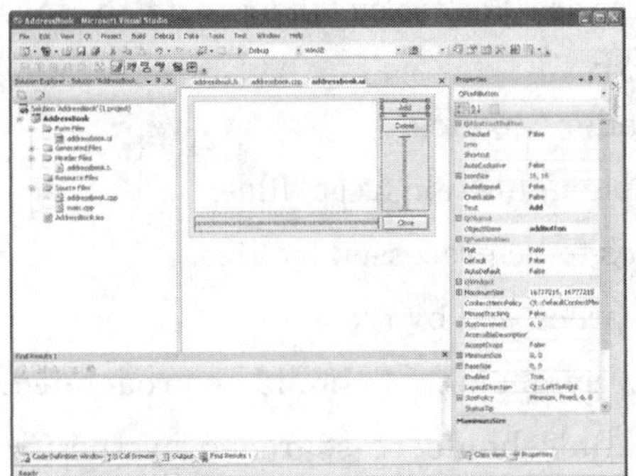

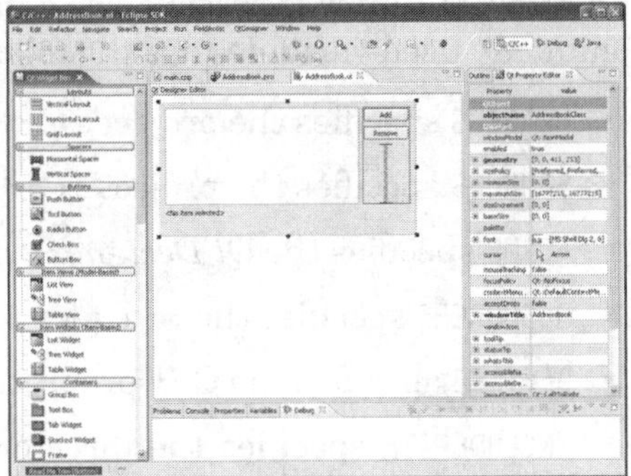

Figure B.1. The Qt Visual Studio and Eclipse integrations in action

Some developers would rather use an IDE to build their applications. Trolltech provides software to integrate with Visual Studio and Eclipse (shown in Figure B.1), and the open source IDEs KDevelop and QDevelop—both written using Qt—provide excellent support for Qt development.

Using qmake

The qmake tool is supplied with Qt. It is used to build Qt itself as well as the tools and examples that accompany it. Throughout the book, we have used qmake project (.pro) files to build our example applications and plugins. In this section, we will study the .pro file syntax in a more systematic (although by no means comprehensive) way, and we will review a few fundamental qmake concepts. For complete coverage, see the qmake manual, available online at http://doc.trolltech.com/4.3/qmake-manual.html.

The purpose of a .pro file is to list the source files that are involved in a project. Since qmake is used for building Qt and its associated tools, it knows Qt very well and can generate rules for invoking moc, uic, and rcc. As a result, the syntax is very concise and easy to learn.

The three main types of project files are app (for stand-alone applications), lib (for static and shared libraries), and subdirs (for recursive subdirectory builds). This can be specified using the TEMPLATE variable, as follows:

```
TEMPLATE = lib
```

The subdirs template can be used for building targets in subdirectories. In that case, we need to specify only the SUBDIRS variable in addition to TEMPLATE = subdirs. In each subdirectory, qmake looks for a .pro file named after the directory and will build that project. The examples.pro file supplied with the examples provided for this book uses the subdirs template to run qmake on the individual examples.

If no TEMPLATE entry is present, the default is app. For app or lib projects, the most commonly used variables are the following:

- HEADERS specifies the project's C++ header (.h) files.
- SOURCES specifies the project's C++ implementation (.cpp) files.
- FORMS specifies the *Qt Designer* .ui files to be processed by uic.
- RESOURCES specifies the .qrc files to be processed by rcc.
- DEFINES specifies the C++ preprocessor symbols that should be predefined.
- INCLUDEPATH specifies the directories that should be searched by the C++ preprocessor for locating global header files.
- LIBS specifies the libraries to link to the project. The libraries are specified either as absolute paths or using the Unix-inspired -L and -l flags (e.g., -L/usr/local/lib and -ldb_cxx).
- CONFIG specifies various project configuration and compiler options.

- `QT` specifies the Qt modules that are used by the project. (The default is `core gui`, corresponding to the *QtCore* and *QtGui* modules.)
- `VERSION` specifies the version number of the target library.
- `TARGET` specifies the base name of the target executable or library, excluding any extension, prefix, or version number. (The default is the name of the current directory.)
- `DESTDIR` specifies the directory in which the target executable should be put. (The default is platform-dependent; for example, on Linux, it is the current directory, and on Windows, it is the `debug` or `release` subdirectory.)
- `DLLDESTDIR` specifies the directory in which the target library file should be put. (It has the same default as `DESTDIR`.)

The `CONFIG` variable is used to control various aspects of the build process. The following options are supported:

- `debug` means that an executable or library with debugging information should be built, and links against the debug versions of the Qt libraries.
- `release` means that an executable or library without debugging information should be built, and links against the release versions of the Qt libraries. If both `debug` and `release` are specified, `debug` wins.
- `warn_off` switches off as many warnings as possible. By default, builds are done with warnings switched on.
- `qt` means that the application or library uses Qt. This option is included by default.
- `dll` means that a shared library should be built.
- `staticlib` means that a static library should be built.
- `plugin` means that a plugin should be built. Plugins are always shared libraries, so this option implies the `dll` option.
- `console` means that the application needs to write to the console (using `cout`, `cerr`, `qWarning()`, etc.).
- `app_bundle` applies only to Mac OS X builds, and means that the executable should be put in a bundle, which is the default on Mac OS X.
- `lib_bundle` applies only to Mac OS X builds, and means that the library should be put in a framework.

To generate a makefile for a project file called `hello.pro`, we type

```
qmake hello.pro
```

After that, we can invoke `make` or `nmake` to build the project. We can also use `qmake` to generate a Microsoft Visual Studio project (`.dsp` or `.vproj`) file by typing

```
qmake -tp vc hello.pro
```

On Mac OS X, we can generate an Xcode project file using

```
qmake -spec macx-xcode hello.pro
```

and makefiles using

```
qmake -spec macx-g++ hello.pro
```

The `-spec` command-line option lets us specify a platform/compiler combination. Normally, `qmake` detects the correct platform, but in some cases it may be necessary to specify it explicitly. For example, to generate a makefile that invokes the Intel C++ Compiler (ICC) for Linux in 64-bit mode, we would type

```
qmake -spec linux-icc-64 hello.pro
```

The possible specifications are located in Qt's `mkspecs` directory.

Although `qmake`'s primary purpose is to generate makefiles from `.pro` files, we can also use `qmake` to generate a `.pro` file for the current directory, using the `-project` option. For example:

```
qmake -project
```

In this mode, `qmake` will search the current directory for files with known extensions (`.h`, `.cpp`, `.ui`, etc.) and produce a `.pro` file that lists these files.

In the rest of this section, we will look in more detail at the `.pro` file syntax. A `.pro` file entry normally has the syntax

```
variable = values
```

where *values* is a list of string values. Comments start with the pound sign (#) and terminate at the end of the line. For example, the line

```
CONFIG = qt release warn_off        # I know what I'm doing
```

assigns the list ["qt", "release", "warn_off"] to the `CONFIG` variable, overwriting any previous values. Additional operators are provided to supplement the = operator. The += operator lets us append values to a variable. Thus, the lines

```
CONFIG  = qt
CONFIG += release
CONFIG += warn_off
```

effectively assign the list ["qt", "release", "warn_off"] to `CONFIG`, just as the previous example did. The -= operator removes all occurrences of the specified values from the variable's current value. Thus,

```
CONFIG  = qt release warn_off
CONFIG -= qt
```

leaves `CONFIG` with the list ["release", "warn_off"]. The *= operator adds a value to a variable, but only if the value is not already in the variable's list; otherwise, it does nothing. For example, the line

```
SOURCES *= main.cpp
```

will add the implementation file `main.cpp` to the project only if it isn't specified already. Finally, the ~= operator can be used to replace any values that match a regular expression with the specified replacement text, using a syntax inspired by `sed` (the Unix stream editor). For example,

```
SOURCES ~= s/\.cpp\b/.cxx/
```

replaces all `.cpp` file extensions with `.cxx` in the `SOURCES` variable.

Inside the list of values, `qmake` provides ways to access the values of other `qmake` variables, of environment variables, and of Qt configuration options. The syntaxes are listed in Figure B.2.

Accessor	Description
`$$varName` or `$${varName}`	Value of qmake variable at that point in the `.pro` file
`$$(varName)`	Value of environment variable when qmake is run
`$(varName)`	Value of environment variable when makefile is processed
`$$[varName]`	Value of Qt configuration option

Figure B.2. Variable accessors available in `qmake`

In the examples so far, we always used standard variables, such as `SOURCES` and `CONFIG`, but it is possible to set the value of any variable and to refer to it later using the `$$varName` or `$${varName}` syntax. For example:

```
MY_VERSION    = 1.2
SOURCES_BASIC = alphadialog.cpp \
                main.cpp \
                windowpanel.cpp
SOURCES_EXTRA = bezierextension.cpp \
                xplot.cpp
SOURCES       = $$SOURCES_BASIC \
                $$SOURCES_EXTRA
TARGET        = imgpro_$${MY_VERSION}
```

The next example combines several of the syntaxes shown earlier and uses the built-in function `$$lower()` to convert strings to lowercase:

```
# List of classes in the project
MY_CLASSES    = Annotation \
                CityBlock \
                CityScape \
                CityView

# Append .cpp extension to lowercased class names, and add main.cpp
SOURCES       = $$lower($$MY_CLASSES)
SOURCES      ~= s/([a-z0-9_]+)/\1.cpp/
SOURCES      += main.cpp
```

```
# Append .h extension to lowercased class names
HEADERS         = $$lower($$MY_CLASSES)
HEADERS        ~= s/([a-z0-9_]+)/\1.h/
```

Sometimes we may need to specify file names that include spaces in a `.pro` file. In that case, we can simply put quotes around the file name.

When compiling a project on different platforms, it might be necessary to specify different files or different options based on the platform. The general syntax for conditionals in `qmake` is

```
condition {
    then-case
} else {
    else-case
}
```

The *condition* part can be a platform name (e.g., `win32`, `unix`, or `macx`) or a more complex predicate. The *then-case* and *else-case* parts specify the values of variables using the standard syntax. For example:

```
win32 {
    SOURCES += serial_win.cpp
} else {
    SOURCES += serial_unix.cpp
}
```

The `else` branch is optional. For convenience, `qmake` also supports a one-line syntax when the *then-case* part consists of only one variable assignment and there is no *else-case*:

```
condition:then-case
```

For example:

```
macx:SOURCES += serial_mac.cpp
```

If we have several project files that need to share some of the same entries, we can factor out the common entries in a separate file and include it in the individual `.pro` files that need it using the `include()` directive:

```
include(../common.pri)

HEADERS        += window.h
SOURCES        += main.cpp \
                  window.cpp
```

Conventionally, project files that are meant to be included by other project files are given a `.pri` (project include) extension.

In a previous example, we saw the `$$lower()` built-in function, which returns a lowercase version of its argument. Another useful function is `$$system()`: It allows us to generate strings from external applications. For example, if we need to determine which version of Unix is being used, we can write

```
OS_VERSION = $$system(uname -r).
```

We can then use the resulting variable in a condition, together with `contains()`:

```
contains(OS_VERSION, SunOS):SOURCES += mythread_sun.c
```

In this section, we have barely skimmed the surface. The `qmake` tool provides many more options and features than we presented here, including support for precompiled headers, for Mac OS X universal binaries, and for user-defined compilers or tools. Refer to the online `qmake` manual for full details.

Using Third-Party Build Tools

Many build tools are available, both open source and commercial, that can be used to build Qt applications. Such tools fall into two broad categories: tools that generate makefiles (or IDE project files) and rely on the standard build system, and tools that are build systems in their own right, with no external build tools necessary.

In this section, we will review three tools, all chosen because they have support for Qt built-in or easily available. The first, CMake, generates makefiles, and the other two, Boost.Build and SCons, are build systems in their own right. In each case, we will see how to build the Spreadsheet application developed in Chapters 3 and 4. Evaluating any new build tool or build system requires some reading up and some experimentation on real applications, but we hope that this brief review of build tools will be illustrative.

CMake: Cross-Platform Make

The CMake tool, available from `http://www.cmake.org/`, is an open source cross-platform makefile generator with support for Qt 4 development built-in. To use CMake, we must create a `CMakeLists.txt` file to describe the project, much like a `qmake .pro` file. Here is the `CMakeLists.txt` file for the Spreadsheet application:

```
project(spreadsheet)
cmake_minimum_required(VERSION 2.4.0)
find_package(Qt4 REQUIRED)
include(${QT_USE_FILE})
set(spreadsheet_SRCS
    cell.cpp
    finddialog.cpp
    gotocelldialog.cpp
    main.cpp
    mainwindow.cpp
    sortdialog.cpp
    spreadsheet.cpp
)
set(spreadsheet_MOC_SRCS
    finddialog.h
    gotocelldialog.h
    mainwindow.h
```

```
    sortdialog.h
    spreadsheet.h
)
set(spreadsheet_UIS
    gotocelldialog.ui
    sortdialog.ui
)
set(spreadsheet_RCCS
    spreadsheet.qrc
)
qt4_wrap_cpp(spreadsheet_MOCS ${spreadsheet_MOC_SRCS})
qt4_wrap_ui(spreadsheet_UIS_H ${spreadsheet_UIS})
qt4_wrap_cpp(spreadsheet_MOC_UI ${spreadsheet_UIS_H})
qt4_add_resources(spreadsheet_RCC_SRCS ${spreadsheet_RCCS})
add_definitions(-DQT_NO_DEBUG)
add_executable(spreadsheet
    ${spreadsheet_SRCS}
    ${spreadsheet_MOCS}
    ${spreadsheet_MOC_UI}
    ${spreadsheet_RCC_SRCS})
target_link_libraries(spreadsheet ${QT_LIBRARIES} pthread)
```

Most of the file is simply boilerplate. The only application-specific items we must put in are the application's name (in the first line), the list of .cpp source files, the list of .ui files, and the list of .qrc files. For header files, CMake is smart enough to figure out the dependencies for itself, so we don't need to specify them. However, .h files that define Q_OBJECT classes must be processed by moc, so we have listed these.

The first few lines set the application name and pull in CMake's support for Qt 4. Then we set up some variables to hold the file names. The qt4_wrap_cpp() command runs moc on the given files, and similarly qt4_wrap_ui() runs uic and qt4_add_resources() runs rcc. To create the executable, we specify all the required .cpp files, including those generated by moc and rcc. Finally, we must specify the libraries to link with the executable, in this case the standard Qt 4 libraries and the threading library.

Once the CMakeLists.txt file is completed, we can generate a makefile using the following command:

```
cmake .
```

This tells CMake to read the CMakeLists.txt file in the current directory and to generate a file called Makefile. We can then use make (or nmake) to build the application, and make clean if we want a fresh start.

Boost.Build (bjam)

The Boost C++ class libraries include their own build tool, called Boost.Build or bjam, available freely and documented at http://www.boost.org/tools/build/v2/. Version 2 of this tool has built-in support for Qt 4 applications but assumes that there is an environment variable called QTDIR that gives the path to the

Qt 4 installation. Some installations of Boost.Build have Qt support disabled by default; for these, we must edit the file `user-config.jam` and add the line

```
using qt ;
```

Instead of relying on `QTDIR`, we can specify the path where Qt is installed by changing the preceding line to something like this:

```
using qt : /home/kathy/opt/qt432 ;
```

Every application built with Boost.Build requires two files: `boost-build.jam` and `Jamroot`. In fact, only one copy of `boost-build.jam` is required for any number of applications, as long as it is in a directory that includes all the applications' directories as subdirectories (no matter how deeply nested). The `boost-build.jam` file needs to contain only a single line, to specify the path to the build system's installation directory. For example:

```
boost-build /home/kathy/opt/boost-build ;
```

The `Jamroot` file needed to build the Spreadsheet application looks like this:

```
using qt : /home/kathy/opt/qt432 ;

exe spreadsheet :
    cell.cpp
    finddialog.cpp
    finddialog.h
    gotocelldialog.cpp
    gotocelldialog.h
    gotocelldialog.ui
    main.cpp
    mainwindow.cpp
    mainwindow.h
    sortdialog.cpp
    sortdialog.h
    sortdialog.ui
    spreadsheet.cpp
    spreadsheet.h
    spreadsheet.qrc
    /qt//QtGui
    /qt//QtCore ;
```

The first line pulls in the Qt 4 support, and we must provide the Qt 4 installation path. Next, we specify that we want to build an executable called `spreadsheet` and that it depends on the files listed. For header files, Boost.Build is smart enough to figure out the dependencies for itself, so normally we don't need to list them. However, `.h` files that define `Q_OBJECT` classes must be processed by `moc`, so we must include them in the list. The last two lines specify the Qt libraries we want to use.

Assuming that the `bjam` executable is in the path, we can build the application using the following command:

```
bjam release
```

This tells Boost.Build to build the application specified in the current directory's Jamroot file using a release build. (If you installed only Qt's debug libraries, this will produce errors; run bjam debug in that case.) The moc, uic, and rcc tools will be run as necessary. To clean up, run bjam clean release.

SCons: Software Construction Tool

The SCons tool, available at http://www.scons.org/, is an open source Python-based build tool that is meant to replace make. It has built-in support for Qt 3, and an add-on to support Qt 4 is available from David García Garzón at http://www.iua.upf.edu/~dgarcia/Codders/sconstools.html. There is one file to download from that site, qt4.py, and this should be put in the same directory as the application. This extension is expected to be included in the official SCons release in due course.

Once qt4.py is in place, we can create an SConstruct file where we specify our build:

```
#!/usr/bin/env python

import os

QT4_PY_PATH = "."
QTDIR = "/home/kathy/opt/qt432"

pkgpath = os.environ.get("PKG_CONFIG_PATH", "")
pkgpath += ":%s/lib/pkgconfig" % QTDIR
os.environ["PKG_CONFIG_PATH"] = pkgpath
os.environ["QTDIR"] = QTDIR

env = Environment(tools=["default", "qt4"], toolpath=[QT4_PY_PATH])
env["CXXFILESUFFIX"] = ".cpp"

env.EnableQt4Modules(["QtGui", "QtCore"])
rccs = [env.Qrc("spreadsheet.qrc", QT4_QRCFLAGS="-name spreadsheet")]
uis = [env.Uic4(ui) for ui in ["gotocelldialog.ui", "sortdialog.ui"]]
sources = [
    "cell.cpp",
    "finddialog.cpp",
    "gotocelldialog.cpp",
    "main.cpp",
    "mainwindow.cpp",
    "sortdialog.cpp",
    "spreadsheet.cpp"]
env.Program(target="spreadsheet", source=[rccs, sources])
```

This file is written in Python, so we have access to all the features and libraries available in the Python language.

Most of the file is boilerplate, with just a few application-specific items needed. We begin by setting the paths to qt4.py and to Qt 4's installation directory. We could avoid copying qt4.py into every application's directory by putting it in a standard location and setting the path to it accordingly. We must explicitly enable the Qt modules we are using, in this case *QtCore* and *QtGui*, and we must specify the files that need to be processed by `rcc` or `uic`. Finally, we list the source files, and set the program's name as well as the source and resource files it depends on. We do not have to specify the `.h` files; the Qt 4 support is smart enough to run `moc` correctly as necessary, by inspecting the `.cpp` files.

Now we can build the application using the `scons` command:

```
scons
```

This builds the application specified in the `SConstruct` file in the current directory. We can clean up using `scons -c`.

- *Getting Started with Qt Jambi*
- *Using Qt Jambi in the Eclipse IDE*
- *Integrating C++ Components with Qt Jambi*

Introduction to Qt Jambi

Qt Jambi is the Java edition of the Qt application development framework. At the heart of Qt Jambi are the C++ libraries that form Qt, made available to Java programmers through the Java Native Interface (JNI). Although considerable effort has gone into making Qt Jambi integrate smoothly with Java and to make its API natural to use for Java programmers, C++/Qt programmers will still find the API familiar and predictable. All the classes are documented using Javadoc at `http://doc.trolltech.com/qtjambi/`.

Until now, Java GUI programmers have had to make do with AWT, Swing, SWT, and similar GUI class libraries, none of which are as convenient to use or as powerful as Qt. For example, in the traditional Java GUI libraries, connecting a user action, such as clicking a button, to a corresponding method involves writing an event listener class; in Qt Jambi, only one line of code is required to achieve the same thing. And Qt's layout managers are much easier to use than Swing's `BoxLayout` and `GridBagLayout`, and they produce better-looking results.

Qt Jambi applications can have main windows with menu bars, toolbars, dock windows, and a status bar, just like Qt applications written in C++. They also have the native look and feel of the platform they are running on, and they respect the user's preferences regarding themes, colors, fonts, and so on. With the full power of Qt under the hood, Qt Jambi applications can take advantage of Qt's powerful 2D graphics architecture (notably the graphics view framework) and of extensions such as OpenGL.

The benefits of Qt Jambi are not limited to Java programmers. In particular, C++ programmers can make their custom Qt components available to Java programmers using the same generator tool that Trolltech uses to make the Qt API available in Qt Jambi.

In this appendix, we will show how Java programmers can start using Qt Jambi to create GUI applications. Then we will show how to make use of Qt Jambi in Eclipse, which integrates *Qt Designer*, and finally we will show how to make custom C++ components available to Qt Jambi programmers. This appendix assumes that you are familiar with C++/Qt programming and with Java. Qt Jambi requires Java 1.5 or later.

Getting Started with Qt Jambi

In this section, we will develop a small Java application that presents the window shown in Figure C.1. Apart from its window title, the Jambi Find dialog has the same appearance and behavior as the Find dialog we created back in Chapter 2. By reusing the same example, we can more easily see the differences and similarities between C++/Qt and Qt Jambi programming. While reviewing the code, we will discuss the conceptual differences between C++ and Java as they arise.

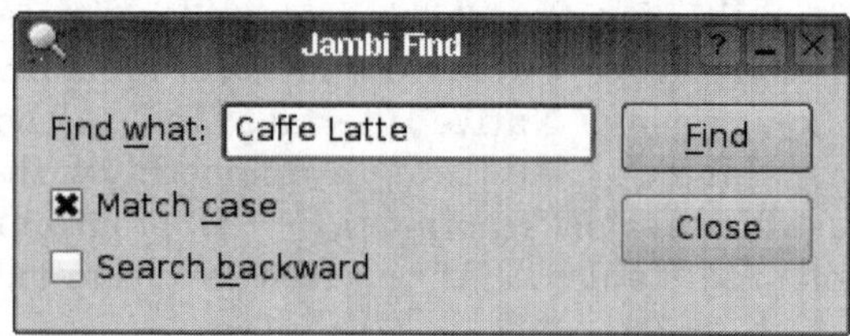

Figure C.1. The Jambi Find dialog

The implementation of the Jambi Find application is done in a single file called `FindDialog.java`. We will review the contents of this file piece by piece, starting with the `import` declarations.

```
import com.trolltech.qt.core.*;
import com.trolltech.qt.gui.*;
```

Between them, these two `import` declarations make all of Qt's core and GUI classes available to Java. Additional sets of classes can be made available with similar `import` declarations (e.g., `import com.trolltech.qt.opengl.*`).

```
public class FindDialog extends QDialog {
```

The `FindDialog` class is a subclass of `QDialog`, like in the C++ version of the example. In C++, we declare signals in the header file, relying on the `moc` tool to generate the supporting code. In Qt Jambi, Java's introspection facilities are used to implement the signals and slots mechanism. But we still need some means of declaring signals, and this is done using the `Signal`*N* classes:

```
    public Signal2<String, Qt.CaseSensitivity> findNext =
            new Signal2<String, Qt.CaseSensitivity>();

    public Signal2<String, Qt.CaseSensitivity> findPrevious =
            new Signal2<String, Qt.CaseSensitivity>();
```

There are ten `Signal`*N* classes—`Signal0`, `Signal1<T1>`, ..., `Signal9<T1, ...,T9>`. The numbers in their names indicate how many arguments they take, and the types `T1`, ..., `T9` specify the types of the arguments. Here, we have declared two signals, each taking two arguments. In both cases, the first argument is a Java `String`, and the second argument is of type `Qt.CaseSensitivity`, a Java enum type. Wherever a `QString` is needed in the Qt API, in Qt Jambi we use a `String` instead.

Unlike the other `SignalN` classes, `Signal0` is not a generic class. To create a signal with no arguments, we use `Signal0` like this:

```
public Signal0 somethingHappened = new Signal0();
```

Having created the signals we need, we are now ready to see the implementation of the constructor. The method is quite long, so we will look at it in three parts.

```
public FindDialog(QWidget parent) {
    super(parent);

    label = new QLabel(tr("Find &what:"));
    lineEdit = new QLineEdit();
    label.setBuddy(lineEdit);

    caseCheckBox = new QCheckBox(tr("Match &case"));
    backwardCheckBox = new QCheckBox(tr("Search &backward"));

    findButton = new QPushButton(tr("&Find"));
    findButton.setDefault(true);
    findButton.setEnabled(false);

    closeButton = new QPushButton(tr("Close"));
```

The only differences between creating the widgets in Java compared to C++ are the small details of syntax. Note that `tr()` returns a `String`, not a `QString`.

```
    lineEdit.textChanged.connect(this, "enableFindButton(String)");
    findButton.clicked.connect(this, "findClicked()");
    closeButton.clicked.connect(this, "reject()");
```

The syntax for signal–slot connections in Qt Jambi is somewhat different than in C++/Qt, but it is still short and simple. In general, the syntax is

```
sender.signalName.connect(receiver, "slotName(T1, ..., TN)");
```

Unlike in C++/Qt, we don't need to specify a signature for the signal. If a signal has more parameters than the slots it connects to, the additional parameters are ignored. Furthermore, in Qt Jambi, the signal–slot mechanism is not limited to `QObject` subclasses: Any class that inherits `QSignalEmitter` can emit signals, and any method of any class can be a slot.

```
    QHBoxLayout topLeftLayout = new QHBoxLayout();
    topLeftLayout.addWidget(label);
    topLeftLayout.addWidget(lineEdit);

    QVBoxLayout leftLayout = new QVBoxLayout();
    leftLayout.addLayout(topLeftLayout);
    leftLayout.addWidget(caseCheckBox);
    leftLayout.addWidget(backwardCheckBox);
```

```
        QVBoxLayout rightLayout = new QVBoxLayout();
        rightLayout.addWidget(findButton);
        rightLayout.addWidget(closeButton);
        rightLayout.addStretch();

        QHBoxLayout mainLayout = new QHBoxLayout();
        mainLayout.addLayout(leftLayout);
        mainLayout.addLayout(rightLayout);
        setLayout(mainLayout);

        setWindowTitle(tr("Jambi Find"));
        setFixedHeight(sizeHint().height());
    }
```

The layout code is practically identical to the C++ original, with the same layout classes working in exactly the same way. Qt Jambi can also use forms created with *Qt Designer*, using `juic` (the Java user interface compiler), as we will see in the next section.

```
    private void findClicked() {
        String text = lineEdit.text();
        Qt.CaseSensitivity cs = caseCheckBox.isChecked()
                ? Qt.CaseSensitivity.CaseSensitive
                : Qt.CaseSensitivity.CaseInsensitive;
        if (backwardCheckBox.isChecked()) {
            findPrevious.emit(text, cs);
        } else {
            findNext.emit(text, cs);
        }
    }
```

The Java syntax for referring to enum values is a bit more verbose than in C++, but it is easy to understand. To emit a signal, we call the `emit()` method on a `Signal`*N* object, passing arguments of the correct types. The type-checking is done when the program is compiled.

```
    private void enableFindButton(String text) {
        findButton.setEnabled(text.length() == 0);
    }
```

The `enableFindButton()` method is essentially the same as the C++ original.

```
    private QLabel label;
    private QLineEdit lineEdit;
    private QCheckBox caseCheckBox;
    private QCheckBox backwardCheckBox;
    private QPushButton findButton;
    private QPushButton closeButton;
```

In keeping with the code in the rest of the book, we have declared all the widgets as private fields of the class. This is purely a matter of style; nothing is stopping us from declaring in the constructor itself those widgets that are referred to only in the constructor. For example, we could have declared `label` and `closeButton` in the constructor since they are not referred to anywhere else, and they would

Using Java's Resource System

Qt Jambi is fully aware of Java's resource system, unlike many of Java's standard classes. Java resources are identified by a `classpath:` prefix. Anywhere a file name could be used in the Qt Jambi API, a Java resource can be specified instead. For example:

```
QIcon icon = new QIcon("classpath:/images/icon.png");
if (!icon.isNull()) {
    ...
}
```

To find the icon, Qt Jambi will look in every `images` directory of every directory or `.jar` file specified in the `CLASSPATH` environment variable. As soon as an image file called `icon.png` is found, the search stops and the file is used.

No exception is raised if the file isn't found. In the above example, if `icon.png` is not found, `icon.isNull()` will return `true`. Classes like `QImage` and `QPixmap`, which have constructors that take a file name argument, have an `isNull()` method that can be tested to see if the file was read successfully. In the case of `QFile`, we can check `QFile.error()` to see if the file was read.

not be garbage-collected when the constructor finishes. This works because Qt Jambi uses the same parent–child ownership mechanism as C++/Qt, so once the `label` and `closeButton` are laid out, the `FindDialog` form takes ownership of them, and behind the scenes it keeps a reference to them to keep them alive. Qt Jambi deletes child widgets recursively, so if a top-level window is deleted, the window in turn deletes all its child widgets and layouts, which delete theirs, and so on, until cleanup is complete.

Qt Jambi makes full use of Java's garbage-collection functionality, so unlike AWT, Swing, and SWT, if the last reference to a top-level window is deleted, the window will be scheduled for garbage collection, and no explicit call to `dispose()` is necessary. This approach is very convenient and works the same as in C++/Qt. The main caveat is that for SDI (single document interface) applications, we must keep a reference to each top-level window that is created, to prevent them from being garbage-collected. (In C++/Qt, SDI applications normally use the `Qt::WA_DeleteOnClose` attribute to prevent memory leaks.)

```
    public static void main(String[] args) {
        QApplication.initialize(args);
        FindDialog dialog = new FindDialog(null);
        dialog.show();
        QApplication.exec();
    }
}
```

For convenience, we have provided the `FindDialog` with a `main()` method that instantiates a dialog and pops it up. The `import com.trolltech.qt.gui.*` declaration ensures that a static QApplication object is available. When a Qt Jambi application starts, we must call QApplication.initialize() and pass it the command-line arguments. This allows the QApplication object to handle the arguments it recognizes, such as -font and -style.

When we create the FindDialog, we pass null as parent to signify that the dialog is a top-level window. Once the main() method is finished, the dialog will go out of scope and be garbage-collected. The call to QApplication.exec() starts off the event loop, and returns control to the main() method only when the user closes the dialog.

The Qt Jambi API is very similar to the C++/Qt API, but there are some differences. For example, in C++, the QWidget::mapTo() member function has the following signature:

```
QPoint mapTo(QWidget *widget, const QPoint &point) const;
```

The QWidget is passed as a non-const pointer, whereas the QPoint is passed as a const reference. In Qt Jambi, the equivalent method has the signature

```
public final QPoint mapTo(QWidget widget, QPoint point) { ... }
```

Because Java does not have pointers, there is no visual distinction in method signatures to indicate whether an object passed to a method can be modified by the method. In theory, the mapTo() method could alter either parameter since they are both references, but Qt Jambi promises not to alter the QPoint argument, since in C++ it is passed as a constant reference. From the context, it is usually clear which parameters are alterable and which are not. In case of doubt, we can refer to the documentation to clarify the situation.

In addition to not altering arguments that are passed by value or as constant references in C++, Qt Jambi also promises that the return value of any non-void method, which in C++ would be returned as a value or as a constant reference, is an independent copy, so altering it will not lead to any side effects.

We mentioned earlier that in Qt Jambi, wherever a QString would be used in C++/Qt, a Java String is used instead. This kind of correspondence also applies to the QChar class, which has two Java equivalents: char and java.lang.Character. There are similar correspondences regarding some of Qt's container classes: QHash is replaced by java.util.HashMap, QList and QVector by java.util.List, and QMap by java.util.SortedMap. In addition, QThread is replaced by java.lang.Thread.

The Qt model/view architecture and the database API make extensive use of QVariant. Such a type isn't needed in Java because all Java objects have java.lang.Object as an ancestor, so throughout Qt Jambi's API, QVariant is replaced by java.lang.Object. The extra methods that QVariant provides are available as static methods in com.trolltech.qt.QVariant.

We have now finished reviewing a small Qt Jambi application, and we discussed many of the conceptual differences between Qt Jambi and C++/Qt programming. Building and running a Qt Jambi application is no different from any other Java application, except that the `CLASSPATH` environment variable must specify the directory where Qt Jambi is installed. We must compile the class using a Java compiler and then we can execute the class using a Java interpreter. For example:

```
export CLASSPATH=$CLASSPATH:$HOME/qtjambi/qtjambi.jar:$PWD
javac FindDialog.java
java FindDialog
```

Here we have used the Bash shell to set the `CLASSPATH` environment variable; other command-line interpreters may require a different syntax. We include the current directory in the `CLASSPATH` so that the `FindDialog` class itself can be found. On Mac OS X, the command-line option `-XstartOnFirstThread` must be supplied to `java` to address a threading issue with Apple's Java virtual machine. On Windows, we execute the application like this:

```
set CLASSPATH=%CLASSPATH%;%JAMBIPATH%\qtjambi.jar;%CD%
javac FindDialog.java
java FindDialog
```

Qt Jambi can also be used within an IDE. In the next section, we will look at how to edit, build, and test a Qt Jambi application using the popular Eclipse IDE.

Using Qt Jambi in the Eclipse IDE

The Eclipse IDE ("Eclipse" for short) is one of the key pieces of software in the Eclipse family of more than sixty open source projects. Eclipse is very popular with Java programmers, and since it is written in Java, it runs on all major platforms. Eclipse displays a collection of panels, called views. Many views are available in Eclipse, including navigator, outline, and editor views, and each particular collection of views is called a perspective.

To make Qt Jambi and *Qt Designer* available inside Eclipse, it is necessary to install the Qt Jambi Eclipse integration package. Once the package is unpacked in the right location, Eclipse must be run with the `-clean` option to force it to look for new plugins, rather than relying on its cache. The Preferences dialog will now have an extra option called "Qt Jambi Preference Page". It is necessary to go to this page and set Qt Jambi's location, as explained in `http://doc.trolltech.com/qtjambi-4.3.2_01/com/trolltech/qt/qtjambi-eclipse.html`. Once the path has been set and verified, Eclipse should be closed and restarted for the changes to take effect.

The next time we start Eclipse and click File|New Project, the New Project dialog that pops up will offer two kinds of Qt Jambi project: Qt Jambi Project and Qt Jambi Project (Using Designer Form). In this section, we will discuss both of these project types by presenting a Qt Jambi version of the Go to Cell example developed in Chapter 2.

To create a Qt Jambi application purely in code, click File|New Project, choose "Qt Jambi Project", and go through each page of the wizard. At the end, Eclipse

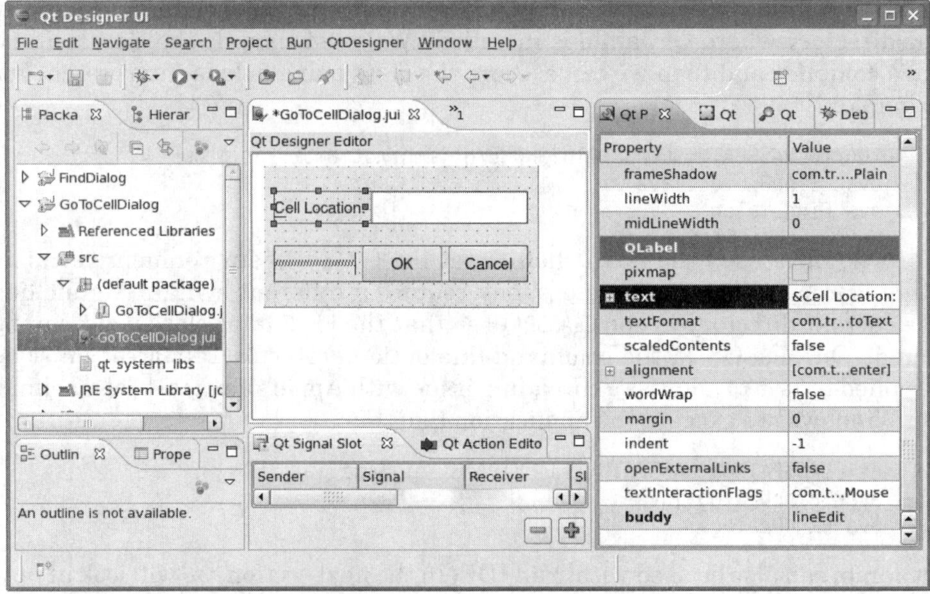

Figure C.2. The Go to Cell dialog in Eclipse

will create a project with a skeleton `.java` file with a `main()` method and a constructor. The application can be run from within Eclipse using the Run|Run menu option. Eclipse shows syntax errors in the left margin of the editor, and shows any errors that occur at run-time in a console window.

Creating a Qt Jambi application that uses *Qt Designer* is very similar to creating a pure code application. Click File|New Project, and then choose "Qt Jambi Project (Using Designer Form)". Again, a wizard will appear. Call the project "JambiGoToCell", and on the last page, specify "GoToCellDialog" as the class name and choose "Dialog" as the form type.

Once the wizard has finished, it will have created `GoToCellDialog.java` and also a Java user interface file `GoToCellDialog.jui`. Double-click the `.jui` file to make the *Qt Designer* editor visible. A form with OK and Cancel buttons will be shown. To access *Qt Designer*'s functionality, click Window|Open Perspective|Other, then double-click Qt Designer UI. This perspective shows *Qt Designer*'s signal–slot editor, action editor, property editor, widget box, and more, as shown in Figure C.2.

To complete the design, we perform the same steps as in Chapter 2 (p. 24). The dialog can be previewed as it could be within *Qt Designer*, and since Eclipse generates skeleton code it is also possible to run it by clicking Run|Run.

The final stage is to edit the `GoToCellDialog.java` file to implement the functionality we need. Two constructors are generated by Eclipse, but we only want one of them, so we delete the parameterless constructor. In the generated `main()` method, we must pass `null` as the parent to the `GoToCellDialog` constructor. Also, we must implement the `GoToCellDialog(QWidget parent)` constructor, and provide a `on_lineEdit_textChanged(String)` method that is called whenever the line editor's `textChanged()` signal is emitted. Here is the resulting `GoToCellDialog.java` file:

```
import com.trolltech.qt.core.*;
import com.trolltech.qt.gui.*;

public class GoToCellDialog extends QDialog {
    private Ui_GoToCellDialogClass ui = new Ui_GoToCellDialogClass();

    public GoToCellDialog(QWidget parent) {
        super(parent);
        ui.setupUi(this);

        ui.okButton.setEnabled(false);

        QRegExp regExp = new QRegExp("[A-Za-z][1-9][0-9]{0,2}");
        ui.lineEdit.setValidator(new QRegExpValidator(regExp, this));

        ui.okButton.clicked.connect(this, "accept()");
        ui.cancelButton.clicked.connect(this, "reject()");
    }

    private void on_lineEdit_textChanged(String text) {
        ui.okButton.setEnabled(!text.isEmpty());
    }

    public static void main(String[] args) {
        QApplication.initialize(args);
        GoToCellDialog testGoToCellDialog = new GoToCellDialog(null);
        testGoToCellDialog.show();
        QApplication.exec();
    }
}
```

Eclipse takes care of invoking `juic` to convert `GoToCellDialog.jui` into `Ui_GoToCellDialogClass.java`, which defines a class called `Ui_GoToCellDialogClass` that reproduces the dialog we designed using *Qt Designer*. We create an instance of this class and keep a reference to it in a private field called `ui`.

In the constructor, we call the `Ui_GoToCellDialogClass`'s `setupUi()` method to create and lay out the widgets and to set their properties and signal–slot connections, including automatic connections for slots that follow the naming convention `on_`*`objectName`*`_`*`signalName`*`()`.

A convenient feature of the Eclipse integration is that it is easy to make `QWidget` subclasses available in the widget box to be dragged on to forms. We will briefly review the `LabeledLineEdit` custom widget, and then describe how to make it available in *Qt Designer*'s widget box.

When we create custom widgets for use with *Qt Designer*, it is often convenient to provide properties that the programmer can change to customize the widget. The screenshot in Figure C.3 shows a custom `LabeledLineEdit` widget in a form. The widget has two custom properties, `labelText` and `editText`, that can be set in

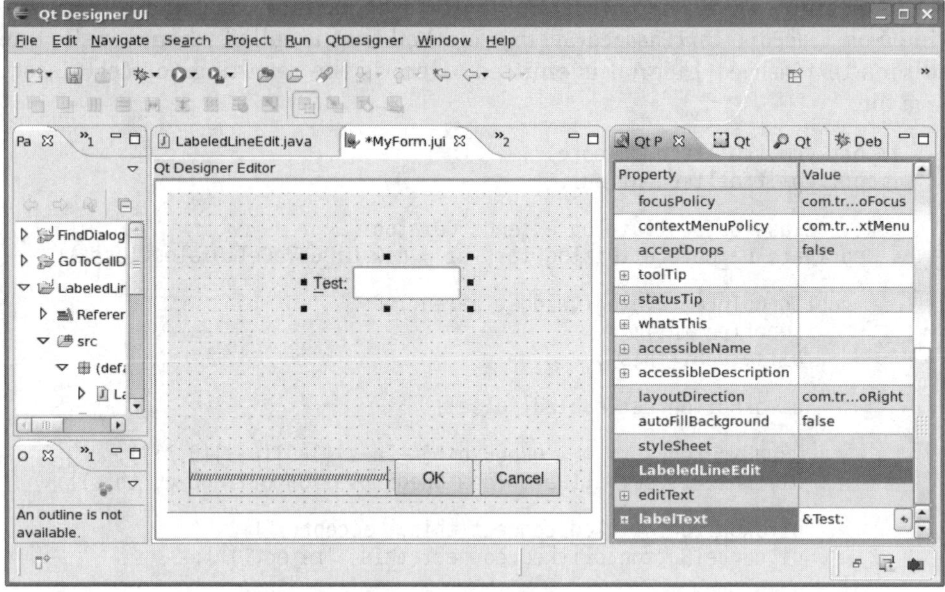

Figure C.3. The `LabeledLineEdit` custom widget in a form

the property editor. In C++/Qt, properties are defined by means of the `Q_PROPERTY()` macro. In Qt Jambi, introspection is used to detect pairs of accessor methods that follow the Qt naming convention `xxx()`/`setXxx()` or the Java naming convention `getXxx()`/`setXxx()`. It is also possible to specify other properties and to hide automatically detected properties using annotations.

```
import com.trolltech.qt.*;
import com.trolltech.qt.gui.*;

public class LabeledLineEdit extends QWidget {
```

The first `import` declaration is needed to access Qt Jambi's `@QtPropertyReader()` and `@QtPropertyWriter()` annotations, which let us export properties to *Qt Designer*.

```
    @QtPropertyReader(name="labelText")
    public String labelText() { return label.text(); }

    @QtPropertyWriter(name="labelText")
    public void setLabelText(String text) { label.setText(text); }

    @QtPropertyReader(name="editText")
    public String editText() { return lineEdit.text(); }

    @QtPropertyWriter(name="editText")
    public void setEditText(String text) { lineEdit.setText(text); }
```

For read-only properties, we can simply use the `@QtPropertyReader()` annotation and provide a getter method. Here we want to provide read-write properties, so each has a getter and a setter. For this example, we could have omitted the annotations, since the accessor methods follow the Qt naming convention.

```
        public LabeledLineEdit(QWidget parent){
            super(parent);

            label = new QLabel();
            lineEdit = new QLineEdit();
            label.setBuddy(lineEdit);

            QHBoxLayout layout = new QHBoxLayout();
            layout.addWidget(label);
            layout.addWidget(lineEdit);
            setLayout(layout);
        }

        private QLabel label;
        private QLineEdit lineEdit;
```

The constructor is quite conventional. To be eligible for use in the widget box, we must provide a constructor that takes a single QWidget argument.

```
        public static void main(String[] args) {
            QApplication.initialize(args);
            LabeledLineEdit testLabeledLineEdit = new LabeledLineEdit(null);
            testLabeledLineEdit.setLabelText("&Test");
            testLabeledLineEdit.show();
            QApplication.exec();
        }
    }
```

Eclipse generates the `main()` method automatically. We have passed `null` as the argument to the `LabeledLineEdit` constructor and added a line to set the label's text property.

Once we have a custom widget, we can add it to a project by copying its `.java` file into the project's `src` in the package explorer. Then we invoke the project's Properties dialog and click the Qt Designer Plugins page. This page lists all the suitable `QWidget` subclasses that are in the project. We just need to check the Enable plugin checkbox for any of the subclasses that we want to appear in the widget box and click OK. The next time we edit a form using the integrated *Qt Designer*, the widgets we have added to the project as plugins will appear at the bottom of the widget box in a separate section.

This concludes our brief introduction to using Eclipse for Qt Jambi programming. Eclipse provides a powerful and functional IDE with many conveniences for software development. And with the Qt Jambi integration in place, it is possible to create Qt Jambi applications, including those that use *Qt Designer*, completely within the Eclipse environment. Trolltech also provides a C++/Qt Eclipse integration with most of the same benefits as the Qt Jambi one.

Integrating C++ Components with Qt Jambi

Qt Jambi lets C++ programmers easily integrate their Qt code with Java. To make our own custom C++ components available to Qt Jambi, we can use the Qt Jambi Generator, which takes a set of C++ header files and an XML file that provides some information about the C++ classes that we want to wrap and produces Java bindings for our C++ components. The Qt Jambi API itself is created using the generator.

Figure C.4 illustrates the process. After running the generator, we obtain some Java files that we must compile using the Java compiler, and some `.h` and `.cpp` files that we must compile into a C++ shared library.

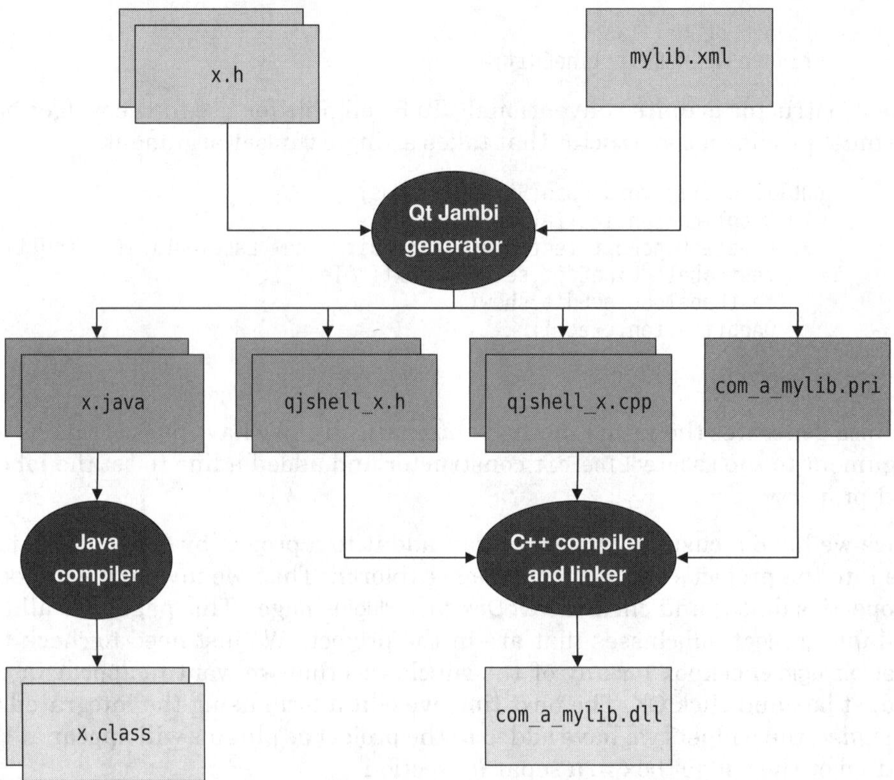

Figure C.4. Making C++ classes available in Qt Jambi

To illustrate the process, we will provide bindings for the data-only `PlotSettings` class and for the `Plotter` widget that we developed in Chapter 5 (p. 121). We will then use the bindings in a Java application. Figure C.5 shows the application running.

The header file we need must define (or include header files that define) all the classes necessary for the library we will build:

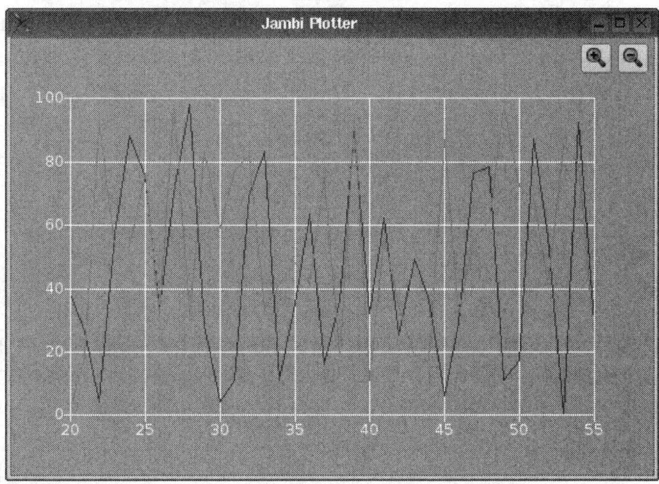

Figure C.5. The Jambi Plotter application

```
#include <QtGui>

#include "../plotter/plotter.h"
```

We assume that the Plotter example code lies in a directory parallel to the Qt Jambi wrapper. We also need an XML file to tell the generator what to wrap and how to wrap it. The file is called `jambiplotter.xml`:

```
<typesystem package="com.softwareinc.plotter"
            default-superclass="com.trolltech.qt.QtJambiObject">
    <load-typesystem name=":/trolltech/generator/typesystem_core.txt"
                     generate="no" />
    <load-typesystem name=":/trolltech/generator/typesystem_gui.txt"
                     generate="no" />
    <object-type name="Plotter" />
    <value-type name="PlotSettings" />
</typesystem>
```

In the outer tag, we specify a Java package name of `com.softwareinc.plotter` for the Plotter component. The `<load-typesystem>` tags import the information concerning the *QtCore* and *QtGui* modules.

The `<object-type>` and `<value-type>` tags specify the two C++ classes we want to make available. We have specified that the `Plotter` class is a C++ "object type"; this is suitable for objects that cannot be copied, such as widgets. In contrast, the `PlotSettings` class is treated as a C++ "value type".

To Qt Jambi users, there is no obvious difference between the two. The distinction is important when the generator maps C++ APIs to Java APIs. For example, if a "value type" is returned from a method, the generator will ensure that a new independent object is returned (to avoid side effects), but if the returned type is an object type, a reference to the original object is returned.

We will need two environment variables, one specifying the path to Qt Jambi, the other to Java. Here is how we set them on Unix systems (using the Bash shell):

```
export JAMBIPATH=$HOME/qtjambi-linux32-gpl-4.3.2_01
export JAVA=/usr/java/jdk1.6.0_02
```

On Windows, we would write

```
set JAMBIPATH=C:\QtJambi
set JAVA="C:\Program Files\Java\jdk1.6.0_02"
```

Naturally, the version numbers and directories may be different for your system. From now on, we will assume that JAMBIPATH and JAVA are available. Once we have the header and XML files, we can run the generator in a console:

```
$JAMBIPATH/bin/generator jambiplotter.h jambiplotter.xml
```

If Qt Jambi has been installed locally rather than system-wide, this may fail on some systems. The solution is to provide a suitable path to Qt Jambi's libraries:

```
export LD_LIBRARY_PATH=$LD_LIBRARY_PATH:$JAMBIPATH/lib
```

Again, we have used the Bash shell's syntax. On Mac OS X, the relevant environment variable is called DYLD_LIBRARY_PATH. On Windows, the equivalent is achieved by adding to the PATH:

```
set PATH=%PATH%;%JAMBIPATH%\lib
```

Now, on Windows, we can run the generator like this:

```
%JAMBIPATH%\bin\generator jambiplotter.h jambiplotter.xml
```

The code generation takes a few moments, and outputs some summary information on the console. For our example, the generator produced the following files, in two parallel directories:

```
../com/softwareinc/plotter/PlotSettings.java
../com/softwareinc/plotter/Plotter.java
../com/softwareinc/plotter/QtJambi_LibraryInitializer.java

../cpp/com_softwareinc_plotter/com_softwareinc_plotter.pri
../cpp/com_softwareinc_plotter/metainfo.cpp
../cpp/com_softwareinc_plotter/metainfo.h
../cpp/com_softwareinc_plotter/qtjambi_libraryinitializer.cpp
../cpp/com_softwareinc_plotter/qtjambishell_PlotSettings.cpp
../cpp/com_softwareinc_plotter/qtjambishell_PlotSettings.h
../cpp/com_softwareinc_plotter/qtjambishell_Plotter.cpp
../cpp/com_softwareinc_plotter/qtjambishell_Plotter.h
```

We must now compile both the Java and the C++ files, but before we do this we should make sure that the CLASSPATH environment variable is set correctly. For example, if we are using the Bash shell, we might do this:

```
export CLASSPATH=$CLASSPATH:$JAMBIPATH/qtjambi.jar:$PWD:$PWD/..
```

Here we have extended the existing `CLASSPATH` with the Qt Jambi `.jar` file, with the current directory, and with the current directory's parent directory. We need the parent directory so that we can access the parallel `com` directory. On Windows, the syntax would be

```
set CLASSPATH=%CLASSPATH%;%JAMBIPATH%\qtjambi.jar;%CD%;%CD%\..
```

We can now compile the `.java` files into `.class` files:

```
cd ../com/softwareinc/plotter
javac *.java
```

After compiling the `.java` files, we must return to the `jambiplotter` directory. Here, the next step is to create the C++ shared library that provides the C++ code for `Plotter` and `PlotSettings`, as well as the C++ wrapper code produced by the generator. We begin by creating a `.pro` file:

```
TEMPLATE      = lib
TARGET        = com_softwareinc_plotter
DLLDESTDIR    = .
HEADERS       = ../plotter/plotter.h
SOURCES       = ../plotter/plotter.cpp
RESOURCES     = ../plotter/plotter.qrc
INCLUDEPATH  += ../plotter \
                $$(JAMBIPATH)/include \
                $$(JAVA)/include
unix {
    INCLUDEPATH  += $$(JAVA)/include/linux
}
win32 {
    INCLUDEPATH  += $$(JAVA)/include/win32
}
LIBS         += -L$$(JAMBIPATH)/lib -lqtjambi

include(../cpp/com_softwareinc_plotter/com_softwareinc_plotter.pri)
```

The `TEMPLATE` variable must be set to `lib` since we want to create a shared library rather than an application. The `TARGET` variable specifies the name of the Java package but with underscores used instead of periods, and `DLLDESTDIR` specifies where the shared library (or DLL) should be put. The `INCLUDEPATH` variable must be extended to include the source directory (since it is not the current directory in this case), the Qt Jambi include path, the Java SDK's include path, and the Java SDK's platform-specific include path. (We cover the `unix` and `win32` syntaxes in Appendix B.) We must also include the Qt Jambi library itself, which we do in the `LIBS` entry. The `include()` directive at the end is used to access the C++ files the generator produced. Once we have the `.pro` file, we can run `qmake` and `make` as usual to build the library.

Now that we have the shared library and suitable Java wrapper code, we are ready to make use of them in an application. The Jambi Plotter application creates a `PlotSettings` and a `Plotter` object and uses them to display some random data. The important point is that they are used just like any other Java or Qt Jambi class. The whole application is quite small, so we will show it in full:

```
import java.lang.Math;
import java.util.ArrayList;
import com.trolltech.qt.core.*;
import com.trolltech.qt.gui.*;
import com.softwareinc.plotter.Plotter;
import com.softwareinc.plotter.PlotSettings;

public class JambiPlotter {
    public static void main(String[] args) {
        QApplication.initialize(args);

        PlotSettings settings = new PlotSettings();
        settings.setMinX(0.0);
        settings.setMaxX(100.0);
        settings.setMinY(0.0);
        settings.setMaxY(100.0);

        int numPoints = 100;
        ArrayList<QPointF> points0 = new ArrayList<QPointF>();
        ArrayList<QPointF> points1 = new ArrayList<QPointF>();
        for (int x = 0; x < numPoints; ++x) {
            points0.add(new QPointF(x, Math.random() * 100));
            points1.add(new QPointF(x, Math.random() * 100));
        }

        Plotter plotter = new Plotter();
        plotter.setWindowTitle(plotter.tr("Jambi Plotter"));
        plotter.setPlotSettings(settings);
        plotter.setCurveData(0, points0);
        plotter.setCurveData(1, points1);
        plotter.show();

        QApplication.exec();
    }
}
```

We import a couple of Java's standard libraries and the Qt Jambi libraries that we need, as well as the `PlotSettings` and `Plotter` classes. We could just as easily have written `import com.softwareinc.plotter.*`.

After initializing the `QApplication` object, we create a `PlotSettings` object and set some of its values. The C++ version of this class has `minX`, `maxX`, `minY`, and `maxY` as public variables. Unless told otherwise, the Qt Jambi generator produces accessor methods for such variables, using the Qt naming convention (e.g., `minX()` and `setMinX()`). Once we have suitable plot settings, we generate two lots of curve data, with 100 random points each. In C++/Qt, the points of each curve are held as a `QVector<QPointF>`; in Qt Jambi, we pass an `ArrayList<QPointF>` instead, relying on Qt Jambi to transform from one to the other as needed.

With the settings and curve data ready, we create a new `Plotter` object with no parent (to make it a top-level window). Then we give the plotter the plot settings, and the data for two curves, and call `show()` to make the plotter visible. Finally, we call `QApplication.exec()` to start off the event loop.

When we compile the application, we must be careful to include not only the normal `CLASSPATH` but also the path to the `com.softwareinc.plotter` package. To run the application, we must also set up a couple of additional environment variables, to ensure that the loader will find Qt Jambi and our bindings. On Windows, we must set `PATH` as follows:

```
set PATH=%PATH%;%JAMBIPATH%\bin;%CD%
```

On Unix, we must set `LD_LIBRARY_PATH`:

```
export LD_LIBRARY_PATH=$LD_LIBRARY_PATH:$JAMBIPATH/lib:$PWD
```

On Mac OS X, the environment variable is called `DYLD_LIBRARY_PATH`. Also, on all three platforms, we must set `QT_PLUGIN_PATH` to include Qt Jambi's `plugins` directory. For example:

```
set QT_PLUGIN_PATH=%QT_PLUGIN_PATH%;%JAMBIPATH%\plugins
```

To compile and run Jambi Plotter on all platforms, thanks to our additions to the `CLASSPATH`, we can simply type this:

```
javac JambiPlotter.java
java JambiPlotter
```

We have now completed the example, and shown how to make use of C++ components in Qt Jambi applications. In fact, the Qt Jambi generator that is the basis of making C++ components available to Java offers many more features than this brief introduction has shown. Although the generator supports only a subset of C++, this subset comprises all of the most common C++ constructs, including multiple inheritance and operator overloading. The generator is documented in full at `http://doc.trolltech.com/qtjambi-4.3.2_01/com/trolltech/qt/qtjambi-generator.html`. We will briefly mention just a few features we didn't need in the example, to give a flavor of what's available.

The key to influencing how the generator works is what we put in the XML file we give it. For example, if we have multiple inheritance in C++, one straightforward way to handle this in Qt Jambi is to identify just one of the classes concerned as an "object type" or "value type" in the type system, and identify all the others as "interface types".

It is also possible to provide more natural method signatures. For example, instead of using an `ArrayList<QPointF>` to pass the points for a curve, it would be nicer to pass a `QPointF` array. This involves hiding the original C++ method and replacing it with a Java method that accepts a `QPointF[]` and calls the original C++ method behind the scenes. We can achieve this by modifying the `jambiplotter.xml` file. We originally declared the C++ `Plotter` type with an entry like this:

```
<object-type name="Plotter" />
```

We will replace the preceding line with a more sophisticated version:

```
<object-type name="Plotter">
    <modify-function
        signature="setCurveData(int,const QVector&lt;QPointF&gt;&amp;)">
        <access modifier="private" />
        <rename to="setCurveData_private" />
    </modify-function>
    <inject-code>
        public final void setCurveData(int id,
                                       com.trolltech.qt.core.QPointF points[]) {
            setCurveData_private(id, java.util.Arrays.asList(points));
        }
    </inject-code>
</object-type>
```

In the <modify-function> element, we rename the C++ setCurveData() method to be setCurveData_private() and change its access specifier to private, thereby preventing access to it from outside the class's own methods. Notice that we must escape XML's special characters '<', '>', and '&' in the signature attribute.

In the <inject-code> element, we implement a custom setCurveData() method in Java. This method accepts a QPointF[] argument and simply calls the private setCurveData_private() method, converting the array to the list that the C++ method expects.

Now we can create and populate QPointF arrays in a more natural manner:

```
QPointF[] points0 = new QPointF[numPoints];
QPointF[] points1 = new QPointF[numPoints];
for (int x = 0; x < numPoints; ++x) {
    points0[x] = new QPointF(x, Math.random() * 100);
    points1[x] = new QPointF(x, Math.random() * 100);
}
```

The rest of the code is the same as before.

In some cases, when classes are wrapped, the generator produces code that uses QNativePointer. This type is a wrapper for C++ "value type" pointers and works for both pointers and arrays. The file mjb_nativepointer_api.log specifies any generated code that uses QNativePointer. The Qt Jambi documentation recommends replacing any code that uses QNativePointer and provides step-by-step instructions for how to do this.

Sometimes we will need to include additional import declarations in the generated .java files. This is easily achieved using the <extra-includes> tag, and is fully described in http://doc.trolltech.com/qtjambi-4.3.2_01/com/trolltech/qt/qtjambi-typesystem.html.

The Qt Jambi generator is a powerful and versatile tool for making C++/Qt classes seamlessly available to Java programmers, and makes it possible to combine the strengths of C++ and Java in a single project.

- *Getting Started with C++*
- *Main Language Differences*
- *The Standard C++ Library*

Introduction to C++ for Java and C# Programmers

This appendix provides a short introduction to C++ for developers who already know Java or C#. It assumes that you are familiar with object-oriented concepts such as inheritance and polymorphism and that you want to learn C++. To avoid making this book an unwieldy 1500 page doorstop by including a complete C++ primer, this appendix confines itself to essentials. It presents the basic knowledge and techniques necessary to understand the programs presented in the rest of the book, with enough information to start developing cross-platform C++ GUI applications using Qt.

At the time of this writing, C++ is the only realistic option for developing cross-platform, high-performance, object-oriented GUI applications. Its detractors usually point out that Java or C#, which dropped C compatibility, is nicer to use; in fact, Bjarne Stroustrup, the inventor of C++, noted in *The Design and Evolution of C++* (Addison-Wesley, 1994) that "within C++, there is a much smaller and cleaner language struggling to get out".

Fortunately, when we program with Qt, we usually stick to a subset of C++ that is very close to the utopian language envisioned by Stroustrup, leaving us free to concentrate on the problem at hand. Furthermore, Qt extends C++ in several respects, through its innovative "signals and slots" mechanism, its Unicode support, and its `foreach` keyword.

In the first section of this appendix, we will see how to combine C++ source files to obtain an executable program. This will lead us to explore core C++ concepts such as compilation units, header files, object files, and libraries—and to get familiar with the C++ preprocessor, compiler, and linker.

Then we will turn to the most important language differences between C++, Java, and C#: how to define classes, how to use pointers and references, how to overload operators, how to use the preprocessor, and so on. Although the C++ syntax is superficially similar to that of Java and C#, the underlying concepts differ in subtle ways. At the same time, as an inspirational source for Java and

C#, the C++ language has a lot in common with these two languages, including similar data types, the same arithmetic operators, and the same basic control flow statements.

The last section is devoted to the Standard C++ library, which provides ready-made functionality that can be used in any C++ program. The library is the result of more than thirty years of evolution, and as such it provides a wide range of approaches including procedural, object-oriented, and functional programming styles, and both macros and templates. Compared with the libraries provided with Java and C#, the Standard C++ library is quite narrow in scope; for example, it has no support for GUI programming, multithreading, databases, internationalization, networking, XML, or Unicode. To develop in these areas, C++ programmers are expected to use various (often platform-specific) third-party libraries.

This is where Qt saves the day. Qt began as a cross-platform GUI toolkit (a set of classes that makes it possible to write portable graphical user interface applications) but rapidly evolved into a full-blown application development framework that partly extends and partly replaces the Standard C++ library. Although this book uses Qt, it is useful to know what the Standard C++ library has to offer, since you may have to work with code that uses it.

Getting Started with C++

A C++ program consists of one or more *compilation units*. Each compilation unit is a separate source code file, typically with a `.cpp` extension (other common extensions are `.cc` and `.cxx`) that the compiler processes in one run. For each compilation unit, the compiler generates an *object file*, with the extension `.obj` (on Windows) or `.o` (on Unix and Mac OS X). The object file is a binary file that contains machine code for the architecture on which the program will run.

Once all the `.cpp` files have been compiled, we can combine the object files together to create an executable using a special program called the *linker*. The linker concatenates the object files and resolves the memory addresses of functions and other symbols referenced in the compilation units.

When building a program, exactly one compilation unit must contain a `main()` function that serves as the program's entry point. This function doesn't belong to any class; it is a *global function*. The process is shown schematically in Figure D.1.

Unlike Java, where each source file must contain exactly one class, C++ lets us organize the compilation units as we want. We can implement several classes in the same `.cpp` file, or spread the implementation of a class across several `.cpp` files, and we can give the source files any names we like. When we make a change in one particular `.cpp` file, we need to recompile only that file and then relink the application to create a new executable.

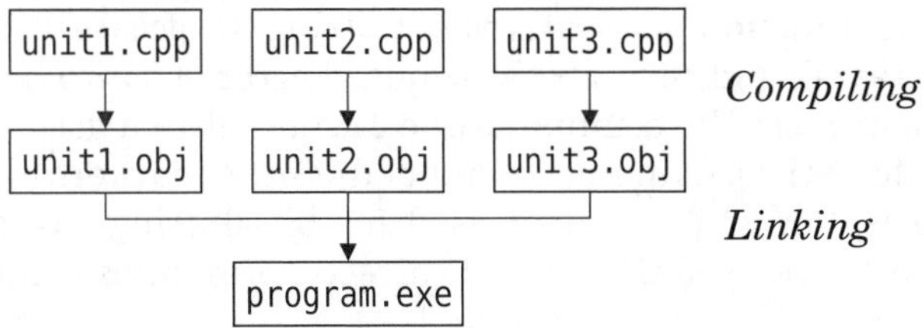

Figure D.1. The C++ compilation process (on Windows)

Before we go further, let's quickly review the source code of a trivial C++ program that computes the square of an integer. The program consists of two compilation units: `main.cpp` and `square.cpp`.

Here's `square.cpp`:

```
double square(double n)
{
    return n * n;
}
```

This file simply contains a global function called `square()` that returns the square of its parameter.

Here's `main.cpp`:

```
#include <cstdlib>
#include <iostream>

double square(double);

int main(int argc, char *argv[])
{
    if (argc != 2) {
        std::cerr << "Usage: square <number>" << std::endl;
        return 1;
    }

    double n = std::strtod(argv[1], 0);
    std::cout << "The square of " << argv[1] << " is "
              << square(n) << std::endl;
    return 0;
}
```

The `main.cpp` source file contains the `main()` function's definition. In C++, this function takes an `int` and a `char *` array (an array of character strings) as parameters. The program's name is available as `argv[0]` and the command-line arguments as `argv[1]`, `argv[2]`, ..., `argv[argc - 1]`. The parameter names `argc` ("argument count") and `argv` ("argument values") are conventional. If the program doesn't access the command-line arguments, we can define `main()` with no parameters.

The `main()` function uses `strtod()` ("string to `double`"), `cout` (C++'s standard output stream), and `cerr` (C++'s standard error stream) from the Standard C++ library to convert the command-line argument to a `double` and to print text to the console. Strings, numbers, and end-of-line markers (`endl`) are output using the << operator, which is also used for bit-shifting. To access this standard functionality, we need the `#include` directives on lines 1 and 2.

All the functions and most other items in the Standard C++ library are in the `std` namespace. One way to access an item in a namespace is to prefix its name with the namespace's name using the `::` operator. In C++, the `::` operator separates the components of a complex name. Namespaces make large multi-person projects easier because they help avoid name conflicts. We cover them later in this appendix.

The declaration on line 3 is a *function prototype*. It tells the compiler that a function exists with the given parameters and return value. The actual function can be located in the same compilation unit or in another compilation unit. Without the function prototype, the compiler wouldn't let us call the function on line 12. Parameter names in function prototypes are optional.

The procedure to compile the program varies from platform to platform. For example, to compile on Solaris with the Sun C++ compiler, we would type the following commands:

```
CC -c main.cpp
CC -c square.cpp
CC main.o square.o -o square
```

The first two lines invoke the compiler to generate `.o` files for the `.cpp` files. The third line invokes the linker and generates an executable called `square`, which we can run as follows:

```
./square 64
```

This run of the program outputs the following message to the console:

```
The square of 64 is 4096
```

To compile the program, you probably want to get help from your local C++ guru. Failing this, you can still read the rest of this appendix without compiling anything and follow the instructions in Chapter 1 to compile your first C++/Qt application. Qt provides tools that make it easy to build applications on all platforms.

Back to our program: In a real-world application, we would normally put the `square()` function prototype in a separate file and include that file in all the compilation units where we need to call the function. Such a file is called a *header file* and usually has a `.h` extension (`.hh`, `.hpp`, and `.hxx` are also common). If we redo our example using the header file approach, we would create a file called `square.h` with the following contents:

```
#ifndef SQUARE_H
#define SQUARE_H

double square(double);

#endif
```

The header file is bracketed by three preprocessor directives (`#ifndef`, `#define`, and `#endif`). These directives ensure that the header file is processed only once, even if the header file is included several times in the same compilation unit (a situation that can arise when header files include other header files). By convention, the preprocessor symbol used to accomplish this is derived from the file name (in our example, `SQUARE_H`). We will come back to the preprocessor later in this appendix.

The new `main.cpp` file looks like this:

```
1 #include <cstdlib>
2 #include <iostream>

3 #include "square.h"

4 int main(int argc, char *argv[])
5 {
6     if (argc != 2) {
7         std::cerr << "Usage: square <number>" << std::endl;
8         return 1;
9     }

10    double n = std::strtod(argv[1], 0);
11    std::cout << "The square of " << argv[1] << " is "
12              << square(n) << std::endl;
13    return 0;
14 }
```

The `#include` directive on line 3 expands to the contents of the file `square.h`. Directives that start with a # are picked up by the C++ preprocessor before the compilation proper takes place. In the old days, the preprocessor was a separate program that the programmer invoked manually before running the compiler. Modern compilers handle the preprocessor step implicitly.

The `#include` directives on lines 1 and 2 expand to the contents of the `cstdlib` and `iostream` header files, which are part of the Standard C++ library. Standard header files have no `.h` suffix. The angle brackets around the file names indicate that the header files are located in a standard location on the system, and double quotes tell the compiler to look in the current directory. Includes are normally gathered at the top of a `.cpp` file.

Unlike `.cpp` files, header files are not compilation units in their own right and do not produce any object files. Header files may only contain declarations that enable different compilation units to communicate with each other. Consequently, it would be inappropriate to put the `square()` function's implementation in a header file. If we did so in our example, nothing bad would happen, because we include `square.h` only once, but if we included `square.h` from several `.cpp` files, we would get multiple implementations of the `square()` function (one per `.cpp` file that includes it). The linker would then complain about multiple (identical) definitions of `square()` and refuse to generate an executable. Conversely, if we declare a function but never implement it, the linker complains about an "unresolved symbol".

So far, we have assumed that an executable consists exclusively of object files. In practice, it often also links against libraries that implement ready-made functionality. There are two main types of libraries:

- *Static libraries* are put directly into the executable, as though they were object files. This ensures that the library cannot get lost but increases the size of the executable.
- *Dynamic libraries* (also called shared libraries or DLLs) are located at a standard location on the user's machine and are automatically loaded at application startup.

For the `square` program, we link against the Standard C++ library, which is implemented as a dynamic library on most platforms. Qt itself is a collection of libraries that can be built either as static or as dynamic libraries (the default is dynamic).

Main Language Differences

We will now take a more structured look at the areas where C++ differs from Java and C#. Many of the language differences are due to C++'s compiled nature and commitment to performance. Thus, C++ does not check array bounds at run-time, and there is no garbage collector to reclaim unused dynamically allocated memory.

For the sake of brevity, C++ constructs that are nearly identical to their Java and C# counterparts are not reviewed. In addition, some C++ topics are not covered here because they are not necessary when programming using Qt. Among these are defining template classes and functions, defining union types, and using exceptions. For the whole story, refer to a book such as *The C++ Programming Language* by Bjarne Stroustrup (Addison-Wesley, 2000) or *C++ for Java Programmers* by Mark Allen Weiss (Prentice Hall, 2003).

Primitive Data Types

The primitive data types offered by the C++ language are similar to those found in Java or C#. Figure D.2 lists C++'s primitive types and their definitions on the platforms supported by Qt 4.

By default, the `short`, `int`, `long`, and `long long` data types are signed, meaning that they can hold negative values as well as positive values. If we only need to store nonnegative integers, we can put the `unsigned` keyword in front of the type. Whereas a `short` can hold any value between -32 768 and +32 767, an `unsigned`

C++ Type	Description
`bool`	Boolean value
`char`	8-bit integer
`short`	16-bit integer
`int`	32-bit integer
`long`	32-bit or 64-bit integer
`long long`*	64-bit integer
`float`	32-bit floating-point value (IEEE 754)
`double`	64-bit floating-point value (IEEE 754)

Figure D.2. Primitive C++ types

`short` goes from 0 to 65 535. The right-shift operator >> has unsigned ("fill with 0s") semantics if one of the operands is unsigned.

The `bool` type can take the values `true` and `false`. In addition, numeric types can be used where a `bool` is expected, with the rule that 0 means `false` and any non-zero value means `true`.

The `char` type is used for storing ASCII characters and 8-bit integers (bytes). When used as an integer, it can be signed or unsigned, depending on the platform. The types `signed char` and `unsigned char` are available as unambiguous alternatives to `char`. Qt provides a `QChar` type that stores 16-bit Unicode characters.

Instances of built-in types are not initialized by default. When we create an `int` variable, its value could conceivably be 0, but could just as likely be -209 486 515. Fortunately, most compilers warn us when we attempt to read the contents of an uninitialized variable, and we can use tools such as Rational PurifyPlus and Valgrind to detect uninitialized memory accesses and other memory-related problems at run-time.

In memory, the numeric types (except `long`) have identical sizes on the different platforms supported by Qt, but their representation varies depending on the system's byte order. On big-endian architectures (such as PowerPC and SPARC), the 32-bit value `0x12345678` is stored as the four bytes `0x12 0x34 0x56 0x78`, whereas on little-endian architectures (such as Intel x86), the byte sequence is reversed. This makes a difference in programs that copy memory areas onto disk or that send binary data over the network. Qt's `QDataStream` class, presented in Chapter 12, can be used to store binary data in a platform-independent way.

* Microsoft calls the non-standard (but due to be standardized) `long long` type `__int64`. In Qt programs, `qlonglong` is available as an alternative that works on all Qt platforms.

Class Definitions

Class definitions in C++ are similar to those in Java and C#, but there are several differences to be aware of. We will study these differences using a series of examples. Let's start with a class that represent an (x, y) coordinate pair:

```
#ifndef POINT2D_H
#define POINT2D_H

class Point2D
{
public:
    Point2D() {
        xVal = 0;
        yVal = 0;
    }
    Point2D(double x, double y) {
        xVal = x;
        yVal = y;
    }

    void setX(double x) { xVal = x; }
    void setY(double y) { yVal = y; }
    double x() const { return xVal; }
    double y() const { return yVal; }

private:
    double xVal;
    double yVal;
};

#endif
```

The preceding class definition would appear in a header file, typically called `point2d.h`. The example exhibits the following C++ idiosyncrasies:

- A class definition is divided into public, protected, and private sections, and ends with a semicolon. If no section is specified, the default is private. (For compatibility with C, C++ provides a `struct` keyword that is identical to `class` except that the default is public if no section is specified.)
- The class has two constructors (one that has no parameters and one that has two). If we declared no constructor, C++ would automatically supply one with no parameters and an empty body.
- The getter functions `x()` and `y()` are declared to be const. This means that they don't (and can't) modify the member variables or call non-const member functions (such as `setX()` and `setY()`).

The preceding functions were implemented inline, as part of the class definition. An alternative is to provide only function prototypes in the header file and to implement the functions in a `.cpp` file. Using this approach, the header file would look like this:

```
#ifndef POINT2D_H
```

```
#define POINT2D_H

class Point2D
{
public:
    Point2D();
    Point2D(double x, double y);

    void setX(double x);
    void setY(double y);
    double x() const;
    double y() const;

private:
    double xVal;
    double yVal;
};

#endif
```

The functions would then be implemented in point2d.cpp:

```
#include "point2d.h"

Point2D::Point2D()
{
    xVal = 0.0;
    yVal = 0.0;
}

Point2D::Point2D(double x, double y)
{
    xVal = x;
    yVal = y;
}

void Point2D::setX(double x)
{
    xVal = x;
}

void Point2D::setY(double y)
{
    yVal = y;
}

double Point2D::x() const
{
    return xVal;
}

double Point2D::y() const
{
    return yVal;
}
```

We start by including point2d.h because the compiler needs the class definition before it can parse member function implementations. Then we implement the functions, prefixing the function name with the class name using the `::` operator.

We have seen how to implement a function inline and now how to implement it in a `.cpp` file. The two approaches are semantically equivalent, but when we call a function that is declared inline, most compilers simply expand the function's body instead of generating an actual function call. This normally leads to faster code, but might increase the size of your application. For this reason, only very short functions should be implemented inline; longer functions should always be implemented in a `.cpp` file. In addition, if we forget to implement a function and try to call it, the linker will complain about an unresolved symbol.

Now, let's try to use the class.

```
#include "point2d.h"

int main()
{
    Point2D alpha;
    Point2D beta(0.666, 0.875);

    alpha.setX(beta.y());
    beta.setY(alpha.x());

    return 0;
}
```

In C++, variables of any types can be declared directly without using `new`. The first variable is initialized using the default `Point2D` constructor (the constructor that has no parameters). The second variable is initialized using the second constructor. Access to an object's member is performed using the `.` (dot) operator.

Variables declared this way behave like Java/C# primitive types such as `int` and `double`. For example, when we use the assignment operator, the contents of the variable are copied—not just a reference to an object. And if we modify a variable later on, any other variables that were assigned from it are left unchanged.

As an object-oriented language, C++ supports inheritance and polymorphism. To illustrate how it works, we will review the example of a `Shape` abstract base class and a subclass called `Circle`. Let's start with the base class:

```
#ifndef SHAPE_H
#define SHAPE_H

#include "point2d.h"

class Shape
{
public:
    Shape(Point2D center) { myCenter = center; }

    virtual void draw() = 0;

protected:
```

```
    Point2D myCenter;
};

#endif
```

The definition appears in a header file called `shape.h`. Since the class definition refers to the `Point2D` class, we include `point2d.h`.

The `Shape` class has no base class. Unlike Java and C#, C++ doesn't provide an `Object` class from which all classes are implicitly derived. Qt provides `QObject` as a natural base class for all kinds of objects.

The `draw()` function declaration has two interesting features: It contains the `virtual` keyword, and it ends with `= 0`. The `virtual` keyword indicates that the function may be reimplemented in subclasses. Like in C#, C++ member functions aren't reimplementable by default. The bizarre `= 0` syntax indicates that the function is a *pure virtual function*—a function that has no default implementation and that must be implemented in subclasses. The concept of an "interface" in Java and C# maps to a class with only pure virtual functions in C++.

Here's the definition of the `Circle` subclass:

```
#ifndef CIRCLE_H
#define CIRCLE_H

#include "shape.h"

class Circle : public Shape
{
public:
    Circle(Point2D center, double radius = 0.5)
        : Shape(center) {
        myRadius = radius;
    }

    void draw() {
        // do something here
    }

private:
    double myRadius;
};

#endif
```

The `Circle` class is publicly derived from `Shape`, meaning that all public members of `Shape` remain public in `Circle`. C++ also supports protected and private inheritance, which restrict the access of the base class's public and protected members.

The constructor takes two parameters. The second parameter is optional and takes the value 0.5 if not specified. The constructor passes the `center` parameter to the base class's constructor using a special syntax between the function signature and the function body. In the body, we initialize the `myRadius` member variable. We could also have initialized the variable on the same line as the base class constructor initialization:

```
Circle(Point2D center, double radius = 0.5)
    : Shape(center), myRadius(radius) { }
```

On the other hand, C++ doesn't allow us to initialize a member variable in the class definition, so the following code is wrong:

```
// WON'T COMPILE
private:
    double myRadius = 0.5;
};
```

The draw() function has the same signature as the virtual draw() function declared in Shape. It is a reimplementation and it will be invoked polymorphically when draw() is called on a Circle instance through a Shape reference or pointer. C++ has no override keyword like in C#. Nor does C++ have a super or base keyword that refers to the base class. If we need to call the base implementation of a function, we can prefix the function name with the base class name and the :: operator. For example:

```
class LabeledCircle : public Circle
{
public:
    void draw() {
        Circle::draw();
        drawLabel();
    }
    ...
};
```

C++ supports multiple inheritance, meaning that a class can be derived from several classes at the same time. The syntax is as follows:

```
class DerivedClass : public BaseClass1, public BaseClass2, ...,
                     public BaseClassN
{
    ...
};
```

By default, functions and variables declared in a class are associated with instances of that class. We can also declare static member functions and static member variables, which can be used without an instance. For example:

```
#ifndef TRUCK_H
#define TRUCK_H

class Truck
{
public:
    Truck() { ++counter; }
    ~Truck() { --counter; }
```

```
        static int instanceCount() { return counter; }

    private:
        static int counter;
    };

    #endif
```

The static member variable `counter` keeps track of how many `Truck` instances exist at any time. The `Truck` constructor increments it. The destructor, recognizable by the tilde (~) prefix, decrements it. In C++, the destructor is automatically invoked when a statically allocated variable goes out of scope or when a variable allocated using `new` is deleted. This is similar to the `finalize()` method in Java, except that we can rely on it being called at a specific point in time.

A static member variable has a single existence in a class: Such variables are "class variables" rather than "instance variables". Each static member variable must be defined in a `.cpp` file (but without repeating the `static` keyword). For example:

```
#include "truck.h"

int Truck::counter = 0;
```

Failing to do this would result in an "unresolved symbol" error at link time. The `instanceCount()` static function can be accessed from outside the class, prefixed by the class name. For example:

```
#include <iostream>

#include "truck.h"

int main()
{
    Truck truck1;
    Truck truck2;

    std::cout << Truck::instanceCount() << " equals 2" << std::endl;

    return 0;
}
```

Pointers

A *pointer* in C++ is a variable that stores the memory address of an object (instead of storing the object directly). Java and C# have a similar concept, that of a "reference", but the syntax is different. We will start by studying a contrived example that illustrates pointers in action:

```
#include "point2d.h"

int main()
{
    Point2D alpha;
    Point2D beta;
```

```
6       Point2D *ptr;

7       ptr = &alpha;
8       ptr->setX(1.0);
9       ptr->setY(2.5);

10      ptr = &beta;
11      ptr->setX(4.0);
12      ptr->setY(4.5);

13      ptr = 0;

14      return 0;
15  }
```

The example relies on the Point2D class from the previous subsection. Lines 4 and 5 define two objects of type Point2D. These objects are initialized to (0, 0) by the default Point2D constructor.

Line 6 defines a pointer to a Point2D object. The syntax for pointers uses an asterisk in front of the variable name. Since we did not initialize the pointer, it contains a random memory address. This is solved on line 7 by assigning alpha's address to the pointer. The unary & operator returns the memory address of an object. An address is typically a 32-bit or a 64-bit integer value specifying the offset of an object in memory.

On lines 8 and 9, we access the alpha object through the ptr pointer. Because ptr is a pointer and not an object, we must use the -> (arrow) operator instead of the . (dot) operator.

On line 10, we assign beta's address to the pointer. From then on, any operation we perform through the pointer will affect the beta object.

Line 13 sets the pointer to be a null pointer. C++ has no keyword for representing a pointer that does not point to an object; instead, we use the value 0 (or the symbolic constant NULL, which expands to 0). Trying to use a null pointer results in a crash with an error message such as "Segmentation fault", "General protection fault", or "Bus error". Using a debugger, we can find out which line of code caused the crash.

At the end of the function, the alpha object holds the coordinate pair (1.0, 2.5), whereas beta holds (4.0, 4.5).

Pointers are often used to store objects allocated dynamically using new. In C++ jargon, we say that these objects are allocated on the "heap", whereas local variables (variables defined inside a function) are stored on the "stack".

Here's a code snippet that illustrates dynamic memory allocation using new:

```
#include "point2d.h"

int main()
{
    Point2D *point = new Point2D;
    point->setX(1.0);
```

```
    point->setY(2.5);
    delete point;

    return 0;
}
```

The new operator returns the memory address of a newly allocated object. We store the address in a pointer variable and access the object through that pointer. When we are done with the object, we release its memory using the delete operator. Unlike Java and C#, C++ has no garbage collector; dynamically allocated objects must be explicitly released using delete when we don't need them anymore. Chapter 2 describes Qt's parent–child mechanism, which greatly simplifies memory management in C++ programs.

If we forget to call delete, the memory is kept around until the program finishes. This would not be an issue in the preceding example, because we allocate only one object, but in a program that allocates new objects all the time, this could cause the program to keep allocating memory until the machine's memory is exhausted. Once an object is deleted, the pointer variable still holds the address of the object. Such a pointer is a "dangling pointer" and should not be used to access the object. Qt provides a "smart" pointer, QPointer<T>, that automatically sets itself to 0 if the QObject it points to is deleted.

In the preceding example, we invoked the default constructor and called setX() and setY() to initialize the object. We could have used the two-parameter constructor instead:

```
Point2D *point = new Point2D(1.0, 2.5);
```

The example didn't require the use of new and delete. We could just as well have allocated the object on the stack as follows:

```
Point2D point;
point.setX(1.0);
point.setY(2.5);
```

Objects allocated like this are automatically freed at the end of the block in which they appear.

If we don't intend to modify the object through the pointer, we can declare the pointer const. For example:

```
const Point2D *ptr = new Point2D(1.0, 2.5);
double x = ptr->x();
double y = ptr->y();

// WON'T COMPILE
ptr->setX(4.0);
*ptr = Point2D(4.0, 4.5);
```

The ptr const pointer can be used only to call const member functions such as x() and y(). It is good style to declare pointers const when we don't intend to modify the object using them. Furthermore, if the object itself is const, we have no choice but to use a const pointer to store its address. The use of `const` provides information to the compiler that can lead to early bug detection and performance gains. C# has a `const` keyword that is very similar to that of C++. The closest Java equivalent is `final`, but it only protects variables from assignment, not from calling "non-const" member functions on it.

Pointers can be used with built-in types as well as with classes. In an expression, the unary `*` operator returns the value of the object associated with the pointer. For example:

```
int i = 10;
int j = 20;

int *p = &i;
int *q = &j;

std::cout << *p << " equals 10" << std::endl;
std::cout << *q << " equals 20" << std::endl;

*p = 40;

std::cout << i << " equals 40" << std::endl;

p = q;
*p = 100;

std::cout << i << " equals 40" << std::endl;
std::cout << j << " equals 100" << std::endl;
```

The `->` operator, which can be used to access an object's members through a pointer, is pure syntactic sugar. Instead of `ptr->member`, we can also write `(*ptr).member`. The parentheses are necessary because the `.` (dot) operator has precedence over the unary `*` operator.

Pointers had a poor reputation in C and C++, to the extent that Java is often advertised as having no pointers. In reality, C++ pointers are conceptually similar to Java and C# references except that we can use pointers to iterate through memory, as we will see later in this section. Furthermore, the inclusion of "copy on write" container classes in Qt, along with C++'s ability to instantiate any class on the stack, means that we can often avoid pointers.

References

In addition to pointers, C++ also supports the concept of a "reference". Like a pointer, a C++ reference stores the address of an object. Here are the main differences:

- References are declared using `&` instead of `*`.
- The reference must be initialized and can't be reassigned later.
- The object associated with a reference is directly accessible; there is no special syntax such as `*` or `->`.
- A reference cannot be null.

References are generally used when declaring parameters. For most types, C++ uses call-by-value as its default parameter-passing mechanism, meaning that when an argument is passed to a function, the function receives a brand new copy of the object. Here's the definition of a function that receives its parameters through call-by-value:

```
#include <cstdlib>

double manhattanDistance(Point2D a, Point2D b)
{
    return std::abs(b.x() - a.x()) + std::abs(b.y() - a.y());
}
```

We would then invoke the function as follows:

```
Point2D broadway(12.5, 40.0);
Point2D harlem(77.5, 50.0);
double distance = manhattanDistance(broadway, harlem);
```

C programmers avoid needless copy operations by declaring their parameters as pointers instead of as values:

```
double manhattanDistance(const Point2D *ap, const Point2D *bp)
{
    return std::abs(bp->x() - ap->x()) + std::abs(bp->y() - ap->y());
}
```

They must then pass addresses instead of values when calling the function:

```
double distance = manhattanDistance(&broadway, &harlem);
```

C++ introduced references to make the syntax less cumbersome and to prevent the caller from passing a null pointer. If we use references instead of pointers, the function looks like this:

```
double manhattanDistance(const Point2D &a, const Point2D &b)
{
    return std::abs(b.x() - a.x()) + std::abs(b.y() - a.y());
}
```

The declaration of a reference is similar to that of a pointer, with `&` instead of `*`. But when we actually use the reference, we can forget that it is a memory address and treat it like an ordinary variable. In addition, calling a function that takes references as arguments doesn't require any special care (no `&` operator).

All in all, by replacing `Point2D` with `const Point2D &` in the parameter list, we reduced the overhead of the function call: Instead of copying 256 bits (the size of four `double`s), we copy only 64 or 128 bits, depending on the target platform's pointer size.

The previous example used const references, preventing the function from modifying the objects associated with the references. When this kind of side effect is desired, we can pass a non-const reference or pointer. For example:

```
void transpose(Point2D &point)
{
    double oldX = point.x();
    point.setX(point.y());
    point.setY(oldX);
}
```

In some cases, we have a reference and we need to call a function that takes a pointer, or vice versa. To convert a reference to a pointer, we can simply use the unary & operator:

```
Point2D point;
Point2D &ref = point;
Point2D *ptr = &ref;
```

To convert a pointer to a reference, there is the unary * operator:

```
Point2D point;
Point2D *ptr = &point;
Point2D &ref = *ptr;
```

References and pointers are represented the same way in memory, and they can often be used interchangeably, which begs the question of when to use which. On the one hand, references have a more convenient syntax; on the other hand, pointers can be reassigned at any time to point to another object, they can hold a null value, and their more explicit syntax is often a blessing in disguise. For these reasons, pointers tend to prevail, with references used almost exclusively for declaring function parameters, in conjunction with `const`.

Arrays

Arrays in C++ are declared by specifying the number of items in the array within brackets in the variable declaration *after* the variable name. Two-dimensional arrays are possible using an array of arrays. Here's the definition of a one-dimensional array containing ten items of type `int`:

```
int fibonacci[10];
```

The items are accessible as `fibonacci[0]`, `fibonacci[1]`, ..., `fibonacci[9]`. Often we want to initialize the array as we define it:

```
int fibonacci[10] = { 0, 1, 1, 2, 3, 5, 8, 13, 21, 34 };
```

In such cases, we can then omit the array size, since the compiler can deduce it from the number of initializers:

```
int fibonacci[] = { 0, 1, 1, 2, 3, 5, 8, 13, 21, 34 };
```

Static initialization also works for complex types, such as `Point2D`:

```
Point2D triangle[] = {
    Point2D(0.0, 0.0), Point2D(1.0, 0.0), Point2D(0.5, 0.866)
};
```

If we have no intention of altering the array later on, we can make it const:

```
const int fibonacci[] = { 0, 1, 1, 2, 3, 5, 8, 13, 21, 34 };
```

To find out how many items an array contains, we can use the `sizeof()` operator as follows:

```
int n = sizeof(fibonacci) / sizeof(fibonacci[0]);
```

The `sizeof()` operator returns the size of its argument in bytes. The number of items in an array is its size in bytes divided by the size of one of its items. Because this is cumbersome to type, a common alternative is to declare a constant and to use it for defining the array:

```
enum { NFibonacci = 10 };

const int fibonacci[NFibonacci] = { 0, 1, 1, 2, 3, 5, 8, 13, 21, 34 };
```

It would have been tempting to declare the constant as a `const int` variable. Unfortunately, some compilers have issues with const variables as array size specifiers. We will explain the `enum` keyword later in this appendix.

Iterating through an array is normally done using an integer. For example:

```
for (int i = 0; i < NFibonacci; ++i)
    std::cout << fibonacci[i] << std::endl;
```

It is also possible to traverse the array using a pointer:

```
const int *ptr = &fibonacci[0];
while (ptr != &fibonacci[10]) {
    std::cout << *ptr << std::endl;
    ++ptr;
}
```

We initialize the pointer with the address of the first item and loop until we reach the "one past the last" item (the "eleventh" item, `fibonacci[10]`). At each iteration, the `++` operator advances the pointer to the next item.

Instead of `&fibonacci[0]`, we could also have written `fibonacci`. This is because the name of an array used alone is automatically converted into a pointer to the first item in the array. Similarly, we could substitute `fibonacci + 10` for `&fibonacci[10]`. This works the other way around as well: We can retrieve the contents of the current item using either `*ptr` or `ptr[0]` and could access the next item using `*(ptr + 1)` or `ptr[1]`. This principle is sometimes called "equivalence of pointers and arrays".

To prevent what it considers to be a gratuitous inefficiency, C++ does not let us pass arrays to functions by value. Instead, they must be passed by address. For example:

```
#include <iostream>

void printIntegerTable(const int *table, int size)
{
```

```
        for (int i = 0; i < size; ++i)
            std::cout << table[i] << std::endl;
    }

    int main()
    {
        const int fibonacci[10] = { 0, 1, 1, 2, 3, 5, 8, 13, 21, 34 };
        printIntegerTable(fibonacci, 10);
        return 0;
    }
```

Ironically, although C++ doesn't give us any choice about whether we want to pass an array by address or by value, it gives us some freedom in the *syntax* used to declare the parameter type. Instead of `const int *table`, we could also have written `const int table[]` to declare a pointer-to-constant-`int` parameter. Similarly, the `argv` parameter to `main()` can be declared as either `char *argv[]` or `char **argv`.

To copy an array into another array, one approach is to loop through the array:

```
const int fibonacci[NFibonacci] = { 0, 1, 1, 2, 3, 5, 8, 13, 21, 34 };
int temp[NFibonacci];

for (int i = 0; i < NFibonacci; ++i)
    temp[i] = fibonacci[i];
```

For basic data types such as `int`, we can also use `memcpy()`, which copies a block of memory. For example:

```
std::memcpy(temp, fibonacci, sizeof(fibonacci));
```

When we declare a C++ array, the size must be a constant.* If we want to create an array of a variable size, we have several options.

- **We can dynamically allocate the array:**

  ```
  int *fibonacci = new int[n];
  ```

  The `new []` operator allocates a certain number of items at consecutive memory locations and returns a pointer to the first item. Thanks to the "equivalence of pointers and arrays" principle, the items can be accessed through the pointer as `fibonacci[0]`, `fibonacci[1]`, ..., `fibonacci[n - 1]`. When we have finished using the array, we should release the memory it consumes using the `delete []` operator:

  ```
  delete [] fibonacci;
  ```

- **We can use the standard vector<T> class:**

  ```
  #include <vector>

  std::vector<int> fibonacci(n);
  ```

* Some compilers allow variables in that context, but this feature should not be relied upon in portable programs.

Items are accessible using the `[]` operator, just like with a plain C++ array. With `vector<T>` (where `T` is the type of the items stored in the vector), we can resize the array at any time using `resize()` and we can copy it using the assignment operator. Classes that contain angle brackets (<>) in their name are called template classes.

- **We can use Qt's QVector<T> class:**

  ```
  #include <QVector>

  QVector<int> fibonacci(n);
  ```

  `QVector<T>`'s API is very similar to that of `vector<T>`, but it also supports iteration using Qt's `foreach` keyword and uses implicit data sharing ("copy on write") as a memory and speed optimization. Chapter 11 presents Qt's container classes and explains how they relate to the Standard C++ containers.

You might be tempted to avoid built-in arrays whenever possible and use `vector<T>` or `QVector<T>` instead. It is nonetheless worthwhile understanding how the built-in arrays work because sooner or later you might want to use them in highly optimized code, or need them to interface with existing C libraries.

Character Strings

The most basic way to represent character strings in C++ is to use an array of `char`s terminated by a null byte ('\0'). The following four functions demonstrate how these kinds of strings work:

```
void hello1()
{
    const char str[] = {
        'H', 'e', 'l', 'l', 'o', ' ', 'w', 'o', 'r', 'l', 'd', '\0'
    };
    std::cout << str << std::endl;
}

void hello2()
{
    const char str[] = "Hello world!";
    std::cout << str << std::endl;
}

void hello3()
{
    std::cout << "Hello world!" << std::endl;
}

void hello4()
{
    const char *str = "Hello world!";
    std::cout << str << std::endl;
}
```

In the first function, we declare the string as an array and initialize it the hard way. Notice the '\0' terminator at the end, which indicates the end of the string. The second function has a similar array definition, but this time we use a string literal to initialize the array. In C++, string literals are simply `const char` arrays with an implicit '\0' terminator. The third function uses a string literal directly, without giving it a name. Once translated into machine language instructions, it is identical to the previous two functions.

The fourth function is a bit different in that it creates not only an (anonymous) array, but also a pointer variable called `str` that stores the address of the array's first item. In spite of this, the semantics of the function are identical to the previous three functions, and an optimizing compiler would eliminate the superfluous `str` variable.

Functions that take C++ strings as arguments usually take either a `char *` or a `const char *`. Here's a short program that illustrates the use of both:

```
#include <cctype>
#include <iostream>

void makeUppercase(char *str)
{
    for (int i = 0; str[i] != '\0'; ++i)
        str[i] = std::toupper(str[i]);
}

void writeLine(const char *str)
{
    std::cout << str << std::endl;
}

int main(int argc, char *argv[])
{
    for (int i = 1; i < argc; ++i) {
        makeUppercase(argv[i]);
        writeLine(argv[i]);
    }
    return 0;
}
```

In C++, the `char` type normally holds an 8-bit value. This means that we can easily store ASCII, ISO 8859-1 (Latin-1), and other 8-bit-encoded strings in a `char` array, but that we can't store arbitrary Unicode characters without resorting to multibyte sequences. Qt provides the powerful `QString` class, which stores Unicode strings as sequences of 16-bit `QChar`s and internally uses the implicit data sharing ("copy on write") optimization. Chapter 11 and Chapter 18 explain `QString` in more detail.

Enumerations

C++ has an enumeration feature for declaring a set of named constants similar to that provided by C# and recent versions of Java. Let's suppose that we want to store days of the week in a program:

```
enum DayOfWeek {
    Sunday, Monday, Tuesday, Wednesday, Thursday, Friday, Saturday
};
```

Normally, we would put this declaration in a header file, or even inside a class. The preceding declaration is superficially equivalent to the following constant definitions:

```
const int Sunday    = 0;
const int Monday    = 1;
const int Tuesday   = 2;
const int Wednesday = 3;
const int Thursday  = 4;
const int Friday    = 5;
const int Saturday  = 6;
```

By using the enumeration construct, we can later declare variables or parameters of type `DayOfWeek` and the compiler will ensure that only values from the `DayOfWeek` enumeration are assigned to it. For example:

```
DayOfWeek day = Sunday;
```

If we don't care about type safety, we can also write

```
int day = Sunday;
```

Notice that to refer to the `Sunday` constant from the `DayOfWeek` enum, we simply write `Sunday`, not `DayOfWeek::Sunday`.

By default, the compiler assigns consecutive integer values to the constants of an enum, starting at 0. We can specify other values if we want:

```
enum DayOfWeek {
    Sunday    = 628,
    Monday    = 616,
    Tuesday   = 735,
    Wednesday = 932,
    Thursday  = 852,
    Friday    = 607,
    Saturday  = 845
};
```

If we don't specify the value of an enum item, the item takes the value of the preceding item, plus 1. Enums are sometimes used to declare integer constants, in which case we normally omit the name of the enum:

```
enum {
    FirstPort = 1024,
    MaxPorts  = 32767
};
```

Another frequent use of enums is to represent sets of options. Let's consider the example of a Find dialog, with four checkboxes controlling the search algorithm (Wildcard syntax, Case sensitive, Search backward, and Wrap around). We can represent this by an enum where the constants are powers of 2:

```
enum FindOption {
    NoOptions      = 0x00000000,
    WildcardSyntax = 0x00000001,
    CaseSensitive  = 0x00000002,
    SearchBackward = 0x00000004,
    WrapAround     = 0x00000008
};
```

Each option is often called a “flag”. We can combine flags using the bitwise | or |= operator:

```
int options = NoOptions;
if (wilcardSyntaxCheckBox->isChecked())
    options |= WildcardSyntax;
if (caseSensitiveCheckBox->isChecked())
    options |= CaseSensitive;
if (searchBackwardCheckBox->isChecked())
    options |= SearchBackwardSyntax;
if (wrapAroundCheckBox->isChecked())
    options |= WrapAround;
```

We can test whether a flag is set using the bitwise & operator:

```
if (options & CaseSensitive) {
    // case-sensitive search
}
```

A variable of type `FindOption` can contain only one flag at a time. The result of combining several flags using | is a plain integer. Unfortunately, this is not type-safe: The compiler won’t complain if a function expecting a combination of `FindOptions` through an `int` parameter receives `Saturday` instead. Qt uses `QFlags<T>` to provide type safety for its own flag types. The class is also available when we define custom flag types. See the `QFlags<T>` online documentation for details.

Typedefs

C++ lets us give an alias to a data type using the `typedef` keyword. For example, if we use `QVector<Point2D>` a lot and want to save a few keystrokes (or are unfortunate enough to be stuck with a Norwegian keyboard and have trouble locating the angle brackets), we can put this typedef declaration in one of our header files:

```
typedef QVector<Point2D> PointVector;
```

From then on, we can use `PointVector` as a shorthand for `QVector<Point2D>`. Notice that the new name for the type appears after the old name. The typedef syntax deliberately mimics that of variable declarations.

In Qt, typedefs are used mainly for three reasons:

- *Convenience*: Qt declares `uint` and `QWidgetList` as typedefs for `unsigned int` and `QList<QWidget *>` to save a few keystrokes.

- *Platform differences*: Certain types need different definitions on different platforms. For example, qlonglong is defined as __int64 on Windows and as long long on other platforms.
- *Compatibility*: The QIconSet class from Qt 3 was renamed QIcon in Qt 4. To help Qt 3 users port their applications to Qt 4, QIconSet is provided as a typedef for QIcon when Qt 3 compatibility is enabled.

Type Conversions

C++ provides several syntaxes for casting values from one type to another. The traditional syntax, inherited from C, involves putting the resulting type in parentheses before the value to convert:

```
const double Pi = 3.14159265359;
int x = (int)(Pi * 100);
std::cout << x << " equals 314" << std::endl;
```

This syntax is very powerful. It can be used to change the types of pointers, to remove const, and much more. For example:

```
short j = 0x1234;
if (*(char *)&j == 0x12)
    std::cout << "The byte order is big-endian" << std::endl;
```

In the preceding example, we cast a short * to a char * and we use the unary * operator to access the byte at the given memory location. On big-endian systems, that byte is 0x12; on little-endian systems, it is 0x34. Since pointers and references are represented the same way, it should come as no surprise that the preceding code can be rewritten using a reference cast:

```
short j = 0x1234;
if ((char &)j == 0x12)
    std::cout << "The byte order is big-endian" << std::endl;
```

If the data type is a class name, a typedef, or a primitive type that can be expressed as a single alphanumeric token, we can use the constructor syntax as a cast:

```
int x = int(Pi * 100);
```

Casting pointers and references using the traditional C-style casts is a kind of extreme sport, on par with paragliding and elevator surfing, because the compiler lets us cast any pointer (or reference) type into any other pointer (or reference) type. For that reason, C++ introduced four new-style casts with more precise semantics. For pointers and references, the new-style casts are preferable to the risky C-style casts and are used in this book.

- static_cast<T>() can be used to cast a pointer-to-A to a pointer-to-B, with the constraint that class B must be a subclass of class A. For example:

  ```
  A *obj = new B;
  B *b = static_cast<B *>(obj);
  ```

```
b->someFunctionDeclaredInB();
```

If the object isn't an instance of B, using the resulting pointer can lead to obscure crashes.

- dynamic_cast<T>() is similar to static_cast<T>(), except that it uses run-time type information (RTTI) to check that the object associated with the pointer is an instance of class B. If this is not the case, the cast returns a null pointer. For example:

```
A *obj = new B;
B *b = dynamic_cast<B *>(obj);
if (b)
    b->someFunctionDeclaredInB();
```

  On some compilers, dynamic_cast<T>() doesn't work across dynamic library boundaries. It also relies on the compiler supporting RTTI, a feature that programmers can turn off to reduce the size of their executables. Qt solves these problems by providing qobject_cast<T>() for QObject subclasses.

- const_cast<T>() adds or removes a const qualifier to a pointer or reference. For example:

```
int MyClass::someConstFunction() const
{
    if (isDirty()) {
        MyClass *that = const_cast<MyClass *>(this);
        that->recomputeInternalData();
    }
    ...
}
```

  In the previous example, we cast away the const qualifier of the this pointer to call the non-const member function recomputeInternalData(). Doing so is not recommended and can normally be avoided by using the mutable keyword, as explained in Chapter 4.

- reinterpret_cast<T>() converts any pointer or reference type to any other such type. For example:

```
short j = 0x1234;
if (reinterpret_cast<char &>(j) == 0x12)
    std::cout << "The byte order is big-endian" << std::endl;
```

In Java and C#, any reference can be stored as an Object reference if needed. C++ doesn't have any universal base class, but it provides a special data type, void *, that stores the address of an instance of any type. A void * must be cast back to another type (using static_cast<T>()) before it can be used.

C++ provides many ways to cast types, but most of the time we don't even need a cast. When using container classes such as vector<T> or QVector<T>, we can specify the T type and extract items without casts. In addition, for primitive types, certain conversions occur implicitly (e.g., from char to int), and for custom types we can define implicit conversions by providing a one-parameter constructor. For example:

```
class MyInteger
{
public:
    MyInteger();
    MyInteger(int i);
    ...
};

int main()
{
    MyInteger n;
    n = 5;
    ...
}
```

For some one-parameter constructors, the automatic conversion makes little sense. We can disable it by declaring the constructor with the `explicit` keyword:

```
class MyVector
{
public:
    explicit MyVector(int size);
    ...
};
```

Operator Overloading

C++ allows us to overload functions, meaning that we can declare several functions with the same name in the same scope, as long as they have different parameter lists. In addition, C++ supports *operator overloading*—the possibility of assigning special semantics to built-in operators (such as `+`, `<<`, and `[]`) when they are used with custom types.

We have already seen a few examples of overloaded operators. When we used `<<` to output text to `cout` or `cerr`, we didn't trigger C++'s left-shift operator, but rather a special version of the operator that takes an `ostream` object (such as `cout` and `cerr`) on the left side and a string (alternatively, a number or a stream manipulator such as `endl`) on the right side and that returns the `ostream` object, allowing multiple calls in a row.

The beauty of operator overloading is that we can make custom types behave just like built-in types. To show how operator overloading works, we will overload `+=`, `-=`, `+`, and `-` to work on `Point2D` objects:

```
#ifndef POINT2D_H
#define POINT2D_H

class Point2D
{
```

```
public:
    Point2D();
    Point2D(double x, double y);

    void setX(double x);
    void setY(double y);
    double x() const;
    double y() const;

    Point2D &operator+=(const Point2D &other) {
        xVal += other.xVal;
        yVal += other.yVal;
        return *this;
    }
    Point2D &operator-=(const Point2D &other) {
        xVal -= other.xVal;
        yVal -= other.yVal;
        return *this;
    }

private:
    double xVal;
    double yVal;
};

inline Point2D operator+(const Point2D &a, const Point2D &b)
{
    return Point2D(a.x() + b.x(), a.y() + b.y());
}

inline Point2D operator-(const Point2D &a, const Point2D &b)
{
    return Point2D(a.x() - b.x(), a.y() - b.y());
}

#endif
```

Operators can be implemented either as member functions or as global functions. In our example, we implemented += and -= as member functions, and + and - as global functions.

The += and -= operators take a reference to another `Point2D` object and increment or decrement the x- and y-coordinates of the current object based on the other object. They return `*this`, which denotes a reference to the current object (`this` is of type `Point2D *`). Returning a reference allows us to write exotic code such as

```
a += b += c;
```

The + and - operators take two parameters and return a `Point2D` object by value (not a reference to an existing object). The `inline` keyword allows us to put these function definitions in the header file. If the function's body had been longer, we would put a function prototype in the header file and the function definition (without the `inline` keyword) in a `.cpp` file.

The following code snippet shows all four overloaded operators in action:

```
Point2D alpha(12.5, 40.0);
Point2D beta(77.5, 50.0);

alpha += beta;
beta -= alpha;

Point2D gamma = alpha + beta;
Point2D delta = beta - alpha;
```

We can also invoke the `operator` functions just like any other functions:

```
Point2D alpha(12.5, 40.0);
Point2D beta(77.5, 50.0);

alpha.operator+=(beta);
beta.operator-=(alpha);

Point2D gamma = operator+(alpha, beta);
Point2D delta = operator-(beta, alpha);
```

Operator overloading in C++ is a complex topic, but we can go a long way without knowing all the details. It is still important to understand the fundamentals of operator overloading because several Qt classes (including `QString` and `QVector<T>`) use this feature to provide a simple and more natural syntax for such operations as concatenation and append.

Value Types

Java and C# distinguish between value types and reference types.

- *Value types*: These are primitive types such as `char`, `int`, and `float`, as well as C# structs. What characterizes them is that they aren't created using `new` and the assignment operator performs a copy of the value held by the variable. For example:

  ```
  int i = 5;
  int j = 10;
  i = j;
  ```

- *Reference types*: These are classes such as `Integer` (in Java), `String`, and `MyVeryOwnClass`. Instances are created using `new`. The assignment operator copies only a reference to the object; to obtain a deep copy, we must call `clone()` (in Java) or `Clone()` (in C#). For example:

  ```
  Integer i = new Integer(5);
  Integer j = new Integer(10);
  i = j.clone();
  ```

In C++, all types can be used as "reference types", and those that are copyable can be used as "value types" as well. For example, C++ doesn't need any `Integer` class, because we can use pointers and `new` as follows:

```
int *i = new int(5);
int *j = new int(10);
*i = *j;
```

Unlike Java and C#, C++ treats user-defined classes in the same way as built-in types:

```
Point2D *i = new Point2D(5, 5);
Point2D *j = new Point2D(10, 10);
*i = *j;
```

If we want to make a C++ class copyable, we must ensure that our class has a copy constructor and an assignment operator. The copy constructor is invoked when we initialize an object with another object of the same type. C++ provides two equivalent syntaxes for this:

```
Point2D i(20, 20);

Point2D j(i);          // first syntax
Point2D k = i;         // second syntax
```

The assignment operator is invoked when we use the assignment operator on an existing variable:

```
Point2D i(5, 5);
Point2D j(10, 10);
j = i;
```

When we define a class, the C++ compiler automatically provides a copy constructor and an assignment operator that perform member-by-member copying. For the `Point2D` class, this is as though we had written the following code in the class definition:

```
class Point2D
{
public:
    ...
    Point2D(const Point2D &other)
        : xVal(other.xVal), yVal(other.yVal) { }

    Point2D &operator=(const Point2D &other) {
        xVal = other.xVal;
        yVal = other.yVal;
        return *this;
    }
    ...

private:
    double xVal;
    double yVal;
};
```

For some classes, the default copy constructor and assignment operator are unsuitable. This typically occurs if the class uses dynamic memory. To make the class copyable, we must then implement the copy constructor and the assignment operator ourselves.

For classes that don't need to be copyable, we can disable the copy constructor and assignment operator by making them private. If we accidentally attempt to copy instances of such a class, the compiler reports an error. For example:

```
class BankAccount
{
public:
    ...

private:
    BankAccount(const BankAccount &other);
    BankAccount &operator=(const BankAccount &other);
};
```

In Qt, many classes are designed to be used as value classes. These have a copy constructor and an assignment operator, and are normally instantiated on the stack without `new`. This is the case for `QDateTime`, `QImage`, `QString`, and container classes such as `QList<T>`, `QVector<T>`, and `QMap<K, T>`.

Other classes fall in the "reference type" category, notably `QObject` and its subclasses (`QWidget`, `QTimer`, `QTcpSocket`, etc.). These have virtual functions and cannot be copied. For example, a `QWidget` represents a specific window or control on-screen. If there are 75 `QWidget` instances in memory, there are also 75 windows or controls on-screen. These classes are typically instantiated using the `new` operator.

Global Variables and Functions

C++ lets us declare functions and variables that don't belong to any classes and that are accessible from any other function. We have seen several examples of global functions, including `main()`, the program's entry point. Global variables are rarer, because they compromise modularity and thread reentrancy. It is still important to understand them because you might encounter them in code written by reformed C programmers and other C++ users.

To illustrate how global functions and variables work, we will study a small program that prints a list of 128 pseudo-random numbers using a quick-and-dirty algorithm. The program's source code is spread over two `.cpp` files.

The first source file is `random.cpp`:

```
int randomNumbers[128];

static int seed = 42;

static int nextRandomNumber()
{
    seed = 1009 + (seed * 2011);
    return seed;
}
```

```
void populateRandomArray()
{
    for (int i = 0; i < 128; ++i)
        randomNumbers[i] = nextRandomNumber();
}
```

The file declares two global variables (`randomNumbers` and `seed`) and two global functions (`nextRandomNumber()` and `populateRandomArray()`). Two of the declarations contain the `static` keyword; these are visible only within the current compilation unit (`random.cpp`) and are said to have *static linkage*. The two others can be accessed from any compilation unit in the program; these have *external linkage*.

Static linkage is ideal for helper functions and internal variables that should not be used in other compilation units. It reduces the risks of having colliding identifiers (global variables with the same name or global functions with the same signature in different compilation units) and prevents malicious or otherwise ill-advised users from accessing the internals of a compilation unit.

Let's now look at the second file, `main.cpp`, which uses the two global variables declared with external linkage in `random.cpp`:

```
#include <iostream>

extern int randomNumbers[128];

void populateRandomArray();

int main()
{
    populateRandomArray();
    for (int i = 0; i < 128; ++i)
        std::cout << randomNumbers[i] << std::endl;
    return 0;
}
```

We declare the external variables and functions before we call them. The external variable declaration (which makes an external variable visible in the current compilation unit) for `randomNumbers` starts with the `extern` keyword. Without `extern`, the compiler would think it has to deal with a variable *definition*, and the linker would complain because the same variable is defined in two compilation units (`random.cpp` and `main.cpp`). Variables can be declared as many times as we want, but they may be defined only once. The definition is what causes the compiler to reserve space for the variable.

The `populateRandomArray()` function is declared using a function prototype. The `extern` keyword is optional for functions.

Typically, we would put the external variable and function declarations in a header file and include it in all the files that need them:

```
#ifndef RANDOM_H
#define RANDOM_H
```

```
extern int randomNumbers[128];

void populateRandomArray();

#endif
```

We have already seen how `static` can be used to declare member variables and functions that are not attached to a specific instance of the class, and now we have seen how to use it to declare functions and variables with static linkage. There is one more use of the `static` keyword that should be noted in passing. In C++, we can declare a local variable static. Such variables are initialized the first time the function is called and hold their value between function invocations. For example:

```
void nextPrime()
{
    static int n = 1;

    do {
        ++n;
    } while (!isPrime(n));

    return n;
}
```

Static local variables are similar to global variables, except that they are only visible inside the function where they are defined.

Namespaces

Namespaces are a mechanism for reducing the risks of name clashes in C++ programs. Name clashes are often an issue in large programs that use several third-party libraries. In your own programs, you can choose whether you want to use namespaces.

Typically, we put a namespace around all the declarations in a header file to ensure that the identifiers declared in that header file don't leak into the global namespace. For example:

```
#ifndef SOFTWAREINC_RANDOM_H
#define SOFTWAREINC_RANDOM_H

namespace SoftwareInc
{
    extern int randomNumbers[128];

    void populateRandomArray();
}

#endif
```

(Notice that we have also renamed the preprocessor macro used to avoid multiple inclusions, reducing the risk of a name clash with a header file of the same name but located in a different directory.)

The namespace syntax is similar to that of a class, but it doesn't end with a semicolon. Here's the new random.cpp file:

```
#include "random.h"

int SoftwareInc::randomNumbers[128];

static int seed = 42;

static int nextRandomNumber()
{
    seed = 1009 + (seed * 2011);
    return seed;
}

void SoftwareInc::populateRandomArray()
{
    for (int i = 0; i < 128; ++i)
        randomNumbers[i] = nextRandomNumber();
}
```

Unlike classes, namespaces can be "reopened" at any time. For example:

```
namespace Alpha
{
    void alpha1();
    void alpha2();
}

namespace Beta
{
    void beta1();
}

namespace Alpha
{
    void alpha3();
}
```

This makes it possible to define hundreds of classes, located in as many header files, as part of a single namespace. Using this trick, the Standard C++ library puts all its identifiers in the std namespace. In Qt, namespaces are used for global-like identifiers such as Qt::AlignBottom and Qt::yellow. For historical reasons, Qt classes do not belong to any namespace but are prefixed with the letter 'Q'.

To refer to an identifier declared in a namespace from outside the namespace, we prefix it with the name of the namespace (and ::). Alternatively, we can use one of the following three mechanisms, which are aimed at reducing the number of keystrokes we must type.

- **We can define a namespace alias:**

```
namespace ElPuebloDeLaReinaDeLosAngeles
{
    void beverlyHills();
```

```
        void culverCity();
        void malibu();
        void santaMonica();
    }

    namespace LA = ElPuebloDeLaReinaDeLosAngeles;
```

After the alias definition, the alias can be used instead of the original name.

- **We can import a single identifier from a namespace:**

```
    int main()
    {
        using ElPuebloDeLaReinaDeLosAngeles::beverlyHills;

        beverlyHills();
        ...
    }
```

  The using declaration allows us to access a given identifier from a namespace without having to prefix it with the name of the namespace.

- **We can import an entire namespace with a single directive:**

```
    int main()
    {
        using namespace ElPuebloDeLaReinaDeLosAngeles;

        santaMonica();
        malibu();
        ...
    }
```

  With this approach, name clashes are more likely to occur. If the compiler complains about an ambiguous name (e.g., two classes with the same name defined in two different namespaces), we can always qualify the identifier with the name of the namespace when referring to it.

The Preprocessor

The C++ preprocessor is a program that converts a .cpp source file containing # directives (such as #include, #ifndef, and #endif) into a source file that contains no such directives. These directives perform simple textual operations on the source file, such as conditional compilation, file inclusion, and macro expansion. Normally, the preprocessor is invoked automatically by the compiler, but most systems still offer a way to invoke it alone (often through a -E or /E compiler option).

- The #include directive expands to the contents of the file specified within angle brackets (<>) or double quotes (""), depending on whether the header file is installed at a standard location or is part of the current project. The file name may contain .. and / (which Windows compilers correctly interpret as a directory separator). For example:

```
#include "../shared/globaldefs.h"
```

- The `#define` directive defines a macro. Occurrences of the macro appearing after the `#define` directive are replaced with the macro's definition. For example, the directive

  ```
  #define PI 3.14159265359
  ```

  tells the preprocessor to replace all future occurrences of the token `PI` in the current compilation unit with the token `3.14159265359`. To avoid clashes with variable and class names, it is common practice to give macros all-uppercase names. It is possible to define macros that take arguments:

  ```
  #define SQUARE(x) ((x) * (x))
  ```

  In the macro body, it is good style to surround all occurrences of the parameters with parentheses, as well as the entire body, to avoid problems with operator precedence. After all, we want `7 * SQUARE(2 + 3)` to expand to `7 * ((2 + 3) * (2 + 3))`, not to `7 * 2 + 3 * 2 + 3`.

  C++ compilers normally allow us to define macros on the command line, using the `-D` or `/D` option. For example:

  ```
  CC -DPI=3.14159265359 -c main.cpp
  ```

  Macros were very popular in the old days, before typedefs, enums, constants, inline functions, and templates were introduced. Nowadays, their most important role is to protect header files against multiple inclusions.

- Macros can be undefined at any point using `#undef`:

  ```
  #undef PI
  ```

  This is useful if we want to redefine a macro, since the preprocessor doesn't let us define the same macro twice. It is also useful to control conditional compilation.

- Portions of code can be processed or skipped using `#if`, `#elif`, `#else`, and `#endif`, based on the numeric value of macros. For example:

  ```
  #define NO_OPTIM          0
  #define OPTIM_FOR_SPEED   1
  #define OPTIM_FOR_MEMORY  2

  #define OPTIMIZATION      OPTIM_FOR_MEMORY

  ...

  #if OPTIMIZATION == OPTIM_FOR_SPEED
  typedef int MyInt;
  #elif OPTIMIZATION == OPTIM_FOR_MEMORY
  typedef short MyInt;
  #else
  typedef long long MyInt;
  #endif
  ```

In the preceding example, only the second `typedef` declaration would be processed by the compiler, resulting in `MyInt` being defined as a synonym for `short`. By changing the definition of the `OPTIMIZATION` macro, we get different programs. If a macro isn't defined, its value is taken to be 0.

Another approach to conditional compilation is to test whether a macro is defined. This can be done using the using the `defined()` operator as follows:

```
#define OPTIM_FOR_MEMORY

...

#if defined(OPTIM_FOR_SPEED)
typedef int MyInt;
#elif defined(OPTIM_FOR_MEMORY)
typedef short MyInt;
#else
typedef long long MyInt;
#endif
```

- For convenience, the preprocessor recognizes `#ifdef X` and `#ifndef X` as synonyms for `#if defined(X)` and `#if !defined(X)`. To protect a header file against multiple inclusions, we wrap its contents with the following idiom:

```
#ifndef MYHEADERFILE_H
#define MYHEADERFILE_H

...

#endif
```

The first time the header file is included, the symbol `MYHEADERFILE_H` is not defined, so the compiler processes the code between `#ifndef` and `#endif`. The second and any subsequent times the header file is included, `MYHEADERFILE_H` is defined, so the entire `#ifndef` ... `#endif` block is skipped.

- The `#error` directive emits a user-defined error message at compile time. This is often used in conjunction with conditional compilation to report an impossible case. For example:

```
class UniChar
{
public:
#if BYTE_ORDER == BIG_ENDIAN
    uchar row;
    uchar cell;
#elif BYTE_ORDER == LITTLE_ENDIAN
    uchar cell;
    uchar row;
#else
#error "BYTE_ORDER must be BIG_ENDIAN or LITTLE_ENDIAN"
#endif
};
```

Unlike most other C++ constructs, where whitespace is irrelevant, preprocessor directives stand alone on a line and require no semicolon. Very long directives can be split across multiple lines by ending every line except the last with a backslash.

The Standard C++ Library

In this section, we will briefly review the Standard C++ library. Figure D.3 lists the core C++ header files. The `<exception>`, `<limits>`, `<new>`, and `<typeinfo>` headers support the C++ language; for example, `<limits>` allows us to test properties of the compiler's integer and floating-point arithmetic support, and `<typeinfo>` offers basic introspection. The other headers provide generally useful classes, including a string class and a complex numeric type. The functionality offered by `<bitset>`, `<locale>`, `<string>`, and `<typeinfo>` loosely overlaps with the `QBitArray`, `QLocale`, `QString`, and `QMetaObject` classes in Qt.

Standard C++ also includes a set of header files that deal with I/O, listed in Figure D.4. The standard I/O classes' design harks back to the 1980s and is needlessly complex, making them very hard to extend—so difficult, in fact, that entire books have been written on the subject. It also leaves the programmer with a Pandora's box of unresolved issues related to character encodings and platform-dependent binary representations of primitive data types.

Header File	Description
<bitset>	Template class for representing fixed-length bit sequences
<complex>	Template class for representing complex numbers
<exception>	Types and functions related to exception handling
<limits>	Template class that specifies properties of numeric types
<locale>	Classes and functions related to localization
<new>	Functions that manage dynamic memory allocation
<stdexcept>	Predefined types of exceptions for reporting errors
<string>	Template string container and character traits
<typeinfo>	Class that provides basic meta-information about a type
<valarray>	Template classes for representing value arrays

Figure D.3. Core C++ library header files

Chapter 12 presents the corresponding Qt classes, which feature Unicode I/O as well as a large set of national character encodings and a platform-independent abstraction for storing binary data. Qt's I/O classes form the basis of Qt's inter-process communication, networking, and XML support. Qt's binary and text stream classes are very easy to extend to handle custom data types.

Header File	Description
`<fstream>`	Template classes that manipulate external files
`<iomanip>`	I/O stream manipulators that take an argument
`<ios>`	Template base class for I/O streams
`<iosfwd>`	Forward declarations for several I/O stream template classes
`<iostream>`	Standard I/O streams (`cin`, `cout`, `cerr`, `clog`)
`<istream>`	Template class that controls input from a stream buffer
`<ostream>`	Template class that controls output to a stream buffer
`<sstream>`	Template classes that associate stream buffers with strings
`<streambuf>`	Template classes that buffer I/O operations
`<strstream>`	Classes for performing I/O stream operations on character arrays

Figure D.4. C++ I/O library header files

The early 1990s saw the introduction of the Standard Template Library (STL), a set of template-based container classes, iterators, and algorithms that slipped into the ISO C++ standard at the eleventh hour. Figure D.5 lists the header files that form the STL. The STL has a very clean, almost mathematical design that provides generic type-safe functionality. Qt provides its own container classes, whose design is partly inspired by the STL. We describe them in Chapter 11.

Header File	Description
`<algorithm>`	General-purpose template functions
`<deque>`	Double-ended queue template container
`<functional>`	Templates that help construct and manipulate functors
`<iterator>`	Templates that help construct and manipulate iterators
`<list>`	Doubly linked list template container
`<map>`	Single-valued and multi-valued map template containers
`<memory>`	Utilities for simplifying memory management
`<numeric>`	Template numeric operations
`<queue>`	Queue template container
`<set>`	Single-valued and multi-valued set template containers
`<stack>`	Stack template container
`<utility>`	Basic template functions
`<vector>`	Vector template container

Figure D.5. STL header files

Since C++ is essentially a superset of the C programming language, C++ programmers also have the entire C library at their disposal. The C header files are available either with their traditional names (e.g., `<stdio.h>`) or with new-style names with a `c-` prefix and no `.h` (e.g., `<cstdio>`). When we use the new-style version, the functions and data types are declared in the `std` namespace. (This doesn't apply to macros such as `ASSERT()`, because the preprocessor is unaware of namespaces.) The new-style syntax is recommended if your compiler supports it.

Header File	Description
`<cassert>`	The `ASSERT()` macro
`<cctype>`	Functions for classifying and mapping characters
`<cerrno>`	Macros related to error condition reporting
`<cfloat>`	Macros that specify properties of primitive floating-point types
`<ciso646>`	Alternative spellings for ISO 646 charset users
`<climits>`	Macros that specify properties of primitive integer types
`<clocale>`	Functions and types related to localization
`<cmath>`	Mathematical functions and constants
`<csetjmp>`	Functions for performing non-local jumps
`<csignal>`	Functions for handling system signals
`<cstdarg>`	Macros for implementing variable argument list functions
`<cstddef>`	Common definitions for several standard headers
`<cstdio>`	Functions for performing I/O
`<cstdlib>`	General utility functions
`<cstring>`	Functions for manipulating `char` arrays
`<ctime>`	Types and functions for manipulating time
`<cwchar>`	Extended multibyte and wide character utilities
`<cwctype>`	Functions for classifying and mapping wide characters

Figure D.6. C++ header files for C library facilities

Figure D.6 lists the C library header files. Most of these offer functionality that overlaps with more recent C++ headers or with Qt. One notable exception is `<cmath>`, which declares mathematical functions such as `sin()`, `sqrt()`, and `pow()`.

This completes our quick overview of the Standard C++ library. On the Internet, Dinkumware offers complete reference documentation for the Standard C++ library at `http://www.dinkumware.com/refxcpp.html`, and SGI has a comprehensive STL programmer's guide at `http://www.sgi.com/tech/stl/`. The official definition of the Standard C++ library is in the C and C++ standards, available as PDF files or paper copies from the International Organization for Standardization (ISO).

In this appendix, we covered a lot of ground at a fast pace. When you start learning Qt from Chapter 1, you should find that the syntax is a lot simpler and clearer than this appendix might have suggested. Good Qt programming only requires the use of a subset of C++ and usually avoids the need for the more complex and obscure syntax that C++ makes possible. Once you start typing in code and building and running executables, the clarity and simplicity of the Qt approach will become apparent. And as soon as you start writing more ambitious programs, especially those that need fast and fancy graphics, the C++/Qt combination will continue to keep pace with your needs.

Index

A

B

D

E

F

G

H

I

M

N

O

P

Q

R

S

T

U

V

W

X

Z

About the Authors

Jasmin Blanchette

Jasmin graduated with a degree in computer science in 2001 from the University of Sherbrooke, Quebec. He did a work term at Trolltech in the summer of 2000 as a software engineer and has been working there continuously since early 2001. In 2003, Jasmin cowrote *C++ GUI Programming with Qt 3*, and in 2005 he cowrote *C++ GUI Programming with Qt 4*. He is the driving force behind Qt 4's container classes and layout system. Jasmin now divides his time between working as one of Trolltech's senior software engineers and completing an M.Sc. thesis in computer science at the University of Oslo.

Mark Summerfield

Mark graduated with a degree in computer science in 1993 from the University of Wales Swansea. He followed this with a year's postgraduate research before going into industry. He spent many years working as a software engineer for a variety of firms before joining Trolltech. He spent almost three years as Trolltech's documentation manager, during which he founded *Qt Quarterly* and cowrote *C++ GUI Programming with Qt 3*. In 2005 he cowrote *C++ GUI Programming with Qt 4*, and in 2007 he wrote *Rapid GUI Programming with Python and Qt*. Mark owns Qtrac.eu and works as an independent trainer and consultant specializing in C++, Qt, Python, and PyQt.

Production

The authors wrote the text using NEdit and Vim. They typeset and indexed the text themselves, marking it up with a modified Lout syntax that they converted to pure Lout using a custom preprocessor written in Python. They produced all the diagrams in Lout and used ImageMagick and KView to convert screenshots to PostScript. The monospaced font used for code is derived from a condensed version of DejaVu Mono and was modified using FontForge. The cover was provided by the publisher. The marked-up text was converted to PostScript by Lout, then to PDF by Ghostscript. The authors did all the editing and processing on Kubuntu and Fedora systems under KDE. The example programs were tested on Windows, Linux, and Mac OS X.

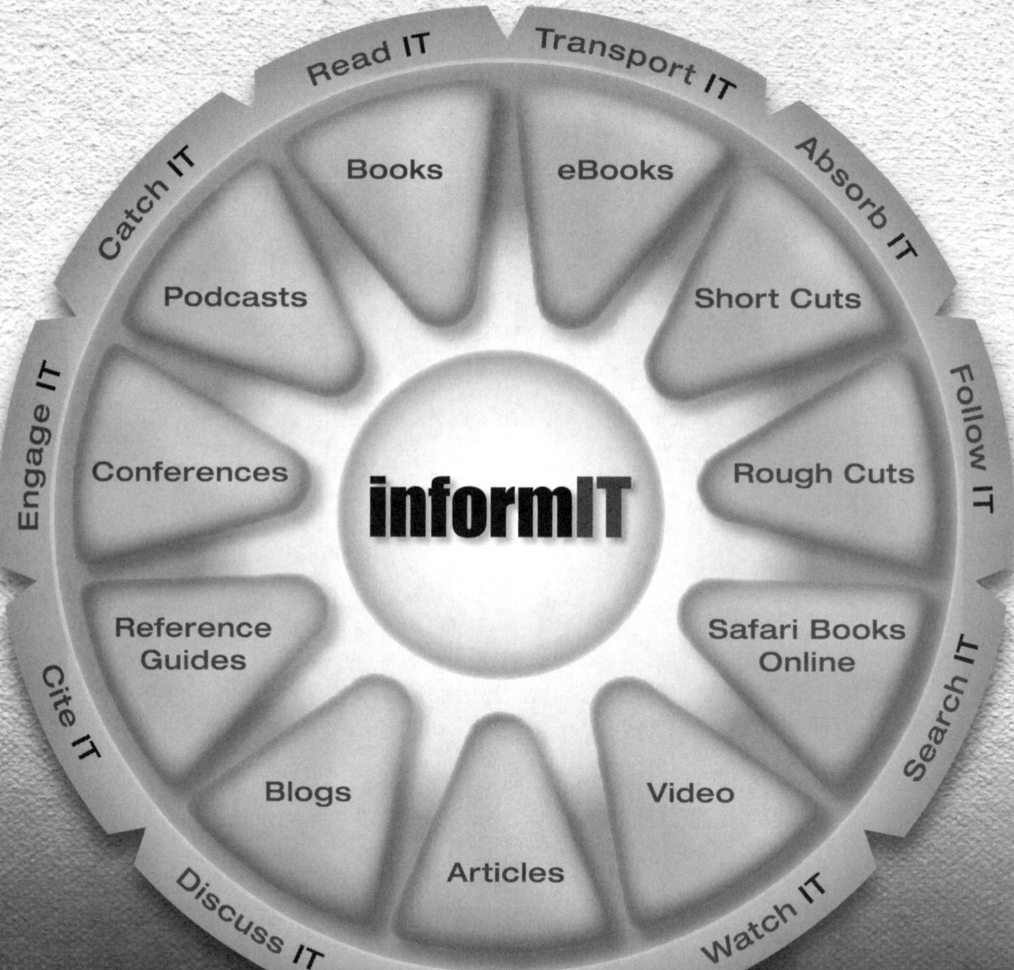

THIS BOOK IS SAFARI ENABLED

INCLUDES FREE 45-DAY ACCESS TO THE ONLINE EDITION

The Safari® Enabled icon on the cover of your favorite technology book means the book is available through Safari Bookshelf. When you buy this book, you get free access to the online edition for 45 days.

Safari Bookshelf is an electronic reference library that lets you easily search thousands of technical books, find code samples, download chapters, and access technical information whenever and wherever you need it.

TO GAIN 45-DAY SAFARI ENABLED ACCESS TO THIS BOOK:

- Go to **informit.com/safarienabled**
- Complete the brief registration form
- Enter the coupon code found in the front of this book on the "Copyright" page

If you have difficulty registering on Safari Bookshelf or accessing the online edition, please e-mail customer-service@safaribooksonline.com.